B.R. 516 (Restricted)

GEOGRAPHICAL HANDBOOK SERIES

FOR OFFICIAL USE ONLY

GREECE

VOLUME I

PHYSICAL GEOGRAPHY, HISTORY, ADMINISTRATION AND PEOPLES

March 1944

NAVAL INTELLIGENCE DIVISION

This book is for the use of persons in H.M. Service only and must not be shown, or made available, to the Press or to any member of the public.

PREFACE

In 1915 a Geographical Section was formed in the Naval Intelligence Division of the Admiralty to write Geographical Handbooks on various parts of the world. The purpose of these handbooks was to supply, by scientific research and skilled arrangement, material for the discussion of naval, military, and political problems, as distinct from the examination of the problems themselves. Many distinguished collaborators assisted in their production, and by the end of 1918 upwards of fifty volumes had been produced in Handbook and Manual form, as well as numerous short-term geographical reports. The demand for these books increased rapidly with each new issue, and they acquired a high reputation for accuracy and impartiality. They are now to be found in Service Establishments and Embassies throughout the world, and in the early years after the last war were much used by the League of Nations.

The old Handbooks have been extensively used in the present war, and experience has disclosed both their value and their limitations. On the one hand they have proved, beyond all question, how greatly the work of the fighting services and of Government Departments is facilitated if countries of strategic or political importance are covered by handbooks which deal, in a convenient and easily digested form, with their geography, ethnology, administration, and resources. On the other hand, it has become apparent that something more is needed to meet present-day requirements. The old series does not cover many of the countries closely affected by the present war (e.g. Germany, France, Poland, Spain, Portugal, to name only a few); its books are somewhat uneven in quality, and they are inadequately equipped with maps, diagrams, and photographic illustrations.

The present series of Handbooks, while owing its inspiration largely to the former series, is in no sense an attempt to revise or re-edit that series. It is an entirely new set of books, produced in the Naval Intelligence Division by trained geographers drawn largely from the Universities, and working at sub-centres established at Oxford and Cambridge. The books follow, in general, a uniform scheme, though minor modifications will be found in particular cases; and they are illustrated by numerous maps and photographs.

The purpose of the books is primarily naval. They are designed first to provide, for the use of Commanding Officers, information in a comprehensive and convenient form about countries which they may be called upon to visit, not only in war but in peace-time; secondly, to maintain the high standard of education in the Navy and, by supplying officers with material for lectures to naval personnel ashore and afloat, to ensure for all ranks that visits to a new country shall be both interesting and profitable.

Their contents are, however, by no means confined to matters of purely naval interest. For many purposes (e.g. history, administration, resources, communications, etc.) countries must necessarily be treated as a whole, and no attempt is made to limit their treatment exclusively to coastal zones. It is hoped therefore that the Army, the Royal Air Force, and other Government Departments (many of whom have given great assistance in the production of the series) will find these Handbooks even more valuable than their predecessors proved to be both during and after the last war.

J. H. GODFREY
Director of Naval Intelligence
1942

The foregoing preface has appeared from the beginning of this series of Geographical Handbooks. It describes so effectively their origin and purpose that I have decided to retain it in its original form.

This volume has been prepared for the Naval Intelligence Division at the Cambridge sub-centre (General Editor, Dr H. C. Darby). It has been mainly written by Dr H. C. Darby, Dr W. A. Heurtley, Mr J. R. James and Miss J. B. Mitchell, with contributions from Professor P. A. Buxton, Mr C. W. Crawley, Mr I. L. Foster, Professor A. G. Ogilvie, Dr Norman White and the Research Department of the Foreign Office. The block diagrams have been constructed by Mrs Gwen Raverat; other maps and diagrams have been drawn mainly by Miss K. S. A. Froggatt, Miss M. Garside, Mrs Marion Plant and Miss J. D. I. Tyson. The volume has been edited by Mr J. R. James.

E. G. N. RUSHBROOKE
Director of Naval Intelligence

March 1944

CONTENTS

APPENDICES:

SUMMARY OF CONTENTS OF HANDBOOK ON GREECE

LIST OF MAPS AND DIAGRAMS

LIST OF PLATES

FACING PAGE

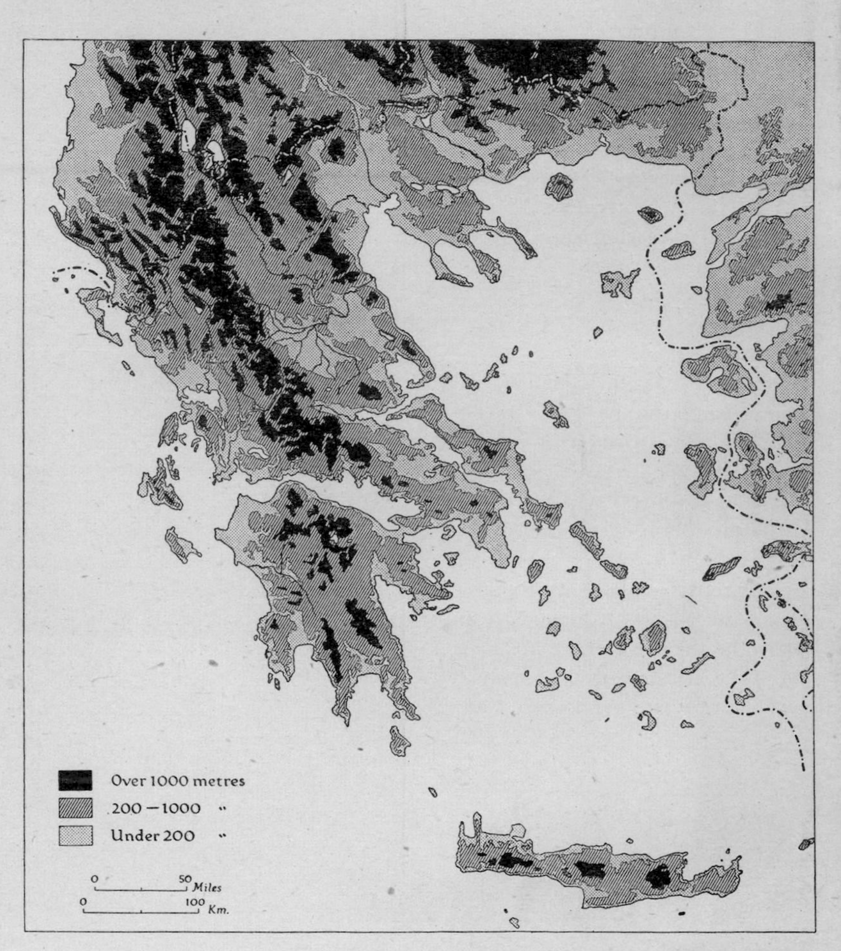

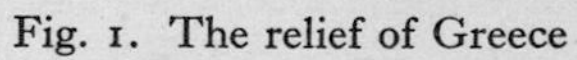
Fig. 1. The relief of Greece

Chapter I

GEOLOGY AND PHYSICAL FEATURES

Geological Structure: Scenery: River Systems: Regional Divisions: The Dividing Mountains: Western Greece: Central Greece: Eastern Greece: North-eastern Greece: The Pelopónnisos: The Ionian Islands: The Thracian Islands: The Northern Sporádhes: The Kikládhes (Cyclades): The Islands of the Eastern Aegean: Kríti (Crete): Bibliographical Note

The area of Greece is 50,147 sq. miles or 129,880 sq. km.; it is thus about the size of England alone. Of this area, the mainland covers 41,328 sq. miles, and the islands, including Kríti (Crete), cover 8,819 sq. miles. The greater part of the country is mountainous, the highest peak (Ólimbos) rising to 9,571 ft. above sea level. It has often been said that 'Greece is a land of the mountains and the sea'. The mountains stretch out as peninsulas which, in many cases, are continued into the Aegean as chains of islands. Gulfs and bays penetrate far inland, and no place in Greece is more than 50 miles from the sea. The coastal plain is usually narrow, but there are also numerous plains in the interior, which have formed regions of settlement from the earliest times.

Geological Structure

The reasons for this variety have been, broadly speaking, as follows:

(1) an old block, built of hard rocks, occupies eastern and north-eastern Greece and has remained relatively rigid since moderately early geological times (see table on p. 7);

(2) younger and weaker rocks, folded during the Tertiary earth-movements, occupy western and southern Greece;

(3) more recent uplift and fracturing affected both the hard block and the folded area, while subsidence produced the sunken basins of the Ionian and Aegean Seas. These movements have continued up to the present day, as successive earthquakes indicate.

These three subjects must be considered separately.

(1) *The Old Block of Eastern and North-eastern Greece*

Ancient folding, probably of Carboniferous age, affected the whole area now occupied by the Balkan mountains and the Aegean Sea

(Fig. 2). The rocks of this area were subjected to great pressure, and were not only intensely folded but were also chemically altered and rendered hard and crystalline. Limestones were changed to

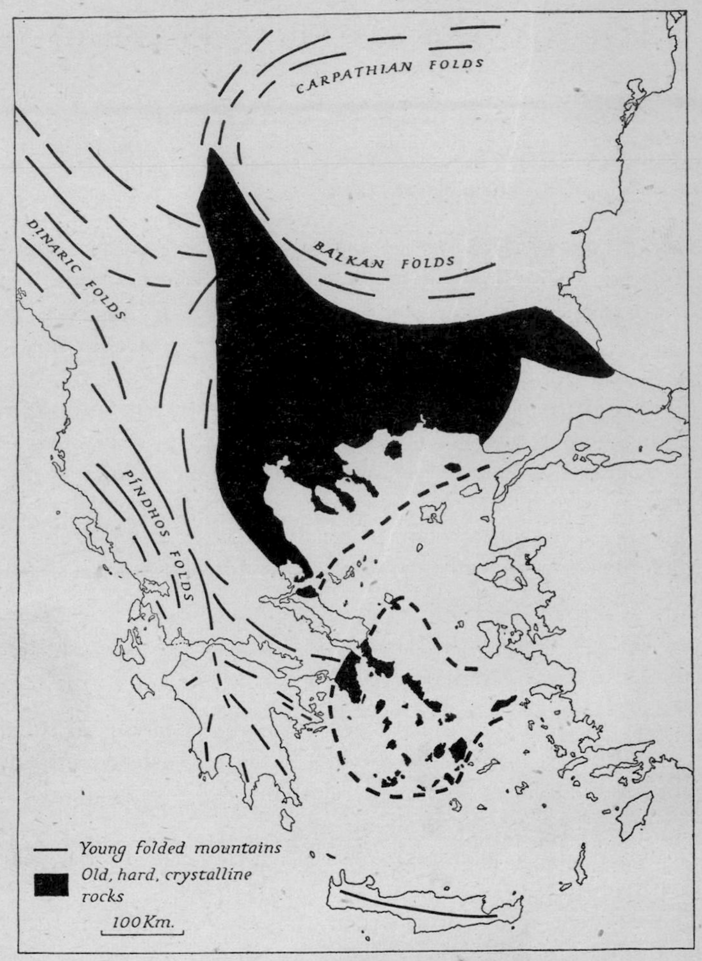

Fig. 2. The structure of the Balkan Peninsula

Based on M. I. Newbigin, *Geographical Aspects of Balkan Problems*, p. 12 (London, 1915) and M. I. Newbigin, *Southern Europe*, p. 399 (London, 1932).

marble; sandstones and clays to schist and gneiss. The region as a whole was then worn down during a lengthy period of erosion, and formed a stable unit around which the later folding of Tertiary times took place. The stresses created by these Tertiary earth movements doubtless caused some fractures both within and around the margins of the old block itself, but the final fracturing which gave shape to the present uplands and plains took place in late Tertiary and even Quaternary times (see below). It was this fracturing, and the subsidence it involved, that produced the Aegean Sea; the Aegean islands are thus the fragmentary remains, above water, of an old land surface.

(2) *The Folded Mountains of Western and Southern Greece*

Throughout western and southern Greece, the structures and rocks present a great contrast to those of eastern and north-eastern Greece. The rocks are all much younger. They were formerly sediments accumulated by rivers, or in lakes and in seas; and sometimes they are of great thickness. All except the most recent of these sedimentary rocks were involved in the Tertiary earth movements. The Illyrian Alps, the Píndhos mountains, the chains of the Pelopónnisos, the mountains of Kríti, as well as the Taurus mountains of Asia, are parts of the great system of Alpine folding that stretches from the Pyrenees right across to south-eastern Asia. In the area that is now Greece, immense lateral pressures folded and overthrust the rocks in a great arc around the old rigid block of the north-east. The folds show in general a north-west to south-east trend, though in detail their direction varies widely. Here and there, as in the Alps themselves, the old crystalline rocks of the foundation project through the folded sedimentary cover.

Within the folded areas, two major groups of rocks may be distinguished, both of which have been altered and hardened by the high temperatures and great pressure developed during folding. In the first place, the muds, sands and gravels—all shallow-water deposits—have sometimes been changed into slates, quartzites and conglomerates. The whole group of non-calcareous sedimentary rocks—shales, sandstones and marls—is known to Alpine geologists as *Flysch*, or 'the sediments that slip'. These rocks, for the most part, are impermeable; streams are therefore numerous, at least during the rainy season, and the land has been easily eroded.

In the second place, the calcareous sediments of the deeper, clearer water have been almost entirely changed into the resistant limestones and marbles that play so great a part in the scenery of Greece to-day. Comparison of Figs. 1 and 4 will show how the highlands of Greece are found mainly on the north-west to south-east bands of limestone, and how the lower ridges and plains are characteristic of the intervening sandstones, mudstones and shales.

(3) *Recent Uplift and Faulting*

After the major folding in western and southern Greece, there was a period of comparative quiescence, during which great masses

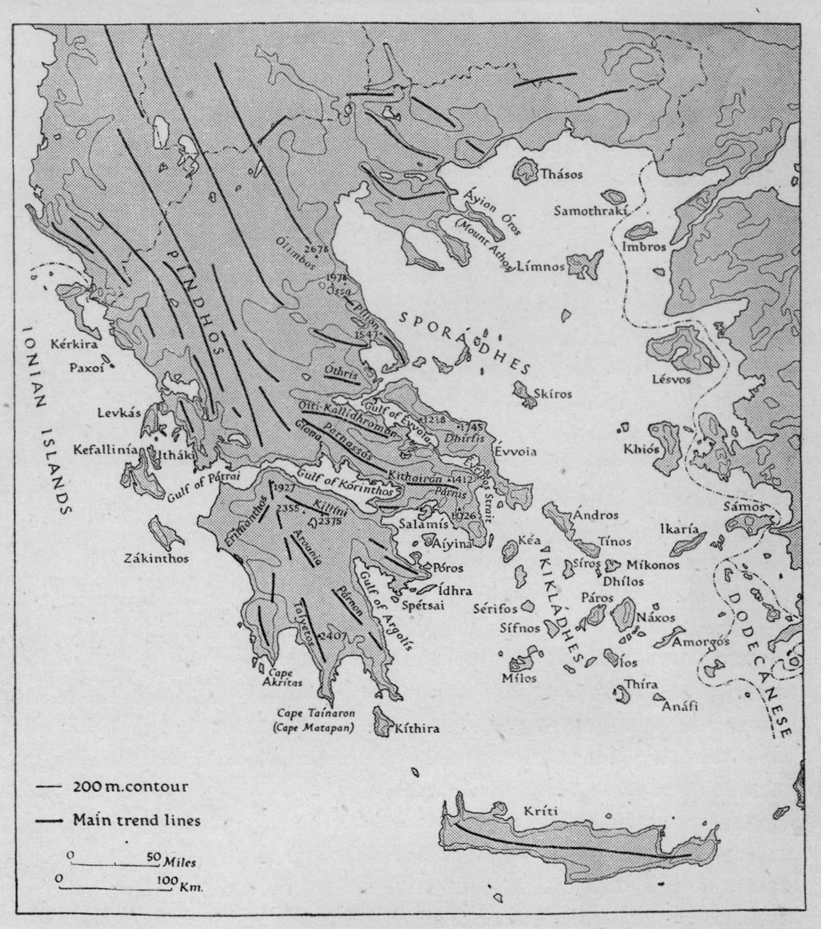

Fig. 3. The main trend lines of relief

Based on J. Sion and Y. Chataigneau, *Géographie Universelle*, Tome VII, Partie 2, Fig. 91 (Paris, 1934). The Dinaric Trend, north-west to south-east, is repeated many times throughout the peninsula; three other trends, NNW–SSE, W–E, and WSW–ENE are also characteristic of southern Greece, and two more, SW–NE and WNW–ESE are seen in the northern part of the country. These trends are shown most clearly by the lines of fracture on Fig. 6.

of material were eroded both from the older lands of the east and from the newer ones of the west. The whole surface seems to have been eventually reduced to a series of rounded and subdued hills of no great height, composed of the more resistant rocks; these were separated by undulating vales corresponding either to weaker rocks or to zones which had been warped downwards. The whole formed what geographers term a 'mature' landscape (Plate 5).

The transition from this 'mature' countryside to the present face of Greece is due to still later earth movements in late Tertiary and Quaternary times. Two stages can be recognized in these later movements. In the first place, there was a general elevation which raised the old 'mature' surface to such a height that its relics are now found at the higher altitudes in the country. An index of the elevation may be gained from the fact that in the Pelopónnisos, some lower Pliocene rocks are now found at nearly 6,000 ft. above sea level.

In the second place, the general uplift was accompanied by great disturbances and faulting movements that affected both the folded areas and the rigid block alike. The earth's crust in this part of the world seems to have yielded to tension and stresses, and this instability has continued up to the present day, as is witnessed by the numerous earthquakes which have occurred with distressing frequency during historical times. Fig. 5 shows the localities of the severe earthquakes recorded between 1501 and 1929. Hot springs, so common in Greece, also provide further evidence of instability.

Much of the present relief of Greece is due to these recent faults. The straight and abrupt edges of many of the mountains, and the unworn aspect of much of the coast, have resulted from fractures that are too recent for the process of erosion to dim or obliterate. Most of these fractures seem to follow definite trends—possible lines of weakness—that are shown on Fig. 6. With this final shattering of the crust, molten igneous rocks of different types were injected into the fractures; volcanoes also appeared, and one of these still remains active in the Aegean islands. A line of volcanic peaks stretches from the dormant cone of Méthana in the Saronic Gulf, through Mílos and Thíra to Kos. The explosion crater of Thíra has been flooded by the sea, but, rising in its centre, the Kaïméni islands are the new cones of a still active volcano (Plate 2).

The Aegean itself owes its very existence to this recent faulting. Here, a portion of the old rigid block has subsided and the sea includes three deep basins, free of islands and bounded by relatively steep slopes. The trends of the edges of these steep slopes harmonize

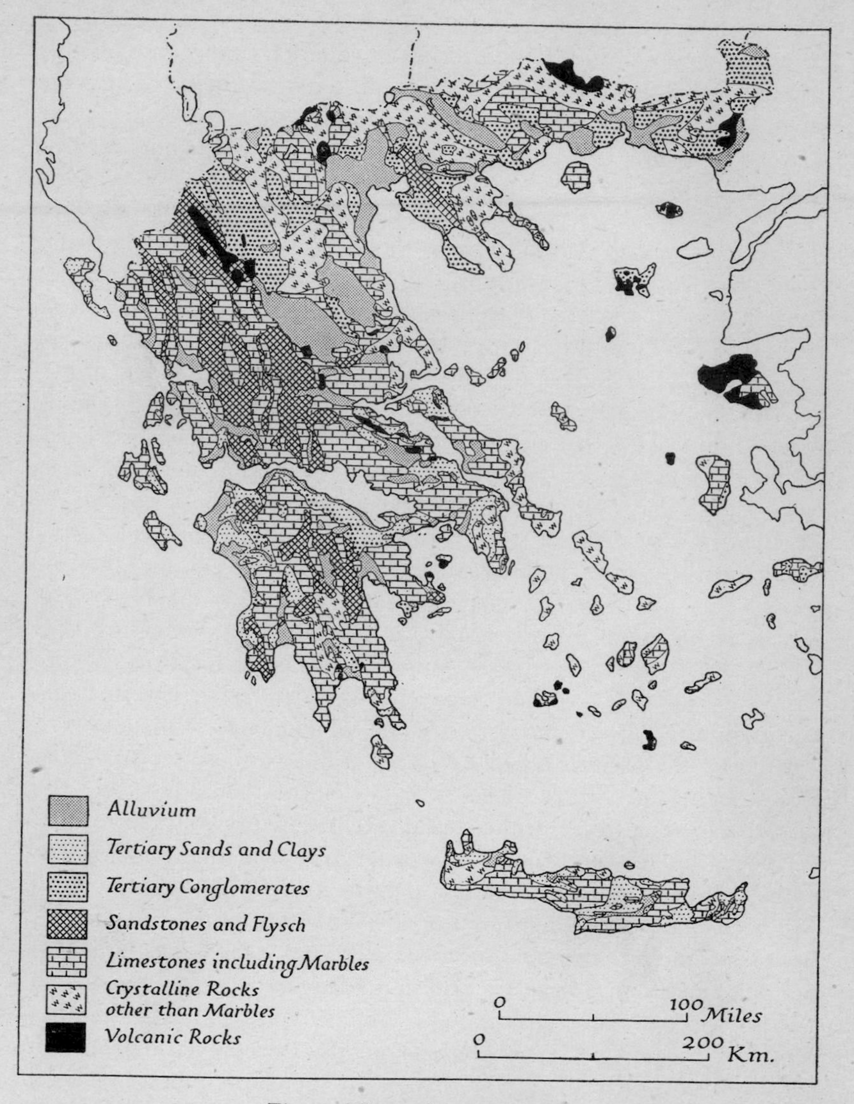

Fig. 4. The geology of Greece

Based on J. Sion and Y. Chataigneau, *Géographie Universelle*, Tome VII, Partie 2, Fig. 91 (Paris, 1934); H. Stremme, 1 : 2,500,000 International Soil Map of Europe (Berlin, 1937); A. Philippson, *Der Peloponnes. Versuch einer Landeskunde auf geoligischer Grundlage.*

Plate 1. Ierissós, after the earthquake of 1932

Earth movements along the coasts of Greece are distressingly frequent. On 28 September 1932, a violent earthquake destroyed the village of Ierissós on the east coast of Khalkidhikí. Mineral springs appeared and changes of altitude occurred.

Plate 2. Thíra (Santorin)

The volcanic island of Thíra, most southerly of the Kikládhes, overlooks the still active vents of the Kaïméni Isles.

Plate 3. The summits of Ólimbos (Olympus)

Ólimbos, the highest mountain in Greece and the traditional home of Zeus, rises in a great fault-scarp to 9,571 ft.

Plate 4. Mount Vardhoúsia

The limestone peak of Vardhoúsia dominates the southern ranges of central Greece. It rises to well over 8,000 ft. and carries snow until far on in the spring.

generally with those of mainland Greece and Anatolia. It seems that the lines of fracture, so evident on the land, are continued out to sea. More detailed soundings than are now available would probably confirm the view that the basin rims mark important lines of dislocation along which the basins themselves foundered.

Table of main Geological Divisions

Quaternary	Recent Pleistocene	Uplift and fracturing
Tertiary	Pliocene Miocene Oligocene Eocene	Alpine folding
Mesozoic	Cretaceous Jurassic Triassic	
Palaeozoic	Permian Carboniferous Devonian Silurian Ordovician Cambrian	Hercynian folding Caledonian folding
	Pre-Cambrian	

SCENERY

Mountainous Districts

A relief map of Greece shows great areas over 3,000 ft. above sea level, and many summits over 6,000 ft. One might, therefore, easily be led to visualize the Greek highlands as a maze of bold ranges and peaks, whereas such features are relatively restricted in extent. There are, in fact, large tracts of highland where the average slopes are gentle, and where even the summits, apart from the highest, are rounded. This comparatively subdued relief of much of the highland is a relic of the old 'mature' landscape: and, despite subsequent changes, much of this former land surface still gives something of its character to the present scenery of the country. A good deal of it can be pieced together by the eye in taking a wide sweep across the horizon.

But although, in looking out over a wide horizon, one often sees a smooth and nearly level surface, every near view shows prominent

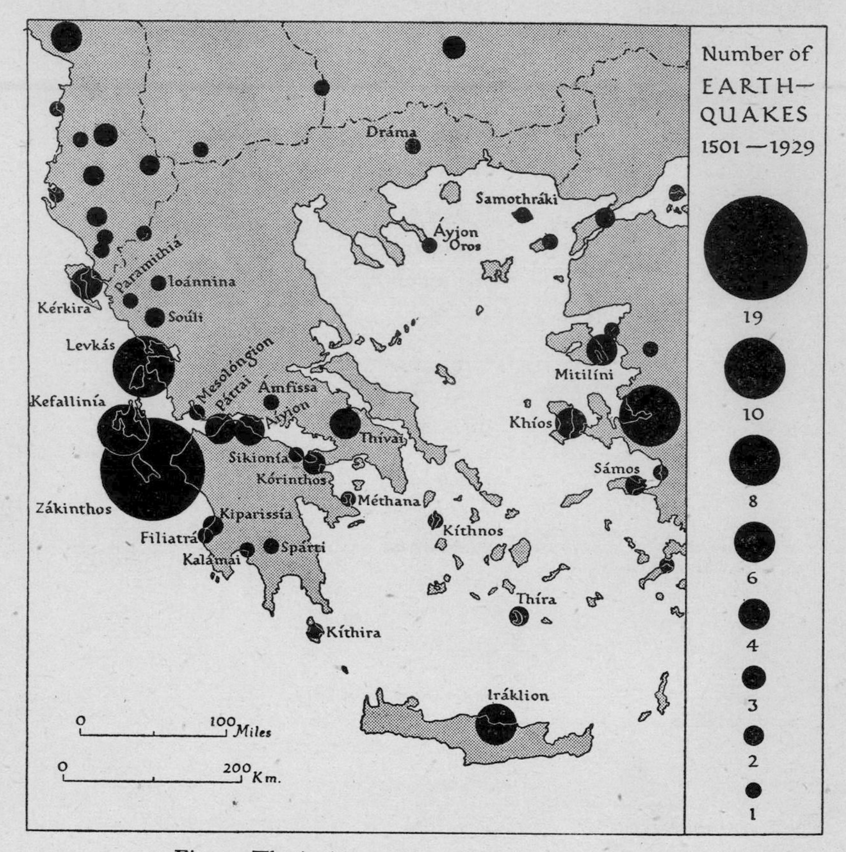

Fig. 5. The incidence of earthquakes, 1501–1929

The map is taken from A. Cavasino, *Publicationi della Commissione Italiana per lo studio delle grandi calamità*, vol. II, reproduced in *Memorie Scientifiche et Tecniche*, vol. II, p. 61 (Roma, 1931).

The distribution suggests that the most disturbed areas are near the intersection of major fractures running north-west to south-east and west to east. There may have been, however, many earthquakes unrecorded during this period, especially on the northern edge of the Aegean Sea.

rugged features. These sharp edges and irregularities occupy a comparatively small area; but, owing to their very nature, they play a large part in the scenery of many districts. This rugged element in

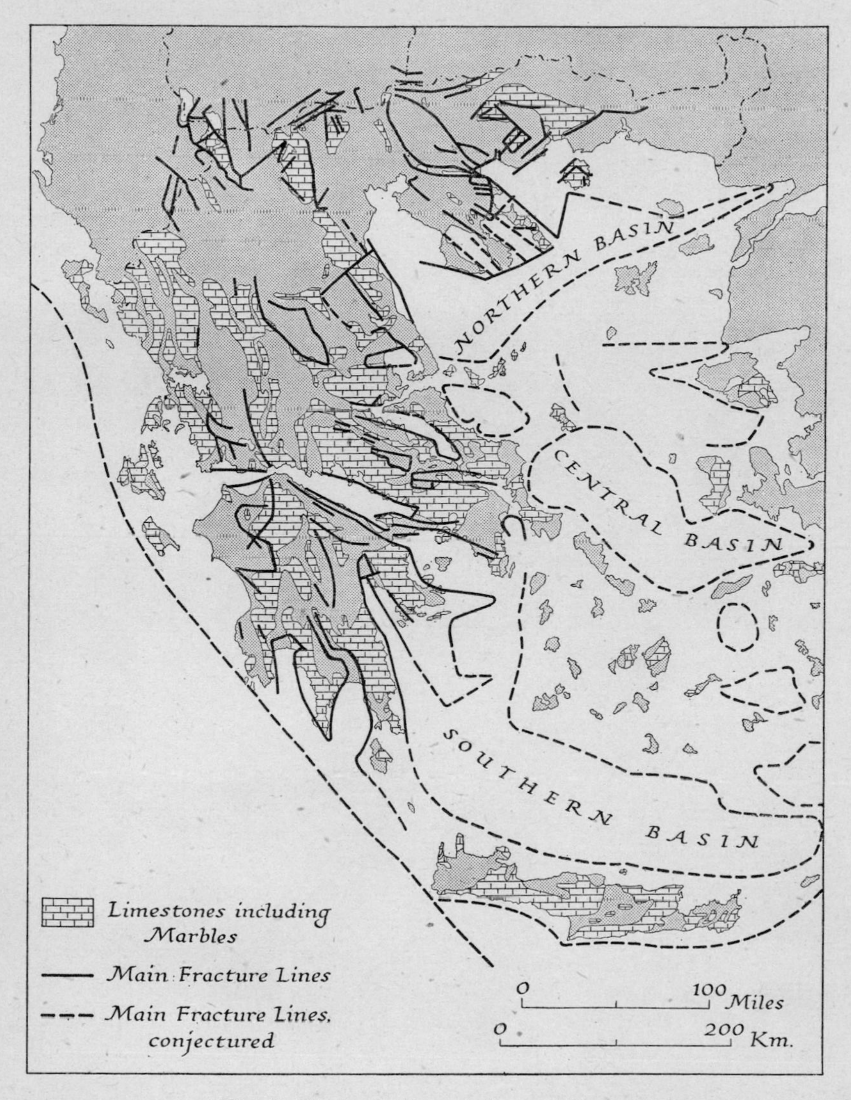

Fig. 6. The main fracture lines of Greece

The lines of fracture follow the dominant features of relief. Those on land have been proved by geological mapping, which, however, has not been carried out systematically in the north-west. The submarine fractures are presumptive, and have been drawn along lines of abrupt slope; some of these prolong the proved dislocations on the land.

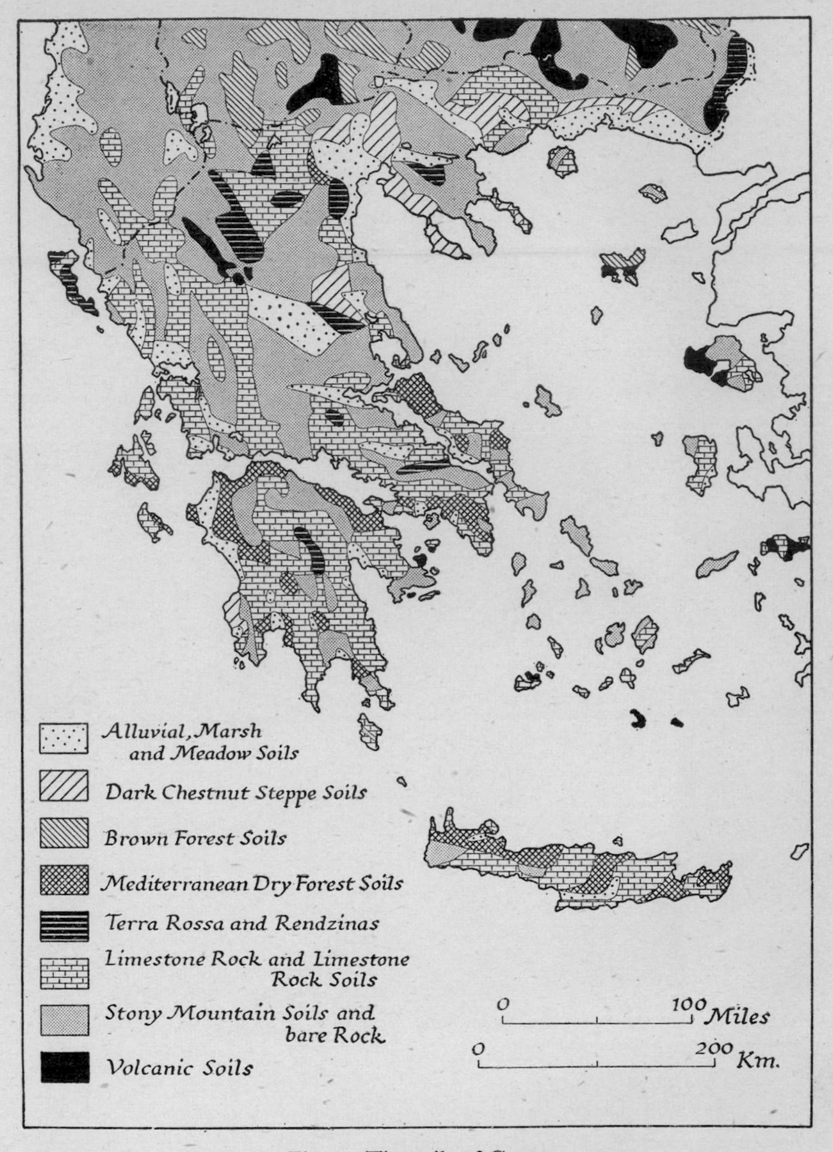

Fig. 7. The soils of Greece

Based on H. Stremme, 1 : 2,500,000 International Soil Map of Europe (Berlin, 1937).

The soils of Greece show great local variety. The nature of the soil is determined primarily by the climate and the character of the parent rock, and thus a general distinction can be made between the soils of the highland and those of the lowland. In general, the mountain soils are thin, poor and stony; the limestone uplands are particularly barren, with little or no soil cover, but here and there in the small basins and narrow valleys, red earth or *terra rossa* develops as the insoluble residue left after the soluble constituents of limestone have been removed. The soils of the plains vary greatly, from widespread fans of infertile, very permeable soil to rather impermeable, fertile clays and loams—the best soils in Greece.

the mountain scenery of Greece is usually due to one or two factors—either to the effects of recent faulting in late Tertiary and Quaternary times, or to the fact that so much of Greece is covered by limestone rocks. These two elements must be examined separately.

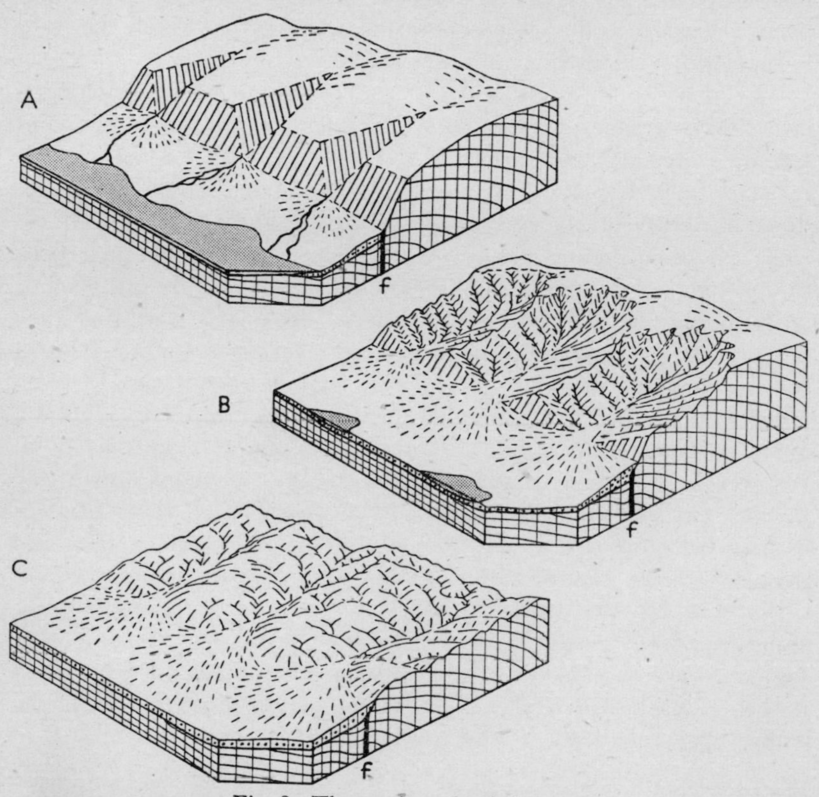

Fig. 8. The erosion of a fault scarp

The abrupt edges that so often bound the 'mature' uplands are usually the direct result of earth movements along a fracture or fault (*f*). The precipitous slopes are known as fault scarps, and the diagrams illustrate the progressive erosion of these scarps from youth (*A*) to maturity (*C*).

The recent faulting and fracturing has resulted in sharp edges and escarpments which have become gashed by the ravines of winter torrents. The formation and subsequent alteration of a fault-scarp is illustrated by Fig. 8. Escarpments of this kind, in different stages of dissection, exist along all parts of the fracture lines shown on Fig. 6. Some of them are immense; for example, that forming the east coast of Thessalía rises from near sea level to 9,571 ft. in Mt

Ólimbos (Plate 3). Almost as imposing is the eastern wall of Taïyetos, overlooking the basin of Spárti, which marks a fault-line parallel to that of Thessalía. The result of the fracturing has been to divide much of the land into blocks, subject to differential movements up and down; and the aspect of some parts of Greece has been compared to that of a badly laid pavement in which the individual blocks are tilted at different angles.

The presence of limestone rocks also results in irregular features, and this is important when it is remembered that there are considerable areas of these rocks in Greece (Fig. 6). Limestone is a resistant rock because it is permeable to water which percolates down any cracks in the surface and widens them by solution. Moreover, the underground rivers of limestone areas enlarge their beds by erosion and solution from mere pipes and tunnels into strings of great caverns. In time, these caverns become so vast that they fall in, thus converting the underground rivers into surface streams flowing at the bottom of gorges that have perpendicular or even overhanging sides. Sometimes the river which caused the solution has abandoned its channel, perhaps to work at yet lower levels in the rock, and the canyon that remains is dry or contains only a tiny stream, too small to have made it. The result of all these features is that the landscape is marked locally by precipitous slopes and deep-cut ravines that present bold and gleaming surfaces to the sun.

To sum up: the gentle contours of the original 'mature' landscape have been broken locally by many irregularities. The smoother highlands are bounded as a rule by long, steep edges, or by narrow gorges. Escarpments and canyon walls together provide most of the really rugged elements in Greek scenery (Plate 18).

Lowland Areas

The lowland element in the Greek landscape is not very considerable, but it has naturally played a very important part in the life of the country. Most of the coastal plains and interior basins were formed during the faulting of late Tertiary and Quaternary times. The complications of coastal movement have depressed some of them below sea level, and then uplifted them again. The surface of these areas is consequently covered by sands, marls and clays; and, where they are gashed by modern streams or by waves, the light colour and weak nature of the strata are obvious. Most of the interior plains have, at one time or another, held lakes, many of which still survived until recently as malarial and unpopulated areas.

Plate 5. Uplands near Ioánnina

Although much of Greece is mountainous, there are large areas of highland where the slopes are gentle and rounded. This is 'mature' landscape.

Plate 6. Spárti and the eastern wall of Taïyetos

The straight eastern edge of the Taïyetos mountains overlooks the basin of Spárti in the Evrótas valley. As in Plate 3, the steep mountain side is an example of a fault-scarp.

Plate 7. The Angítis (Angista) Gorge

The gorge lies immediately north of the Pangaíon mountains. Limestone is resistant to weathering and erosion; it allows water to percolate down its many joints or cracks, and its surface is therefore largely waterless.

Plate 8. Olimbía from the south bank of the Alfiós

Beyond the alluvial plain of the Alfiós is a low terrace which marks the one-time level of the river. In the background the terraces are higher and more deeply dissected.

Fig. 9 illustrates a lake basin formed by faulting, and surrounded by terraces that mark the spasmodic decline of the water level; the higher terrace lands, with their weak sediments, are usually much dissected by deep ravines (Plate 8).

Finally, on the slopes of all plains and basins, recent deposits of river gravels and alluvium add their own characteristic forms to the landscape. Weathering, denudation and deposition take place at a relatively rapid rate in Greece, partly because of climatic conditions

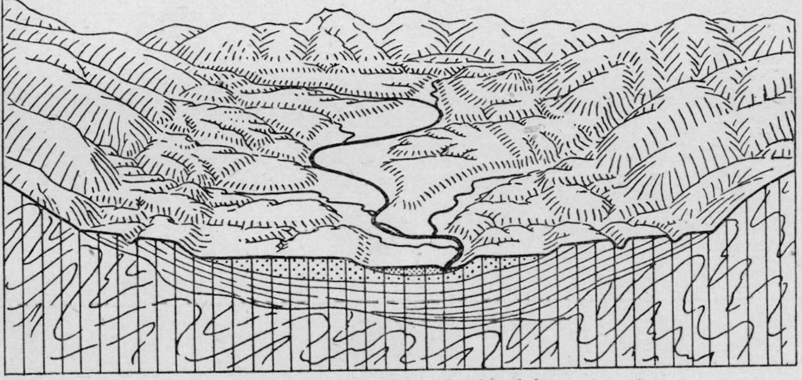

Fig. 9. A dissected basin plain

The diagram shows a flat flood plain and dissected terraces at two different levels. Most of these plains are thickly covered with the debris of erosion brought down from the surrounding mountains. Near the hill foot these deposits are usually coarse and stony; on the flood plain they are the fine alluviums laid down by the main river.

and partly because of the sudden transitions from high to low ground. The rapid variations in diurnal temperature quickly break up the bare rock surfaces exposed by the sparseness of the vegetation. The heavy rains of winter, the short torrential downpours of summer, and the steep slopes help the rapid transport of material, which is ultimately brought by heavily laden streams to form extensive fans and deltas in the lowlands (Plate 23).

River Systems

The major rivers of Greece show certain features in common. In their upper courses, their valleys are often wide and gently sloping; here are the relics of the former 'mature' landscape (Fig. 16). In their middle courses, narrow deep gorges alternate with plains. In their lower courses, meanders develop across the small coastal plains, and the rivers sometimes reach the sea through deltas. The juxtaposition of uplifted areas and depressed basins, due to faulting, has naturally given rise to many peculiarities of drainage, and abrupt

Fig. 10. The drainage of Greece

Based on the 1 : 1,000,000 G.S.G.S., Series 2758: Europe, and corrected from the 1 : 250,000 G.S.G.S., Series 4088: The Balkans. Many of the rivers of Greece are short, swift-flowing streams—a serious barrier to communications after heavy rains, but mere trickles during the long, dry summers.

bends due to river capture are characteristic (Fig. 11). Moreover, the presence of considerable areas of limestone has further complicated the river system. Sink-holes (*katavóthra*), underground streams, and

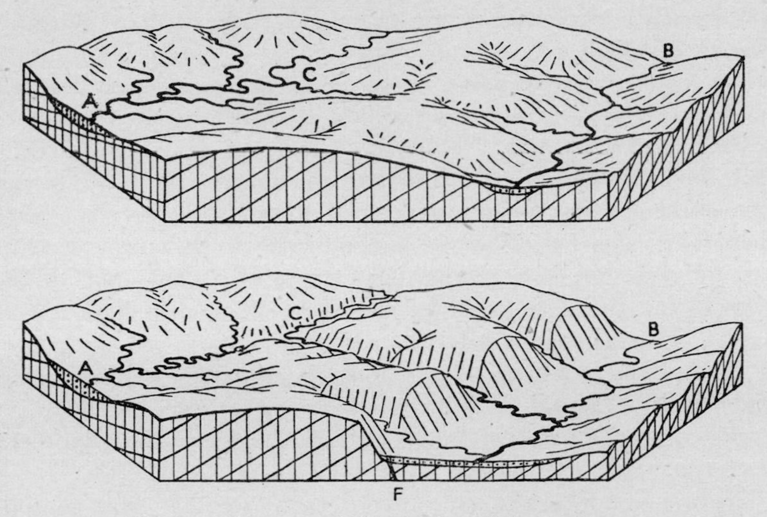

Fig. 11. Diagrammatic illustration of river capture

The diagram shows one of the causes of river capture. After the area drained by the river *B* was lowered by faulting (*F*), a tributary of *B* became much more vigorous (rejuvenated). Eventually this tributary tapped river *A* at *C*, there forming an 'elbow of capture'.

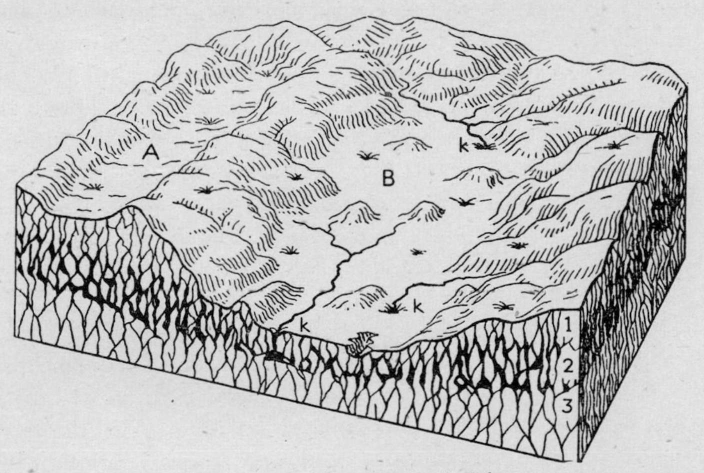

Fig. 12. Karstic hills and plains

The term *karst* is applied to limestone country that is partly, or wholly, without superficial drainage. In the course of time three hydrographic zones are developed underground: 1 is a dry zone, 2 is a zone, intermittently dry and wet, 3 is a zone with constant circulation in the fissures. Corresponding to these hydrographic zones, the surface of the plain *A* will be dry, and that of *B* intermittently dry and wet. Other features are also developed in pure limestone country by the solvent action of runnels of rain water. These flute the surface, and at points of marked weakness, deep shafts or sink-holes, known in Greek as *katavóthra* (*k*), are produced.

bare waterless areas (*karst*) are all characteristic of many localities (Fig. 12 and Plate 9).

The major rivers of north-western Greece are strongly flowing, well-fed streams, as is sometimes indicated by their names: Árakhthos means 'to smite or dash'; Thíamis comes from the verb 'to rush'. Their longest reaches are parallel to the north-west to south-east grain of the country, and are developed on sandstone, or shale beds. These long parallel stretches are joined by shorter transverse sections that, for one reason or another, cut across the main grain of the country; the rivers as a whole, therefore, frequently have zigzag courses. The transverse stretches are usually deep, narrow gorges cut through the limestone ranges, and it is probable that these rivers were powerful enough to maintain their old courses as the ridges developed. The Thíamis of Ípiros and the Mégdhova of the southern Píndhos are good examples.

The drainage of eastern and north-eastern Greece is more complicated in pattern. The river systems have been greatly affected by the subsidence of the Aegean basins and of the mountain enclosed basins to the north and west (Fig. 6). Great plains with slow, sluggish rivers are joined by narrow ravines with turbulent torrents. The Kifissós, the Sperkhiós, and above all the Piniós, show these characteristic features. Many of the great rivers of this region follow what appear to be most difficult courses. They continue to run along lines inherited from the old surface of low relief, even though these smooth slopes have since been broken up by great fractures and differential movement. The Piniós, cutting between the mountains of Ólimbos and Óssa, has maintained its old course, despite the present barrier of high coastal mountains. The Axiós, Strimón and the Néstos of Makedhonía are also older than the mountains which hem them into their defiles (Plates 10, 11, 12).

The rivers of the Pelopónnisos have varied characters. Those of the north coast are short, simple torrents which have cut deep, straight valleys. The course of the Evrótas has been complicated by the transverse faulting of the basin plains of Lakonía. The Alfiós river, the longest in the Pelopónnisos, pursues a very curious course (Fig. 17). It has inherited part of its course from an older land surface, and it has changed direction as a result of recent faulting; it wanders across sediment-filled plains and cuts through resistant rock ridges. It is an epitome of river development in Greece.

There are, finally, a number of small areas characterized by interior drainage, most of which owe their origin to faulting. Three

Plate 9. The emergence of the river Krushovítis from underground

In common with many rivers in limestone regions the river Krushovítis runs for part of its course as a subterranean stream.

Plate 10. Incised meanders of the river Néstos (Mesta)

The Néstos, like the Strimón, is much older than the mountains through which it flows.

Plate 11. The river Piniós near Goúnitsa

The Piniós enters the fertile plain of Lárisa at Goúnitsa. Here, the river is seen cutting through the low plateau that bounds the plain on the west.

Plate 12. The river Strimón in the Rúpel Gorge

The broad and swift flowing Strimón enters Greece by the Rúpel Gorge. The view is looking upstream, about 2 miles north of the railway bridge over the river.

main areas stand out: (1) the Kifissós-Kopaïs basin of central Greece (60 × 25 miles); (2) the Trípolis basin of the central Pelopónnisos (43 × 16 miles); and (3) the Vegorrítis-Ptolemaïs basin in northern Greece (42 × 27 miles). Other smaller, but still important areas, are the Margarítion basin, the high basin of Ioánnina, the Lake Préspa basin, all in the north-west; the Doïrán basin and the Nevrokópion basin in Makedhonía.

Regional Divisions

The major physical regions of mainland Greece, shown on Fig. 13, are described under the following headings:

A. *The Dividing Mountains.*

B. *Western Greece.*
(1) The Ridges and Furrows of Ípiros.
(2) The Hills and Plains of Akarnanía.

C. *Central Greece.*
(1) The Highlands of Voiotía and Attikí.
(2) The Blocks and Basins of Voiotía and Fokís.

D. *Eastern Greece.*
(1) The Western Lowland Zone.
(2) The Western Mountain Belt.
(3) The Eastern Lowland Zone.
(4) The Eastern Mountain Belt.

E. *North-eastern Greece.*

F. *The Pelopónnisos.*
(1) The Northern and Eastern Highlands.
(2) The Central Corridor and North-western Pelopónnisos.
(3) The South-western Highlands and the Plain of Messinía.

The islands of Greece, shown on Fig. 3, are described under the following headings:

The Ionian Islands.
The Thracian Islands.
The Northern Sporádhes.
The Kikládhes (Cyclades).
The Islands of the Eastern Aegean.
Kríti (Crete).

A. The Dividing Mountains

The central mountain belt, extending southwards from Albania to the Gulf of Kórinthos, forms the backbone of northern Greece and a most effective barrier to communications. For the most part, it is

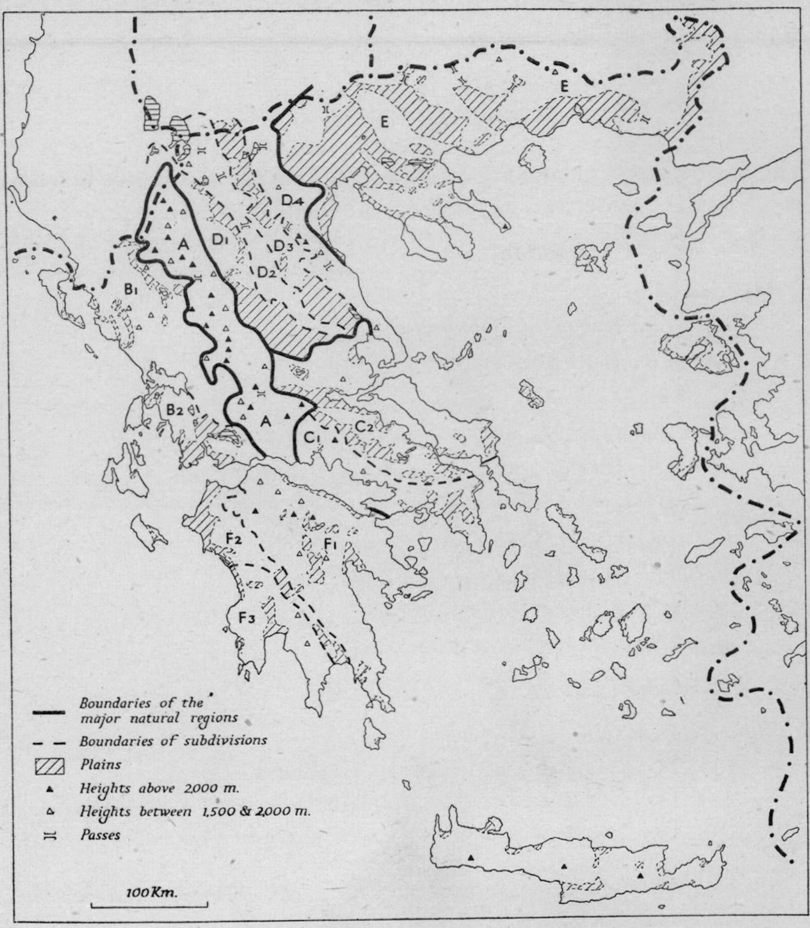

Fig. 13. The major physical regions of Greece

Key map to indicate the areas described in the text.

a gently rolling plateau, some 6,000 ft. high; but here and there, rugged escarpments and deep ravines break the general smoothness of the landscape. The region forms the watershed between the rivers draining into the Ionian Sea and the Aegean respectively; but the river Mégdhova, rising in the east, penetrates all the chains as it flows south-westwards in a series of profound ravines to join the Akhelóös. This exceptional river in no way modifies the effectiveness of the barrier, since its ravines are impassable. The mountains themselves are crossed by only two important passes: in the north, the Métsovon pass leads from Kalabáka to Ioánnina; in the south, a narrow pass near Mt Timfristós leads from the headwaters of the Sperkhiós valley to Karpenísion (Fig. 14). These two passes conveniently divide the mountains into three regions.

The northern region, lying between Albania and the Métsovon pass, has two main subdivisions. In the west is an area known as the Vlach Highlands, where impermeable rocks (shales and sandstones) have weathered into broad upland valleys and gently sloping hills (Fig. 15). To the east lies the main watershed of this northern

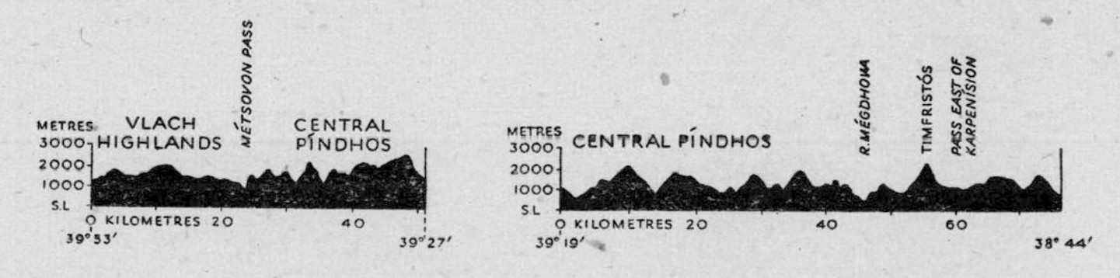

Fig. 14 A highland profile of northern Greece

Based on the 1 : 250,000 G.S.G.S., Series 48048: The Balkans. The vertical exaggeration is just over three times.

region, for the most part lower than the Vlach Highlands, but rising to the high Grámmos mountains (8,265 ft.) on the Albanian frontier.

The central region, lying between the Métsovon pass and Mt Timfristós, forms the Píndhos mountains proper. They are built largely of limestone and have an average width of some 20 miles. The eastern edge is comparatively straight, and is separated from the plain of Thessalía by a fairly continuous belt of foothills. The western edge, by contrast, is far from straight; limestone bastions stand out from the main range and fall in cliffs to the deep gorges of the Akhelóös and its tributaries.

The southern region, lying between Timfristós and the Gulf of Kórinthos, broadens to over 50 miles, for the main watershed bends south-eastwards and becomes parallel to the Gulf, while secondary ranges continue due south to the coast. The dominating heights are formed by the limestone blocks of Panaitolikón, Khelidhón and Vardhoúsia, between which lie belts of less impressive uplands, weathered from sandstones and slates. The whole region is exceedingly difficult to cross, for it is deeply cut by the winding affluents of the Mégdhova in the north, and tributaries of the Évinos and Mórnos in the south-west (Plate 4).

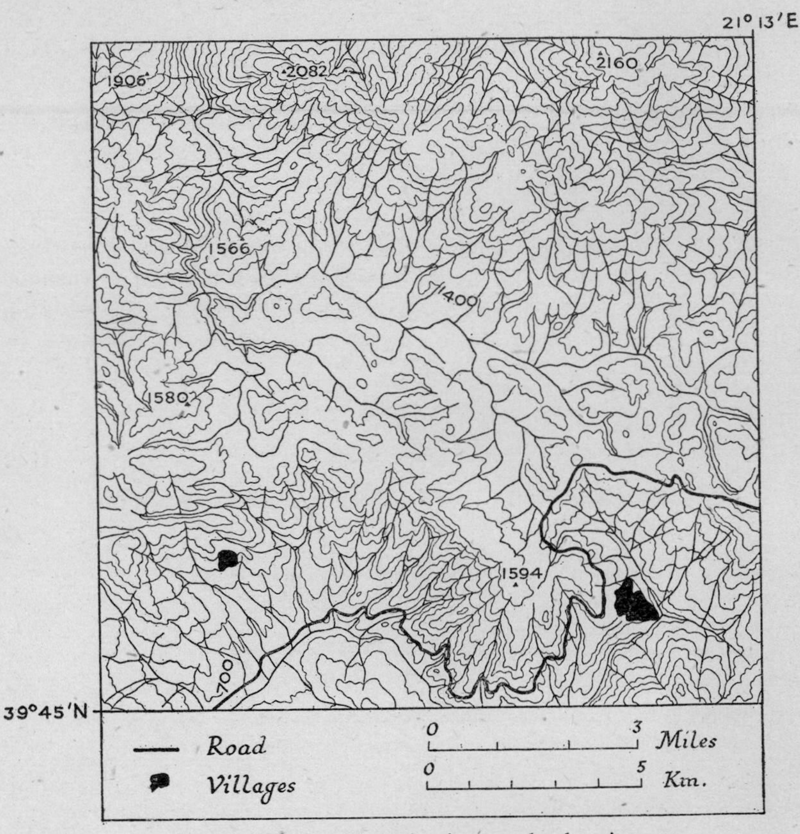

Fig. 15. Mature dissection in an upland region

Based on the 1 : 100,000 *Epitelikós Khártis tis Elládhos*, Ioánnina sheet, IV Z (1934).

The contour interval is 100 m. The area is part of the Vlach Highlands and contains the headwaters of rivers that flow respectively south-west to the Gulf of Amvrakía, north-west to Albania, and north-east to the Gulf of Thérmai. Each of these rivers begins its course in a comparatively broad upland valley, but later passes through several profound gorges.

B. Western Greece

(1) *The Ridges and Furrows of Ípiros* (Figs. 20, 21, 37 and 38)

Between the Albanian frontier and the Gulf of Amvrakía is the administrative region of Ípiros. For the most part it is peculiarly

Plate 13. Métsovon

Métsovon, in the northern Píndhos mountains, lies on the main route from Ioánnina to Kalabáka.

Plate 14. Mount Smólikas

The limestone pyramid of Smólikas rises to 8,636 ft. and dominates the Vlach Highlands to the south-east. The corrie, in shadow, is a typical feature of glaciated highlands. The photograph also shows the upper limit of fir forest.

Plate 15. Ioánnina

The plain of Ioánnina, with its lake, lies to the west of the Métsovon Pass. The basin is one of the most notable areas of subterranean drainage in northern Greece.

Plate 16. The plain of Mesolóngion

The flat and malarial lands near Mesolóngion are almost constantly flooded.

inhospitable, less because of its elevation, which is rarely above 6,000 ft., than because of its greatly varied relief. Outcrops of resistant limestone form parallel mountain chains, narrow, serrated, and with imposing precipices: between them, belts of sandstones, shales and slates form deep valleys, usually unsuitable for cultivation or for settlement.

Although there is a broad similarity of relief throughout the region, there are certain local variations upon the general pattern of ridge and furrow. In the north, beyond the river Thíamis, the ridges are higher than those to the south. On the other hand, the valleys are more open and inviting, communications are somewhat easier, and there has consequently been reciprocal penetration of this frontier region by Greeks and Albanians. The river Thíamis rises in the broad upland basin of Ioánnina, some 1,600 ft. above sea level; the lake of Ioánnina itself has no visible outlet, and is drained underground. In summer, when the lake contracts, large areas of moist, alluvial soils are left exposed for cultivation (Plate 15).

South of the Thíamis, the main rivers of Ípiros flow southwards to the Gulf of Amvrakía. The Árakhthos runs in gorges throughout its upper course, cut for the most part in impermeable rock. It therefore carries a tremendous load of detritus, which is constantly being laid down near its mouth. In this way the alluvial plain of Árta has been built up. The river Loúros also runs southwards to the gulf, but it flows in a deep valley through limestone and its waters are relatively clear. While this river has played little part in the building of the plain, it contributes to the swampy character of the lowland. Within recent years there has been considerable irrigation of the plain of Árta, and its flatness and fertility have produced a distinctive physical unit.

East of the Gulf of Amvrakía and the lowland of Árta, the land rises rapidly to a high plateau of sandstones and shales, deeply cut by the Akhelóös and its tributaries.

(2) *The Hills and Plains of Akarnanía* (Figs. 21, 22 and 38)

From the Gulf of Amvrakía in the north to the Gulf of Pátrai in the south, the province of Akarnanía presents five distinct types of countryside: (1) In the north-west is a limestone region, for the most part dry and barren, but in places yielding a cultivable soil. Its general level is little more than 2,000 ft. high, but in the centre it rises to 5,187 ft. (2) Southwards, the plateau gives way to broad and swampy lowlands, traversed by the rapid and silt-laden Akhelóös.

(3) In the north-east, limestones are still in evidence, but here they alternate with less resistant rocks, broken up by a multitude of impassable ravines. (4) In the south-east, the Arákinthos hills, just over 3,000 ft. in height, overlook the lagoons and marshes of Mesolóngion. (5) Finally, there is a complex depression, formed when the whole of this region was severely fractured in late Tertiary and Quaternary times. The main depression runs from the south-eastern corner of the Gulf of Amvrakía to the Mesolóngion lagoons, and contains lakes Amvrakía and Ozerós; a subsidiary trough lies to the north of the Arákinthos mountains and holds lakes Angelókastron and Trikhonís (Plate 31).

C. Central Greece

(1) *The Highlands of Voiotía and Attikí* (Figs. 24, 29, 40 and 45)

The physical characteristics of this region epitomize the geography of Greece. In the west are the massive limestones so characteristic of northern and western Greece; in the east are the crystalline rocks of more ancient times, representing the western margin of the old

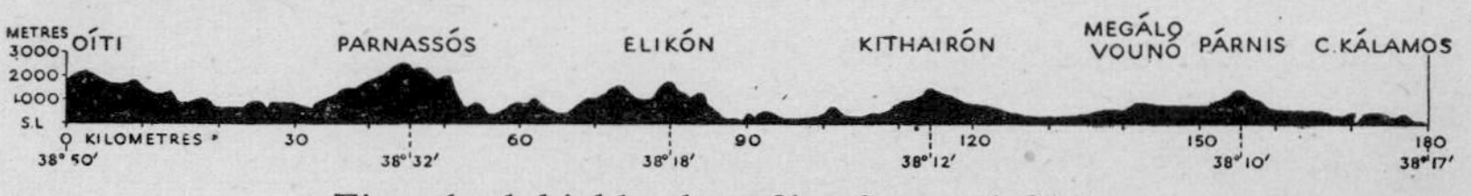

Fig. 16. A highland profile of central Greece

Based on the 1 : 250,000 G.S.G.S., Series 4088: The Balkans. The vertical exaggeration is just over three times. The profile has not been drawn in a continuous straight line; changes in direction are indicated where points of latitude are marked.

hard rocks of the Aegean. The trend of the mountains and coasts has largely been determined by faulting, and the gulfs and peninsulas are intricately locked.

The region is essentially a highland, not so much a continuous range of imposing heights as a series of separate mountain blocks. From Parnassós in the west, the series continues with few real gaps through Elikón, Kithairón and Párnis to the Gulf of Évvoia (Fig. 16). Even the lower blocks, with their bare rock surfaces and many bold cliffs, are impressive; and the whole line presents a long and somewhat winding escarpment to the north (Plate 17).

South of this line of limestone rocks comes the peninsula of Attikí, which structurally is a relic of the old blocks of eastern and north-eastern Greece. It was the crystalline marbles of this district that made possible the sculpture of ancient Athens; the main quarries were those of Pendelikón and Imittós. The less resistant rocks of this old block (usually schists and slates) form the lower regions, while the undulating plain of Mesóyia and the floor of the Kifisós valley are covered with Tertiary sediments. It was in the Kifisós valley that the city of Athens grew.

(2) *The Blocks and Basins of Voiotía and Fokís* (Figs. 30, 31 and 47)

To the north of the highlands of Voiotía and Attikí, the recent faulting has resulted in the close juxtaposition of plains and plateaux. From south to north these are the Kifissós valley, the mountains of Lokrís, the Sperkhiós valley, and the Óthris mountains; these last are continued into the island of Évvoia.

The river Kifissós is noteworthy in that it has no natural outlet to the sea. It flows through a highly productive and well-peopled valley, until it eventually enters the flat plain of Kopaïs; most of this plain was once occupied by Lake Kopaïs, but to-day its waters are led artificially through the small lakes of Ilikí and Paralímni to the sea. To the north of the Kifissós valley rise the steep cliffs of the Lokrís mountains, which are about 4,500 ft. above sea level. North of the Lokrís mountains is the great fault trough drained by the Sperkhiós, a remarkable feature, even on a small-scale map. The alluvial plain of this river, flanked by gently sloping fans and terraces, leads from the heart of central Greece to the Maliaic Gulf. This gulf, together with the Straits of Oreoí and Tríkeri, continues the line of the fault trough eastwards (Plate 18).

The highlands that bound the Sperkhiós valley to the north reach their highest point in the mountains of Óthris. Culminating in Mt Yerakovoúni (5,669 ft.) their rounded summits dominate the whole region. The highest land is built of limestone; but farther north, where slates and igneous rock crop out, there are rolling and even flat-topped plateaux some 3,000 ft. high. Chief of these are the Narthákion hills, rising to 3,316 ft.

Throughout the greater part of central and northern Évvoia, the mountain ranges lie almost parallel to the trend of the island. Many of them are typical limestone plateaux, cut by deep ravines. The greatest ranges are in the central part: the Pixariá mountains rise from the Aegean coast to 4,436 ft., and above them towers the pyramid of Mt Dhírfis, 5,726 ft. This bare peak, only 4 miles from the coast, has no mountain of similar height within 55 miles and is therefore an outstanding landmark. The narrow limestone mountains of Kandhílion present high precipices to the Gulf of Évvoia, and are continued northwards by the Xirón range.

The lowlands of Évvoia are mostly covered with late Tertiary sediments, and are rarely flat—here and there a small alluvial plain offers a richness of soil, unequalled elsewhere in the island.

D. Eastern Greece

Between the dividing mountains (A) and the Gulf of Thérmai is a region of ridge and furrow, similar in pattern to that of western Greece. In the west, howevever, the variations in relief are due to the erosion of folded rocks of unequal resistance, whereas in eastern Greece they are due to fracture and unequal uplift. There are, in all, two belts of highlands (D (2) and D (4)) and two of lowlands (D (1) and D (3)), trending from north-north-west to south-south-east, and roughly equal in length and in breadth. The high belts form almost continuous mountain ranges, while the low belts are interrupted here and there by sills or by bolder plateaux.

(1) *The Western Lowland Zone*

This narrow strip of lowland runs from Korçe (Koritza) in south-eastern Albania to the plains of Thessalía in central Greece. From the frontier to the small town of Karperón, the corridor is drained by the Aliákmon, a powerful river which has converted the once smooth floor of this lowland into a minutely dissected plain. Farther south the Khasiá plateau rises steeply to 4,000 ft., separating the drainage area of the Aliákmon from that of the Piniós, and providing the one serious barrier to communications throughout the region. The plain of Upper Thessalía is covered by alluvial deposits from the Piniós and its many tributaries, coarse-grained near the mountain rims, but merging into fine silts where the one-time marshes have been drained.

(2) *The Western Mountain Belt*

A series of high plateaux extends northward from the Gulf of Pagasaí to the shores of Lake Préspa on the frontier. In the south, the first of these uplands is not impressive, but beyond the Piniós defile there is a rapid rise to a massive and rolling plateau of ancient crystalline rocks. Farther north, beyond the gorge of the Aliákmon, the mountains gradually increase in altitude and in grandeur: their rugged sides rise precipitously to heights of over 6,000 ft., and the

Plate 17. Parnassós

The highest summit of Parnassós rises to 8,064 ft. at the southern end of a north-south ridge. The upper slopes are almost completely bare of vegetation, except for a few tufts of grass on which sheep are pastured in summer.

Plate 18. The gorge of the Asopós in the Oíti mountains

The high limestone mountains of Oíti rise abruptly from the flat floor of the Sperkhiós valley, seen in the distance.

Plate 19. Lacustrine beds of clays and marls

These easily eroded rocks fringe the damp plain, known as the 'Lake Corridor', that stretches from Thessaloníki to the Gulf of Strimón. The corridor is bounded by smooth plateaux of crystalline rocks. The bush cover is pseudo-maquis.

Plate 20. The plain of Almopía (Enotia)

The plain of Almopía, in Pélla, is backed by the eroded fault-scarp of the Páïkon mountains. Mountain rimmed plains are common throughout north-eastern Greece.

whole region forms a formidable barrier to communication. Nevertheless, there are two low passes, that of Siátista (2,250 ft.), and in the north, Klisoúra (3,800 ft.). The last pass in Greece, Pisodhérion, lies just to the west of Flórina, and from it the imposing Baba Range crosses into Yugoslavia.

(3) *The Eastern Lowland Zone*

From Bitolj in Yugoslavia southwards to the plain of Lárisa there is a remarkable series of lowlands, providing a comparatively easy route-way between the two countries. The lowlands are not continuous, but form a series of five major basins, separated from each other by thresholds of varying heights. The most northerly is the basin of Flórina, drained through the Monastir Gap to Yugoslavia. Next come the basins of Eordhaía, which at one time must have been occupied by a lake of considerable size. To-day, only vestiges of this lake remain, in the numerous isolated lakes and marshes. Farther south is the transverse vale of the Aliákmon, bounded by the abrupt slopes of the Kamvoúnia and Piéria mountains. These in turn overlook the basin of Elassón, drained southwards through a series of deep gorges to the plain of Lárisa. This last lowland is one of the greatest and most important in peninsular Greece. Although nearly flat it contains several minor depressions below the general level of the plain, evidence of the unequal subsidence which affected the whole of this region. One of these minor depressions holds the residual lake Voïviïs which receives the overflow of the Piniós.

(4) *The Eastern Mountain Belt* (Figs. 31, 32, 47 and 48)

Bordering the Gulf of Thérmai is an almost continuous belt of highlands, throughout which there are considerable variations of relief. These differences are due mainly to the various degrees of upheaval that followed upon the fractures of late Tertiary and Quaternary times. The ranges are lowest in the south, where they form the peninsula of Magnísia. Here the gently rounded summits again provide evidence of the old mature surface, and they are markedly different from the steep fractured slopes that descend to the sea. The graceful Mt Pílion (5,308 ft.) and the limestone pyramid of Óssa (6,409 ft.) dominate the landscape farther north. Beyond the vale of Témbi, cut through the coastal mountains by the river Piniós, are the broader ranges of Ólimbos. Ólimbos, itself (9,571 ft.), is the highest peak in Greece, rising abruptly from the narrow coastal plain in a great fault-scarp (Plate 3). From it there stretches to the north a remarkably continuous mountain barrier, which gradually trends away from the coast. The widest part of this barrier is formed by the ancient crystalline rocks of the Piéria mountains, over 6,000 ft. in height, which overlook the almost inaccessible gorge of the Aliákmon. Northwards, the younger limestones of the Vérmion mountains rise abruptly from the broad plain of Kambanía to a high, barren plateau. The three towns of Véroia, Náousa and Édhessa have grown up on interesting sites. They lie at the junction of mountain and plain, on terraces of calcium carbonate, known as calc-sinter. These terraces, which are steadily growing higher, have been built by deposition from the rivers cascading down the steep slopes of the limestone plateau.

E. North-eastern Greece (Figs. 33–5 and 49–51)

North-eastern Greece is made up of a series of plains and plateaux, which have been formed by the differential fracturing of the old crystalline rocks. The intricacies of the fracturing can be gauged from the curious shapes of the peninsula of Khalkidhikí. The tilted plateau blocks have relatively smooth surfaces, which vary in height from less than 3,000 ft. in Khalkidhikí to over 7,000 ft. in the Alí Butús mountains on the northern frontier. The straight edges of the plateaux drop steeply to the plains, but their regularity is broken by ravines and gullies; they form, in fact, dissected fault scarps. The borders of the uplands of Khalkidhikí, Pangaíon, Kroúsia and Belashitsa all show this abrupt descent into the plain. Structurally, the island of Thásos is a similar block to Pangaíon, surrounded by sea instead of alluvium. North of Dráma the fractured blocks do not form such distinctive entities, but merge into the general mass of the Rodhópi mountains.

The plains which lie between these blocks are covered by recent deposits, laid down by the five great rivers of northern Greece. In the west, the deep and clear Aliákmon and the more turgid Axiós flow through the Kambanía of Thessaloníki. Here, the lake of Yiannitsá with its surrounding marshes once occupied a considerable area, but this has now been drained to provide land for the settlement of refugees from Turkey. Farther to the east is the plain built up by the Strimón, a broad, swift-flowing river which enters Greece at the Rúpel Pass. Here, too, marshes and the one-time lake Akhinós have been converted into rich agricultural land. The Strimón valley is connected to the plain of Dráma by the narrow fault trough trenched by the Angítis. Still more to the east are the broad coastal lowlands of Dhitikí Thráki which form two distinct regions, the plain of Xánthi to the west, drained by the Néstos, and the plain of Komotiní to the east. Finally, the Évros with its low, marshy valley, forms the frontier with Turkey (Plates 7, 24).

F. The Pelopónnisos

The Pelopónnisos, with an area of 8,356 sq. miles (21,643 sq. km.), is for the most part a region of wild and rugged highlands of limestone, fringed on the north and west by a zone of sandstone foothills and by a narrow coastal plain. The folds of the peninsula have been cut off from those of central Greece by the great fractures which produced the Gulfs of Pátrai and Kórinthos. Strabo described the Pelopónnisos as a plane leaf, in which the mountains form the ribs of the leaf, the southern gulfs the indentations of its edge, and the promontory between Pátrai and Aíyion the stalk attachment.

The lowlands are few and isolated, but there are a number of enclosed upland plains. Most of these contain variable lakes due to imperfect subterranean drainage (e.g. the basin of Trípolis). The division of the Pelopónnisos into three physical units (Fig. 13) is based largely upon the great structural depression (F (2)), drained by the Alfiós and the Evrótas. To the east of this depression are the northern and eastern highlands (F (1)), to the west, the south-western highlands and the plain of Messinía (F (3)).

(1) *The Northern and Eastern Highlands* (Figs. 23, 24, 28, 40 and 44)

The great belt of highlands, parallel to the Gulf of Kórinthos, includes the three limestone massifs of Erímanthos (Olonós), Aroánia (Khelmós) and Killíni (Zíria), all of which are over 7,000 ft. high. The northern face of the mountains towers high above the gulf, and is perhaps the most imposing escarpment in Greece. The river valleys of the region are short and steep, for the most part flowing directly to the sea, and carving profound ravines into the highland.

The highland peninsula of Argolís is a limestone plateau, its rolling summits rising to over 3,600 ft., its surface pitted by sinkholes and small basins, and its sides cleft by deep gorges. At the broad south-eastern end of the peninsula, the Adhéres hills are made of sandstone, flanked on the north by the lava dome of Méthana, and on the south by the limestone islands of Ídhra and Dhokós.

The backbone of the eastern highlands is formed by the long ridges of Maínalon and Málevon which run south-south-east in heights reaching well over 6,000 ft. They broaden at places into extensive plateaux, highest in the central Pelopónnisos where the general altitude is about 4,000 ft. Most of this region is deeply cut into by an elaborate system of valleys, but the remarkable basin of Trípolis is an exception, and forms one of the largest areas without superficial drainage in Greece.

(2) *The Central Corridor and North-western Pelopónnisos* (Figs. 25, 39 and 41)

The great structural depression that divides the highlands of south-western Pelopónnisos from those to the north-east is drained by the Alfiós to the north and the Evrótas to the south. In Pliocene times much of the floor of this corridor was submerged, in part by the sea and in part by several large lakes. The sediments of these remain to-day in the river basins. It was only after the most remarkable changes that the Alfiós developed its present drainage basin, and became the largest river in the peninsula (Fig. 17).

North of the Alfiós are the comparatively broad plains of Ilía, which are separated from the high limestone regions of Akhaïa by ranges of foot-hills, some 2,000 ft. high. The coast has been formed by festoons of sand bars topped by dunes, and behind this shield the rivers have laid down their load as a flat coastal plain.

(3) *The South-western Highlands and the Plain of Messinía* (Figs. 26, 27, 42 and 43)

The south-western highlands fall into three main regions; in the east, the high chain of Taïyetos, continued by the peninsula of Máni; in the west, the hill groups extending into the peninsula of Messinía; and finally the hills north of the peninsula.

The Taïyetos range is a narrow ridge of crystalline rocks, rising abruptly on its faulted eastern edge to over 7,000 ft. The western face is less steep, climbing from a coastal terrace to a tangle of hills, before the last ascent to the finely sculptured crest. The peninsula of Messinía is essentially a low platform standing less than 1,000 ft. above sea level; from this platform, hill masses rise to heights of over 3,000 ft. The third highland region lies to the north, and rises to 4,659 ft. in its highest summit, Tetráyi.

The basin of Messinía comprises two plains: the larger, southern plain is marked by faulted terrace lands, between which are the ill-

Plate 21. Highlands north of Sérrai

The view from the Acropolis in Sérrai looks north over a maturely dissected plateau. To the south is the recently drained plain of the Strimón.

Plate 22. Alistráti, on the road from Sérrai to Dráma

The main road from Sérrai enters the plain of Dráma at the small town of Alistráti, at the south-eastern foot of the Menoíkion range.

Plate 23. The Erímanthos in the dry season

The Erímanthos flows south across impermeable rocks to join the Alfiós. When stripped of their vegetation, these rocks are rapidly eroded and present finely chiselled slopes. The turgid flood waters of the river leave the bed clogged with detritus.

Plate 24. The mouth of the Évros (Maritsa)

The Turkish port of Enez stands on the east bank of the Évros. The grass fringing the water is *Phragmites*, commonly found in wet places in England.

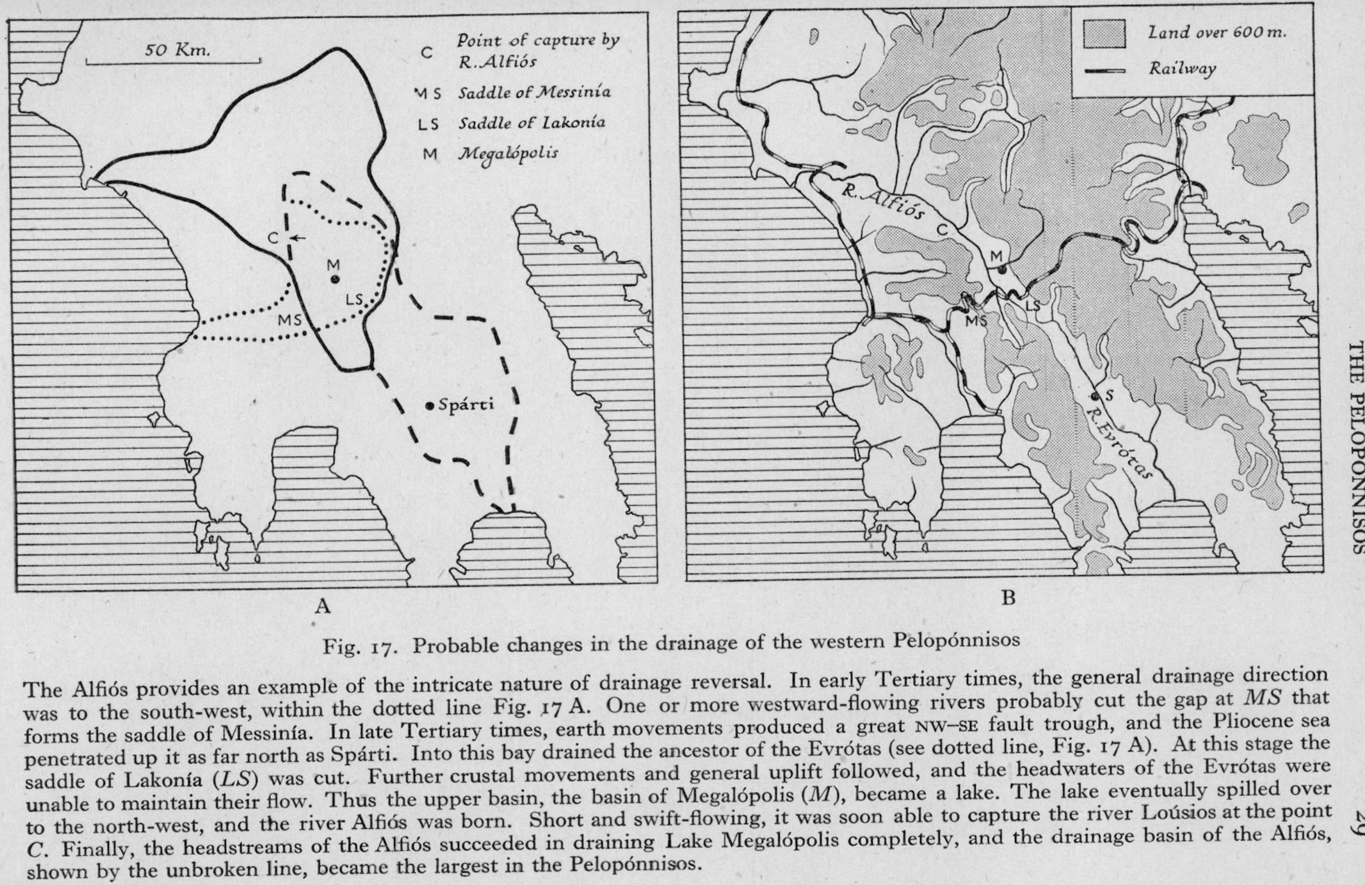

Fig. 17. Probable changes in the drainage of the western Pelopónnisos

The Alfiós provides an example of the intricate nature of drainage reversal. In early Tertiary times, the general drainage direction was to the south-west, within the dotted line Fig. 17 A. One or more westward-flowing rivers probably cut the gap at *MS* that forms the saddle of Messinía. In late Tertiary times, earth movements produced a great NW–SE fault trough, and the Pliocene sea penetrated up it as far north as Spárti. Into this bay drained the ancestor of the Evrótas (see dotted line, Fig. 17 A). At this stage the saddle of Lakonía (*LS*) was cut. Further crustal movements and general uplift followed, and the headwaters of the Evrótas were unable to maintain their flow. Thus the upper basin, the basin of Megalópolis (*M*), became a lake. The lake eventually spilled over to the north-west, and the river Alfiós was born. Short and swift-flowing, it was soon able to capture the river Loúsios at the point *C*. Finally, the headstreams of the Alfiós succeeded in draining Lake Megalópolis completely, and the drainage basin of the Alfiós, shown by the unbroken line, became the largest in the Pelopónnisos.

drained alluvial flats of the river Pámisos; the smaller, northern plain is flanked by steep limestone hills from the base of which numerous springs emerge.

The Ionian Islands

The Ionian islands lie off the west coast of Greece, and are closely related in structure to the folded mountains of Ípiros. For the most part they are composed of limestone, which is primarily responsible for the mountainous nature of so much of their surface. Elsewhere, the less resistant rocks known as *Flysch* (see p. 3) are exposed, especially in the regions of low hill country. Finally, on the narrow coastal plains and in the small river valleys there are deposits of young Tertiary material.

There are five principal islands. In the north is Kérkira (Corfu), with the greatest extent of lowland, but rising in the north to Mt Pandokrátor, 3,000 ft. above sea level. Levkás (Santa Maura), almost attached to the mainland of Akarnanía, is much more mountainous. The highest peak, Stavrotós, is 3,744 ft. in height, and the high western edge of the island falls abruptly to the sea. Kefallinía (Cephalonia), the largest island of the group, lies opposite the entrance to the Gulf of Pátrai. Irregular in outline, and wholly mountainous in character, its most magnificent scenery is in the south, where the forest-clad slopes of Aínos rise to 5,315 ft. Off the north-eastern coast is the dry and rocky island of Itháki (Ithaca), the legendary home of Odysseus (Ulysses). Lastly, Zákinthos (Zante) lies off the north-western coast of the Pelopónnisos. In its western half a broad limestone belt of highland rises to a maximum altitude of 2,768 ft. and contrasts strongly with the lowlying country to the east.

The Thracian Islands

In the northern Aegean are the four islands of Thásos, Samothráki, Límnos and Áyios Evstrátios. The first two are outlying fragments of north-eastern Greece. Thásos is a picturesque mountain mass of marble and schist, rising to 3,419 ft., with steep, fir-clad slopes and a bare crest. There are, however, narrow strips of fertile coastal plain, especially in the north-west. Samothráki (Samothrace) is chiefly composed of volcanic material and rises steeply to a rocky peak, 5,249 ft. in height. Límnos and Áyios Evstrátios are the visible fragments of the submarine ridge that runs north-eastwards from the Northern Sporádhes. The desolate nature of the low and almost featureless interior of Límnos is partly offset by the magnificent harbour of Moúdhros on the south coast. Áyios Evstrátios (Ai Strati) is only 20 sq. miles in area and consists of a low range of wooded hills, dissected by well-watered valleys.

The Northern Sporádhes

These islands fall into two main groups. In the north is a narrow chain of five main islands: Skíathos, Skópelos, Iliodhrómia, Pélagos and Yioúra, the largest of which is only 36 sq. miles in area. They repeat the crystalline character of the mountainous peninsula of Magnisía, and their steep and indented coasts usually climb to a rugged interior. There are, however, fertile and sheltered valleys, especially in Skíathos and Skópelos. The second group of islands lies to the south, and consists of Skíros and numerous islets and rocks. Skíros, famous for its marble, has an area of 80 sq. miles; in the south it is barren and mountainous, rising to 2,671 ft., but farther north there are pine-covered hills and small fertile plains.

The Kikládhes (Cyclades)

To the Ancient Greeks, the many islands of the Kikládhes were regarded as a circle arranged around the sacred island of Dhílos, but to the geologist they are seen as the seaward continuation of the mountains of central Greece. Thus, the mountains of southern Évvoia are continued through the northern chain of islands, Ándros, Tínos and Míkonos, with Yioúra, Síros and Dhílos as southerly fragments of this arc. Farther south the mountains of Attikí are continued seawards through Kéa, Kíthnos, Sérifos, Sífnos, Amorgós, and so on to the Dodecanese. Outlying fragments of this southern chain are the large islands of Páros and Náxos to the north, and the small islands of Folégandros, Síkinos, Íos and Anáfi to the south. Both chains are made up of very diverse material, but they are chiefly composed of ancient crystalline rocks such as marble, granite, gneiss, and schists. Finally, on the southern rim of these old hard rocks is a line of volcanic activity, curving south-eastwards from the Méthana peninsula in the Saronic Gulf, through the island of Mílos, to the still active vent of the Kaïméni islands in the explosion crater of Thíra.

The Northern Chain

Ándros, the second largest island in the Kikládhes, has an area of 146 sq. miles. Its straight south-western coast rises abruptly to a high limestone ridge (3,199 ft.), from which four great spurs extend north-eastwards. Tínos is a continuation of Ándros to the south-east, but is much lower and flatter in outline. Míkonos is a dry and barren plateau of granite with an extremely irregular outline. Yioúra, Síros and Dhílos are small and infertile, but the central position of Síros and its port of Ermoúpolis have brought considerable wealth to the island (Plate 26).

The Southern Chain

Kéa rises steeply to 1,876 ft. in well-wooded slopes, but like Kíthnos and Sérifos to the south it has little scenic value or fertility. Sífnos, on the other hand, has a small and highly cultivated plain in the south-east. Amorgós, much farther to the east, has a long narrow ridge as its central backbone, rising in its eastern end to 2,562 ft. There are, however, numerous small plains on the indented north coast. Páros, famous in antiquity for its marble quarries, rises from a fertile maritime plain in the north to three central peaks, one of which is 2,530 ft. above sea level. Farther to the east is the island of Náxos, the largest of the Kikládhes and 170 sq. miles in area. The dominating peak is Mt Zevs (3,294 ft.), which rises in bare, towering crags from the central mountain range. In the west and north-west of the island there are low, rolling hills and broad, fertile plains. Náxos is famous for its emery, or corundum, the hardest known material after diamond, and the close proximity of this mineral to the marble of Páros may well have been critical in the history of sculpture. To the south of the southern chain, the small islands of Folégandros, Síkinos, Íos and Anáfi are composed chiefly of bare marble, rising to mountainous interiors from bold and inhospitable coasts.

The Volcanic Rim

Mílos is shaped like an irregular ring, broken on the north coast by a channel that leads to the central bay. The island is built of young volcanic material overlying ancient crystalline rocks, and it rises from marshy and lowlying plains in the east to a height of 2,536 ft. Thíra (Santorin) is a crescent-shaped island, bare and waterless, which towers above the great basin that once formed the centre of

Plate 25. Límnos
The view shows the eastern harbour of Kástron, looking from the fort.

Plate 26. Síros (Ermoúpolis)
The church of Saint George, at an altitude of 590 ft., crowns the older and higher part of the town. Ermoúpolis is the chief island port of the Aegean.

Plate 27. Párga

Párga is one of the few ports on the coast of Ípiros. The citadel is built on a limestone promontory that separates two small bays.

Plate 28. The Straits of Préveza

The shallow straits, now less than 1,000 yards wide, lead into the Gulf of Amvrakía (Árt
from the Ionian Sea.

the volcano. Within the basin are the active Kaïméni or 'Burnt' Islands.

THE ISLANDS OF THE EASTERN AEGEAN

The three large islands of Lésvos, Khíos and Sámos lie near the coast of Asia Minor and are detached portions of the peninsulas of that country. Lésvos, often called Mitilíni, has a variety of structure, with bare volcanic rocks in the west, and ancient metamorphic rocks in the centre and east. It has an area of 627 sq. miles, and most of its surface is a confused and rather featureless mass of hills. The highest point, 3,214 ft., is in the south-east, but towards the west the country becomes gentler and lower. Khíos, 320 sq. miles in area, is built mainly of shales and limestone, but in the south-east there is an outcrop of young Tertiary rocks. The island is crossed from north to south by a high, broken range which reaches a maximum altitude of 4,156 ft. in Mt Pelinaíon. Spurs, valleys and wide undulating plateaux descend from this range to a narrow coastal plain. Sámos, 193 sq. miles in area, is composed mainly of crystalline schists and limestone, which give rise to wild, mountainous country. In the east, however, Tertiary sediments are dominant, and the landscape changes to one of low hills and plains.

There are, in addition, the small island of Psará off the north-west coast of Khíos, the elongated and mountainous island of Ikaría south-west of Sámos, and finally, the almost uninhabited group of Foúrnoi islets between Ikaría and Sámos.

KRÍTI (CRETE)

Kríti, with an area of 3,200 sq. miles, is by far the largest of the Aegean Islands and the fifth largest in the Mediterranean, being somewhat smaller than Corsica. The island owes its fundamental structure to the Alpine earth storm, its height to the vigorous upheavals of late geological time, and its strikingly bold scenery to the wide development of limestone. In structure and landscape, therefore, it is closely related to western and southern Greece.

The relief consists mainly of four mountainous areas, which resemble four islands when seen from a distance. From west to east these are the Lévka Óri or White Mountains, rising to 7,904 ft., Mount Ídhi (Ida), 8,195 ft. and the highest point in the island, Dhíkti Óri, 7,166 ft., and the less impressive Sitía mountains, 4,851 ft. They have many features in common. The amount of upheaval was greatest in the south, and the result is that these highland masses present an abrupt slope to the almost harbourless south coast, while to the north the land falls in a succession of terraces and comparatively gentle valleys to the indented coast. Secondly, the mountains are composed mainly of limestones, and the deforested and soilless surface is exposed to the weather. Rapid weathering of the bare rock has resulted in serrated crests and huge litters of sharp boulders below the cliffs. There are also the many features due to solution—caves of all sizes and shapes, unroofed caverns forming impassable ravines (some of those leading down to the south coast are nearly 3,000 ft. in depth), and enclosed depressions that vary from small sink-holes to large flat-floored plains surrounded by high precipices. The best examples of these circular depressions are the plain of Omalós, in the Lévka Óri region, the Nídha plain just south of Mount Ídhi, and the plain of Lasíthi north-west of the high crests of Dhíkti Óri.

The limestones rest with a gently domed structure upon a great variety of older rocks, all of them impermeable. These mica-schists, slates, shales, quartzites and sandstones are not widely exposed, except in the western and eastern ends of the island, but they are everywhere responsible for bringing a liberal supply of water to the surface on the lower slopes.

The lowlands of Kríti are largely covered by sediments of the Pliocene Sea, but even in these areas isolated outcrops of limestone are frequent, and the smoothness of the plain is broken. Moreover, the weak sediments are deeply cut into by numerous streams, so that throughout the island the low, flat land is limited to small alluvial plains near the north coast, and to one greater strip, the Mesará, in the south. Curiously enough, the plain of Mesará forms the watershed between the two largest rivers in the island, the Yeropótamos draining west, and the Anapodháris draining south-east.

BIBLIOGRAPHICAL NOTE

1. The fullest general and modern account of the physical features of Greece is found in Otto Maull, *Länderkunde von Südeuropa* (Leipzig u. Wien, 1930), which is vol. XXVI of the *Enzyklopädie der Erdkunde*. This contains a full bibliography and references to previous research. Less complete descriptions are to be found in:

(*a*) M. I. Newbigin, *Southern Europe* (London, 1932).

(*b*) J. Sion et Y. Chataigneau, *Méditerranée Péninsules Méditerranéennes* (Paris, 1934) which forms vol. VII, part 2, of the *Géographie Universelle*.

2. Works dealing with the Greek coasts are given in the bibliographical note to Chapter II, p. 77.

Plate 29. The north-east coast of the Gulf of Amvrakía (Árta)
The steep and uninviting slopes of Makrinorós are covered with Valona oak forests.

Plate 30. Vónitsa Bay
The bay is in the south-west of the Gulf of Amvrakía. The fort, shown in the foreground, stands on a rocky hill, immediately west of the town. The view looks north-west.

Plate 31. Lake Amvrakía and the Gulf of Amvrakía

This infra-red photograph shows the northern end of the great depression that leads from the Mesolóngion lagoons to the south-eastern corner of the Gulf of Amvrakía. In the distance are the highlands of north-western Greece, visible to the Albanian frontier.

Plate 32. The northern entrance to the Levkás Channel

The mainland coast, in the foreground, is only separated from the island of Levkás by narrow mud banks. The dredged channel is navigable by vessels drawing 14 ft.

Chapter II

COASTS

General Features: Ípiros: The Gulf of Amvrakía: The West Coast of Aitolía and Akarnanía: The Gulf of Pátrai: The Gulf of Kórinthos: The West Coast of the Pelopónnisos: The Gulf of Messinía: The Gulf of Lakonía: The Gulf of Argolís: The Saronic Gulf: The Gulf of Petalioí and the Southern Gulf of Évvoia: The Northern Gulf of Évvoia: The Maliaic Gulf, Oreoí and Tríkeri Straits: The Gulf of Pagasaí (Vólos): The Western shores of the Gulf of Thérmai: Khalkidhikí: South-eastern Makedhonía and Dhitikí Thráki: Bibliographical Note

General Features

In geologically recent times, there was a great subsidence of the land over large areas of south-eastern Europe, accompanied by a corresponding encroachment of the sea. To this are due the irregular coastline of Greece, with its many gulfs, and the countless islands and sunken rocks of the Aegean. Thus the Kikládhes are simply the continuation, out to sea, of the mountain chains of the mainland. Even to-day, the process of subsidence is not complete; earthquakes are still common along the coasts of Greece, and while they may not lead to displacements of great size, they recur with considerable frequency (Fig. 5 and Plate 1).

The coasts, owing their origin to so recent a submergence, have not been modified to any great extent by subsequent wave erosion and weathering. Cliffs, therefore, which are the result of long-continued erosion by the sea, are not a common feature of the Greek coasts, although bold and rocky headlands are frequent. Moreover, the coastal mountains are mainly composed of limestone, a resistant rock which has largely withstood wave attack.

A broad distinction can be made between the coasts of eastern and southern Greece, the coast of western Greece, and the coast east of the Khalkidhikí peninsula. In eastern and southern Greece—the only part of the country where lowlands of any extent come down to the sea—the coast is dissected and island-fringed in a fashion unique in Mediterranean Europe. The submergence of the land has formed deep gulfs and peninsulas of fantastic shape: the gulfs are continued landwards into plains, and conversely, the mountain ridges of the interior can be followed into the peninsulas bounding the sunken areas. Thus the Gulf of Thérmai leads into the lowlands of Kambanía, the Maliaic Gulf into the plain of the Sperkhiós, and the Taíyetos and Párnon ranges of southern Greece are prolonged into finger-like peninsulas (Fig. 1). The islands, in harmony with the increasing dissection of the mainland coasts, become more numerous as one passes southwards, and tend to direct coastal traffic along certain well-defined lines.

In western Greece, however, the coast follows, or is only slightly transverse to, the trend of the high Píndhos mountains, and although broken by the Gulfs of Amvrakía and Pátrai, the Ionian shores are for the most part regular and inhospitable. Moreover, they look out beyond the few Ionian islands to an island-free sea. In the western Pelopónnisos this regularity of shoreline has not been achieved by fracturing and subsidence, but by the smoothing action of waves and currents upon detritus. Here, sand dunes, backed by lagoons, attain their fullest development in Greece; and to-day, as in ancient time, the shoreline has little significance in the lives of the people.

East of Khalkidhikí, the coasts of Makedhonía and Dhitikí Thráki are smooth and almost harbourless, lacking both the variety of promontory and bay so characteristic of the southern Aegean shores and also the rugged boldness of Ípiros. It is nevertheless true that when this northern coast first foundered, great inlets appeared and the coast was much more broken than it is to-day; but it was in these troughs that subsequent deposition was most rapid, and they now represent marshy lowlands between ancient plateaux.

To the Greeks, the sea has always been the natural medium of travel, uniting diverse and widely separate regions. Roads across the high and mountainous country are almost all of very poor quality, and even the better roads are but second or third class by western European standards. The *Routes Nationales* are few, but fit for motor traffic; the tracks are many, but for the most part fit only for mules. The difficult gradients of the interior, and the lack of adequate finances, have also limited the construction of railways.

This chapter is concerned only with the coasts of the mainland and of closely neighbouring islands. For convenience, the coast is divided into seventeen sections (Fig. 18), each of which is treated under three headings: (1) general description, (2) detailed description, (3) communications.

The coasts of the Greek islands are described in vol. III.

(1) ÍPIROS (EPIRUS)

General Description (Figs. 20, 37)

The main features of the north-west coast of Greece have been determined by the subsidiary ranges of the Píndhos mountains, whose imposing and well-defined chains are visible from a very

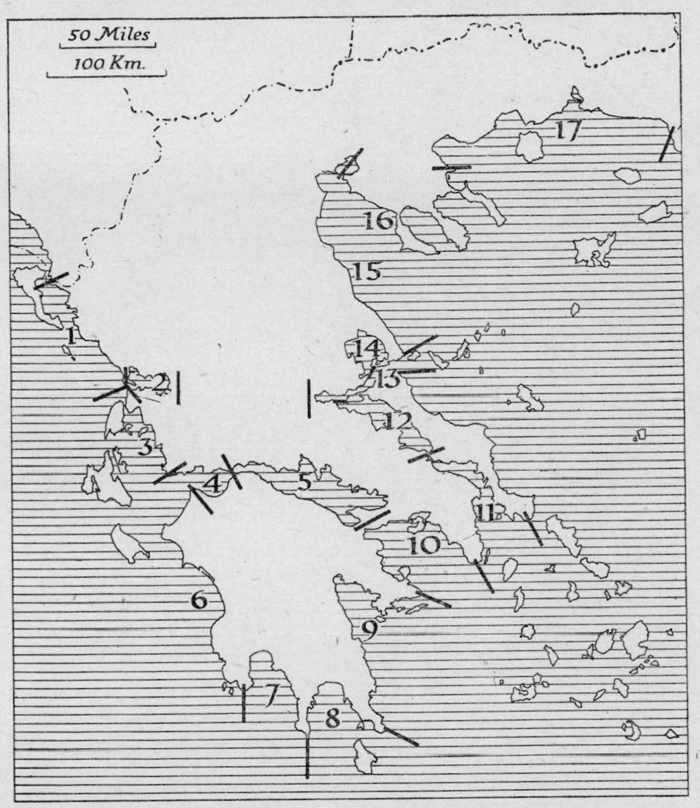

Fig. 18. A key map to coastal descriptions

considerable distance out to sea. These ridges run almost parallel to the coast, and since they are little inferior in height to the main range, they present most formidable barriers to communication inland (Fig. 20). Throughout the region the land is unproductive, sparsely populated, and ill-provided with roads.

For the most part the coast is steep and rocky, without any good landing places, but here and there the submergence of transverse valleys has resulted in bays. The formation of deltas has considerably reduced the size and depth of the more sheltered of these bays, so that even here, quays and piers at which vessels of any size can get alongside are rarely to be found. Fortunately, the prevailing calm of the sea facilitates the landing of goods and passengers from small boats.

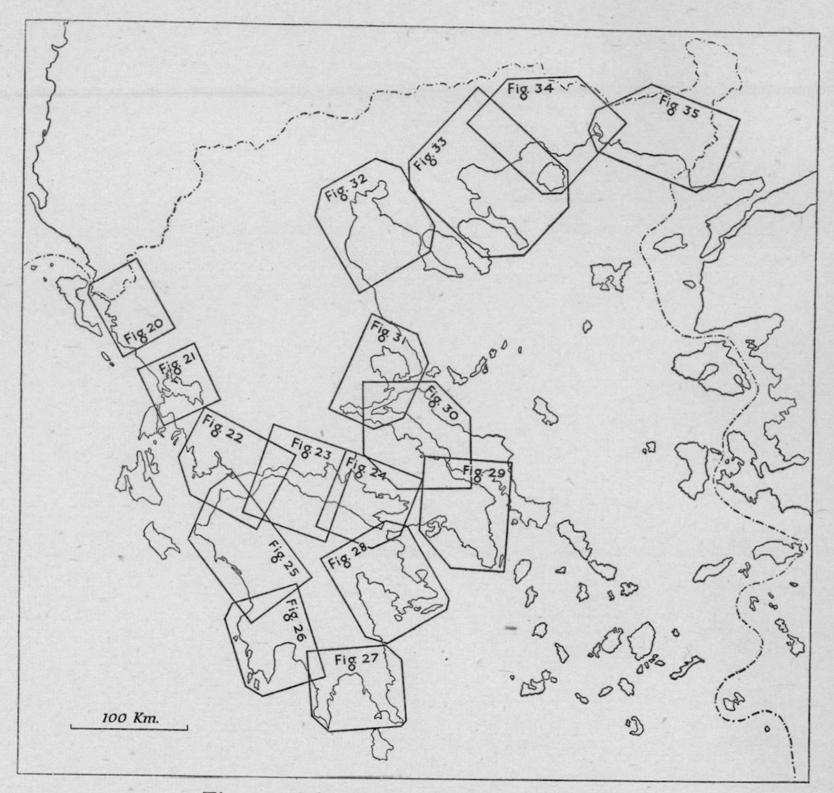

Fig. 19. A key map to landscape diagrams

The series of landscape diagrams, Figs. 20–35, have been based chiefly upon the 1 : 100,000 *Epitelikós Khártis tis Elládhos* (Athínai, 1925–). Information has also been obtained from Greek and British Admiralty charts, from G.S.G.S. 1 : 250,000, Series 4088: The Balkans, and from numerous photographs. The vertical exaggeration is approximately 2½ times.

Detailed Description

From the low promontory of Cape Stílos on the Albanian side of the frontier to Sayiádha Bay, 12 miles to the south-east, the coast is rocky, steep and indented. Offshoots from the main limestone ridge come down to the sea, forming bold promontories, and giving shelter to the partially enclosed bays. For example, the promontory

Plate 33. The north-west coast of Levkás

The bare limestone ridges of western Levkás have been strongly attacked by wave action, resulting in sea cliffs.

Plate 34. Cape Doukatón

The bold promontory of Doukatón ends the almost unbroken line of sea cliffs along the west coast of Levkás.

Plate 35. The Gulf of Zavérdha

The flat and well-cultivated plain at the head of the gulf leads northwards to Vónitsa on the Gulf of Amvrakía. The small port of Pálairos lies on the eastern, or far, side of the plain.

Plate 36. Astakós Bay (Dragoméstі)

Astakós Bay is the most southerly of the mountain rimmed bays on the coast of Akarnanía.

that ends in Cape Stílos protects the irregular inlet of Port Fteliá, and some 5 miles to the south-east, a hook-shaped peninsula shelters Port Paganiá from all but westerly winds. Sayiádha Bay is also open to the west, and on the flat strip of shoreland at its head is the first settlement of importance on the Greek coast.

South of Sayiádha the mountains are farther inland, and the coast is formed by the deltaic and partially cultivated plain of the river Thíamis. Yet even here the villages lie at some distance from the sea, for the shores are too marshy for settlement and the sea is too shallow for any but the smallest craft. South of the delta, the limestone ridges again approach the coast, running out north-westwards as lofty peninsulas. Thus the promontory, which drops from 1,100 ft. in bluff and wooded slopes to Kodramoúrto Point, separates the fine sandy bay of Igoumenítsa in the north from Platariá Bay in the south.

From the thickly wooded island of Sívota and the neighbouring islet of Áyios Nikólaos, the coast resumes its south-easterly trend to Préveza over 40 miles away; and since it runs more or less parallel to the folds of the Píndhos mountains, there are few indentations of any importance. Although the coastal ranges rise steeply to heights of over 1,500 ft., their forested sides have a more gentle appearance than the bare, dissected slopes of the northern ridges. Occasional tiny bays, each with its strip of sandy shore, offer some shelter to small craft: the most important are Moúrtos, Pérdhika and Aríla, but apart from Moúrtos, the associated villages lie slightly inland.

To the east of the bold promontory of Cape Keládhio is Port Párga, with its citadel commanding the bays on either side (Plate 27). Both are suitable only for small vessels, and of the two, the eastern is the better. Exports of tobacco, fruit, olives and wine come from the fertile valleys which here converge upon the sea. A further 3 miles to the east, bold limestone hills rise abruptly from the rock-girt shores of Áyios Ioánnis Bay, and southwards, low red cliffs continue to the small bay of Fanári where the rivers Akhéron and Kokkitós enter the sea by a common mouth.

The coast is rocky for some distance southwards from Fanári, and then small headlands separate sandy beaches, as far south as Cape Kastrosikiá. Coastal ranges tower behind, culminating in peaks over 3,000 ft. high. From the low red bluff of Kastrosikiá to Cape Mítika, the highlands are not such a pronounced feature of the landscape, and the smooth line of the intervening bight is backed only by a low chain of hills (Fig. 38). South from Mítika the olive-clad slopes come down gently to low cliffs and a sandy beach, while the whole shoreline to the Straits of Préveza is fringed with a continuous chain of rocks.

Communications

Roads. Two major roads lead inland from the coast, and are alone suitable for motor traffic in all weather. The more northerly runs from Igoumenítsa to Ioánnina (60 miles), and for the most part follows the winding course of the Thíamis: the more southerly runs from Préveza via Néa Filippiás (27 miles) to Árta, crossing the marshy ground of the Loúros by means of a causeway. A branch from this second route runs north-westwards to Ioánnina. In addition, there are roads possible in dry weather for light cars from Sayiádha to Filiátes (10 miles) and from Párga to Paramithiá (9 miles). The many good roads on the island of Kérkira date from the British occupation (1814–64).

Railways. None.

(2) THE GULF OF AMVRAKÍA (ÁRTA)

General Description (Figs. 21, 38)

The Gulf of Amvrakía is an enclosed depression, some 20 miles long and 13 miles wide, with a low irregular coastline: within it are a few scrub-covered islets (Fig. 21). It is protected from the open sea by the composite peninsula terminating in Préveza. The low and narrow limestone ridges forming the backbone of the Préveza peninsula have been extended by terrace-like deposits of recent geological age, by wave-built accumulations, and by subsequent uplift. Similar wave action and possible emergence have also extended the coast of Aitolía northwards to form the peninsula of Áktion (Actium), so that the gap between the two peninsulas, the Straits of Préveza, is now less than 1,000 yards wide and is very shallow (Plate 28).

The northern shore of the gulf is rendered almost unapproachable by the silt of two rivers, the Loúros and the Árakhthos, which flow across the one large plain in Ípiros. The Árakhthos, draining across impermeable rocks, carries the greater load and has been the more active in its deposition. It has built a considerable fan at its mouth, and most of the eastern part of the plain across which it flows is high enough to be dry, well-peopled and cultivated. The Loúros, on the other hand, fed by many tributaries and springs from the

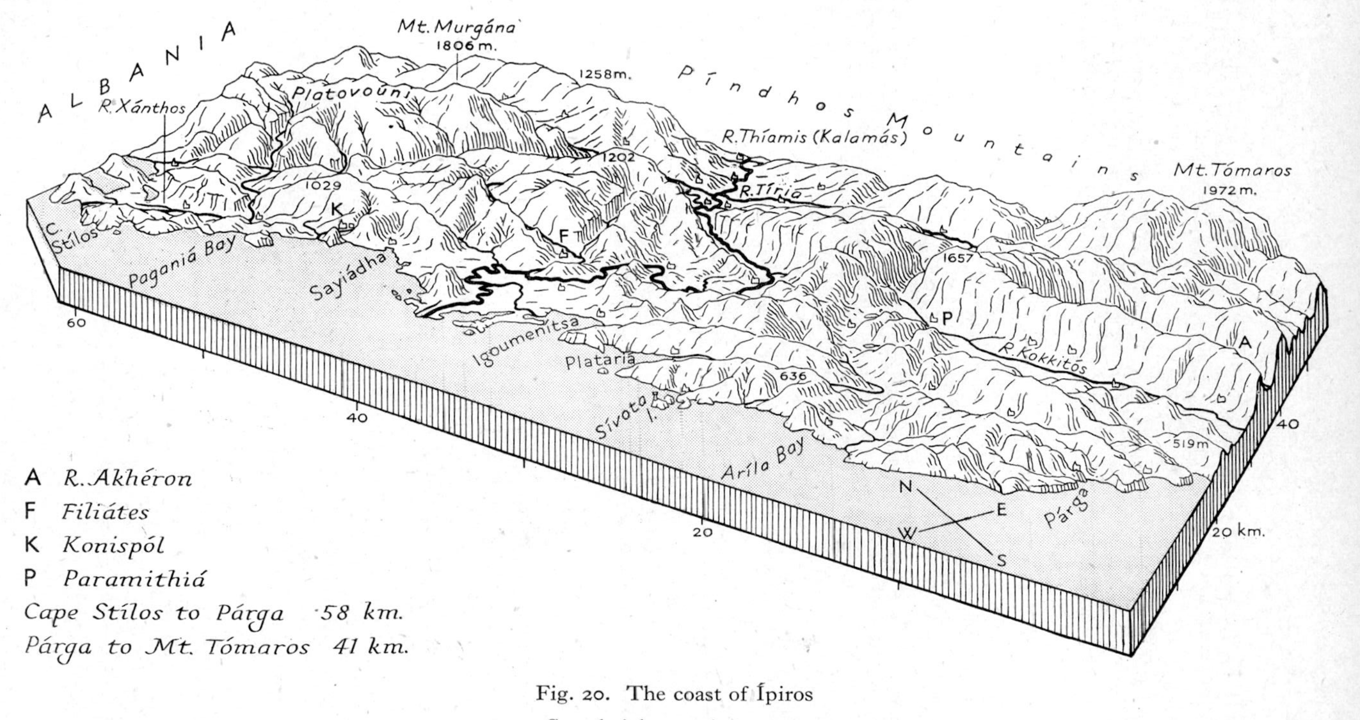

Fig. 20. The coast of Ípiros
Spot heights are in metres

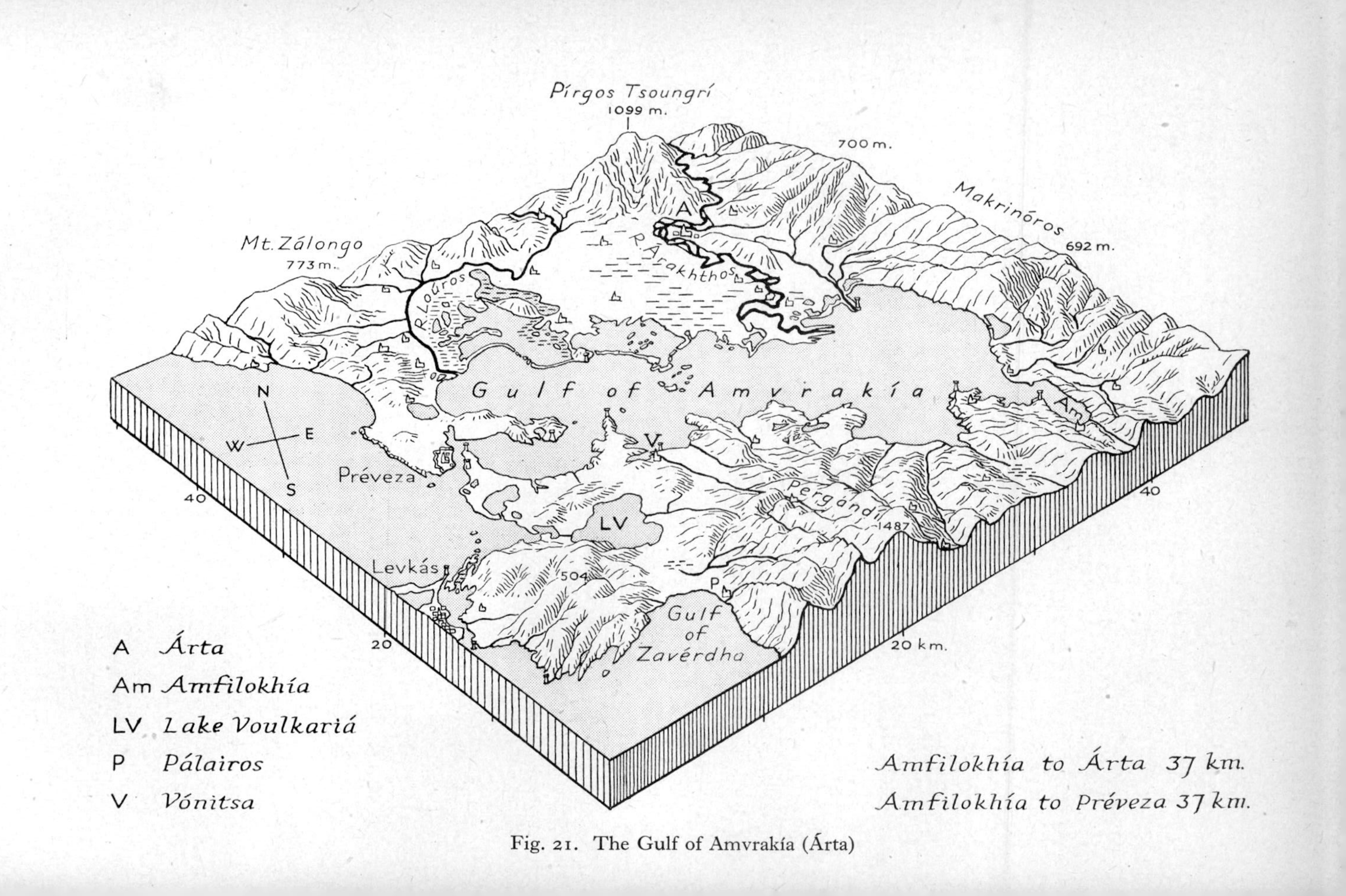

Fig. 21. The Gulf of Amvrakía (Árta)

limestone ridges to the west, carries much water but little silt, and there are marshes along its lower course. The waves of the gulf have built a series of spits which, by way of two intervening islets, link the deltas of the two rivers. By contrast, the southern shore is indented with bays of considerable depth, and limestone hills coming down to the sea give a bold and picturesque appearance to much of the landscape. Thus the gulf serves Akarnanía better than Ípiros, for it is only on the south coast that there are deep and sheltered harbours (Plate 31).

Detailed Description

The Straits of Préveza which trend north-east and then east into the gulf are barred almost completely by extensive flats of coarse sand, gravel and sea-weed. On the inner and north shore is the town of Préveza, with just under 9,000 inhabitants, engaged chiefly in the export of agricultural produce from the surrounding plains. Although the chief port of Ípiros it possesses few harbour facilities beyond a short quay.

East from Préveza cultivated hills come down gently to a sand and shingle beach, but from Cape Laskára the direction and nature of the shoreline change and the west coast of the Gulf of Amvrakía is bold and precipitous until Mázoma lagoon is reached. From here an irregular stretch of swamp, marsh and lagoon extends along the northern shore, in many places only separated from the water of the gulf by a narrow strip of sand and mud. The marshes are infested by snakes and reptiles, the lagoons abound in fish and prawns, and swarms of mosquitoes are troublesome everywhere. Here, too, are vast numbers of aquatic birds, including flocks of pelicans.

On the north-east coast of the gulf the high ridge of Makrinóros falls steeply to the sea and boats can land only at the sandy mouths of deep-cut ravines. Southwards the small villages of Arápis and Boúka, backed by low and swampy country, lie on either side of the isolated hill, Mavrovoúni (black mountain). Karvasará Bay, with its deep water, bold coast, and sheltered position in the south-east corner of the gulf, affords anchorage to coastal vessels calling regularly at the village of Amfilokhía near the head of the bay (Plate 29).

Along the south coast rocky headlands, sometimes extended seawards by low sandy points, form a series of broad bays. For the most part the steeply rising sides are thickly wooded and offer little opportunity even for small boats to land, while here and there the coast is rock-fringed. By contrast the heads of the bays are low and sandy and invite settlement, except where marshes extend to the sea. From east to west the most important bays are Loutráki, Roúga, Vónitsa and, finally, the Gulf of Préveza itself (Plate 30).

Communications

Roads. One of the principal arterial roads in Greece, although kept in a very bad condition, skirts the eastern shores of the gulf and connects Árta in the north with Agrínion in the south. The road is liable to flooding, especially in the winter months. Several less important roads strike across the drained plain north of the gulf from Kópraina, Komméno and Salaóra Bay to converge upon Árta. From Vónitsa on the south coast, a road runs south-west to Lévkas (12 miles) and a second road follows a broad valley south to Pálairos (Zavérdha) (10 miles).

Railways. None.

(3) The West Coast of Aitolía and Akarnanía

General Description (Figs. 21, 22 and 38)

From the Straits of Préveza the coast of western Greece trends in irregular fashion for some 50 miles to the Gulf of Pátrai. It consists of two types: to the north the minor folds of the Píndhos mountains result in bold coastal features; to the south deposition from the Akhelóös, largest of all rivers in Greece, has formed broad swampy lowlands behind an indented shore.

The general run of the coast is from north-north-west to south-south-east, but in detail there are two recurring directions: the longer stretches are from north to south, parallel to the limestone ridges of the interior; the shorter stretches are transverse, cutting eastwards across the mountain folds. As a result, a series of great bays have been formed in the angle between these directions. At the heads of these inlets there are alluvial plains, giving comparatively easy communication northwards. By contrast, communications to the east are extremely difficult.

Detailed Description

From the Straits of Préveza to the northern tip of Levkás island, the coast recedes to form the shallow and rock-strewn bay of Dhermatá. At first, low marshy shorelands predominate, but gradually they give way to high cliffs and eventually to a consolidated shingle beach lying off extensive mud flats (Plate 32).

Levkás. The island of Levkás is built of lofty limestone ridges between which there are valleys of considerable fertility. These give the coast its characteristic features of cliffed promontories and deep inlets. In the north-east the island is separated from the mainland only by mud banks, crossed by the Levkás channel. The west coast of the island runs south-south-west for 22 miles in an almost unbroken line of high cliffs, eventually terminating in the bold promontory of Cape Doukáton. Along the whole of this coast, the limestone ridges have been sharply faulted and subjected to powerful erosion from the Ionian Sea (Plates 33, 34).

On the south coast numerous bays lie in the shelter of long, bare promontories; the largest, Vasilikí Bay, provides excellent shelter and good anchorage, while to the east are the deep, but less important, bays of Aftéli, Sívota and Roúdha. Off the south-east coast is the hilly island of Meganísi with rugged cliffs, broken here and there where some richly cultivated valley slopes gently to the sea. On the east coast of Levkás occasional fertile plains break the line of bold, coastal mountains, and in the north the long inlet of Dhrépanon Bay separates the island of Levkás from the mainland. From this bay the Levkás channel leads northwards for almost 4 miles to Dhermatá Bay and is navigable by vessels drawing 14 ft.

The Mainland. To the east of Dhrépanon is the first great inlet on this stretch of coast. This is the semicircular Gulf of Zavérdha, from the head of which a cultivated plain gives easy communication northwards to the Gulf of Amvrakía. Coasting vessels call at the village of Pálairos on the eastern shore of the gulf (Plate 35).

The coast trends southwards from Pálairos in an almost unbroken line, offering no shelter to shipping. But at Cape Kamiláfka begins the second of the great embayments along this coast, partially sheltered on the south-west by the mountainous island of Kálamos. The gulf is divided into two bays by a low sandy point: the more westerly, known as Mítika Bay, is sandy and steep-to, and is frequented by coasting vessels: that to the east, Voúrkos Bay, is less important.

From Voúrkos Bay the coast again resumes its southerly trend to Cape Krithotí, 11 miles away. Everywhere the dissected limestone ridges rise abruptly from considerable depths. The land is sparsely inhabited and is thickly covered with wild olive and Valona oakwoods. The cliffed coasts are still in evidence on either side of Astakós Bay, the last of the three great embayments on this western coast. The eastern side of the bay is more indented than the north-western and the hills rise less abruptly inland. The town of Astakós, lying at the head of the bay, has a small port, through which passes the agricultural produce of the fertile interior (Plate 36).

The rocky indented coast, beyond the harbour of Platiyiáli, gives way southwards to a swampy plain, covered with reeds and intersected by creeks. Occasionally, from the flatness of this deltaic region, hills rise abruptly to considerable heights, isolated areas which are used for grazing cattle. Such are the Khounovína hills, 545 ft. high, separated from the mountainous island of Petalás by shallow, sandy flats. Port Petalás, at the southern end of the island, is frequented by vessels engaged in the timber trade.

On the mainland coast the broad plain of the lower Akhelóös extends south to the Gulf of Pátrai. In winter the river inundates the whole plain near the sea, and it was to drain this area that Hercules is alleged to have confined the irregular current by dams and dikes. There is a depth of less than 2 ft. at the mouth of the river, so that it is not navigable, although it is 300 ft. across some 30 miles from the sea. Immediately south of the Akhelóös delta, and partially sheltered on the south-west by the mountainous island of Oxiá, is the broad bay of Oxiá. The isolated hills of Mt Koutsouláris rise abruptly from its eastern shores.

Communications

Roads. No motor road follows the mainland coast and very few lead inland. The main routes are four in number: from Levkás to Vónitsa (12 miles), skirting the south side of Dhermáta Bay and the north shore of Lake Voulkariá; from Pálairos to Vónitsa (10 miles); from Astakós northwards to Vasilópoulon (6 miles); and from Astakós south-east to the ferry town of Katokhí, 9 miles from the mouth of the Akhelóös. On the island of Levkás, metalled roads are more numerous, and an important road runs along the east coast.

Railways. None.

(4) The Gulf of Pátrai (Patras)

General Description (Figs. 22, 39)

The Gulf of Pátrai, separating Aitolía in the north from Akhaïa in the Pelopónnisos, extends from the Ionian Sea for some 30 miles to the Gulf of Kórinthos. The narrow plain that borders the gulf in the north is almost wholly formed by river deposits; it is never more than 4 miles wide and is generally very much less. It widens

Plate 37. Mesolóngion

The town of Mesolóngion lies on the northern shores of the shallow Mesolóngion lagoons. It is connected by a road, built on a causeway, to the islet of Tourlís.

Plate 38. Pátrai (Patras)

Pátrai, the third largest port of Greece, looks north-west across the Gulf of Pátrai. The imposing and deeply eroded mountains are characteristic of the north coast of the Pelopónnisos.

Plate 39. Itéa

Itéa, port for Dhelfoí (Delphi), lies at the head of the Gulf of Kríssa, a great inlet on the north coast of the Gulf of Kórinthos. The high massif of Parnassós lies to the north-east.

Plate 40. The Gulf of Kórinthos

The indented northern shores of the Gulf are everywhere backed by steep limestone mountains. The infra-red photograph shows the Gulf of Kríssa with snow-capped Mt Vardhoúsia on the left (west) and the Parnassós massif on the right.

towards the west, because the Akhelóös brings down more silt than the Évinos (Fídharis). Thus the rough hill country which comes down to the gulf in the east gradually gives way to a complex system of shallow lagoons in the west (Fig. 22). These extensive stretches of lagoons and marshes are only separated from the gulf by narrow, broken strips of sand and mud, scarcely above sea level. Offshore, the water is everywhere too shallow for the anchorage of large vessels, and the deposition of sediment is slowly pushing the shoreline southwards. On the other hand, the coastal waters off the Pelopónnisos offer anchorages in case of necessity; and although the shores are generally low and sandy, they are free from marshes.

Detailed Description

The north coast trends eastwards for 30 miles, from Oxiá Island to Cape Andírrion. For the first 7 miles the low shorelands are diversified only by brush-covered sand hills, behind which are lagoons with fisheries. Eastwards are the two sandy islets of Áyios Sóstis and Tourlís, and the extensive stretch of Mesolóngion lagoon, with its numerous islets and mudbanks. The lagoon is so shallow that only boats of the lightest draught can cross it, except for a narrow channel with a minimum depth of 17 ft. This has been dredged from Tourlís to the harbour of Mesolóngion on the eastern shore of the lake, thus allowing direct communication by steamer from Pátrai. The name of the town, which means 'in the midst of a waste of wood and marsh', is descriptive of its site, for apart from the vineyards it is surrounded by swamp. Northwards the waste extends to the narrow depression enclosing Lake Aitolikón; southwards the coastal plain is little better than a marsh, covered with tall reeds which almost conceal the villages from sight.

Where the Évinos joins the sea the coast is low and cultivated, but upstream, cultivation gives way before marsh and then pine forests. To the east of the river the higher ground leading to Mount Varásovon is thickly clothed with olive groves, while on the coast, too, the shore is wooded to Kalidhón Bay. This bay, which gives anchorage only to small vessels, lies under the south-western face of Mount Varásovon, a rugged mass of limestone rising 3,000 ft. sheer from the gulf. Eastwards a richly cultivated vale meets the sea at Vasilikí Bay and separates Varásovon from the limestone precipices of Mount Klókova, 3,412 ft. in height. Finally, a low and narrow strip of cultivated plain lies between the rough hill country to the north and the shallow offshore waters of the gulf.

The south coast of the gulf forms a great semicircular bay from the low shingle spit of Cape Pápas in the west to the promontory of Cape Ríon in the east. Throughout its 24 miles, the smooth line of the shore presents no sheltered inlets, although in case of necessity anchorage can be found anywhere along the coast. Pátrai, the largest town of the Pelopónnisos, with a population of over 110,000 in 1940, and the second passenger port in Greece, looks north-westwards over the gulf; but it gains its importance from the fertility of the surrounding country rather than from any natural advantages as a harbour.

A fertile, cultivated plain, varying considerably in breadth, is hemmed between the sandy shore and the low plateau and mountains of the interior. There are occasional woods of dwarf oak and pine close to the sea, while large prosperous villages, vineyards and olive groves, orchards and tilled fields are evidence of the productivity of the alluvial plain.

Communications

Roads. From Cape Andírrion a coastal road skirts the southern slopes of Mt Klókova and then turns north to avoid Mt Varásovon. From here it follows the Évinos valley until it is joined by a motor road from the small port of Krionéri to the south. The road then crosses a marshy plain to Mesolóngion and strikes north-west to Aitolikón and Agrínion as one of the arterial roads of Greece. The islet of Tourlís is connected to Mesolóngion by a road built on a causeway.

In the Pelopónnisos a good metalled road follows the coast from Cape Ríon, through Pátrai to Káto Akhaïa. Here it leaves the sea, but the broad triangle of land with its apex at Cape Pápas has a complicated network of second and third class roads.

Railways. A single-track, metre-gauge railway runs north-west for 38 miles from Krionéri to Agrínion; from Aitolikón there is a 6 miles branch line westwards to Katokhí. The Pelopónnisos railway, single tracked and metre gauge, roughly follows the shores of the Gulf of Pátrai throughout its length. There are no branch lines inland.

(5) THE GULF OF KÓRINTHOS (CORINTH)

General Description (Figs. 23, 24 and 40)

The Gulf of Kórinthos is over 70 miles long, and considerably more than 12 miles across, in its broadest part. There is a striking contrast between its two shores. On the south coast the charac-

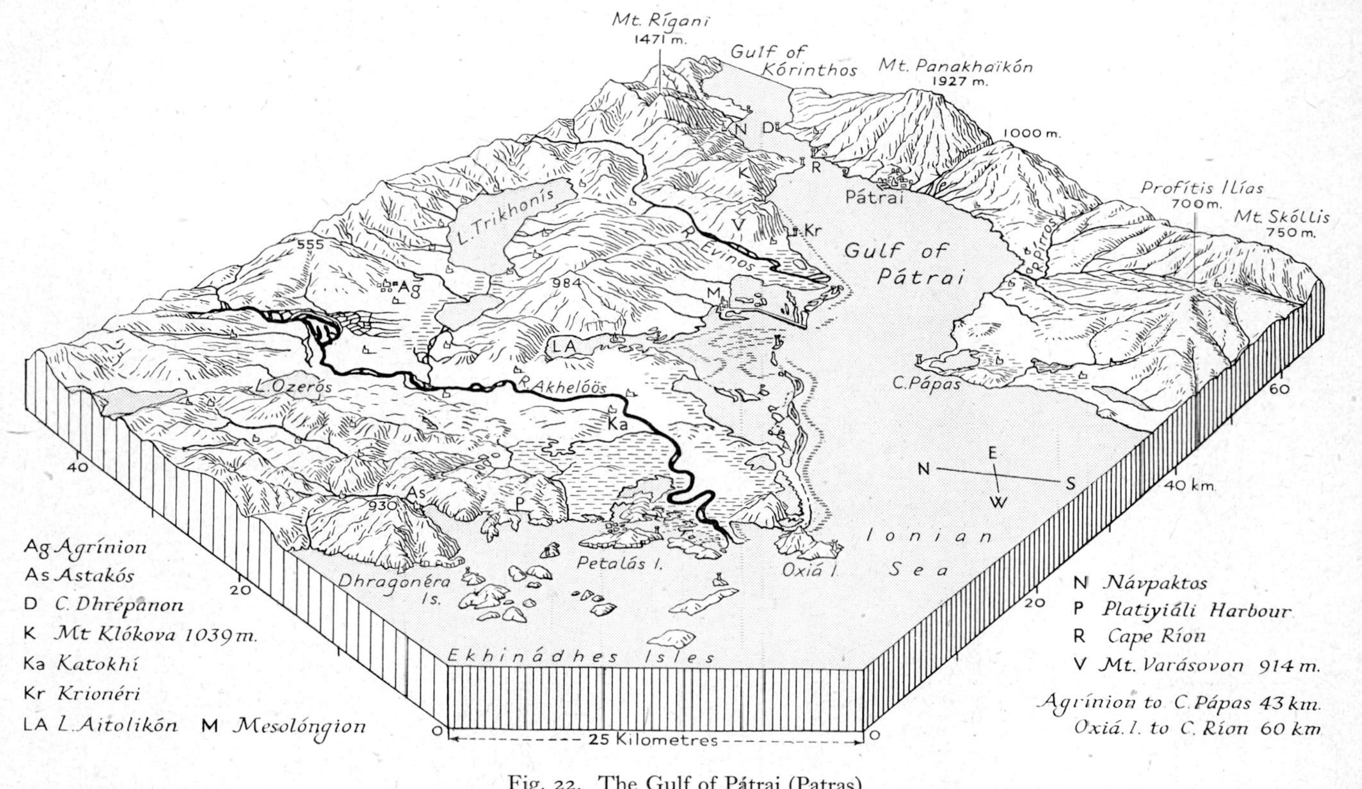

Fig. 22. The Gulf of Pátrai (Patras)

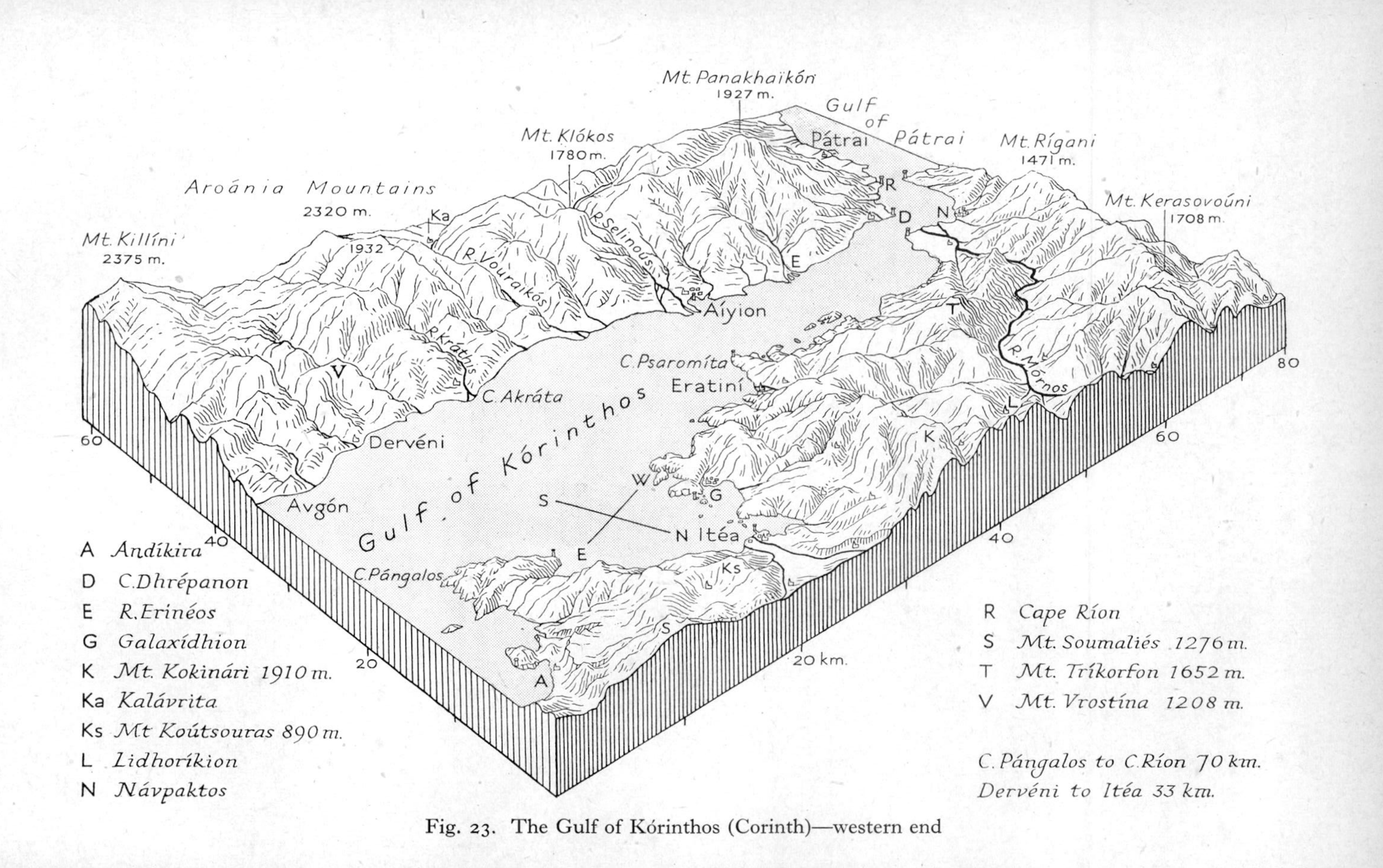

Fig. 23. The Gulf of Kórinthos (Corinth)—western end

teristic feature is the belt of fertile land that descends from the mountains to the sea in two terraces of varying width. The lower or northern terrace is a narrow irregular fringe of gravels, deposited by the numerous torrents which rush down at right angles to the line of the coast: the higher terrace is composed of marl, carved into sharp forms by these same rivers. Westwards the marl formation decreases in width, until both terraces disappear completely and the mountains fall steeply to the sea (Figs. 23, 24). The green strip of flat land near the shore is closely dotted with villages and towns: the plain is farmed intensively and vineyards are the most prominent feature of the coastal plain.

On the north coast, by contrast, bare, limestone mountains come down abruptly to the gulf. Denudation has long ago removed their thin soil cover, and deposition of sediment has been too scanty to form a continuous strip of flat land along the shore. The arid mountains are almost without inhabitants; here and there a village may be seen clinging to the slopes, but it is only on the alluvial plains of the Mórnos and at the head of the Gulf of Kríssa that there are settlements of any size (Plates 39, 40).

W. M. Leake* has left an account of the impressions made upon him by the Gulf of Kórinthos (Corinth): 'I doubt whether there is anything in Greece, abounding as it is in enchanting scenery and interesting recollections, that can rival the Corinthiac Gulf. There is no lake scenery in Europe that can compete with it. Its coasts, broken into an infinite variety of outline by the ever-changing mixture of bold promontory, gentle slope, and cultivated level, are crowned on every side by lofty mountains of the most pleasing and majestic forms; the fine expanse of water inclosed in this noble frame, though not so much frequented by ships as it ought to be by its natural adaptation to commerce, is sufficiently enlivened by vessels of every size and shape to present at all times an animated scene. Each step in the Corinthiac Gulf presents to the traveller a new prospect, not less delightful to the eye than interesting to the mind, by the historical fame and illustrious names of the objects which surround him.'

Detailed Description

North Coast. A shingle beach runs north-east from Andírrion to the town of Návpaktos on the west side of the Mórnos delta. Beyond the swampy shores of the river mouth the mountains again rise

* W. M. Leake, *Travels in the Morea*, vol. III, pp. 397–8 (London, 1830).

abruptly from the sea, and except for narrow, deep valleys ending in tiny strips of alluvium, as at Eratiní, the coast presents a steep and barren aspect until the Gulf of Kríssa is reached. Here the olive-covered plain of Itéa recedes inland; elsewhere the gulf is surrounded by high mountains, culminating north-eastwards in Mount Parnassós (8,064 ft.). On the western side of the gulf is the harbour of Galaxídhion, which has regular steamer connexion with neighbouring ports, while near the delta, the bay of Itéa also offers anchorage to coasting vessels. The small town of Itéa, at the head of the bay, is the chief port of the district (Plate 39).

A mountain spur, running southwards to Cape Pángalos, separates the Gulf of Kríssa from the deep and well-sheltered Gulf of Andíkira, near the head of which lies the small port of Andíkira. From its eastern shores Mt Verseníkos rises boldly to a height of 2,326 ft., and the coast is everywhere uninviting.

To the south-east lies the double head of the gulf, the very deep Gulf of Alkionídhes in the north and Kórinthos Bay in the south, separated from each other by the long and steeply rising peninsula formed by the Yeránia mountains. The southern shores of Alkionídhes are comparatively unbroken, but in the north the coast is deeply indented, for high spurs run out seawards at right angles to the grain of the country. Between them are sheltered bays, of which the largest is Domvraína, a landlocked stretch of water, partially sheltered in the south by three rocky islets, and enclosed on the east by the striking mountain Korombíli (2,976 ft.). At the head of the gulf is Yermenós Bay, where the forms of the boldly rising mountains are softened by forest cover (Plate 41).

South Coast. On the south side of the gulf a sandy beach, backed by a terrace of highly cultivated alluvium, extends north-east from Cape Ríon to Cape Dhrépanon. Inland, plane trees and oleanders flourish in the small valleys, and Aleppo pines and a great variety of flowering shrubs cover the mountain ridges. Just beyond Dhrépanon, the mountains reach the sea, and from here a bold coastline, fringed by a pebbly beach only a few yards wide, runs almost due east. The even line of the shore is broken by small inlets into which short mountain torrents have deposited debris. The streams are mere trickles during summer, but in winter they are a serious hindrance to communication.

From the delta of the Erineós the line of the coast changes to south-east, the hills recede from the shore, and the coastal plain with its numerous villages reappears. Aíyion is the largest town,

Plate 41. Domvraína Bay

The almost landlocked bay is on the north-east coast of the Gulf of Kórinthos. The photograph provides a very good example of a 'submerged shoreline'.

Plate 42. The Kórinthos (Corinth) Canal

The canal cuts across the Isthmus of Kórinthos for a distance of a little over 3 miles. Its bottom width is not less than 69 ft., and its depth is not less than $26\frac{1}{4}$ ft. The view is looking towards the Saronic Gulf from the railway bridge.

Plate 43. The coastal plain of the western Pelopónnisos

The view shows the highly cultivated plain to the east of Agoulinítsa Lagoon. The single-track metre-gauge railway in the foreground runs from Pírgos to Kiparissía.

Plate 44. Navarínon Bay

The sandy northern head of the bay, as shown in the photograph, is backed by extensive lagoons and marshes. The bay is the largest and safest harbour in the Pelopónnisos.

and its harbour is the best in the Gulf of Kórinthos. Beyond the plain of Aíyion, largely devoted to currant growing, the strip of alluvium lying between the mountains and the sea is seldom more than 400 yd. broad. Moreover, it is frequently interrupted by north-projecting ridges which fall steeply to the gulf. Here and there, as at the mouths of the Selinoús and the Kráthis, the deposition of sediment breaks the regularity of the shoreline by forming low points of gravel and alluvium.

From the white conical peak of Avgón, the narrow coastal plain continues unbroken to Kórinthos, 34 miles to the south-east. At first hemmed in by well-wooded mountains, and in places less than 300 yd. wide, the lowland later broadens out, beyond Dhimínion, to form a fertile district 2–3 miles in width. The lowland villages in this area are peculiar in that they are inhabited only during the winter; in summer most of the people move to the cooler and healthier pasturelands of the uplands. Everywhere the coast is clear of dangers, but there are no sheltered harbours, only open roadsteads, where coasting vessels collect the produce of the country.

The Bay of Kórinthos is a deep bight terminating the Gulf of Kórinthos. Its northern coast is mountainous, its southern coast is a fertile plain, rising inland in a series of terraces. On its northern shores is the fashionable watering place of Loutráki, with a casino and comfortable hotels. At its head is the port of Kórinthos, in a commanding position on the isthmus and 1·5 miles to the south-west of the canal.

Communications

Roads. Main roads leading inland from the north coast are few, and the only ones of importance begin at the small ports of Návpaktos and Itéa. From Návpaktos a coastal road runs south-west to Cape Andírrion and an inland route traverses hilly country to Agrínion in the north-west. A new road, reported to be in good condition (1942), follows the Mórnos valley north-east to Lidhoríkion (38 miles). From Itéa a road capable of taking heavy traffic runs north across a wide, olive-covered plain to Ámfissa (8 miles) and then continues to Brállos and Lamía. A second road, of less importance, leads to Dhelfoí and then proceeds east to Levádhia. It is joined from the south by a bad road with many hairpin bends, running from the small port of Andíkira. Finally, from the open roadstead and village of Alepokhóri at the head of the Gulf of Alkionídhes, a poor motor road leads across the isthmus to Mégara. It would have considerable military importance in the event of the Kórinthos canal being closed.

A metalled road of varying width and quality runs the full length of the south coast, and from it motor roads lead south for limited distances up the numerous valleys. The coastal road, with its large numbers of bridges and culverts is vulnerable both to freshets and demolition. Arterial roads run south from Kórinthos to Árgos and east across the isthmus to Athínai (Athens).

Railways. There are no railways on the north coast. In the south, the Pelopónnisos railway follows the shores of the gulf closely: at Dhiakoftó a 750 mm. (2 ft. 5½ in.) gauge, single-track line runs southwards for 14 miles to Kalávrita. Kórinthos is the junction of the Pelopónnisos coastal route and the Trípolis branch of the Piraiévs-Athínai-Pelopónnisos (P.A.P.) Railway.

(6) The West Coast of the Pelopónnisos

General Description (Figs. 25, 26, 41 and 42)

The west coast of the Pelopónnisos is the only part of the peninsula where the nature of the shoreline has not been determined by faulting (Fig. 6). Here, the most characteristic feature of the coast is the long line of sand dunes, stretching almost uninterruptedly from Cape Pápas in the north to Kiparissía some 100 miles to the south (Fig. 25). Most irregularities in the coastline have also been smoothed out by the deposition of sand bars, so that there are few harbours of any importance. The planting of pine forests has helped to fix the dunes, thus preventing their advance on the fertile plains of the interior. Behind the dunes are a number of brackish or salt-water lagoons, while occasionally there are local salt-pans. Few of the lagoons have any outlet to the sea, and they abound with fish.

South of Kiparissía, however, the maritime plain narrows and the coast becomes steeper and more indented as one approaches Cape Akrítas. The greatest of these indentations is that of Navarínon Bay, which forms the largest harbour in all the Pelopónnisos.

Detailed Description

From Cape Pápas to Cape Killíni, 23 miles to the south-west, the coast forms a shallow bight. There are no harbours, except where the small rocky hill of Cape Kounoupéli breaks the even line of the low, sandy shore and gives partial shelter to a tiny bay. Just south

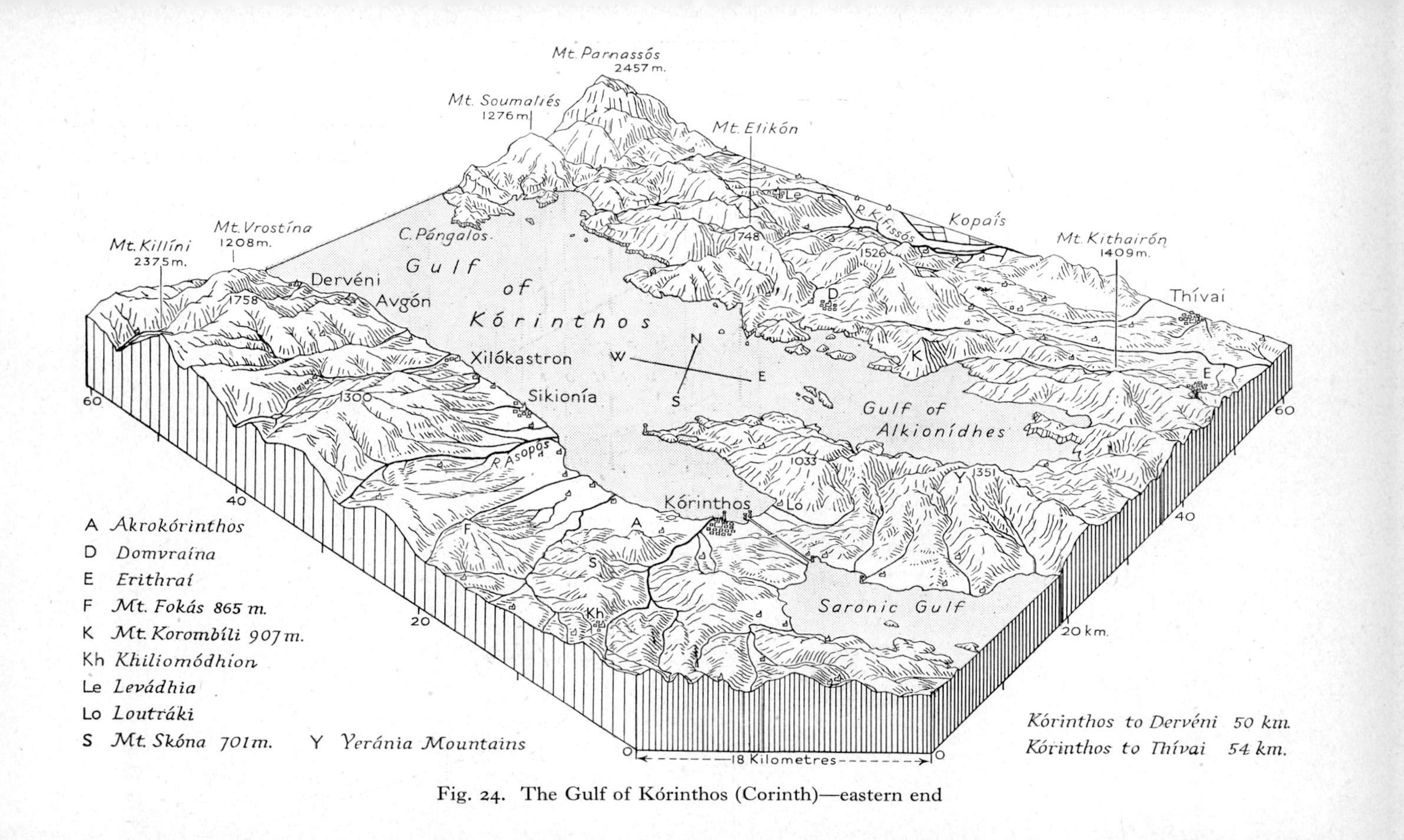

Fig. 24. The Gulf of Kórinthos (Corinth)—eastern end

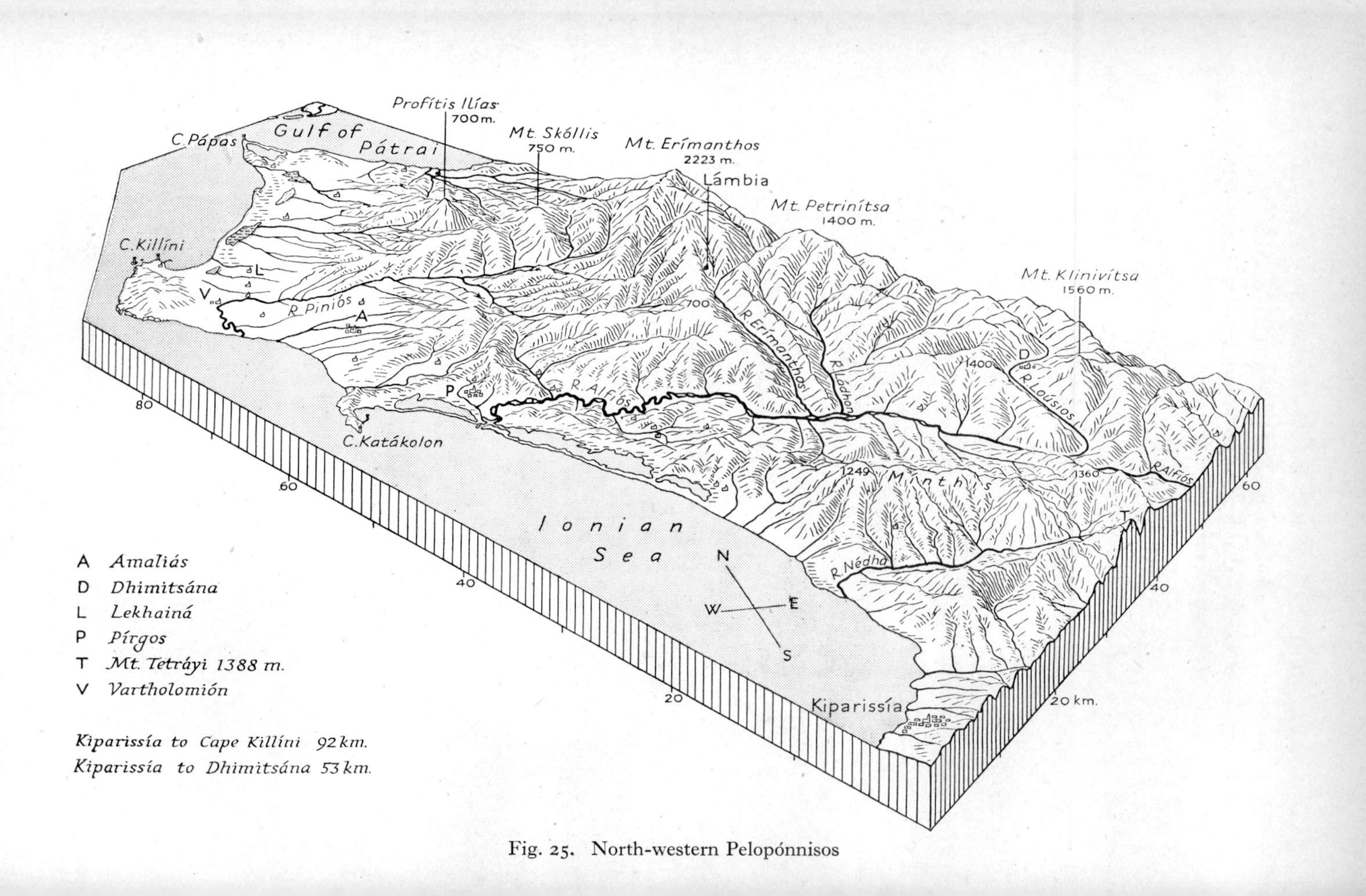

Fig. 25. North-western Pelopónnisos

of Cape Pápas the rounded dark hills of Mavrovoúni approach close to the sea; elsewhere the shore is fringed with sand dunes, which hinder drainage from the broad coastal plain. The largest of the lagoons so formed is Lake Kotíkhi, important for its fisheries and salt-pans.

Between Cape Killíni and Cape Tripití, 8 miles farther south, a high and dissected plateau falls steeply, in places by cliffs, to a sandy beach, thus breaking the chain of sand dunes and separating the fertile plains of Ilía from the sea. In the shelter of Cape Killíni is the small port of the same name, through which pass currants, olives and lemons from the cultivated interior.

The direction of the coast now changes and forms a large open bay between Cape Tripití and the low point of Cape Katákolon, 19 miles to the south-east. In its northern part the fertile plains drained by the River Piniós come down to a smooth sandy shoreline, but farther south hills approach close to the sea, scattered rocks appear offshore, and numerous small bays break the regularity of the coast. Katákolon lies on the north-eastern side of the Katákolon peninsula and has steamer connexion with other Greek ports.

The Gulf of Kiparissía forms a great bight between Cape Katákolon and Cape Koúnellos, almost 40 miles to the south-south-east. For the greater part the coast is a sandy beach, backed by pine-covered sand dunes and a series of lagoons, most evident in the north where they form an almost continuous chain of water for 17 miles. The Alfiós, the largest river in the Pelopónnisos, alone has the power to make its way to the sea in this northern stretch. Farther south the smooth sandy beach is crossed by many streams, and high mountains come close to the shore. The largest town, Kiparissía, lies at the foot of these mountains ½ mile from the sea, and its port is protected by a breakwater, 300 yd. in length (Plate 87).

Southwards to Navarínon Bay the coast, while still low, is more indented and rocky, with a few sandy bays where mountain streams enter the sea. The coastal plain, barely more than 1 or 2 miles in width, is highly cultivated and supports numerous villages. Próti island, lying ½ mile west of the small harbour of Marathópolis, has cliffed coasts, except on the north-west. Its shores are steep-to, rising to a brush-covered and rocky plateau, nearly 650 ft. high.

Navarínon Bay, almost completely sheltered on the west by the long-cliffed island of Sfaktiría, is the largest and safest harbour in the Pelopónnisos. It was here, during the War of Independence, that Admiral Codrington in command of twenty-six men-of-war annihilated the greater part of the Turkish fleet in barely two hours. In the north, at the smooth head of the bay, the shore is sandy with extensive lagoons and marshes close behind, and in the east the bay is shallow for a considerable distance off the cultivated and undulating lowlands. The small harbour of Pílos lies in the south and is formed by a mole about 100 yd. in length (Plate 44).

The coast from Navarínon Bay trends southwards for 6 miles to Methóni, and is rocky and steep-to throughout, subject to westerly swell and without any satisfactory anchorage. Methóni, the site of an ancient Venetian fortress, has a little harbour affording shelter to small vessels. To the east and south the coastline forms a series of bays sheltered partly by high and rocky promontories and partly by the group of three islands, Sapiéntza, Ayía Mariáni and Skhíza.

Communications

Roads. A road of widely varying quality follows the coast, at some slight distance inland, throughout the length of the western Pelopónnisos. From north to south it falls into four distinct sections: from Káto Akhaía to Lekhainá (23 miles) it is a narrow, unmetalled track; from Lekhainá to Pírgos (25 miles) it is metalled, but sometimes impracticable for wheeled traffic; from Pírgos to Kiparissía (37 miles) it is a track only possible for cars in dry weather; and from Kiparissía via Pílos to Methóni (44 miles) it is rough but metalled. It is linked by track to every small harbour, but only that from Pírgos to Katákolon is a first-class road. To the east arterial routes branch out across the Pelopónnisos from Pírgos, Pílos and Kiparissía.

Railways. The Pelopónnisos railway cuts across the base of the peninsula of Pápas from Káto Akhaía and runs south to Kaló Neró, roughly following the trend of the Ionian shores, though several miles inland. A branch line continues south to Kiparissía, but the main line from Kaló Neró turns due east and then south to Kalámai. Killíni, Loutrá and Katákolon are all connected by branch lines to the main railway (Plate 43).

(7) The Gulf of Messinía

General Description (Figs. 26, 42)

The Gulf of Messinía is the more westerly of two great inlets on the south coast of the Pelopónnisos. On either side of the gulf, long south-jutting peninsulas fall steeply to the sea, but there are contrasts between the east and west coasts (Fig. 42). That to the east is longer, more indented, rugged and inhospitable; sea cliffs, although comparatively rare in Greece, are here frequent, evidence perhaps of the great force with which the sea breaks against these coasts during south-westerly winds. At the foot of the cliffs there is usually a narrow shingle beach, and above them a scree slope leading to the precipitous, faulted sides of the Taïyetos mountains, or their southerly continuation into the Máni peninsula.

The west coast also owes its major features to faulting and subsidence, but it is not so much indented and the water offshore is not so deep as on the east. Moreover, the relief of the peninsula, while mountainous, is more subdued than the Taïyetos range, and the more gently sloping land is carefully cultivated, supporting numerous settlements. But it is only at the head of the gulf that there is any broad development of lowland, and here, as a result of deposition, the shoreline is smooth and the water offshore is shallow. The broad valley of the Pámisos leads south to the gulf and provides the one natural routeway in the southern Pelopónnisos which can be followed by road and rail.

Detailed Description

The west coast of the gulf trends north-east for 7 miles from the steep and rugged promontory of Cape Akrítas to Cape Livádha. Sea cliffs terminate minor promontories and smooth, sandy bays lie between. Mími Bay is the largest of these and affords some shelter from north-easterly winds. Beyond Cape Livádha is the small harbour of Koróni, dominated still by the impressive ruins of a Venetian castle; but farther north, the coast runs in an almost unbroken line for about 10 miles to Petalídhion Bay. Along this stretch of coast the eastern slopes of Mt Likódhimos fall steeply to the sea, except where some stream forms a small maritime plain. The lower slopes of the hills and the plains are covered with olive plantations and the land is well cultivated, supporting many villages. The village of Petalídhion stands on the shore of a small shallow bay, frequented by coasting vessels.

The head of the gulf, from Petalídhion to Almirós Bay, is backed by a coastal plain, and into it drains the Pámisos and many seasonal rivers. Messíni, the administrative centre of its province, stands 2 miles upstream on the right bank of the Pámisos and at the foot of Mt Ithómi, a prominent landmark and the citadel of the ancient city of Messene. Marshes lie on either side of the river, but farther east, as one approaches Kalámai, the land becomes drier and the town is surrounded by vineyards and olive groves. The smooth line of the shore is slowly being pushed southwards, and the artificial harbour at Kalámai is only maintained by constant dredging. It was from this port that over 8,000 men of the Allied forces were evacuated on the night of 26–27 April 1941.

The east coast of the gulf is more than twice the length of the western coast, extending almost 60 miles from Cape Taínaron (Matapan) to Almirós Bay. Taínaron, composed of dark grey marble, is the most southerly point of mainland Greece, and the termination of the Máni peninsula. It was off this cape that the British fleet under Admiral Sir Andrew Cunningham fought the successful action against the Italian fleet on the night of 28 March 1941. The scenery in this peninsula is extremely wild; the villages, hedged in by thickets of cactus, cling to almost inaccessible cliffs and are reached only by the roughest of footpaths. There are no springs, streams dry up in summer and water is obtained only from cisterns. The many indentations of the rock-fringed coast of the Máni peninsula form innumerable small bays, usually of considerable depth. Of these, Liménion provides the best natural harbour in the Gulf of Messinía, and the village has steamer connexion with other Greek ports. Northwards the coast is rugged, barren and less indented. Here and there, as at Selínitsa and Kardhamíli, there is a small harbour and village, but nowhere is there any broad development of coastal plain until the bay of Almirós is reached, near the head of the gulf.

Communications

Roads. Little information is available about the west coast route from Koróni to Kalámai (27 miles), but it is certainly suitable for motor traffic during dry weather. At the head of the gulf, a wide and good road leads from Kalámai to Messíni (6 miles), where a first-class road strikes north-east to Trípolis (49 miles), and a steep, narrow and rough-surfaced road runs south-west to Pílos. From Kalámai a car road runs north-eastwards to Ladhá (5 miles) and in 1940 was under construction via the Langádha pass to Spárti. A second road rounds the north-eastern head of the gulf from Kalámai to Almirós (4 miles).

The dividing peninsula between the gulf of Messinía and Lakonía is crossed by only one road. It runs from Liménion to Yíthion (15 miles), following a low saddle at the southern end of the Taïyetos mountains.

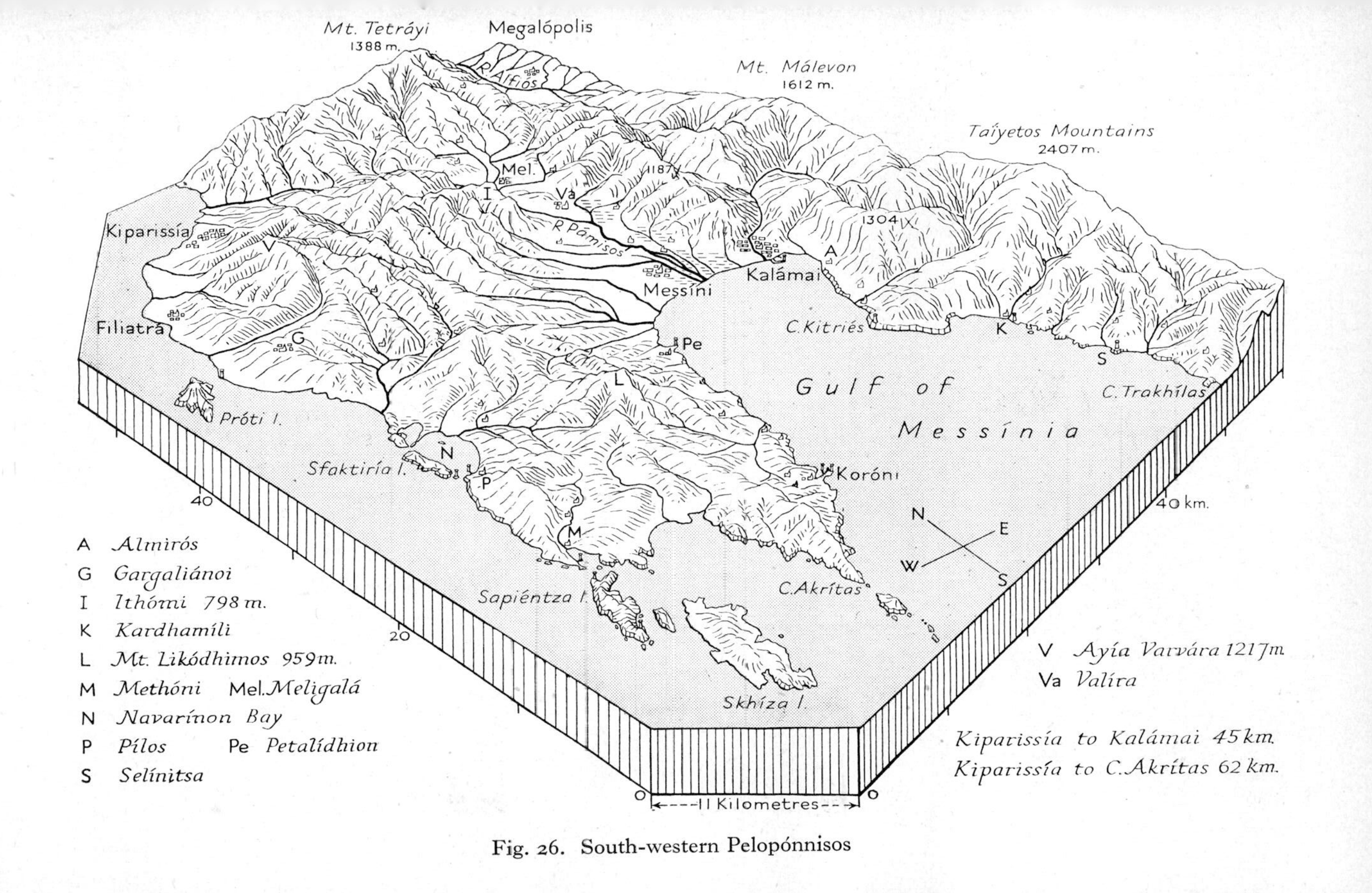

Fig. 26. South-western Pelopónnisos

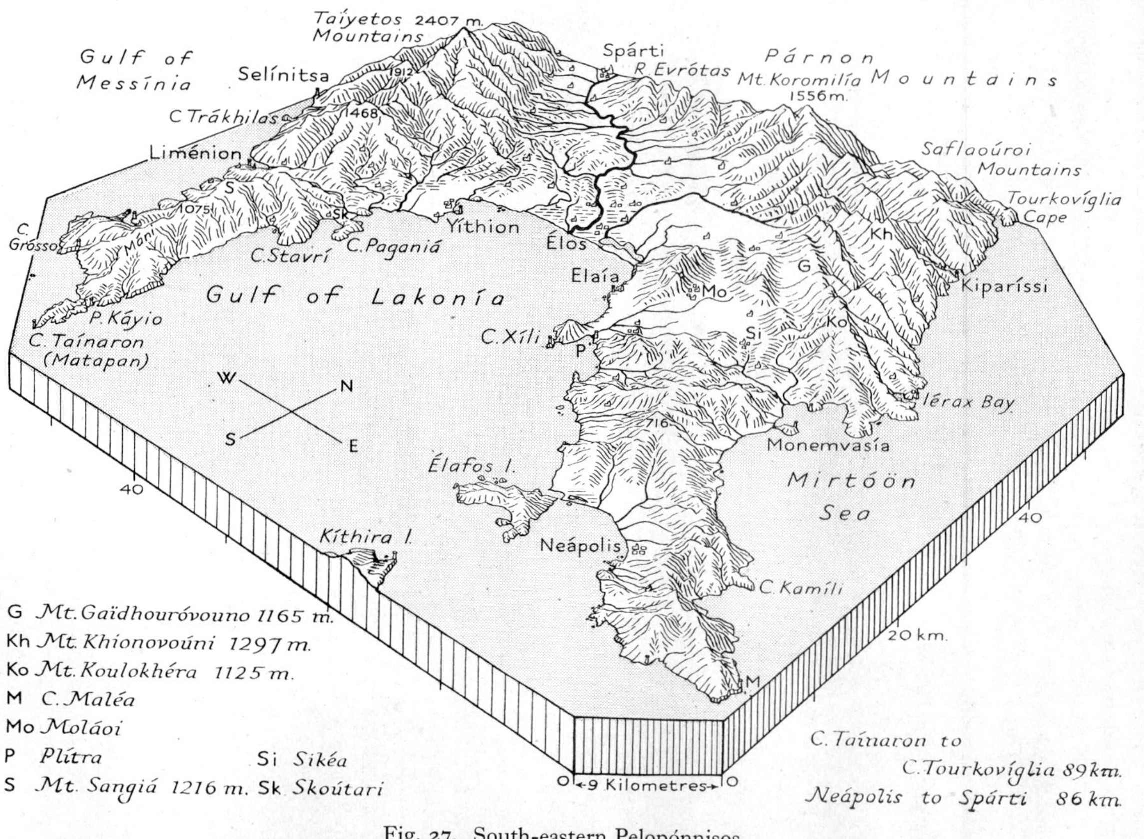

Fig. 27. South-eastern Pelopónnisos

Railways. The Pelopónnisos railway leads north from Kalámai, first along the edge of deltaic flats and then across the plain of Messinía to the gap town of Zevgolatió, junction of the west coast and Trípolis routes. Asprókhoma, near Kalámai, is the junction of a 3-mile branch running westwards across several delta channels to Messíni.

(8) THE GULF OF LAKONÍA

General Description (Figs. 27, 43)

The Gulf of Lakonía is the more easterly of the two great inlets on the south coast of the Pelopónnisos, and, like the Gulf of Messinía to the west, it has been formed by comparatively recent submergence. The similarities of position, geological history and climate have led to coastal characteristics which are common to both gulfs. Both possess high, rocky and indented coasts with few good harbours; drowned valleys are frequent, and the water immediately offshore is of considerable depth, except near the head of each gulf. Here the deposition from large south-draining rivers, coupled with wave and current action, has resulted in smooth shores of a low and marshy nature (Fig. 27).

Detailed Description

The west coast trends northwards from Cape Taínaron (Matapan) for over 40 miles. The marble headland of Taínaron, connected to the Máni peninsula by a narrow isthmus, is much indented and anchorage can be found at Asómatos, Vathí, and Pórto Káyio (Plate 46). Káyio is the best of the three bays, and although restricted in space by rocky shoals, it is frequented by steamers from Piraiévs. The mountain slopes which almost encircle the harbour are terraced and under cultivation, but in general this southern region is the most sterile of all the lands bordering the gulf. Farther north, the high peaks of Mts Kakó and Sangiá (3,990 ft.) lie some 2 or 3 miles inland, and their steep and rocky sides are but sparsely covered with vegetation. There are, however, small and scattered villages on the lower slopes and on the high coastal terraces which at one stage in the geological history of the area were cut into the hard limestone rock. A few tiny coves alone break the monotony of the high and uninviting coast, but depths close inshore are usually too great for satisfactory anchorage, and the coves are used only by small coasting craft. Northwards, two large peninsulas jut out to the south-east, that to the south ending in Cape Stavrí, and that to the north in Cape

Paganiá. They partially enclose two broad bays, but only Skoútari Bay, which lies between the peninsulas, is of importance. Here, shelter from all but south-easterly winds and a good holding ground in the mud bottom provide the best anchorage in the Gulf of Lakonía.

To the north of Paganiá is a broad bight with low sandy beaches, and beyond, in the shelter of a small promontory, is the busy and crowded port of Yíthion. It is the chief and almost the only port of Lakonía, and has steamer connexion with Piraiévs and Pátrai.

The head of the gulf fronts the deltaic plain of the river Evrótas, low and marshy near the sea, but cultivated farther inland. Navigation up the Evrótas is hindered by a shallow bar at the mouth, beyond which the river can be used by flat-bottomed boats. The harbourless coast trends almost due east for 9 miles in an unbroken line, depths being less than 3 fm. for more than ½ mile from the shore.

The east coast of the gulf and the southern tip of the Élos peninsula trend roughly north-west from Cape Maléa. For the most part, arid and sterile mountains fall quite steeply to the sea, and the coast immediately offshore is fringed by a narrow, rocky bank. Off the south coast, the barren and indented island of Élafos is separated from the mainland by a tortuous boat-channel, in parts barely 1 fm. in depth. Farther south still is the larger volcanic island of Kíthira, and between it and the mainland is Élafos Strait the most direct channel for vessels proceeding to the Grecian archipelago from the west.

From Cape Maléa the high and irregular coast trends westwards, and then recedes north to form the large bight of Vatíka Bay. The port of Neápolis lies on its indented and steep eastern shores; to the west the coast is low and swampy, with a cultivated plain behind. Northwards, the many large inlets are minutely indented at the mouths of mountain streams, which drain into the sea only after heavy rains. The most northerly of these large inlets is Xíli Bay, with the sheltered anchorage of Plítra at its head. The submergence of the ancient town of Plítra is perhaps evidence of the coastal movements which still affect Greece. From Cape Xíli to the head of the gulf the only harbour of note is at Elaía, a small and exposed anchorage, but, nevertheless, the principal port of the district.

Communications

Roads. The lands on either side of the gulf are extremely ill-supplied with roads. One leads north from Yíthion to Spárti (28 miles); a second, still in course of construction, from Yíthion to

Plate 45. Trakhíla

The tiny village of Trakhíla, at the head of Trakhíla Bay, is one of the few small ports on the east coast of the Gulf of Messínia. The southern end of the Taÿetos range is seen in the distance.

Plate 46. Pórto Káyio Harbour

Pórto Káyio, on the south-west coast of the Gulf of Lakonía, has regular steamer connexion with Piraiévs. The harbour is open to the east.

Plate 47. Andikíthira (Cerigotto)

The small island of Andikíthira lies midway between Kíthira and Kríti. Potamós, its chief town, is at the head of the bay shown in the photograph.

Plate 48. Ídhra (Hydra)

The chief town of Ídhra stands on barren slopes dominating the best harbour on the indented north coast of the island.

Skála on the Evrótas, and a third from Elaía on the east coast to Moláoi.

Railways. None.

(9) The Gulf of Argolís

General Description (Figs. 27, 28, 43 and 44)

The Gulf of Argolís is a deep and sheltered arm of the sea: to the west are the high and rugged mountains of the Párnon range; to the east are the extremely arid mountains of Argolís. At the head of the gulf is the plain of Argolís, once a bay of the sea, which has gradually been filled up by the alluvial deposits brought from the surrounding mountains.

The drowned coastline provides several good harbours, but all suffer because of their distance from any fertile and well-populated district. Only Návplion, near the head of the gulf, can claim importance, and here the water offshore is so shallow that large steamers have to anchor at some distance from the shore.

Detailed Description

The west coast. From Cape Maléa, the south-eastern extremity of the Greek mainland and, indeed, of Europe, the irregular and steep-to coast trends northwards and is extremely rugged and inhospitable. Monemvasía, a lofty and precipitous peninsula, which gave its name to Malmsey wine, lies 9 miles to the north of Cape Maléa. During medieval times this was one of the strongest fortresses in the Pelopónnisos and one of the chief ports engaged in Levantine trade, but to-day the citadel lies in ruins and the modern town, which huddles on the south-eastern slopes, is but rarely visited by trading vessels.

North of the anchorage of Palaiá Monemvasía the coast continues to the head of the gulf, mountainous, abrupt and indented. At first, the southern spurs of the Párnon ridge descend to the sea and end in bold capes; between them are small bays, each with a strip of sandy shore and perhaps a tiny coastal plain. The villages of Iérax (Yeráki) and Kiparíssi at the head of two such inlets have attained importance, but communication inland hardly exists. Farther north the slightly irregular and high coast is broken at two places only, where broad bays are in part backed by small plains. On the more southerly stands the port of Pláka which has steamer connexion with Návplion and Piraiévs: it serves the town of Leonídhion, some 2 miles inland. The more northerly bay is that of Ástros, behind which is a restricted strip of lowland, in part cultivated and in part marshy. The town of Ástros is 2 miles to the west of its port, Parálion Ástrous. Apart from the unhealthy nature of the marshy plain, the alluvium is impregnated with salt, streams are brackish, and the only water supply is collected rain water.

The head of the gulf, as far as Návplion Harbour in the east, is very shallow, and the gently shelving bottom prevents a near approach to the low smooth shores by any vessel of deep draught. Despite this, Návplion is a busy seaport and one of the leading cities of Greece, for the broad alluvial plain of Argolís, which it serves, is well peopled and conveniently situated for trade with the Archipelago. The ready access to the open sea, afforded by the Gulf of Argolís, early facilitated the import of goods and ideas from Crete and Egypt, and later, the profitable piracy of the Homeric princes. Of the three fortified towns, Tiryns, Argos, and Mycenae, whose wealth once marked the greatness of early Greek civilization on this plain, Árgos alone has retained importance as a modern city. Návplion and the small port of Tolós to the south were embarkation centres during the final stages of the 1941 campaign in Greece.

The east coast. From Cape Skíllaion, which terminates the arid mountainous ranges of the peninsula of Argolís, the coast trends west-south-west, at first high and unbroken, but becoming more indented as one passes westwards. Clear, deep channels separate the mainland from the many bare and rocky islands to the south. Ídhra, the largest island, is rugged and irregular, and the chief town is built on the barren northern slopes overlooking its port. It has steamer connexion with Piraiévs and other Greek ports. To the west of Ídhra are Spétsai and Spetsopoúla, lying in the eastern entrance to the Gulf of Argolís. They, like Ídhra, were important naval bases in naval operations during the War of Independence; and to-day, a striking proportion of all Greek shipping is owned by residents of these islands. Opposite Spétsai, the coast of the mainland swings north-west to the head of the gulf in a series of broad indentations, namely, Khéli, Veveréntza, Koilás, Vourliá and Khaïdhári. But while anchorage can be found here and in the shelter of the small but bold islands of Ipsilí, Platía and Tolós, the barrenness of the interior has prevented the growth of any large port.

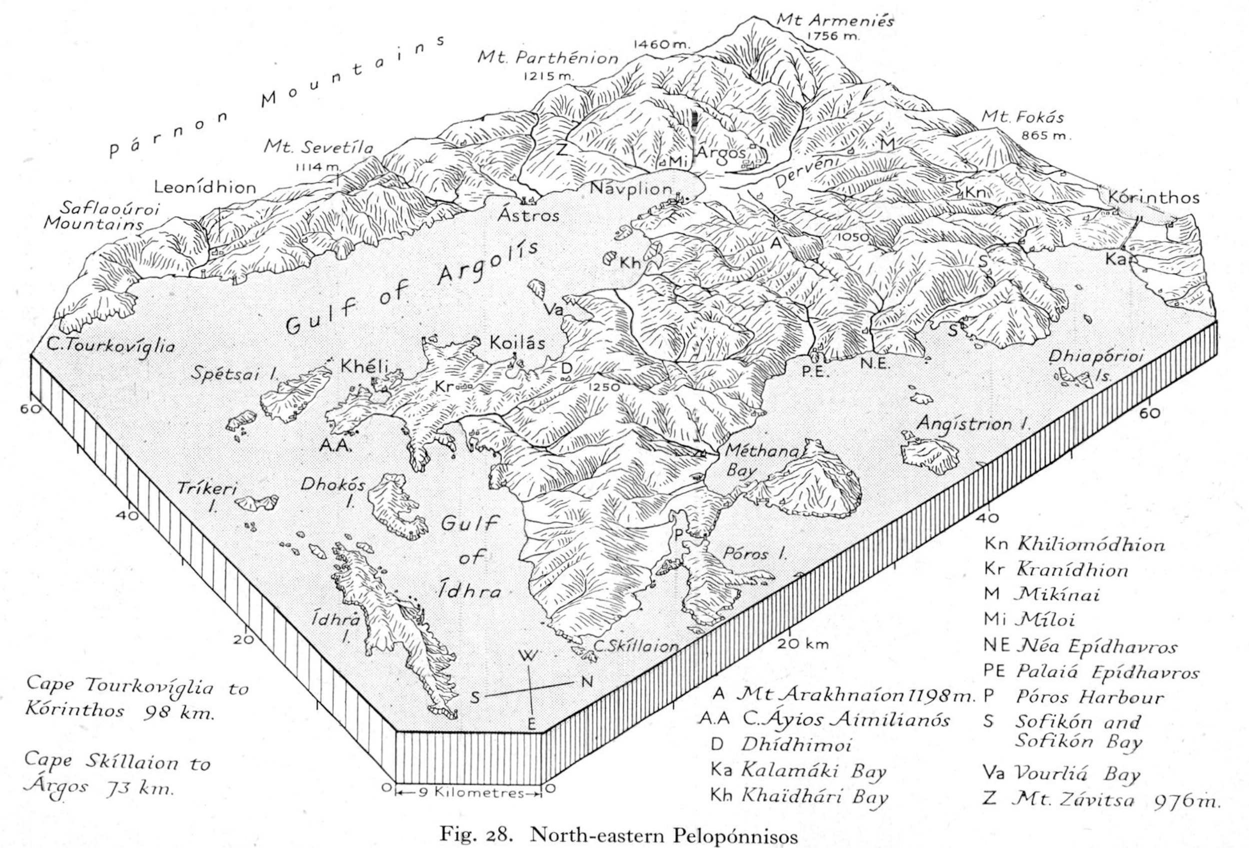

Fig. 28. North-eastern Pelopónnisos

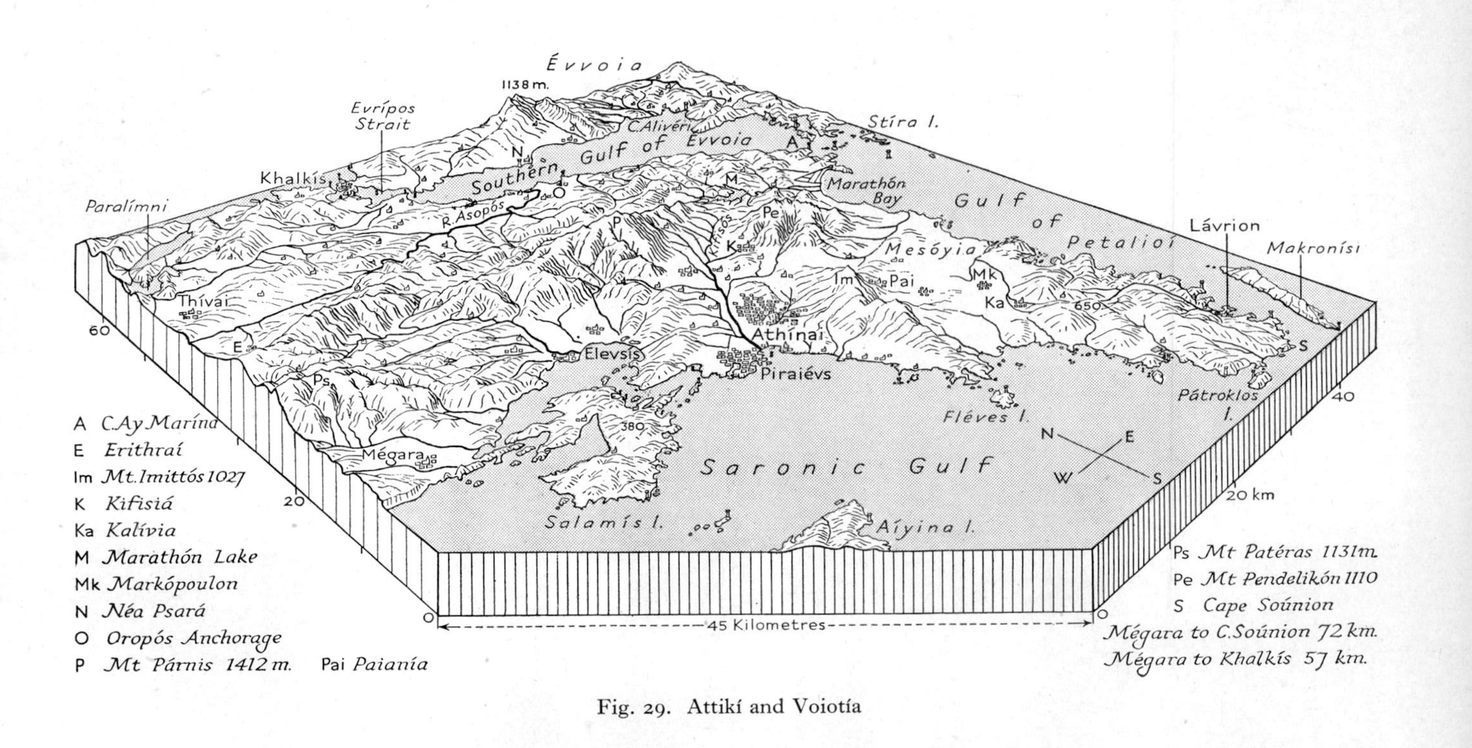

Fig. 29. Attikí and Voiotía

Communications

Roads. The road network in the plain of Argolís is the densest in the Pelopónnisos. Metalled roads connect Míloi and Návplion with the large towns of the plain, and arterial roads lead north to Kórinthos and west to Trípolis. By contrast, there are practically no motor roads elsewhere in this region, and what few there are, are of poor quality. One climbs a narrow valley from Monemvasía to Angelóna, and then descends gently to the plain of Moláoi; a second, by avoiding the coast, connects Khaïdhári with Návplion, and a third joins Pórto Khéli to Kranídhion.

Railways. The Pelopónnisos railway, passing through Árgos from Trípolis, gently ascends the plain of Árgolis and the Dervéni valley, and then, by way of sharp twists and steep gradients, enters the Lévkon valley leading to Kórinthos. A 7 miles branch line from Návplion runs north-west to Árgos.

(10) The Saronic Gulf

General Description (Figs. 28, 29, 44 and 45)

The Saronic Gulf is a broad arm of the Aegean which separates the peninsula of Attikí in the north from the peninsula of Argolís in the south. While the scenery of its coasts has been described by Leake as 'one of unmitigated sterility and rocky wildness exhibited in every possible form of mountain, promontory, and island', the geographical position of the gulf has made it the busiest thoroughfare in Grecian waters. Ocean-going vessels and the many ships of the Greek mercantile marine frequent the port of Piraiévs, the fourth greatest port in the Mediterranean.

Both in the north and the south, the much indented and island-fringed shores of the gulf are steep-to, rising boldly to coastal mountains which follow no one trend: but while on the south-west coast there is little lowland, there are in Attikí (Attica) the broad plains of Mesóyia and Athínai, and farther west the Elevsís and Mégara lowlands (Fig. 29).

Detailed Description

The south-western shores of the Saronic Gulf (Saronikós Kólpos) are very much broken and rise steeply to the bold and arid mountains of Argolís. From Cape Skíllaion the highly indented coast trends north-west to Póros, in the shelter of which lies an almost land-locked harbour, considered one of the finest in Greece for capacity, convenient depths and shelter. The town of Póros, site of a naval training school and important for its government dockyards, lies on the eastern shores of the bay. North-west of the island is the bold and rocky headland of Méthana, the whole peninsula made up of sharp mountain ridges radiating from the central volcanic peak of Mt Khelóna, 2,431 ft. high. Water is scarce, and apart from a little terrace cultivation, Méthana is desolate. Nevertheless, it is noted for its medicinal waters and is becoming a fashionable watering place.

From the high isthmus which unites the peninsula to the mainland, the coast resumes its north-westerly trend. Here it is very bold, the mountains rising abruptly to a great height from the sea; but at Palaiá Epídhavros, the coastal range is broken by a little plain, covered with lemon groves. A rocky peninsula, the site of the ancient Epidaurus, juts out to sea and forms two bays, the more northerly of which is the better sheltered. From Epídhavros to the head of the gulf, the numerous inlets of the steeply shelving shores, such as Sofikón and Kalamáki, afford indifferent anchorage to small vessels.

The head of the gulf is formed by the isthmus of Kórinthos which unites the Pelopónnisos on the south to the mountainous district of Mégara and central Greece on the north. The isthmus is a low neck of land, rising from the south in a series of steep terraces to a central plateau, less than 300 ft. high. For the most part its surface is waterless and barren; elsewhere it is overgrown with stunted shrubs and dwarf pines, and its thin stony soils provide little opportunity for agriculture. The Kórinthos canal leads north-westwards from the head of Kalamáki Bay, across the narrowest part of the isthmus, a distance of just over 3 miles (Plate 42).

The north-east coast at first trends westwards from Cape Soúnion, the southern tip of the Attikí peninsula, and both Soúnion cove and Legrainá Bay offer shelter to small craft. But from Cape Katafiyí the coast swings to the north, first to the shallow harbour of Anávissos and then to a shoal and rock-encumbered bight. The inland plain of Mesóyia leading down to the bight is bounded on the west by the furrowed range culminating in Mt Imittós. Steep and rough grey limestone slopes, in parts overgrown by stunted shrubs, but elsewhere bare of cover, come down to the sea in three rocky promontories and are continued offshore in the island of Fléves. Northwards is the densely peopled plain of Athínai (Athens), served by Fáliron Bay and the ports of Piraiévs and Pérama, and beyond are

Plate 49. The Attikí Peninsula near Cape Soúnion

The view shows the 'cape and bay' coast with its maquis vegetation, typical of Attikí. To the north-east the long island of Makronísi can be seen.

Plate 50. Piraiévs and Salamís

In the foreground is Zeás Harbour, behind which are Piraiévs and the main harbour. Across the Saronic Gulf to the west is the mountainous island of Salamís with its naval base barely discernible on the north-east coast. In the far distance are the Patéras mountains, rising to 3,583 ft.

Plate 51. Coastal road near Skaramangá
A good road, by Greek standards, runs from Piraiévs to Elevsís.

Plate 52. Elevsís
The small town lies on the alluvial plain of Thriásion. The view across the gulf shows the north coast of Salamís.

the low limestone hills which separate the plain from the land-locked Gulf of Elevsís (Plate 50).

Shut in to the south by the clear-cut mountains of Salamís island and to the north by the smooth sweep of the mainland coast, the Gulf of Elevsís has access to the Saronic Gulf only by narrow winding channels. It was used by the Greek navy as a submarine exercise area. Elevsís, a small port serving the Thriásion plain, lies on the northern shores of the gulf (Plate 52). To the west of the town is a chain of wooded hills, which advances south from Mt Kithairón and alone breaks the smooth line of the coast, for farther west again the olive and vine-clad plain of Mégara comes gently to the sea. On the east coast of Salamís, the shores of a broad, but sheltered, inlet are used as a government dockyard.

From Mégara, a low saddle gives easy access westwards across the isthmus of Kórinthos; but on the coast, the high and beetling slopes of the Yeránia mountains, known as the Skironian Cliffs, make the interior inaccessible from the sea. Although limited in extent, they are a most formidable barrier, and both road and railway are literally carved from their face. Between the Skironian Cliffs and Kalamáki Harbour at the head of the Saronic Gulf, the hills again rise gently from the water and there are many smooth beaches.

Aíyina is a large hilly island in the centre of the Saronic Gulf, the hills culminating in a central peak, 1,752 ft. high. For the most part the island is barren, though cultivation of olives and vines is important in the western valleys and plains. Aíyina, the capital and chief port of the island, is a town of some 2,000 people on the north-west coast and has regular steamer connexion with Piraiévs.

Communications

Roads. The influence of Athínai on road development is clearly shown in Fig. 45. Good roads radiate in all directions from the capital, but they soon lose their first-class quality. An excellent motor road leads west from Athínai to the Gulf of Elevsís, continues as an indifferent road around the northern shores of the gulf to Mégara, and then runs on to Kórinthos. A second road also runs westwards from Mégara to Alepokhóri, on the Gulf of Alkionídhes. The port of Piraiévs is linked to the capital by a good two-way road, and also to the small oil port of Pérama, but from Pérama to the naval base of Skaramangá the motor road is rough. Lastly, a good motor road runs from Piraiévs, south-east along the coast, to Vouliagméni, but there is no direct road connexion between here and Soúnion.

On the south coast, metalled roads are extremely rare; thus a track, not suitable for motor traffic, leads inland from Palaiá Epídhavros to Ligoúrion, from which a rough, narrow, metalled road continues to Návplion. This is the easiest route across the peninsula of Argolís.

Railways. The Piraiévs-Athínai-Pelopónnisos railway climbs a 1 : 40 gradient from Kórinthos to the 300 ft. bridge over the Kórinthos canal and then, having crossed the isthmus obliquely to Kalamáki, is later forced along the precipitous slopes of the Skironian Cliffs. It continues close to the sea through Mégara to Elevsís, climbs a broad col and descends eastwards to Áno Liósia and Athínai.

From Piraiévs, terminus of one of the branches of the Orient Express route, a standard-gauge railway runs north-east through Athínai to Oinóï and so to northern Greece. An electrified railway also runs from Piraiévs to Athínai (5·3 miles), while a westward extension of the Hellenic Electric Railway connects Piraiévs to Pérama (6 miles): both are standard gauge. Finally, an electrified metre-gauge line runs north-east from Athínai to Kifisiá (9 miles).

There are no railways in the peninsula of Argolís.

(11) The Gulf of Petalioí and the Southern Gulf of Évvoia (Euboea)

General Description (Figs. 29, 45 and 46)

Between the south-west coast of Évvoia and the mainland coast of Attikí is a long stretch of water which leads to the port of Khalkís in the narrow Evrípos Straits.* The southern half is known as the Gulf of Petalioí, the northern as the Gulf of Évvoia.

The structural history of the gulfs is of interest. The peninsula of Attikí and the southern half of Évvoia are related to the Kikládhes. They are all composed of crystalline rocks and their folds trend from north-west to south-east. After the folding, offshore fractures, parallel to the mountain grain, led to submergence. The Kikládhes to the south-east formed two chains of islands, which can be seen continuing the lines of Évvoia and Attikí, while the deeply indented coasts of the Gulf of Petalioí show the typical features of a recently submerged shoreline. The many promontories are the result of minor folds, transverse to the main north-west to south-east trend. Farther

* In *Mediterranean Pilot*, vol. IV and on the relevant Admiralty charts, the name Evrípos Straits is applied, not only to the restricted channel at Khalkís, but also to the southern Gulf of Évvoia.

north, the Gulf of Évvoia runs west-north-west to east-south-east, for here the line of submergence followed the trend of the Kithairón, Párnis and Pendelikón mountains. These are offshoots from the great Píndhos range, sweeping east-south-east from the main range to terminate at Capes Kálamos and Ayía Marína.

Detailed Description

The west coast stretches northwards for some 30 miles in an ever-repeating scene of rocky promontory and smooth bay. There is an alternation too in the offshore depths, in harmony with the coastal features; the headlands plunge steeply to considerable depths, the plains shelve gently to shallow seas. Many of the numerous bays, though spacious and beautiful, are enclosed by barren mountains and offer only indifferent anchorage to shipping. Their shores, sometimes sandy and sometimes marshy, are usually backed by a narrow stretch of plain, growing cereals, olives, and evergreen oaks. Apart from Lávrion (Laurium), which owes its importance to the shipment of ores from surrounding mines, there are no large settlements, but there are several small villages, engaged in fishing and farming. Chief of these are Rafína and Pórto Ráfti, little harbours which played a very important part in the evacuation of Allied forces from Greece in late April 1941. One of the largest plains is that of Marathón, near the head of Petalioí. It is a crescent-shaped stretch of flat land curving round the shores of a wide bay and bounded on the landward side by a semicircle of steep mountains. The shore is a shelving, sandy beach, free from rocks and shoals, and overgrown with pine trees. The bay of Marathón was carefully chosen as a landing beach by the Persians in 490 B.C., for a back-door assault on Athens.

Some few miles off the west coast is the island of Makronísi. Its shores are everywhere indented and the land rises steeply to the mountainous north-south backbone of the island. This is especially the case on the west, where the coast is cliffed for long stretches (Fig. 29).

The north-west coast of the Gulf of Évvoia extends from Cape Ayía Marína (near Kálamos) to the Evrípos Straits, a distance of some 30 miles. The coast line is now comparatively straight and there are no sheltered anchorages for the first 20 miles. In this region, parallel chains of hills run from Mt Párnis to the high, steep coast. The first and almost the only harbour is that of Oropós Bay which lies between two low points, some 2 miles apart. It is backed by a small plain on which stands the hamlet of Skála Oropoú.

The east coast of the Gulf of Petalioí, with its many bays and headlands, is even more indented than the coast of Attikí. Numerous islands lie offshore, rising steeply from considerable depths. Of these, the group known as Petalioí, mountainous and sparsely inhabited islands, give their name to the gulf. On the south coast of Évvoia is the broad bay of Káristos, exposed to southerly winds and with the harbour of Káristos lying at its head. Farther north the many bights give to this part of the island a character entirely different from any other region in Évvoia. Coastal mountains, scored by seasonal torrents, rise steeply from the shore.

On the north-eastern side of the Gulf of Évvoia the coast is lower and less irregular, and apart from Alivérion Bay in the east there are no major inlets. The small but fertile coastal plain is served by the two little ports of Váthia and Néa Psará (the ancient Eritria). Towards the west, the mountains recede inland and the gulf narrows to Búrji Channel, which in turn leads into Khalkís outer harbour (Plate 54).

Communications

Roads. Several roads strike inland from the east coast of Attikí and converge upon the capital. From Cape Soúnion a good road, wide enough for two-way traffic, skirts the coast to Lávrion (6 miles) and then continues north-west to Athínai (38 miles); from Pórto Ráfti a metalled road goes west to Markópoulon, where it joins the Lávrion-Athínai route; and from Marathón a motor road traverses the coastal plain to the south, rounds Pendelikón and also continues west to the capital (26 miles). Similarly, good motor roads connect Skála Oropoú and Kálamos to Athínai, while a road from Khalkís crosses the Evrípos Straits by a swing bridge, 130 ft. long, and continues as a two-way road in a fair state of repair (1941) to Thívai (19 miles).

In Évvoia, the only motor road of importance follows the coastal plain from Khalkís to Alivérion. It then runs due north across the island to Kími, the terminal of a ferry to the island of Skíros.

Railways. The metre-gauge Attikí railway runs from the port of Lávrion to Thorikón on Thorikón Bay and then climbs the narrow Potamós valley before turning north-west across the Mesóyia plain to make use of the gap between Pendelikón and Imittós. At Áno Iráklion it joins the electrified line to Kifisiá. From the shores of

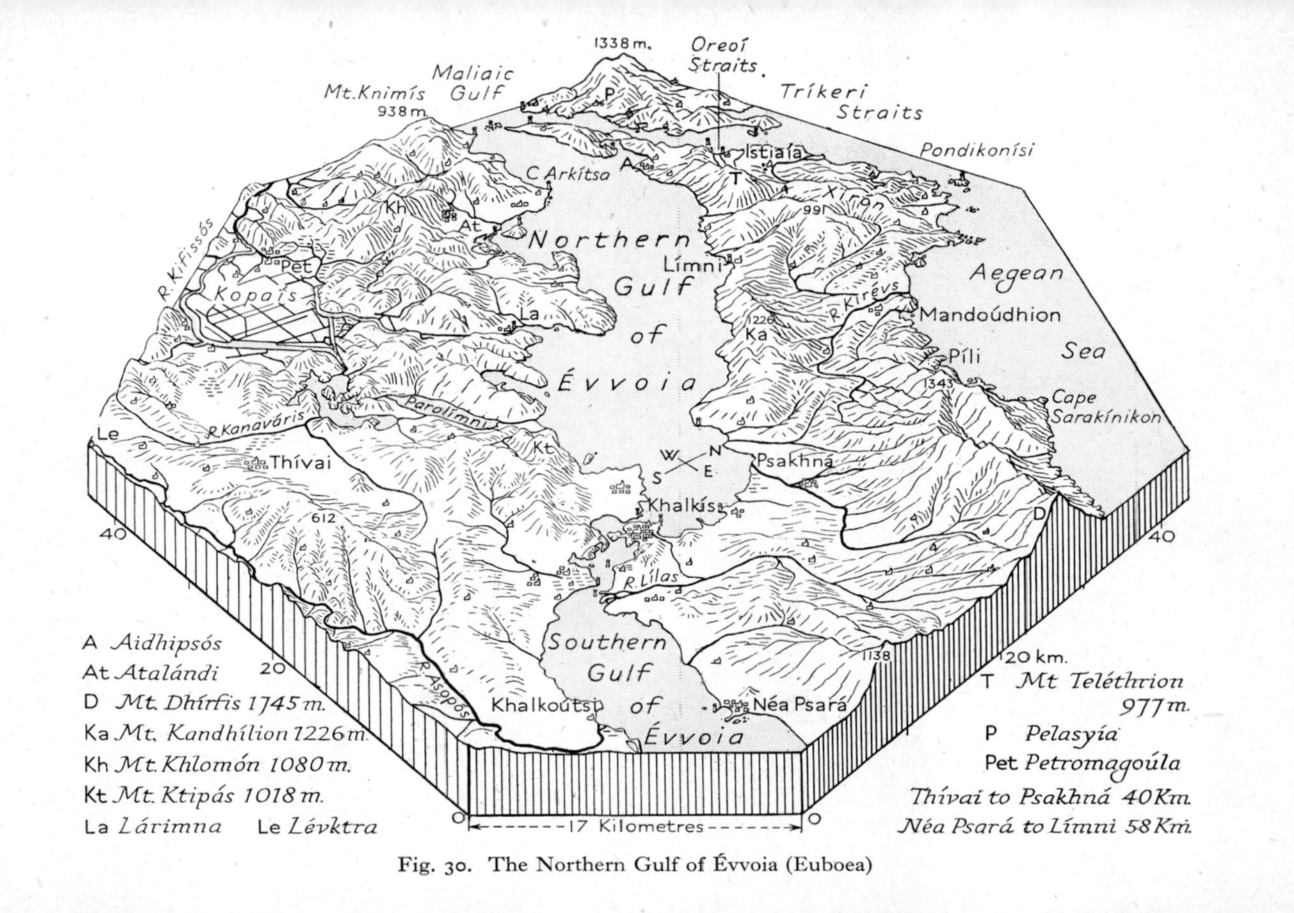

Fig. 30. The Northern Gulf of Évvoia (Euboea)

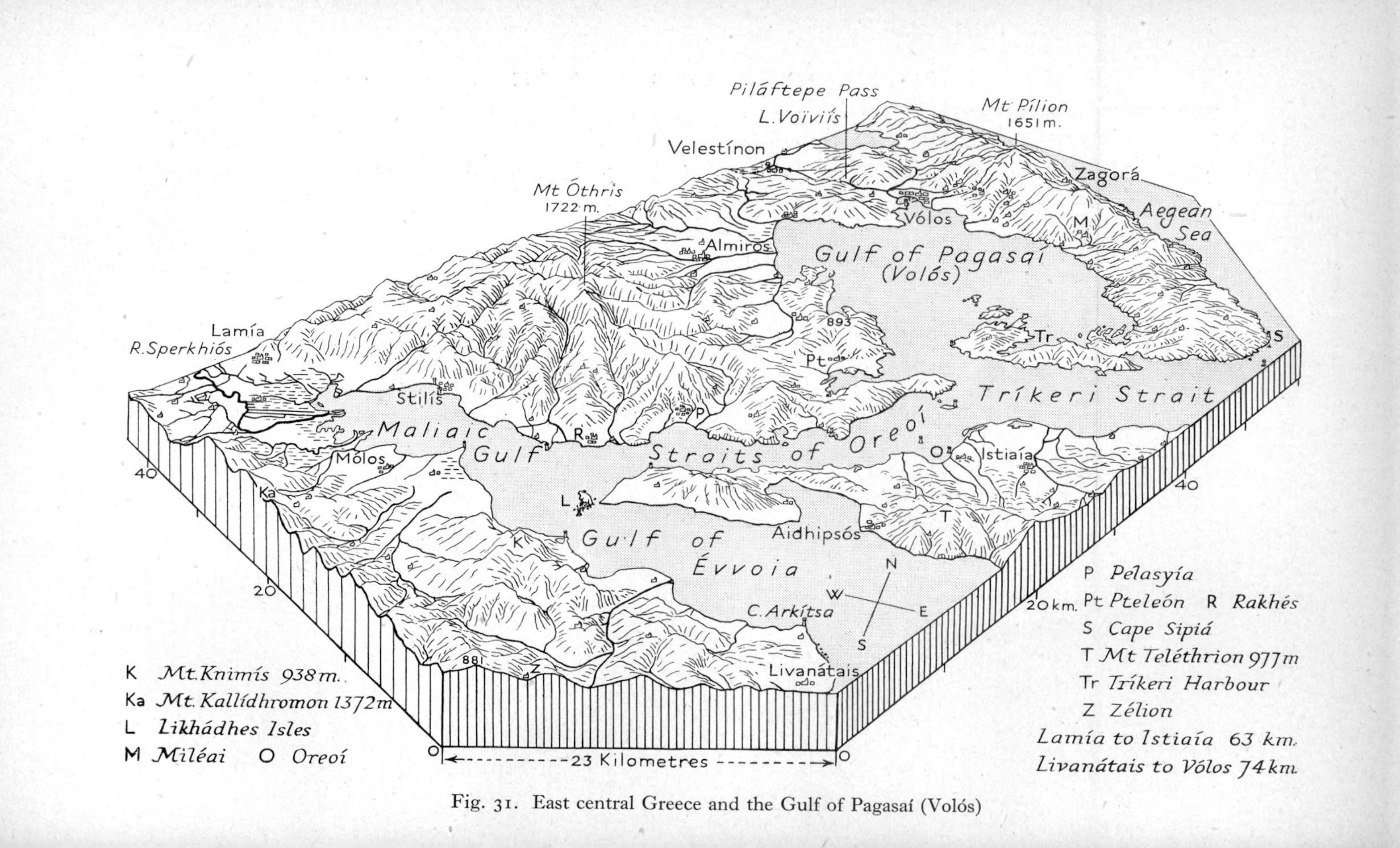

Fig. 31. East central Greece and the Gulf of Pagasaí (Volós)

the Evrípos Straits opposite Khalkís a standard-gauge of the Piraiévs-Platí line (Hellenic State Railways) runs south to Oinóï.

There are no railways in Évvoia.

(12) THE NORTHERN GULF OF ÉVVOIA (EUBOEA)

General Description (Figs. 30, 31, 46 and 47)

The northern part of the Gulf of Évvoia separates the island of Évvoia from the mainland of central Greece, and extends north-west for 50 miles from Evrípos Straits to the Likhádhes islands. It owes its origin to great fractures, followed by subsidence. Movements along these fractures are still liable to occur, giving rise to minor coastal features. Thus, in 1897 a low cliff up to 5 ft. in height and more or less continuous for 34 miles suddenly appeared along the western side of the gulf.

Although both coasts owe their origin to subsidence and are for the most part backed by high land, there is a clear distinction between them. On the east, the grey mountains of Évvoia are close to the shore; there are no large inlets, and sheltered anchorages are not to be found (Fig. 30). Even the minor bays offer little protection, for they are subjected to furious gusts of winds from the neighbouring mountains. On the west, there is a greater development of coastal plain and three great inlets offer protection to shipping. Here, too, there are numerous settlements, served by coastal roads.

Detailed Description

The south-west coast forms the seaward edge of Fthiótis-Fokís. From the exceedingly narrow straits of Evrípos, commanded by Khalkís, the coast extends north-west for 6 miles to the low promontory of Cape Gáïdharos. At first the low and indented shore is backed by sand hills, but farther west the coast is steep-to and the mountain-enclosed bays of Skroponéri and Lárimna (Lármes) afford good anchorage. From Lárimna the minutely indented coast sweeps round in a great curve to Cape Kérata, beyond which is Atalándi Bay, open to the north, but otherwise well sheltered. To the west the shore is sandy and a coastal plain begins which widens slowly as the Maliaic Gulf is approached.

The north-east coast is everywhere steep-to, except in the south, where a cultivated plain shelves gently seawards. Northwards, however, the Kandhílion mountains approach close to the shore and there are no pronounced inlets. Farther north still is the Gulf of

Aidhipsós, which provides the only shelter along the whole coast; but the depths in the central part of the gulf are too great for good anchorage.

Communications

Roads. A metalled road, mostly in bad condition, runs north-west from Lárimna to Atalándi (20 miles) and then follows the coast via Livanátais (25 miles) and Mólos (45 miles) to Lamía (68 miles) across the swampy plain of the Sperkhiós. A motor road strikes south-west from Livanátais for 19 miles, to join the arterial route from Lamía to Athínai. Communication with the interior is also provided by a good-weather road from Lárimna to Akraífnion; thence an all-season road leads on to Thívai.

In Évvoia, a short coastal road joins Khalkís with Psakhná (9 miles), where one branch continues to Politiká and the other crosses the island to Mandoúdhion. This latter town can also be reached by a metalled road from Límni.

Railways. None.

(13) The Maliaic Gulf, Oreoí and Tríkeri Straits

General Description (Figs. 31, 47)

The general trend of the mountains and coasts in the east of central Greece is from north-west to south-east, but cutting across this line is a long and narrow arm of the sea. From the Aegean in the east, the Tríkeri Straits lead to the Straits of Oreoí, which in turn give access to the Maliaic Gulf. The faulted depression does not end here, for the long and narrow plain of the Sperkhiós extends to the foot of the Píndhos mountains (Fig. 1).

There is a progressive change in the type of coast as one passes from east to west. After the formation of the depression, sedimentation was rapid wherever the enclosing mountains allowed the development of major rivers. Thus, in the Tríkeri Straits, where submergence was most pronounced, and where the streams running into the sea are short and seasonal, the effects of deposition are barely to be seen. This is especially the case on the northern shores, where the watershed of the Tríkeri range is exceptionally close to the sea, and where the hills plunge steeply to the indented and rocky coast. On the south side of the channel, the streams draining from Évvoia are longer, and small plains have developed, giving a smoother

Plate 53. Rafína Harbour

The harbour is one of a number of small fishing centres on the east coast of Attikí.

Plate 54. The coast of Évvoia near Néa Psará

The road on the right follows the coastal plain westwards to Khalkís.

Plate 55. Áyios Ioánnis at the foot of Mount Pílion

The western shores of the Gulf of Thérmai offer few sheltered harbours: small fishing boats are drawn up on to the open sandy beach.

Plate 56. The Sithoniá Peninsula

The rocky and indented coasts shown in the photograph are typical of Sithoniá, centra[l] peninsula of Khalkidhikí.

edge to the land. Towards the west, where submergence has not been so great and where the rivers are longer, the coastal plains broaden to several miles and the depth of water decreases gradually towards the head of the Maliaic Gulf.

Detailed Description

The Maliaic Gulf (Maliakós Kólpos) extends westwards for some 10 miles, and provides good anchorage in depths of from 10 to 16 fm. The southern shore, indented with broad and very shallow bights, is backed by a low, marshy plain. Villages avoid the coastal lowlands and lie at the base of the steeply rising Kallídhromon mountains about 2 miles inland. Swiftly flowing streams have cut deeply into the highland, only to lose their well-defined courses amidst marshes, when their valleys flatten abruptly to the alluvial plains. Near the head of the gulf is the delta of the Sperkhiós which alone has the volume to make its way direct to the sea, but on either bank, and especially to the north, are large tracts of marshland. On the northern shores of the gulf the mountains are closer to the sea, but here, too, broad bays are backed by a cultivated plain of varying width. The large village of Stilís, at the head of the most westerly of these bays, is the one important settlement on the coast, and even here the harbour can only be approached through a narrow dredged channel.

The Straits of Oreoí lead east-north-east from the Maliaic Gulf to the Tríkeri Straits, forming a deep trough which separates the narrow peninsula of northern Évvoia from the mainland. Even its broadest part is rarely more than 3 miles across, yet depths are almost everywhere between 30 and 40 fm., slowly deepening towards the east. There are marked contrasts between the northern and southern shores of the straits. In the north-west, deposition from the many streams draining the southern slopes of the Óthris mountains, coupled with wave and current action, has had the usual effect of smoothing the shoreline. Here and there isolated plains are separated by rocky and indented promontories, where cliffed edges are not uncommon. Farther east, however, the mainland runs out to sea in the peninsula of Tragovoúni and the mountains fall steeply to a sinuous and rock-girt shore. By contrast, it is the western half of the southern shore which is rocky and indented, whereas to the east a broad and cuspate plain has been built up. There are no protected anchorages on this comparatively smooth and sandy stretch of coast, except for the partial shelter offered by Oreoí Bay.

The Straits of Tríkeri lie between Évvoia to the south and the mainland to the north, attaining an average width of about 5 miles and a general depth of from 40 to 50 fm. High land rises steeply from the much indented north coast and there are consequently no villages of importance. Plataniá Bay, backed by a strip of sandy beach, gives the best anchorage. On the south coast the shoreline is less broken and the slope seawards from the mountains of Évvoia is comparatively gentle. Towards the east, however, the small plains give way to the hilly north-eastern tip of Cape Artemísion. Opposite the mouth of the straits is the mountainous island of Skíathos, the most westerly of the nine major islands which form the Northern Sporádhes.

Communications

Roads. From Lamía a coastal road of variable quality skirts the southern slopes of Óthris, and then strikes north to Pteleón. Lamía is also joined to Atalándi by a comparatively good road. In Évvoia the port of Oreoí is connected to Istiaía and Aidhipsós, but elsewhere motor-roads are practically non-existent.

Railways. From Stilís on the northern shores of the Maliaic Gulf a standard-gauge branch line of the Piraiévs-Platí railway runs west to Lamía and then on to the junction town of Lianokládhion.

(14) The Gulf of Pagasaí (Vólos)

General Description (Figs. 31, 47)

The Gulf of Pagasaí is the most northerly of the great inlets in central Greece. It is a circular sheet of water, some 20 miles across, bounded on the west by the slopes of the Óthris mountains and the confined plain of Almirós, on the south-east by the curving Tríkeri peninsula, and on the east by the steeply rising peninsula of Magnisía (Fig. 31). To the north it is separated from the fertile plains of Thessalía by a series of broad hill ranges. Land approaches are difficult and communications are poor, although road and railway cut through the enclosing hills to the port of Vólos. To the south the narrow Straits of Oreoí lead to the gulf from Évvoia and the mainland, while the straits of Tríkeri give access from the Aegean.

Detailed Description

The west coast consists of two distinct types—the indented and steep-to coast of the south, and the smooth, gently shelving shores of the north. From Cape Stavrós, terminating the peninsula of

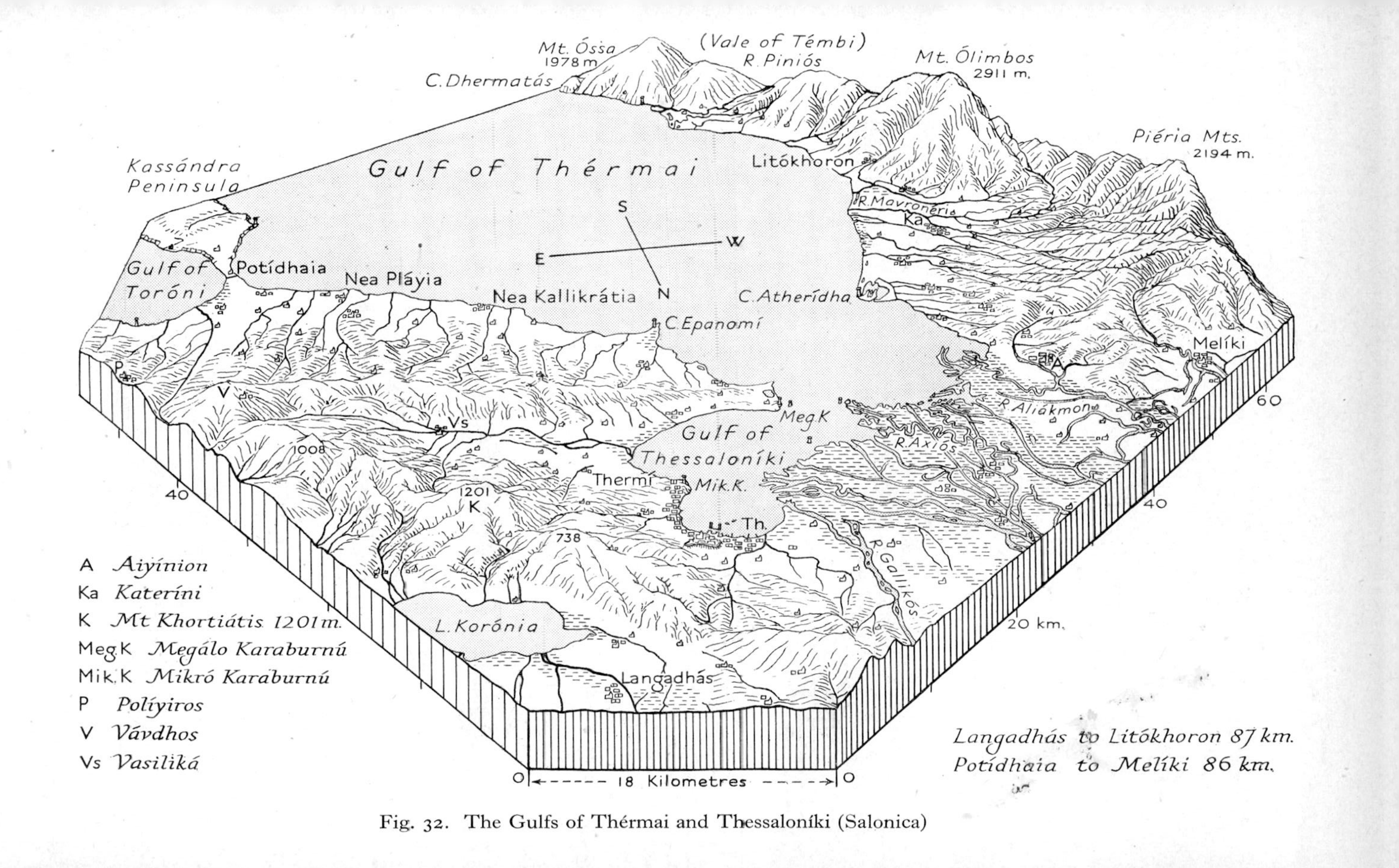

Fig. 32. The Gulfs of Thérmai and Thessaloníki (Salonica)

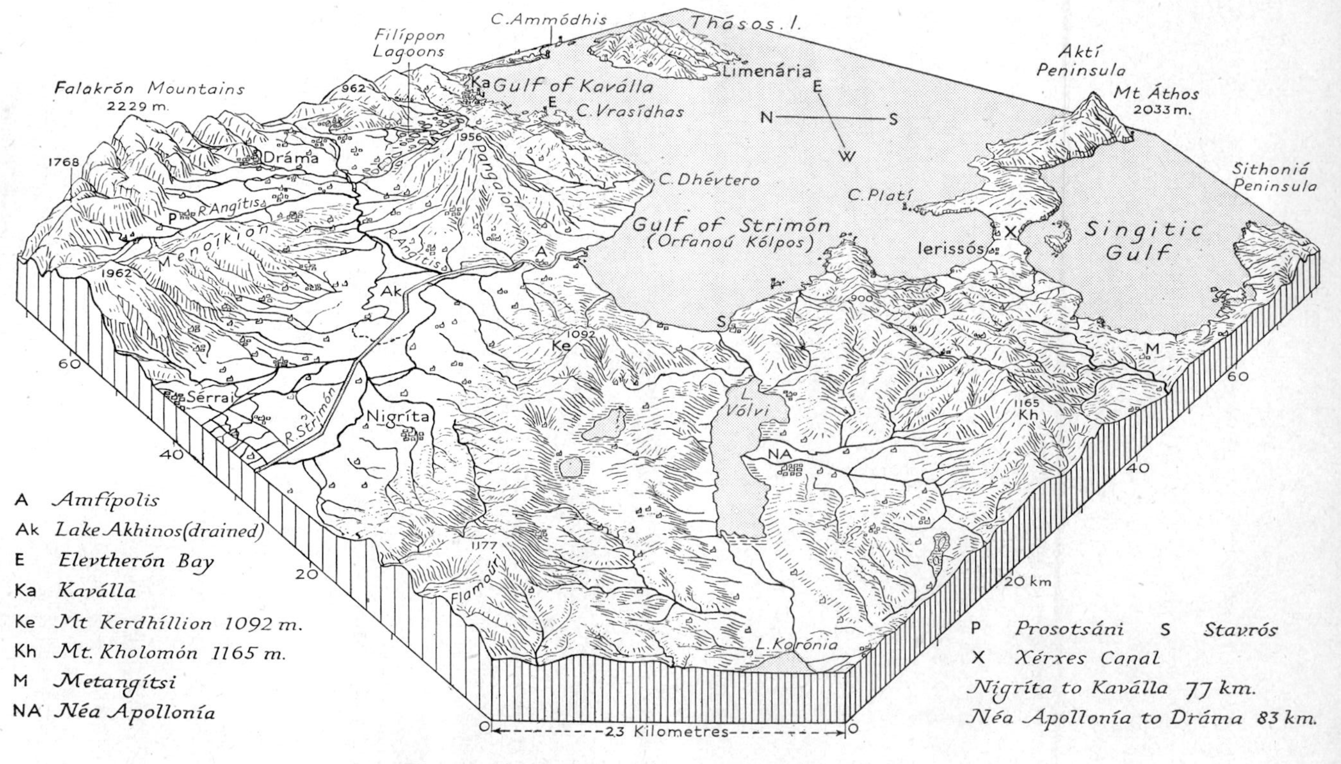

Fig. 33. Eastern Khalkidhikí and the Gulf of Strimón

Tragovoúni and marking the western entrance to the Gulf of Pagasaí, a series of sheltered inlets indent the coast. The most important from south to north are Pteleón, Niés, Mitzélla and Soúrpi, each with its small settlement near the head of the bay. Although open to winds from a northerly quarter, they offer temporary anchorage to shipping. Except at the heads of these bays mountains fall steeply to the coast and there are no large settlements. Then to the north there is an abrupt change. The alluvial plain of Almirós, crossed by many rivers, comes gently to the low and marshy shore. Tiny deltas alone break the smooth line of the northward-sweeping shore and there are no sheltered anchorages and no coastal villages. Some 4 miles inland the settlements are more numerous, and Almirós, the largest town, forms the regional centre of the plain.

The north coast is divided into two by the Gulf of Vólos, and it is only on the shores of this inlet that plains attain any breadth; that to the west tends to be flooded in winter, but the plain to the east is under extensive olive groves. The Gulf of Vólos is well protected, except from the south, and the port at its head thrives with the trade of the fertile lowlands of Thessalía. To the west of the gulf the sinuous line of the rocky shore provides a succession of tiny coves where winter torrents run to the sea. To the east, the slopes of Pílion approach the shore, but they are separated from the sea by a narrow coastal plain of varying width.

The east coast of the Gulf of Pagasaí trends north-north-west to south-south-east to the well-sheltered bay of Vathoúdhi. In the north, near Kalá Nerá, there is a restricted coastal plain, but elsewhere the land plunges rapidly from the high ridge of the peninsula to deep water immediately offshore. Nevertheless, villages are more numerous on this western-facing side of Magnisía than on the deeply incised and longer slopes towards the Aegean.

The south coast is greatly indented and fringed with islands, the largest of which are Alatás and Palaió Tríkeri. Long, bold peninsulas extend north-north-east, falling steeply to the many deep-water bays. Of these, Vathoúdhi Bay offers the best anchorage and is almost completely protected by an enclosing rim of high land. Farther west Tríkeri Harbour is the largest inlet, but here the depths are inconveniently great for anchorage.

Communications

Roads. An all-weather road leads north-west from Vólos, ascending the low ridge which connects the Óthris and Pílion mountains.

Farther inland, on the way to Lárisa, it deteriorates rapidly. A coastal road, reported in 1942 to have been widened and improved, runs south-west from Vólos to Almirós and Pteleón, while another road follows the coast south-eastwards to Miléai.

Railways. From Vólos a metre-gauge line, with a maximum gradient of 1 : 48, climbs to the Piláftepe pass and then crosses the Thessalian plain to Lárisa. Vólos is also connected by the junction town of Velestínon to Kalabáka, again by single-track, metre-gauge railway. The line round the north-eastern head of the gulf, from Vólos to the small harbour of Agriá (5 miles) and then inland to Miléai (17 miles), is only 600 mm. (1 ft. 11$\frac{5}{8}$ in.) gauge and is sometimes called the 'steam-tramway'.

(15) The Western shores of the Gulf of Thérmai

General Description (Figs. 32, 47 and 48)

From the Gulf of Pagasaí to Thessaloníki (Salonica) the coast runs, roughly north-westwards for about 125 miles, and in the north forms the western edge of the Gulf of Thérmai. The shoreline is smooth and inhospitable throughout, whether it is backed by the imposing mountains of the south or the broadening maritime plain of the north. The only facilities for landing are provided by tiny bays, each with its narrow strip of open sandy beach. These bays offer partial shelter to small boats and are indicated on large-scale maps by the word *skála* (small port). The villages rarely lie close to the beach, and in general the shores are bare of settlement and without roads (Fig. 48).

Detailed Description

The coast can be clearly divided into a northern and a southern section, similar in length, but very distinct in character. In the south, the magnificent ranges of mountains, of which Pílion and Óssa are the most noteworthy heights, rise abruptly from the sea (Fig. 32). Pílion rises in a broad and rounded outline to 5,308 ft., and is clothed in beech forests, said to have provided Jason with timber for the Argos. Óssa or Mt Kíssavos is a conspicuous peak rising steeply to 6,409 ft., and about 7 miles inland, from the lofty headland of Cape Dhermatás. The mountains extend south-east from these more lofty heights to form the long, hook-shaped peninsula of Magnisía. From the shores of the Aegean the land rises

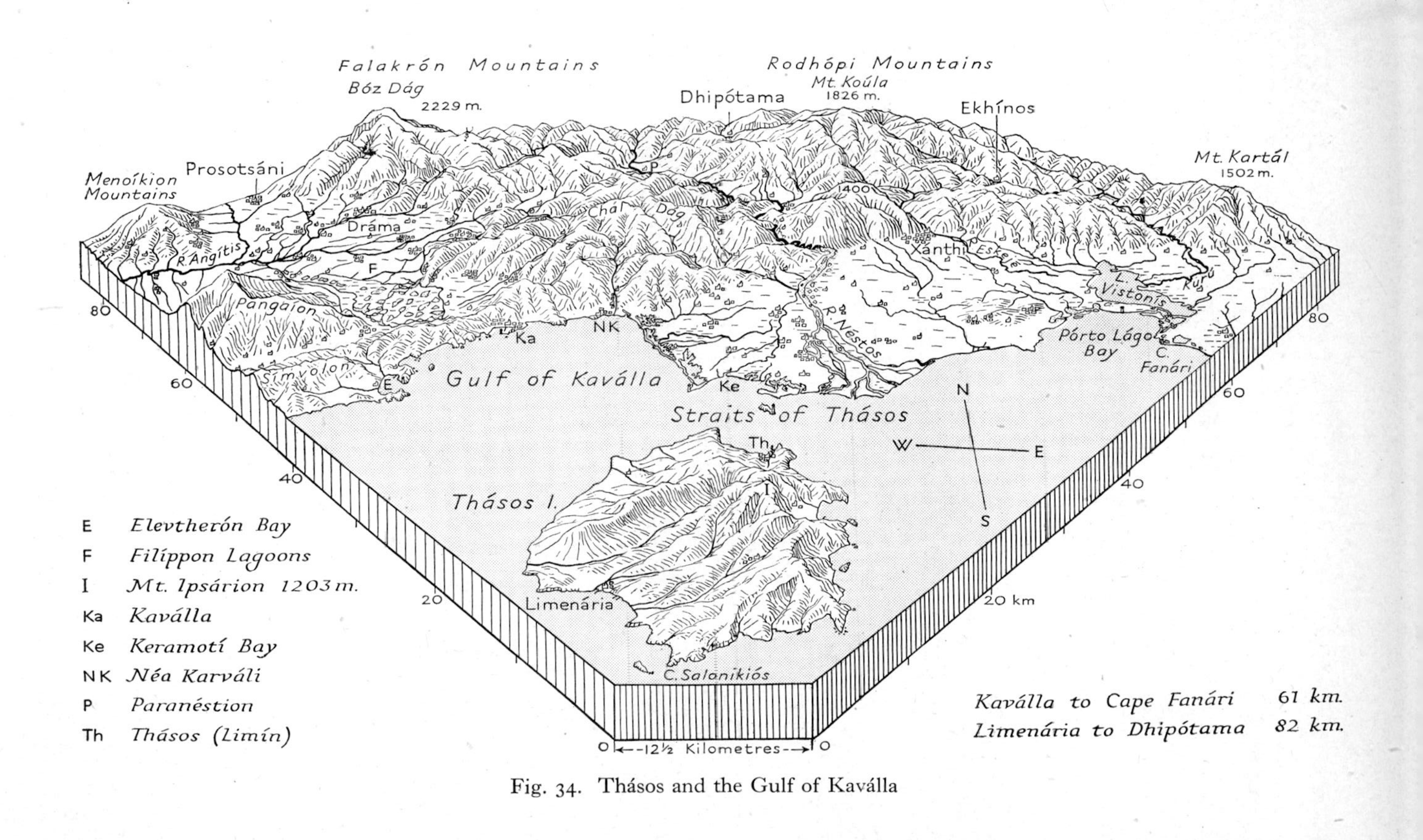

Fig. 34. Thásos and the Gulf of Kaválla

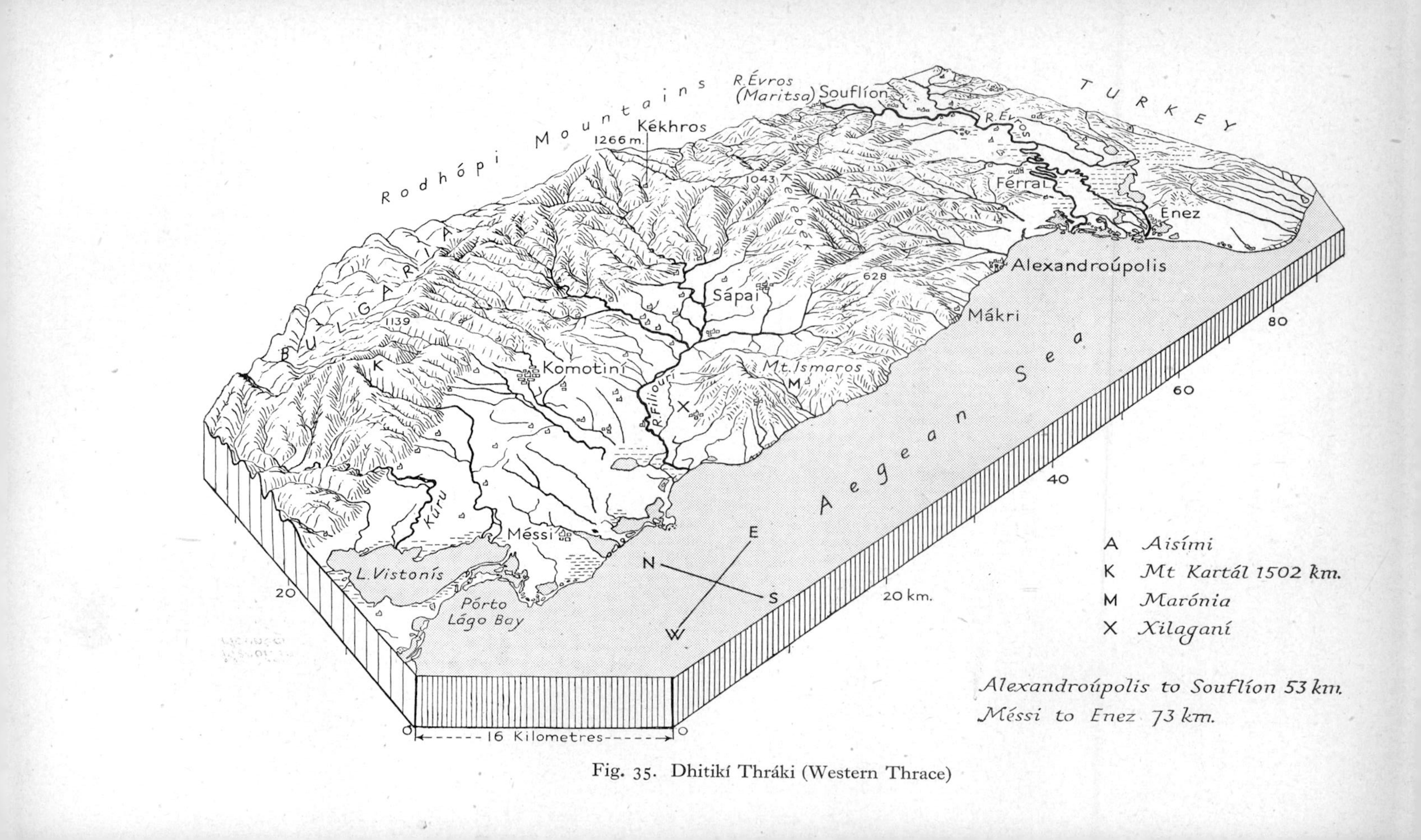

Fig. 35. Dhitikí Thráki (Western Thrace)

steeply to the uneven and sharp crest of the peninsula. Numerous streams leading down to small bays have cut deeply into the mountains, thereby making land travel difficult. The dislocations which affected the whole of this region so profoundly are responsible for the even line of the shore and the north-north-west to south-south-east trend of the coast. Settlements are few, and isolated coves alone provide anchorage for small craft.

In the north, beyond Óssa, the river Piniós cuts its way through the coastal ranges by the beautiful vale of Témbi (Tempe), to enter the sea by a delta. From this point the high ground trends gradually away from the coast, leaving between it and the sea an ever-widening belt of lowland, fronted by a sandy beach. The last landmark of these mountains is Mount Ólimbos (9,571 ft.), snow-capped for most of the year, composed of bare, light-coloured rocks and rising in a series of abrupt precipices cut by deep, thickly wooded ravines. The low coastal lands now broaden considerably, and an almost continuous series of sand bars separates fresh and salt-water marshes or small lagoons from the sea. They are responsible for the particularly smooth line of the shore and for the absence of anything approaching a good harbour. Tiny bays, some of them little better than open beaches, serve the villages and small towns which stand on the drier and firmer land several miles from the shore. Thus Skála Leptokariás serves Leptokariá, a small town some 3 miles distant, at the junction of mountain and plain. Skála Litokhórou serves Litókhoron which lies in a similar geographical position, 4 miles south-west of its harbour, and there are many other examples (Plate 55).

Towards the head of the gulf, the river Aliákmon and Axiós cross wide marshy lowlands: they are constantly edging farther and farther south and are therefore rapidly extending the area of their deltas southwards. As a result the coastline at the mouth of these rivers is undergoing continual change and should be approached with caution. Within recent years there has been considerable drainage of these marshy lowlands.

Communications

Roads. There are practically no roads either along this coast or leading inland which are suitable for motor traffic in all weather. From Thessaloníki, however, good roads strike out in all directions, apart from the south-west. Ayiá on an upland plain near Óssa is connected to the shores of the gulf by track and to Lárisa by a metalled road. Farther north a motor road runs westwards from

Vromeróskala to Kateríni, but not far beyond this town, towards Elassón, it deteriorates into a dry-weather track.

Railways. The Piraiévs-Platí standard-gauge line from Lárisa (Hellenic State Railways) uses the gorge cut by the Piniós to reach the shores of the Gulf of Thérmai. It then follows the coastline for 19 miles before turning inland to Kateríni in order to avoid sand dunes and salt-pans. North of Cape Atherídha the line again comes close to the shore until it is driven inland to Platí by the deltaic marshes of the Aliákmon.

From Thessaloníki the standard-gauge Flórina line runs westwards to Platí and Véroia, then on to Flórina and Bitolj in Yugoslavia. A second line, the Thessaloníki-Idhoméni standard gauge, leaves in a north-westerly direction and then runs northwards along the Axiós valley to Skoplje and Beograd (Belgrade). Finally the Thessaloníki-Alexandroúpolis standard-gauge railway, after running parallel to the Idhoméni line, strikes northwards up the Gallikós valley.

(16) Khalkidhikí

General Description (Figs. 32, 33, 48 and 49)

The most striking feature of the Khalkidhikí peninsula is the great length of coastline compared with the small land area. In the north the neck of the peninsula is formed by a strip of lowland extending from the Gulf of Thessaloníki eastwards to the head of the Gulf of Strimón. Immediately to the south there rises a broad region of crystalline mountains from which the three peninsulas of Kassándra, Sithoniá and Aktí project south-eastwards into the Aegean.

For the most part the land rises abruptly to the interior, and the steep face of the land represents the faulted edges of ancient plateaux. These faults, which run from north-west to south-east, have determined the main trend of the coastline; they are of very recent origin and coastal movements of considerable magnitude still occur. It is to this fact that the youthful configuration of the coast is due: there are practically no coastal plains, streams are short, straight and swift-flowing, and villages close to the sea are often a considerable height above it. Here and there, well-sheltered inlets may form natural harbours, but the landward approach to them is always difficult, and there is no port of any size. Where coastal routes exist they are very near to the shore, while inland tracks are forced to climb high crests and difficult passes.

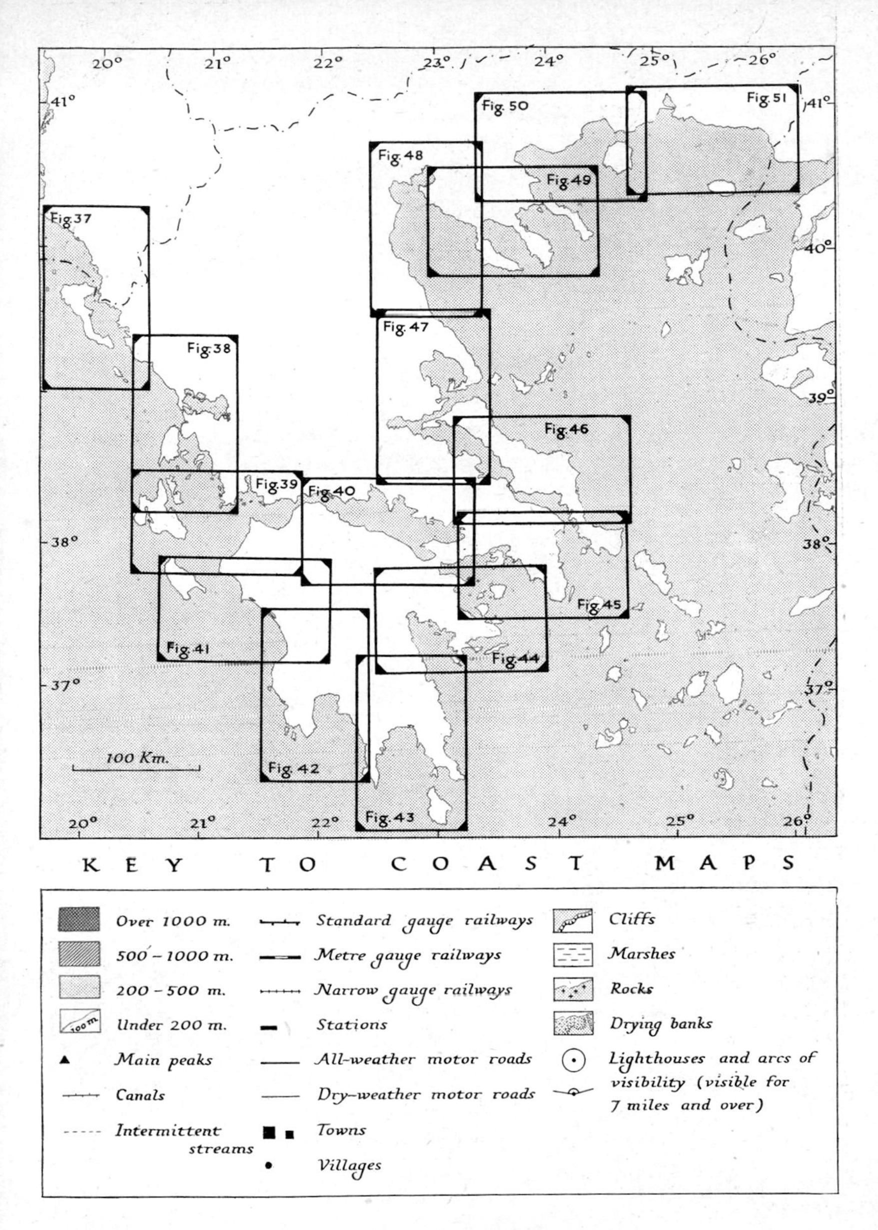

Fig. 36. Key for sequence of coastal maps

For sources of coastal maps see Bibliographical Note, p. 77.

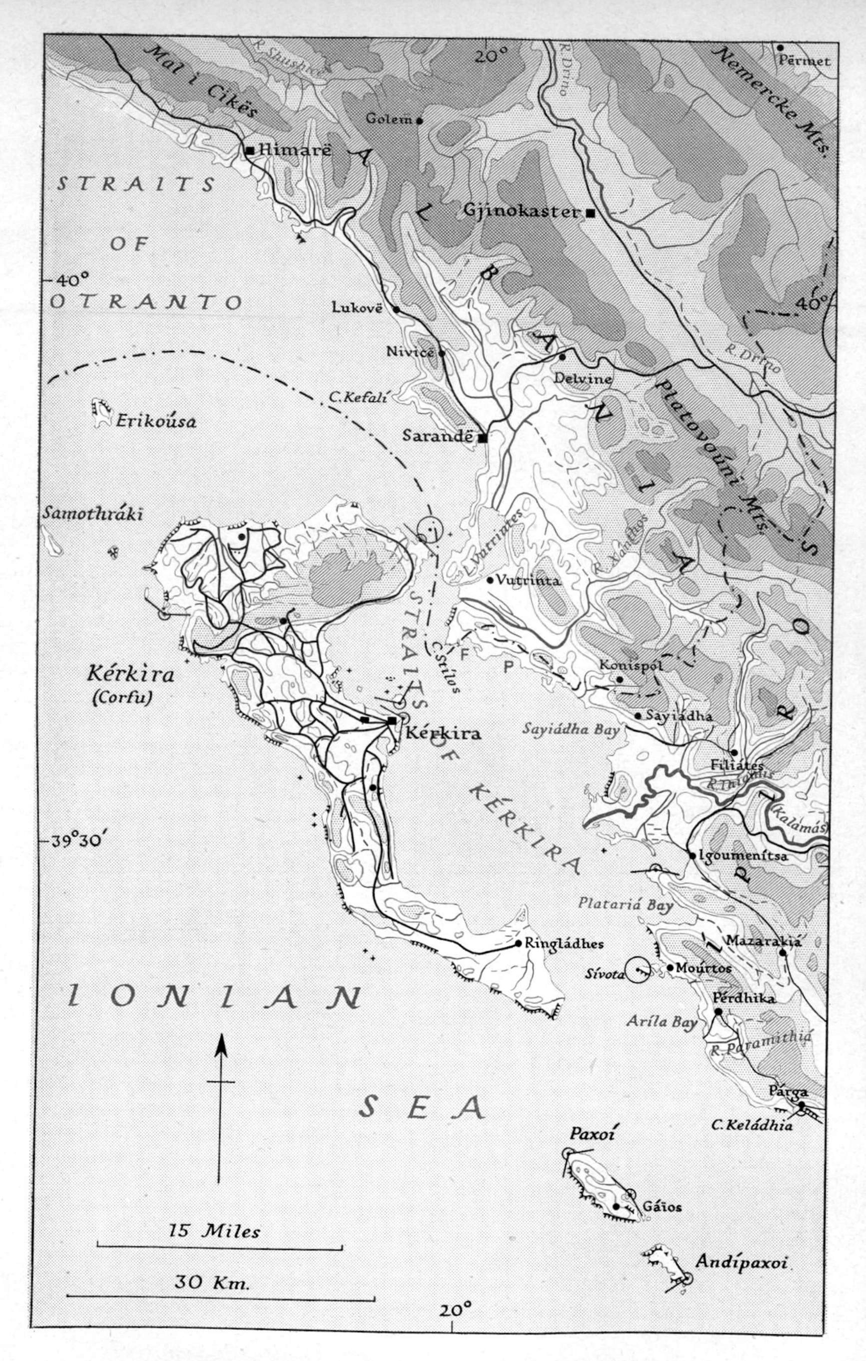

Fig. 37. Kérkira and Ípiros (Epirus)

F, Fteliá Bay; *P*, Paganiá Bay.

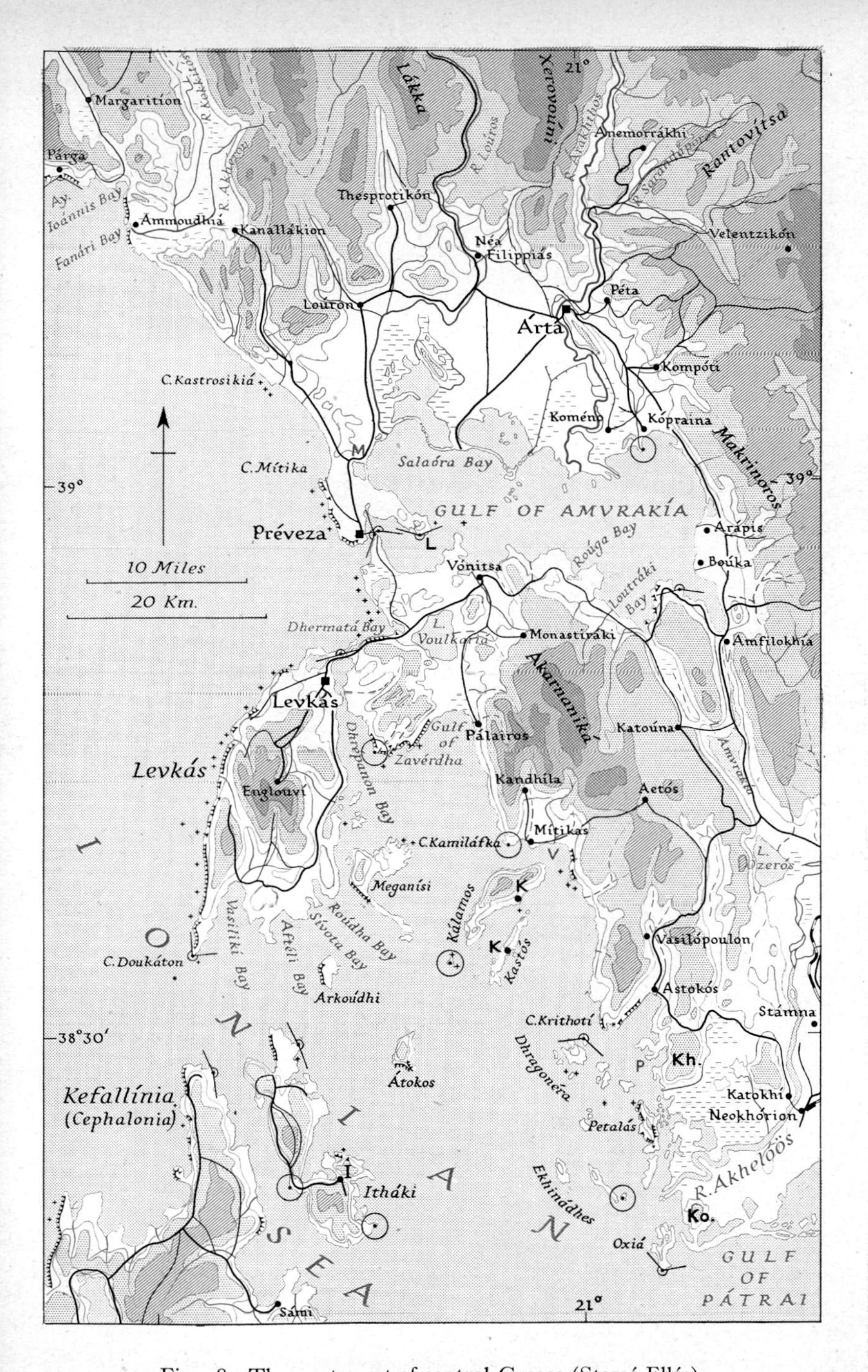

Fig. 38. The west coast of central Greece (Stereá Ellás)

Kh, Khounovoúna Hills; *Ko*, Mt Koutsouláris; *L*, Cape Laskára; *M*, Mázoma Lagoon; *P*, Platiyiáli Bay; *V*, Voúrkos Bay.

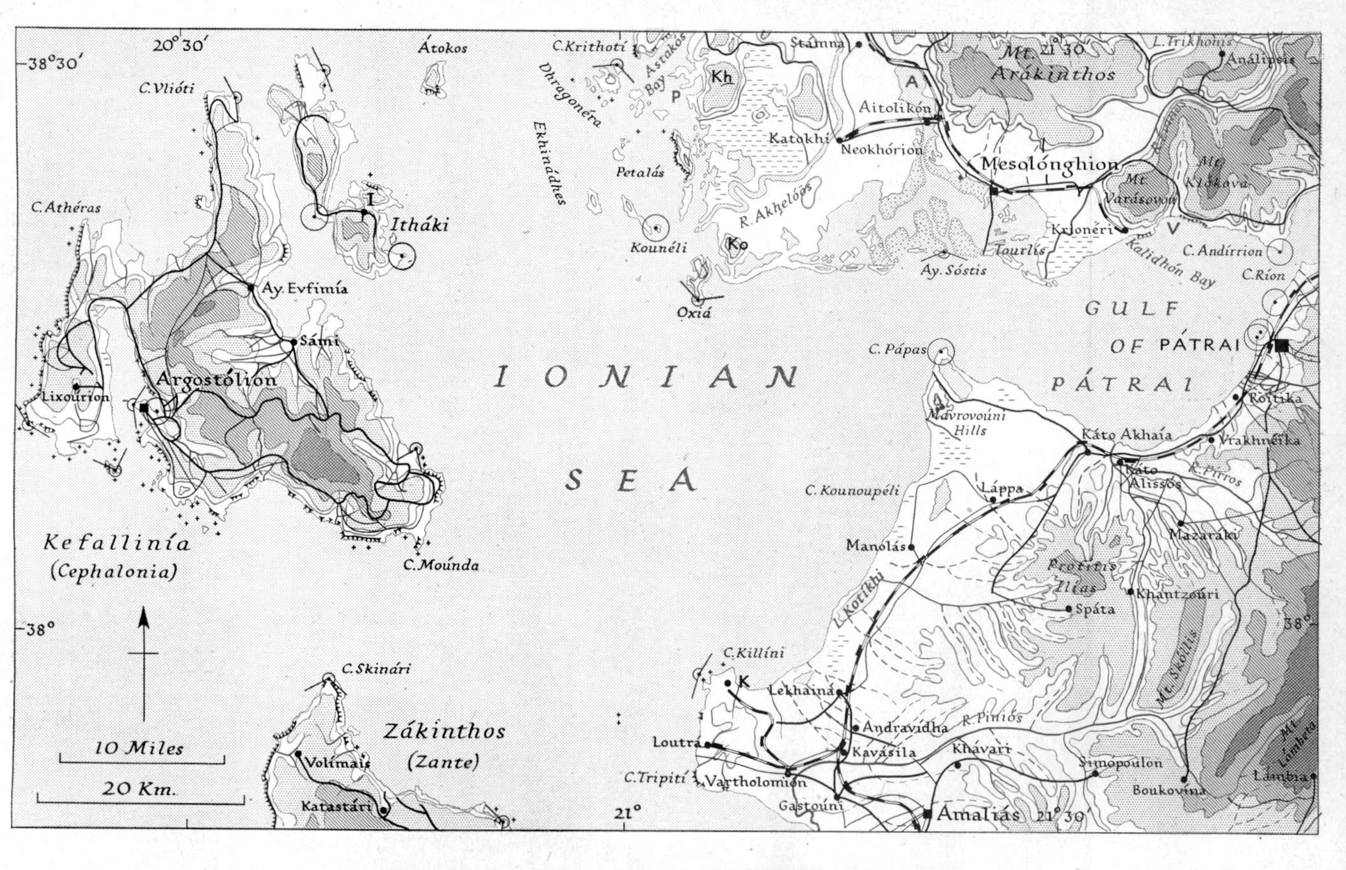

Fig. 39. Kefallinía and the Gulf of Pátrai (Patras)

A, Lake Aitolikón; *Kh*, Khounovoúna Hills; *K*, Killíni; *Ko*, Mt Koutsouláris; *P*, Plativiáli Bay; *V*, Vasilikí Bay.

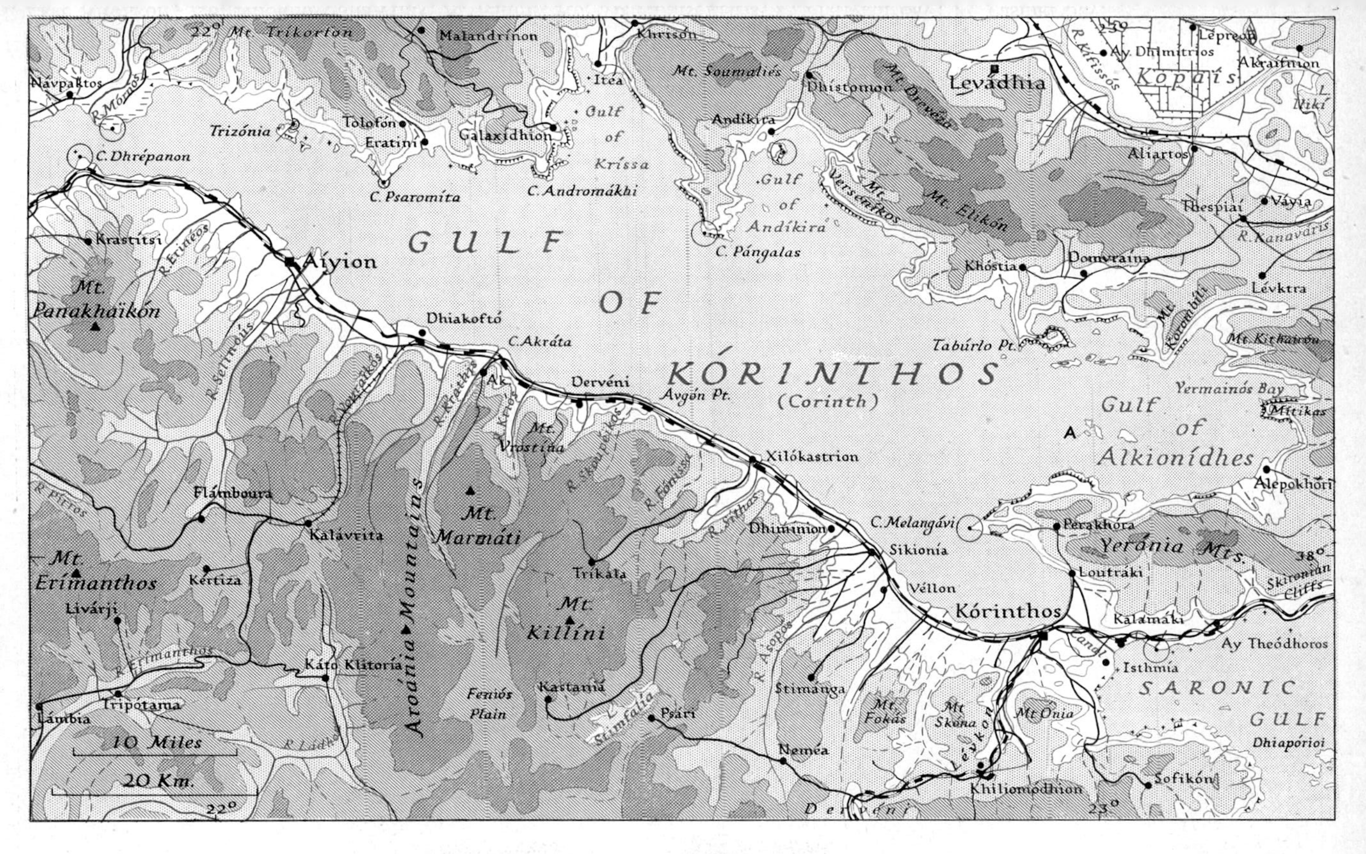

Fig. 40. The Gulf of Kórinthos (Corinth)

A, Alkionídhes Islands.

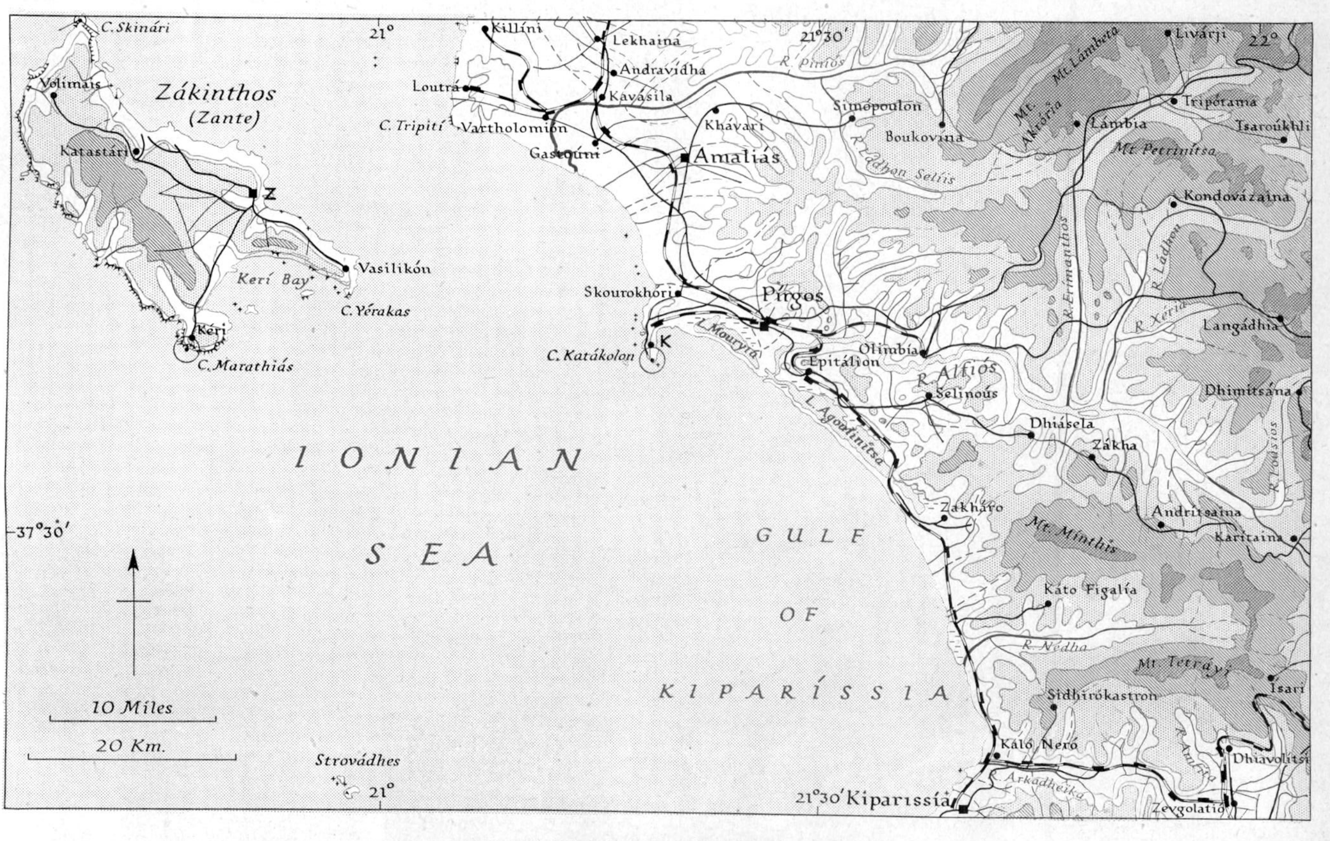

Fig. 41. North-western Pelopónnisos

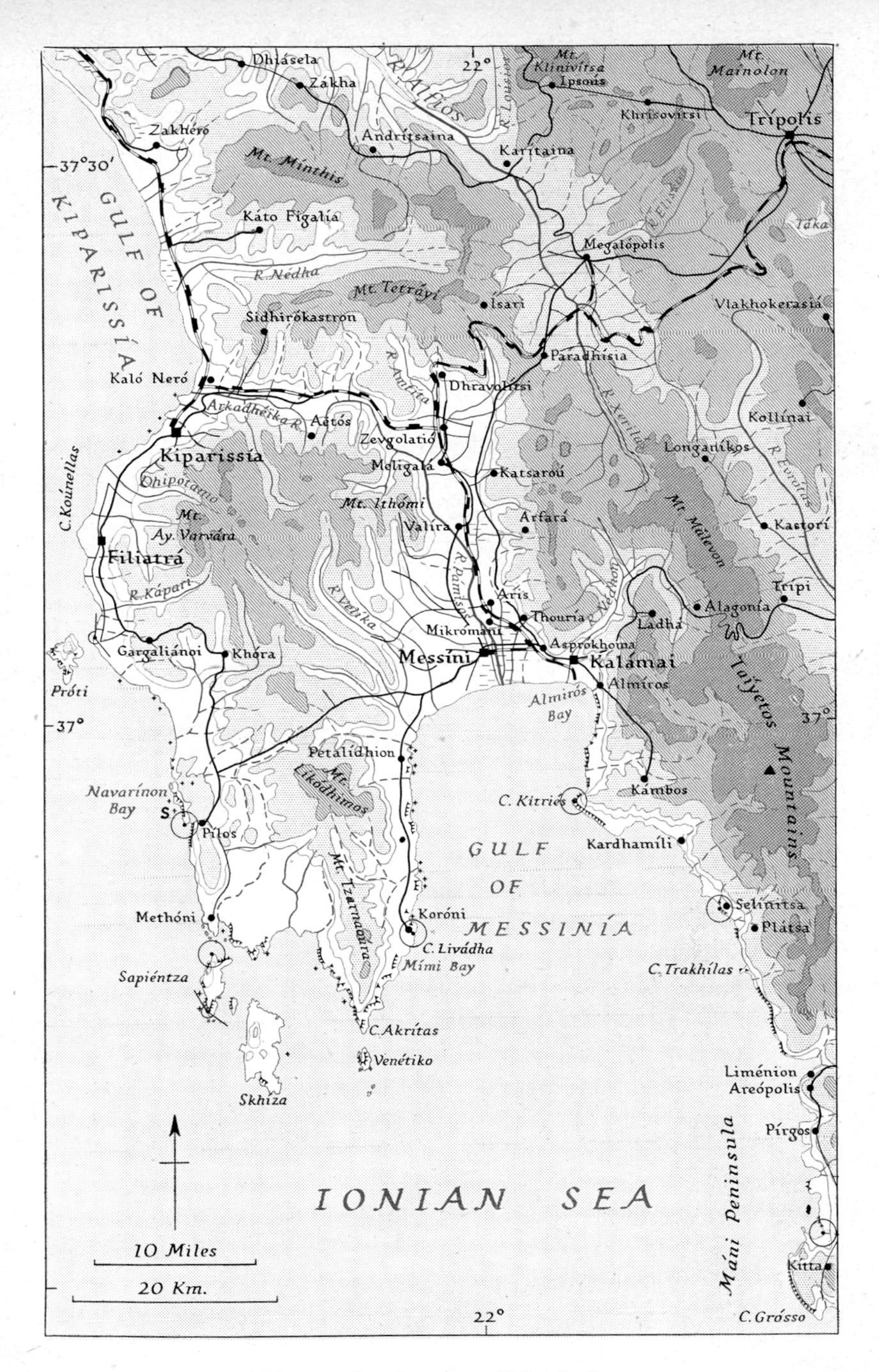

Fig. 42. South-western Pelopónnisos

S, Sfaktiría Island.

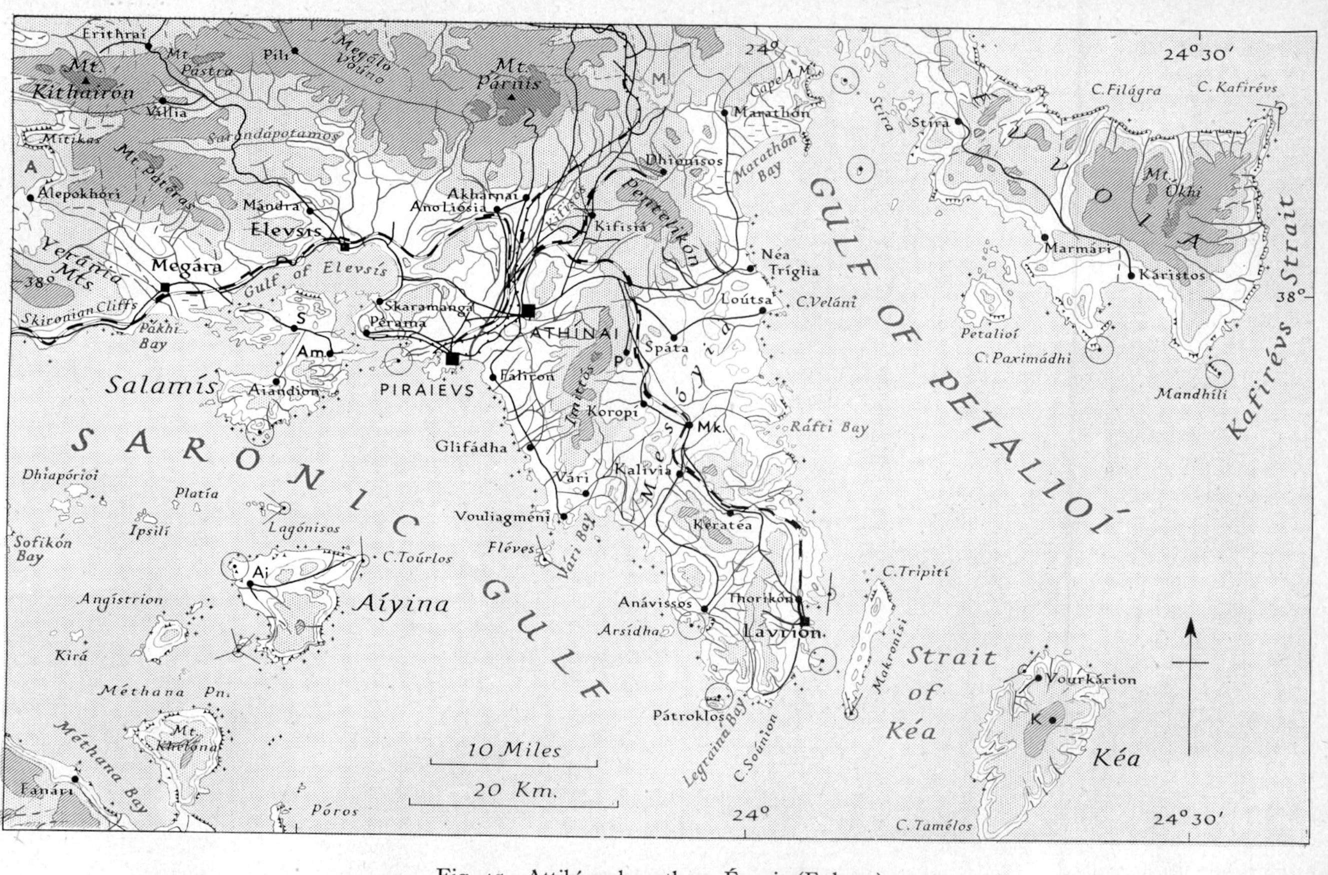

Fig. 45. Attikí and southern Évvoia (Euboea)

A, Gulf of Alkionídhes; *Am*, Ambeláki; *Cape A.M.*, Cape Ayía Marína; *M*, Marathón Lake; *Mk*, Markopoulon; *P*, Paianía; *S*, Salamís.

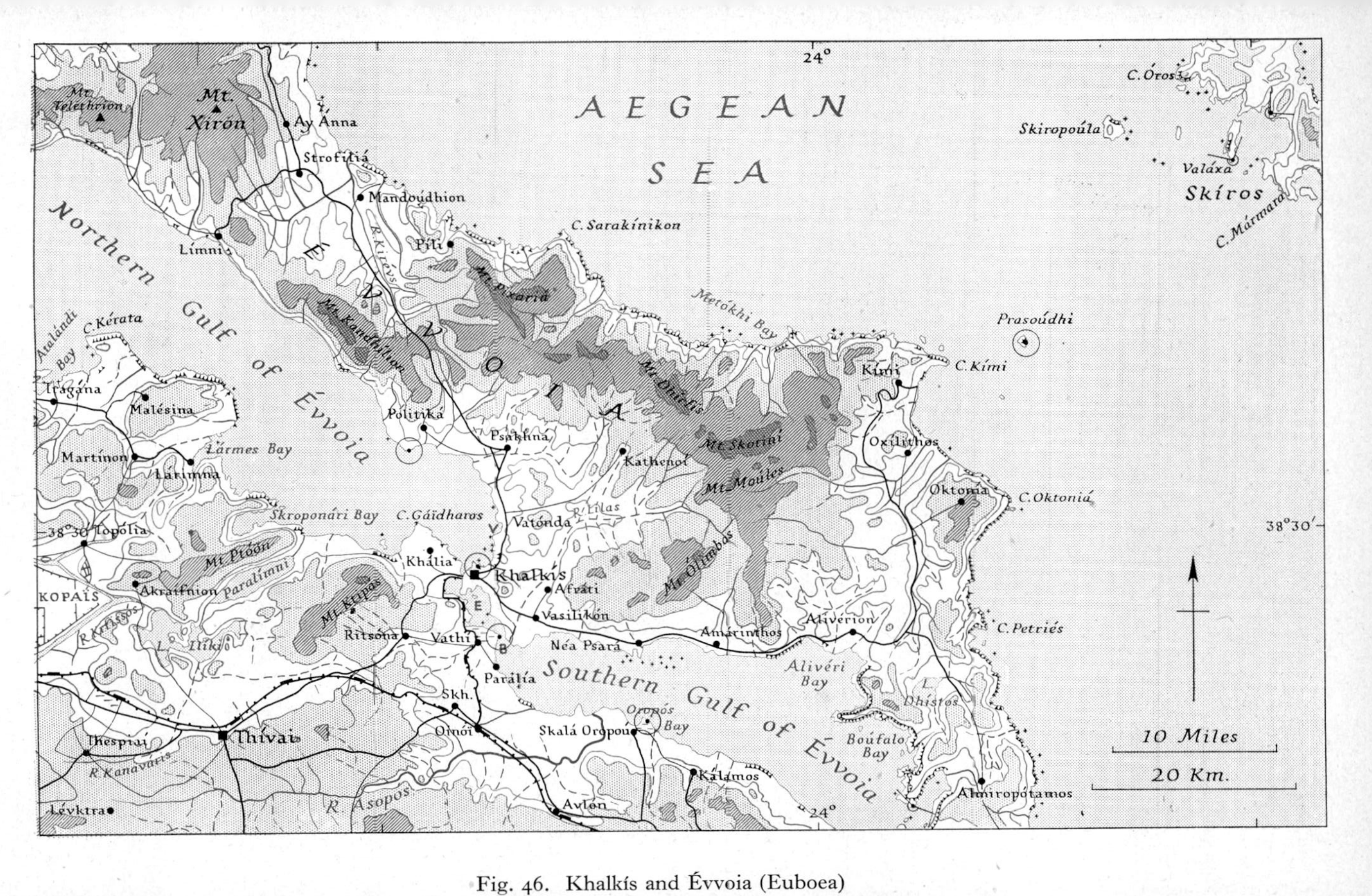

Fig. 46. Khalkís and Évvoia (Euboea)

B, Búrji Channel; *E*, Evripós Strait; *Skh*, Skhimatárion; *V*, Vatónda Bay.

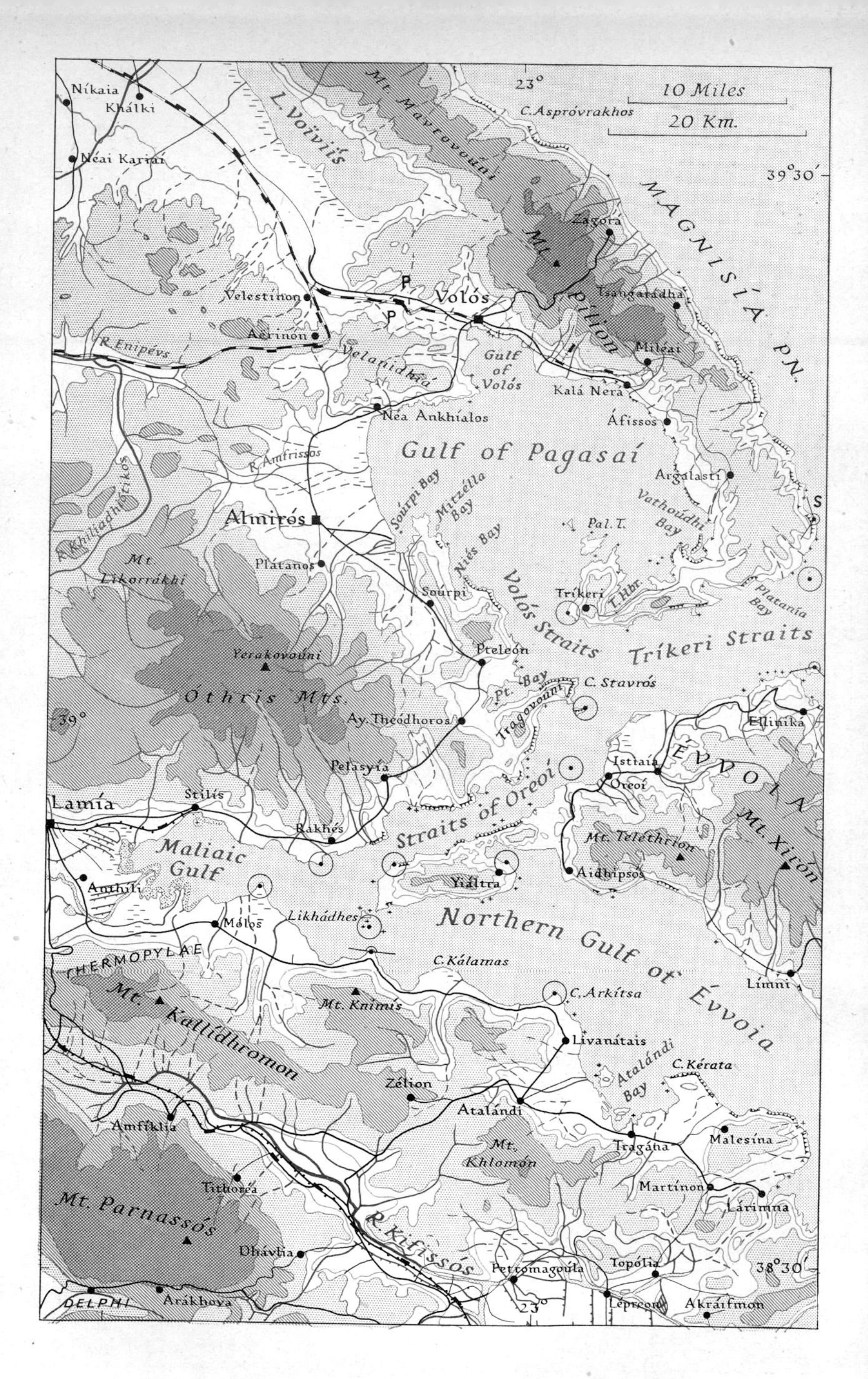

Fig. 47. East central Greece and the Gulf of Pagasaí (Vólos)
P, Piláftepe Pass; *Pal. T*, Palaió Tríkeri; *S*, Cape Sipía.

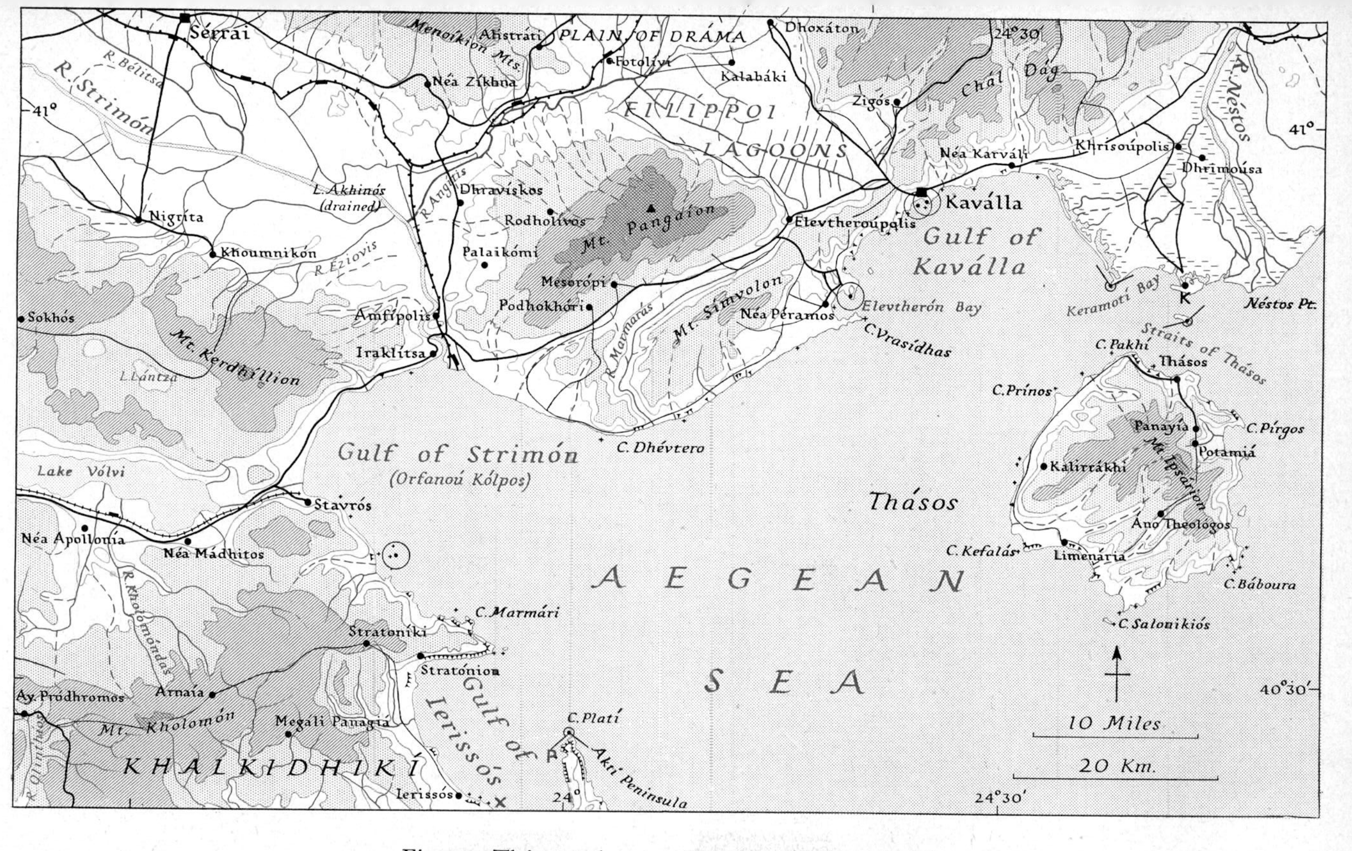

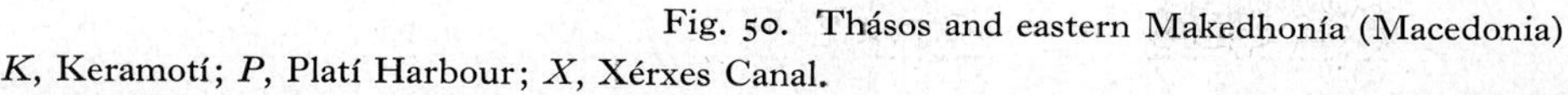

Fig. 50. Thásos and eastern Makedhonía (Macedonia)

K, Keramotí; *P*, Platí Harbour; *X*, Xérxes Canal.

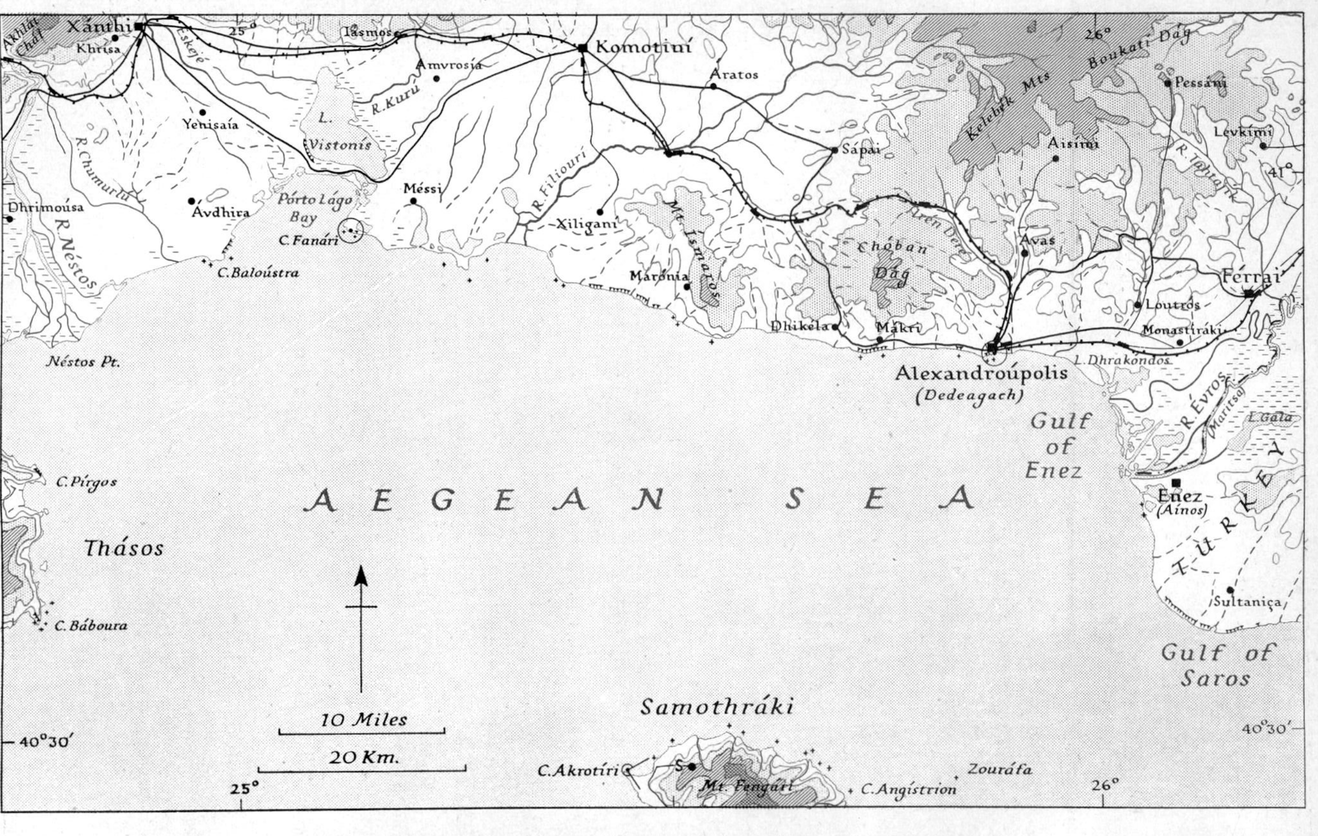

Fig. 51. Samothráki and the coast of Dhitikí Thráki (Western Thrace)

Detailed Description

The north-western coast has many distinctive features. The old and highly altered rocks which give a bold and inaccessible character to so much of Khalkidhikí are here replaced by relatively soft undisturbed rocks. Thus, although the trend of the eastern shores of the Gulf of Thérmai has been determined by faulting, the coastal lands are low, terraced and comparatively well populated. The shoreline is smooth, except for the cliffed bluffs of Mikró Karaburnú and Megálo Karaburnú, and farther south the low sand-spits of Cape Túzla and Cape Epanomí.

The peninsula of Kassándra, which curves south-eastwards for 34 miles, is the most westerly of the three finger-like peninsulas of Khalkidhikí. Once an island it is now linked to the mainland by a sandy isthmus, across which the Potídhaia canal, 128 ft. wide and 7 ft. deep, was being cut in 1937. South of the canal there are low sea cliffs, but for the most part the shore is a beach, smooth in outline and without good anchorages.

The peninsula of Sithoniá, 25 miles in length, rises boldly from the sea to a mountainous and forested interior. The peninsula trends to the south-east and is connected to the mainland by a narrow isthmus. To the south the shoreline is irregular in outline, offering many good anchorages, and sea cliffs are a common feature. The difficulty of land communications and the poverty of the interior have prevented the development of any ports (Plate 56).

The peninsula of Aktí, which forms the autonomous province of Áyion Óros, trends south-eastwards for 31 miles. It is linked to Khalkidhikí by the Xérxes Isthmus which has risen at least 45 ft. since a canal was cut across it in 480 B.C. by the Persian general, Xerxes. To the south, and especially on the west coast, the rugged and thickly wooded mountains rise abruptly from the sea and the numerous monasteries are often perched on the high sea cliffs (Plate 91). The east coast is less impressive and there are numerous small bays backed by intensively cultivated gardens and orchards. The beaches, fringing the bays, provide good landing places for the neighbouring monasteries. Near the tip of the peninsula, Áyion Óros (Mount Áthos) rises in a sharp cone to 6,660 ft. and is one of the most widely visible peaks in the Aegean (Fig. 33).

Communications

Roads. Apart from the major roads which make use of the 'Lake Corridor', most roads in Khalkidhikí are dirt tracks fit only for motor traffic in dry weather. From Thessaloníki a broad tarmac road runs north-east to Laïná, where one road continues to Sérrai and another swings south-east skirting the southern shores of Lakes Korónia and Vólvi to Stavrós. A second road, two-way and macadamized, runs south from Thessaloníki to Kalamariá and follows the coast to Angelokhóri and Epanomí. Just south of Kalamariá an asphalt road turns inland to Políyiros, the chief town of Khalkidhikí, and from this centre a motor road leads south to the small port of Yerakiní at the head of the Gulf of Kassándra.

Railways. The Saraklí-Stavrós narrow-gauge railway (600 mm. or 1 ft. 11$\frac{5}{8}$ in.) makes use of the 'Lake Corridor' and is isolated from the rest of the Greek rail system.

(17) South-eastern Makedhonía (Macedonia) and Dhitikí Thráki (Western Thrace)

General Description (Figs. 33, 34, 35, 50 and 51)

The coasts of south-eastern Makedhonía and Dhitikí Thráki trend approximately eastwards for 170 miles from the Gulf of Strimón to the Turkish frontier. Broad open bays with comparatively smooth shores succeed one another, and there are no good natural harbours. Immediately inland, extensive lowlands are traversed by sluggish rivers, or crystalline plateaux rise steeply from narrow coastal plains. This coast is markedly different from that of peninsular Greece, lacking the innumerable tiny coves and many harbours of the latter. The contrasts arise from the different physical features of the two regions (see pp. 1–3).

In the north-east the main features of the coast have been determined by the great dislocations, which, in recent geological time, shattered the old crystalline plateaux. More or less vertical movements took place, isolating many of the plateau blocks. Thus the islands of Thásos and Samothráki became separated from the mainland, and their steep faces rise boldly above the sea. A period of rapid sedimentation followed upon the dislocations, partly filling some of the troughs between the crystalline plateaux, and extending the coastal plains southwards with the detritus brought from the highland areas. This had the effect of smoothing the shoreline, although the process is by no means complete, as, for example, where the depression occupied by Lake Vistonís and Pórto Lágo still divides the plain of Xánthi from that of Komotiní (Figs. 34 and 35). Wave action is also playing its part in this smoothing action, as on the east coast of the Gulf of Kaválla where sand bars choke the mouths of rivers and so form many small lagoons. The plains are crossed by rivers which have built deltas of varying sizes; but it is only the Néstos which has a pronounced delta. To the west the Strimón basin is almost shut off from the sea by low hills and deposition has therefore taken place across the lower valley and not at the river mouth; to the east, the Évros has so far only had time to build up a deltaic plain in the trough separating the Rodhópi mountains from the mountains of Turkish Thrace.

The broad stretches of coastal lowlands, composed of sand, mud or silt, are almost always flat, badly drained and marshy, and it is because of the malarial nature of much of this country that there are few settlements on the coast itself. The ports of Kaválla and Alexandroúpolis serve the drier and well-populated plains farther inland; but both ports are small and their harbours are artificial and ill-equipped for considerable traffic. Arterial roads and railways avoid the coast mainly for military reasons.

Detailed Description

The Gulf of Strimón (Orfanoú Kólpos) is a broad bay in the angle between Khalkidhikí on the south-west and the mainland on the north (Fig. 50). There are few coastal settlements, and on the south-west mountains rise steeply inland in terraced and heavily wooded slopes. Approaching the village of Stavrós near the head of the gulf, the very narrow coastal plain broadens to more extensive lowlands, and over a low threshold to the west of the village is the 'Lake Corridor' leading to Thessaloníki. From Stavrós to the small delta mouths of the Strimón the coast is low and sandy, while inland the coastal plain soon gives way to the wooded slopes of Kerdhíllion, a much dissected plateau separating the 'Lake Corridor' from the valley of the Strimón. To the west of the delta is the village of Iraklítsa (Tsáyezi) and to the east, and some little way upstream, is the newly created naval or military harbour of Amfípolis.

From the delta to Cape Dhévtero the coast trends south-east and is backed by fertile terraces with numerous villages, while in the distance the forest-clad Pangaíon mountains are clearly visible. On rounding the broad headland of Dhévtero there is a sudden change in the type of country, for the coast, rising steeply to the thickly wooded and heavily eroded Símvolon mountains, is practically without settlement and certainly without any good anchorage.

The Gulf of Kaválla is the second of the great embayments along the north-eastern coast. On the west the submergence of the land has resulted in many small coves which are well sheltered by surrounding hills; on the east is the low and swampy salient of the Néstos delta where sand bars fringe numerous small lagoons (Fig. 50). The port of Kaválla lies at the head of the gulf and serves as the outlet for the well-populated plain of Dráma (Plate 58).

Thásos island is a forested mountain block lying immediately south of the Néstos delta. It is roughly hexagonal in shape, but there are many small bays which break the smooth line of the shore. At the head of each bay there is usually a strip of cultivated lowland, while on the north-east coast there is a narrow coastal plain. Elsewhere, gleaming white cliffs are backed by dark forest-clad mountains.

The Plains of Xánthi and Komotiní together form a broad lowland belt extending eastwards for some 55 miles to the Chobán Dag (Fig. 51). They are divided from each other by the Bay of Pórto Lágo and Lake Vistonís, where the subsidence along a north-north-east axis has been greater than that which affected the plains on either side. In general the shoreline is smooth, and deposition from the numerous, but intermittent, streams which cross the plains has resulted in shallow banks offshore. The coast of the plain of Xánthi is low, malarious and without settlement, but farther inland there are occasional areas of higher and drier ground where villages are frequent. On either side of Pórto Lágo Bay and on the western shores of the Komotiní plain, wave action has built a series of sand dunes, behind which are many lagoons rich in bird life. Farther east beyond the river Filiourí, the ground rises steeply and healthier conditions prevail. The steep seaward face of these hills continues to Alexandroúpolis, just to the west of the uninhabited and marshy lands of the Évros delta.

Samothráki, like Thásos farther to the west, is a mountainous island composed chiefly of ancient rocks. There are few harbours, and except for a low sandspit on the west, the coasts rise steeply to the shrub-covered interior (Plate 60).

Communications

Roads. This region is comparatively well supplied with good metalled roads, which lead northwards from the principal ports to the large towns of the inland basins. Thus, Amfípolis is connected to Sérrai, Kaválla to Dráma, Pórto Lágo to Xánthi and Komitiní, and Alexandroúpolis to Edirne (Adrianople). In addition, a tarmac road from Amfípolis crosses the Strimón by a first-class bridge

Plate 57. Kalamítsa Point

The promontory marks the western entrance to the Gulf of Kaválla. The two islets in the background lie close together about 300 yards to the south-south-east.

Plate 58. Kaválla

Kaválla, with a population of over 60,000 people, is the chief port of north-eastern Greece. The old town, encircled by walls, is built on the steep slopes of the promontory on the east side of the bay. The photograph shows part of the fine Byzantine aqueduct of two, and in some places of three, tiers of arches.

Plate 59. Limenária on the island of Thásos

Limenária lies on the south-west coast of the island. With strong southerly winds it is frequently impossible to land at the village.

Plate 60. Khóra on the island of Samothráki

The mountainous island offers few facilities for landing.

(maximum load 14 tons) and closely follows the coast to Stavrós. A second road, narrow, but in a good state of repair (1940), runs south from Amfípolis and then uses the broad upland valley between the Pangaíon and Símvolon mountains to reach Elevtheroúpolis (30 miles) and Kaválla (37 miles). A new, well-graded tarmac road runs north-west from Elevtherón Harbour to Elevtheroúpolis. Numerous dirt roads, suitable for motor traffic in dry weather, provide a fairly close network in most coastal regions.

Railways. A standard-gauge railway, completed in May 1940, runs northwards along the lower course of the Strimón from Amfípolis to Miríni (12 miles), where it joins the Thessaloníki-Alexandroúpolis line (Hellenic State Railways). Alexandroúpolis is also connected by the Franco-Hellenic Railway with Edirne (Turkey) and Svilengrad (Bulgaria).

BIBLIOGRAPHICAL NOTE

1. The main sources for an account of the structure and relief of the Greek coasts are given in the bibliographical note to Chapter 1.

2. Much descriptive material, of unequal value, is to be found in the numerous travel books and papers on Greece. Of these, one of the most valuable is W. M. Leake, *Travels in the Morea*, 3 vols. (London, 1830), and *Travels in Northern Greece*, 4 vols. (London, 1835); these provide useful and detailed topographical descriptions. Far more widely read is J. G. Frazer's delightfully written book, *Studies in Greek Scenery, Legend and History* (London, 1931), which was first published in 1900 under the title *Pausanias and other Greek Sketches*. A paper by A. W. Gomme, 'The Scenery of Greece', in *Geographical Journal*, vol. LVII, pp. 418–30 (London, 1921), gives, in short space, a clear picture of the infinite variety of form and colour in Greek scenery. The coastal descriptions in *Les Guides Bleus—Grèce* (Paris, 1935) and *Baedeker's Greece* (Leipzig and London, 1909) are useful, but far from comprehensive.

3. From a navigational point of view, the most accessible material is to be found in the following publications of the Hydrographic Department, Admiralty:

(*a*) *Mediterranean Pilot*, vol. III, 7th ed. (London, 1943).

(*b*) *Mediterranean Pilot*, vol. IV, 7th ed. (London, 1941).

(*c*) *The Admiralty List of Lights, Fog Signals and Visual Time Signals*, 1941, Part V, 'Mediterranean, Black and Red Seas' (London, 1941).

More complete, however, are the four volumes of *Naviliakí, Odhiyíi ton Ellinikón, Aktón* [Greek Sailing Directions] A, B, Γi and Γii (Athínai, 1937–9), published by the Hydrographic Service of the Royal [Hellenic] Navy. They are very fully illustrated with charts of small areas, harbour plans, and sketches.

4. The coastal maps have been drawn mainly from G.S.G.S. 1 : 250,000 Series 4088: *The Balkans* (Ordnance Survey, 1940). The detail and accuracy of this map are considerably greater in northern Greece than in the Pelopónnisos, but the information has been checked, wherever possible, from the Greek Army Geographical Staff, 1 : 100,000, *Epitelikós Khártis tis Elládhos* (Athínai, 1925–41), and from other official maps of Greece (see pp. 399–403). British Admiralty charts have also been used fully as well as Greek charts Nos. 1–12, 14–48 (Athínai, 1917–39) (see pp. 406–9).

Roads and railways have been drawn from Greek Government maps.

Chapter III

CLIMATE

Introduction: General Character of the Climate: Pressure and Winds: Temperature: Rainfall: Snow and Snow-cover: Humidity: Visibility: Sunshine and Cloudiness: Climatic Regions: Bibliographical Note

Introduction

The main characteristics of the climate of Greece are due to three major features: the general pressure conditions, the position of the area, and its relief.

The General Pressure Conditions. In winter (Fig. 52) the great anticyclone of central Asia extends over south Russia and often over the Danubian plains to the northern mountains of the Balkan peninsula: thus a strongly developed and very persistent high-pressure system lies north of Greece. To the south of Greece a less intense, but nevertheless persistent, belt of high pressure is found over north Africa, Cyrenaica and Egypt, leaving a region of relatively lower pressure between these northern and southern systems. Along this relatively low-pressure belt the depressions of winter pass eastwards. In summer (Fig. 52) the dominant features are the development of a great low-pressure area over the plains of north-west India and the Persian Gulf, and the northward movement of the Azores high. Throughout the summer these conditions cause steady north winds over the eastern basin of the Mediterranean.

The Location of Greece. The position of Greece between the land mass of eastern Europe, with its varied relief and climatic extremes, and the southern basin of the eastern Mediterranean sea, gives to the climate of Greece something of a transitional character. In spite of its latitude and peninsular form, the climate of parts of mainland Greece shows variations from the pure Mediterranean type; features characteristic of the continental climate of eastern and central Europe appear in addition to the distinguishing marks of the Mediterranean regime.

The Relief. The distribution of mountains and lowlands and the indented nature of the coast emphasize the effect of location. On the one hand, the mountainous character of much of the area carries continental conditions southward; on the other hand, numerous bays and gulfs allow the influence of the Mediterranean sea to penetrate

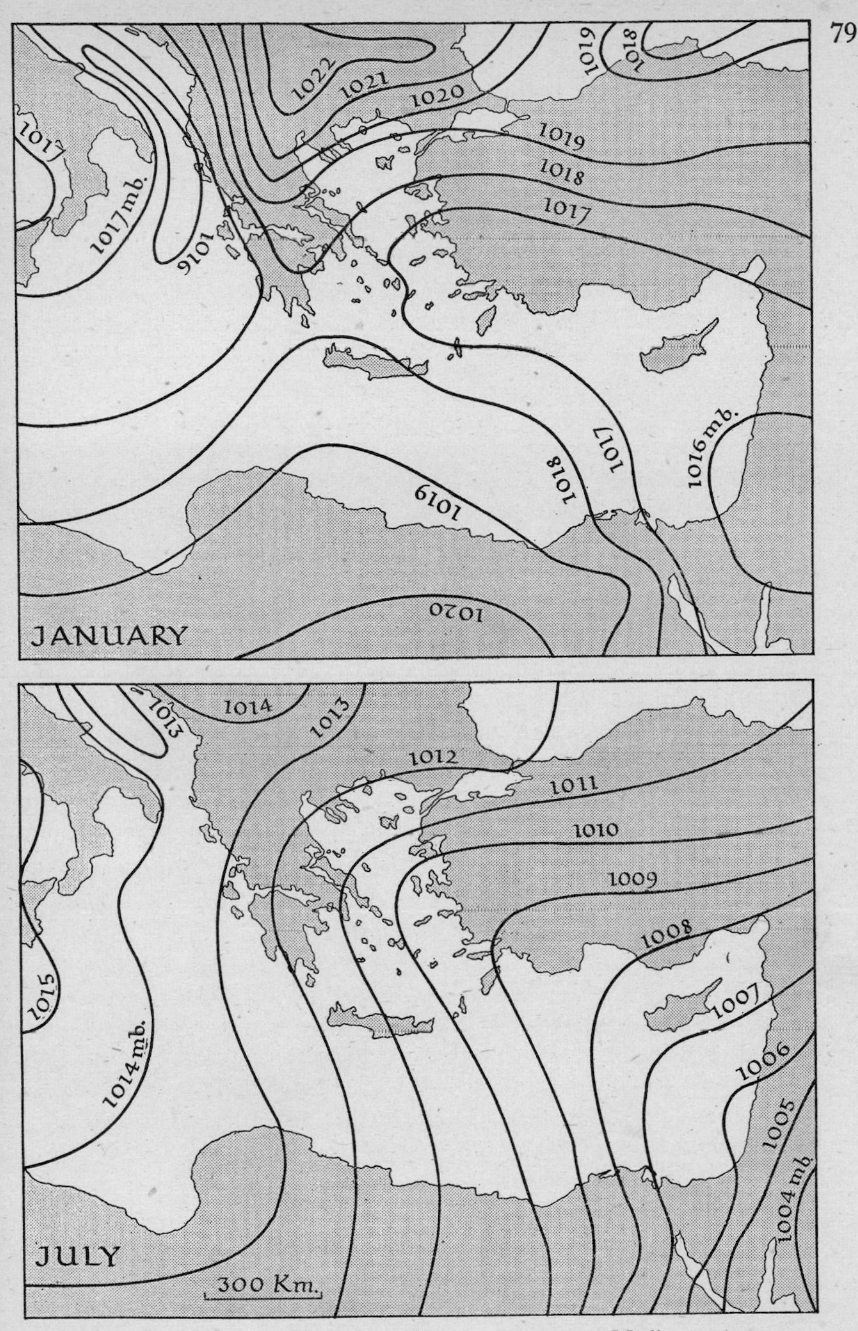

Fig. 52. Isobars for January and July in the eastern Mediterranean

Based on I.D. 1117. *The Climate of the Eastern Mediterranean &c.*, Plates I and III (London, 1916).

The high-pressure systems north and south of Greece in winter, and the very low-pressure system of south-west Asia in summer are controlling factors in the climate of the eastern Mediterranean.

in places far into the highlands. An effect of the relief is seen in the variety of local climates.

The marked differences in climate and weather, between neighbouring areas, makes it necessary to generalize with caution about climatic conditions in Greece and the Aegean. Meteorological stations are few and for the most part confined to lowland areas (Fig. 53), while records are often short and incomplete. Thus there is a danger in giving too wide a significance to data which may reflect only local conditions or exceptional seasons.

General Character of the Climate

In general, Greece has the warm wet winters and hot dry summers typical of Mediterranean countries. The winter and summer seasons are well marked, with a very brief spring and a longer autumn. But many local variations, determined largely by altitude and distance from the sea, are superimposed on this well-defined seasonal pattern.

Spring. This is perhaps the most enjoyable season in the lowlands, especially in western Greece; it is short, for winter is often tardy, particularly in the eastern plains, and in most years only March and April have soft agreeable weather. During March warm winds from the south sometimes bring rain, but in April the heat of the land is sufficient to make them dry. Temperature changes are frequent at this season and often large in amount. Near the mountains and in enclosed valleys the drop in temperature at night is very marked; the cold air from the higher slopes flows down after sunset bringing low temperatures during the night and early mornings.

Summer. The heat of summer begins to be felt in the plains by the middle of May, and before the end of the month the temperature is rising rapidly: Maximum temperatures are experienced in July and August, and in the interior and in sheltered situations the heat may be intense. The coasts and islands are tempered by cooler breezes. In the mountains the heat is not great until July, and August is usually the hottest month, but even in this month the temperatures are lower than in the plains.

Autumn. Like spring, autumn is a transition season marked by variable conditions which begin late in August. One day the air is calm and the sky serene, the next day the temperature drops, squally winds blow and there are heavy showers. Except in the north the increase of rainfall is not great until late October, and many autumn days are as lovely as those of spring. In eastern Greece autumn may be prolonged; the cold is usually not severe until mid-December, and the rainstorms though torrential are short. Here, autumn is a very pleasant season for travel, in many years better than spring which may be cold and wet.

Winter. Although winter is the wet season, rain does not fall for long at a time, and in most areas there is an average of only ten or

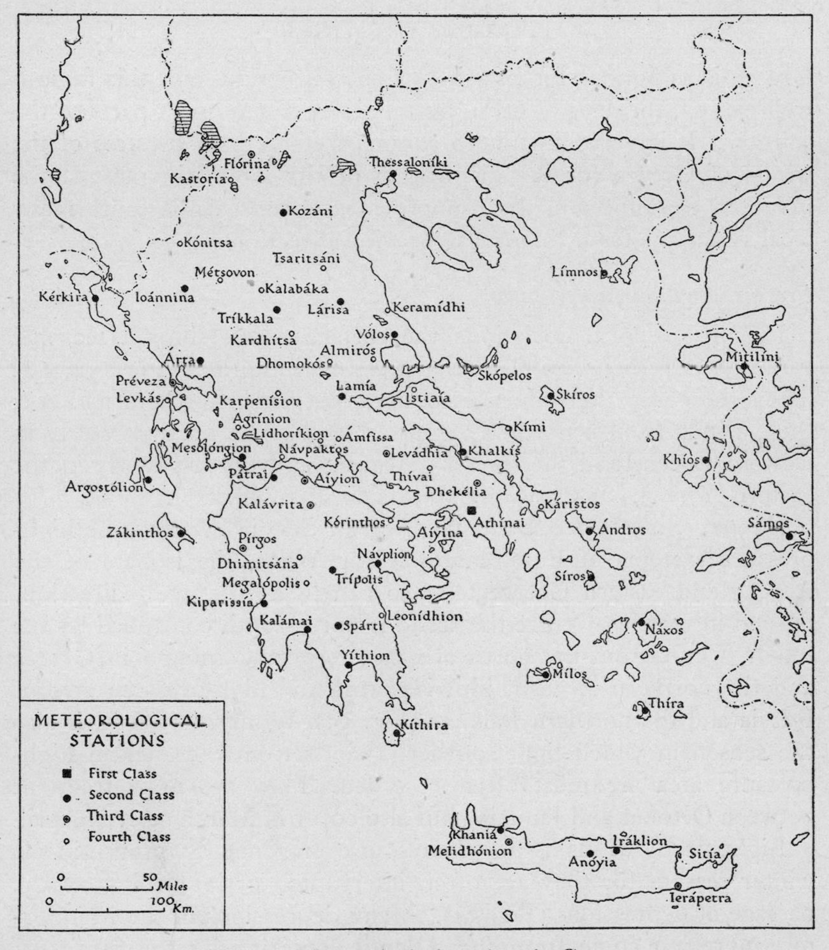

Fig. 53. Meteorological stations in Greece

Meteorological stations are classified according to the number of climatic elements which they record. A fourth-class station records rainfall only. Although Greece is predominantly mountainous, it should be noted that almost all meteorological stations are below 400 m. (1,300 ft.). The altitude, latitude and longitude for these stations are given in Appendix IX, Table I.

twelve rain days a month. Winter rainfall conditions are well established by November, though the weather remains soft until mid-December and the period of greatest cold is usually in January. Even then, in the coastal plains, the temperatures are by no means really low. By February, temperatures are beginning to rise again and spring flowers appear in more sheltered places.

Pressure and Winds

Greece is as famous for its winds as its clear skies and this fame is well earned, for days of calm are relatively few in most parts of the country. It is very difficult to summarize the main features of the winds of Greece for the disposition of the mountain masses, the indented coastline and the numerous scattered islands cause many local variations from the prevalent wind directions.

Pressure and Surface Winds

In spite of local deviations the surface winds show a seasonal variation in response to changing pressure conditions (Figs. 52, 55). They show also the influence of the arrangement of land and sea; thus, winds from a northerly quarter tend to be north-westerly in western Greece and the western Aegean, and north-easterly in the eastern Aegean. South winds show a similar deflexion.

Winter. Since Greece and the Aegean Sea lie between the high-pressure systems of Eurasia and north Africa, the isobars of the Aegean and eastern Greece tend to run in an east-west direction, though in western Greece the trend is north-south controlled by the relief. Winds from the north are therefore predominant in Greece and the northern Aegean, blowing from the high-pressure area of Russia and the northern Balkans (Fig. 55). Winter, however, is also the season in which light southerly winds from the African high-pressure area are most often recorded. They are most frequent between October and January, but also occur in March or even April.

Light steady winds do not always, or even generally, prevail in the winter season, for they are often interrupted or intensified by the passage of depressions (Fig. 54). Many depressions of the Mediterranean region come from the Atlantic, entering by the Straits of Gibraltar or across the lowland of south-west France. Others develop over the Mediterranean, especially over the Tyrrhenian and Adriatic Seas where cold winds from central and eastern Europe blow down from the neighbouring mountains, thus forming sharp surfaces of discontinuity with warm damp air moving across the Mediterranean. These depressions, moving from west to east, are diverted south in winter by the high pressures ruling in the Danubian plains and north Balkans, and they pass in frequent succession over the Greek peninsula and the Aegean Sea. Alternatively, and especially in spring when a tongue of high pressure often unites the high-pressure region of the Balkan mountains with that of Anatolia, the depressions pass to the south, via Cyprus and the Gulf of Alexandretta, to the Euphrates. The effects of the passage of depressions over Greece are clearly marked. With the approach of a depression, the sky clouds and the

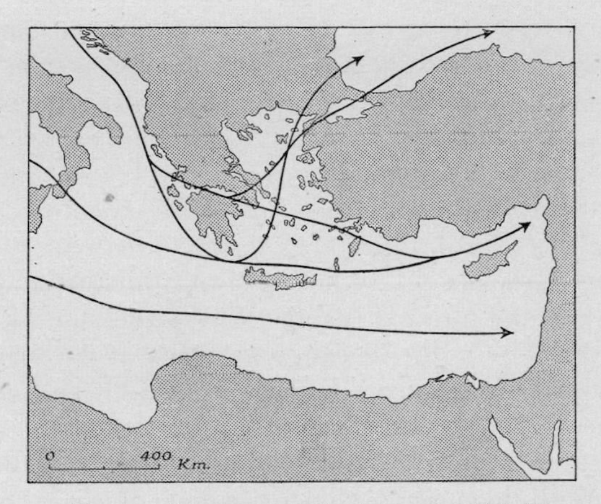

Fig. 54. Tracks of depressions in the eastern Mediterranean

The lines are highly generalized, and show only the most frequent paths followed by depressions. Depressions are numerous in the winter half year, almost unknown in the summer.

winds blow from a northerly quarter if the centre of the depression is to the south, or from a southerly quarter if the centre is to the north. The frequency with which depressions pass between Kríti and the mainland gives to Kríti prevailing winds from the south in winter in contrast with the rest of Greece. As the centre of the depression approaches, the temperature rises, the strength of the wind increases, and there is widespread and heavy rainfall. In the rear of the depression the temperature falls sharply as the north-east winds, usually cold for the time of the year, become established.

Spring. Pressure over the Mediterranean as a whole falls in spring. Centres of low pressure develop over the Tyrrhenian Sea and north Africa, while a marked fall of pressure occurs in the Levant. Thus a high-pressure ridge, sometimes to be seen in winter stretching from the Balkans to Cyrenaica, is accentuated at this season and effectively divides the eastern from the western basin of the Mediterranean, since it forms a barrier to the passage of depressions.

Summer. Pressure continues to fall over the Levant, Red Sea and Persian Gulf area, until, in July, the isobars run almost north and south across Greece with a steep pressure gradient towards the east (Fig. 52). The winds are variable in May and early June, as also in the autumn, but by mid-June the steady northerly winds, known as the Etesian winds, have become established, blowing along the isobars (Fig. 55). The Etesians thus tend to be north-west in the Ionian Sea and western Aegean; from the north in the central Aegean and north-east in the eastern Aegean. Since depressions are rare in summer, these northerly winds are seldom interrupted and blow with great constancy in June, July and August over the sea and islands; they are of considerable strength, frequently exceeding force 5 of the Beaufort scale, and sometimes reaching gale force. Near the coasts and over the land, local relief controls the wind direction and the Etesians may not be felt. The southward inclination of the trees on some of the more forested islands bears witness to the strength of the Etesian winds over the Aegean Sea. Many of the islands are also exposed to winter gales; trees do not grow well, and vegetation is sparse on the higher ground. Navigation off the coasts is difficult at all seasons, and for short periods landing is frequently impossible.

Autumn. With the onset of colder weather, pressure rises over the south Russian steppes and Anatolia, and the isobars tend to change again to an east and west direction over the Black Sea, north Aegean and Anatolian plateau. At the same time, pressure increases again over north Africa, and the isobars of the eastern Mediterranean in October foreshadow the arrangement of the winter season.

Gales

Most winds of gale force (over 7 in Beaufort scale) occur during winter, and winds strong enough to cause a rough sea in the Aegean blow almost exclusively between north-east and north-west or between south-east and south-west.

Northerly gales are associated with an intensification of anticyclonic conditions in the northern Balkans. At such times there is a very sudden transition from the exceptionally high pressures over the land to the lower pressures over the sea. In other words, there is a steep pressure gradient and cold air from the highlands pours into the Aegean in a violent though shallow air current of gale force and squally character. These gales are often stronger than the pressure gradient alone would suggest, since their force is increased by descent from high mountains. They may last for days since they are due to

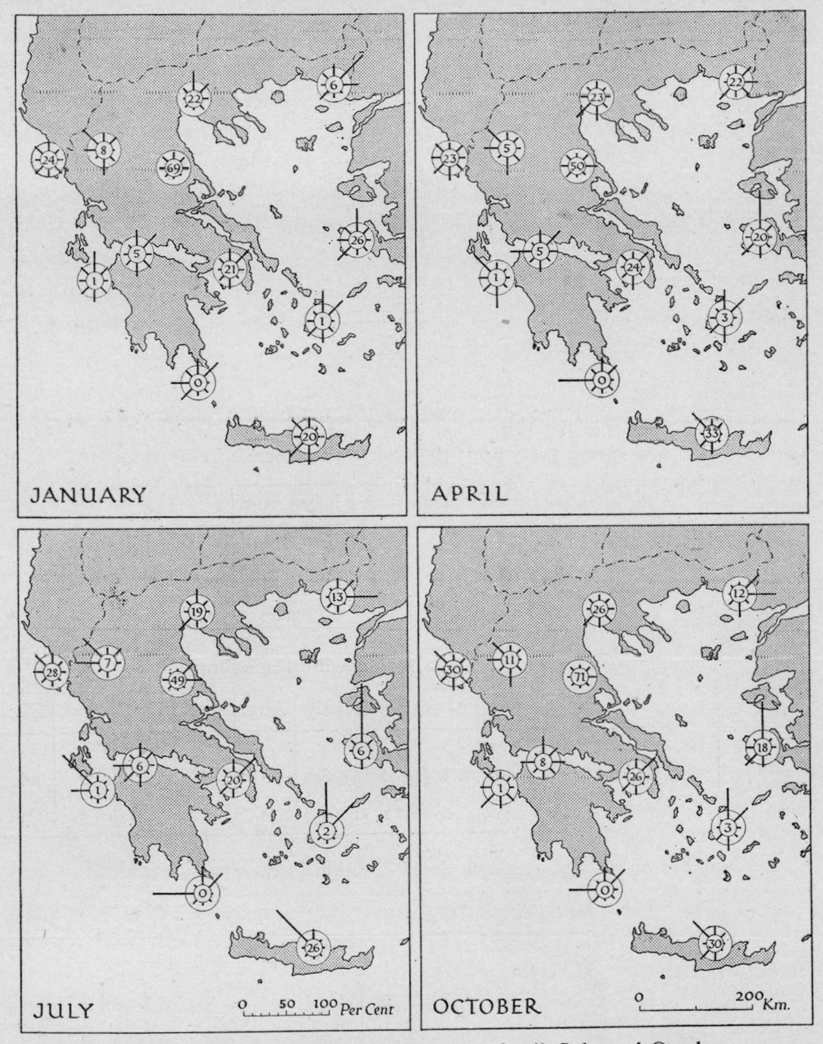

Fig. 55. Wind-rose maps for January, April, July and October

Based on E. G. Mariolopoulos and A. N. Livathinos, *Atlas Climatique de la Grèce* (Athènes, 1935).

The figure in the inner circle shows the percentage of observations when calms were experienced; the outer circle indicates a wind frequency of 10 %.

the establishment of a persistent high-pressure area. Six or seven days of northerly gales have been recorded, but gales of three or four days' duration are more usual. The weather may be fine and cold with clear skies, but when depressions pass south of the Aegean Sea at the same time as intense anticyclonic conditions are developed to the north, there are frequent heavy showers of rain or snow. Local weather observations may give no hint of the near approach of northerly gales, though the pressure conditions shown on synoptic charts may indicate the probability of their development. Southerly gales are also a winter phenomenon and are due exclusively to the passage of exceptionally deep depressions over northern Greece and the north Aegean Sea. A depression usually takes one to two days to pass, but if it is of unusual size or if two deep depressions succeed one another rapidly the gales may blow for three or four days. As a rule, southerly gales are fewer in number, shorter in duration and less severe than those from the north.

Frequency of Northerly and Southerly Gales, 1902–13

Average number of days with wind force 8 or 9

	Jan.	Feb.	Mar.	Apr.	May	June	July	Aug.	Sept.	Oct.	Nov.	Dec.
Northerly gales	3·2	2·5	2·3	1·6	1·1	1·1	1·2	1·0	1·5	1·0	1·5	1·9
Southerly gales	0·9	0·3	0·5	0·7	0	0	0	0	0	0·1	1·5	1·2

Greatest number of days with wind force 8 or 9

	Jan.	Feb.	Mar.	Apr.	May	June	July	Aug.	Sept.	Oct.	Nov.	Dec.
Northerly gales	7	6	5	4	4	4	3	5	4	4	5	4
Southerly gales	4	2	2	4	0	1	0	0	1	1	5	3

Number of gales of over two days' duration in the period 1902–13

	Jan.	Feb.	Mar.	Apr.	May	June	July	Aug.	Sept.	Oct.	Nov.	Dec.
Total number of gales	8	5	3	5	2	5	11	8	6	5	5	6
Longest duration of gales in days	7	4	4	4	3	5	7	5	8	5	5	3

Source: *Weather in the Mediterranean*, vol. II, part 10, p. 24 (Meteorological Office, London, 1936).

In summer gales are rare: but if they lack the frequency and violence of winter storms they are often of considerable duration. They blow almost entirely from northerly quarters and are due to a temporary steepening of the pressure gradient normal for the time of the year. Thus they have the steady quality of the Etesian winds.

The frequency and duration of these northerly and southerly gales and their characteristic winter distribution are seen in the above table, which refers to the Aegean Sea between Athínai and Smyrna.

Local Winds

Local winds are of great importance in Greece and very misleading ideas on the general air circulation would result from observations at coastal stations only, especially if confined to a particular time of day.

The Effect of Relief. Local winds due to relief are very numerous. They develop where the land surface forms a barrier to the prevailing winds: the air banks up behind an obstacle and then flows round or over it by the easiest route, giving rise to a wind of considerable force and constancy often coming from an anomalous direction. Thus the highlands of Évvoia, Ándros and Tínos hold up the northerly Etesians. Even when the Etesians are weak, sufficient banking of the air takes place to cause strong air currents wherever there is a gap. The Kafirévs Channel between Ándros and Évvoia is one such gap and the strong north or north-east winds of this channel are notorious. They scarcely cease for about four months in the summer and often reach gale force. Except at the gaps the prevailing wind is diverted; wind observations at the meteorological station on the east coast of Ándros show that the northerly Etesians of the central Aegean are here diverted into a strong north-west wind. Local winds of a very squally character are frequent on the lee shore of many islands where the Etesians bank up on the windward side, overtop the summit, and blow strongly down the steep lee slopes. These winds often churn up the sea into white foam and hence their name 'white squalls'.

Certain areas in the lee of highlands experience local winds due to relief of another character. The rush of cold air down the valleys of Makedhonía and Thráki gives rise to a local wind called the *vardarac*, analogous to the *mistral* of the Rhône and the *bora* of the Adriatic. The warm drying wind of Thessalía, the *livas*, analogous to the *föhn*, is due to adiabatic heating of the air current descending the eastern slopes of the Píndhos mountains. The air has already been warmed by release of latent heat due to condensation as the west wind rises up the western slopes.

Land and Sea Breezes. Land and sea breezes are very well developed on the islands and in coastal areas in the summer months. During the day, under the glare of the summer sun the land warms up relatively to the sea at a rapid rate, especially if the vegetation cover is sparse. The air in contact with the land surface rises and the pressure falls locally, drawing in the damp cooler air from the sea. These sea breezes are often of considerable strength by the early afternoon, but they bring no rain, since the temperature of the air increases on contact with the heated land sufficiently to counteract the effect of adiabatic cooling of the rising air currents. During the clear night rapid radiation takes place from the land surfaces, the temperature of the air in contact with it falls quickly and the cool air rolls down to the sea, giving rise to well-marked land breezes from the early hours of the evening until dawn. These land and sea breezes greatly modify summer heat in the islands and are especially well developed in the Gulfs of Návplion, Thessaloníki and Smyrna. The Turkish name *imbat* is still widely used in Greece for these sea breezes.

Winds of the Upper Air

Very little information relating to winds of the upper air is available for Greece and the Aegean. Observations carried out at Léros (1933–5), and over short periods during the war of 1914–18 at Thessaloníki, Dráma and Smyrna, have been published.

In so far as any general conclusions can be drawn from the very scanty data, it seems that below about 1,800 m. the winds tend to vary in direction and force with the season and time of day as at the surface. Above 1,800 m. there is a closer approximation to the planetary wind system, winds tending to be westerly or somewhat north of westerly, especially in the summer months when few depressions disturb atmospheric conditions in this area.

Temperature

Temperature in Greece with rare exceptions is not extreme: the cold of winter, except in the mountains, is modified by coastal influences, and the heat of summer is tempered by sea breezes or northerly winds. The diurnal rise of temperature at many stations ceases as early as noon, due to the local development of cooling winds. A characteristic of the Greek climate is the variability of the temperature. Sudden and great changes occur from day to day or even within the same day, and the strong relief causes great irregularities from place to place. There are marked differences between mountains and plains, between the interior and the coast, between west and east coasts of the mainland, between north and south coasts of the islands and even between different parts of the same coast according to the degree of shelter. In general the temperature in Greece shows an increase from north to south at all seasons, the winter isotherms follow the latitude, those of summer the relief.

Winter. January is usually the coldest month and the lowest temperatures are to be found in the upland basins where dense cold air seeps down from the surrounding mountains, often causing temperature inversion. The lowest mean temperature for January is recorded at Flórina (620 m.) 0·8° C. on the northern frontier of Greece, a town of a high level plain flanked by the Píndhos mountains. Kozáni (667 m.) 2·2° C., Lárisa (76 m.) 5·4° C., Tríkkala (114 m.) 5·5° C. and Thessaloníki (39 m.) 5·6° C. all bear witness to the cold of north-eastern Greece in January. Trípolis (661 m.) has a January mean temperature of 5·1° C.; here altitude and the basin-like situation modify the effect of a southerly position (Appendix IX, Table 3). Absolute minimum temperatures of considerably less than −10° C. have been recorded at Flórina (−23° C.), Kozáni (−19° C.), Tríkkala (−19° C.), Trípolis (−17° C.) and Lárisa (−13° C.) (Appendix IX, Table 4).

Frost may occur in all months of the year, even in southern Greece, but it is only common from November to May, with a maximum number of frost days at many stations in January and February (Appendix IX, Table 5). Frost is more common in western Greece, the Ionian islands and in Thíra than in eastern Greece and the northern Aegean islands. Severe frost, with the thermometer remaining below freezing point all day, occurs only in northern Greece and in the mountain districts. All day frosts are recorded, usually in January or February, at stations in Ípiros, Thessalía, Makedhonía and Thráki.

Spring. The temperature rises slowly in February and March and more rapidly in April and May. The sudden change from winter cold to summer heat is a feature common to all Greece.

Summer. The highest mean monthly values occur in July at most stations in eastern Greece, e.g. Návplion, Athínai, Vólos, Tríkkala and

23°C =72°F

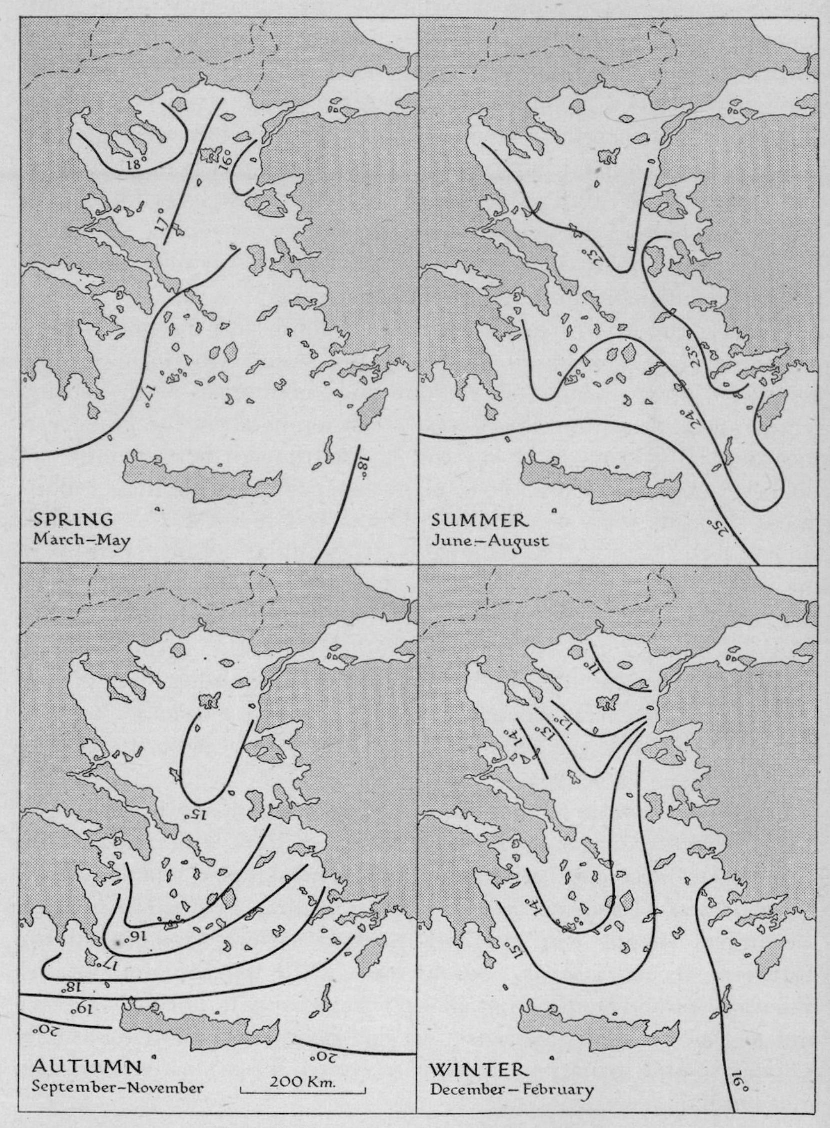

Fig. 56. Sea temperatures in the Aegean

Based on *Weather in the Mediterranean*, vol. II, part 10, pp. 10–16 (London, 1936). The temperatures (°C.) are those of the surface water.

Thessaloníki, but in eastern Makedhonía and Thráki, August is slightly hotter. July and August are equally warm both in western Greece and in most of the islands. In Kíthira and Kríti, however, August is the hottest month. Throughout Greece maximum temperatures seem to occur late in July or early in August: absolute maxima of more than 44° C. have been recorded for many stations in all parts of Greece. At Lárisa and Kalámai 45° C. has been reached, 45·7° C. at Iráklion and the highest temperature ever recorded was 48° C. at Trípolis on 6 and 12 August 1896.

Autumn. The temperature falls sharply in the autumn; the fall is most pronounced at northern stations, but is also marked in the islands. At Athínai and in the eastern Aegean islands the autumn transition period is longer, and a warm autumn is usually experienced.

The Range of Temperature

The seasonal range of temperature is much greater over the mainland than in the islands. This is due largely to the greater winter cold in the highlands of the peninsula; in summer there are no great differences between the mean temperatures of continental stations and those of the archipelago. The diurnal range of temperature is greatest in highland Greece and least in the islands. There is also a marked difference between the east and west coastal areas; the east coast has more extreme temperatures than the west.

Sea Temperatures

The temperature of the water of the Aegean Sea is much affected by that of the neighbouring lands and islands and by the prevailing winds. The temperature of the water on the whole decreases from south to north (Fig. 56), and the gradient is steep in the southern Aegean in the autumn and in the northern Aegean in the winter. The broken nature of the coastline, the numerous islands and the great variations in the depth of the sea cause marked differences in the temperature of the sea water from place to place. The Etesian winds, by removing the surface water which is replaced by deeper water, tend to keep the inshore waters along the north Aegean coasts relatively cool. The same effect occurs temporarily in winter after strong *vardarac* winds. This, coupled with the lower salinity of the gulf, accounts for the occasional freezing of the shore waters about Thessaloníki.

Rainfall

The depressions of the winter season cause by far the greater part of the rainfall of Greece, but, even in the absence of depressions, some rainfall is brought by the southerly winds blowing from the African high-pressure area. The winds pick up moisture as they cross the Mediterranean and their relative humidity is high. As they move north they are cooled and their relative humidity is increased. When the winds are further cooled by rising over the Greek land mass, condensation takes place. Thunderstorms contribute also to the rainfall total. Since the winds of the summer season are mainly northerly and continental, summer rainfall is slight or absent apart from thunderstorm rain (Fig. 57).

Pátrai, Návplion and Kalámai in the Pelopónnisos and all the island stations (Fig. 58) show the true Mediterranean rainfall regime, with a winter maximum in November, December and January, and an almost rainless summer; June, July and August at all these stations have an average rainfall of less than 25 mm. In the south Aegean islands and at Návplion the five months of May to September are all dry, while at the southernmost stations, Náxos, Thíra and Kíthira, the season with less than 25 mm. rainfall extends from April to September and at Thíra from April to October.

In central Greece Athínai (Fig. 58) has the characteristically dry summer from April to September. Winter is the wet season with a slight autumn maximum and November in many years is the wettest month. In northern Greece, in Thessalía, Makedhonía and Thráki, though the winter wet period is still dominant, there are slight autumn and spring maxima and a less well-marked summer drought, since convectional showers in summer are frequent.

The total amount of rainfall shows marked differences in distribution throughout Greece (Fig. 59). In general, rainfall diminishes from west to east and from north to south, but there are many variations. Since the greater part of the rainfall is brought by the south and west winds of the depressions, the west coasts receive the greater amount. The high figures for December rainfall at Kérkira (200 mm.), Zákinthos (234 mm.) and Khíos (164 mm.) offer a marked contrast to those recorded at eastern stations, Vólos (55 mm.), Khalkís (72 mm.), Athínai (68 mm.) and Návplion (92 mm.). The west coast has an average rainfall of about 1,100 mm. per annum, the east coast about 500 mm. The seaward slopes of the mountains of Thessalía and the islands of the Northern Sporádhes are an

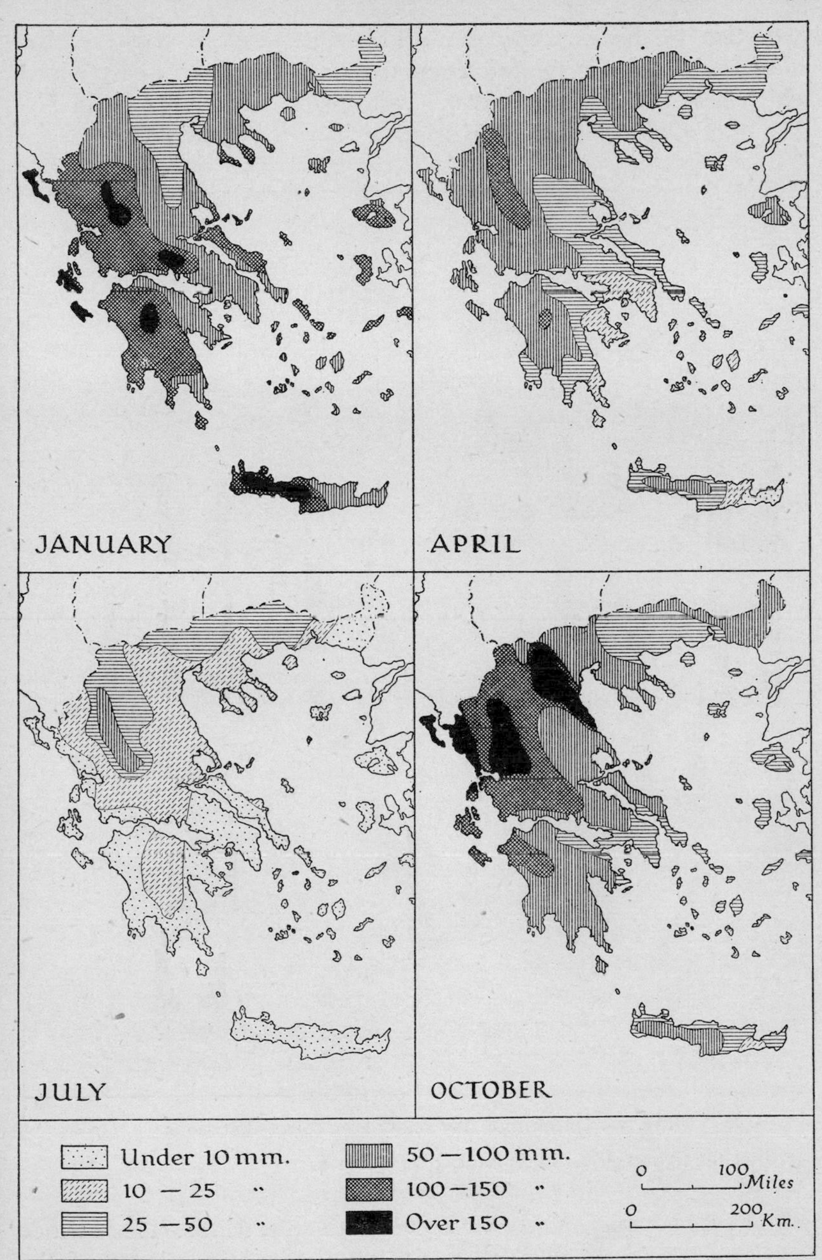

Fig. 57. The seasonal distribution of rainfall

Based on E. G. Mariolopoulos and A. N. Livathinos, *Atlas Climatique de la Grèce* (Athènes, 1935).

exception to this generalization. This north-eastern coast receives considerable winter rainfall from the prevailing north-east winds, which here blow onshore after passing over the north Aegean Sea. The shores of the Gulf of Kórinthos have a low rainfall since the

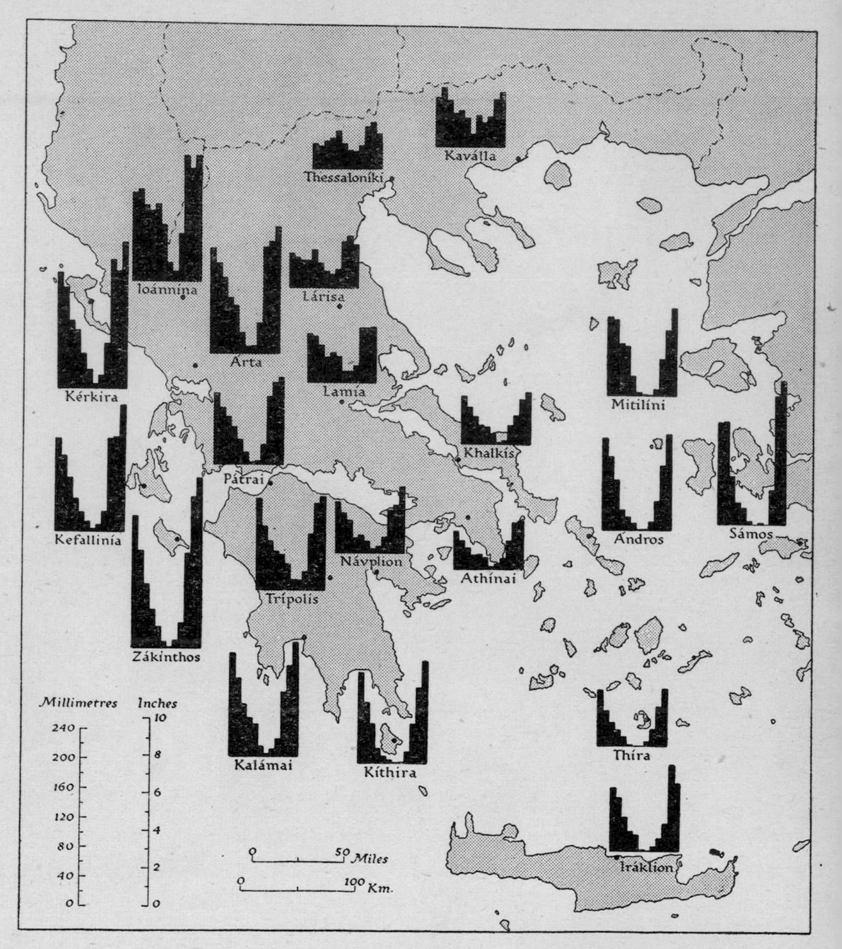

Fig. 58. Mean monthly rainfall for selected stations

Based on the figures given in Appendix IX, Table 6.

gulf affords a passage to the west and south-west winds. These winds keep their moisture until they rise up the western slopes of the mountains of Attikí. The south Aegean islands have a slightly heavier rainfall than the east coast stations, but much less than the Ionian islands. Rainfall, especially summer rainfall, increases markedly with increasing altitude.

The rain usually falls in heavy showers often of great intensity, but usually of short duration. The fine, long-continued rain of northern countries is exceptional, though heavy, continuous rain for a short time is experienced with the passage of the warm front of a depression. Rain, even in winter, rarely falls all day; the number of rain days varies considerably from year to year, but the average number is small compared to the total rainfall (Appendix IX, Table 7).

It is thus the seasonal distribution and the character of the rainfall rather than the total amount which makes Greece a dry land. In addition, the total amount of rainfall is not reliable, large variations occurring from year to year. Records of rainfall at Athínai show a variation from more than double the normal amount to less than one-third the normal (Fig. 60), but there seems to be no periodicity in the occurrence of these wet and dry years.

Thunderstorms

The frequency of thunderstorms in Greece compared with other Mediterranean lands is not high. Two types of thunderstorms occur; some are associated with the passage of the cold fronts of depressions, which are therefore mainly winter storms; others are due to convection currents set up by unequal heating of the land and therefore occur mainly in summer.

In winter the maximum number of thunderstorms occurs in north-west Greece, the Ionian islands, the islands off the Anatolian coasts and in the mountains of Kríti. The greater frequency of thunderstorms in these areas is due to the fact that the instability of the rising air in the rear of depressions is here further favoured by the relief of the land. The southern Aegean has a greater number of thunderstorms than the northern Aegean at this season, since depressions are most numerous along tracks that pass in the direction of Cyprus, and thus the northern Aegean lies in the more stable northern sector of the depressions. In late spring, depressions move along more northerly tracks and it is in April and May that the north Aegean has its greatest number of storms. The frequency of thunderstorms in Akarnanía and Ípiros also increases at this season, for the same reason.

Summer thunderstorms are most numerous in northern Greece where continental conditions favour the heating of the land and thus the formation of local rising currents of air. A secondary area of maximum frequency extends at this season from the interior of the Pelopónnisos through Argolís to Attikí.

Ípiros shows the highest annual frequency of thunderstorms in Greece, since it experiences both winter and summer storms.

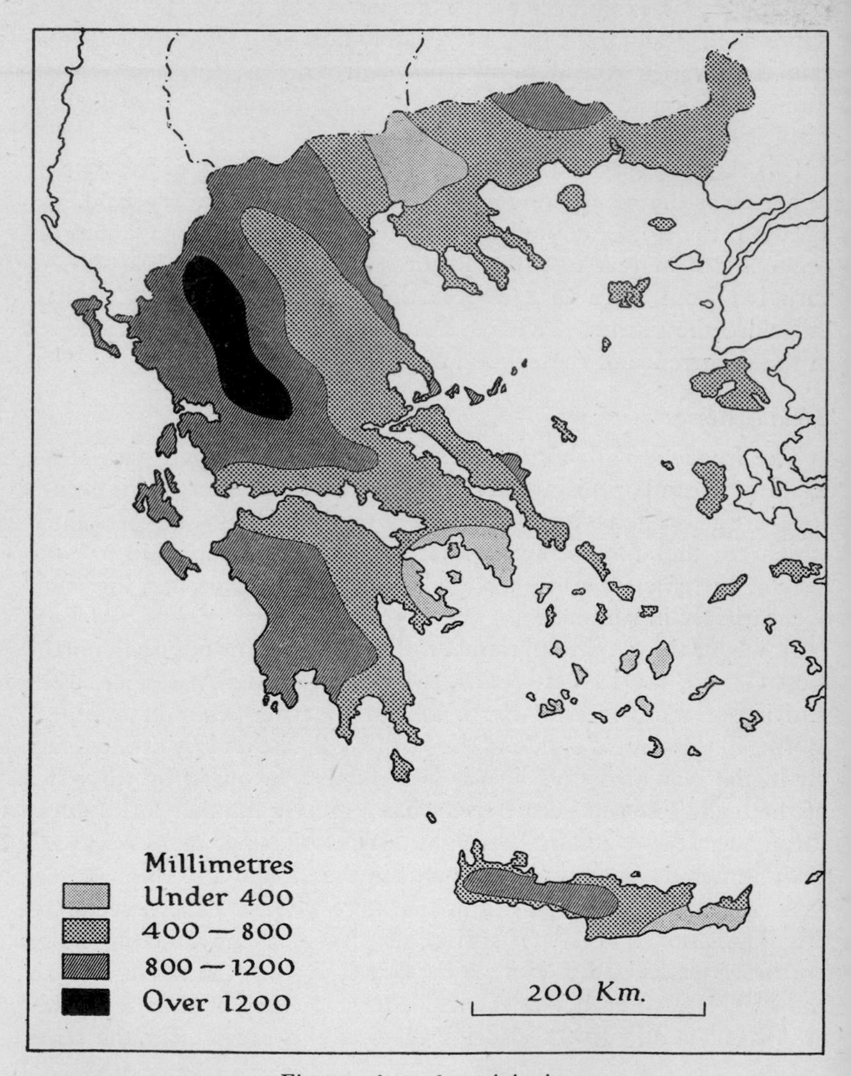

Fig. 59. Annual precipitation

Based on E. G. Mariolopoulos and A. N. Livathinos, *Atlas Climatique de la Grèce* (Athènes, 1935).

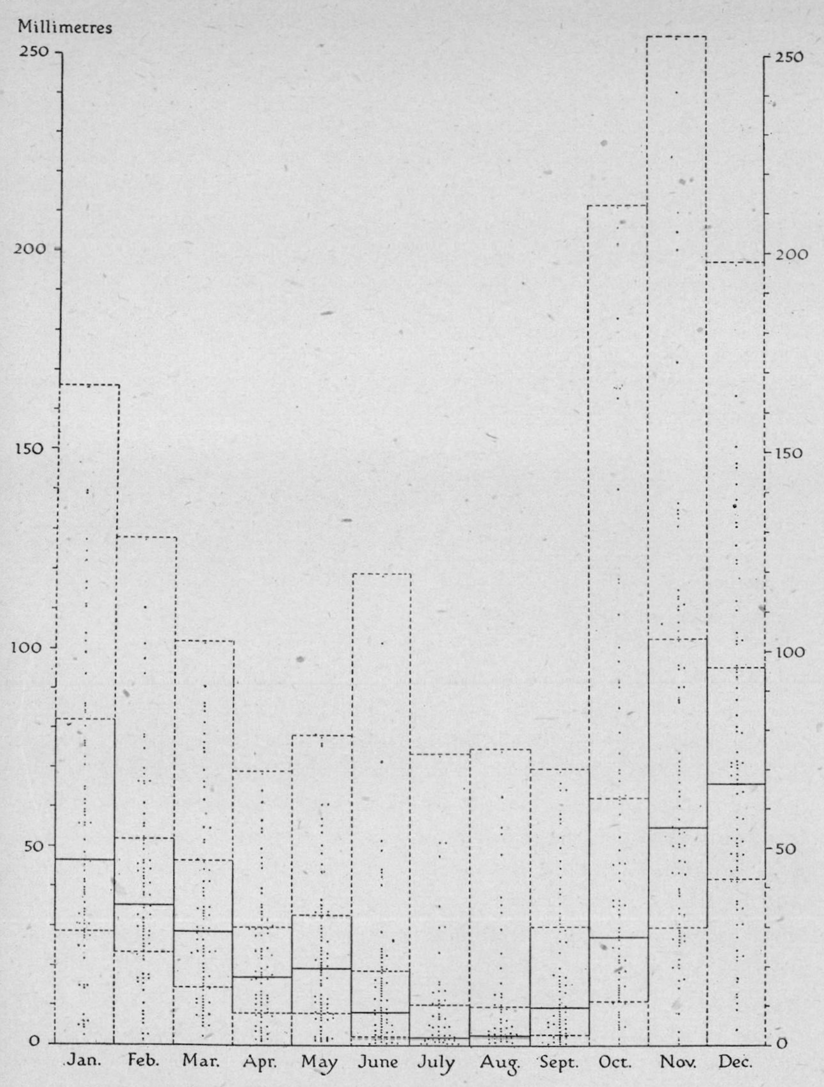

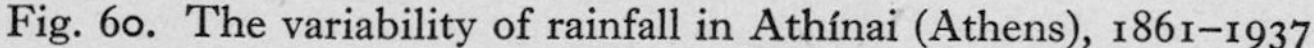

Fig. 60. The variability of rainfall in Athínai (Athens), 1861–1937

Based on statistics, pp. 419–20, *Annuaire Statistique de la Grèce*, 1938 (Athènes, 1939).

The figure, known as a dispersion diagram, shows the variability of rainfall for each month of the year from 1861 to 1937. For example, in the column for January, each dot represents the actual amount of rainfall which fell during the January of one particular year, and the height of the column indicates the maximum rainfall ever experienced in that month throughout the 77 years. The continuous line drawn across the column is known as the median, and it is of much greater climatic significance than the figure for average monthly rainfall. In any January the chances are exactly equal that there will be more, or less, rainfall than the amount indicated by the median. Average amounts, on the other hand, are often distorted by freak conditions, e.g. periods of exceptionally heavy rainfall. The broken lines across each column are further refinements, and are known as quartiles. For a fuller consideration of this method of rainfall representation, reference should be made to P. R. Crowe, 'The analysis of rainfall probability, a geographical method and its application to European data', *The Scottish Geographical Magazine*, vol. XLIX, no. 2, pp. 73–91 (Edinburgh, 1933).

Makedhonía, which has the greatest number of summer storms, has the next highest annual total. In general, western Greece has more thunderstorms than eastern Greece, and the islands off the Anatolian coast more than the Ionian islands. The fewest thunderstorms occur along the coastal plains of the south-eastern Pelopónnisos and in Voiotía (Appendix IX, Table 9).

Hail falls more often in western than eastern Greece and in southern than northern Greece. It is a winter phenomenon often associated with winter thunderstorms. July and August are generally the months most free from hail.

Snow and Snow-cover

Falls of snow are recorded at meteorological stations, but details of snow-cover are lacking and the following conclusions must be regarded as somewhat tentative.

Falls of snow may be expected in Greece at any time between November and April (Appendix IX, Table 8) and are associated most frequently with northerly winds in the rear of depressions. On the coastal plains and in the islands snow is of more frequent occurrence than is generally supposed; it falls here on an average of one to four days per annum, but it usually melts as it falls and never lies for long. In all inland areas, the ground in most years may be seen white with snow sometime during the winter; the duration of the snow-cover and the frequency with which it occurs increases from south to north, from west to east, and with increasing altitude. It is not possible to take any one contour as the approximate snow-line, since the plane above which snow lies tilts markedly towards sea level to north and east.

The snow-line in spring decreases in height from the west to the east coast; throughout the winter rain falls more often and more heavily on the west, while the snowfall associated with depressions over the Aegean Sea is heavier on the east. Further, the southerly aspect, the strong sunshine, and the dry air are responsible for a marked difference in the height of the snow-line between the northern and southern slopes, especially in the late winter and the spring. The conditions of snow-cover may best be considered in relation to a lower, an intermediate, and a higher tilted plane.

Below 450 m. in southern Greece and 150 m. in central Greece, a day with snow-cover is rare; even in northern Greece, in maritime regions below 300 m. the temperatures are too high for snow to lie long.

At intermediate levels, from 600 to 900 m. in southern and western Greece, from 300 to 600 m. in central and eastern Greece, and from sea level to 300 m. in inland situations in northern Greece, the ground is covered with snow for short periods in most years. Any one snowfall rarely lies for more than a few days, but in the aggregate the ground is covered intermittently with snow from five to thirty days each winter, with a considerable variation from year to year. Extensive snow-cover is most likely to be found in January and February. The roads and tracks at these levels are not often blocked for long, though immediately after a fall of snow travellers may be temporarily delayed. At the same time it is perhaps in these areas that the effects of an abnormally severe winter would perhaps be felt most, since no routine arrangements are made to meet them.

At higher levels, for which there are no systematic records, falls of snow in the winter months are obviously frequent and heavy. Above 900 m. in the south and along the west coast, about 600 m. in the centre and east, and above 300 m. near the northern frontier, the amount of snow and the duration of snow-cover increase rapidly. At about 1,350 m. in the south and 1,000 m. in the centre, snow-cover is persistent for about three months from mid-December to early March, and it is probable that tracks at this level are completely blocked during this period. In the Pelopónnisos travellers have reported snow-drifts at 1,500 m. and an extensive snow-cover at 1,800 m. in mid-April; the last drifts on the highest summits disappear about the beginning of June. In Kríti the winter snowfall at higher levels is heavy and the conditions appear to be similar to those observed in the Pelopónnisos. In central Greece continuous snowfields were seen at 2,000 m. in mid-May with drifts down to 1,600 m.; Parnassós loses its snow-cap only in June. In northern Greece fresh snow has been noted on 1 June down to 1,800 m.; small patches of snow may remain into July in the shade of the highest summits.

Humidity

The mean annual relative humidity throughout Greece lies between 60% and 75%, but there are strong seasonal and diurnal variations especially at coastal stations on the mainland (Appendix IX, Table 10).

Greece has a reputation for great dryness of the air and this is due to the low summer rainfall of eastern Greece. Attikí in the dry season is one of the driest regions of Europe, the relative humidity sometimes falling to as low as 5%. It is this dryness which gives the extreme blue colour to the sky and makes the heat of the Thessalian and Attic plains much more bearable than the damp heat of the western coast.

In winter, however, the reputation for dryness is by no means justified; from November to March the relative humidity throughout Greece is in general very high. With southerly winds and mild cloudy weather in front of a depression the relative humidity may rise to 100%, though it falls sharply with the arrival of dry northerly winds. The maximum values are particularly high on the west coast of Greece and in the Ionian islands on the approach of a depression.

Visibility

Visibility in Greece is normally very good, the air is transparent and clear on many days at all seasons and the limpid light gives to Greek scenery much of its charm. There is a tendency to regard a visibility of less than 5 miles as 'poor', and this must be borne in mind when reading local descriptions, unless they are based on distance observations graded according to the international scale. Even above the towns and cities in Greece, the atmosphere is remarkable for its clarity, a reflexion of the almost complete lack of industry, and of the small amount of fuel burned even in private houses. The one exception is the Athínai-Piraiévs area, in which a certain amount of industry has developed in the past twenty years.

Mist. True fog is rarely experienced in Greece, and then only in winter, but ground mist is common. Its geographical and seasonal distribution is very varied: it is very common in the mountains especially in spring, and the peaks and higher ridges are apt to be wreathed in mist for several days at a time. In the coastal areas, morning mist is frequent in spring, early summer and autumn after fine calm nights with dew, but it is soon dispelled as the sun gains power. Mist in the mornings is often seen on many of the islands, probably due to the contact of warm moist sea air with the land surface cooled by radiation during a clear night.

Haze, caused by dust and heat shimmer, is very frequent during the summer months and in the mid-day hours. Throughout northern Greece, low visibility except near dawn and dusk is a persistent feature of the summer weather.

Sunshine and Cloudiness

Greece has a very high figure for annual insolation, ranging from 2,200 to 3,100 hours per annum (Appendix IX, Table 11). The maximum figure is recorded at Zákinthos (3,107 hr.), followed by Mitilíni (3,053 hr.), and the minimum figures are Tríkkala (2,228 hr.) and Ioánnina (2,316 hr.). All stations with sunshine records have more than 300 hr. sunshine in both July and August. The great amount of sunshine is a most striking feature of the Greek climate to visitors from north-west Europe. In contrast with the figures recorded at Greek stations, Eastbourne, one of the sunniest places in Britain, has only 1,833 hr. sunshine in an average year.

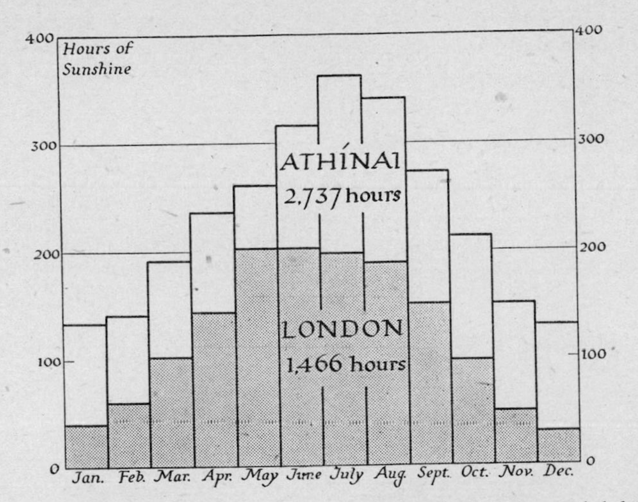

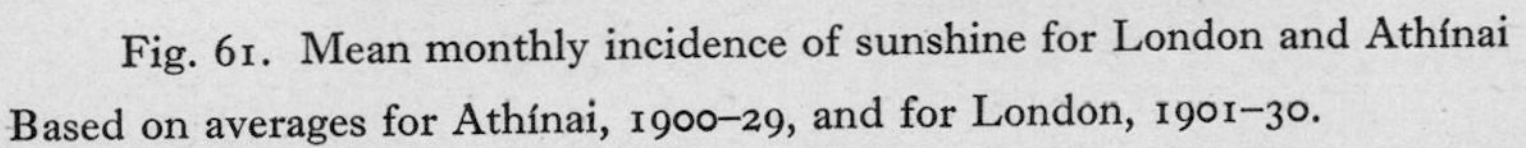

Fig. 61. Mean monthly incidence of sunshine for London and Athínai

Based on averages for Athínai, 1900–29, and for London, 1901–30.

Cloud. Since the prevailing winds of Greece and the Aegean are continental, the area as a whole has clear skies. The maximum annual cloudiness (55 %) is found in Ípiros and Makedhonía, and the minimum cloudiness (32–35 %) in the southern islands of the Ionian Sea, in parts of south-eastern Pelopónnisos and in the southern islands of the Aegean Sea.

Winter is the cloudy season, when the sky is as a rule about half covered; wholly covered skies are rare. The mean number of days per annum of wholly covered skies varies from 24 at Piraiévs to 91 at Tríkkala. In summer, the sky is completely clear for days on end; the mean number of days per annum with clear skies varies from 82 at Tríkkala to 165 at Mitilíni. The curves of the isonephs from May to October approximately follow the latitude, cloudiness increasing at this season with rainfall from south to north. In winter the isonephs show strong deviations from the latitude, because of the frequency of depressions along certain tracks.

THE CLIMATIC REGIONS OF GREECE

The separate elements of climate have been shown to vary throughout the country, and when these are studied together a considerable variety of climatic types is found to exist within the limited area of Greece. The climatic regions will be seen to depend upon position in relation to land and sea, and upon the relief of the land. Climatically Greece may be divided thus (Fig. 62):

A. *The Mediterranean Climate of Central Greece and the Pelopónnisos:*

(1) The Western Region.
(1 *a*) The Ionian Islands.
(2) The Eastern Region.
(2 *a*) The Kikládhes.

B. *The Modified Mediterranean Climate of Northern Greece:*

(1) Thessalía.
(1 *a*) The Northern Sporádhes.
(2) Makedhonía and Thráki.
(2 *a*) The Northern Islands of the Aegean.
(3) The Eastern Islands of the Aegean.

C. *The Mountain Climate:*

(1) The Píndhos Region.
(2) The Highlands of the Pelopónnisos.

A. *The True Mediterranean Climate.* This type of climate is confined to the lowlands of central and southern Greece. The region however is not uniform and a distinction can be made between the mainland and the islands and between east and west coasts. The western region (Fig. 62) of the mainland has a much heavier winter rainfall, a more complete but shorter summer drought, and a lower range of temperature; the differences between both the diurnal and seasonal maxima and minima are less. The climate of the Ionian islands resembles that of the western region, the climate of the Kikládhes that of the eastern region, modified by insularity. Compared with that of the neighbouring part of the mainland the

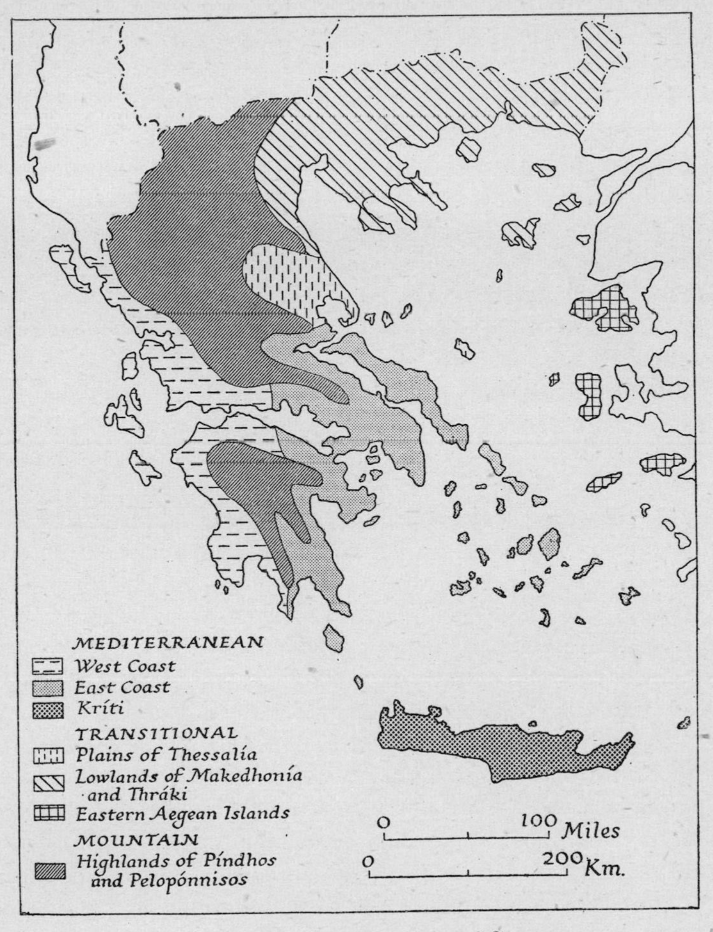

Fig. 62. The climatic regions of Greece

It is interesting to compare this division of Greece with that shown on Fig. 64.

climates of the islands are more equable, the total rainfall is higher but the summer drought more complete; the winds are stronger and there is a greater frequency of winds from the northern quarters.

B. *The Modified Mediterranean Climate.* A modified type of the Mediterranean climate is found in the coastal and interior plains of

Thessalía, Makedhonía and Thráki. The temperature and rainfall figures for meteorological stations in northern Greece show some features which are continental in type. The seasonal range of temperature, especially inland, is much greater than farther south. The summers are very hot, almost suffocatingly so when the Föhn-like wind, the *livas*, blows down from the mountains. The winters are rigorous, frost is common, and again a local wind, known in Makedhonía as the *vardarac*, bringing very cold air from the northern high-pressure areas intensifies the seasonal variation. Thunderstorms are frequent in the summer season and thus a secondary rainfall maximum, or at some stations even the primary maximum occurs in June or July. Nevertheless, the Mediterranean character of the climate is sufficiently preserved for olive trees and maquis to grow in sheltered situations on the coastal fringe.

The Northern Sporádhes have an insular variety of the climate of Thessalía and the northern Aegean islands of Thásos, Samothráki and Límnos are similarly related to the climate of Makedhonía and Thráki. The climate of the eastern islands of Lésvos, Khíos, Sámos and Ikaría is essentially Aegean, though it reflects to some extent the influence of the neighbouring land mass of Anatolia.

C. *The Mountain Climate of Greece.* Highlands introduce into the Mediterranean a climate similar to the continental type of central Europe. The Píndhos region and the chief mountain masses of western Makedhonía and Dhitikí Thráki have a true mountain climate. The summer rainfall and winter snowfall is much higher than in the lowlands and the greater part of the precipitation in the highest areas probably falls in the summer months. The air, as in the Alps, is dry, clear and invigorating; great temperature differences occur between sunny and shady slopes. Mountain and high plateaux of the Pelopónnisos have a mountain climate in modified form. Here again, the altitude modifies the summer heat and lowers the winter temperature sufficiently for much of the precipitation to fall as snow. The seasonal distribution of rainfall is transitional in type: though summer is the season of minimum rainfall, the summer drought is not complete; rain storms break all the year round on the higher ranges and the altitude decreases the length of the dry season. Summer rain falls in showers, heavy and continuous rain is frequent in autumn and winter.

BIBLIOGRAPHICAL NOTE

1. A general introduction to the climate of Greece is to be found in W. G. Kendrew, *The Climates of the Continents* (3rd ed. Oxford, 1937) and in J. Sion and Y. Chataigneau, *Méditerranée Péninsules Méditerranéennes* (Paris, 1934), which is vol. VII, part 2 of the *Géographie Universelle.*

2. The fullest and most recent account has been written in Greek by E. G. Mariolopoulos, *The Climate of Greece* (Athínai, 1938). A paper in French, by the same author, gives a brief introduction to this work, 'Aperçu sur le climat de la Grèce', in *Bulletin de la Société belge d'Astronomie, de Météorologie et de Physique du Globe*, nos. 11 and 12 (Bruxelles, 1934). Other useful papers are: H. Renier, 'Die Niederschlagsverteilung in Südosteuropa', *Memoires de la Societé de Géographie de Belgrade*, vol. I (Belgrade, 1933); A. N. Livathinos and E. G. Mariolopoulos, 'Jahrlicher Gang und geographische Verteilung des Gewitters in Griechenland', *Beiträge zur Geophysik*, vol. XXIV, parts 2–3 (Leipzig, 1929).

3. Detailed information about the climate and weather conditions of Greece and the Aegean is to be found in the following publications of the British Meteorological Office: M.O. 391*b*, *Weather in the Mediterranean*, vol. II, parts 7–12 (London, 1936); M.O. 391*c*, 'Aids to Forecasting', *Weather in the Mediterranean*, vol. III (London, 1937).

4. The Royal Observatory in Athínai publishes statistics and maps in *Bulletin mensuel météorologique de l'Observatoire nationale d'Athènes*, and in *Annales de l'Observatoire nationale d'Athènes.* One of the most valuable publications is E. G. Mariolopoulos and A. N. Livathinos, *Atlas Climatique de la Grèce* (Athènes, 1935). The text of these is in Modern Greek and French.

Chapter IV

VEGETATION

Introduction: Herbaceous Communities: Forests: Brushwood Communities: Bibliographical Note

Introduction

The flora of Greece is closely related to that of the rest of the Balkan peninsula, and, via the numerous Aegean islands, to the flora of Anatolia (Fig. 63). Plant migration has been on the whole from western Asia to the Balkans and thence to central and north-western Europe. Only a few species found on the high mountains appear to have migrated south from the Alps and the Carpathians.

The character of the natural vegetation is primarily determined by the climate. In the lowlands, temperature is high enough for plant growth all the year round; trees and many shrubs with sufficiently long roots to tap the soil waters at all seasons are evergreen. The leaves, however, are suited to reduce water loss under the strong summer sun. They are often small and narrow, sometimes mere spines. Some are protected by thick shiny skins, others by a close felting of hairs, and yet others store water and are thick and succulent. Many herbaceous plants have a winter season of growth. Flowers may be found throughout the winter, but autumn and more especially spring are the flowering seasons of most plants. The hot dry summer is the resting season. The vegetation of these areas is thus Mediterranean in type, with the plants able to withstand the summer drought. In the highlands of southern and central Greece, and at lower altitudes in the north, the character of the vegetation changes as summer rainfall and winter cold increase. Special protection against drought is no longer necessary, but low winter temperatures impose a resting period. Deciduous trees appear on the middle slopes; still higher, conifers predominate, and at the highest altitudes pastures or a rock flora, often rich in endemic species, replace forest. The herbaceous plants of the highlands and of the more continental northern lowlands have a short period of spring and summer growth and the majority flower in early or mid-summer.

The character of the soil to a lesser extent plays a part in determining the natural vegetation types. The supply of soil water is influenced by the permeability of the rock; thus there is a marked difference between the limestone soils, which emphasize the dryness of a region, and the heavier clays which mitigate it. A species is often to be found growing on calcareous and siliceous soils alike, where temperature is high and rainfall sufficient, but the same species may be limited to siliceous soils at higher altitudes or in drier areas, where the climatic conditions are more rigorous. Thus, though at a given altitude there may be a distinction between the Tertiary clays, the crystalline schists and the limestones, the

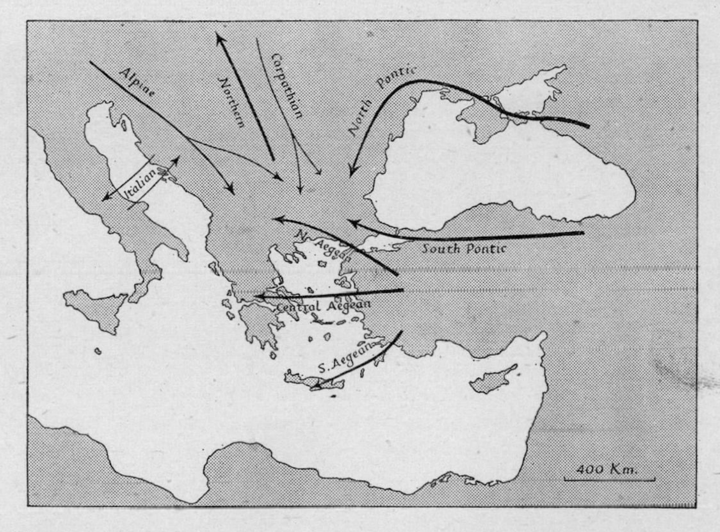

Fig. 63. The chief routes of plant migration into south-eastern Europe

Based on W. B. Turrill, *The Plant Life of the Balkan Peninsula*, p. 426 (Oxford, 1929).

distinction may well be due to resulting differences in the amount and temperature of the soil water and air, rather than to differences of soil chemistry.

Though climate and soil are the most important natural factors determining the vegetation type, it is impossible to consider the natural vegetation of Greece without emphasizing the effect of man's activities in modifying its character. He has drained much marshland, and, by cutting the trees and encouraging grazing animals, he has reduced the natural forests and extended the scrub.

Since climate and soil conditions and the accessibility of areas to the depredations of man and his animals vary with altitude, the

Table showing Plant Communities of the Different Altitude Zones, with Subdivisions according to Geographical Regions

Region	Type of vegetation	Dominant species
0–200 m. Coastal belt and lowlands	Mediterranean, transitional and central European areas Largely cultivated Natural vegetation types: 1. Grove and field weeds 2. Sand-dune vegetation 3. Salt-marsh vegetation 4. Fresh-water marsh vegetation 5. River-bank vegetation	(1–4) Very numerous species (5) *Nerium Oleander, Vitex Agnus-castus, Platanus orientalis, Populus* spp.
200 m.—700–1,000 m. Hill and foot-hill zone	**Mediterranean area:** Evergreen woods ⇢ Maquis ⇢ Phrygana **Transitional area:** Oak and mixed woods ⇢ Pseudomaquis ⇢ Phrygana / Shiblyak **Central European area:** Deciduous ⇢ Shiblyak	**Mediterranean area:** *Pinus halepensis, Quercus Ilex, Q. Aegilops* ⇢ Maquis: *Arbutus Unedo, A. Andrachne, Myrtus communis, Spartium junceum, Quercus coccifera* ⇢ Phrygana: *Poterium spinosum, Coridothymus capitatus, Genista acanthoclada* **Transitional area / Central European area:** *Quercus conferta, Q. lanuginosa, Castanea sativa, Fraxinus Ornus, F. excelsior* ⇢ Pseudomaquis: *Juniperus* spp., *Quercus coccifera, Q. macedonica, Buxus sempervirens* ⇢ Phrygana / Shiblyak: *Paliurus Spina-Christi, Cotinus coggygria*
1,000–1,500 m. Montane zone	**Mediterranean area:** Fir forest **Transitional and central European areas:** Deciduous forest	**Mediterranean area:** *Abies cephalonica* **Transitional and central European areas:** *Fagus sylvatica, Quercus* spp.
1,500–2,000 m. High mountain zone 1,500–1,700 m.	**Mediterranean area:** Fir and pine forest **Transitional and central European areas:** Fir, pine and beech forest	**Mediterranean area:** *Abies cephalonica, Pinus nigra* **Transitional and central European areas:** *Abies cephalonica, A. alba, Fagus sylvatica*
1,700–2,000 m.	Mountain brushwood Mountain pasture	*Juniperus communis, Daphne oleoides, Prunus prostata* and numerous other species
Above 2,000 m.	Stony meadow and rock plants	*Medicago* spp., *Silene* spp., *Alyssum* spp., *Coronilla* spp., *Campanula celsii* *Sedum* spp., *Silene* spp., *Saxifraga* spp., *Sempervivum* spp.

Note. The arrows ⇢ show the links between the plant communities. Forest when cut down is replaced by brushwood; maquis when cut or overgrazed is replaced by phrygana or in colder areas by shiblyak.

vegetation zones of Greece can be broadly differentiated in terms of height above sea level.

Within this division there is also regional variation, higher latitude to some extent having the same effects as increasing altitude. The regional variations in vegetation correspond very closely to the regional variations in climate, as a comparison of Fig. 64 with Fig. 62

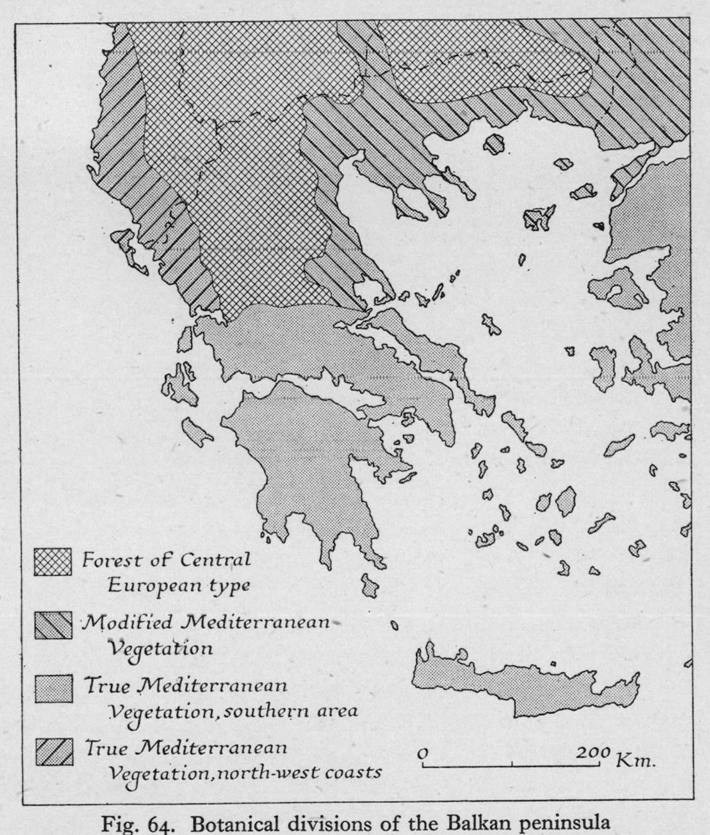

Fig. 64. Botanical divisions of the Balkan peninsula
Based on W. B. Turrill, *The Plant Life of the Balkan Peninsula*, p. 350 (Oxford, 1929).

reveals. The most marked variations are between south and central Greece, which in vegetation as in climate are true Mediterranean in type, eastern Thessalía and lowland Makedhonía and Thráki which are transitional in character with a strong Mediterranean bias, and the Píndhos Mountains and the highlands of Makedhonía and Thráki, which show central European affinities in vegetation, both in character and species.

Herbaceous Communities*

The fertile soils of the coastal lowlands and of the inland plains and river valleys are regions of luxuriant vegetation, but most of the land is under crops. In addition to field crops, olives, figs, almonds, pomegranates, walnuts and mimosa, valued for their fruits or their shade, grow in groves or along the edges of the fields. The practice of fallowing and the wide spacing of cultivated trees in groves allow a rich weed flora. The plants are mostly spring flowering and make carpets of colour in March and April. On dry banks, often forming a rough hedge, two natives of Mexico flourish, the agave (Plate 69) and the prickly pear. Introduced by the Venetians into Greece, these two plants have become completely naturalized and grow freely over wide areas. The prickly pear was sometimes planted round Frankish castles to serve as natural 'barbed wire'.

Hill sides are often terraced where conditions permit, especially those facing seawards, and the sunny slopes of mountain valleys. Both in northern and southern Greece it is common to find slopes with a southerly or south-westerly aspect terraced and carefully cultivated, while, in the same valley, the shady slopes are covered with forest or scrub.

While it is true that the greater part of Greece would under natural conditions be covered with more or less continuous woody communities of forest and tall brushwood, and before the advent of man probably was so covered, open communities dominated by low scrubby and herbaceous plants now occupy much of the area not under cultivation. Such communities are best called 'semi-natural', since they are composed, with very local exceptions, of native plants, but the structure of the vegetation is due primarily to the destruction of trees and shrubs by man, and to the prevention of regeneration of forest and brushwood by the flocks of sheep and goats. Herbs, annual and perennial, are naturally present in the lower strata of all except the densest forests and brushwoods, and a rich herb flora occurs at the margins of woods, in clearings, and in situations too steep or rocky for full tree growth. It is doubtless from such sources that species have spread in the course of past centuries to cover much larger areas, concomitant with the destruction of trees and bushes.

* The botanical name of a plant is given when it is first fully discussed: the common English name if one exists is used subsequently. Appendix VII, p. 474, gives a list of the plants mentioned in the text with their botanical name, their common English name if any, and their common Greek name if known.

In many areas of pseudomaquis, phrygana and shiblyak (brushwood communities) the number of species of herbs far outnumbers the species of woody plants. Many herbs are protected from summer drought, and even more from the attacks of grazing animals, by growing in the clumps of kermes oak, Christ's thorn, and other spiny or prickly plants (Plate 71). Others survive because they are poisonous (as species of spurge) or unpalatable (as species of mullein) to grazing animals. Destruction of woody plants has often been so great that herbs dominate the vegetation and the secondary communities so formed are themselves of an open type, varying in floristic composition not only with altitude and latitude but with local conditions. In the lowlands, the herbs are mostly members of typical Mediterranean genera with a certain number of species limited to the eastern Mediterranean lands. On the mountains, however, there are a large number of Greek endemics (that is, of species not found in any country other than Greece), and often these have only a very limited range. Most of these high mountain plants are related to lowland species of Mediterranean distribution, and central European 'alpines' are rare. Towards the northern boundaries, in Ípiros, Makedhonía, and Thráki, there are larger numbers of south-eastern and central European types than there are in southern Greece.

Herbaceous vegetation of stony ground covers wide areas at all altitudes in southern Greece and the islands. Turf- or mat-forming grasses are rare, and meadows or closed pasture-lands at all comparable to those of central and western Europe appear only very locally. This is partly due to the dry summers and partly to the prevalence of limestone. Many of the species of grasses are annuals which avoid the summer drought by an ephemeral development in spring, or are structurally adapted for living under dry conditions, at least for a part of the year. An unusually large number of herbs other than grasses have bulbs, tubers, corms, or other forms of underground stems. Thus there are many species of grape hyacinth (*Muscari*), star of Bethlehem (*Ornithogalum*), crocus (*Crocus*), fritillary (*Fritillaria*), *Scilla*, *Romulea*, *Narcissus*, *Iris*, garlic (*Allium*), tulip (*Tulipa*), autumn crocus (*Colchicum*), *Gladiolus*, etc. These, together with many members of the buttercup, poppy, pink, crucifer, and pea families, amongst others, flower in the early spring or, in a less number, in the autumn. In spring, the stony ground may be, for a short time, a mass of colour from multitudes of such plants as these. Later, members of the daisy, deadnettle, borage, and mullein families tend to predominate but without giving mass effects. Special mention should be made of pinks (*Dianthus*), campions (*Silene*), mulleins (*Verbascum*), thymes (*Thymus*), and knapweeds (*Centaurea*) which abound on stony hill slopes. In some parts eradication of utilizable plants, including those palatable to grazing animals, has been carried so far that much of the ground is bare or occupied only by species of spurge (*Euphorbia*), *Asphodelus*, and a few other plants which have not been exploited (Plate 64).

The vegetation on rocks varies according to exposure and the nature of the substratum. The flora is particularly rich on partly shaded limestone rocks such as occur in some gorges. It is naturally in the hills and mountains that bare rock is most exposed and in limestone districts this tends, after forest destruction, to develop *karst* features (see p. 16) which are maintained by excessive grazing. The list of plants of rocky habitats is too long to give here, but a few striking or especially characteristic plants are: campanulas, saxifrages, violas, species of *Potentilla*, *Sedum*, *Achillea*, *Draba*, *Asperula*, *Lotus*, *Acantholimon*, *Ranunculus*, *Silene*, *Dianthus*, *Cerastium*, *Minuartia* (Plate 63), *Astragalus*, and *Arabis*.

Areas of sandy soil occur only locally in Greece and then usually in valleys in other than limestone districts. Thus, in some parts of Makedhonía there are deep deposits of sandy debris washed down from the hills and covered with a loose vegetation of grasses, clovers and other legumes, knapweeds (*Centaurea* spp.), knotgrasses (*Polygonum* spp.), and other plants.

The waste lands within the cultivated areas are of three types: the coastal dunes, the salt marshes and the fresh-water marshes, and spreads of stony gravel along the rivers. Coastal sand dunes are sporadic; there are considerable sandy areas near Préveza on the Gulf of Árta and on the west coast of the Pelopónnisos, and sand dunes along parts of the shores of Attikí, Makedhonía and Thráki. The dunes for the most part are bare except for xerophytic plants, usually of a creeping habit, and in southern and central Greece isolated stone pines and Àleppo pines. Salt marshes are often developed behind sand dunes in many areas, around the Gulf of Árta, along the west coast of the Pelopónnisos, at Marathón and Fáliron (known here as *alípeda*), and in Makedhonía and Thráki. Although the central areas of inland plains around the *katavóthres*, which would be marshy in a natural state, are now largely drained, fresh-water marshes are locally extensive. There is a rich marsh vegetation in the lower river plains of Thráki and Makedhonía, in Thessalía, in the Sperkhiós valley, around the Gulf of Árta, in Attikí and

Lakonía. The characteristic plants of the sand dunes and of the salt and fresh-water marshes do no differ greatly from area to area or from those of similar habitats in other parts of Europe (Figs. 65, 66). River courses, as a rule, are not marshy but stony along the banks, and planes, poplars, willows, oleanders and terebinths grow there.

Sea level

Sand dunes	Salt marsh	Fresh-water marshes	River bed	Well
Cakile maritima	*Linum maritimum*	*Typha angustifolia*	*Tamarix* spp.	
Eryngium maritimum	*Euphorbia pubescens*	*Alisma plantago-aquatica*	*Nerium oleander*	*Populus* spp.
Medicago marina	*Lavatera cretica*	*Scirpus tabernaemontani*	*Vitex agnus-castus*	
Euphorbia peplis	*Spergularia salina*	*Scirpus maritimus*	*Laurus nobilis*	
Polygonum maritimum	*Frankenia hirsuta*		*Platanus orientalis*	
Salsola kali			*Salix* spp.	
Cyperus kali			*Populus* spp.	
Pinus pinea				

Fig. 65. Characteristic plants in sand dune and marsh communities in Attikí
Based on W. B. Turrill, *The Plant Life of the Balkan Peninsula, passim* (Oxford, 1929).

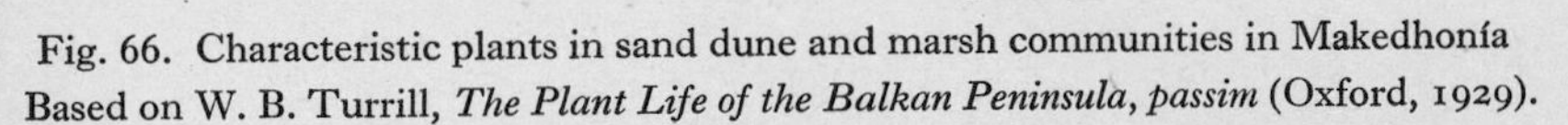

Sea level

Pebble beach	Sand dunes	Salt marsh	Fresh-water marsh	River bed	Pseudomaquis
Eryngium creticum	*Carex divisa*	*Salicornia fruticosa*	*Phalaris arundinacea*	*Salix alba*	
Eryngium maritimum	*Eryngium creticum*	*Limonium virgatum*	*Iris pseudacorus*		
Matthiola tricuspidata	*E. maritimum*	*Limonium vulgare*	*Eleocharis palustris*		
Cakile maritima	*Pancratium maritimum*	*Goniolimon collinum*	*Orchis palustris*		
Salsola kali	*Marsdenia erecta*	*Juncus acutus*	*Lythrum salicaria*		
Salicornia fruticosa		*Polygonum maritimum*	*Scirpus maritimus*		
		Echinophora tenuifolia	*S. holoschoenus*		
		Frankenia hirsuta	*Cyperus longus*		
			Juncus bufonius		

Fig. 66. Characteristic plants in sand dune and marsh communities in Makedhonía
Based on W. B. Turrill, *The Plant Life of the Balkan Peninsula, passim* (Oxford, 1929).

Forests

From 200 m. to the greatest heights in Greece forest and scrub cover the greater part of the surface. Woods are relatively more open in Mediterranean lands than in central Europe and therefore the undergrowth is richer. At all heights much land once forested is now bare, but three forest types are clearly differentiated, the Mediterranean evergreen, the mixed deciduous, and the fir. The altitude limit of different trees varies widely in Greece; the rule that the higher the mountain mass the higher the limit of the trees holds good if allowance is made for latitude. Aspect is also an important factor, especially in relation to rain-bearing winds. In the main the tree limit is lowest in north-eastern Greece and highest on the well-watered western slopes of the Píndhos Mountains, the mountains of the Pelopónnisos and those of the Ionian islands (Fig. 67).

Though few lands have suffered more severely from deforestation than Greece, trees, especially in the remoter mountain districts far from the sea, still cover large areas. *The Annuaire Statistique de la Grèce*, 1938, gives the extent of forest land in 1937 in sq. km. as follows:

Dhiamerísmata (regions)	Total area	State forest	Other forests	Timber	Copse	Mixed
1. Stereá-Ellás and Évvoia	4,598	2,490	2,108	1,330	1,146	2,122
2. Pelopónnisos*	2,725	1,998	727	1,178	284	1,263
3. Kikládhes	—	—	—	—	—	—
4. Ionian Islands	98	18	80	25	49	24
5. Thessalía*	2,250	975	1,275	700	1,480	70
6. Makedhonía	6,145	4,216	1,929	1,643	3,573	929
7. Ípiros	1,023	738	285	292	538	193
8. Kríti	160	—	160	50	60	50
9. Aegean Islands	450	15	435	314	47	89
10. Thráki	1,730	1,622	108	284	1,111	335
Total sq. km.	19,179	12,072	7,107	5,816	8,288	5,075

Dhiamerísmata (regions)	Greek fir	Black pine	Aleppo pine	Beech	Chest-nut	Deci-duous oaks	Broad leaved and ever-green oaks
1. Stereá-Ellás and Évvoia	1,104	18	1,861	26	8	583	997
2. Pelopónnisos*	685	176	1,235	—	7	266	357
3. Kikládhes	—	—	—	—	—	—	—
4. Ionian Islands	20	—	27	—	—	3	48
5. Thessalía*	350	145	—	390	65	985	315
6. Makedhonía	36	399	541	1,255	1	3,177	536
7. Ípiros	92	121	1	43	2	303	461
8. Kríti	—	—	100	—	—	—	60
9. Aegean Islands	—	16	367	—	—	20	47
10. Thráki	—	2	65	215	—	1,380	68
Total in sq. km.	2,287	877	4,197	1,929	283	6,717	2,889

* The *Annuaire Statistique de la Grèce*, 1938 has, by error, transferred the figures for the Pelopónnisos to Thessalía, and those of Thessalía to the Pelopónnisos. This mistake has been corrected in the tables given above.

Makedhonía and Thráki have well-wooded highlands, mixed deciduous forests on the lower slopes, beech and coniferous forest at greater heights. Ólimbos, Óssa and Pílion are wooded with oak, chestnut and pine: the Píndhos Mountains carry oaks and chestnuts on their middle slopes, firs and pines at higher altitudes: the

Óthris Mountains have extensive oak forests. The accessible slopes of Attikí have been almost completely deforested, but Aleppo pines occur at low altitudes especially in the north-east, and the upper slopes of Párnis, Kithairón and Elikón are fir covered. The forests of the Pelopónnisos are more restricted: the higher mountain slopes are largely covered with Greek fir and Black pine, but the oak and chestnut woods of the middle slopes are fragmentary. Aleppo pines and stone pines are the characteristic trees of the north and west coastal plains, but here also extensive forests, apart from the great oak wood of Manoládha, are absent. Of the islands, Thásos and the Northern Sporádhes are still well wooded, the mountains of Lésvos, Khíos, and Sámos have broken forests of oak and pine. Límnos and the Kikládhes are very bare; such forests as they may once have had have long since been cut down.

Mediterranean Evergreen Forest

The woods from sea level to about 600 m. are chiefly formed of Aleppo pine, stone pine and evergreen oaks.

The Aleppo pine (*Pinus halepensis*) is a fairly large tree when growing in fertile soil and favourable conditions. It is of shapely, rather wide, pyramidal habit. However, it is often found on thin dry soils and much exposed to wind, and then becomes small, twisted and misshapen. It is not confined to any one type of soil and it grows on limestones, sandstones and crystalline schists and on the sandy stretches of the coast. The Aleppo pine is the chief forest tree of the coastal lowlands of the Mediterranean and is not found far inland or at great heights. It grows best at altitudes below 400 m., but on coastal ranges it climbs to 1000 m. and more; at great heights, however, it is often reduced to a bush. The Aleppo pine usually forms rather open woods; it does not cast a dense shade so that the ground under and between the trees is sunbaked and bare, or if the trees are widely spaced, covered with scrub undergrowth. The resin is used locally, to-day, as in Ancient Greece, to preserve wine, and the wine of Attikí and of many districts of the Pelopónnisos is very highly resinated, and is called *retsína* or *retsináta*. The tree occurs widely in Greece; it is absent from the southern part of the Pelopónnisos, but it is abundant along the west coast of Ilía, the north coast of Akhaïa, on the isthmus of Kórinthos and the coasts of Argolís. In central Greece it is the characteristic tree of the eastern slopes of Pendelikón, of the lower slopes of the Párnis-Kithairón-Elikón mountain group, and good forests of it grow on the Tertiary hills of northern Évvoia.

The lower seaward slopes of Pílion, Óssa, and Ólimbos also have Aleppo pine trees, and it is the dominant tree of the islands of the Northern Sporádhes. It is found locally in sheltered places on the coasts of Thráki and Makedhonía, especially in the eastern peninsulas of Khalkidhikí. The barbarous method used by the Greeks in collecting resin from the Aleppo pine has stunted and deformed a large proportion of the pines of southern mainland Greece. This is especially evident when one compares the tapped pines of the open hill-side with the untapped trees in protected areas such as the Royal Gardens, or the Grove at Olympia (Olimbía).

The stone pine (*Pinus pinea*) belongs, like the Aleppo pine, to the Mediterranean area, but is much more limited in distribution. The young trees have a characteristically spherical habit; as they get older the lower branches die leaving a long straight trunk topped by a wide flat crown, hence the popular name 'umbrella pine'. The tree casts a strong shadow and thus, when it grows in close woods, there is little or no undergrowth; the heat is tempered but the light is insufficient for good herbaceous growth. In Greece the tree is rarely a forest builder, though probably its natural area has been reduced by deforestation. It is usually found singly or in small groups, is much more strictly confined to the seashore than the Aleppo pine, but occurs in the same areas as the latter tree.

Two oaks are also important trees in the lowlands—the ilex oak or the holm oak (*Quercus Ilex*) and the Valona oak (*Quercus Aegilops*). These oaks, and most others in Greece, have recognizable acorns, but their leaves are very different from those of the English oak.

The Valona oak grows on a variety of soils and forms extensive forests on the lower slopes of the hills, usually below 300 m. Exceptionally, especially on well-watered western slopes, it forms forests to 700 m. The woods are generally open and are often used as grazing grounds. They are found in Thráki, on the lower wetter slopes of the mountains of western Greece, and in the Pelopónnisos. Valona oak grows over large areas in Akarnanía, south of the Gulf of Árta; this area once supplied the French navy with much of its timber, and acorns are still one of the main exports of the region. Two great forests occur in the Pelopónnisos: one in the extreme north-west stretches from Káto-Akhaïa to Manolás, landwards from the pine zone of the coast; the other is north of Yíthion on the north-west shore of the Gulf of Lakonía. In Lésvos the Valona oak forms considerable woods in the north-west and around the Gulf of Kalloní. The island of Kéa is noted for its Valona oaks; here they are

Plate 65. Forested valley near Sérrai

This valley, 3 miles north-east of Sérrai, is typical of many of the deep gorges in the highlands of north-eastern Greece. The right-hand slope is heavily forested, probably with deciduous oaks; the left-hand slope has open scrub, with a group of planted cypresses.

Plate 66. *Abies cephalonica* on the central Píndhos mountains

This spruce takes its name from the island of Cephalonia (Kefallinía) where it is abundant on the mountain slopes. The trees in the foreground are young; those behind are older.

Plate 67. Fully-grown *Pinus Nigra*

This pine is commonly found over much of central and southern Europe and exists in a number of forms, e.g. the Corsican Pine and the Austrian Pine. The tree is frequently planted in England.

Plate 68. Stunted *Pinus Nigra*

Goats grazing on upland pastures destroy most of the vegetation and damage young pines. The pine in the foreground owes its peculiar shape to heavy grazing by these animals.

trees of cultivation and commerce. Elsewhere, though the tree is not cultivated, the woods are protected since the cups of the acorns are much used in tanning. The acorns have a sweet and nutty flavour and are eaten locally either raw or roasted.

The ilex oak has a wide distribution and is found in numbers in the lower river valleys in most parts of Greece. Oriental planes, white poplars and black poplars occur mixed with the oaks in the river valleys, and planes, and sometimes poplars, mark wells and springs to an altitude of 1,300 m. They often stand out conspicuously in an otherwise bare countryside and, easily identified from a distance, these groups of planes give a useful indication of the presence of water (Plate 70).

Mixed Deciduous Forests

The woods of Mediterranean type give place on the middle slopes of the mountains in central and southern Greece to deciduous trees, among which deciduous oaks and chestnut are dominant. In areas where the climate is not purely Mediterranean, deciduous oak woods replace the Aleppo pine and evergreen oak woods even at low altitudes, and it is these areas which are considered transitional in vegetation type (Fig. 67).

Deciduous oak woods are well developed below 1,200 m. *Quercus lanuginosa*, an oak with downy leaves, grows in nearly all parts of Greece in hill and montane zones. *Q. conferta* is another widespread species and is not confined to the true Mediterranean domain. It is the dominant tree of the sandstone belts of the Píndhos, of many of the woods of north-western Thessalía, and is found in south Makedhonía. In some islands oaks are important trees; in Náxos there are traces of former oak woods, in Samothráki oaks occur frequently on the middle slopes, here again the relics of an extensive forest. In Sámos the forest trees are mainly oak and pine. On the *karst* lands of Ípiros mixed manna-ash and oak woods are common. The manna-ash (*Fraxinus Ornus*) is often found locally dominant mixed with oak, *Quercus lanuginosa*, the Durmast oak (*Q. sessiliflora*) and the Turkey oak (*Q. Cerris*), and with hornbeam (*Carpinus orientalis* and *C. Betulus*). Of more limited distribution the Macedonian oak (*Quercus macedonica*) occurs in parts of Ípiros and Makedhonía as a dominant tree associated with the same species as the manna-ash. The manna-ash woods and the Macedonian oak woods are characteristic of the area with a transitional type of climate and a certain summer rainfall.

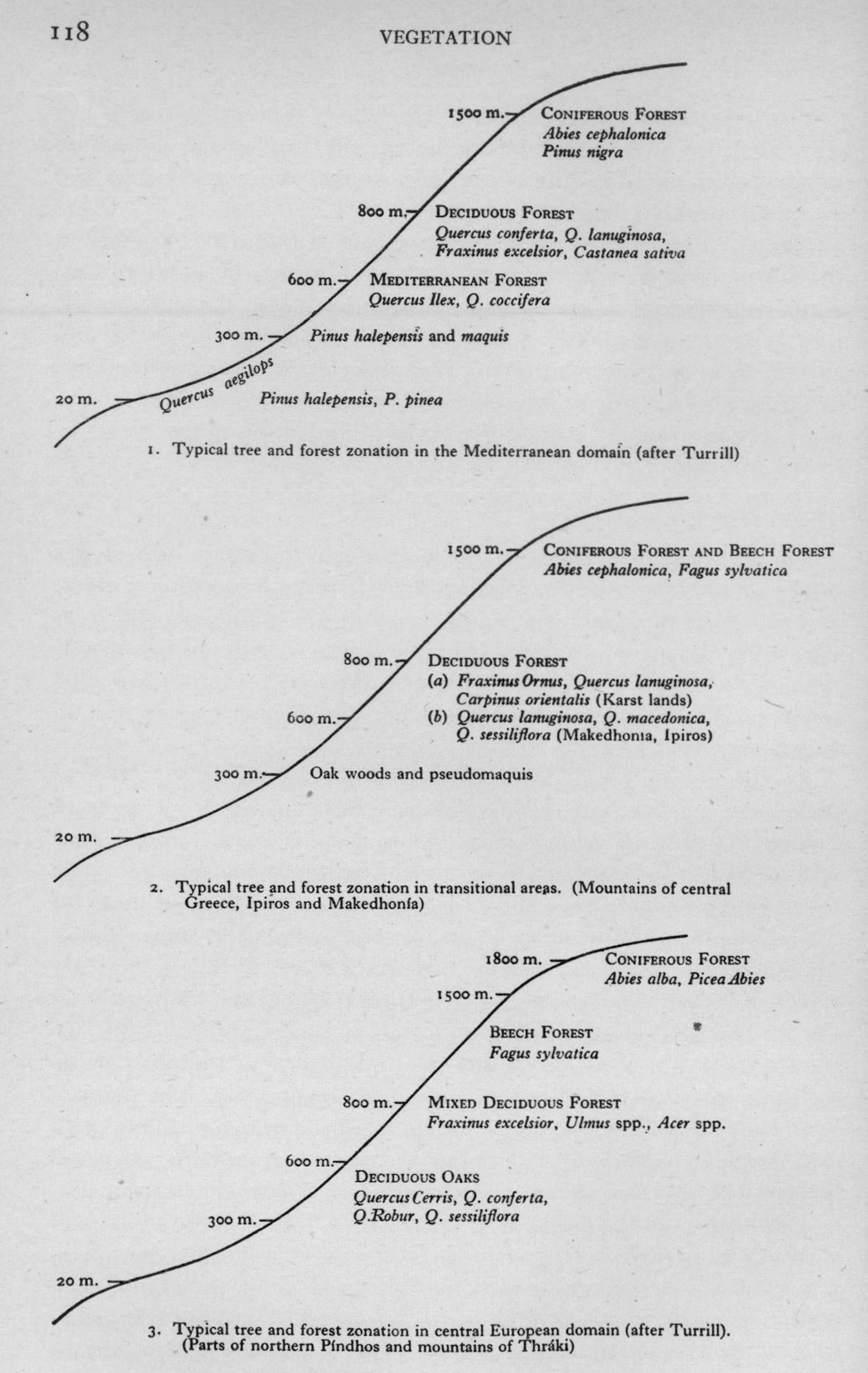

1. Typical tree and forest zonation in the Mediterranean domain (after Turrill)

2. Typical tree and forest zonation in transitional areas. (Mountains of central Greece, Ipiros and Makedhonía)

3. Typical tree and forest zonation in central European domain (after Turrill). (Parts of northern Píndhos and mountains of Thráki)

Fig. 67. Forest communities in Greece

Based on W. B. Turrill, *The Plant Life of the Balkan Peninsula*, p. 136 (Oxford, 1929).

The Spanish chestnut (*Castanea sativa*) grows best on siliceous soils, the crystalline schists of eastern Greece and the slates and sandstones of the folded mountain area of the west. Chestnut woods occur in southern Makedhonía, on the middle slopes of Ólimbos, Óssa and Pílion, and Dhélfi in Évvoia. It is found in the Sperkhiós valley and, mixed with the English species of hornbeam, ash, and beech, it is the dominant tree of many of the upper Píndhos valleys. In the Pelopónnisos, extensive chestnut woods are found on the outcrops of sandstone and conglomerates on the western flanks of the mountains of Akhaïa and on the crystalline rocks of the Párnon and Taÿetos ranges. An especially large forest gives its name to Kastanítsa, a village on the eastern slopes of Párnon.

The horse chestnut (*Aesculus Hippocastanum*) has a limited distribution in montane woods of Ípiros, Thessalía and Fthiótis.

Woods of beech (*Fagus sylvatica*) occur widely only on higher slopes where climatic conditions are similar to those of central Europe. The beech is not found in southern Greece even in the mountains, and the mixed beech-oak woods on the slopes of Mt Oíti and the Oxiá Mountains are said to be the most southerly in Europe.

The deciduous woods have a considerable undergrowth. The sumac (*Rhus coriaria*) is a common tree of the underwood, especially on dry stony slopes between 650 and 1,000 m. in the Pelopónnisos. The Judas tree (*Cercis siliquastrum*), *Ostrya carpinifolia*, a small tree with leaves and male catkins like those of the hornbeam and with female catkins resembling hops, wild pear (*Pyrus communis*) and the bay tree (*Laurus nobilis*), are common in oak woods. Most of the common plants of the pseudomaquis occur too; indeed, especially on the *karst* lands, there is no well-defined limit between woods and scrub. In the oak woods of the central Pelopónnisos the common bracken grows very thickly and to a great height. In both the deciduous and coniferous forests, gorges, ravines, rock surfaces and clearings provide a favourable habitat for flowering bulbs and other herbs. Crocuses, irises, tulips, fritillaries, asphodels, campanulas, anemones, veronicas, and a host more make sheets of colour on the mountain sides in spring and summer.

Coniferous Forest

The dominant tree of the high altitude forests of Greece is the fir. At about 600 m. the fir replaces the deciduous trees in limestone areas of Mediterranean climate, and above 1,400 m. covers large tracts on all soils in northern as well as southern Greece. The altitudinal limit of the firs varies widely and is probably related to the dominant winds, the rainfall maxima, the height of the mountains and their accessibility to man.

Woods of Greek fir (*Abies cephalonica*) and its varieties, and of intermediates between the Greek and white fir (*Abies alba*), clothe the higher slopes of the Áthos peninsula, the mountains of Makedhonía, Ípiros, Thessalía, and are also markedly characteristic of the high calcareous mountains of central and southern Greece. Kefallinía has magnificent forests of these firs; the limestone belts of the central Píndhos range carry forests of firs; the upper forests of the Óthris mountains, and their continuation, the mountains of central Évvoia are fir-clad. So also are the broad high shoulders of Parnassós, with here and there a splendid specimen of the Greek fir (Plate 66) often standing isolated. Firs succeed pines and oaks on the upper slopes of Elikón and Párnis. The fir is the dominant tree of the high mountains of the Pelopónnisos: the limestone regions of Erímanthos, Aroánia and Killíni, the mountains of central Arkadhía and the calcareous massif of Párnon all have extensive fir forests. Most of the Aegean islands do not reach the fir forest belt, but Thásos has fir forests which cover all the upper slopes except the highest peaks.

The only other forest-forming tree of these altitudes is the Black pine (*Pinus nigra*), found almost exclusively on siliceous soils from 700 to 1,700 m. It is a tall dark tree with a straight trunk much in demand for ship masts. The Black pine, since it avoids limestone areas, is less widespread than the firs, but it is found, sometimes mixed with firs, sometimes alone, forming thick forest on the crystalline massifs. It forms the high forest of Ólimbos, and of the mountains of northern Évvoia; it occurs in the Píndhos region in Ípiros, and in Stáklia, Aitolía. In the Pelopónnisos the Black pine is found on the outcrops of crystalline schist of Killíni and Párnon and forms thick forest over large areas in the Taïyetos mountains. The mountains of Sámos carry forests of Black pine, and it forms the dominant tree of the forested heights of Lésvos between the Gulfs of Yéras and Kalloní (Plates 67, 68).

The thick pine and fir forests have little or no undergrowth, but, where the trees are more openly spaced, juniper, hawthorn, and a small-leaved lime, stunted to a low bush, form a shrub layer. Plants with conspicuous flowers are still numerous at these heights: crocus, tulips, scilla, cyclamen, irises, gentians, campanulas and anemones appear in spring and summer.

Brushwood Communities

A brushwood type of vegetation covers more than half the land surface of Greece, and it is significant that the dominant plants of these communities have common names in modern Greek (see Appendix VII).

Brushwood is found on once forested land; forest fires, long-continued cutting for timber and fuel, and over-grazing by animals have caused extensive deforestation. Natural regeneration of forests is difficult. The annual variation of precipitation is great; moreover, the total amount is barely adequate for tree growth on porous soils. If

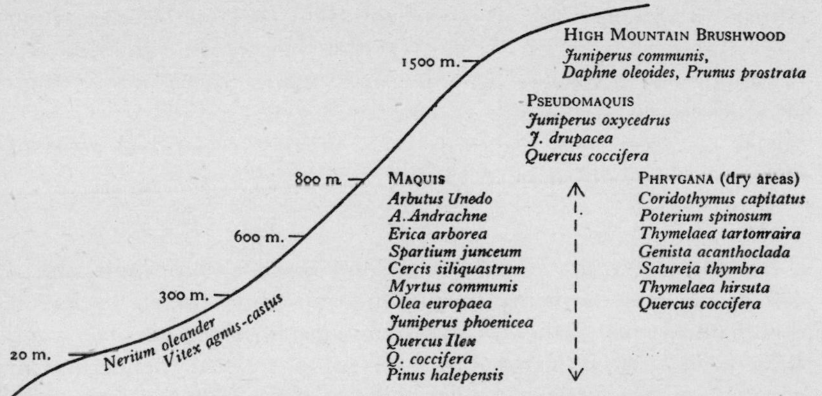

Fig. 68. Brushwood communities in southern and central Greece

Based on W. B. Turrill, *The Plant Life of the Balkan Peninsula, passim* (Oxford, 1929). Phrygana replaces maquis where the vegetation is much cut or heavily grazed, especially on dry soils. Pseudomaquis replaces both at about 800 m.

rainfall is below the average for one or two seasons many young trees die, and even in normal years many more are eaten by voracious goats.

The plants of the brushwood are able to withstand dry conditions; they have deep or spreading roots, small leaves, some with leathery or waxy coverings, while spines, thorns and aromatic sap occur in many species.

The brushwood communities vary widely in character; some are dense and impenetrable, others are open and sparse; in some the plants are 2–3 m. high, in others they form tight cushions growing close to the ground. Four types of scrub may be distinguished in Greece: maquis, pseudomaquis, phrygana and shiblyak (Figs. 68, 69).

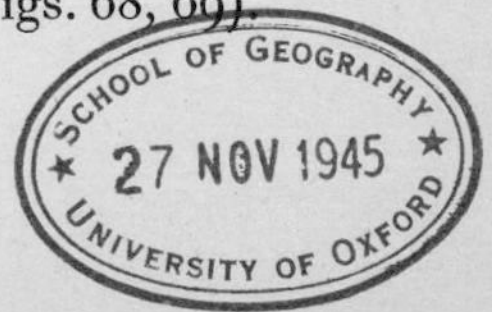

True maquis occurs generally in the same regions as the Mediterranean forest which it replaces—that is, on lower slopes near the coast, though it extends some way inland and to fairly high altitudes in southern and central Greece. Its upper limit is not clearly defined though it is usually well developed only below 1,000 m. Pseudomaquis, formed of hardier shrubs, replaces maquis at higher altitudes in the south and even at low levels in the north. Where the vegetation is kept down by browsing sheep and goats and by the cutting of brushwood for fuel both maquis and pseudomaquis degenerate into phrygana, a term given to areas covered by low-growing and widely spaced bushes. Phrygana is found especially where soils are thin and poor, but it is doubtful whether it is ever a climax vegetation type. It corresponds to the type of vegetation known as *garrigue* in the western Mediterranean. The shiblyak is a community of deciduous woody plants and is found only at high altitudes in the Mediterranean climate of south and eastern Greece, but it is common in the hill zones of the transitional areas of Thessalía, Makedhonía and Thráki.

Maquis

Maquis can form a complete ground cover 2–3 m. high, and if one or more of the many thorny and spiny and prickly species is dominant, it may make an almost impenetrable region. Here and there from a sea of evergreen bushes rises a tree, an Aleppo pine or a tall specimen of the ilex oak. Many of the common plants of the maquis have very varying habits.

Maquis grows best on the siliceous soils and in the better watered areas, and is found more highly developed and over greater areas in western than eastern Greece. It is restricted in Makedhonía and Thráki to limited coastal areas protected from the north winds; it is found here and there along the Aegean coast of Thráki, on the lower slopes of Mt Áthos, and in southward-facing bays of the Khalkidhikí peninsula. The deforested lower slopes of the crystalline mountains of Ólimbos, Óssa and Pílion and the crystalline schists of southern Évvoia are covered with dense maquis. This is a region of locally higher rainfall, since the prevalent north-east winds are here onshore (Fig. 59). In Ípiros true maquis does not extend high or far inland except in sheltered river valleys; the limiting effects of the cold winds of the Píndhos show clearly. In Akarnanía and Aitolía it is well developed on the slate and sandstone belts, and large areas of dense maquis occur around the Gulf of Amvrakía and along the coasts of

Aitolía. It is a vegetation form found extensively in the Pelopónnisos, in the Argolís peninsula and in the Párnon region. In the north and east Aegean islands thick maquis covers the deforested zones. It is well developed in the North Sporádhes, Thásos and Samothráki, and covers large tracts of volcanic rocks in southern Lésvos. Very thick aromatic scrub is also found in eastern Sámos.

Characteristic Plants of the Maquis. The maquis is a mixed community, one plant is rarely dominant though particular groups of plants are characteristic of particular areas. Along the watercourses, on the pebbles brought down by the torrents, oleander maquis flourishes. The oleander (*Nerium Oleander*) is the dominant species of this community, and in summer many river valleys are ribbons of rose red blossoms across bare rock country. With the oleander, the bay tree (*Laurus nobilis*), the strawberry tree (*Arbutus Unedo*), and the ilex oak are usually found. The Chaste tree (*Vitex Agnus-castus*) is a low bush with scented aromatic leaves and most commonly with deep blue flowers, though these may be pink or white. It is also common on stony ground along river beds especially near the sea. It has supple stems used all over Greece for basket weaving.

The drier slopes of the hills have at low altitudes a great variety of maquis plants. The commonest plants are the myrtle (*Myrtus communis*), the lentisc (*Pistacia Lentiscus*), Spanish broom (*Sparteum junceum*), the tree heath (*Erica arborea*), the heath (*E. verticillata* Forsk.), *Calycotome villosa*, the Kermes oak (*Quercus coccifera*), the wild olive, the Judas tree, and numerous species of cistus. The lentisc grows from sea level to about 900 m. and yields a sticky resin, the much-valued gum-mastic. The gum is used commercially as an ingredient of varnish for oil paintings; locally it is used to flavour the liqueur *mastika,* and mixed with sugar is eaten as a sweetmeat. The Spanish broom is more strictly confined to lower slopes, and is rare above 600 m. The heaths grow to greater heights, but almost always avoid limestone soils. The tree heath at its maximum development is about 3 m. high; it is rarely found in tree form above about 300 m., but persists to great heights far beyond the maquis zone, eventually reduced to minute proportions. The heath, *Erica verticillata,* is a smaller plant, and its bright pink flowers in autumn and spring are a valued source of honey for bees. It grows to 1,000 m. in Attikí and to 2,000 m. in Kríti, and it is commoner in northern Greece than the tree heath. *Calycotome* is a gorse-like plant growing about 2 m. high and armed with formidable spines. It grows freely on rocky hillsides and makes them a blaze of yellow in the spring. The Kermes oak is a most ubiquitous plant; it grows on every soil in every situation and is not only common in many maquis communities but is one of the most widespread dominants of the pseudomaquis and is found also in phrygana. This prickly-leaved oak may be of any size from a tall shapely tree 15 m. high to a small cushion. It derives its name from a scarlet berry, really a gall produced by an insect, which it bears as abundantly as acorns. The 'berry' was an important article of commerce as the source of a scarlet dye much used by Byzantine and Italian dyers.

Pseudomaquis

Beyond the climatic limit of true maquis a plant community often differentiated as pseudomaquis is found. It occurs above the maquis in central and southern Greece in all the regions mentioned, and often succeeds phrygana at altitudes high enough to give protection from human interference. Pseudomaquis is much more widespread than maquis in northern Greece and covers wide areas on the hills of Makedhonía.

Plants of the Pseudomaquis. The pseudomaquis is not a degenerate form of maquis, and is often quite as luxuriant as maquis in growth. The hardier species of the maquis are common to both communities, but the myrtle, arbutus, heath lentisc and wild olive disappear while the Macedonian oak, box (*Buxus sempervirens*), terebinth (*Pistacia terebinthus*), *Juniperus excelsa*, *Jasminum fruticans* and the cherry-laurel (*Prunus laurocerasus*) are common in pseudomaquis but rare in maquis.

The pseudomaquis, like the maquis, is a mixed community, but unlike maquis it usually has one plant very definitely dominant in one area. The dominant plant, however, varies from place to place. The Kermes oak is the dominant plant in many areas, and the lower slopes of the hills behind Thessaloníki have impenetrable thickets of this prickly oak. Junipers are also common dominants; *Juniperus oxycedrus* is a plant of wide distribution and almost pure communities occur in many areas. *J. excelsa* is a common dominant of the pseudomaquis in Makedhonía and Thráki and *J. drupacea* in central and southern Greece. The Macedonian oak builds pseudomaquis communities in parts of Ípiros and Makedhonía. Climbing plants are common: *Clematis cirrhosa*, *Hedera Helix* and *Smilax aspera* twine themselves about the taller plants and add greatly to the difficulty of passage through the brushwood.

Ecologically, pseudomaquis stands between maquis and shiblyak, and in parts of Makedhonía the one passes into the other with no marked division.

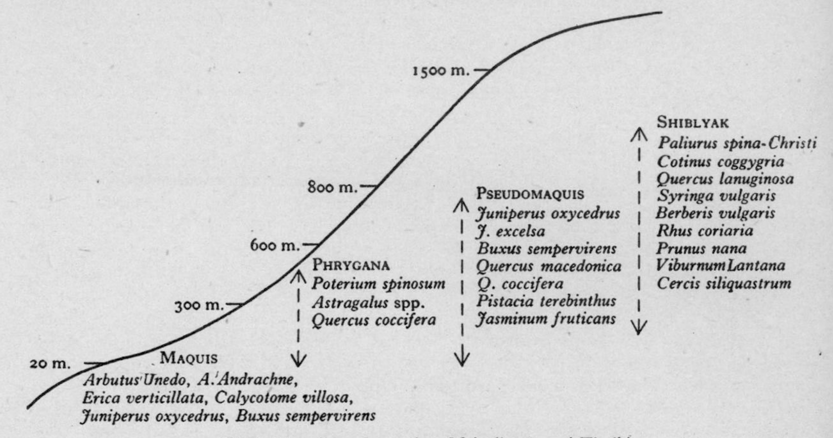

Fig. 69. Brushwood communities in northern Greece

Based on W. B. Turrill, *The Plant Life of the Balkan Peninsula, passim* (Oxford, 1929). The brushwood communities of Makedhonía and Dhitikí Thráki show more variation than in the south. Maquis occurs only in sheltered places near the coast. Pseudomaquis replaces maquis and phrygana inland and at greater altitudes; deciduous shiblyak replaces pseudomaquis in higher regions.

Phrygana

Wherever conditions are adverse to luxuriant plant growth the maquis and pseudomaquis are replaced by phrygana. Thorny and woody plants, with thick and spiny leaves, grey-green in colour, and with resinous and often aromatic sap, grow in low bushes with bare

Plate 69. Agaves, olives and cypresses

The photograph shows the road from Mistrás on the plain of Lakonía, with the Taïyetos mountains in the background. On the right are *Agave americano* and olives; in the centre cypresses, and behind them, *Thuyas.*

Plate 70. Oriental plane

The Oriental plane is a tree commonly found near wells and villages. Its lofty, wide-spreading branches provide welcome shade in the hot, clear summers. It is occasionally planted in England.

Plate 71. *Quercus coccifera*, on the slopes of Ólimbos

Quercus coccifera grows to a height of 20 ft. in favourable situations. Here, as in most of the Mediterranean region, it exists in the form of a low bush—the result of cutting for firewood, burning, grazing and exposure at high altitudes.

Plate 72. Alpine meadowland

The view shows part of the plateau of Ólimbos at a height of about 7,500 ft. Note the tussocky character of the vegetation.

patches of rock between them. The phrygana, if not in flower, hardly colours the mountain slopes, but it does provide some sparse pasture for sheep and goats, some herbs for *saláta* for man and a little fuel and litter.

This type of vegetation occurs widely in Greece. On the lower hill slopes of Thráki, Makedhonía, and Thessalía it replaces pseudo-maquis on dry and accessible sites. Phrygana vegetation is typically developed on the hills of Attikí, where tree and shrub cutting from classical times has destroyed both forest and maquis. Imittós, Pendelikón, and Elikón have poor maquis vegetation at the best, and true phrygana covers most of their lower slopes. In parts of Aitolía, and on the isthmus of Kórinthos the limestone soils, even at sea level, have an almost desert barrenness, broken only by clumps of grey-green plants. Phrygana vegetation covers much of the surface of the Ionian islands and of the Kikládhes. Here the summers are long and dry, and the slopes in many islands are so steep that the soil is washed away by winter rains. Thus the vegetation, constantly exploited by man, cannot form a continuous cover. Skíros, Yíoura, and some of the other small islands of the Sporádhes, show true phrygana vegetation, while the limestone plateau of Khíos supports only such plants as marjoram, thyme and *Poterium spinosum*.

Plants of the Phrygana. The most common dominant plants of the phrygana are thyme and a small bush of the rose family, *Poterium spinosum*. Cretan thyme (*Coridothymus capitatus* Reichb.) is a stiff under-shrub usually about ½ m. high, but where goats are absent it grows to twice that height and forms a rounded shapely bush. *Poterium spinosum* L. grows ½–1 m. high, and its flowers are rather like those of the common burnet. It is a very prickly plant, and growing knee high it makes walking unpleasant if it is at all thick. It is cut and used as fuel, and in some places, where wine is exported, as packing for bottles.

Many smaller plants of low-growing bushy habit are associated with these two. Marjoram (*Origanum onites* L.) is very common in central and southern Greece: it is known in Greece as *rigáni*. Kermes oak, reduced to small bush in size, and many cistuses belong to this community as well as to the maquis. *Cistus salviifolius* L., *Cistus creticus* L., *Cistus monspeliensis* L. and *Cistus parviflorus* Lam. are all common in Attikí. French lavender (*Lavendula Stoechas* L.), Genista (*Genista acanthoclada* DC.), Stachys (*Stachys cretica* L.) Savory (*Satureia Thymbra* L.), two little shrubs of the Daphne family (*Thymelaea hirsuta* L., and *Thymelaea tartonraira*), are all usual plants of the dry bare areas.

Shiblyak

Shiblyak is a Serbian word used in variant forms throughout the Balkans to describe deciduous brushwood of central European type. In central and southern Greece it is only found at high altitudes, but in the more continental climate of Makedhonía and Thráki it is sometimes found in the lowlands. Dense thickets of the Christ's thorn occur in parts of the Axiós and Strimón plains, sometimes replaced higher up the slopes, where the soil is drier, by pseudo-maquis dominated by the Kermes oak and *Juniperus oxycedrus*.

The most common dominant of shiblyak vegetation within Greek boundaries is the Christ's thorn (*Paliurus spina-Christi*). It grows to 3 m. in favourable situations and, with its long curved spines, makes impenetrable thickets. Other characteristic plants are *Cotinus coggygria*, *Quercus lanuginosa*, lilac (*Syringa vulgaris*), the common barberry (*Berberis vulgaris*), and sumac (*Rhus coriaria*).

Vegetation above the Tree Limit

Only a small area in Greece lies above the limit of tree growth. High mountain brushwood occupies part of this region, a community dominated by the common English species of juniper (*Juniperus communis*) and *Daphne oleoides*. In northern Greece high mountain meadowland is well developed, especially in the Píndhos region, and is much valued as summer pasture for flocks. In southern Greece true mountain pastures are rare, and the limestone peaks are bare except for rock vegetation growing in the cracks. Here species of *Campanula*, *Silene*, *Alyssum* and stonecrop when in flower make streaks of colour against the bare surface of the rock (Plate 72).

BIBLIOGRAPHICAL NOTE

The most comprehensive description of the vegetation of Greece is W. B. Turrill, *The Plant Life of the Balkan Peninsula* (Oxford, 1929). A general account is given in A. F. W. Schimper, *Pflanzengeographie auf physiologischer Grundlage*, 3rd ed. edited by F. C. von Faber, Band II (Jena, 1935). Both of these books give selected bibliographies of the more important specialised works on the region. A more up to date account may be found in M. Rikli, *Das Pflanzenkleid der Mittelmeerländer* (Bern, 1942).

Chapter V

ANCIENT GREECE

Prehistoric Greece: The Beginnings, about 3000 B.C.; The Minoan and Mycenean Civilizations, 3000–1100 B.C.; The Dorian Invasions, 1100–800 B.C.
The Rise of the Greek City States: The Growth of the City State, after 800 B.C.; Greek Colonization, 770–550 B.C.; The Rise of Hellenic Civilization.
Classical Greece: The Persian Wars; The Athenian Empire and the Peloponnesian War; The Civilization of the Fifth and Fourth Centuries B.C.
Macedonian and Hellenistic Greece: The Empire of Alexander the Great; Political History after the death of Alexander, 323–146 B.C.; Hellenistic Civilization.
Roman Greece: Graeco-Roman Political and Economic Development; Graeco-Roman Civilization.
Bibliographical Note.

PREHISTORIC GREECE

Greek history, properly speaking, begins about 800 B.C., but Greek origins go back for more than two thousand years before that date. Civilizations had succeeded one another and had left material remains. Though it is not possible to speak of a historical background to those remains, it is possible, by piecing together the evidence of archaeology, mythology, tradition and legend, to gain a more or less coherent picture, at least in outline, of the general course of events. For the earlier phases, the principal evidence is, for obvious reasons, supplied by archaeological excavation, but the interpretation of this evidence is naturally somewhat speculative.

The Beginnings, about 3000 B.C.

The earliest inhabitants of Greece of whom we have any knowledge were in a pre-metal stage of civilization. Their settlements extended from Thessaly, where they were most densely concentrated, through Boeotia at least as far south as Corinth. Their tools and weapons were of stone, and their pottery, both plain and painted, was of exceptionally fine quality. The origin of this civilization remains obscure in the absence of a close parallel elsewhere.

A second phase of the pre-metal civilization followed, during which settlement was more widely distributed, covering many parts of Macedonia, Thessaly, Boeotia, Corinthia; and there was one settlement, at least, in Arcadia (Fig. 70). Many of the earlier sites continued to be occupied, but since the pottery was now quite different, and since a new style of house was in use, the arrival of a new people has been inferred. From detailed resemblances between their pottery, tools, and utensils, to those in use farther north, especially in the region

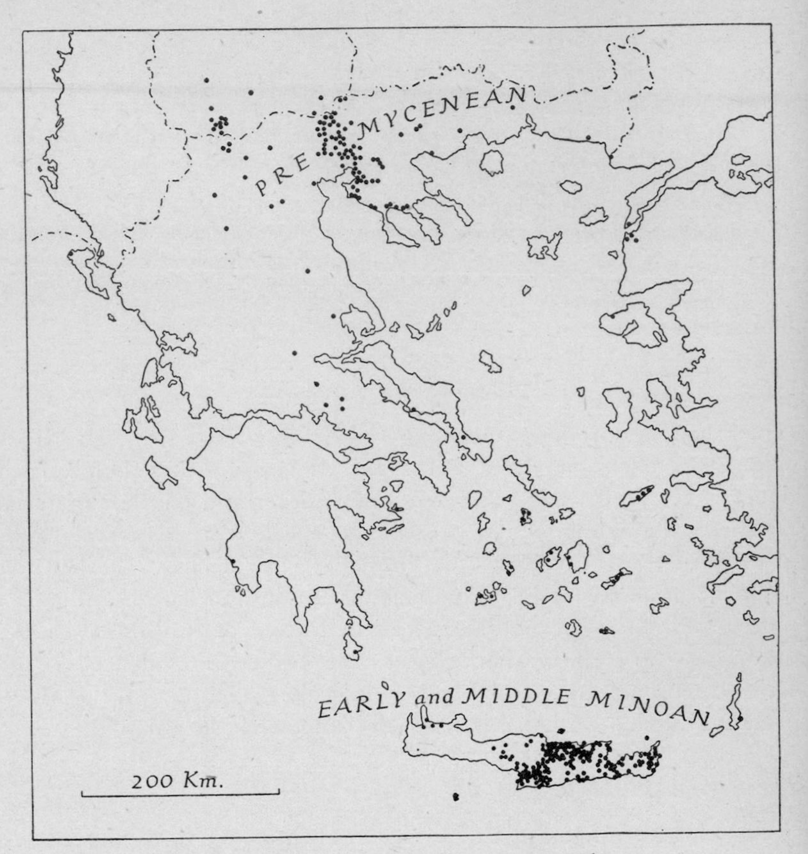

Fig. 70. Prehistoric sites in Greece, 3000–1600 B.C.

Based on: (1) S. Casson, *Macedonia, Thrace and Illyria*, folding map (Oxford, 1926); (2) D. Fimmen, *Die Kretisch-Mykenische Kultur*, plate 1 (Leipzig und Berlin, 1921); (3) W. A. Heurtley, *Prehistoric Macedonia*, p. xxii (Cambridge, 1939); (4) J. D. S Pendlebury, *The Archaeology of Crete: an introduction*, pp. 36, 278 and 282 (London 1939).

The mainland sites are pre-Mycenean; those of Crete and the islands are Early and Middle Minoan.

of the Middle Danube, it has been further deduced that this civilization originated in that part of Europe, and spread southwards to Greece.

The Minoan and Mycenean Civilizations, 3000–1100 B.C.

The use of metal (first copper, then bronze), already long familiar in the East, had been spreading westwards and had reached the coast of Asia Minor. From here, it was carried, early in the third millennium B.C., by what seems to have been a mass migration of people to Greece, overland through Macedonia into Thessaly, and by sea via the islands to central Greece and Crete.

The Minoan Civilization. This third civilization carried with it the seeds of development, which reached their full flowering in Crete. The geographical position of the island favoured intercourse with Egypt and the East, and, owing to this intercourse and to their own natural talents, the Cretans made a rapid advance in knowledge and skill. In their spacious palaces, designed for comfort and convenience, life seems to have been easy and serene. The arts flourished, especially those of the lapidary, the goldsmith, the worker in ivory, the fresco painter and the vase painter; and such a degree of excellence was reached in these arts that Cretan civilization can be compared with, and in some respects surpasses, that of Egypt or Sumeria. The centre of all this splendour was the great palace of Cnossus; other palaces were at Phaestus, Ayía Triádha, and Mállia. That the Cretans were familiar with the art of writing is proved by the hundreds of clay tablets, inscribed either with pictographs which may represent words or (and these are later) with linear signs which may represent syllables, found in the ruins of Cnossus.

The Minoan civilization, so called after the legendary king Minos, seems to have been based on sea power and on sea-borne trade; and evidence has been found of Minoan contacts not only with Greece, Syria and Egypt but with lands as far distant as Sicily and Spain. Perhaps it was the sense of security given them by their navy which allowed the islanders to leave unfortified their palaces and the towns which clustered around them. Consequently, when invasion came, after a thousand years of peaceful development, it found them unprepared.

The Mainland Civilization. On the mainland, development was much less rapid. The immigrants of the early third millennium B.C. settled in the neighbourhood of Corinth, in Argolis, and on the island of Aegina. From here they spread northwards into Boeotia and the Sperchios valley and southwards as far as Messenia, and, eventually, westwards to Ithaca and Levkas in the Ionian islands (Fig. 71). Their standard of living was not high; and their settlements were small, not more than villages, and only rarely fortified. Their potters produced vases of extraordinarily fine quality, but usually undecorated: simple gold ornaments have been found in their tombs.

The Achaeans. About 2000 B.C. signs of upheaval appear on the mainland. At some sites, marks of a general conflagration, houses of a new type built on the debris of the earlier, new styles of pottery, and different burial customs, indicate a change of population. Converging lines of evidence make it likely that this upheaval was caused by the entry into central and southern Greece of the Achaeans, a Greek-speaking people, perhaps from Thessaly or Macedonia, or even from beyond. The earlier civilization collapsed and the new, which was to prevail for four hundred years, took its place. It seems to have been materially poorer than the civilization which it displaced; its plain pottery is characterized by a dull uniformity; its painted pottery is lifeless; and there is no sign of progress anywhere.

The Mycenaean Civilization. The contact of this Achaean civilization with that of Crete produced great changes, and, from about 1600 B.C. onwards, palaces very like the Minoan were being built for the Achaean nobles of the mainland; Minoan artists were decorating them and Minoan craftsmen were supplying objects of luxury. Thus arose the civilization known as Mycenaean, which was Minoan material civilization taken over wholesale by people who had little of their own. Some adaptation was bound to be made, and this is illustrated by the difference between the palaces and tombs of the mainland and those of Minoan Crete itself. The Minoan palace is rather a confused medley of rooms and corridors which seems to have grown rather than to have been planned. The Mycenaean palace, on the other hand, gives the impression of having been planned; and planned in relation to the *megaron* or hall, in which stood the hearth; the hall was approached by a series of vestibules, broad stairways and ramps leading directly from the main gateway in the circuit wall. The reason for this arrangement was probably religious, the hearth having a sacred and symbolic character, and being the focus of the life of the palace. Mycenaean palaces too, in contrast to Minoan, were strongly fortified in conformity with the quasi-feudal character of Achaean society.

There are differences also between the shape and structure of Mycenaean and Minoan tombs; the former are beehive in shape, the latter are rectangular. Mycenaean gold ornaments, especially those found in profusion in the shaft graves at Mycenae, though the patterns of their decoration are often derived from Minoan art, have a barbaric appearance, which is quite un-Minoan, and suggests that the Minoan goldsmiths made them in that particular way in order to satisfy the tastes of their Mycenaean employers. Vase painters, too, departed from Minoan standards, both by adopting

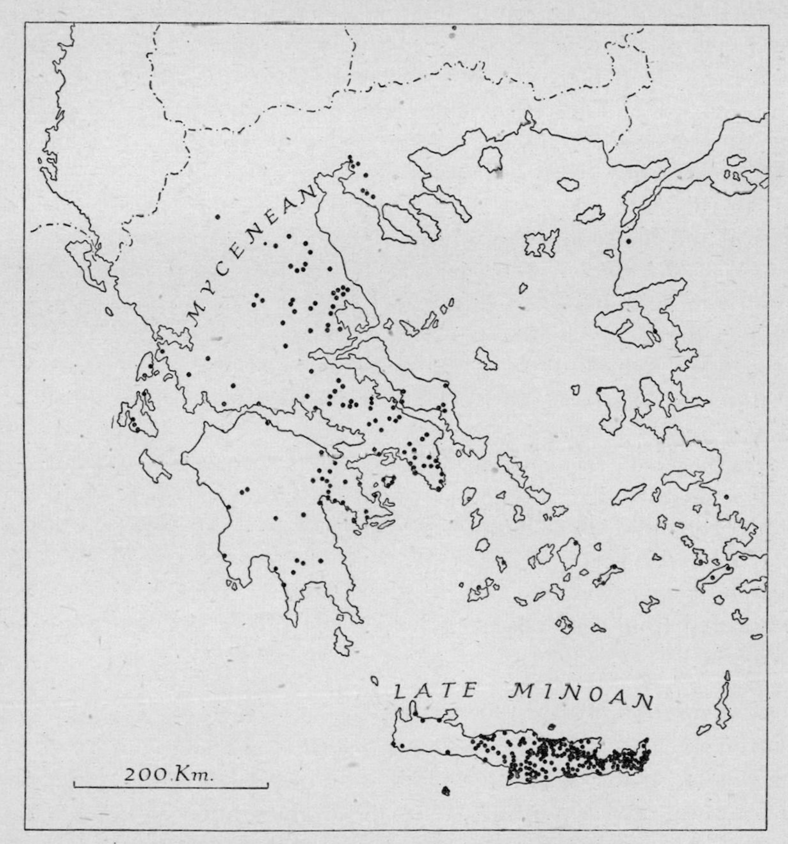

Fig. 71. Prehistoric sites in Greece, 1600–1200 B.C.

Based on: (1) S. Casson, *Macedonia, Thrace and Illyria*, folding map (Oxford, 1926); D. Fimmen, *Die Kretisch-Mykenische Kultur*, plate 1 (Leipzig und Berlin, 1921); (3) J. D. S. Pendlebury, *The Archaeology of Crete: an introduction*, pp. 284 and 288 (London, 1939).

The mainland sites are Mycenean; those of Crete and the islands are Late Minoan.

Achaean shapes for their vases, and by adding human and animal figures to Minoan patterns.

The increasing luxury and magnificence of Achaean society, which seems to have reached its climax about two hundred years after the first contact with Crete, presupposes great wealth, acquired in all probability by conquest or piracy, or both. So far, relations with Crete seem to have been peaceful, but given a society like the Achaean, acquisitive and military, and Minoan society, also acquisitive but relying on sea power, an ultimate clash was inevitable. That such a clash occurred can be inferred from the wholesale destruction and sack of the Cretan palaces, which took place, on archaeological evidence, about 1400 B.C., and which can hardly be attributed to any but Achaeans. The enlargement and embellishment of the palaces of Mycenae and Tiryns, the strengthening of their fortifications, and the construction of the 'Treasury of Athens', all of which occurred about this date, was probably a natural sequel to the destruction of a rival and the acquisition of new riches.

The Trojan War. Achaean power, now heir to the Minoan, continued to expand for the next two hundred years. About 1200 B.C. an expedition in which most of the Achaean nobility took part was launched. Ostensibly it sought to avenge the abduction of Helen, the wife of Menelaus, king of Sparta, by Alexander (Paris) of Troy, but in reality it aimed at obtaining control of the commercial advantages which the position of Troy, at the entrance to the Dardanelles, commanded. Here was the key to the rich Black Sea trade. The expedition achieved its immediate object, the capture of Troy, and left a profound impression on Greek folk memory; but, ultimately, it turned out to be a disaster, for the Achaean power never recovered from the exhaustion which the protracted campaign had involved.

The Dorian Invasions, 1100–800 B.C.

Almost as great an impression was left by another event or series of events, which occurred within the 'third generation' after the Trojan war, and which completed the disintegration of the Achaean power. This event was the 'coming of the Dorians'. The Dorian invasion formed part of wider movements which were taking place beyond the northern frontiers of Greece, and which had the effect of shifting southwards Greek tribes already established in northern Greece, who, in their turn, displaced others. Aided by weapons of iron, the Dorians pushed through to the Peloponnese, dispossessed the Achaeans, destroyed their strongholds, and drove them overseas or into the mountains. This movement was long drawn-out, and the unsettled conditions of the time were unfavourable to civilization.

The art of the 'Dark Ages', as this period has not inappropriately been named, is known chiefly from the gigantic painted vases which

Plate 73. The 'treasury of Atreus', Mycenae, thirteenth century B.C.

This is the largest of the bee-hive tombs. Sculptured half-columns of marble stood on either side of the doorway, and sculptured marble slabs filled the triangular space above the door.

Plate 74. The temple of Hera, Olympia, seventh century B.C.

This is one ot the earliest Doric temples.

Plate 75. Metope from the Temple of Zeus, Olympia

One of the twelve labours of Hercules is represented on this work of the early fifth century B.C. Hercules, aided by Athena, supports the world on his shoulders, while Atlas offers him the golden apples of the Hesperides.

Plate 76. Panathenaic votive vase

have been found associated with tombs or sanctuaries. On the mainland of Greece, the last phase of Minoan-Mycenaean vase painting lingered sufficiently long for some of its elements to be incorporated in the new style which succeeded it. The vase-painters' repertoire now consisted almost exclusively of rectilinear designs, which, in Attica, came to be symmetrically disposed with mathematical precision over the whole surface of the vase. Votive offerings made of bronze, which often take the form of figurines of men or animals, have been found in sanctuaries, notably at Olympia. The art of this period is known under the generic name of 'Geometric'.

The Rise of the Greek City States

The Growth of the City State, after 800 B.C.

The years following the arrival of the Dorians, from 800 B.C. onwards, were marked by recovery after invasion and by the rise of the city state. The beginnings of this characteristic Greek institution date from the later days of Achaean rule, when, mainly for reasons of security, the inhabitants of a district moved from their scattered villages and took up their abode beneath the walls of the neighbouring castle. Thus, in Attica, these villages or groups of villages were originally independent, and it was only when the lords of the Acropolis had obtained a certain pre-eminence that the villages surrendered their independence and merged their governments in a single government with its centre at Athens. By this arrangement, Athens became the head of a united state, which included all Attica, and of which all the inhabitants of Attica became citizens. The political rights of citizenship could be exercised at any time by going to Athens, and the duty of the state to protect its citizens in time of danger was recognized by allowing them to shelter within the walls. The other city states developed on more or less similar lines, but the villages of Boeotia were never welded into complete unity with the leading city of Thebes; and in the Peloponnese the city of Sparta always remained dominant in relation to the other settlements, whose inhabitants had no political rights in the Spartan state.

The years following the formation of the city state formed essentially a period of experiment in methods of government. Athens, for instance, soon passed from monarchy to oligarchy; next, an attempt to establish a 'tyranny' (the Greek term for the unconstitutional rule of an individual) in 630 B.C. failed; then the rich industrialist, Solon, was given dictatorial power to introduce constitutional and social reforms on democratic lines (594 B.C.); from 561 to 528 B.C. the 'tyrant' Peisistratus was in power, a period incidentally of great building and artistic activity; finally in 507 B.C., the reforms of Cleisthenes introduced a genuinely democratic constitution, in which the Assembly of citizens had sovereign power. The other states, after somewhat similar experiments, arrived at some kind of democratic government, with the exception of Sparta, which retained its peculiar dual kingship and constitution based on a rigid military code, attributed to the semi-legendary lawgiver Lycurgus.

Despite their democratic character, slavery was a common institution in the Greek city states, especially in the fifth and fourth centuries B.C. It was justified by the Greeks on the grounds of necessity; without it, citizens would be unable to devote their time to serving the state. The slaves were mostly Thracians, Scythians and Asiatics, and only rarely Greeks. For the most part they were either purchased or captured in war or piracy. They were employed in domestic work, in agriculture, in industry (conditions in the silver mines of Laurium were very bad), and in public service as roadmen, clerks and policemen. There have been very varied estimates about the number of slaves in Greece, and it has even been said that the slave population of fifth-century Athens outnumbered the freemen.

All the city states had this in common, that in relation to their neighbours they were sovereign and independent. Between them, boundaries were fixed, war or peace declared, ambassadors exchanged, treaties and alliances made. All the apparatus, in fact, which has been employed throughout history by large countries or empires in their mutual relations, is here seen in full employment by tiny states, most of them smaller than an English county. The process of world history, exhibited in microcosm, gives a peculiar value to Greek history.

It has been said with truth that there is no history of ancient Greece, only a history of separate Greek states. But despite this political dismemberment and despite their local antagonisms, the Greeks were spiritually one. The rise of the great sanctuaries at Delphi and Olympia, the institution of periodic festivals and games, the peculiar position of the Delphic oracle described as the 'common hearth of Greece'—all these stand for the Greek consciousness of a common heritage, and for a strong sense of unity.

Greek Colonization, 770–550 B.C.

Commercial enterprise went hand in hand with political experiment. This commercial development was earliest and greatest not in mainland Greece, but among the Ionian cities of western Asia Minor, peopled, so tradition ran, by Greeks from Attica in the days of the Dorian invasions. These cities were aided in their early development by contacts with the rich inland state of Lydia. The leading city, Miletus, opened up the Black Sea trade. Phocea and Samos similarly opened up trade with the western Mediterranean. A great movement of colonization was thus inaugurated between 770 and 550 B.C. (Fig. 72).

Commerce, however, was not the only motive for founding colonies. Discontented with conditions at home, especially in those states

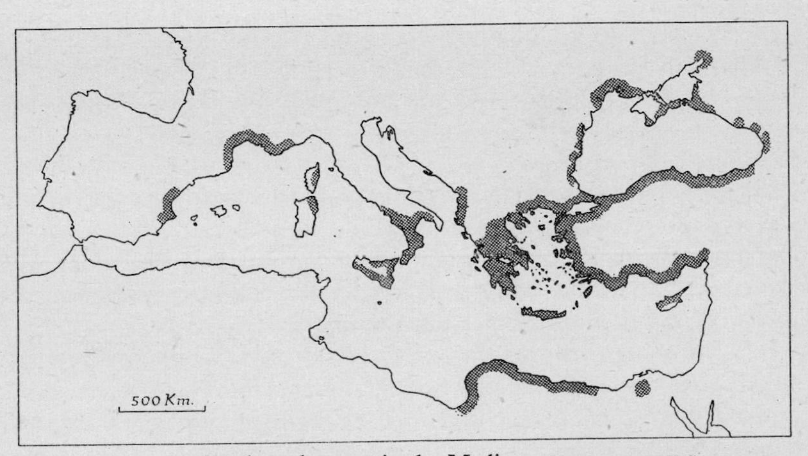

Fig. 72. Greek settlements in the Mediterranean, *c.* 550 B.C.
Based on W. R. Shepherd, *Historical Atlas*, p. 12 (London, 1930).
Note the absence of Greek settlements in north-west Africa and south-east Spain —areas occupied by the Carthaginians.

where a defective land system made it difficult for many to get a living, or impelled merely by a spirit of adventure, groups of citizens set sail to try their fortunes overseas. Once founded, these colonies remained politically independent but in as close touch with their mother cities as circumstances permitted; they sent representatives to the Pan-Hellenic games, and never lost consciousness of being Hellenic cities and outposts of civilization among barbarians. Some of these cities have vanished, but many have survived; Syracuse, Taranto and İstanbul, for example, were originally Greek colonies.

As their trade expanded, Greek merchants were brought into relations with Phoenician merchants of the Syrian coast towns, who had for some centuries monopolized the trade of the Mediterranean, and who already had trading stations in Greece, on the coast of Asia Minor, in Sicily and North Africa and beyond. The result of Greek competition was to deprive these Phoenicians of their Aegean and of some of their Sicilian markets, and to confine them to the eastern and western corners of the Mediterranean and the African coast.

Trade was revolutionized in the early seventh century by the invention of coinage, values having previously been estimated in heads of cattle. This invention was due to the Lydians of Asia Minor, and was adopted from them by their neighbours, the Ionian Greeks, from whom it passed to the other city states.

The Rise of Hellenic Civilization

The early importance of Ionian Greece on the western shores of Asia Minor was evident not only in colonizing activity but also in artistic development. It was here, too, that the beginnings of Greek literature and philosophy were to be found. Some have called this early development 'the springtime of Greece'; others have named it 'Greece before Greece'; and it has also been said that 'Greece was educated by Ionia'. This early development was at one time obscure, but it is now evident that the role played by Lydia in the evolution of the Ionian cities was an important one.

Vase painting. In the Ionian cities, in Cyprus and in Crete, the Minoan-Mycenaean civilization had not come so near to vanishing point as on the mainland; and now, quickened by contact with the civilizations of Egypt and the East, metal working, vase painting and other arts revived. From Cyprus and Crete the products of these schools soon found their way to the mainland where similar local schools experimented with the new elements, each in its own way. 'Geometric' art was revolutionized. For about a century and a half, that is from about 700 to 550 B.C., Corinthian vases dominated the market, and were exported in large quantities to Sicily and Italy, but around 550 the monopoly had passed to Athens, on account of the superiority of her potters and painters, and the great period of Attic vase painting now began. Many of the pictures painted, or rather sketched, on these vases are masterpieces, and exhibit the finest qualities of Greek art. The cutting of dies in the mints of many of the Greek city states also gave Greek craftsmen an opportunity for the exercise of their amazing skill and sense of beauty in the production of coins.

Sculpture. Among the earliest subjects of Greek sculpture, standing figures, male and nude, are very frequent. They have been found at various sanctuaries on the mainland and in some of the islands, and were dedications, set up in the precincts of temples, according to Greek religious custom. Terra-cotta prototypes of these figures, dating from about 700 B.C., have been located in Crete, where, indeed, Greek tradition itself placed the origin of Greek sculpture. The life-size figures of this type, in stone and later in marble, in the rest of Greece and the islands, belong mostly to the sixth century and are the products of local schools, but many show strong Ionian influences.

Architectural sculpture during this period is represented in the Acropolis Museum by some remarkable sculptured groups from the pediments (gables) of temples or shrines on the Acropolis destroyed by the Persians. These figures are of coarse local stone and, except for the flesh parts, are painted in bright colours. Sculpture in relief was also popular, either in the form of architectural ornament or of tombstones. Finds in bronze and ivory also show considerable technical development.

Architecture. In this period was fixed the type of the Greek temple, based on the Mycenaean *megaron*, to which, in course of time, more and more columns were added. The closed central part (*sikos*) was divided into a vestibule, a hall (*naos*) in which was the statue of the god, and a room at the back (*opisthodomos*) reserved for the temple treasure or votive offerings. A row of columns ran round the *sikos*. The altar at which offerings were made stood outside the temple in the open air. The temple and its altar stood in a walled enclosure (*ieron*), which might include other temples with their altars, small shrines and votive statues, as at Delphi, for instance, or Olympia. Architecturally, Greek temples are of three 'orders', the Doric, the Ionic and the Corinthian, readily distinguished by differences in their columns (Fig. 73).

Literature. In this period, too, Greek literature, philosophy and science had their beginnings, and these, as in the case of the visual arts, must be looked for outside Greece. Homer, the earliest Greek poet and perhaps the greatest, is believed to have composed his famous epics, the *Iliad* and the *Odyssey*, in Ionia. These epics reflect, in some measure the civilization of his own day, but they are concerned with events, which had occurred some four centuries earlier—the Trojan war and its aftermath. The mature perfection of their technique, and their elaborate rules and conventions, presuppose a school of epic poetry with a long tradition behind it. This school may, conceivably, have had its origin in the lays sung

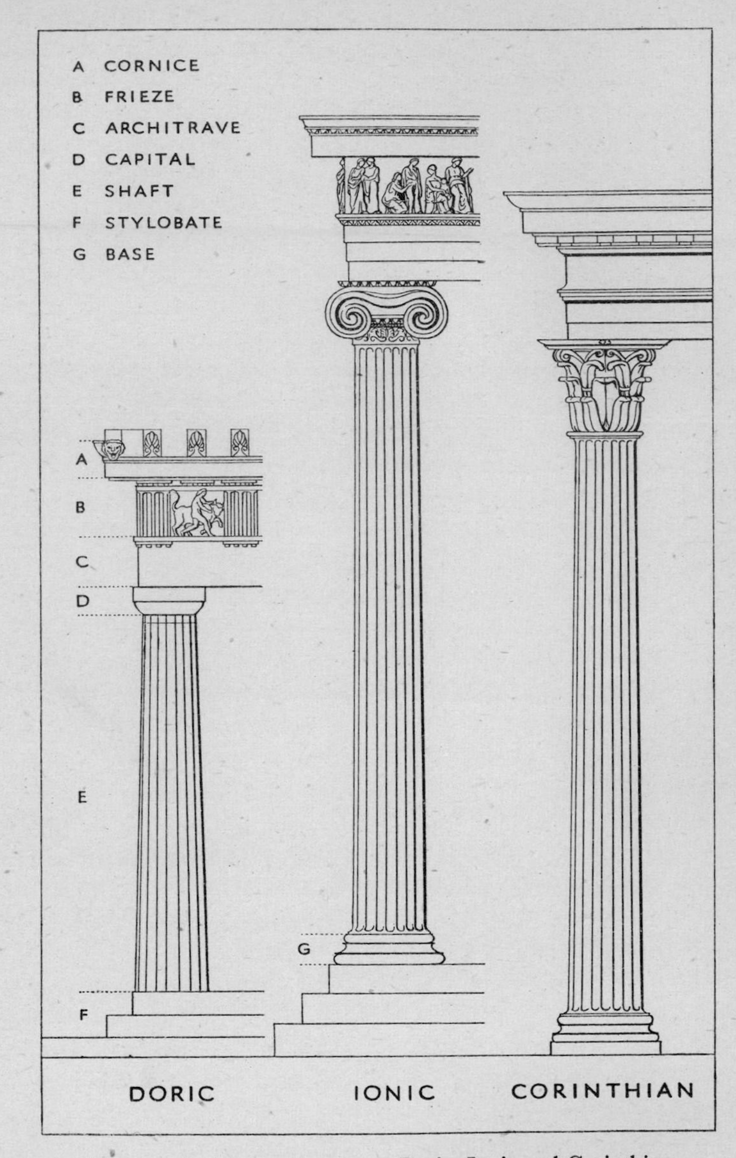

Fig. 73. Architectural orders—Doric, Ionic and Corinthian

Doric, based on the Parthenon, Athens; Ionic, from the Erechtheum, Athens; Corinthian, from the Temple of Olympian Zeus, Athens (Plates 79, 106).

Only a general impression of the chief characteristics of the three orders can be given on such small-scale drawings.

by minstrels at the courts of Achaean nobles. The first authors of the rare fragments of lyric poetry which have survived and which show no less distinction in this more intimate class of poetry were also the eastern Greeks of Asia Minor. Thales, the first of the long line of brilliant Greek thinkers, who sought to solve the problem of the universe, was a Greek of Miletus. Other Ionian thinkers were Anaximander, Pythagoras and Hecataeus.

Classical Greece

The Persian Wars

Towards the end of the sixth century B.C. there came an event which was to have a profound influence on Greek history. In order to understand this, it is necessary to consider the historical events which had formed a background to the high civilization of Ionia on the western shores of Asia Minor. The relations between the Greek settlements there and their inland neighbours had been fairly good, at least until the seventh century, when they fell under the control of the inland state of Lydia. The Lydians, in turn, were defeated by the expanding state of Persia in 546 B.C., and the Greek cities of Ionia automatically became part of the vast Persian empire, now stretching to the borders of India. But in 499 B.C., the Greek cities of Ionia revolted, and it was this revolt which was to have far-reaching effects on their fellow-Greeks in the west, for Athens had assisted the Ionian Greeks, and Darius, the Persian king, determined to punish the insignificant little city which had defied him. He sent a fleet of transports to the coast of Attica (490 B.C.); the troops disembarked in the bay of Marathon and were attacked by a small force of Athenians who had marched out from Athens. After a short engagement, the Persians were routed and hastily re-embarked for home. Ten years later, Xerxes, the successor of Darius, dispatched another expedition. The army came by land through Macedonia, and the fleet sailed along the coast. The army was halted at the pass of Thermopylae (see p. 444) by a small force of Spartans, whose heroic resistance was, however, soon overcome, and the Persians pressed on to Attica. They took Athens and destroyed all the buildings on the Acropolis. The Greek fleet, however, more than half of which was Athenian, defeated the Persian fleet in the Bay of Salamis. In the following year the army, which had withdrawn to an entrenched camp on the north slope of Mt Cithaeron near the town of Plataea, was routed by a confederate Greek army. Salamis and Plataea, both in 480 B.C., were decisive, and the Persian menace was thus effectively removed.

By this time, the pattern of Greece as it was to be during the next three centuries had taken shape. The five city states, Athens, Sparta, Thebes, Argos and Corinth, had each acquired that individuality with which they were henceforth to be associated in later times. The subsequent history of Greece until the time of the Roman conquest was to be, in a great measure, the history of the interrelations of these five city states.

Curiously enough, the Cretans, who had played such a great part in the prehistoric period, scarcely appeared in the affairs of classical Greece. Thus they took no part either in the Persian or in the Peloponnesian wars, nor in any of the conflicts of the Hellenistic period. The internal history of Crete during these years, as Polybius (202–120 B.C.) has told us, was one long series of bitter civil wars. The leading cities involved were Cnossus, Gortyn and Cydonia, though, in alliance with these, there were many other independent cities.

The Athenian Empire and the Peloponnesian War

The prestige acquired by Athens, from her share in the defeat of the Persians, enabled her to found a maritime confederacy with its headquarters and treasury in the island of Delos, and later to transform the confederacy into an empire based largely on tribute (Fig. 74). The treasury was shortly afterwards removed to Athens 'for security' (454 B.C.), and some of the money was used to pay for the ambitious building programme of the statesman, Pericles, now leader of the Athenian democracy. This high-handed action on the part of Athens provoked hostility throughout Greece, and many of the city states prepared to range themselves on the side of Sparta, between whom and Athens rival interests and 'ideology' would, it was clear, inevitably lead to a collision.

In 431 B.C. the Peloponnesian war broke out, a war in which most of the city states took part. The conflict has become more famous than perhaps its importance and the numbers engaged in it would seem to justify, because detailed description of it has been left by a historian of genius, Thucydides, himself a contemporary and a participant. Moreover, the war is of peculiar interest to a student of sea power, because, as well as exemplifying a struggle between rival political ideologies, it is a fine example on a small scale of how a war waged between a maritime and a continental power tends to be conducted.

Pericles himself had a clear vision of the strategy involved. To the Athenians he said: 'The visible field of action has two parts, land and sea. In the whole of one of these you are completely supreme.... Your naval resources are such that your vessels may go where they please.' Of the Spartans he wrote: 'In a single battle the Peloponnesians and their allies may be able to defy all Hellas,

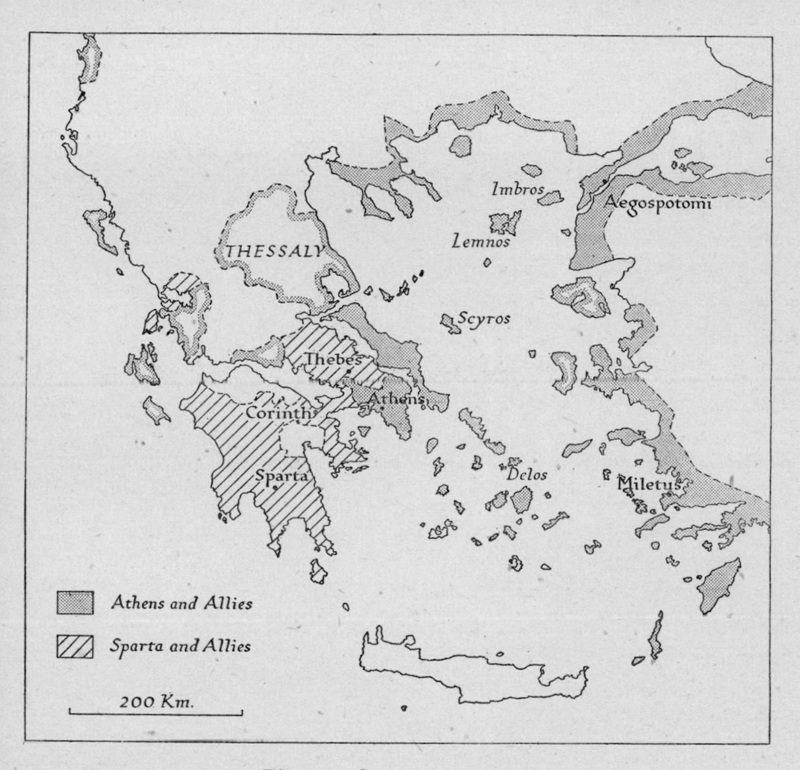

Fig. 74. Greece in 431 B.C.

Based on: (1) J. B. Bury, *A History of Greece*, p. 396 (London, 1924); (2) W. R. Shepherd, *Historical Atlas*, p. 17 (London, 1930).

The areas of the non-tributary allies of Athens (e.g. Thessaly) are not completely shaded.

but they are incapacitated from carrying on a war against a power different in character from their own.... Familiarity with the sea they will not find an easy acquisition.' As a maritime power with only a small army, Athens was obliged to avoid large-scale engagements on land, and to seek out those parts of the theatre of war where her navy could most effectively damage Spartan interests by detaching Spartan allies either by force or persuasion. This accounts for the fighting off the western coasts of Greece and in Sicily. Sparta, on the other hand, as a continental power with only a weak navy, was obliged to direct her blows at the continental possessions of Athens. Thus the invasion of Attica and destruction of the crops right up to the walls of Athens formed the routine part of each year's campaign, and there was much fighting in Thrace, where Athens had powerful tributary allies. It is little wonder therefore that, with the opponents fighting in different spheres, the struggle dragged on for years in an indecisive fashion.

The weakness of the Athenian position was that she depended for her food supply on imported corn, and should her 'life-line' be cut, she would be faced with starvation. The main source of her corn supply was south Russia, and Athenian interest in the route to the Black Sea was correspondingly great; the islands of Scyros, Lemnos and Imbros marked the way. Whenever the Athenian Assembly met, the agenda always contained the item 'Respecting corn'. Thus ten times a year attention was officially drawn to this vital question. At length in 405 B.C. Athenian power was crushed at its weakest spot. The Athenian navy was caught by surprise and destroyed at Aegospotami in the Hellespont itself. The Spartans had succeeded in fitting out an adequate fleet with the aid of Persia, and it was by sheer good fortune that they had in Lysander an exceptionally competent admiral. In the following year, Athens was blockaded and forced by famine to surrender. Treachery also contributed to the Athenian downfall, and this is not surprising, for there were in almost every city state discontented factions, prepared to assist the common enemy if, by so doing, they could destroy their political rivals or upset the existing constitution.

Despite Spartan predominance, Athens later succeeded, amidst the complicated rivalries of the Greek city states, in recovering something of her lost empire. It is interesting to note which three islands she bargained for and obtained—Scyros, Lemnos and Imbros. At last by the Peace of Callias in 371 B.C., the two states agreed to recognize each other's predominance, that of Athens on sea and that of Sparta on land. During the struggle, Corinth, at first dreading the development of Athenian trade, had been on the side of Sparta; but after 395 B.C. the domineering attitude of Sparta forced her into alliance with Athens.

But already new forces were rising in the Greek world. Thebes became prominent for a time, but, by now, the political life of Greece was in great confusion. The mutual rivalries of the city states were intense, and within each city the rivalry of parties was so great that it often endangered the life of the state. Into this confusion the new power of Macedonia was soon to arrive.

The Civilization of the Fifth and Fourth Centuries B.C.

Much more important than the political history of Greece was the Greek contribution to the art and thought of later times. The intense life of the small communities of the Greek city states brought artistic achievement to its highest point. The architecture of fifth-century Athens reached a splendour unknown in Europe up till then and perhaps unsurpassed since; and in this glorious setting the writers and thinkers of the city produced works that have become the inspiration of later times.

Architecture. The great period of classical Greece, the fifth and fourth centuries B.C., was one of great building activity. During these years the Greek temple reached and passed its zenith. In the fifth century the Parthenon, the Erechtheum, and the Theseum were built at Athens; the great temple of Zeus at Olympia; the temples at Bassae, Sunium, and Aegina; and the round temple at Delphi. To the fourth century B.C. belong the temple at Tegea, and the new temple of Apollo at Delphi. Of secular buildings, the Propylaea on the Acropolis were built in the fifth century, and the monument of Lysicrates in the fourth. To the fourth century also belong many of the theatres, of which that of Epidaurus (Plate 105) is the most noteworthy, and many of the secular buildings attached to the great sanctuaries, as, for instance, the Leonidaeum at Olympia, and the Gymnasium at Epidaurus. Some of the finest examples of fortifications, too, were built in the fourth century—at Eleutherae, Messene and elsewhere.

Sculpture. Outstanding examples of architectural sculpture of the fifth century are the pediment groups from the temples of Aegina, Olympia and the Parthenon. Separated from each other in point of time by intervals of about twenty years, they illustrate stages in the process by which Greek sculptors were ridding themselves of certain conventions and coming to see 'things as they are'. The Parthenon groups have been acclaimed as the noblest achievement of Greek sculpture and their place is assured, but some modern critics prefer the Olympian. Among the famous statues of the fifth century were the colossal gold and ivory figures of Athena in the Parthenon, and of Zeus at Olympia, both works of the Athenian sculptor Phidias.

What these were like can only be conjectured from small-scale copies or representations on coins. But large-scale copies of works by two other renowned sculptors, Myron and Polycleitus, are familiar in European collections, e.g. the Disc-thrower (Discobulus) of Myron, and the Athlete with a spear (Doryphorus) of Polycleitus.

Fourth-century architectural sculpture is well represented in the National Museum at Athínai by fragments from the pediment sculptures of the Temple of Athena at Tegea, and from the Temple of Asclepius at Epidaurus. The former are probably by Scopas, the architect of the temple. Other great sculptors of the period were Praxiteles and Lysippus who made many bronze statues of athletes.

Literature. The classical period of Greek architecture and sculpture was also the classical period of Greek literature and thought. The works of Homer had become known in mainland Greece in the course of the sixth century, and their influence had been immediate and decisive. But before that, a school of epic poetry had existed on the mainland, though its origins are obscure. The Boeotian, Hesiod, had used the same metre as Homer but without Homer's mastery. His theme, too, was not war and adventure, but husbandry and the sorrows of the peasant. The influence of Homer is plain, however, in the great lyric odes of Pindar (*c.* 522–450 B.C.), composed in honour of victories in the Olympic and other games and intended to be recited in the cities from which the victors came.

Attic drama had its remote origins in the religious songs and dances performed at the temples of gods or the tombs of heroes, and this religious character was never lost; so that when these primitive songs and dances had developed into plays, performed in theatres before large audiences, the plots were still concerned with the gods and heroes of mythology, and, as such, were familiar to the audience. Interest was, thus, not so much in the plot as in the author's handling of it. The plays were produced in daylight, without elaborate costumes or scenery, before highly critical and intelligent spectators. The great age of Greek tragedy was the fifth century, and the three great tragedians, Aeschylus, Sophocles, and Euripides, had no successors. Aristophanes, the greatest of the comic dramatists, belongs also to this age.

Prose of the fifth century is represented by Herodotus and Thucydides. Both were historians, the former a naïve but entertaining collector of information, in which fact and fable were indiscriminately mixed; the latter endowed with a critical sense, a philosophic outlook, great powers of description, and a fine style. When it is realized

Plate 77. The Acropolis from the north-west

Plate 78. The Erechtheum, south side.
The photograph shows the Portico of the Maidens, fifth century B.C.

Plate 79. The Parthenon from the south-west

Plate 80. The Theseum, or Temple of Hephaistos, fifth century B.C. This is the most complete of all Greek temples.

that this kind of descriptive writing was in its infancy, that no official reports were available, and that his material had to be laboriously collected by word of mouth, Thucydides's *History of the Peloponnesian War* must be regarded as a work of genius.

Literary activity of the fourth century reflects the contemporary spirit of inquiry in numerous works of philosophy and science, and in technical treatises. Oratory was brought to a fine art, and speeches for delivery either in the Assembly or in the law courts were prepared with the same elaborate care as poems. Many of the speeches of Demosthenes, the protagonist of Greek independence against the kings of Macedonia, have been preserved and have the permanent value of great literature.

In this age of inquiry the same religious and social problems which vex the modern mind were being discussed with the utmost freedom. Freedom was, however, held to have gone too far in the case of Socrates, whose perpetual questioning of everything in heaven and on earth was considered by the orthodox to be sapping the foundations of the state. He was tried and condemned to death in 399 B.C. His work was continued by his disciples who, however, never forgave democracy for the treatment of their master, so that the ideal constitution envisaged by the greatest of them, the philosopher Plato, was almost an absolutism on the Spartan model. Aristotle, the other great figure in Greek philosophy, was born in 384 B.C. After having been tutor to Alexander the Great, he settled in Athens in 335 B.C. where he founded the Lyceum, which soon supplanted Plato's institution, the Academy. His works on the science of ethics, politics and metaphysics place him among the greatest thinkers of all time.

Macedonian and Hellenistic Greece

The Empire of Alexander the Great

Macedonia had hitherto played but a small part in Greek affairs. It had lagged behind the development of southern Greece, but, amidst the confused condition of Greece in the middle of the fourth century, the rising state of Philip of Macedon (359–336 B.C.) had decided advantages. It was unexhausted by long wars and it possessed natural resources, in cereals, gold and timber, greater than those of any of the city states to the south. Under Philip the northern area was consolidated into a strong unit that extended into Thessaly, and the confused politics and divisions of the south provided ample opportunity for interference. At length, at the battle of Chaeroneia

(338 B.C.), Philip defeated an army of Athenians, Thebans and others, induced to join together by the new threat of this northern power. It was the hatred of Philip that inspired the famous 'Philippics' of the Athenian orator Demosthenes. But in the following year all the Greek states, with the exception of Sparta, had answered an invitation to send representatives to a Pan-Hellenic Congress under Philip's presidency at Corinth. In 336 B.C. Philip was assassinated, and his son Alexander succeeded him. It was this Alexander who was to become 'the Great' by turning against Asia and conquering what seemed almost the whole world, or at any rate that part of it which mattered.

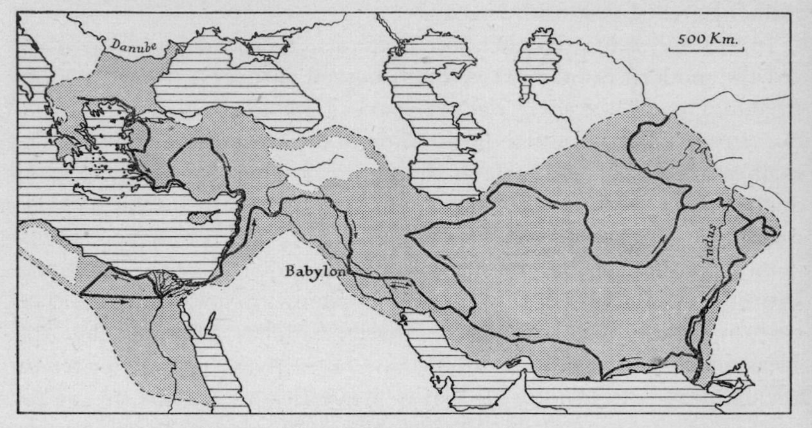

Fig. 75. The empire of Alexander, 323 B.C.
Based on W. R. Shepherd, *Historical Atlas*, pp. 18–19 (London, 1930).
The route of Alexander's march is indicated by a heavy line.

That the Greeks should attempt an attack on the vast Persian empire and succeed might seem an almost impossible feat, unless the state of the Greek world and of the Persian empire is remembered. Among the Greeks the idea of an attack on Persia had long been current. During the fourth century there had grown up the idea that any dominant power in Hellas would be obliged by self-interest and by racial duty to turn its arms against Asia, to rescue the Ionian Greeks of Asia Minor, and to conquer an empire. Many Greek writers had dwelt upon the theme. Then, in the second place, the condition of the Persian empire invited an aggressor. The emperor, no longer powerful, was by now little more than a titular lord over ever-rebelling provinces. Treachery or lack of resources had brought one rebel after another to disaster, but an empire, whose high officers dared such adventures, was clearly nearing its death. The Persians, too, had become involved more than once in the politics of the Aegean world, and there had been a number of invasions of Asia Minor by Spartan forces. Philip of Macedon had been planning an invasion, and had announced his design at the Congress of Corinth in 337 B.C. His son Alexander now inherited the idea, and, two years after the death of his father, he crossed into Asia Minor with a force of about 35,000 infantry and 4,500 cavalry.

The account of the victorious march of Alexander to Egypt and right across Persia over the Khyber Pass to India itself reads like a legend (Fig. 75). In the midst of his work of organization, and while planning new conquests, he contracted a fever and died at Babylon in 323 B.C. The great empire he had created broke up with his death, but his work was far from being transitory in character. He had carried the seeds of Greek culture to the East. The Greek language and Greek ideas were spread right over the Near East, and became an important factor in the political and religious history of these lands. As for Alexander himself, his name passed into the legendary cycles of medieval Europe.

Political History after the death of Alexander, 323–146 B.C.

Several states arose upon the ruins of Alexander's empire. The Ptolemies ruled in Egypt; the Seleucids in Syria and for a time in Persia itself. Various smaller states arose in Asia Minor. In Greece itself, Macedonia remained a powerful kingdom in the north, but was not again to dominate the world; while in the south, the Greek city states acquired varying degrees of freedom.

These years were characterized by the formation of coalitions or 'leagues' among the Greek states, of which the purpose was to offer a united front against the interference of Macedonia. This united front was seldom achieved, and the leagues even took to fighting one another. In the course of the rather confused history of the period, Athens was twice occupied by Macedonian troops, once in the year after Alexander's death and again in 262 B.C. when she took the wrong side in one of the numerous disputes for the Macedonian throne. An outstanding event of this period was the appearance before Delphi of a band of Gauls, a detachment from the main body which was on the move towards Asia Minor. They were thrown back by the Aetolians, now the official guardians of the sanctuary. The Aetolian cities, hitherto some of the most backward and least heard of in Greece, had formed themselves into a league after the death of Alexander, and were prominent in Greek affairs throughout the third century. In 220 B.C. they went to war with the Achaean League, a coalition founded forty years earlier, which had defended Greece against Macedonia, but which was now supported by Macedonia against the Aetolians. By this time, however, events in the west were casting their shadow over Greece, and the war was brought to an end in 217 B.C.

During the Second Punic War between Rome and Carthage, Philip V of Macedonia allied himself with Hannibal (215 B.C.), and, to offset this, the Romans secured the alliance of the Aetolians and Spartans. The Romans, who had, some years before, been recognized as honorary Hellenes, in return for clearing the Illyrian Sea of pirates, thus acquired a firmer footing in Greece. In the second of the three Macedonian Wars which followed, Philip was defeated (197 B.C.), and the victorious Roman consul Flamininus in a moving scene at the Isthmian Games of 196 B.C. declared Rome the 'protector of Greek freedom'.

The third Macedonian War ended in the defeat of Philip's son and successor, Perseus, at the battle of Pydna (168 B.C.) and the dissolution of the Macedonian empire. Anti-Roman elements continued to be active both in Macedonia and Greece, so that in 148 B.C. the Romans made Macedonia a Roman province, and Sparta, Rome's ally, gave the Romans a pretext for suppressing the Achaean League and adding Greece to her empire as a dependency of Macedonia (146 B.C.). Crete, however, was not subdued until 67 B.C. and only then after a campaign of three years.

Hellenistic Civilization

Architecture. Greek building activity in this period was largely in the lands to which Hellenism had spread, following the wake of Alexander's conquests. In Egypt, Syria and in Asia Minor, Greek architects were busy laying out new cities and erecting secular and religious buildings which Greek sculptors were embellishing. The most impressive monuments of the Hellenistic Age, as this period is called, is the great altar of Zeus at Pergamum in Asia Minor, adorned with sculpture in the rather florid style characteristic of the Pergamene school. In Greece itself, a number of monumental secular buildings were erected, for example, the Portico of Attalus, and the 'Tower of the Winds', both at Athens; and the Portico of Echo, and the Palaestra at Olympia. At Delos, too, there are many buildings of this period, and domestic architecture is represented there as nowhere else. The finest mosaic of the period is that recently discovered in the 'Roman Villa' at Corinth. Fortifications continued to be built, and the hills of Aitolía are still crowned with walls, towers and gates recalling the days of the Aetolian League. At Oeniadae, in Akarnanía, the remarkable harbour works, still to be seen, were constructed by Philip V of Macedonia in 219 B.C.

Sculpture. The sculpture of the Hellenistic Age exhibits the characteristics of an art that has passed its best period, but is, nevertheless, full of life and vigour, and there was no falling off in technical skill. The chief schools of sculpture were those of Pergamum, Rhodes and Ephesus; in Greece itself, little was produced. Well-known works of this period are the Aphrodite of Melos, the Apollo Belvedere (known only from copies), the Dying Gaul, and the 'Victory', all of Samothrace. Portraits were extremely popular and there was a great demand for busts of famous persons, living and dead, to adorn public buildings, libraries and the like.

Literature. The schools of philosophy at Athens remained open, but intellectual pre-eminence passed to Alexandria. Here, though the creative genius which had characterized Attic writers of the fifth and fourth centuries was spent, the Attic literary tradition was carried on by scholars and men of learning attracted by the great library. Historians, grammarians, commentators and scientists predominated, and even poetry acquired a flavour of learning. Epicurus (341–270 B.C.) taught at Athens during the earlier part of the period. Poets also cultivated an artificial but often charming simplicity, and the pastoral idylls of Theocritus, and many epigrams (a form of poetry which became popular at this time) are among the most beautiful things in Greek literature. Epic poetry, also, was revived with some success.

Roman Greece

Graeco-Roman Political and Economic Development

As part of the Roman state, Greece entered upon a period of peace such as she had not before known in her history. The Romans treated the Greeks in a generous manner, and the *Pax Romana* was regarded by most Greeks as a relief from the confusion of the Hellenistic period. As the contemporary historian Polybius wrote, 'If we had not perished quickly, we should not have been saved.' The Achaean League was dissolved and, fearing a competitor, the Romans destroyed the city of Corinth. For administrative purposes, the Greek states were subordinated to the Roman province of Macedonia, but Athens and Sparta were given special privileges. The quiet of the new Roman province was disturbed, however, when in 88 B.C. Athens and some other cities unwisely allied themselves with Mithridates, king of Pontus in Asia Minor, who was in conflict with Rome. For her share in the war, Athens was sacked by the Roman general Sulla, and the walls of the Piraeus were levelled.

During the last decades of the Roman republic (up to 27 B.C.), Greece was scarcely affected by the wider events of Roman policy, yet two civil wars were fought out on Greek soil or in Greek waters, and many Greeks took sides in the conflicts. The struggle between Caesar and Pompey was decided at Pharsalus in Thessaly in 48 B.C., and although the Greeks had supplied Pompey with a fleet, the victorious Caesar treated them leniently; individual cities, however, received severe punishment. Greece also became involved in the struggle between Mark Antony and Octavian until the great naval victory of Actium (31 B.C.) in which Octavian was triumphant. The geographer Strabo, who was in Greece two years later, has left a melancholy account of the effects of civil war upon the countryside; large tracts of country remained desolate and many notable cities stood in ruins.

Under the Roman emperors, from Augustus (Octavian) onwards, Greece was specially favoured. Augustus himself separated Greece from Macedonia and formed it into the separate province of Achaia with its capital at Corinth which had been refounded by Caesar in 44 B.C. Nero thought a Greek audience was 'the only one worthy of himself and his accomplishments'. The results of the liberality of Hadrian are still to be seen at Athens (see p. 152). Marcus Aurelius, too, found time to visit Athens where he established a university in A.D. 176. Large numbers of Romans were attracted to the country—to visit its sanatoria, to admire its artistic treasures, and to study at Athens. In return, Greek culture was having considerable influence upon Roman thought and writing; indeed many Romans were complaining that Rome itself was becoming 'a Greek city'. Captive Greece was taking her barbarian captors captive. But already a new ingredient was being added to the combined civilizations of Greece and Rome, for about the year A.D. 54 St Paul had visited Athens and Corinth. It was at Corinth that the two Epistles to the Thessalonians were written. Subsequently, the Epistles to the Corinthians show something of the life of the most flourishing city of Roman

Greece. Some believed, but, for long, the new faith made little progress, and the beginnings of the Christian Church were small.

A picture of the Greek countryside under the Roman empire is given in the famous 'Description of Greece' written by Pausanias about the years A.D. 160–80. Compared with Strabo's time, the land was much more prosperous, but much of it was still in a desolate state, and the economic life of the country was not as flourishing as its intellectual and social pre-eminence might imply. It is true that new luxury industries (marble, textiles, table delicacies) were springing up to meet the needs of Rome, but the only cities with a really flourishing trade were Corinth and Patras.

The Roman peace was broken in A.D. 175 by the Costoboci, a northern tribe who raided into central Greece. They were defeated by the local militia, and retired beyond the Roman frontier. This was the first hint of northern interference that was to prove so important a factor in later Greek history. A more serious invasion was that of the Goths. They appeared on the frontier about A.D. 250, and the Emperor Valerian caused the walls of Athens to be rebuilt and other fortifications to be put across the Isthmus. But these precautions did not save Athens, for the Goths captured and pillaged the city in A.D. 267. Ultimately they were repulsed and retired beyond the Danube, and Greece was spared another Gothic invasion for over a century (see p. 156).

In the reign of Diocletian there were considerable administrative changes. The Roman empire was now divided into two halves (A.D. 285), and Diocletian himself usually resided at Nicomedia on the shores of the Sea of Marmora. Thus the way was prepared for the foundation of Constantinople by Constantine about A.D. 330, and for the ultimate division into eastern and western empires. It is impossible to say when the Roman empire 'ended' and the Byzantine empire 'began', but the foundation of 'New Rome' about A.D. 330 may be taken as a convenient beginning for the story of Byzantine Greece.

Graeco-Roman Civilization

Architecture. The Graeco-Roman style which now came into being was fundamentally Greek, but a certain loss of fineness may have been due to the Roman element or to an inherent tendency already perceptible in Hellenistic work. However that may be, the principal cities and sanctuaries of Greece now received magnificent additions in the way of monuments and public buildings in this style. Such are almost all the buildings of Corinth. The damage and loss inflicted by Mummius, Sulla and Nero were to some extent offset by the enlightened liberality of the Emperor Hadrian (A.D. 117–38), who showed his deep interest in Greece by repairing and adding to old buildings, and erecting new ones. He completed the magnificent temple of Zeus at Athens, built the library, and also the arch known by his name; and, in more questionable taste, he erected many statues of himself at Olympia and other places. Another individual who has left memorials of his liberality was Herodes Atticus, a rich citizen of Marathon (A.D. 101–77). At Athens he built the Odeum, still named after him; at Corinth he enlarged and beautified the Peirene fountain and built the Odeum; at Olympia he built an aqueduct to conduct water into the sacred enclosure. At Olympia, too, a palace and a triumphal arch were built by the Emperor Nero.

Sculpture. After the sack of Corinth, hundreds of works of Greek art, especially statues, were shipped to Rome; Sulla and the Emperor Nero carried off more. When the demand for originals could no longer be satisfied, Greek sculptors produced copies to take their place, and it is from these copies that our conception of much of Greek sculpture is formed. Greek sculptors also made portrait busts for Roman families. The extreme realism of these portraits was no doubt demanded by Roman patrons, who wanted a portrait to be before all things a likeness, but it had been anticipated in portraits of the Hellenistic Age.

Literature. Greek had now become a cosmopolitan language; educated Romans made a point of learning it, and Greek slaves, imported to Rome, introduced a knowledge of it into Roman families. Thus it came to have a profound influence upon Latin literature. The numerous treatises on scientific subjects, medicine, philosophy and the like, which Greek scholars continued to produce, created a vocabulary of abstract terms which became international and are still in use. The two outstanding historians of the period were Polybius (202–120 B.C.), whose *History* was originally designed to record the dramatic rise of Roman supremacy in the Mediterranean, and Plutarch (A.D. 46–120), famous for his *Lives.* Christianity directed Greek thought into new channels, and, in the language of the Greek philosophers, theologians found ready to hand an instrument well adapted to express the fine distinctions which the definition of Christian doctrine required.

BIBLIOGRAPHICAL NOTE

1. Greek legends had preserved the memory of a king in Crete (Minos) and of the heroes of the Trojan War, but it seems that even the ancient Greeks themselves were unaware of the remarkable civilization that had preceded their own. It was not until the archaeological discoveries of Heinrich Schliemann at Troy, Mycenae and Tiryns (from 1870 onwards), and the work of Sir Arthur Evans in Crete (from 1893 onwards), that the early history of the Aegean world was revealed. The great work by Sir Arthur Evans, *The Palace of Minos at Knossos*, 4 vols. (London, 1921–35), not only gives a detailed description of the discoveries at Knossós, but covers the whole field of Minoan civilization, and is particularly rich in illustrations.

Shorter surveys of this early civilization and its archaeological remains are given in the following books:

A. R. Burn, *Minoans, Philistines and Greeks* (London, 1930).

G. Glotz, *La Civilisation Égéenne* (Paris, 1923); translated by M. R. Dobie and E. M. Riley as *The Aegean Civilization* (London, 1925).

H. R. Hall, *The Civilisation of Greece in the Bronze Age* (London, 1928).

J. D. S. Pendlebury, *The Archaeology of Crete: an introduction* (London, 1939). The same author has written an excellent *Guide to the Palace of Minos* (London, 1933).

A small book by C. H. and H. B. Hawes, *Crete the Fore-runner of Greece* (London, 1909), gives a very readable account of the Minoan civilization.

Convenient books in English on the prehistory of mainland Greece are rare, but H. D. Hansen's *Early Civilisation in Thessaly* (Baltimore, 1933) can be recommended to the non-specialist.

2. The authoritative bibliographies of *The Cambridge Ancient History* (Cambridge, 1923–39) indicate the vast literature that is available about the history of classical Greece.

One of the most comprehensive of the shorter histories is J. B. Bury's *A History of Greece to the Death of Alexander the Great* (London, 1900, 2nd ed. 1913). This provides a clear narrative of events, but the earlier section on prehistory is now out-of-date.

An interesting account of the most characteristic political institution of the Greeks is given in G. Glotz, *The Greek City and its Institutions*, translated from the French by N. Mallison (London, 1929).

Another book, also by Glotz, gives an account of the economic history of Greece up to the Roman Conquest—*Ancient Greece at Work*, translated by M. R. Dobie (London, 1926). This may be supplemented by M. I. Rostovzeff's *A History of the Ancient World* (St Petersburg, 1899), translated from the Russian by J. D. Duff (Oxford, 1926, 2nd ed. 1930).

Finally, one of the most attractive of all books dealing with Ancient Greece is Sir Alfred Zimmern's *The Greek Commonwealth: Politics and Economics in Fifth-century Athens* (Oxford, 1911, 5th ed. 1931). This gives a picture of ancient economic and social history in the light of the geographical conditions of the Greek lands, and can be strongly recommended.

3. Various aspects of Greek civilization form the subject of the following works whose titles are explanatory. All present authoritative summaries of their respective subjects:

E. A. Gardner, *A Handbook of Greek Sculpture* (London, 1896, 2nd ed. 1915).

W. Lamb, *Greek and Roman Bronzes* (London, 1929).

A. de Ridder and W. Deonna, *L'Art en Grèce* (Paris, 1924) translated by V. C. C. Collum as *Art in Greece* (London, 1927).

D. S. Robertson, *Greek and Roman Architecture* (Cambridge, 1929).

L. Robin, *Greek Thought and the Origins of the Scientific Spirit*, translated from the French by M. R. Dobie (London, 1928).

C. T. Seltman, *Attic Vase-painting* (Cambridge, Mass., 1933).

C. T. Seltman, *Greek Coins: a history of metallic currency and coinage down to the fall of the Hellenistic kingdoms* (London, 1933).

A collection of essays, edited by R. W. Livingstone, provides a summary of many aspects of Greek civilization.—*The Legacy of Greece* (Oxford, 1921). A brief and readable survey is S. Casson's *Ancient Greece* (London, 1922).

Chapter VI

MEDIEVAL AND TURKISH GREECE

BYZANTINE GREECE

The Eastern Roman Empire

The Roman emperors had for some time felt the need of a new administrative centre when in A.D. 285 the empire was divided into two by Diocletian—an eastern and a western half. Diocletian took up his residence in the east, at Nicomedia near the Sea of Marmora, where he could keep in close touch with the critical frontiers on the Danube and the Tigris, and where oriental ideas of sovereignty could be developed unhampered by the republican traditions of Rome itself. Early in the next century, Constantine reunited the two halves, but fixed the capital in the east, and between 328 and 330 he enlarged the old town of Byzantium to form the city of 'New Rome which is Constantinople'. Soon the whole empire was divided again, and what had started as an administrative partition became after 395 a more fundamental separation.

The fates of the two empires in east and west respectively were very different. Whereas the western empire collapsed under the strain of the Barbarian invasions, the Roman empire in the east continued for centuries as a permanent factor amidst the changing political geography of Europe and the Near East. The wealth of the eastern provinces, the strategic position of the capital, and the intelligent policy of successive emperors, explain this contrast between east and west, and account for the survival of the eastern provinces as an imperial entity.

The eastern or Byzantine empire was thus a continuous development of the Roman empire, and was characterized by the fusion of two traditions—Greek and Roman. In language, literature and theology, Greek influence was paramount. In law, diplomacy and military tradition, the Roman tradition was important.

The administrative reorganization of Diocletian and Constantine was but part of wider changes that were transforming the old pagan empire of Rome into the medieval Christian empire called Byzantine. The religious attitude of Constantine had been as momentous as his imperial policy. Christianity now became the recognized religion of the empire. Soon, the minor bishopric of Byzantium became the patriarchate of Constantinople, and a Council of 381 gave it first place in the Eastern Church, directly after the see of Rome. It had to face the opposition of the older patriarchates of Antioch, Alexandria and Jerusalem until these were engulfed in the advancing tide of Islam during the seventh century. There remained the problem of relations with Rome, and, after a chequered history, varied by schisms and heresies, the final break came in 1054, when the two great leaders of the Christian Church put each other under a ban.

The separation of the eastern and western empires had meant that Greek interests were henceforward identified with those of the Byzantine emperors. This was in some senses a gain, in others a loss. On the one hand, Greek became the language of the court, and Greek culture became an important element in the Byzantine civilization. On the other hand, the imperial city grew at the expense of Greece; Constantinople, rather than Athens, became the important factor in Greek life, and Greece became increasingly provincial. The Greeks themselves now became known not as 'Hellenes' but as 'Romaioi'. It was Justinian too, who, in 529, virtually abolished the University of Athens, the stronghold of pagan philosophy. Christianity was now spread throughout the whole of Greece, save in the mountain regions of Laconia, which did not become Christian until well into the ninth century.

The Danube Frontier

The Byzantine emperors had continually to face two groups of frontier problems, to the east and north respectively (Fig. 76). The former were concerned with the attacks of the Moslems upon the Asiatic provinces of the empire; but it was not until the rise of the Ottoman Turks in the fourteenth century that the Greek lands themselves were threatened by this eastern peril. The other frontier problems were caused by the restless tribes beyond the Danube, and Greece was affected by these from an early date.

This Danube frontier was an old problem that had frequently confronted the Roman emperors. In the third century some Goths had raided as far as Athens (see p. 151). These newcomers proved to be but a vanguard. Towards the end of the fourth century, the Visigoths (the western branch of the Goths), fearing the Huns of the steppe-lands behind them, had defeated the imperial generals, and had poured into peninsular Greece (378–95). But their destiny lay in the west, and, before the end of the century, they had moved north-

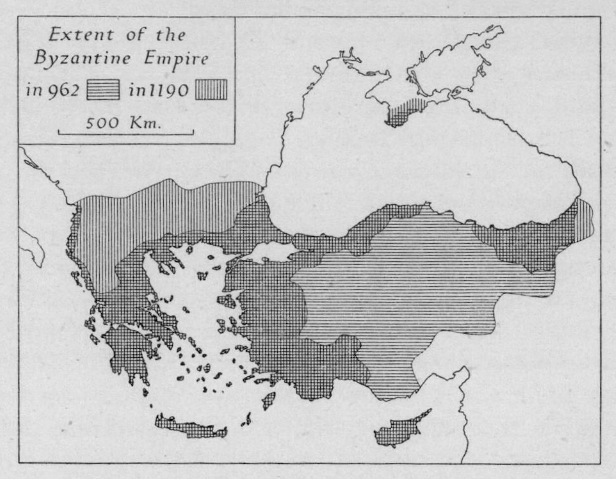

Fig. 76. The Byzantine Empire, A.D. 962–1190

Based on R. L. Poole, *Historical Atlas of Modern Europe*, plates 5 and 6 (Oxford, 1902).

This shows the reaction of the Byzantine frontiers to attacks from Europe and Asia. The strength of the empire lay in its seaward margins. Compare, for example, with Fig. 78.

wards, and so into Italy; by 412 they had reached Spain. The Huns themselves raided the empire up to the gates of Constantinople itself (446), and in 482 the Ostrogoths raided the country. But neither in the fourth nor fifth centuries was there any large-scale settlement of northerners on the lands of the empire.

These raids of Goths and Huns were only a prelude to far greater movements of peoples from beyond the river. Indeed, one of the most important factors in the history of Greece from the sixth to the twelfth century was the complete breakdown of the Danube frontier. The ethnography of the northerners that came swarming southwards is not always clear. The Byzantine chroniclers speak of Slavs, Antae (also Slavs), Bulgars, Huns (by whom they may have meant Bulgars), Avars, Cumans and Patzinaks; the vague names of 'Getae' and 'Scythians' are also mentioned. Of these, the two peoples that had direct effect upon the fortunes of medieval Greece were the Slavs and the Bulgars.

The Slavs

Of all the northerners the Slavs were the most important to Greece. Expanding from their homeland in the Pripet marshes, the Slavs reached the lands immediately to the north of the Danube by, at latest, the third century, but there is no sure evidence that they had penetrated (at any rate in considerable numbers) southwards into the peninsula before the end of the fifth century. Early in the sixth century their raids became frequent, and Macedonia, Thessaly and Epirus were repeatedly devastated; and with the reign of Justinian (527–65), conditions along the Danube deteriorated. Despite the fierce resistance put up by the imperial troops, hordes of Slavs and Bulgars crossed the river almost every year to raid and loot. In 540, they raided Greece as far south as the Isthmus of Corinth, and Justinian was forced to organize defensive measures on a large scale. Large numbers of new forts were set up, and old ones were strengthened. From the river Sava to the Black Sea, some eighty castles were built or restored, and behind these some hundreds of fortified positions provided a 'defence in depth'. Despite these efforts, the raids continued. It is unlikely that they led to permanent settlements on any large scale, but their influence upon the countryside was very marked. The historian Procopius, who lived during the first half of the sixth century, compared the ravaged lands of Greece to the 'Scythian deserts', and he described how the inhabitants fled into the mountains and the forests for safety.

In the latter part of the sixth century, after the death of Justinian, the Slav raids grew in intensity, and about the year 578 an army of some 100,000 'Slavonians' poured into 'Hellas' and Thessaly. A contemporary chronicler, John of Ephesus, tells of the horror that now fell upon Thrace and Illyricum, and it is from this time that we must date the arrival of Slav settlers in considerable numbers into Greece. Raiding had passed definitely into settlement. To the north, the lands of what is now Yugoslavia were likewise open to the penetration of other Slav peoples (Slovenes, Croats and Serbs) during the first half of the seventh century.

The widespread incursions of the Slavs were reinforced by those of the Avars, a nomad group prominent in the northern lands during the sixth and early seventh centuries. Moreover, in the early years of the seventh century, the main effort of the Byzantine empire was engaged in a struggle with the Persians, and the European provinces were thus left exposed. The Byzantine diplomats spoke of lands occupied by the Slavs in Thrace, Macedonia and Greece as grants made through the generosity of the emperor; the frontier might therefore be placed either at the Danube or at no great distance from the Aegean Sea according to the imperial or the Slav point of view. Some dates stand out. In 597, and again in 609, Salonica, protected by its strong walls and by its Saint Demetrius, had managed to withstand the assault of the surrounding Slav tribes in Macedonia. In 623, Slavs were raiding Crete. In 626, a united horde of Avars, Slavs and Bulgars were besieging Constantinople, not for the first time, but they failed to take the city. The Avar power ceased to be important after about 630, but Slav pressure southwards continued. Thus in 674 a body of Slavs seized the opportunity of an Arab siege of Constantinople to settle in the rich plain of Thessaly, where the place-name of Velestínon still recalls the name of one of their tribes (the Velegezêtes).

It is difficult to form a clear picture of the extent of Slav settlement in Greece during these years, and the subject has aroused much controversy. A contemporary encyclopedist, Isidore of Seville (*d.* 639), summed up the situation by saying that 'the Slavs took Greece from the Romans', but it is certain that the large towns, at any rate, did not fall to the Slavs. Athens was still in Greek hands, nor, wrote J. B. Bury, 'had the country yet become Slavised, as it is said to have become in the following century'.* There is little evidence about the relations of the immigrant Slavs and the Greeks at this time, but it seems likely that the newcomers were easily converted to Christianity and that they lived more or less under the suzerainty of the Byzantine emperor.

It is not surprising that, in view of these incursions, the command of the imperial army in Greece was an important office. The system of themes, or districts under military organization (*thema* = regiment), that had been found necessary to meet the Persian and Arab wars of the seventh century, was now extended under the Emperor Leo III (717–40) from Asia to Europe. The number of themes

* J. B. Bury, *A History of the Later Roman Empire*, 395 A.D. *to* 800 A.D., vol. II, p. 280 (London, 1889).

varied, but by the tenth century they comprised about thirty, of which eight covered what is now Greece and the Aegean islands.

It was during the eighth century that Slav influence became greatest in Greece. In 746 a great plague breaking out in the Near East reached Monemvasia in the Peloponnese, and, from there, spread over the whole empire. The population of Greece suffered heavily, and was then further reduced by the migration of many skilled workmen to Constantinople; whole families left both the mainland and the islands. Empty districts were thus left free to be colonized by the Slavs who now pressed southwards in greater numbers than ever. In the words of the imperial historian, Constantine Porphyrogenitus, 'all the open country was Slavonized and became barbarous, when the plague was devouring the whole world'. According to W. Miller, this is the real explanation of the Slav colonization of Greece. Whatever be the truth, the Slavs had by now certainly spread widely over the Greek lands. So widespread were their settlements that in the eighth century the southern Balkan lands and mainland Greece were known as 'Sclavinia' (Fig. 77).

The central government at Constantinople, alarmed at this influx, dispatched the general Staurakios to deal with the newcomers, and they were reduced and forced to pay tribute (783). But early in the following century, when the imperial forces were being threatened by Saracens and Bulgars, the Slavs of the Peloponnese rose in revolt, and, conspiring with the Saracens, they attacked the fortress of Patras (807). But the siege was raised, and, after some time, the rebellion was put down. There was a fresh rising in the Peloponnese about the year 849, which was again suppressed, and military colonists were established here as in northern Greece. Special terms were made with two Slav tribes in the south near Mount Taygetos—the Milings and the Ezerites, who agreed to pay tribute. These two tribes were in rebellion again in the middle of the tenth century, and, although they were once more reduced to obedience, it is apparent that they still retained a large measure of independence.

The military reduction of the Slavs prepared the way for their assimilation, and in this work the Church played a great part. With the foundation of monasteries and churches went on the active work of assimilation. The Orthodox religion and the Greek language regained the ground they had lost, and by the tenth century many people of Slav descent were occupying high positions in the empire. But even in the thirteenth century, some Slav tribes still lived apart from the Greeks, and maintained their old customs in the mountainous districts of Elis and Arcadia. The Milings remained separate longest, possibly even until the eve of the Ottoman conquest.

The Slavs have left evidence of their settlement in the numerous Slavonic place-names that are to be found in Greece to-day. Over much of the Peloponnese a Slavonic place-name can be found every three or four miles (Fig. 95).

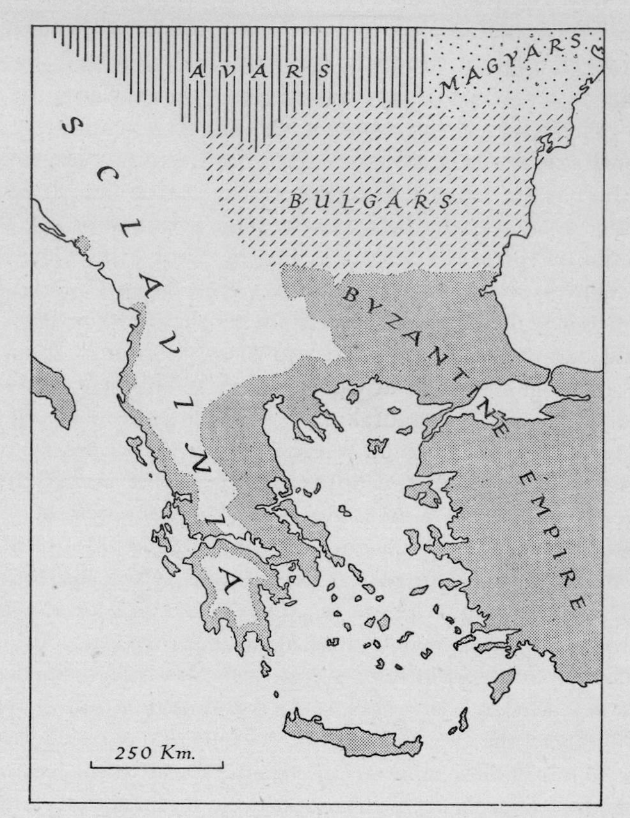

Fig. 77. The Balkan Peninsula about A.D. 800

Based on R. L. Poole, *Historical Atlas of Modern Europe*, plate 4 (Oxford, 1902). This map shows dominant political groupings rather than ethnic distributions; thus Slavs were also to be found in the areas marked as 'Avars' and 'Bulgars'. For the Byzantine frontier against the Slavs, see p. 158.

The Bulgars

The Bulgars, like the Huns and the Avars before them, were peoples from the Asiatic steppes who during the sixth century were to be found in the country north of the Black Sea. Their early history in Europe is obscure, but it seems fairly certain that they took part in some of the attacks of the Slavs and the Avars against Salonica and Constantinople during the sixth and seventh centuries. Towards the end of the seventh century, the main body moved southwards and, in 679, established themselves between the Danube and the Balkan Mountains. The river definitely ceased to mark the northern frontier of the Byzantine empire.

South of the Danube, the newcomers found the land already peopled with Slavs, and the new state that came into being was the result of fusion between Bulgars and Slavs. The two centuries that followed 679 were marked by intermittent warfare with the Byzantine emperors. In order to check the growth of the Slav and Bulgar population in Thrace and Macedonia, the emperors established Syrian and Armenian colonists there in the eighth and ninth centuries. Later emperors followed the same policy, and from the eleventh to the thirteenth century colonies of Uzes, Patzinaks and Cumans from the lands to the north of the Black Sea were introduced.

Although continually raiding the empire, the Bulgars were culturally its children, and in 865 they officially adopted the Greek form of Christianity. Under Simeon the Great (893–927) the Bulgar state greatly extended its frontiers westward over the Slavs of Serbia and southward into northern Greece (Fig. 78). In Macedonia and in Epirus, the empire was able to keep only the coastlands, and Bulgar raids penetrated even as far south as the Isthmus. The new Bulgarian realm soon broke into two owing to revolt in the western Serb provinces. In 972, eastern Bulgaria came to an end, and by 1018 the now independent western unit had also been recovered by the empire. From 1018 to 1186, the Bulgars ceased to form a separate state. The second Bulgarian empire, which came into existence as the result of revolt of Bulgars and Vlachs (see p. 360), once more included a part of northern Greece within its territory, but it lasted only for a short time (1186–1258), and was ultimately succeeded by Serb domination in the Balkan peninsula (Fig. 79).

Although Macedonia and the lands around had passed from Bulgar control, Bulgars continued to be an important element in the population of the area. Unlike the Slavs of peninsular Greece, however, the Bulgars and Slavs of these areas were not assimilated by the Greeks, and they remained distinct groups. Linguistically separate from the Greeks, they were to form a complicating factor in the 'Macedonian problem' of later times.

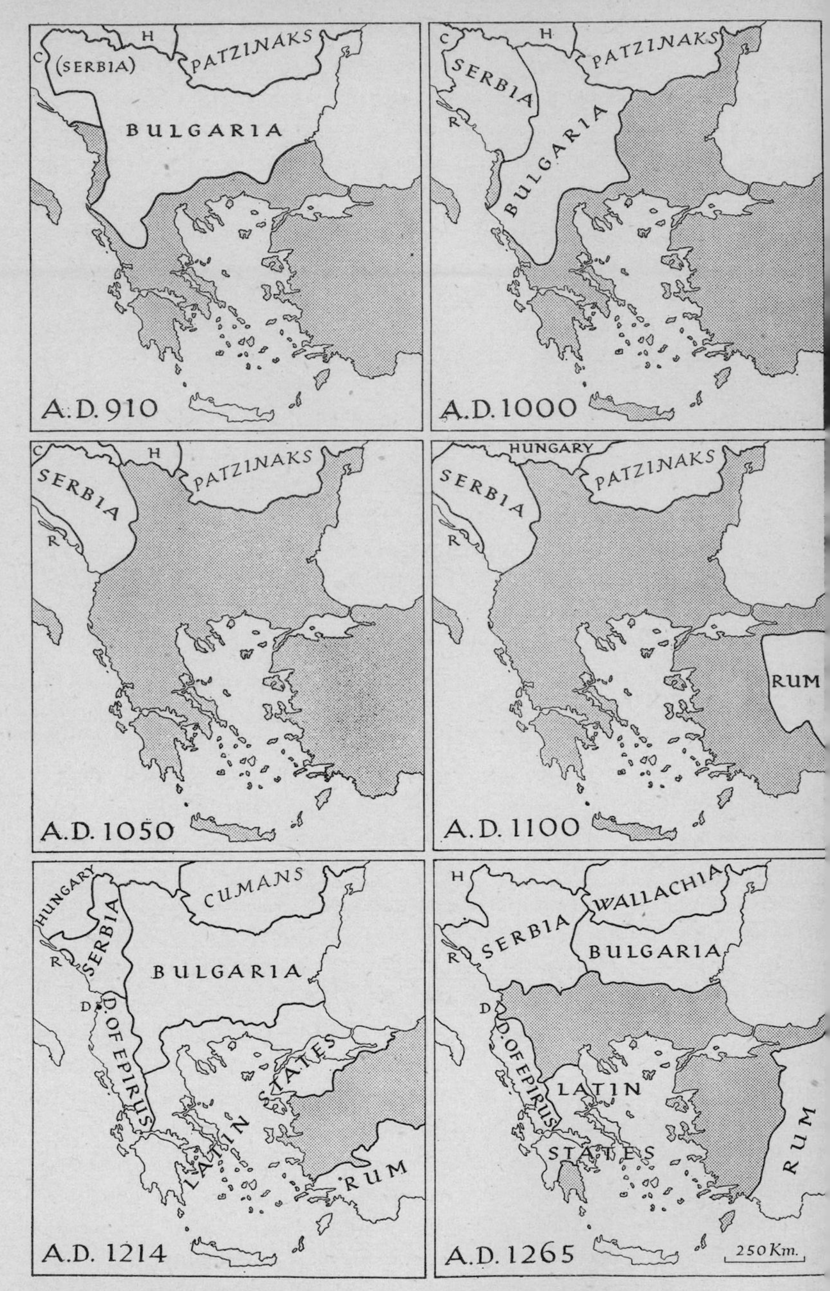

Fig. 78. The Balkan Peninsula, A.D. 910–1265

Based on: (1) E. A. Freeman, *Atlas to the Historical Geography of Europe*, map 34–37 (London, 1903); (2) W. Miller, *The Latins in the Levant*, p. 81 (London 1908); (3) W. R. Shepherd, *Historical Atlas*, pp. 59, 67, 89 (London, 1930).

The area included in the Byzantine empire is stippled. *C* = Croatia; *D* = Durazzo *H* = Hungary; *R* = Ragusa.

The Vlachs

Apart from the Slavs and the Bulgars, another non-Greek people emerge in the history of medieval Greece. Their language is a dialect of Romanian and is therefore derived from Latin; and it is generally admitted that they are descended from Roman colonists and Latinized provincials in the areas north and south of the Danube.* Their existence may be inferred from records as early as the sixth century in date, but the first definite mention of them was not until the year 976. During the next two centuries, reference to them became frequent, but they were intermingled with other peoples in such a way that it

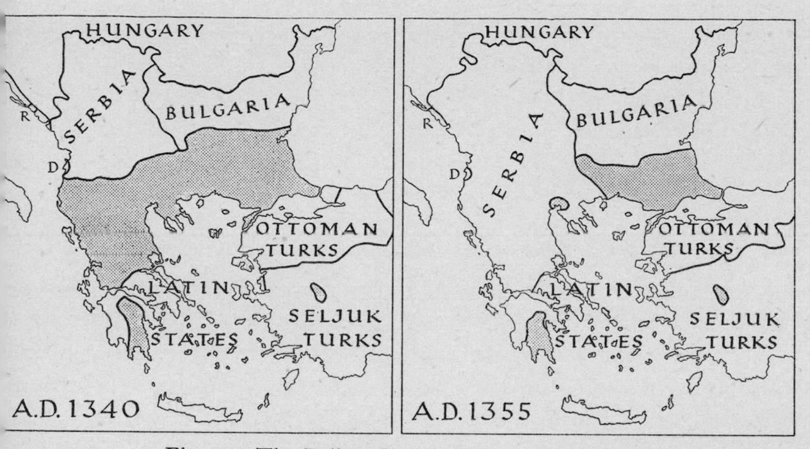

Fig. 79. The Balkan Peninsula, A.D. 1340–1355

Based on: (1) E. A. Freeman, *Atlas to the Historical Geography of Europe*, maps 40 and 41 (London, 1903); (2) W. R. Shepherd, *Historical Atlas*, p. 89 (London, 1930). The area included in the Byzantine empire is stippled. *D* = Durazzo; *R* = Ragusa.

is difficult to form any clear idea of their distribution. Several districts were called after them; thus 'Great Vlachia' was the name given to Thessaly, and 'Little Vlachia' to Acarnania and Aetolia, while there were Vlachs also in Bulgaria and to the north. These last were involved in the revolt against the Byzantine empire which led to the establishment of the second Bulgarian empire in 1186 (see p. 161).

In the eleventh-century *Strategicon* by Cecaumenos, there is a description of the Vlachs around Trikkala and Larissa, in Thessaly.

* The Vlachs, or Wallachs, called themselves *Romans*; the name 'Vlach' was applied to them by their neighbours; its origin is identical with the English 'Wealh' or 'Welsh' (i.e. stranger), and represents a Slavonic adoption of a general term applied by Teutonic peoples to Roman provincials in the fourth and fifth centuries.

Their mode of living then seems to have been very similar to wha it is to-day; from April to September they lived with their flock in the mountains, and descended to the plains only in winter. Ther is also reference, in the same account, to the appointment of Byzantine official to administer the Vlachs. Towards the end of th eleventh century, these southern Vlachs were mentioned by th Byzantine historian Anna Comnena, who referred to nomadic foll 'commonly called Vlachs' in the mountainous region of Thessaly About the year 1170, Benjamin of Tudela described them thus 'Here are the confines of Wallachia, a country of which the in habitants are called Vlachi. They are as nimble as deer and descen from their mountains into the plains of Greece committing robberie and taking booty. Nobody ventures to make war on them, nor ca any king bring them to submission.' At the division of the Byzan tine empire in 1204, Great Vlachia was included in the kingdom o Salonica under Boniface, but it soon reappeared as an independen principality under its old name (see p. 173).

The Economic Development of Byzantine Greece

If it is difficult to obtain any detailed evidence about the coming o Slavs and Bulgars into the Greek lands, it is even more difficult t form a clear picture of the domestic history of Greece in the Byzan tine empire from the death of Justinian in 565 to the fall of Constanti nople in 1204. Certain facts, however, stand out: something can b said about the economic condition of the area, and especially abou its commerce; some evidence is also available about the interna political condition of the Greek themes during the twelfth century the advent of western armies into Greece, culminating in the grea invasion of 1204, is comparatively well documented; and, lastly there are archaeological remains which speak for themselves of th former Byzantine influence in the land (see Appendix II).

Until the coming of the ships of the western cities of Venice, Geno and Amalfi, in the eleventh century, the Greeks were to a great exten the carriers of the eastern Mediterranean. Though the land was fille with Slav immigrants, the Greek cities of the coast were still abl to maintain their mercantile connexions. A great movement o exchange centred on Constantinople itself and, in the ninth an tenth centuries Byzantine trade was at its height. It is true that th advance of Islam had restricted trade in the eastern Mediterranea but the Black Sea trade was important; amber, furs and metals cam from Russia and the northern shores of Asia Minor. Greek ship also carried much of the trade between Constantinople and the west, but the Italian merchant fleets gradually shut out the Greeks from western waters. The Italian cities, at first the rivals, were soon the superiors of the Greeks in wealth and industry, and they came ultimately to dominate the carrying trade of the Aegean.

One great hindrance to Aegean shipping was piracy. In 823, some Saracens, who had migrated from Spain to Alexandria, fell upon Crete, at that time recovering from an earthquake, and conquered it. Their control was marked by religious toleration which reconciled the inhabitants to their rule; and in the years that followed, Christians helped to man the ships of the Moslem corsairs who menaced the coasts and islands of the Aegean. Cretan pirates became the terror of the eastern seas, and Crete grew into a great centre for traffic in slaves. At last, after many attempts, the island was restored to Christian rule in 961. Some of the Moslems left; others sank into serfdom. As in the Peloponnese, the missionary followed the soldier, and many Greek and Armenian Christians were attracted here. The Christian recovery of the island was in the main successful, though not a few Moslems kept their religion. But the recovery of Crete did not mean the abolition of piracy in the Aegean. The chronicle ascribed to our English Benedict of Peterborough states that in 1191 piracy was still rife; some of the Aegean islands were uninhabited for fear of the pirates; in other islands, they themselves lived. Despite their depredations, however, commercial activity, though interrupted, never broke down, and, indeed, with the coming of the Italian cities, it greatly increased.

An important item in Greek trade was silk. About the year 550, two Persian monks had smuggled some eggs of the silkworm into the Byzantine empire, and from these precious eggs were derived all the varieties of silk-worm that stocked the western world for over a thousand years. The silks of the Byzantine empire became famous throughout medieval Europe, and the cities of central and southern Greece shared greatly in this prosperity. Thebes in particular became an important centre. No silk is now made at Thebes and there are no mulberry trees there, but the plain around the town is still known as 'Morokampos' from the mulberry trees which once gave the town its prosperity.

Though the carrying trade was passing into the ships of the west, the Greek cities did not lose their prosperity. Some indication of conditions in Greece in the twelfth century is furnished by the large numbers of Jewish communities in the area. Benjamin of Tudela, writing about 1160, provided a list of the Jewish communities. The great city of Thebes had about 2,000 Jews who were 'the most skilled artificers in silk and purple cloth throughout Greece'. Salonica, 'a very large city' on the Via Egnatia from Durazzo to Constantinople, had about 500 Jews; Armylo (Almirós), another 'large city', had 400; Corinth had 300; Egripo (Khalkís) was 'a large city upon the sea-coast where merchants come from every quarter', and it had about 200 Jews. There were also many smaller Jewish communities.

The Political Condition of Greece in A.D. 1200

Though the economic circumstances of the Greek cities in the twelfth century seem to have been moderately prosperous, the political condition of Greece was far from happy. The financial oppression of the Byzantine government was heavy, and money that should have been spent on the defence of the country went instead to support the ostentation of the imperial capital. Byzantine officials regarded the country, in the words of a contemporary, as an 'utter hole', to be exploited as much as possible; the imperial governors received no salaries, but made their office self-supporting. Besides this, the Greek population had to endure the exactions of native tyrants. Under the Comneni dynasty of the twelfth century, feudalism had made considerable progress. Large tracts of land were under the control of families whose quarrels disturbed the life of the country. The historian Niketas speaks of these notables (*archontes*) as 'inflamed by ambition against their own fatherland, slavish men, spoiled by luxury, who made themselves tyrants, instead of fighting the Latins'.

Beset by imperial exactions, disturbed by internal feuds, raided by pirates, occupied in part by Vlachs, threatened by the rising second empire of Bulgaria, it is little wonder that the condition of Greece seemed ripe for western interference. The raids of western princes in the twelfth century and the ever-growing strength of the western cities (especially of Venice) in the Aegean Sea, formed but a prelude to the great disaster that fell upon the Byzantine world in 1204.

Western Interference up to 1204

The Norman conquerors of southern Italy, seeking to match the exploits of William the Conqueror in England, seized a pretext to invade the Byzantine provinces that lay so near across the narrow Straits of Otranto. Between 1081 and 1084, they occupied Corfu, took Durazzo, and penetrated as far as Larissa in Thessaly. They retired only to return again in 1106, but without success. For forty years Greece was left alone, until the expedition of Roger of Sicily in 1146. In that year, a landing was made at Itea on the north of the Gulf of Corinth, and the Normans marched to Thebes. The city was looted and many of its silk weavers were sent back to Sicily. From Thebes, the invaders marched to Corinth, plundered it, and then sailed home with their booty. In the years that followed, the Normans became increasingly involved in the domestic intrigues of the empire, and after 40 years a Norman army once again marched across Greek soil (1185). Starting from Durazzo, it made for Salonica, and a fleet was sent by sea to help in the siege of the city. After successfully looting the city, the Normans were defeated and returned home.

Faced with the Norman peril in the eleventh century, the emperor had sought aid from Venice whose wealthy merchants were now trading in eastern waters. The price of assistance was free trade throughout the empire, and a charter of 1082 laid the sure foundation for Venetian supremacy in the commerce of the Aegean and the Black Seas. 'On that day', says one historian, 'began the world commerce of Venice.'* The Venetians were soon everywhere. Their very success, however, aroused distrust, and, to counteract Venetian influence, succeeding emperors granted commercial privileges to Pisa, Genoa and Amalfi. During the twelfth century the empire and Venice were sometimes at war and sometimes acting together, according to the exigencies of the moment; but all the while the antagonism between the two powers was developing. It is this antagonism together with Norman raids of the twelfth century that provided the background for the spectacular events of 1204 which inaugurated a new period in the history of Greece.

FRANKISH AND VENETIAN GREECE

The Fourth Crusade

From the end of 1199 onwards, a fourth crusade was preached in France and Germany. Its leading members were French feudal lords like Baldwin of Flanders; its goal was Jerusalem; and its immediate strategic objective was the heart of Moslem power in Egypt. The Venetians agreed to provide transport, and, by August 1202, the army was assembled at Venice, but the crusaders then found it

* C. Diehl, *Une république patricienne: Venise*, p. 33 (Paris, 1915).

impossible to pay the sum agreed upon. The Venetians therefore proposed that payment be postponed in return for help against the Adriatic city of Zara which had been occupied by the Hungarians. In spite of papal protests against this attack on a Christian city, the crusading fleet sailed in November 1202, and Zara was successfully taken. But this diversion to Zara was only a preliminary to a much greater diversion. For a long time, many in the west had looked with hatred towards the Byzantine empire, and, during the preparations

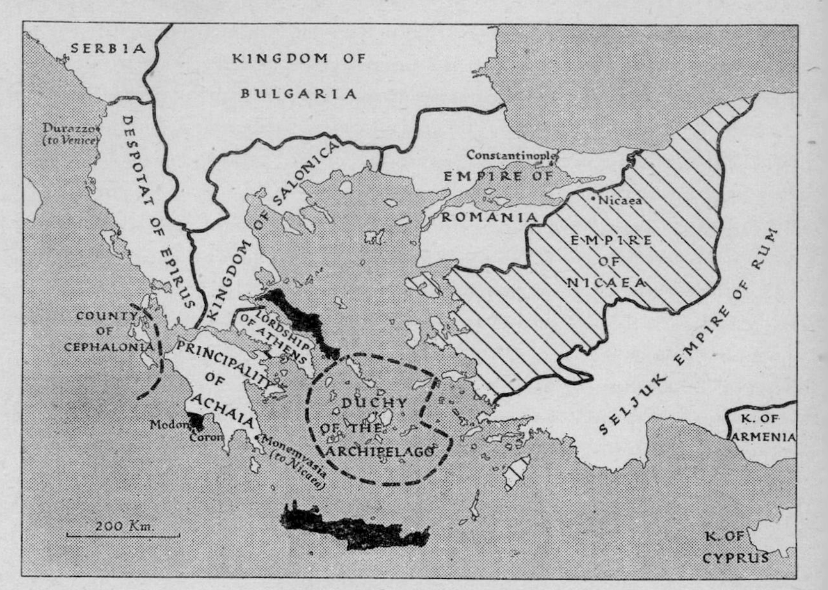

Fig. 80. Greece in A.D. 1214

Based on: (1) *The Cambridge Medieval History*, vol. 4, map 43 (Cambridge, 1923); (2) W. Miller, *The Latins in the Levant*, p. 81 (London, 1908).

Venetian possessions are shown in black. The empire of Trebizond lay along the south-eastern shores of the Black Sea—off this map.

of 1200–2, the crusading plan had become involved in a series of complicated motives which led the crusaders ultimately not against the infidel but to Constantinople. Venice in particular had everything to gain by an attack on its great commercial rival in the east. The details of this great diversion are obscure and have been the subject of controversy, but the result is clear enough. In June 1203, the crusading fleet appeared outside the harbour of Constantinople, and the crusaders were very soon in possession of the city. Involved in disputes about the imperial throne, they decided to divide the empire amongst themselves. A new emperor was to be elected with control over one-quarter of the empire. The remaining three-quarters were to be divided, one-half to the Venetians and one-half to the crusaders. The year 1204 is one of the great landmarks in European history.

Count Baldwin of Flanders was elected emperor to rule over a restricted Latin empire that included the territory on either side of the Sea of Marmora together with some nearby islands. Venetian nobles occupied many other islands, and Venice assumed direct sovereignty over a number of other areas. Rewards for the Frankish adventurers were found on the mainland of Greece. Representatives of the old Byzantine emperors remained only in three areas—in the territory around Nicaea in Asia Minor, in Epirus, and in Trebizond on the Black Sea coast (Fig. 80). Although the Latin empire at Constantinople lasted only for 57 years, some of the Venetian and Frankish states continued for two or three hundred years. From 1204 onwards until the coming of the Turk, the history of the Greek lands lost its unity, and became the story not of one but of many separate states. The units that thus arose in the Greek world fall conveniently into the following groups, each of which must be considered separately (Fig. 80):

(1) The Latin empire of Romania, 1204–61.
(2) The Greek empire of Nicaea, 1204–1453.
(3) The Latin kingdom of Salonica, 1204–23.
(4) The duchy of Athens, 1205–1460.
(5) The principality of Achaia, 1205–1432.
(6) The duchy of the Archipelago, 1207–1566.
(7) The county palatine of Cephalonia, 1194–1483.
(8) The despotat of Epirus, 1204–1336.
(9) Scattered Venetian possessions, various dates from 1204 to 1715 in the Aegean and to 1797 in the Ionian Islands.
(10) Scattered Genoese possessions, various dates from 1261 to 1566.
(11) The Knights of Rhodes, 1309–1522.

The Latin Empire of Romania, 1204–61

The Latin empire, lying athwart the Sea of Marmora, soon began to shrink both in Thrace and in Asia Minor. In Thrace, it had to face the attacks of the Bulgars, and in Asia Minor it had a rival in the Greek empire of Nicaea which still maintained the Byzantine tradition. Only the rivalries of the states around kept it alive for as long as 57 years, and it fell to the Nicaean Greeks in 1261. The last of the emperors to reign, like the first, was named Baldwin. He fled to the west where the empty title of 'Latin Emperor' continued until the death of its last holder in 1383.

The Greek Empire of Nicaea, 1204–1453

The Latin empire of Constantinople was never able to make much progress in Asia Minor. There, in the prosperous city of Nicaea,

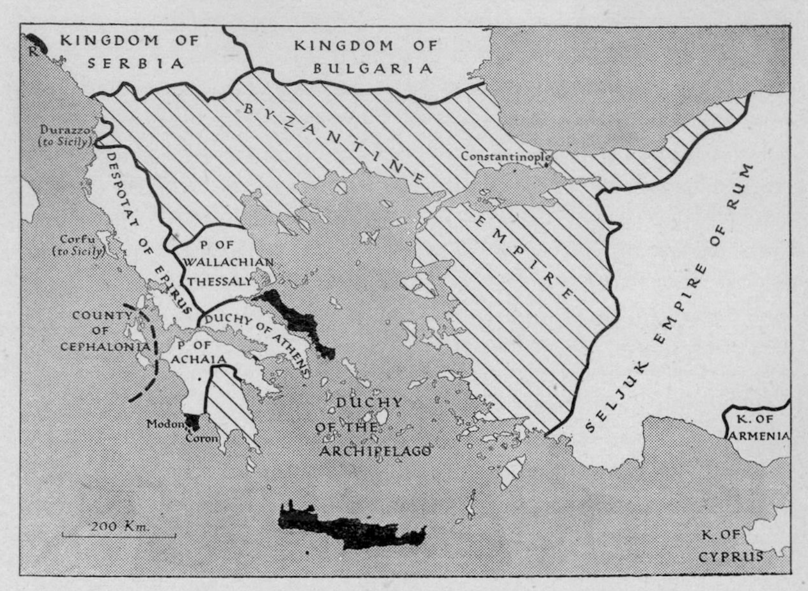

Fig. 81. Greece in A.D. 1265
Based on W. R. Shepherd, *Historical Atlas*, p. 89 (London, 1930).
Venetian possessions are shown in black; *R*=Ragusa.

Theodore Lascaris, the son-in-law of a former Byzantine emperor, established a court that soon became the centre of a small but reviving Greek empire. Under Theodore and his successors, the new empire was organized efficiently and its frontiers were extended in Asia Minor and over the islands of Lesbos, Chios, Samos and Icaria. Soon, it recovered ground in Europe, and the Maritsa became its northern boundary against Bulgaria. In 1246, much of the Epirot empire of Salonica was annexed and the Byzantine frontier was carried to the Adriatic itself (Fig. 81).

The Lascarid dynasty was replaced by the noble family of Palaeologus in 1259, but this involved no change of external policy, and at last, in 1261, Constantinople itself was captured. It was the culmination of a steady progress since 1204. Now, after an interval of 57 years, the empire of Nicaea became merged in that of Constantinople. The revival had not recovered the whole of Byzantine territory, but, at any rate, it had got back the heart and centre of the empire, together with a substantial extent of territory.

The revived Byzantine empire was to last another two hundred years, and its European must be distinguished from its Asiatic history. In the Peloponnese, in 1262, it recovered Monemvasia together with Mistra and Maina (see p. 175), and during the fourteenth century this southern base became a most important element in the empire (Fig. 83). By 1432, the whole Peloponnese had been restored to Byzantine rule, with the exception of some coastal stations held by Venice (see p. 177). The story of Byzantine recovery in northern Greece was different. For a time the frontiers of the empire continued to expand. The greater part of Thessaly (Wallachian Thessaly) was added in 1318 (see p. 173), and in 1336 the despotat of Epirus itself was won (see p. 179). But at this very moment of success, the great resurgence of Serbia under Stephen Dushan wrested a great part of these possessions from Byzantine rule. Stephen's empire stretched to the Gulf of Corinth, and all that remained to Constantinople in the north was Thrace and the district around Salonica (Fig. 82). It is true that the Serbian state soon broke up into fragments; these, however, did not return to Byzantine rule, but passed to a new power, the Turks, who were soon to engulf the whole Aegean world.

In Asia Minor, the Byzantine empire had started to shrink almost as soon as its centre had been transferred from Nicaea to Constantinople. Various Turkish powers encroached on imperial territory until only a narrow strip remained along the Sea of Marmora. With the rise of one of these powers, the Ottoman Turks, the loss was accelerated, and, by the middle of the fourteenth century, only a few isolated Byzantine points were left in Asia Minor. But the Ottomans did not restrict their activities to Asia. By 1356 they had landed in Europe, and in 1361 they transferred their capital to Adrianople. What Stephen Dushan had torn from Byzantine territory, the Ottomans were now to inherit—and more. By the two battles of the Maritsa (1371) and Kossovo (1389), the power of the Bulgarians and the Serbians was broken, and their territories passed into Turkish hands; by 1390, the Turks had reached the Danube. In 1393, they conquered Thessaly and Neopatras. At the end of the century, the Byzantine empire consisted only of Salonica, the Peloponnese and Constantinople. In 1453, the great city itself fell. What the Fourth Crusade had started in 1204, the Ottomans now completed, and by 1461 they were masters of almost all mainland Greece. The islands of the Aegean, however, held out for over another century, and, not until the duchy of the Archipelago fell in 1566, was Ottoman supremacy as complete in the islands as on the mainland (see p. 178).

The Latin Kingdom of Salonica, 1204–23

The leader of the crusaders, Boniface of Montferrat, obtained, as his share of the spoil, the title of king and a grant of land including Macedonia, Thessaly and much of central Greece. He set out in the

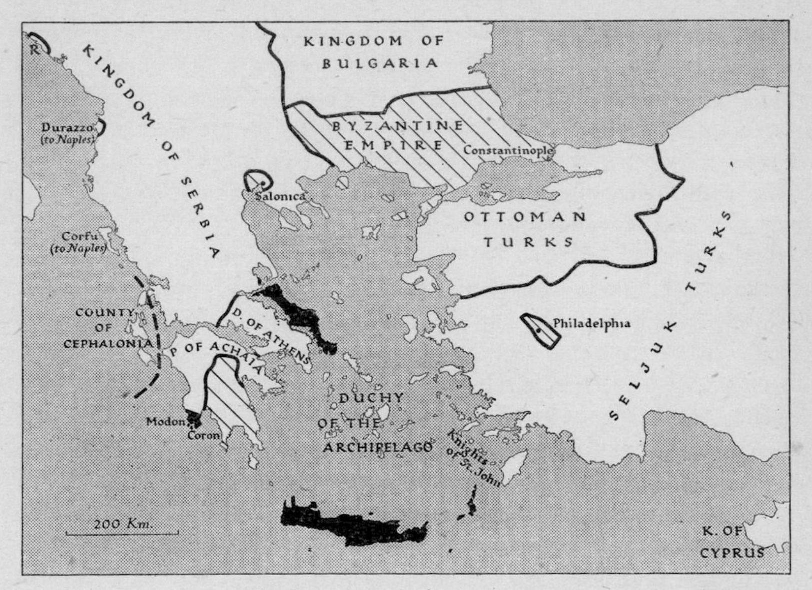

Fig. 82. Greece about A.D. 1355

Based on W. R. Shepherd, *Historical Atlas*, p. 89 (London, 1930).

Venetian possessions are shown in black; *R* = Ragusa. The island of Santa Maura (Levkás) was not united to the county of Cephalonia until 1362.

autumn of 1204 to take possession of his kingdom and to parcel it out among his barons. Thus Larissa became the fief of a Lombard noble; Velestino passed into the hands of a Rhenish count; the commanding position of Boudonitza, near the pass of Thermopylae, was assigned to the Pallavicini family from near Parma, and their ruined castle still looks down on the countryside around. The new kingdom was not destined to last very long. The reluctance of the king to acknowledge the overlordship of the emperor of Romania was a source of weakness; and the attacks of the Bulgars was another weakness. In 1223, the kingdom was occupied by the despot of Epirus, and it remained under Epirote control until the reviving Greek empire of Nicaea annexed the greater part of it in 1246 (see p. 170).

A branch of the Epirote dynasty continued, however, to rule in Thessaly, for one of its members had married the heiress of the hereditary chieftain of the Wallachians (see p. 179). This principality, sometimes independent, and sometimes in alliance with one of the surrounding states, was known variously as 'Great Wallachia' or the 'Duchy of Neopatras' (Fig. 81). When the line of the Wallachian princes became extinct in 1318, their territories were divided. The greater part of the rich Thessalian plain was annexed by the Byzantine empire. The southern area, including the city of Neopatras itself, in the valley of the Spercheus, was conquered by the Catalan Company, then dominating Athens, and this enlarged state became known as the 'duchies of Neopatras and Athens' (see p. 174).

The Duchy of Athens, 1205–1460

One of the associates of Boniface was a Burgundian noble named Othon de la Roche who, in 1205, received the territories of Athens and Thebes in the south of the kingdom of Salonica. This unit in central Greece maintained its identity long after the Latin kingdom of Boniface had disappeared, and it became one of the most permanent of the Frankish states in Greece. At first its ruler was known merely as 'Sire' or 'Megaskyr' (Great Lord), but from the middle of the thirteenth century onwards he became the 'duke' of Athens. After twenty years' rule, Othon, with his wife and his two sons, left Greece for ever to return to his native land (1225), and he bequeathed his domain of Thebes and Athens to his nephew Guy who carried on his work. Under the tolerant Frankish regime, the silk manufacture of Thebes once again prospered; Athens, too, was prosperous. 'The splendour of the Theban Court and the excellent French spoken at Athens struck visitors from the West.'*

But at the beginning of the fourteenth century this prosperous Frankish rule was cut short from an unexpected quarter. A band of

* W. Miller, *Essays on the Latin Orient*, p. 29 (London, 1920).

Catalan mercenaries, after fighting in Sicily and in Asia Minor, was employed by the duke of Athens against the neighbouring principality of Neopatras, but they soon proved dangerous allies. Disputes about payment culminated in the overthrow of the Franks. On a fatal day in the spring of 1311 the Catalans were outstandingly victorious on the plain of Boeotia, and only a few Frankish knights survived the battle; the widows of the fallen provided wives for the newcomers. The Catalan mercenaries surprised by their own sweeping victory, which so struck the imagination of their contemporaries, sought a ruler outside their own ranks, and turned to their former employer, Frederick II of Sicily. Thus it was that for over half a century the duchy of Athens was ruled in name by absentee dukes of the Sicilian House, while the real power was wielded by a vicar-general appointed to represent them. To the north, the Catalans conquered the southern part of the Wallachian duchy of Neopatras, including the city of Neopatras itself (1318), and the double title of 'dukes of Athens and Neopatras' was borne by the kings of Aragon, the successors of the Sicilian rulers, long after the Catalan duchy had disappeared.

The sons of the mercenaries did not possess the fighting qualities of their fathers; and in 1388, Athens was occupied by a Florentine family of bankers named Acciajuoli who were prominent in the affairs of the Peloponnese to the south. Thus began the third chapter in the history of the medieval duchy of Athens (Fig. 83). The Catalans vanished from the scene almost as completely as the Franks before them, and the next half-century saw many Florentine families in the area. But the independence of the duchy was difficult to maintain before the rising tide of Turkish successes. In June 1456 the Turks occupied Athens, and Thebes fell four years later. From 1460 onwards, central Greece remained Turkish, apart from two brief intervals when the Venetians occupied Athens (1466 and 1687–8).

By the time of the arrival of the Turks, a new element had been added to the population of Attica and Boeotia. Towards the end of the Catalan regime, the area had been disturbed by civil war, and, to repair the ravages, Albanian settlers were invited to colonize the waste lands (*c.* 1380). After the occupation of Epirus by the Tocco family in 1418, still more Albanians came in under the Florentine dukes. The settlement had permanent results. From these colonists of the fourteenth and fifteenth centuries are descended many of the Albanians of Attikí and Voiotía who still speak Albanian as well as Greek (see p. 362).

Plate 81. The Temple of Apollo, Bassae
The temple was built in the fifth century B.C. by Ictinus, architect of the Parthenon.

Plate 82. A Byzantine church of the twelfth century, Daphni
The photograph shows the east end of the monastery church.

Plate 83. The church of Áyios Elevthérios, Athens, ninth century A.D.
Sculptures taken from earlier buildings are incorporated in the walls. In the background is the modern Cathedral.

Plate 84. The Kapnikaréa, Athens
The Kapnikaréa is a Byzantine church of the twelfth century, with additions of later periods.

The Principality of Achaia, 1205–1432

Just before the conquest of Constantinople, Geoffrey de Villehardouin, nephew and namesake of the historian of the conquest, was driven by bad weather into the port of Modon in the Peloponnese. While he was staying there and becoming involved in the local quarrels, the great drama of the break-up of the Byzantine empire was taking place. In the winter of 1204, Boniface was taking possession of his kingdom of Salonica, and Geoffrey accordingly made his way to the headquarters of Boniface. There he outlined to an old friend from Champagne, William of Champlitte, a scheme for the conquest of the Peloponnese, promising to acknowledge William as his overlord. The two men, with only a few hundred soldiers, won almost the whole of the peninsula in a single battle. The newly won land was partitioned into twelve baronies among their followers, the ruins of whose baronial castles can still be seen standing in strong positions. William, recalled by affairs in France, died on his way home, and Geoffrey then became 'prince of Achaia' in his stead.

There were two areas which Villehardouin was unable to acquire. One was the territory around the Venetian ports of Modon and Coron, guarding the sea route to the east; occupied in 1206, they remained in Venetian possession until 1500. The other was the southern rock of Monemvasia, 'the Gibraltar of Greece', under the flag of the Byzantine state of Nicaea; this, however, was conquered in 1246, but only with the aid of Venetian galleys, and only after a siege of three years. Then, in the south, the fortress of Mistra was built to overawe the Slavs of Taygetos and the restless people of Maina. But Monemvasia was not kept for long. The third of the Villehardouins, William, became involved in disputes between the despotat of Epirus and the reviving empire of Nicaea; captured by the Nicaean Greeks, he was restored to freedom only in return for the fortresses of Monemvasia, Mistra and Old Maina (1262). It was the gain of this southern territory that paved the way for the ultimate restoration of Byzantine authority in the Peloponnese (Fig. 81).

William de Villehardouin left no male heir, and the marriage of his daughter Isabella to the son of Charles I of Naples united the fortunes of the principality with those of the Angevin power at Naples. After William's death in 1278, the principality was ruled by deputies appointed from Naples, for Isabella, though young, was already a widow. She next married Florenz of Hainaut, a young

Flemish nobleman who thus became prince of Achaia, and, after this, many Flemings appeared in Greece. Widowed for a second time, Isabella married a prince of the House of Savoy, and the Flemings were replaced by Piedmontese. The newcomers were so unpopular,

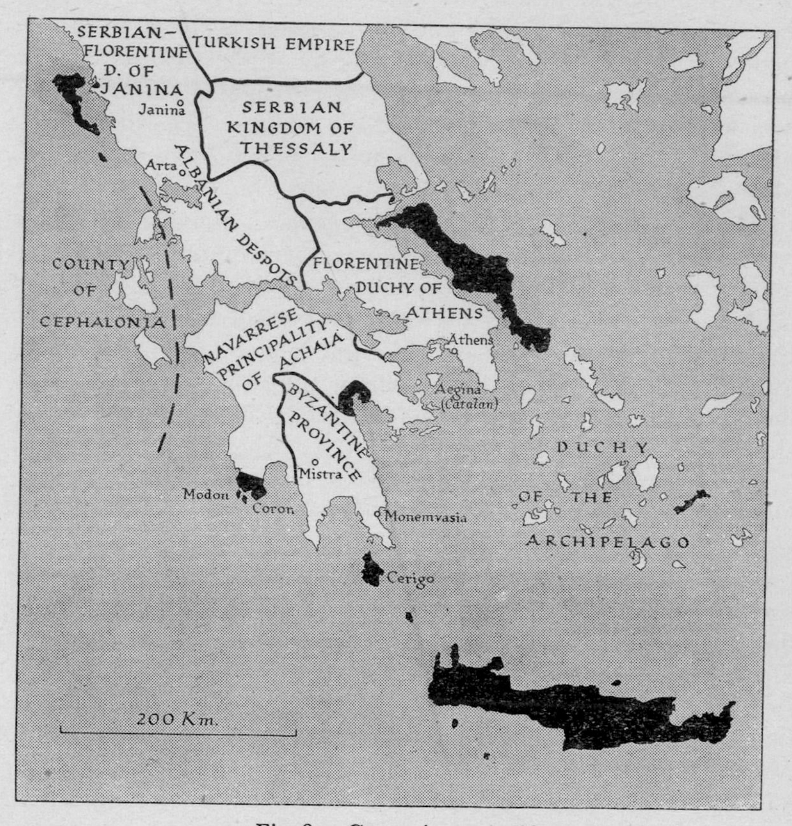

Fig. 83. Greece in A.D. 1388

Based on W. Miller, *The Latins in the Levant*, p. 332 (London, 1908).

Venetian possessions are shown in black. The southern portion of the despotat of Epirus was now under the control of an Albanian chieftain (Ghin Boua Spata) at Arta; the northern portion, centred on Janina, had been held by a Serbian chieftain (Thomas Preliubovitch), but he died in 1385 and his widow married Esau Buondelmonti, a Florentine noble.

however, that Isabella and her husband left Greece for ever, and the government lapsed to the Angevin power at Naples. A disputed succession followed, and the barren title of 'prince of Achaia' continued to pass from one absentee to another.

This unsatisfactory state of affairs continued during the fourteenth century, until a band of mercenaries did for Achaia what the Catalans had done for Athens in 1311. The origin of the Navarrese Company is obscure. They had been employed by the king of Navarre in his struggle with Charles V of France; and, seeking adventures farther afield, became involved in the complications of the succession to Achaia. They soon occupied much of the peninsula, and, in 1386, their leader declared himself 'vicar' of the principality; he became 'prince' ten years later (Fig. 83). It was from his widow's nephew that the Byzantine emperor was able to take the whole of the Peloponnese by 1432 (see p. 171), apart from a few points held by Venice; for to Modon and Coron, the Venetians had added Argos (1388), Nauplia (1388) and Lepanto (1407). But the Byzantine reconquest was not to last long. By 1461 the advancing tide of Turkish success had engulfed the whole of the Peloponnese up to the limits of the Venetian colonies (see p. 172).

In the middle of the fourteenth century, the Byzantine rulers of the Peloponnese had strengthened their army by recruiting large numbers of Albanians. These mercenaries were followed by colonists, and a large number of Albanians then settled upon the waste lands of the province, where their descendants remain to this day.

The Duchy of the Archipelago, 1207–1566

At the partition of 1204, the Greek islands had been allotted to Venice, but the government of the republic decided to leave their occupation to private citizens. Accordingly, Marco Sanudo, a nephew of the doge, set out with some companions to win a principality among the islands of the Cyclades (1207). They succeeded in founding a state that was in some ways the most stable of all those brought into being by the Fourth Crusade. Sanudo kept Naxos and some other islands for himself, and partitioned the surrounding islands amongst his fellow-freebooters. Thus at Andros and elsewhere arose those feudal castles whose ruins still dominate the landscape.

Sanudo had no wish to become merely a local governor under the republic, and so he acknowledged the overlordship of the Latin emperor who formed the islands into a duchy known sometimes as the duchy of Naxos, of the 'Dodekannesos' and of 'the Archipelago'. The nominal suzerainty was later transferred to Achaia (1261) and then to Naples (1267), though Venice more than once claimed overlordship. The duchy survived the revival of Byzantine power (see p. 172), and the Sanudo dynasty continued until 1383, when it was replaced by that of the usurper Francesco Crispo, a member of a Lombard family who had come to have possessions in Melos. The Crispi remained in power for the next two centuries.

Under the rule of the Crispi, Venetian influence became increasingly important in the affairs of the island barons, and Venice more than once took over the government of Andros, Naxos and Paros. But not even Venetian interference was able to save the islands from the Turkish raids which grew increasingly frequent. At last, in 1566, the Turkish conquest took place; for thirteen years a Jewish favourite of the Sultan, Joseph Nasi, ruled as an absentee duke, until the final incorporation of the duchy into Turkey in 1579. Nowhere else in Greece did Latin rule leave so many traces as among these islands of the Cyclades—in memorials, in language and in religion and the Roman Church has remained important here up to this day

The County Palatine of Cephalonia, 1194–1483

Even before the Fourth Crusade, Matteo Orsini, a member of an Italian family, had made himself master of the islands of Cephalonia, Zante and Ithaca (1194). During the Venetian occupation of Corfu (1206–14), he acknowledged the supremacy of Venice, but afterwards transferred his allegiance to the prince of Achaia. His descendants became involved in the politics of Epirus, and ruled over that province from 1318 until it was reunited to the Byzantine empire in 1336 (see p. 179). Meanwhile, in 1324, the islands had been annexed outright by the Angevins to Achaia, and the county was not granted out again until 1357. It was then given to the Tocco family from Beneventum who united Santa Maura (Levkás) to the other islands. By 1418 the Tocci had also revived the continental dominion of the Orsini, and had made themselves masters of the country south of Janina (Fig. 86). The court of Cephalonia during these years was described by Froissart as a second fairyland. But family dissensions soon enabled the Turks to interfere; Janina was lost in 1430, and by 1449 Arta, Aetolia and Acarnania had also become Turkish. The islands likewise fell to the Turks in 1479, although with the exception of Santa Maura they were soon recovered by Venice and held for over three hundred years (*c.* 1482–1797); Santa Maura did not become Venetian until 1684.

The Despotat of Epirus, 1204–1336

While the Byzantine empire was being appropriated by the crusaders, the difficult country of Epirus was seized by a representative

Plate 85. The plain of Marathón

[T]he plain is the scene of the defeat of the Persians by the Athenians in 490 B.C. Cultivated [l]owlands lead gently to a shelving sandy beach on the east coast of Attikí. In the back[g]round are the limestone foothills of Pendelikón.

Plate 86. Monemvasía

[M]onemvasía is connected to the mainland of eastern Lakonía by a long stone bridge. In [th]e 13th–16th centuries it was successively held by Villehardouin, the Pope, the Vene[ti]ans, and the Turks.

Plate 87. Kiparissía

The picturesque castle, now in ruins, offered a vigorous resistance to the Frankish conquerors in 1205; it was afterwards in the possession of Geoffroy de Villehardouin, 'Prince of Morea'. The town was destroyed by Ibrahim Pasha in 1825.

Plate 88. Návplion (Nauplia)

The rocky hill in the background is crowned by the (partly) Venetian fortress of Palamidi The foreground shows the P.A.P. railway from Árgos.

f the imperial family, Michael Angelus Comnenus, who maintained is newly acquired territory against all comers. The court of Arta ecame, like that of Nicaea, a refuge for Greeks against the Latin nvaders of the Aegean world. The second 'despot' of Epirus conuered the neighbouring kingdom of Salonica in 1223, and founded new Greek empire of Salonica. This success both alarmed the 'ranks and also offended the rival Greek empire of Nicaea. In 1246, he Nicaean emperor was able to conquer the province of Salonica, ut the Wallachian principality of Neopatras, to the south, was left ndependent until 1318 (see p. 173).

In the west, Epirus itself still remained free until the last of the irect line from Michael Angelus was killed, in 1318, by a member f the Orsini family of Cephalonia who then maintained the indeendence of the despotat until it was reunited to the Byzantine mpire in 1336. Soon, however, the area was annexed by the exanding state of Serbia under Stephen Dushan (1349), and a large art of northern Greece fell under the control of the Serbs. On the reak-up of the Serbian empire after Stephen's death in 1355, there vas great confusion; Epirus was disputed by Serbs, Albanians and thers (Fig. 83) until the southern portion was acquired by the 'occo family from Cephalonia in 1418 (see p. 178). By 1449, howver, the area had passed under Turkish control, and with it the bscure people of Albania who, in the fourteenth century, had been xpanding southwards towards Acarnania and Aetolia and even into 'hessaly where the Vlachs had hitherto formed the bulk of the opulation.

'enetian Possessions, 1204–1797

Before 1204 Venice already occupied a commanding position in ne eastern Mediterranean trade that played so great a part in the conomic life of medieval Europe. That she could undertake the ransport of the Fourth Crusade is in itself a measure of her power. Ier gains at the partition of 1204 reflected these maritime interests, nd marked a turning point in her history. While the Frankish dventurers occupied the mainland of Greece, Venetian influence vas predominant in the islands and coasts of the Aegean. Modon nd Coron, 'the right eye' of the republic, were important stations n the eastern route; Crete, purchased in 1204, was held, despite nany insurrections, till 1669; Euboea, gained in 1209, was Venetian ntil 1470, and early in the fifteenth century large numbers of .banians were induced to settle on the uncultivated lands of the island. But a map of territorial possessions does not do justice t Venetian enterprise in the Aegean, for, frequently, Venice acquire influence and trading rights without actual dominion and administra tive responsibility. The Venetians who created the duchy of th Archipelago owed allegiance to the Latin empire; elsewhere, to

Fig. 84. Venetian possessions in the Greek lands

Based mainly on *The Cambridge Medieval History*, vol. IV, pp. 476–7 (Cambridg 1923).

It is difficult to construct a really satisfactory map of Venetian possessions becau sovereignty was sometimes not clearly defined, and Venice frequently acquire influence and control without administrative responsibility. Venetian citizens, to held land from other powers, e.g. in the case of the duchy of the Archipelago (s p. 178). The dates on the above map, moreover, do not take account of some chang in status, e.g. Venice paid tribute to the Turks for Zante from 1485 to 1699. N is any attempt made to indicate the occupation of the Peloponnese between 1685 and 1715 (Monemvasia was not taken until 1690). In Crete, after 1669, Venice st retained Grabusa (*G*) until 1691, and the island in Suda Bay (*S*) and Spinalon (*Sp*) until 1715.

Venetian citizens held lands from other powers; thus a member of the Zorzi family of Venice in 1355 became marquess of Boudonitza, a dependency of the principality of Achaia.

In the centuries that followed the Fourth Crusade, Venice increased her colonies in the Aegean and the Peloponnese by purchase and by conquest. 'Never', are we told, 'was there a state so dependent on the sea.' Structurally, the Venetian empire was coming to consist of a series of strategic points, calling stations, islands, and merchant quarters in cities, all of which were strung along the greatest of medieval trade routes. Although these possessions fluctuated, the net result was an increase in dominion until, in the fifteenth century, Venetians and Turks were meeting at every point. The defence of the Aegean against the Turk had fallen to Venice. The first Turkish war lasted from 1464 to 1479, and thereafter there was intermittent warfare, with many oscillations in Venetian sovereignty (Fig. 84). Though Morosini in 1685 acquired the Peloponnese for a brief spell, the province was finally lost to the Turk in 1718. In that year, too, the last island that Venice held in the Aegean—Tenos—was also lost; the Ionian islands, however, she kept until 1797 (see p. 194).

Genoese Possessions, c. 1261–1566

Genoa played a less important part than Venice in the history of the Aegean. She had no Byzantine tradition to pull her eastward, but soon, like Venice, she was benefiting by the carrying trade of the Crusades; the earliest treaty between Genoa and the Byzantine empire is dated 1155. Genoa took no part in the Fourth Crusade which brought so rich a gain to Venice in 1204, but with the overthrow of the Latin empire in 1261 came the opportunity of the Genoese. In return for assisting the Greek empire of Nicaea, they exacted commercial privileges; the price was free trade throughout the empire, a monopoly of shipping in the Black Sea, and permission to found colonies in the Aegean. In the city of Constantinople, now restored to Byzantine hands, they were assigned the suburb of Galata as their special quarter, and they also obtained the rich city of Smyrna in Asia Minor. From the events of 1261, then, dates the rise of Genoa as an Aegean power (Fig. 85).

Genoese families now appeared in the islands. The Zaccaria were soon exploiting the alum mines of Phocea (1275) and the rich mastic plantations of Chios (1304); the latter island passed ultimately into the control of a Genoese chartered company whose partners, abandoning their own names, became known as 'the Giustiniani'.* The rich island of Lesbos passed in 1355 into the hands of the Gattilusio family which became connected by marriage with the Byzantine imperial house, and which extended its control to the nearby islands of Thasos, Lemnos, Samothrace and Imbros, as well as to Phocea in Asia Minor and to Aenos on the mainland of Thrace.

Fig. 85. Genoese possessions in the Greek lands
Based on *The Cambridge Medieval History*, vol. IV, p. 477 (Cambridge, 1923).

The vicissitudes of these and the other Genoese islands were many; and the rivalry between Venice and Genoa, breaking at times into open war, was the main key to the local politics of the Aegean world. But as the fourteenth century drew to a close, a new factor overshadowed this rivalry—the coming of the Turks. Though each city negotiated commercial treaties with the new enemy, they sometimes sank their differences in an attempt to meet this menace to western interference in the Aegean. One after another, the Genoese

* This is the only example of this method of control by Latins in the Aegean. The company was known as the *maona*. Other examples of Genoese companies were the *maona* of Cyprus founded in 1374, and that of Corsica founded in 1378.

islands passed into Turkish hands. With the loss of Chios in 1566, Genoese sovereignty disappeared from the Aegean.

The Knights of Rhodes, 1309–1522

At the break-up of the Byzantine empire in 1204, Rhodes was seized by a Greek noble, Leon Gabalas, but it was soon under the control of Italian adventurers, who, during the thirteenth century, were compelled at times to acknowledge the overlordship of the emperor of Nicaea. Raided frequently by the Turks, it was occupied in 1309 by the Knights of St John, who, since the fall of the Holy Land, in 1291, had lived in Cyprus. The dominion of the Knights soon stretched over the neighbouring islands which were governed on feudal principles. The strategic situation of the islands in the eastern Mediterranean was important, for they formed a great fortress against the Turks. Many monuments still tell of their prosperity in the fourteenth century, despite Turkish raids. At length, in 1522, the Turks succeeded in occupying Rhodes, and the Knights were allowed to withdraw to Malta.

Frankish Civilization in Greece

The Frankish occupation formed a curious episode in the history of Greece. The newcomers from the west—Italians and Frenchmen, Catalans and Navarrese, Germans and Flemings—established a feudal constitution in all the states they founded. Thus, below the twelve barons of Achaia, for whom most information is available, there were greater and lesser vassals, then freemen, then serfs. Elsewhere there were variations, but the same general features of feudal society were to be found. To this land of opportunity came the younger sons of French noble houses seeking adventure and fortune. Of the court of Geoffrey de Villehardouin's successor in Achaia, the Venetian historian, Marino Sanudo, wrote: 'Knights came to the Morea from France, from Burgundy, and above all from Champagne, to follow him. Some came to amuse themselves, others to pay their debts, others again because of crimes, which they had committed.' Pope Honorius III in the thirteenth century, could well speak of Greece as 'New France'. The social life of this feudal society, with its brilliant courts and gay tournaments, was a bright one; and a picture of the fine array of western chivalry has been preserved for us in the anonymous *Chronicle of the Morea*, versions of which exist in French, Italian, Aragonese as well as in Greek. The Greeks, apart from those in Crete, seem to have accepted the occupation with tameness, which contrasts with the frequent rebellions they raised under the Turks. Occasionally, especially in Achaia, old native families were to be found holding fiefs under the western barons.

At first, the Franks took over the existing Greek ecclesiastical organization, but installed Roman Catholic churchmen everywhere. There were fruitless attempts to reunite the churches of Rome and Constantinople, but the Roman faith made very little headway among the Greeks. Later on, towards the end of the fourteenth century, the Greek Church recovered a good deal of ground, and some Orthodox bishops were allowed to return to their sees. The Greek people found in them an ally against their foreign rulers. It was in the Ionian islands, and in the Cyclades that Roman Catholic influence was most permanent, and it survives up to the present day.

The Frankish occupation has left many traces upon the countryside, in great castles and isolated towers, but it made little mark upon the Greek people and their institutions. Conquerors and the conquered never really amalgamated except to produce some despised half-castes (*Gasmouli*) who usually sided with the Greeks. The newcomers did not come in sufficient numbers to obtain a firm grip on the country, and they remained to the end a series of garrisons in a foreign land. Their conquest became an episode, not a formative factor in the life of Greece. 'New France' was to pass away for ever before the advance of the Turk, leaving behind not much more than archaeological remains to recall the brilliant interlude of western chivalry.

TURKISH GREECE

The Ottoman Advance

It was at the request of a Byzantine emperor that the Ottoman Turks first came into Europe to fight against the Serbs. But having defeated the Serbs, they refused to return to their Asiatic homeland, and, in 1354, established themselves on the European shores of the Dardanelles. A long and successful campaign in Thrace followed: Adrianople was captured in 1360, and the Turkish capital was then moved to this city from Brusa in Asia Minor. From this base in Thrace the Turkish conquest of south-eastern Europe began. The desperate effort of the Serbs, the Bulgars, the Vlachs and the Albanians to stay the progress of the Turks was shattered at Kossovo in 1389. The chronology of the Turkish advance is sometimes confusing, as the Christian states were frequently defeated and became tributary some years before they were completely annexed (Fig. 86).

The Latin states fell one after another during the next century. Macedonia (except for Salonica) was occupied by 1380; Salonica itself may have resisted until 1430. In 1393, Thessaly was annexed. The duchy of Athens was occupied in 1456–60; and by 1461, the Turks were also in complete control of the Peloponnese, apart from some coastal points held by the Venetians (see p. 177). In the north,

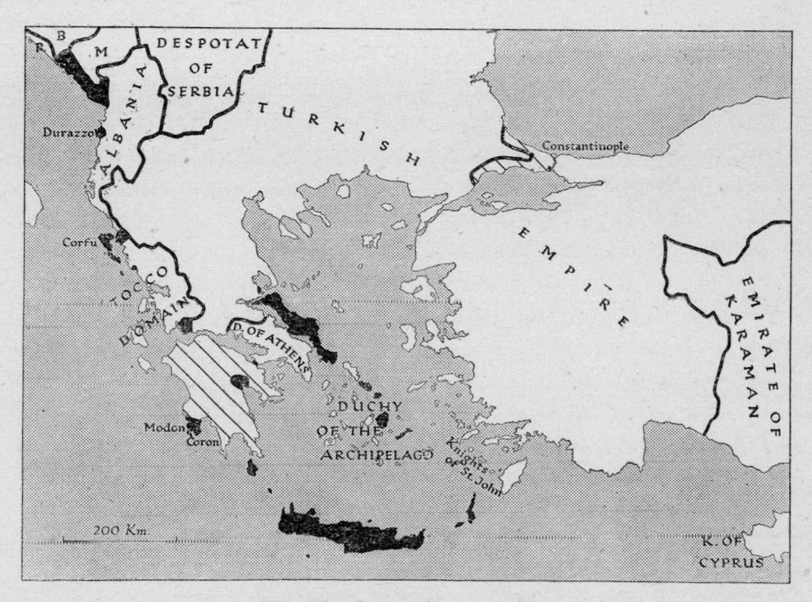

Fig. 86. Greece in A.D. 1440

Based on: (1) E. A. Freeman, *Atlas to the Historical Geography of Europe*, map 43 (London, 1903); W. R. Shepherd, *Historical Atlas*, p. 93 (London, 1930). Venetian possessions are shown in black; *B* = Bosnia; *M* = Montenegro; *R* = Ragusa.

Janina fell in 1430; the continental domain of the Tocco family had completely disappeared by 1449; and in 1479 the Turks extended their rule to the nearby Ionian islands, but they did not keep these for very long; Zante went to Venice in 1482, and Cephalonia and Ithaca in 1500; Santa Maura, however, except for a brief period (1502–3), did not become Venetian until 1684.

By the time that Constantinople itself had fallen in 1453, the Turks were in control of almost all the Greek mainland. Soon, the Aegean islands were mastered also. Lemnos, Imbros, Samothrace and Thasos were acquired in 1456–7, Lesbos in 1462, Euboea in 1470. But over a century was to elapse before Turkish control was complete. Not until the duchy of Naxos and the island of Chios had fallen in 1566 were the Turks in as complete control of the Aegean Sea as of the Greek mainland; Crete itself did not fall until 1669, and the island of Tenos lingered on under Venetian sovereignty until as late as 1715. In the Aegean islands, a number of Albanians were settled, especially in the latter half of the sixteenth century, as part of a scheme of colonization.

Turkish Control of Greece

The Greek lands, divided among so many sovereignties since 1204, found unity once more in a foreign rule centred at Constantinople. The main features of the political organization of the Turkish lands were simple. The whole area was under the administration of the *beglerbeg* (lord of lords) of Rumili (European Turkey) stationed at Sofia. In 1470, the Greek lands comprised six 'sanjaks' organized on a military basis: (1) Morea, (2) Epirus, (3) Thessaly, (4) Salonica, (5) Euboea, Boeotia and Attica, (6) Aetolia and Acarnania. Other sanjaks were added as the islands and Crete were acquired. Each sanjak was divided into 'cazas' or subdistricts, of which, for example, there were twenty-three in the Morea. A great deal of the local administration, however, was left in the hands of the Greek 'archontes', or notables, of every town and even of every hamlet; these undertook, for example, the farming of taxes and the work of policing.

Greeks were used not only for local administration but also for more general administrative purposes. It was a feature of Turkish policy to use Christians themselves to hold together and govern the vast Turkish empire, and this policy reflected itself in the Church, in the army and in the civil service.

The Church. The Turks did not attempt any wholesale conversion of the Greeks to Islam, but sought to manage the Christian population through its own Church. Indeed, some Orthodox Christians had been in favour of the change by which a Turkish sultan replaced a Byzantine emperor inclined to reunion with Rome. As Voltaire said, the Greek clergy 'preferred the turban of a Turkish priest to the red hat of a Roman Cardinal'. This hatred of the western Church enabled the sultan to interfere, and even to appear as a patron of the Orthodox faith. The Greek Patriarch was treated with great respect, and freedom of Christian worship was guaranteed. Here was an insurance against the possibility of a western and

Catholic crusade to deliver the eastern lands. It is true that the Patriarch came more and more under the control of the Turkish authorities, but then the Christians themselves were soon intriguing and bidding for the office. It is true also that many Christian churches, even St Sophia itself, were converted into mosques wherever Moslems were numerous, and minarets have only lately disappeared from Macedonia and Thessaly. But still the fact remains that the Turkish regime was, with but few exceptions, a tolerant one.

The great financial distinction between true believers and Christians was the payment of the 'haratch', or capitation tax, by every male unbeliever over ten years of age (except by priests, by the blind, by the maimed and by old men). A Christian had also to pay twice the duty paid by a Moslem (5 % as against 2½ %) on imports and exports. Hardship, however, arose not from the legal taxes, but from various illegal exactions by the provincial governors, so much so that in 1691 the central government prohibited the exaction of additional taxes on the plea of local necessity. Despite this, the Christians continued to suffer from the corruption of Turkish administration, but then so did their fellow-Moslems. Many Christians escaped either into Venetian territory or overseas. Some entered the Venetian employ as mercenaries, and the Greek 'stradioti' were known all over Europe. Numerous Epirote families settled across the waters in Calabria.

The Janissaries. There is a good deal of obscurity about the origin and working of the *corps d'élite* of the Turkish army, the janissaries (*yeni-tscheri* = new troops). About the year 1330 the corps was formed, recruited entirely from Christian children, taken at an early age (at about six or seven) and brought up as Moslems in a sort of military brotherhood, in which marriage was prohibited. From then on, every Christian father was compelled, at intervals of five years, or oftener, to make a declaration of the number of his sons, and one boy out of every five, or one out of every family, was taken by the officers of the sultan. The recruitment was enforced in all parts of the Ottoman empire in Europe, but mainly in Bosnia, Bulgaria and Albania. It is surprising that of the many insurrections against Turkish rule, only one (the Albanian agitation of 1565) seems to have been roused by this terrible tribute.

By the sixteenth century the janissaries numbered about 12,000–20,000, and had grown into a powerful and favoured corps; what was at first a curse came to be regarded by many parents as a blessing. There is even record of Moslems who lent their children to Christians so they might become members of so powerful a body. Creatures of the sultan, the janissaries in turn imposed their yoke upon him; they mutinied more than once, and in 1566 extorted the privilege of legal marriage, and membership of the body became to some extent hereditary. They lasted as a corps until 1826, but long before this they had ceased to be recruited from tribute-children; the last regular levy on children was in the year 1676. The result both of the levy, and of the migration of Greeks into Venetian territory and overseas, was a considerable diminution in the numbers of Greeks in the Greek lands. Indeed, by the end of the seventeenth century the time had come when 'a taxable infidel seemed a more valuable asset than a less remunerative believer'.*

The Civil Service. The genius of the Turks was for conquest rather than administration, and so they used their conquered subjects to run the machinery of their empire. Some Greeks rose to high office; many even rose to the rank of Grand Vizier. Indeed, in the middle of the sixteenth century, the Venetians were reporting that the great offices in the Sultan's service were usually filled by Greeks and that many Turks were complaining of the favour shown to the Greeks. For some time the condition of this advancement was conversion to Islam, but about the middle of the seventeenth century the religious test was abolished for a number of the important offices of state, and in the following century the Grand Dragoman of the Porte (a secretary of state) was usually a Greek; so was the Grand Dragoman of the Fleet; and the Morea, too, was placed under a native governor.

Greek and Venetian Resistance

Although individual Greeks prospered in the Turkish empire, the Greek cause suffered; and when national and private interests clashed, the former only too often were sacrificed. This is not to say that all Greeks patiently endured the foreign yoke. Immediately after the conquest, assistance from the west had seemed possible, and there were many later proposals for a western crusade against the Ottoman power, but all these suggestions brought no substantial relief. A Spanish expedition in 1532, under the Genoese Andrea Doria, captured Coron and a great part of the Morea, but the Spaniards were expelled in the following year, and the Greeks were treated with great severity. Throughout the whole period of the

* W. Miller, *Essays on the Latin Orient*, p. 366 (Cambridge, 1921).

Turkish occupation, Christian bandits known as 'klephts' maintained a semi-independent existence in the more mountainous regions north of the Isthmus. They preyed upon the more peaceful people of the plains, and to combat them the Turks organized a Christian gendarmerie known as 'armatoli'. The exploits of both are recorded in the ballad poetry of Greece.

The Christian defence now fell upon Venice. The first Venetian-Turkish war of 1463–79, which cost Venice both Argos and Euboea, was followed by repeated outbursts of hostilities for over two and a half centuries. Modon, Coron and Lepanto were lost in 1500, and, with the Turkish capture of Nauplia and Monemvasia in 1540, the last foothold of Venice in the Peloponnese disappeared; on the other hand, the Venetians had acquired a hold upon the Ionian islands of Zante (1482), Cephalonia and Ithaca (1500). In the Aegean, the Northern Sporades, Myconos and Aegina were lost in the war of 1537–40. All that then remained to Venice were Crete, Tenos and the Ionian possessions.

Up to the middle of the sixteenth century, most of the islands of the Aegean, however, were still in western hands. The fall of the duchy of the Archipelago in 1566, and the capture of Chios from the Genoese in the same year, meant that the Turks were now in as complete control of the islands as of the mainland. The Turkish attack on Cyprus in 1570 produced a fresh outburst of warfare, and a large Christian fleet was collected with the help of the Papacy and of Spain. The Christian victory in the naval engagement off Lepanto (1571), famous though it has become, brought little relief to Greece. Roused by the prospect of help, the Greeks of the Peloponnese had risen to arms; but Christian counsels were divided; the last Greek resistance in Maina was quelled, and in 1573 the Venetians made a peace with the Turks that lasted until 1645.

During the seventy years of peace there were occasional Greek risings. In 1585 there was revolt in Acarnania and Aetolia, and again in 1611 there was another revolt around Janina. Early in the seventeenth century the restless people of Maina were also in rebellion and they were not reduced, in name at any rate, until 1614. During these years, and indeed during the whole period 1460–1684, piracy was a more important source of disturbance than revolt. The corsairs of North Africa, of Catalonia, Dalmatia, Genoa, Malta, Sicily and Tuscany, repeatedly plundered the coasts of Greece; some were Christians, some were Moslems, but, in any case, that made no difference to their victims. 'The unparalleled rapacity of these pirates devastated the maritime districts to such a degree that, even at the present day, many depopulated plains on the coasts of the Archipelago still indicate the fear which was long felt of dwelling near the sea.'*

During the Cretan war (1645–69) between Venice and the Turks, two rebellions were prompted by the Venetians in Greece. The Albanians of the Peloponnese rose in 1647, and in 1659 the people of Maina (who, incidentally, sold Christians to Turks as well as Turks to Christians) were able to sack Kalamata. By taking advantage of local feuds, the Turks were able to reduce the Mainates, many of whom fled the country to Italy and to Corsica, where their descendants still live around Cargese. These diversions in the Morea could not prevent Crete from falling into Turkish hands in 1669, except for the three fortresses of Grabusa, Suda and Spinalonga (Fig. 84).

The renewal of war between Venice and Turkey in 1684 brought greater success to the Christian cause. In 1683, the Turks had been repulsed from Vienna; their best soldiers were engaged in Hungary, and the moment seemed ripe for western interference in Greece. The Venetian forces were under Francesco Morosini, and he entered into negotiation with the peoples of the two historic centres of resistance to the Turk—Epirus and Maina. In 1684, he captured the Ionian island of Santa Maura, and by August 1687 he was the possessor of all the Peloponnese, except Monemvasia (not reduced until 1690). He marched north of the Isthmus and captured Athens, but failed in an attack on Euboea. After long negotiations, the Treaty of Carlowitz in 1699 gave Venice the whole of the Peloponnese.

The new province was in a sorry condition. Much of the land had gone out of cultivation; the neglect under Turkish administration had been aggravated by the destruction of war and by pestilence. According to one estimate, the population had fallen from over 200,000 inhabitants before the war to under 100,000. Venetian policy restored prosperity to the area; agriculture was improved; colonists were settled on empty lands, and many thousands of families arrived from the northern shores of the Gulf of Corinth. It has been estimated that the population of the province rose from 116,000 in 1692 to 177,000 in 1701, and to over 250,000 in 1708; and these figures are probably underestimates.† But although Venice improved the land, she failed to keep the sympathies of its people. The commercial policy of the Republic hampered the trade of the area; Venetian

* George Finlay, *A History of Greece*, vol. VII, p. 57 (Oxford, 1877).

† W. Miller, *Essays on the Latin Orient*, p. 418 (Cambridge, 1921).

soldiers were quartered on its inhabitants; there were religious difficulties between Roman Catholics and Orthodox. Soon, the Christian inhabitants of the peninsula forgot the evils of the old regime. In 1710, one French traveller found the Greeks of Modon wishing for their return under Turkish domination, and envying the lot of those Greeks who still lived under it.*

Such were the conditions, when, in 1714, the Turks, having defeated Russia, were free to attempt the recapture of the peninsula. The campaign of 1715 was marked by striking Turkish victories and by mutinies in the Christian garrisons. Even Maina acknowledged the Turk; Tenos, the last Venetian island in the Aegean, also surrendered; and, in Crete, the last Venetian fortresses were likewise lost. By the treaty of Passarowitz in 1718, Venice relinquished her claim to the Peloponnese. Her most eastern possessions were now the islands of Cerigo and Cerigotto. Although she still held the Ionian Islands and four nearby places on the mainland, she ceased, from this time onward, to be an important factor in the fortunes of Greece.

But although Venice was no longer a decisive influence in the Greek world, the Venetian interlude was not without result. The material prosperity of the Greek lands continued to improve, and Turkish policy henceforward made a conscious attempt to placate the Greek subjects of the empire. The people of the Peloponnese were exempted from the land tax for two years. Immigrants were exempted for three years, for the Turks were anxious to attract newcomers to settle on the wasted lands, and from this period dates another immigration of Albanians. At the heart of the empire, in Constantinople, an administrative aristocracy was developing among the Greek officials. Known as Phanariotes, from the 'Phanar' quarter of the city, these Greeks played an increasingly important part in administrative affairs during the eighteenth century. The four great Phanariote officers were those of dragoman of the Porte, dragoman of the Fleet, prince of Moldavia and prince of Wallachia. Around these great ones were crowds of minor Greek officials.

Moreover, if Venetian power was declining, so was Turkish power, despite the victory of 1718. The Turkish failure to take Vienna in 1683 marked the transition from an expanding to a declining Turkey. In the north-west, Austria, and in the north-east, Russia, were soon to press back the Turkish frontiers. With the eighteenth century, too, came the beginnings of an effort to make the Greek lands independent.

* A. de La Motraye, *Travels*, vol. 1, p. 333 (London, 1723).

Russian Interference

Of the two rising enemies of the Turk, Russia was to exercise the most decisive influence upon Greek affairs. Russian interest in south-east Europe was a natural corollary to the expansion of the Russian state under Peter the Great (1689–1725) and his successors, and the Russo-Turkish wars were an inevitable consequence of a Russian Black Sea policy. Russian imperial agents appeared in various parts of European Turkey to prepare their fellow-Orthodox Christians for the day of liberation. The possibility of active resistance, however, did not come until after the middle of the century. In the sixties, Russian agents were busily stirring up trouble in the historic centre of disaffection at Maina, and an English visitor to Greece in 1767 heard people frequently talk of their approaching deliverance through Russian aid. The Sultan appears to have shown but a careless contempt for these intrigues.

In 1768, Russo-Turkish war broke out over the question of Poland, and two brothers named Orloff at once proceeded to Greece to organize an insurrection. The hopes of Catherine the Great were so high that Voltaire even thought it possible that Constantinople might soon become the capital of the Russian empire. But the small Russian force that landed in the Peloponnese in 1769 failed to rouse Greek national feeling. Many Greeks had no wish to exchange one foreign ruler for another, and were not prepared to swear allegiance to Catherine. The result was a complete defeat of the Russo-Greek forces by the Turks at Tripolitsa. But if the Russians had failed in the Peloponnese, they had been successful north of the Danube; and, too, the Russian fleet that appeared in the Aegean succeeded in occupying many of the Cyclades, which were greatly depopulated owing to corsairs and emigration. The war was ended in 1774 by the Treaty of Kutschuk Kainardji, by which Russia secured a firm grip upon the north shore of the Black Sea, and obtained also an international sanction for the rights of the Orthodox Christians of the Turkish empire. This vague stipulation was to provide a pretext for Russian interference in the domestic affairs of the Turkish empire.

During the early years of the peace, both Greeks and Turks suffered greatly from bands of Albanians who had been employed in the Turkish army but who now ravaged far and wide, both in the Peloponnese and to the north of the Isthmus. The condition of much of the countryside was desperate. The population of the Peloponnese (excluding Maina) had again been reduced to 100,000, and it was estimated that about 80,000 people had either died or emigrated; many had gone to the Crimea; over 12,000 had gone to Istria. The Albanian marauders were not put down until the dispatch of a Turkish expedition to the Peloponnese in 1779; some Albanians were induced to settle peacefully, others were exterminated. After this there was considerable improvement in the countryside; even the restless Mainates were induced to pay regular tribute. Despite the plague of 1781–5, the population of the Peloponnese had almost trebled itself by the end of the century.

Russian interest did not abate after 1774. Catherine at one time suggested a restoration of the Byzantine empire, under her grandson, with Constantinople as its capital. Russian propaganda continued to be active in the Greek lands; a military academy for Greeks was established in Russia, and its pupils were selected from the principal Greek families by the Russian consuls. In 1783, a commercial treaty with the Sultan gave Greeks the right to trade under the Russian flag. From now onwards, Greek shipping spread actively over the Mediterranean, and increasing commercial prosperity contributed to the new sense of Hellenic unity that was developing during the years.

In 1787, Russo-Turkish antagonism once more flared into war over the question of the Crimea, and Russian agents scattered manifestos throughout Greece, inviting co-operation against the Turk. This succeeded in rousing the Albanian Christians around Suli, but it was evident that they were not sufficiently strong to provide a major diversion in the war. Nor were the exploits of pirates in the Aegean, infamous though they were, sufficient to turn the scales of warfare against the Turk. In 1792, Catherine, without consulting her Greek supporters, concluded the Treaty of Jassy with the Sultan; this treaty extended the Russian frontier to the Dniester in the north, and provided for a general amnesty for all Greeks involved in the war. By this time, however, a new factor in the form of the French Revolution had appeared to complicate the policies of all European states.

The Rise of Greek National Feeling

The struggle for Greek independence was to come about not merely as an instrument of Russian policy but as a result of rising national self-consciousness among the Greeks themselves. The French Revolution, breaking out in 1789, was a powerful stimulus to every people in Europe, and the enthusiasm of its rallying cries—Liberty and Freedom—found a responsive answer in Greece. One of the warmest supporters of the new ideas was Constantine Rhigas (1760–98), born at Velestino. It was he who wrote the famous Greek version of the Marseillaise, paraphrased by Byron as 'Sons of the Greeks, arise'. It was he, too, who founded the 'Hetaerea', a society to promote Greek patriotic sentiment and to provide the Greeks with arms. Believing that the influence of the French Revolution would shortly lead to action in the Balkans, he went to Vienna to organize the movement among exiled Greeks and their sympathizers. From here, he published many Greek translations of foreign works not in classical Greek but in the common tongue. He also formed a collection of national songs which, though not published until sixteen years after his death, was passed from hand to hand in manuscript, arousing patriotic enthusiasm everywhere in Greece. His work was cut short, for he was handed over by the Austrian government to the Turks and was shot in 1798.

The death of Rhigas did nothing to abate the intellectual ferment that was active among the Greeks, and one indication of this was the work of Adamantios Korais (1748–1833). He was the son of a merchant at Smyrna, though from 1782 onwards he lived in France (in Paris itself after 1788). Inspired by the French Revolution he devoted himself to furthering the cause of Greek independence. Laying great stress on the classical inheritance of the Greeks, he sought to methodize the written language of his country in accordance with classical tradition (see p. 320). The result, something between the classical tongue and the common speech, was not merely of academic interest; for, in Greece as in other countries, the codifying of the written language, so that it became intelligible to all peoples and classes, was a powerful factor in calling into being a new nation, and the name of Korais must ever remain an important one in the story of the Greek revolt. Nor was Korais the only man to work along these lines. In the Ionian islands, a school of writers was busily at work collecting folk songs to feed Greek patriotism with memories of its past glory and heroism. It is true they wrote in the popular tongue and did not follow the systematization of Korais, but both schools of thought were symptoms of an educational revival and of the new feeling of nationality in Greece.

Despite the great influence of the French Revolution upon Greece, the Revolutionary and Napoleonic wars hardly touched Greece itself. In 1797, the Venetian Republic was extinguished and the Ionian islands were occupied by the French as a stepping stone to the East. The general commanding the French troops was instructed: 'Be careful in issuing proclamations to the Greeks to make plenty of reference to Athens and Sparta'. Napoleon himself addressed the Mainates as 'worthy descendants of the Spartans who alone among the ancient Greeks knew the secret of preserving political liberty'. The common fear of French interference in Greece even drew together for a short time those irreconcilable foes, the Tsar and the Sultan; France was forced to evacuate the Ionian islands in the following year, and in 1800 they became a federal republic under the joint protection of Russia and Turkey. But the unnatural allies were soon at war, and in 1807 the islands were ceded to France. They were taken by the British in 1809–10, and emerged in 1815 as a protectorate under British control, and so they remained until 1864.

The Congress of Vienna in 1815 did not attempt to solve the problem of south-eastern Europe, and Greece remained part of the Sultan's domain. There were, however, signs everywhere of the new spirit of Greek nationality. The 'Hetaerea' of Rhigas had been revived at Odessa in 1814, and its influence now extended throughout European Turkey. Thus the Albanians in Greece felt as Greek as the Greeks, and were to play a great part in the liberation to come. A feeling of expectancy was evident among the Phanariotes of Constantinople as well as among the bishops of the Orthodox Church. Travellers who returned from Greece brought away the impression that a crisis was at hand.

In the meantime, Turkish administration continued steadily to decline. Inefficiency and corruption were to be met with everywhere. The local officials of the empire were straining after independence, and a series of rude shocks prepared the way for the Greek insurrection. Serbia had been in revolt since 1804, and an Albanian adventurer, Mehemet Ali, had become virtually independent in Egypt. Another Turkish official, Ali Pasha of Janina, had also become independent in Albania, and, with Turkish action against the rebel, a favourable moment had arrived for the war of liberation. The first outbreak against the Turk in Moldavia and Wallachia (1821) was soon quelled. But before this northern revolt was over, the Greeks of the Peloponnese had risen and the struggle for Greek independence had begun.

BIBLIOGRAPHICAL NOTE

1. It was at one time the fashion to decry the Byzantine empire, and Gibbon poured contempt upon it. Since then a large number of writers have reassessed the part played by the empire in the history of Europe and the Near East. An authoritative account, complete with exhaustive bibliographies, will be found in *The Cambridge Medieval History*, vol. IV (Cambridge, 1923). The volume is entitled *The Eastern Roman Empire* (717–1453), and is devoted entirely to the empire. A short attractive summary of the main features of the Byzantine civilization is given by Norman H. Baynes in *The Byzantine Empire* (London, 1925).

The following two books are particularly useful for a scholarly assessment of the evidence relating to the Slav immigration into Greece: J. B. Bury, *A History of the Later Roman Empire*, 395–800 A.D., 2 vols. (London, 1889); J. B. Bury, *A History of the Eastern Roman Empire*, A.D. 802–867 (London, 1912).

2. Much was done to rehabilitate the history of Byzantine and later Greece by the English scholar George Finlay who spent many years in Greece. His *History of Greece*, published between 1844 and 1862, opened a field that had hitherto been neglected by English writers. A new edition, revised by himself and edited by H. F. Tozer, was later published in 7 vols. (Oxford, 1877).

3. Not many English scholars have followed in Finlay's footsteps, but an outstanding exception is W. Miller. Like Finlay he lays stress on the fact that 'contemporary Hellas owes as much, or more, to the great figures of the Middle Ages as to the heroes of classical antiquity'. His *The Latins in the Levant* (London, 1908) is a detailed authoritative work covering the period 1204–1566. Another detailed work by the same author is *Essays on the Latin Orient* (Cambridge, 1921). This is a collection of articles and monographs originally published elsewhere. It deals mainly with Frankish Greece, but also has articles on Roman, Byzantine and Turkish Greece. A short and useful summary by the same author is *The Latin Orient* (S.P.C.K. London, 1920).

Another account of Frankish Greece, which summarizes earlier work on the subject, is Rennell Rodd's *The Princes of Achaia and the Chronicles of Morea*, 2 vols. (London, 1907).

4. An account of Turkish Greece may be found in vol. v of Finlay's *History of Greece* (see above). This may be supplemented by two articles on Turkish and Venetian Greece up to 1718 in W. Miller, *Essays on the Latin Orient* (see above), and by a short summary, *The Turkish Restoration in Greece*, 1718–97 (S.P.C.K. London, 1921), also by W. Miller.

An account of the general setting of the history of Turkish Greece can be found in J. A. R. Marriott, *The Eastern Question* (Oxford, 1924).

5. Of the many travel books written about Greece, two, by W. M. Leake, give an excellent and detailed picture of conditions in Greece between the years 1804–1810: *Travels in the Morea*, 3 vols. (London, 1830); *Travels in Northern Greece*, 4 vols. (London, 1835). These also contain a good deal of material about a number of other topics, e.g. the Slavs in Greece, the Frankish period.

Chapter VII

MODERN GREECE, 1821–1943

The War of Independence, 1821–1832: The Reign of Otho I, 1833–1862: The Reign of George I, 1863–1913: The Crisis of 1912–1923: Domestic Affairs, 1923–1941: Foreign Affairs, 1923–1941: Enemy Occupation, May 1941–December 1943: Bibliographical Note

The War of Independence, 1821–1832

The Preparation for War

The literary and classical revival of the late eighteenth century was merged with the ferment of ideas produced by the 'Enlightenment' and the French Revolution. But the rise of Russia at the expense of Turkey led the Greek clergy and people to renew an older and simpler dream of freedom, in which the expulsion of the Turks and possession of land were more prominent than the purification of language or ideas. The Greeks had never been fully disarmed: the *klephts* of the Peloponnese, half brigands and half patriots, had become more daring than ever. Napoleon sent emissaries from Italy to the Peloponnese in 1797, and hundreds of peasant warriors enlisted in the Ionian regiment of the French Republic, which had momentarily annexed these islands. Many Greeks looked also to Ali Pasha of Janina, who was conducting, with French backing, a spirited struggle for his own independence in Epirus. Finally, the Greek (and Albanian) sailors, particularly those of the islands of Hydra and Spezzia (Spétsai) off the eastern coast of Argolis, were rising in wealth and confidence, and felt little fear of the Turkish navy, which was manned by unreliable Greek crews and commanded by Turkish officers often ignorant of the sea.

The men who revived a more or less secret society, *Filikí Hetairía*, at Odessa in 1814 were rather revolutionary than traditionalist in temper; but their agents glorified Russia as the expected leader of a crusade. The meeting between Napoleon and the Tsar at Tilsit (1807) had been followed by a new Russian war against Turkey; and the Peace Treaty of Bucharest (1812) between Tsar and Sultan left a number of still unsettled disputes which might lead to a diplomatic rupture at any time. It was true that the statesmen at Vienna in 1814–15 agreed on a conservative system in Europe, and could ill afford an upheaval in the Balkans. But the Quadruple Alliance did not include any guarantee of the Turkish empire; while the Holy Alliance, and the character of Alexander I who initiated it, implicitly excluded any such idea. The Greek patriots expected help from the Tsar or at least from his Corfiot minister, Capo d'Istria. In spite of appearances, therefore, the Levant was in no such state of tranquillity as the Sultan, Metternich, and most of the European merchants desired.

The Struggle, 1821–1827

The War of Independence could not have been won by the Greeks without the armed intervention of foreign Powers; but, equally, the movement could hardly have been permanently suppressed if these Powers had held aloof. The Powers were led to intervene, partly in order to remove the deadlock which threatened constant disturbance and piracy in the Aegean, but also by the pressure of public opinion at home; and the very success of the Greeks in creating this deadlock was due rather to the spirit which animated them than to their physical resources in so unequal a struggle.

The signal for revolt was given in March 1821 by a raid upon Jassy and Bucharest from Russian territory; but this ill-considered enterprise was disavowed by the Tsar, and was finally suppressed in June without eliciting any sympathy from the Romanian peasantry. Meanwhile, in April, a spontaneous but ill-coordinated rising in the Peloponnese, led by the clergy, the 'primates' (landowners and magistrates) and many armed chieftains, began with a wholesale extermination of the Turks. Turkish reprisals, including the execution of the Patriarch at Constantinople, led to the departure of the Russian ambassador and a formal rupture of relations. For the next four years the other Powers attempted, with diminishing success, to prevent the revolt in Greece from becoming the occasion of a general attack by Russia upon Turkey, which might be followed by an upheaval all over Europe. England, no less than Austria, was anxious to keep the Tsar quiet; but, whereas Metternich hoped to see the revolt soon quietly suppressed, Canning began to see an opportunity either of intervening alone to England's advantage or, if that were impossible, of joining hands with the Tsar in order to keep some control over the issue. In either case, the Greeks were likely to profit.

In spite of personal, sectional and regional quarrels, much savage cruelty and a great lack of discipline, the Greeks showed themselves to be brave soldiers and skilful sailors. The Peloponnese was nearly cleared of the Turks, who failed to open the way for its reconquest either by way of Attica and the Isthmus or across the Gulf of Corinth. The Turks underrated their enemies and failed at first to secure the coasts and islands against the Greek ships under Andreas Miaoulis. During this respite the Greeks were unable to organize their government on a firm basis. An assembly, not recognized by rival bodies, produced in January 1822 a little-heeded 'Constitution of Epidaurus', and elected the Phanariote Alexander Mavrokordato as President. The military chieftains resented the attempt to form a regular government. But the 'European' Greeks had on their side both the wealthy islanders and the European Committees which were collecting funds (in England chiefly under Byron's influence); between them, they held the purse-strings, and by the end of 1824, their authority seemed to be well established.

Meanwhile, the Sultan purchased the help of his nominal vassal, Mehemet Ali, Pasha of Egypt, by allowing him to subdue and occupy Crete and by promising further rewards for the conquest of the Peloponnese. Miaoulis was no longer able to deny the sea passages to their combined fleets. Early in 1825, Mehemet's stepson Ibrahim landed an Arab army of more than 10,000 men at Modon in the south, and soon overran a great part of the Peloponnese, without, however, being strong enough to reduce it systematically. North of the Isthmus, Missolonghi (Mesolóngion) held out in the west until April 1826, two years after Byron's death there, and the Moslem forces could not recover Attica until the French philhellene Fabvier was forced to surrender the Acropolis in June 1827. By this time the prospect of foreign intervention was at last taking shape.

Foreign Intervention, 1827–1829

At the eleventh hour the Greek provisional government had just agreed on a compromise between the factions: the 'Russian' party of Kolokotronis and the chieftains secured in April the election of Capo d'Istria (henceforward known as Capodistrias) as President for seven years; the choice of Sir Richard Church and of Lord Cochrane to command the Greek forces on land and at sea was a concession to the 'English' party of the islanders and some of the primates; the 'French' party of Kolettes, whose support came mainly from north of the Isthmus, was satisfied by the publication in May 1827 of the extremely democratic 'Constitution of Troizen'. Nauplia was still in Greek hands, and Ibrahim, when he took the field again in April, still found so many centres of armed resistance that he adopted a new policy of systematic devastation among the vineyards of Messenia and Elis.

Before his death in December 1825, Tsar Alexander I had already ceased to discuss the Greek question with his continental allies, and leaned towards the more active policy which his successor Nicholas I was to pursue more resolutely. Canning disliked the double prospect of an Egyptian occupation in Greece and of Greek piracy in the Aegean, but he was hardly in a position to move alone in response to a Greek appeal for British protection (June 1825). The upshot was the Protocol signed by the duke of Wellington at St Petersburg on 4 April 1826. The two governments agreed to impose on both parties, by means of joint or separate mediation, a settlement giving to the Greeks, within unspecified boundaries, an autonomous but tributary status, with compensation for the Turkish proprietors. On 29 April the Assembly made a formal request for mediation on this basis, but staked out its claim for the future by arguing for the inclusion of every region, subdued or not, that had taken up arms during the revolt.

Even before the Protocol was signed, the Tsar sent an ultimatum to the Sultan requiring negotiation on outstanding Russo-Turkish disputes, and the resulting Convention of Akkerman (October 1826) was a diplomatic success for Russia. The Bourbon government of France, to whom a section of the Greeks had also appealed, desired to share, not in a revolution, but in a crusade. This prolonged but enlarged the negotiations. The tripartite Treaty of London (6 July 1827), signed during Canning's brief premiership, added little to the proposals of the Protocol, but an additional article provided for sending a combined fleet to Greek waters in order to enforce an armistice on both parties—'without however taking any part in the hostilities'. Both parties accepted the armistice, but neither Ibrahim on land, nor the English philhellene Hastings at sea, ceased operations. Stratford Canning at Constantinople went a little beyond his instructions by referring in a private letter to cannon-shot as the final arbiter; this was repeated by Admiral Codrington to his captains. By such ambiguities the governments were able to avoid direct responsibility for the decisive conflict in the Bay of Navarino on 20 October, when the Turkish and Egyptian fleets were destroyed by the naval squadrons of England, Russia and France. Metternich might call this encounter a 'frightful catastrophe', and Wellington, who came into office in January 1828, might describe it as an 'untoward event'; but the ambassadors had already left Constantinople, and England was not released from her obligations under the Treaty even if Russia should separately pursue the quarrel to the point of war.

The Egyptians soon evacuated the Peloponnese, after a mere show of resistance to a French force, which arrived in the name of the three Powers and which stayed there from 1828–33. But the Sultan would not yield. He had denounced the Convention of Akkerman and almost invited the Russian declaration of war (April 1828); nothing but a disastrous second campaign forced him to accede to the Treaty of London as part of the peace treaty signed at Adrianople (14 September 1829) in the presence of a Russian army.

The New Kingdom, 1829–1832

The future status and the frontiers of Greece were still undetermined. Wellington thought that a small independent state under a European sovereign would be less open to Russian influence than a larger territory still tributary to Turkey. As President, Capodistrias was somewhat unjustly suspected by England and France of being a tool of the Tsar. His services to Greece have been underrated, but in attempting personal rule he had not sufficient means of enforcing it; faction and anarchy culminated in his assassination (October 1831). Meanwhile Prince Leopold of Saxe-Coburg, soon to be the first king of Belgium, accepted and then declined the throne of Greece (February–May 1830); it was accepted in May 1832 by King Louis I of Bavaria, an enthusiastic philhellene, for his younger son Otho, then aged 17 (see table on p. 206). Delegates from Thessaly, Epirus, Chios and Crete attended the fourth National Assembly (August 1829), but these regions were in full Turkish occupation. Wellington wanted at first to liberate only the Peloponnese and the lesser islands, excluding even Euboea; but the three ambassadors in conference at Poros (December 1828) had recommended a more generous settlement, and public opinion could not conceive a Greece without Athens at least. The northern frontier, as offered to Leopold in 1830, ran south-westwards from the Gulf of Zeitoun to the mouth of the Aspropotamos; but Palmerston was able to secure for Otho in 1832 the line proposed at Poros in 1828, from the Gulf of Volos in the east to the Gulf of Arta (Amvrakía) in the west, including Acarnania but leaving the northern shore of both gulfs (and the southern point of the latter) in Turkish hands (Fig. 87). A Turkish garrison remained in the Acropolis until March 1833, and Athens was a mere village when it became the capital of Greece.

Among the islands, the ambassadors had proposed to include both Samos and Crete, with the support of Palmerston in opposition. But Palmerston in office could not or would not reverse the decision of 1830, which was based on the view that Samos (like Chios and Mitylene) was too near the coast of Asia Minor, and Crete too rich

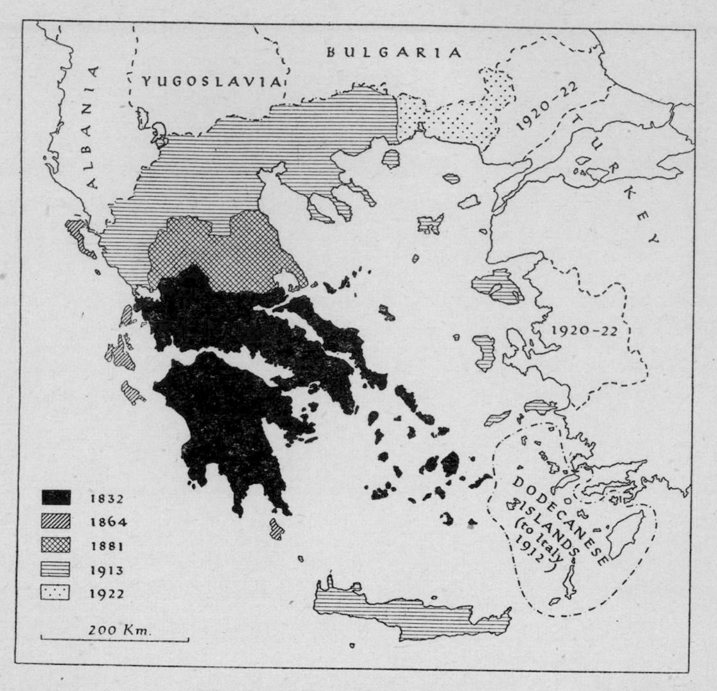

Fig. 87. The growth of Greece

Based on (1) R. Muir and G. Philip, *Historical Atlas*, p. 86, 6th ed. (London, 1924); (2) I. Bowman, *The New World*, pp. 403 and 515, 4th ed. (New York, 1928).

The frontier of 1881 was modified in 1897 when a number of small points were retroceded to Turkey. The Treaty of Sèvres (August 1920) gave Greece the greater part of Eastern Thrace and also Smyrna, the latter subject to a plebiscite in five years' time. These provisions came to nothing after the disaster of September 1922 (see p. 220), and were cancelled by the treaty of Lausanne (July 1923).

and distant a prize, with its strong Turkish minority, to be entrusted to the infant state. Samos obtained, and Chios recovered, a tolerably autonomous status, though Samos was badly misgoverned and Chios never recovered its old prosperity after the Turkish massacre of the islanders in 1822. Crete was restored to the Sultan in 1840 after fifteen years under Egyptian rule; two generations of periodical risings passed before the Turkish garrison was removed in 1898, and the Cretan Greeks' desire for full union with Greece was not satisfied until 1912.

The Reign of Otho I, 1833–1862

Since Leopold's withdrawal had been grounded partly on rumours of opposition, the Powers did not consult the Greeks in advance about their next choice. Russia stipulated against any Constitution as a condition of advancing her share of the promised loan of 60,000,000 francs from the three Powers. The Bavarian Regents for the young King Otho, who landed at Nauplia on 6 February 1833, determined to administer the country from the centre, giving office only to the most 'European' Greeks such as Trikoupis, Kolettes and Mavrokordato. Bavarian ministers soon gave place to Greeks; but, on coming of age in 1835, Otho himself presided over his Cabinet. Much was gained in the first ten years of Bavarian rule, but the leaders and veterans of the revolution were ill content, and some of them kept the tradition of local insurrections alive for many years. Officials nominated and removable by the Crown filled the place that had been occupied under the Turks by the primates and clergy in a crude form of local self-government. The establishment of an autocephalous state Church was unpopular, lacking the consent of the Patriarch until 1852, and coming from a king for whom as a Roman Catholic no Orthodox rite of coronation was possible. Centralization, police supervision, taxation and statistics became the order of the day.

Although the bloodless revolution of September 1843, which forced the king to promise a Constitution, was managed by the military men, Orthodox and Russian in their sympathies, the first prime ministers under the Constitution of 1844 were Mavrokordato, who was associated with the 'English' party, and then his rival Kolettes, who was favoured by the French. Both of them shared the official belief in centralization; but, whereas the former wanted the Greeks to put their modest house in order before looking to expand, the latter shared the more popular view that expansion was the first condition for improvement. Wearing the national dress and surrounded by patriots of the 'national party', Kolettes gained the sympathy of the king, and still more of the energetic queen. After his death in 1847, memories of the War of Independence were kept alive in the names of succeeding ministers. It was intended that the nominated Senate

(Yerousía) of twenty-seven members should be a conservative check upon the Chamber of Deputies (Voulí) elected by universal manhood suffrage, but in practice the Senate soon became a platform for criticism by the Opposition.

Nationalist sentiment was stirred by Palmerston's over-hasty blockade of the Piraeus in 1850 for the sake of dubious monetary claims (a proceeding endorsed by a small majority in the Commons but censured in the House of Lords), and more permanently by the rising agitation in the Ionian islands for union with Greece. Since the islands had come under British protection in 1815, successive governors had done much to improve their material prosperity, already proportionately much greater than that of Greece itself. But the constitutional reforms of 1849, greatly relaxing the constraints imposed in 1817, did no more than past coercion to allay unrest. The Greek character of the islands emerged from beneath the upper layer of Italianate society on which the English government, like its Venetian predecessors, had hitherto relied for support.

The progress of nationalist and democratic feelings was not in itself a danger to the dynasty. The king and queen were now thorough 'Greeks', and were never so popular as when their impulse to support insurrections in Epirus and Thessaly during the Crimean war was rudely checked by an Anglo-French military occupation of the Piraeus (1854–7). But after 1859 the Greek desire to imitate Garibaldi could hardly be shared by the German king, although he would not agree to renounce future attempts against Turkey as the condition for accepting Lord John Russell's offer of the Ionian islands. At the same time, a new generation of politicians was growing up, nursed at the University of Athens in the principles of the French Revolution; the rising spirit of opposition was heralded by the election of Epaminondas Delegeorges to the Chamber in 1859. In October 1862 a rising in Acarnania, following a revolt in February of the garrisons at Nauplia and elsewhere, brought the king and queen hurriedly back in their yacht from a voyage round the coastal ports, only to find the garrison of Athens in revolt and a provisional government already set up. They sailed away on 24 October and retired to Bamberg, where the ex-king died four years later.

Otho was somewhat pedantic and Amalia often impulsive; but later generations have given a more generous recognition both to their sincerity and to the progress of Greece under their rule. In thirty years, population and shipping had alike been doubled, and foreign trade (no doubt at its lowest ebb in 1833) had been more than quadrupled, only to be more than doubled again in the next decade. Athens had grown from a village into a small city, and Piraeus from nothing into a busy port. Without repudiating a special relation to the protecting powers, the king had done his best to make Greece a state more nearly independent in fact; and, without adding to its territory during his reign, he had rather encouraged than repressed the assertion of its future claims.

The Reign of George I, 1863–1913

The revolution itself was bloodless, but faction spread into minor civil war, while the three Powers tried to find a new ruler. In order to exclude a nephew of the Tsar, who was favoured by the Russians and the French, the British government insisted on respecting the Protocol of 3 February 1830, which disqualified members of the Powers' reigning families. In spite of this, the National Assembly ratified an overwhelming plebiscite in favour of Prince Alfred, Queen Victoria's second son; but three months later they accepted the second son of the heir to the Danish throne, whose supporters in the plebiscite (like those in favour of a Greek by birth) had numbered only six. This settlement was embodied in a Treaty between Denmark and the three Powers (13 July 1863); in October, after 30 years, the Greeks again welcomed a stranger aged 17 as their king (see table on p. 206).

A speculative hope, which had moved many to ask for Prince Alfred, had become a public assurance with the proposal for the Danish Prince—England's free consent to the union of the Ionian islands with Greece (Fig. 87). The cession of the islands, completed by a Treaty between Greece and the three Powers on 29 March 1864, was partly a sacrifice, but also a means of escape from a diplomatic deadlock and a relief from trying to govern in face of a Greek unionist Assembly. The islanders gained at first moral rather than material satisfaction; the upper classes were ill content, and the clergy objected to the inevitable transfer of authority from the Patriarch at Constantinople to the Synod in Athens. Yet the cession was an unprecedented gesture by a Great Power, and an immense gain to Greece in wealth, population and prestige, and also in the admixture of an aristocratic culture which had never been subjected to the Turks and was rooted in centuries of Venetian rule.

The title of George I as 'King of the Hellenes' (not 'King of Hellas') indicated that he must be a constitutional or even a democratic

MODERN GREECE: DYNASTIC TABLE

(1) *Bavarian House*

Maximilian I, Elector (1799), then first king (1805) of Bavaria, d. 1825

Louis I, King of Bavaria, abd. 1848

Maximilian II, King of Bavaria

Otto = Amalia of Oldenburg
b. 1816. OTHO, King of Greece, 1833. abd. 1862, d. 1866

(2) *House of Schleswig-Holstein-Sonderburg-Glücksburg*

Christian IX, King of Denmark, b. 1818, d. 1906

Frederick VIII,
King of Denmark

Alexandra = Edward VII,
King of England

b. 1846, William = Olga of Russia
became GEORGE I, King of the Hellenes, 1863;
assassinated, 1913

CONSTANTINE = Sophia of Prussia
b. 1868, King of the Hellenes, 1913
Compelled to withdraw, 1917, in favour of Alexander
Returned, 1920, on Alexander's death
Abd. 1922, in favour of George, who had withdrawn with him in 1917; d. 1923

George, High Commissioner
in Crete, 1898–1906

3 other sons
1 daughter

b. 1890, GEORGE II = Elizabeth of Romania
King of the Hellenes, 1922
Withdrew, Dec. 1923, without abdicating

ALEXANDER
King of the Hellenes,
1917, d. 1920

Paul

(REPUBLIC, 1924–1935)

George II Restored, 1935. Withdrew during German invasion, 1941; set up Greek Government in England and, later, in Cairo.

ruler. It is a tribute to his tact that he was able for nearly fifty years to keep his footing in the system set up by the Constitution of 1864 (see p. 239), with only occasional resort to the dismissal of an undefeated ministry or to his right of forming an extra-parliamentary Cabinet. The first crisis of the reign was occasioned by the condition of Crete. Behind the tale of fiscal, judicial and educational grievances was the desire for union or at least for autonomy, which inspired the desperate struggles of the insurrection of 1866. The proposal of Napoleon III and the Tsar for an open Cretan plebiscite was supported by all the Powers except England; but neither Derby nor Gladstone would contemplate anything more than autonomy. The Sultan formulated an Organic Statute which became the nominal law for the next ten years. Feeling in Athens had been running high in favour of combining support for the Cretans with a new bid for Thessaly and Epirus; but in February 1869 a new premier had to agree, under pressure from the Powers in conference, to a declaration renouncing aggression against Turkey. Another set-back for Greek ambitions was the creation of the Bulgarian Exarchate in 1870 by the Turks at the prompting of the Russians (see p. 353): for different reasons, both saw the advantage of isolating Orthodox Slavs in European Turkey from the Greek influence of the Patriarch. About the same time, internal quarrels were aggravated by nice questions of constitutional legality.

Factious passions, easily aroused, were as easily forgotten in a common wave of patriotic feeling during the Russo-Turkish War of 1877–8. But the Greeks had little sympathy for the Slavs in revolt, and still less for the increasingly Pan-Slav policy of Russia. Their public resolution 'to occupy the Greek provinces of Turkey' (2 February 1878) came too late, and was followed so quickly by an armistice between Russia and Turkey that the Greek army never marched. Volunteers supported a short-lived movement in Epirus; the more serious risings in Thessaly and Crete were brought to an end by the mediation of British consuls and by the Turkish undertaking at San Stefano to adhere more strictly to the Organic Statute in Crete and to extend its principles to the provinces of Turkey in Europe. At the Congress of Berlin, which undid the Slav character of the Russian Treaty of San Stefano (Fig. 88), England unsuccessfully supported the Greeks' claim to direct representation, but secured for them an undertaking by the Powers to press upon the Sultan an improvement in their northern frontier so as to run from the mouth of the Salamvrias (Piniós) to that of the Kalamas (Thíamis) opposite Corfu.

The Turks were resigned to the loss of Thessaly, the richer but more indisputably Hellenic region; but they clung to Janina, Preveza and Arta in the west—a region which they and the Moslem minority described as part of 'Albania', while to the Greeks it formed a part (and only the southern part) of 'Epirus'. Finally a Conference, from which Greece was excluded, led to a Convention (24 May 1881)

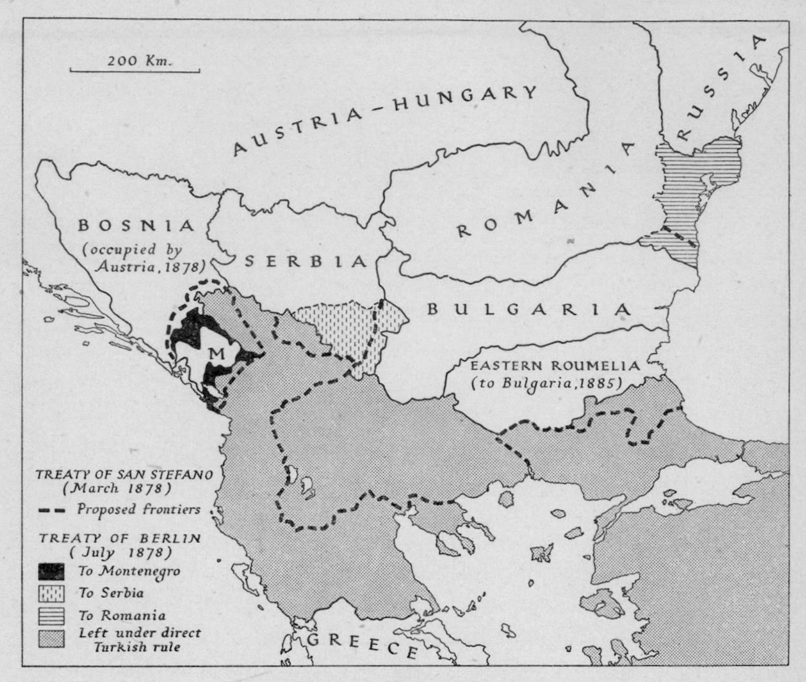

Fig. 88. The Balkans in 1878

Based on (1) *The Cambridge Modern History Atlas*, map 119, 2nd ed. (Cambridge, 1924); (2) C. Grant Robertson and J. G. Bartholomew, *An Historical Atlas of Modern Europe*, plates 23–25, 2nd ed. (Oxford, 1924).

It is interesting to compare this with Fig. 98 showing the limits of the Bulgarian Exarchate created in 1870, and with Fig. 99 showing the ethnographic limits of Bulgarians according to a Bulgarian source. *M* indicates Montenegro.

which left Janina and Preveza to Turkey but gave to Greece the town and district of Arta as well as almost the whole of Thessaly (Fig. 89). The Cretan Christians were for the moment not ill-satisfied with the concessions made in the Pact of Halepa (October 1878). The Greeks of Cyprus, who had unexpectedly become British subjects in 1878, were as yet more grateful for liberation from Turkey than critical of the fiscal burdens and constitutional restrictions of virtual Crown Colony rule.

Fruitless mobilizations, in 1881 and again in 1886, only added to the public debt. The bellicose Deligiannis, premier for the first time in 1885, was ousted by his senior and more realistic rival Trikoupes, whose periods of office, now as earlier, were spent in trying to make good by economic reforms the expenses of the 'National Party's' policy of expansion. Trikoupes lived to appease the beginnings of a

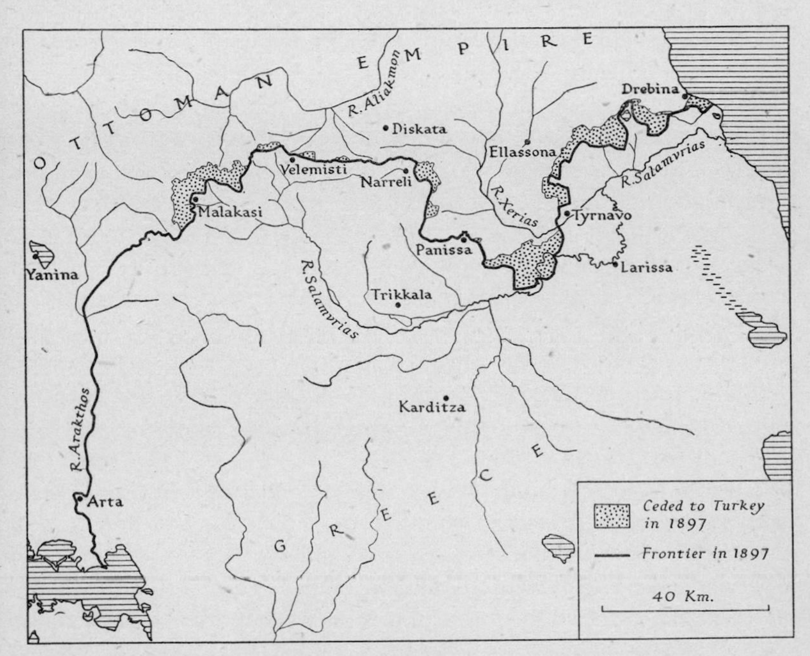

Fig. 89. Rectification of the Turco-Greek frontier, 1897

Based on 'Map to illustrate the rectification of the Turco-Greek Frontier in 1897'. Lithographed at the Intelligence Division, W.O., Feb. 1898 (I.D.W.O. no. 1317): the map is on a scale of 1 : 400,000.

new outbreak in Crete (1889), but died in 1896, at the moment when the inability of Turkish governors to restrain the Moslem minority produced the final insurrection. This time, in spite of the Powers, Deligiannis was supported by the king as well as by all parties in arming for war, both in Crete and on the continent. Turkey replied to the incursion of irregular bands into Macedonia by a declaration of war (April 1897): a month later, the Powers had to intervene to save the nation from defeat and the dynasty from overthrow in a conflict undertaken against their advice. Certain strategic points along the northern frontier were retroceded to Turkey, and the Powers instituted a Commission of Control over sufficient Greek revenues to serve the interest of the indemnity to Turkey and of older national debts also. One half of the Cretan problem was settled (November 1898) by a four-Power occupation of the chief towns and by appointing as High Commissioner the Greek king's second son, Prince George, who did much to pacify the island and to make its autonomy a reality. After a disagreement with his Cretan councillor, Eleutherios Venizelos, and a proclamation of union with Greece by the Cretan opposition, Prince George resigned in 1906: the island was being rapidly and peacefully hellenized under his successor, and the remaining international troops had just been withdrawn, when the Near-Eastern crisis of 1908 produced another but still premature proclamation of union.

In Macedonia, the Sultan had discovered an ideal method of fostering Balkan rivalries by showing favour in turn to the different 'nationalities', which he there misgoverned. After the creation of the Exarchate in 1870, Bulgarian churches and schools had been at first encouraged. But the creation of a virtually independent Bulgaria in 1878, and the inclusion of Eastern Roumelia in 1885, followed by the growing violence of Bulgarian agitation after 1895, led the Sultan to show some favour to the Serbs of Macedonia, and also to the Vlachs, whom the Romanians had lately begun to claim as their kinsmen. It suited the Turks in 1905 for the first time to give the Vlachs distinct privileges, in such a way as to instigate a diplomatic rupture between Romania and Greece (see p. 361). Of the rival claims in Macedonia, the Sultan most feared those of the Greeks and made fewest concessions to them. In spite of the Powers' programme of reforms (1903), the reign of terror of the Bulgarian Macedonian Committees became so bad that in 1904 the Greeks organized rival armed bands under klephts and even army officers. In 1905, the Sultan was forced by a naval demonstration to accept the measures of international control, which had been arranged by the Powers and were later prolonged in March 1908 for six years. But the experiment had done little to pacify the province before it became the starting point of a novel and momentous revolution.

Since the suspension in 1878 of the Turkish Constitution, hastily conceded two years earlier, Abdul Hamid had enjoyed an Indian summer of bureaucratic power. Administrative despotism and foreign control were alike resented by a party of 'Young Turkish' reformers;

their secret 'Committee of Union and Progress', founded at Geneva in 1891, was transferred to Paris and then in 1906 to Salonica, where it spread rapidly among the army officers, with the sympathy of the Jews and Freemasons. When Enver Bey proclaimed the Constitution in Macedonia and threatened to march on Constantinople, the Sultan gave way the next day, 24 July 1908, and the Powers optimistically agreed to withdraw their controls. But the proclamation of Prince Ferdinand as independent 'Tsar of the Bulgarians', and the simultaneous annexation of Bosnia and Herzegovina by Austria (5–7 October 1908), combined with dissensions in the Young Turkish Parliament to produce a counter-revolution at the capital (13 April 1909). Thereupon the Committee's Macedonian army marched on Constantinople, deposed Abdul Hamid (27 April 1909), and came to terms with Bulgaria and Austria at the expense of the Serbs, whose friends in Russia failed them.

The Greek government stood aloof from this crisis in the history of the Turks and the Balkan Slavs, and also dared not accept the renewed proclamation of union made by a Cretan provisional government. Although the remaining European troops left the island, the Young Turks insisted on forcing Greece under threat of war to disavow the agitation in Crete, Macedonia and Epirus, and to place the future of Crete once more in the hands of the Powers (August 1909). This humiliation led to the seizure of power at Athens by the newly formed Military League of officers, who were dissatisfied with the handling of the Cretan question; they invited to Athens the Cretan leader Venizelos, who was technically a Greek subject. Victorious in the elections which followed his appointment (18 October 1910) as prime minister, Venizelos succeeded in persuading the Military League to dissolve itself in return for such a revision of the Constitution of 1864 as should make military intervention in politics unnecessary; this was carried out (January–June 1911) by the 'Second Revisionary National Assembly' (see p. 241). The elections for the next ordinary Chamber (25 March 1912) gave him 150 out of 181 members, including all but one of those from north of the Isthmus: always his popularity was to be greatest in the newest and frontier regions, and least secure in the conservative Ionian Islands.

Venizelos's advent to power began a stormy period of triumphs and disasters, of which King George I lived only to see the beginning: on 18 March 1913 he was assassinated by a Greek in the newly occupied city of Salonica, after the virtual union of Crete to Greece and a few months before the fiftieth anniversary of his accession. Between the unhappy Turkish war of 1897 and the appointment of Venizelos as prime minister in 1910, the king's prudent restraint prevented criticism of the dynasty from becoming serious; before and after those dates he had been generally popular. During his reign, the Ionian islands, Thessaly and Arta, and finally Crete, had been incorporated (Fig. 87); population had been trebled and its density doubled; foreign trade and the tonnage of merchant shipping had alike been more than trebled. Brigandage had been much reduced, nearly 4000 km. of roads and over 1000 km. of railway constructed, and the way was now opening at last for connexion by rail with Europe. Unfortunately, the corruption of politics and the violent intervention of the army had not been eliminated by the surgical operation of 1911.

The Crisis of 1912–1923

The Balkan Wars, 1912–1914

The First Balkan War. The Balkan peoples soon perceived that the Young Turks were more nationalist than liberal. Then in September 1911 the Italians took occasion to make war on Turkey for the possession of Tripoli and Cyrenaica, which they had long coveted; they brought pressure to bear by occupying Rhodes, Kos, Leipso and ten islands of the Dodecanese (April–May 1912). A congress of island delegates declared, however, for union with Greece, and the Treaty of Lausanne (18 October 1912), which ended the war with Turkey, provided (in vain) that the Italians should leave these islands as soon as the Turkish evacuation of the two African provinces (now known as Libya) should be complete (see p. 221). Thus the Turkish revival, and the ambitions of Italy, gave the Greeks new reasons for thinking that no time must be lost in making sure of their share in the 'Turkish inheritance'.

Venizelos had already renewed relations with Romania and made overtures to Bulgaria. Bulgaria first negotiated with Serbia a Treaty of Alliance (13 March 1912), followed by a Military Convention (12 May), envisaging offensive action against Turkey and providing for the division of the spoils; her Treaty with Greece (29 May) remained defensive in form, but was soon followed by a Military Convention. By September 1912, Montenegro had also come to understandings with the three larger Balkan States. Early in October she declared war on Turkey, the other three States sent an ultimatum which could have but one answer, and the Greek Chamber completed the annexation of Crete by admitting its deputies and appointing a governor. On 17 October Turkey declared war on Montenegro, Bulgaria and Serbia, but made a bid for Greek neutrality. Venizelos, however, with his eyes on Macedonia, fulfilled his obligations to Bulgaria by declaring war on Turkey (18 October). The Greeks took a full share in the sweeping victory of the Balkan Allies. The army of the Crown Prince Constantine cleared southern and western Macedonia and entered Salonica on 8 November, only to be joined there by a rival and suspicious Bulgarian force. The armistice signed on 3 December 1912 did not include the Greeks, but the Turks acquiesced, under pressure from the Powers, in the full demands made by the Allies at the London Conference. Thereupon Enver Bey overthrew the government, repudiated the terms and renewed the war on 3 February 1913; but Janina surrendered to the Greek Crown Prince on 6 March (twelve days before he became king Constantine), Adrianople fell to the Bulgarians, and Scutari to the Montenegrins. By the Treaty of London (30 May 1913) Turkey ceded collectively to the Balkan Allies all her territory in Europe (apart from Albania), except Constantinople and its approaches within a line drawn from Enez (Aínos) on the Aegean to Midia on the Black Sea. Crete was finally ceded to Greece, but the fate of the Turkish Aegean islands and of Albania was to be settled by the Powers.

The Second Balkan War. The previous decision of the Powers (20 December 1912), under pressure from Austria and Italy, to accept the principle of an independent Albania, thus depriving Montenegro of Scutari, Serbia of access to the Adriatic, and Greece of 'Northern Epirus', led directly to the second Balkan War. The partition of Macedonia became more crucial than ever. In face of Bulgarian provocations, Serbia and Greece made an alliance on 2 June, and replied to a Bulgar attack at the end of the month by a general advance. In a short but bloody campaign, the Serbs invaded Bulgaria, the Greeks seized the whole of Macedonia and most of the Thracian coast, and the Romanians took the opportunity to occupy the southern Dobrudja without firing a shot. By a Treaty with Bulgaria signed at Constantinople on 29 September 1913, Turkey recovered Enez, Adrianople and Kirk-Kilisse, which it had already reoccupied, and also pushed the frontier a little northwards from Midia on the Black Sea. The Treaty of Bucharest (10 August 1913) between Bulgaria and her Balkan enemies gave most of Macedonia to the Greeks; the eastern frontier now reached the Aegean at the mouth of the Mesta (Néstos), excluding Xanthe but including the coveted tobacco port of Kavalla (Fig. 90).

The peace treaty between Greece and Turkey (14 November 1913) left to the decision of the Powers the two most important questions of the islands and Albania. Among the Turkish Aegean islands, nine had been occupied by the Greeks during the war; in addition, the

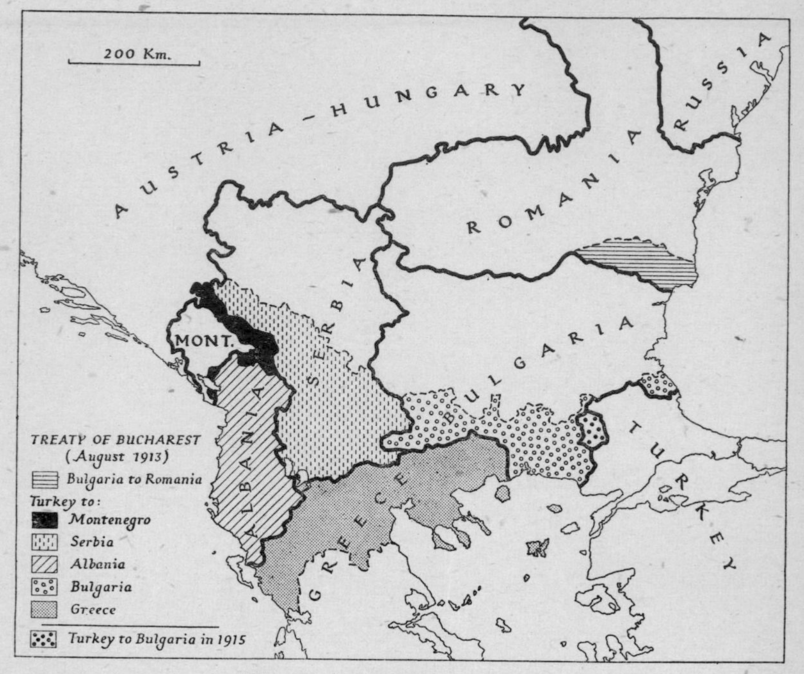

Fig. 90. The Balkans, 1912–13
Based on C. Grant Robertson and J. G. Bartholomew, *An Historical Atlas of Modern Europe*, plate 25, 2nd ed. (Oxford, 1924).

Assembly of Samos, which had often been in conflict with its princes, proclaimed union with Greece, and was officially annexed by a Greek force on 15 March 1913. In February 1914 the Powers recognized Greek sovereignty over all these islands except Tenedos and Imbros; but for the Italians, the Greeks would no doubt have occupied the Dodecanese also during the Balkan War. The Powers made it a condition of their award that the Greeks should withdraw from those districts of northern Epirus (Santi Quaranta, Chimarra, Argyrokastro and Koritza) which they had occupied during the war but now had to surrender to the new state of Albania. But before the

Greek troops had gone, the Greeks in these districts obtained a limited autonomy under international supervision by an arrangement made at Corfu on 17 May. Prince William of Wied, the chosen ruler of Albania, who arrived at Durazzo in March, had no authority outside that port and little enough within it.

The War of 1914–1918

Thus the outbreak of the European War in August 1914 was for the Greeks, as for their Balkan neighbours, only the intensification of a crisis which had begun two years earlier. The first signs of the fateful rift between King Constantine and Venizelos appeared at once. Both men were popular, Venizelos as architect of the Balkan alliance and Cretan union, Constantine for his leading part in the Balkan campaign. But their sympathies in the war, as well as their expectations of its outcome, were sharply opposed. The king admired the German army, and declined with regret an invitation from his brother-in-law the Kaiser to join the Central Powers. The Cretan statesman was more impressed by the naval power of the Entente countries (also the original guarantors of Greece), by their economic ties with Greece, and by the strength of their case in the eyes of the world. Having assured Serbia that, although he could not move against Austria, he would help her to repel any Bulgarian attack, he made it clear (23 August) that Greece would be ready to join the Entente Powers against a Turkish attack in return for a guarantee against the Bulgarian danger. A fortnight later, having got their leave to reoccupy northern Epirus, he advised the king to concert plans with the Allies for an occupation of Gallipoli; but Greece remained neutral when England declared war on Turkey (5 November). In two further memoranda to the king (January 1915), he supported England's invitation to reconstitute the Balkan alliance by surrendering Kavalla to the Bulgarians in return for Allied promises of 'important compensations' on the coast of Asia Minor. In February, he persuaded a Crown Council of former prime ministers to recommend the dispatch of one division to Gallipoli.

Dismissed by the king (6 March), Venizelos kept a majority of nearly 60 at the elections held on 13 June, returned to office on 23 August, and at once renewed his pledges to Serbia against a Bulgarian attack. When Bulgaria mobilized in September, he persuaded the reluctant king to mobilize too, and to invite France and England to supply the army that Serbia lacked; before Constantine could change his mind, French troops began to disembark at

Salonica. On 4 October the king again dismissed him, and again dissolved the Chamber after it had defeated the new ministry. This government, controlled by the Palace and the General Staff, was pledged to 'benevolent neutrality' towards the Allies and to the view that the Treaty with Serbia applied only to a purely Balkan conflict. Serbia was overrun before Allied help could reach her, and Venizelos's liberal party abstained from the elections (19 December). A Bulgarian force was allowed to occupy Fort Roupel, one of the keys to eastern Macedonia (May 1916).

Greek confidence in the Allies' intentions had not been improved by the Treaty of London (26 April 1915), which was known to have assigned the Dodecanese to Italy in full sovereignty, and to have arranged a partition of Albania more favourable to Italy than to Greece. Confidence in the Allies' power was also weakened by their inability to help Serbia or to force the Dardanelles. With the fall of Venizelos, the Allies, distrusting the king's no longer benevolent neutrality, introduced martial law at Salonica, replaced the Greek troops in Epirus by Italians, and demanded the demobilization of the Greek army, a 'non-political' government and fresh elections. Venizelos sailed for Crete, appealed to the Greeks to 'save what may still be saved', landed at Salonica (5 October 1916) and there organized a provisional government which soon declared war on Germany and Bulgaria.

Greece now had two governments: that of Venizelos, supported throughout the newly won regions, but not yet formally recognized by the Allies beyond the limits of its actual authority; that of Constantine, supported by his League of Reservists in the provinces of old Greece, and behaving so as to make itself intolerable to the Allies. The king gained by Athenian resentment at the drastic measures of the Allies, who expelled the enemy legations from Athens, obtained full control of the Piraeus and of the recently completed railway to Salonica, and punished Greek resistance to a landing party (1 December) by blockading the coasts and insisting on the removal of all Greek troops and equipment to the Peloponnese. America's entry into the war (April 1917), and the failure of the king's appeals to Berlin for an attack on Venizelist Macedonia, forced him to show less open hostility to the Allies; but they in turn had lost patience, and presented an ultimatum requiring his immediate abdication, and intimating also that the Crown Prince George, suspected of pro-German sympathies, would not be acceptable. The next day (12 June 1917) King Constantine appointed his second son

Alexander in his place, avoiding a formal abdication, and left Greece with his family for Switzerland. The French deported some of his supporters to Corsica, and occupied Athens.

At the end of June 1917 Venizelos, as prime minister of a reunited government, declared war on the Central Powers and recalled the Chamber of June 1915, all but ten of whose members joined in a vote of confidence. A large number of anti-Venizelist civil servants and officers were removed, and, although most of the former had been

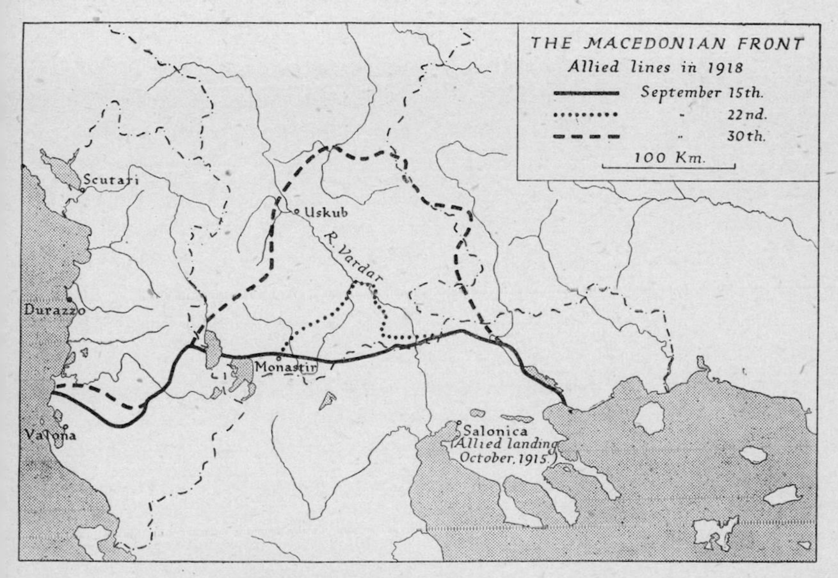

Fig. 91. The Macedonian Front, 1918

Based on H. W. V. Temperley, *A History of the Peace Conference*, vol. IV, p. 14 (London, 1921).

The allied line was held by Italians, French, Greek, Serbian and British troops; facing them were Germans west of the valley of the Vardar and Bulgarians to the east.

reinstated by 1920, many of the latter remained as an irreconcilable and dangerous element in politics. The Allied army had been pinned at Salonica for a year after landing there in October 1915. With the help of Serbian forces brought there from Corfu, they had been able in November 1916 to recover at Monastir a small corner of Serbian territory; in July 1917 a pact signed at Corfu announced the projected union of the Yugoslavs in a single state. By the spring of 1918, 250,000 Greeks had been remobilized. But it was not until September 1918 that the combined French, English, Greek and

Serbian armies began the offensive which led to the capitulation of Bulgaria, the abdication of King Ferdinand (4 October), the recovery of Belgrade, and the signature of an armistice by Turkey on 30 October 1918 (Fig. 91).

The Peace Settlement, 1919–1923

The personality of Venizelos impressed itself strongly at the Peace Conference. Once more Bulgaria paid dearly for the miscalculations of her rulers: by the Treaty of Neuilly (27 November 1919) she was partly disarmed and had to restore the southern Dobrudja to Romania, while Greece not only recovered eastern Macedonia but also cut Bulgaria off from the Aegean by obtaining western Thrace with the small port and railway of Dedeagach (renamed Alexandroúpolis). The Treaty stipulations for giving Bulgaria economic outlets to the sea were to be a cause of endless argument: while the Bulgarians looked for the recovery of Dedeagach, and the Greeks offered alternative facilities by rail westwards to Salonica, both parties were too suspicious to agree upon the natural solution—a direct and not very difficult outlet by rail from Sofia down the Struma valley to Salonica.

In spite of the armistice terms, the Turks could not easily be disarmed in Asia Minor, and the final settlement with them was long delayed by dissensions among the Powers, by the rashness of the Greeks, and by the revolution which was recreating Turkey herself. The Greeks wanted to keep the future of Constantinople open by making it an international city, and were represented in the Allied garrison there. Asking for a large part of the coast of Asia Minor, they were allowed in May 1919 to occupy Smyrna and in December to reoccupy northern Epirus. Early in 1920, in view of the unexpected strength of the hostile Kemalist movement, the Allied Supreme Council decided to keep the Sultan at Constantinople but to allow the Greek army to pacify both Thrace and Asia Minor northwards from Smyrna to the Dardanelles.

The Treaty of Sèvres (signed on 10 August 1920 but never ratified) was highly favourable to Greek ambitions: Greece was to obtain Adrianople and all eastern Thrace to Chatalja within 20 miles of the capital, together with Gallipoli and the northern shore of the Sea of Marmora (subject to an International Commission for the Straits). Smyrna and its hinterland were placed under Greek administration, with provision for a local parliament which might opt after five years for incorporation in Greece (Fig. 87): Venizelos's aim was to provide a check on Turkish nationalism and a refuge for the Greeks of Asia Minor (scattered, but numbering a million or more) in case of oppression. Turkey ceded all the Aegean islands which had already been occupied, but the fate of some remained uncertain until 1923 (see below).

The population of Venizelist Greece had swollen in eight years from under three to six and a half millions. But the triumph was short-lived. The country was exhausted by war and prolonged mobilization, and exasperated by the corruptions of adventurers attached to Venizelos's party and profiting by his absorption in making war or peace. Six weeks after the Chamber had unanimously endorsed the treaties, the accidental death of King Alexander (25 October 1920) fatally revived the one issue that Venizelos most wished to avoid. His preference was for a constitutional monarchy, and he offered the Crown to Constantine's third son, Prince Paul; but Paul refused it, as properly belonging to his father or his elder brother George. Venizelos's opponents then all combined to defeat him by more than two to one at the elections (14 November), and, after his departure and the removal of his officials, arranged a plebiscite (5 December) in which the Venizelists abstained and all but a handful of over a million Greeks voted for the return of King Constantine. A fortnight later the king reached Athens after more than three years of exile. Probably the revival of Turkey and the jealousy of Italy would have deprived even a Venizelist Greece of the full harvest of the Treaty of Sèvres; in addition, the Allies now refused to recognize Constantine and withdrew their financial support. France made haste to secure herself in Syria by a reconciliation with Ankara (20 October 1921). In England, Mr Lloyd George's pro-Greek policy was feared, not only in official quarters as likely to offend Moslem sentiment in India, but also by the public as likely to delay complete demobilization.

Meanwhile the three Powers (England, France and Italy) which met in London (February–March 1921) to discuss a revision of the Treaty of Sèvres in Turkey's favour, were confirmed in their views by the failure of a preliminary Greek attack (March–April). In a second offensive, the Greek army came within 60 miles of Ankara (July), but had to retreat again after a costly defeat at the River Sakaria (26 August). Constantine, who had rejected Allied offers to mediate in the spring, now placed the fate of Greece unconditionally in the hands of Lord Curzon and the Powers (December 1921), and carried on at home a policy of revenge against the Venizelists. His minister Gounaris ignored one defeat in the Chamber (March 1922); and, although he resigned in May when he could no longer conceal the Powers' proposals (note of 26 March) for the evacuation of Asia Minor, he formed a new coalition. At the end of August the Turks took the offensive and entered Smyrna a fortnight later (9 September 1922). Most of the city was burned to the ground amid the confusion of escaping Greek civilians and soldiers (see p. 378). Before resigning, the Greek government ordered demobilization of the demoralized army.

The consequence of this disaster haunted Greek politics for fifteen years or more. When Colonel Plastiras headed a revolution among units of the army assembled in Chios, King Constantine abdicated (September 1922) in favour of his eldest son George II (who had been excluded as pro-German by the Powers two years earlier), and died next year at Palermo. Six of his leading advisers, including his prime minister and commander-in-chief, were among those tried by a revolutionary court martial of eleven officers (only two of whom, however, were Venizelists), and were shot on 29 November 1922. This unusual violence was due to panic, and to revulsion in Athens against a government which had long concealed by grandiose promises the real weakness of Greece's changed situation. The execution of civilian politicians shocked those of other countries, but Lord Curzon, presiding over the Conference which had just met at Lausanne, did not break off relations with the revolutionary government.

The settlement with Kemalist Turkey was at last completed by the Treaty of Lausanne (24 July 1923). For the most part, the treaty merely confirmed the changes in the Treaty of Sèvres already brought about by intervening events or decisions of the Powers. The elimination of the Greeks from Asia Minor was a fact which the Powers, themselves in part responsible for the adventure, could only temper by the arrangements made for an exchange of populations (see p. 379). A revision of the frontier in Thrace had already been settled at Paris in March 1922, and Turkey now recovered the line of the Maritza which she held in 1914. In November 1921 the Conference of Ambassadors had restored northern Epirus to Albania, with the frontier of 1914. Tenedos and Imbros, reserved for Turkey in 1914 but occupied by the Powers during the war and handed over to Greece after the Treaty of Sèvres, were now to be demilitarized along with the Greek islands of Lemnos and Samothrace.

An agreement, wrung from Italy by Venizelos at the height of his power (29 July 1919) and confirmed in 1920 by the Treaty of Sèvres, had assigned to Greece the islands of the Dodecanese, with the important exception of Rhodes which was to exercise an option by plebiscite within five years (1919) or fifteen years (1920) after the supposed case of the cession of Cyprus to Greece by England. This agreement was repudiated by Italy in 1922, the Treaty of Sèvres being still unratified; and at Lausanne all these islands were ceded by Turkey unconditionally to Italy. The Italians argued that their first conditional promise of evacuation, made to Turkey in 1912, was overridden by the Allies' offer of the islands to Italy in the Treaty of London (April 1915) and by the state of war with Turkey which followed; and that their second promise of evacuation, made in 1919–20 in favour of Greece, was overridden by the non-ratification and general revision of the Treaty of Sèvres, and by the non-fulfilment of the condition which applied only to Rhodes. But the real reason lay in their *de facto* occupation since 1912 and in their intention, carried out gradually, of developing naval and air bases there. The islands remained directly under the Italian Foreign Office, and the inhabitants had no chance of expressing any desire for union with Greece.

Cyprus, with about 350,000 inhabitants (one-fifth Turks), had been occupied by England in return for her services to Turkey in 1878, annexed in 1914 when she declared war on Turkey, and momentarily offered to Greece in October 1915 on the unfulfilled condition that Greece would immediately enter the war. But England promised France in 1916 not to alienate Cyprus (so near to Syria) without French consent; its cession by Turkey to England at Sèvres was confirmed at Lausanne and it became a Crown Colony in name, as it had long been in effect, by Letters Patent of 10 March 1925. At the same time the number of elected members of the Legislative Council was increased, but not so as to give an elected Greek majority. The annual tribute of about £93,000, due to Turkey by the Convention of 1878, had been assigned from the first to the service of the Ottoman debt; proving a heavy burden on the island, it was soon partly offset by variable grants from the Treasury (fixed in 1910 at £50,000), and then wholly remitted (1928) in return for a small annual contribution of £10,000 for imperial defence. The island was not used as a strategical base, and was somewhat neglected. In 1925 and 1929 the elected members petitioned for redress of grievances and for union with Greece; the decisive rejection of the latter demand by both Conservative and Labour governments did not put an end to financial and educational grievances. A budget dispute in 1931

led to riots at the capital and demonstrations involving about one-third of the villages. As a result of this episode, the Legislative Council was suspended. The agitation for union, which hardly existed before 1919, met with some sympathy in Greece, but no encouragement from Venizelos; it was hampered by the islanders' knowledge of the much heavier financial burdens laid on post-war Greece.

The Treaty of Lausanne put an end to an almost continuous foreign crisis of more than ten years' duration. The Greeks, discouraged but acquiescent, began to see that their 'Great Idea' could hardly be realized in full and that defence of their gains by reconcilation with their neighbours was more urgent than further expansion. In spite of recent set-backs, those gains were great indeed. But reconciliation abroad was bound to be slow in coming, at least while the domestic crisis was still unsolved.

Domestic Affairs, 1923–1941

The Republic of 1923–1935

After the abdication of Constantine in September 1922, the country had to face the issue between Republicans and Royalists—an issue easily confused with that between Venizelists and anti-Venizelists (see p. 242). The Populists, who favoured a democratic monarchy, abstained from the elections (December 1923), in which the Venizelists won 200 and the Republicans 120 seats; but the latter had such energetic backing from officers of the army and navy that the young King George II left Greece without formally abdicating. Invited by the National Assembly, Venizelos made a brief reappearance as prime minister (January 1924), but returned to Paris when his proposal for a plebiscite, to be followed by a general election, was opposed by the Republicans. Supported by the Republican Officers' League, the new premier Papanastasiou first used a vote of the Assembly to proclaim the Republic on 25 March 1924 and then held a plebiscite (13 April) in which more than two-thirds of the voters confirmed his action.

In June 1925 the leader of this Officers' League, General Pangalos, overthrew the next ministry, dissolved the Assembly which had completed the draft of a Constitution, issued by proclamation a modified Republican Constitution (30 September 1925), and promised to submit it for ratification after fresh elections. But in January 1926 he announced his intention to concentrate all executive and administrative powers in his own hands, postponed any election indefinitely, and suspended the whole of the new Constitution except the first Article which declared Greece to be a Republic. Security of tenure for the civil service was suspended, and newspapers were forbidden to publish any protests. Without extolling dictatorship in principle, Pangalos professed to be overriding Athenian party politics in the interests of the country as a whole, and promised to revive the Constitution with increased powers for the President shortly to be elected. By skilful manœuvres he secured his own election as President in April 1926. Four months later he was overthrown by General Kondilis, a former associate whom he had exiled. After dissolving the Republican Guard of Pangalos by force, Kondilis thereupon offered to dissolve his own party (National Republicans) and to give up the premiership after the general election fixed for November 1926. This example of public spirit made possible a Coalition government of leading Royalists and Republicans to match a Chamber in which the latter had only a small majority. Under Republican pressure, and working on the previous Assembly's draft of 1925, the new Chamber at last adopted the final text of the Republican Constitution on 2 June 1927 (see p. 243). But the resignation of the Royalist Tsaldaris, and then of the Republican leader Papanastasiou, soon weakened a hitherto surprisingly successful coalition.

Venizelos still corresponded with friends and supporters in Greece, and his figure loomed large. After a long visit to Crete he came to Athens in March 1928, reassumed the leadership of his old party, and on 3 July took office once more, forming a government which was supported by two-thirds of the new Chamber. Once more his record during four and a half years of power (1928–1932) was to be one of striking success in foreign policy and of growing difficulties at home. At home, his construction of a Senate under the Constitution of 1927 had no popular appeal, he was unable to promise lower taxation, and his wise reconciliation with Turkey in 1930 (see p. 227) was denounced by Royalists as betraying the interests of Greece. In principle a constitutional monarchist, he thereby lost the full confidence of the Republicans; in practice friendly to the republican experiment and long opposed to the restoration of any member of Constantine's family, he was thereby exposed to the unjust imputation of being nothing more nor less than a Venizelist. The currency crisis of 1931 began a ding-dong struggle in which Venizelos was first momentarily defeated by the Republicans in the Chamber and then lost ground in two successive elections (September 1932, February 1933) to the 'Populist' party of the moderate Royalist Tsaldaris. When Venizelos resigned for the third and last time in nine months, Tsaldaris once more formed a government (10 March 1933), restoring the decided Royalist Metaxas as Minister of the Interior and the anti-parliamentary, now almost Royalist, Kondilis as Minister of War, but dropping Papanastasiou, the symbol of republicanism in the last two Cabinets.

Tsaldaris remained in office for two and a half years, and presided over the transition to monarchy. His party held a majority in the Chamber, but the Venizelists in opposition controlled the Senate, which was thus able to block measures passed by the Chamber. The opposition argued that in such a case a joint meeting of Senate and Chamber was obligatory; the Government, that it was merely permitted (see p. 244). Extreme Royalists like Metaxas were in favour of suspending the Constitution, on the ground that the Senate's obstructive tactics made government impossible. On the other side, the Republicans alleged, not without reason, that ministers supported by the Populist party were undermining the Republican Constitution by favouring the movement for restoration of the monarchy. General Plastiras, who had begun the revolution in Chios in 1922, twice attempted a Republican military coup (March 1933 and March 1935). On the second and more serious occasion, the insurgent officers were overpowered in Athens, and Plastiras's own movement in Macedonia was forestalled at Salonica. When the cruiser *Averoff* put to sea with some smaller ships and joined the movement, Venizelos, who was in Crete, was momentarily persuaded to lead it, but he soon withdrew to Rhodes and thence to Paris, while the warships surrendered themselves to the government. This episode probably convinced him that the Royalists had the upper hand; he was to give a provisional blessing to the restored monarchy before his death on 18 March 1936. The attempted coup was followed by some death sentences, and by a purge in the civil service and the army. The Chamber was then dissolved, the Senate abolished, and the security of tenure of judges and civil servants suspended. The Liberals and Republicans abstained from the elections held on 9 June 1935, so that the monarchists almost monopolized the new Chamber; but the extreme Royalists were still a minority among them.

A fifth National Assembly for constitutional revision empowered the government to hold a free plebiscite; but General Kondilis, backed by the most decided enemies of the Republic, first forced Tsaldaris to declare himself openly for a monarchy, then replaced him as prime minister (10 October), got the new Chamber to declare in favour of the monarchical form of government and the Constitution of 1911, and himself became regent in the name of King George II. After all this, the plebiscite (3 November 1935), in which 97% of the votes were said to have been cast in favour of the king's return, was merely a matter of form. The Republicans alleged that the secrecy of the ballot was not observed, and that many Royalists cast more than one vote. Against this, it was argued that the Greeks were tired of the Venizelist feud with Constantine's family, and had postponed a change until now only through fear of civil war and loss of political liberties. But, with their rapidly increasing economic dependence on Nazi Germany (which hurt the towns but benefited the peasantry), the tide was setting not only against the Republic but against constitutional monarchy too.

King George II and General Metaxas, 1935–1941

King George II, who had lived mostly in England since he left Greece in 1923, attempted reconciliation by discarding the parties which had secured his return in November 1935. He insisted on a general amnesty, got rid of Kondilis, who died shortly afterwards, and dissolved the Chamber with a view to constitutional revision by a new National Assembly. But the free elections held in January 1936 produced a deadlock like those of 1933, exposing incidentally the unreliability of the recent plebiscite: fifteen Communists held the balance between 143 Monarchists and 142 Liberals, Republicans and Agrarians (see p. 250). On the death of the king's non-party premier Demertzig in April, General John Metaxas, who did not share the king's belief in the value of parliament, obtained the consent of the Chamber to an adjournment for five months, governing meanwhile by decree. His path was smoothed by the death of several political veterans—not only Kondilis (31 January) and Demertzig (13 April), but also Venizelos (18 March) and Tsaldaris (15 May). Konduriotis, the first President of the Republic (1924–1929), had died in August 1935; his successor, Zaimis, who had also formerly been ten times prime minister, died in September 1936 at the age of 81. Nevertheless, Metaxas met with obstruction from the political parties and from the recently appointed legislative commission of forty deputies. The Communists' appearance of strength was accidental, but he used their threat of a general strike to convince the king that constitutiona monarchy was impossible in Greece and to get his consent to decree dissolving the Chamber and declaring martial law (4 August 1936) No date for new elections was fixed, and constitutional guarantees o liberty of the subject were suspended (see p. 247).

The virtual dictatorship inaugurated by General Metaxas, i imitation of Mussolini and Hitler, was still unshaken when he die in January 1941, successfully defending his country against th Italian attack, and before the onrush of the German invaders. Hi dictatorship was more intelligent than that of General Pangalos te years earlier. In a broadcast address (10 August 1936) he began b appealing to the youth of Greece against outworn politicians, partie and parliaments. He announced and partly carried out a programm of social reforms, coupled with rearmament. Without pursuing hi initial suggestions for a 'corporative State', he introduced minimun wages, insurances and maternity benefits, organized youth move ments and started a ten-year programme of public works (see p. 338) Since the depression which started in 1929, the Greeks had alread doubled wheat production and increased industrial output by mor than 50%, in an effort to reduce imports and so offset the fallin market for their two main export crops—tobacco and currants Clearing agreements with Germany enabled them to sell these crop at high prices in Reichsmarks; but these marks remained in German as a credit fund with which Greece might buy (also at high prices such armaments and industrial products as Germany could spare— not always what Greece most wanted. Finding a large unused credi in Reichsmarks, Metaxas had no choice but to buy from Germany but he declared his readiness to trade with England if she woul undertake to buy a definite quantity of tobacco or currants.

Opposition to the new regime continued for a time. The Athenian disliked a censorship which affected not only the press but Universit studies and even the speeches of Pericles, or Antigone in the theatre moreover, a form of government which silenced opposition wa certainly distasteful in principle to the country as a whole. But afte some critics had been banished to the islands in 1938, there was n more trouble. The Greeks knew that it was not easy for them t combine political liberties with unity, in face of dangers fron authoritarian neighbours. When war came, the Republican officer were allowed to rejoin the army and the Greeks were united as the had never been during the war of 1914–18.

Foreign Affairs, 1923–1941

Relations with Turkey

The problem of migration and resettlement, which overshadowed all else for some years after 1922, was partly domestic and partly international. Few countries have had to undergo such an upheaval as this migration, which suddenly increased the population of Greece on balance by about 20% without adding to its territory and within a few months of military defeat and political revolution (see p. 368).

The gradual absorption of the refugees made possible the reconciliation with Turkey which was the main achievement of Venizelos during 1928–1932. The negotiations, begun in 1929, were hindered by fears of naval rivalry, which Venizelos allayed by advising the Chamber to build light craft only. A final Convention about the exchange of populations (10 June 1930) prepared public opinion for his visit to Ankara and signature there of a Treaty of neutrality, conciliation and arbitration, a Protocol on parity of naval armaments, and a commercial Convention (all signed 30 October 1930 and ratified 5 October 1931). The Greek people followed his lead and ceased to look on the Turks as their natural enemies. Old ambitions were tacitly abandoned. 'The ghost of the Roman Empire, which had so long haunted the Near East, was finally exorcised.' Relations continued to improve: in 1932 Greece warmly supported the admission of Turkey to the League of Nations, and a ten-year agreement for consultation and guarantee of frontiers was signed on 14 September 1933. Nor did Greece make any objection to the Montreux Convention of 20 July 1936, by which Turkey recovered full strategical control of the Straits, and Greece incidentally regained the right to fortify the islands of Lemnos and Samothrace.

Relations with the Balkan Powers

The Pact of 1930 between Greece and Turkey was preceded by other Balkan agreements. Both parties acknowledged the help of Italy, which had already made its own pacts with Turkey (30 May 1928) and with Greece (23 September 1928). Greece already had a pact with Romania (21 March 1928); in announcing the pact with Italy, Venizelos declared that the question of the Dodecanese no longer existed, and soon afterwards (November 1928) he made an agreement with Albania. By the treaties of November 1926 and November 1927 Albania had become almost a protectorate of Italy; Mussolini was anxious to strengthen his position there by promoting

Balkan pacts under Italian patronage rather than under that of France, Yugoslavia and the Little Entente. The Yugoslav government, fearing isolation in the Balkans, ratified at last its conventions of 1924 and 1925 with Italy, and accepted Venizelos's offer (October 1928) to negotiate on outstanding differences. Yugoslavia had taken offence in 1924 at the terms of a Greek agreement with Bulgaria about minorities, and had denounced the alliance of 1913; negotiations for its renewal had failed in 1925. A settlement (1926) of Yugoslav claims relating to port and railway facilities at Salonica was rejected by the Greek Chamber in 1927; but the initiative of Venizelos led at last to the signature of six protocols relating to these claims, and of a pact between the two countries (27 March 1929). Yugoslavia was linked with Romania in the Little Entente, and had a pact with Turkey dating from 1925. A Bulgarian Treaty with Turkey (6 March 1929), and an agreement with Yugoslavia on frontier questions only (26 September 1929 and 14 February 1930), added to the links in this chain of pacts, which was greatly strengthened by the reconciliation between Greece and Turkey; Bulgaria, the one 'unsatisfied' Balkan state, was still on bad terms with Greece and had no general pact with Yugoslavia; the differences between them were hard to bridge, and public opinion was suspicious in all three countries. With this exception, the moment seemed favourable for discussion of a Balkan entente or even of a Balkan federal pact. Common economic problems pointed in the same direction.

In October 1930 the first of a series of unofficial 'Balkan Conferences' was held at Athens. Greek, Turkish, Yugoslav, Romanian, Albanian and Bulgarian delegations were present, together with observers sent by the governments. The initiative came from Papanastasiou, the Republican leader, and Venizelos gave it his blessing. The Conference agreed on a regular constitution, chose a Balkan flag and hymn, advocated an annual meeting of foreign ministers, and set up a committee to draft a Balkan pact against war, and for mutual help. Other committees suggested postal union and co-operation in the fields of social legislation and economics. But Bulgaria protested, with sympathetic Italian comment, because the agenda excluded concrete applications of minority questions and confined discussion to the general principles. A second unofficial Balkan Conference was held in October 1931, when 200 delegates were welcomed by the Turkish government at İstanbul and afterwards by Kemal himself at Ankara. This Conference initiated a Balkan Chamber of Commerce but made little progress in the direction of a draft Balkan pact: the Bulgarians reopened the minorities question, and even threatened to raise the still more thorny question of revision of frontiers. The third Conference met at Bucharest in October 1932, and the fourth at Salonica in November 1933, both continuing the non-political discussions, but avoiding consideration of a political pact. A fifth Conference, arranged for Belgrade in 1934, was cancelled owing to Yugoslav fears that it might endanger the progress of their separate negotiations with Bulgaria, which had just produced a commercial treaty in May 1934. Official discussions between Greece and Bulgaria had been confined mainly to the subject of financial claims; a temporary settlement made in 1927 was upset by the Hoover moratorium on war debts (1931), and a final settlement, discussed in 1933, was delayed by Bulgaria's refusal to abandon her claims for revision of the peace treaties.

The modest success of these unofficial Conferences, and still more the need to resist revisionist claims which had the support of Italy and Germany, led Greece, Turkey, Yugoslavia and Romania, in spite of Bulgarian abstention, to sign a Pact (9 February 1934), including a mutual guarantee of frontiers and promise of consultation. A protocol explained that the obligations of the Pact would arise if any Balkan state should join another Power in aggression against one of the signatories. But the force of this protocol was lessened by declarations which excluded any obligation for Turkey to fight Russia or for Greece to fight any greater Power; the Turks feared that revisionist Bulgaria might join Russia in attacking Romania, the Greeks that she might join Italy in attacking Yugoslavia. With these reservations the Pact was ratified by the Greek Senate, and registered at Geneva in October 1934. Meeting again at Ankara in the autumn, the same states adopted statutes for a Balkan Entente, modelled on those of the Little Entente—a combination equally opposed to revision of the peace treaties.

The Balkan Pact of 1934 reflected a certain distrust of Italy, which was deepened by the Franco-Italian agreement of January 1935; Greek opinion in particular was very hostile to Italy throughout the Abyssinian dispute. When 'sanctions' had been withdrawn in July 1936, Italy assured these states that she intended no retaliation; but the visit of Dr Schacht to Athens in June, and German press discussion of collaboration between Germany and Italy in the Balkans, made the value of such assurances doubtful. Nevertheless, General Metaxas, in power since April 1936, was generally considered to be an admirer of Italy and Germany; in the Balkan Conference at Belgrade (May 1936) he showed that he was anxious to minimize the commitments of Greece under the pact, at least until his programme of rearmament should have made some progress. He was well aware that Greece must take account of the British navy, as well as of the German or Italian army, and showed less readiness than Bulgaria to submit completely to German economic predominance. But in Balkan politics he preferred isolation, at the risk of having to fight Bulgaria without support, to far-reaching security pacts involving the danger of conflict with the Axis Powers. Holding that the interests of Greece were Mediterranean, not continental, he clung to the friendship of Turkey and tried to avoid giving offence to the protagonists in the impending conflict. Romania also leaned towards isolation after the fall in August 1936 of M. Titulescu, a leading exponent of 'collective security'. The mood in the Balkan capitals began to be that of *sauve qui peut*.

It was natural that Yugoslavia, conscious that the solidity of both the Little Entente and the Balkan Entente was weakening, should seek to reinsure herself elsewhere. Her pact with Bulgaria (24 January 1937), although vague and brief, was intended to have the same symbolic importance as the pact between Greece and Turkey seven years earlier. Her political and commercial treaties with Italy (25 March 1937) were more warmly welcomed in the Italian than in the Yugoslav press. For the sake of breaking up the Little Entente, it cost Italy nothing to make reassuring statements about her intentions in Albania, and it was worth while for Germany to relax for a time in Italy's favour her own economic hold on Yugoslavia. In spite of being partly responsible for it, both Greece and Romania felt misgivings about the new Yugoslav policy, but they made the best of it by joining next year with Yugoslavia and Turkey in coming to terms with Bulgaria. This Pact of Salonica (31 July 1938) appeared to restore and extend the common front of the Balkan States; but the four 'satisfied' states, whose Pact of 1934 had originally been directed against Bulgaria, now had to admit her on terms which showed how the successes of the revisionist 'Axis Powers' had weakened their own position. Bulgaria still did not undertake to guarantee existing frontiers, and legalized her own rearmament by getting release from the military clauses of the Treaty of Neuilly (1919) in return for nothing more than a promise not to seek revision by force.

Relations with Italy and Germany

Revision by force soon became the order of the day. When Mussolini followed up Hitler's destruction of Czechoslovakia by suddenly incorporating Albania, England and France came forward with unilateral guarantees to Greece and Romania (13 April 1939). These were followed, first by Anglo-Turkish and Franco-Turkish joint declarations (May–June) for mutual aid against aggression which might lead to war in the Mediterranean area, and then (after the outbreak of war) by the tripartite Treaty of 19 October 1939 for the same purpose; but a protocol released Turkey from any obligation which might involve her in war with Russia. This treaty indirectly linked Greece, as the friend of Turkey, with France and England. But the Greek government did nothing to provoke Italy, accepting an assurance (10 April) of her 'intention to respect absolutely the integrity of both the Greek mainland and islands', and agreeing in September to reaffirm the principles of the pact of 1928 between the two countries. At the same time Metaxas made it quite clear that Greece would defend her territory against attack from any quarter.

After the outbreak of war in Europe, the Greek press was confined by the censorship to a strict neutrality, but public opinion was very hostile to Italy, and friendly towards the British and American democracies, however strongly impressed by the continental power of Germany. The collapse of France so weakened the position of England and Turkey in the Mediterranean that Italy made bold to enter the war; and at the end of June 1940, Romania's forced surrender of Bessarabia to Russia destroyed the whole structure of the Balkan Entente, which had been reaffirmed at its Conference in February. Mussolini's reiterated assurances of his friendly intentions towards Greece began to be blended with threats and accusations that Greece was allowing England to violate her neutrality. The Greek government was bombarded by Italian complaints, Greek ships were attacked by 'unknown' aircraft, and on 15 August the light cruiser *Helle*, bedecked with flags in the harbour of Tenos for the Feast of the Assumption, was torpedoed by an 'unknown' submarine. This outrage completed the conversion of Greek opinion to the cause of England even in her darkest hour, and the Greek government began to mobilize unobtrusively, supported by Turkey and by a renewed British guarantee (5 September). While Germany encouraged Bulgaria and Hungary to carve up Romania, and then sent her own troops to occupy the remnants, Metaxas could still prove his neutrality by fresh commercial negotiations with Germany and by a private appeal to Hitler to restrain his Italian ally. But after the meeting between Hitler and Mussolini at the Brenner Pass on

4 October, the German press began to talk openly of a military occupation of all the Balkan states as the prelude to an assault on Egypt.

At 3 a.m. on Monday, 28 October 1940, the Italian Minister in Athens presented an ultimatum, demanding free passage for Italian troops, 'with full respect of Greece's sovereignty'. He was surprised when Metaxas refused, and astonished when the Greeks actually resisted the Italian forces, which crossed the frontier in Epirus half an hour before the ultimatum expired at 6 a.m. Outnumbered, and hampered by very great difficulties of supply, the Greeks not only maintained their own ground but pushed forward on to ground almost as familiar and equally difficult. In November, the still 'neutral' German Legation in Athens was sporting a flag in honour of the fall of Koritzá to the Greeks. On 6 April 1941 the German armies, assembled in Bulgaria, crossed the Greek frontier without notification, and entered Athens three weeks later; not until then did the Greek army in Epirus surrender to the Italians. The British expeditionary force, which the Greeks dared not invite until the last moment, had done its best under impossible conditions before the greater part of it was re-embarked with difficulty towards the end of April. Metaxas had died on 29 January 1941, and his successor as President of the Council (Korizis) took his own life in despair; but the king and his government still hoped to carry on the struggle on Greek soil with the British forces in Crete. Before the end of May, however, he and they had to leave the last of the Greek islands for Egypt. The Germans began their attack on Crete on 20 May, and on 1 June came the decision to withdraw British forces from the island.

Enemy Occupation, May 1941–December 1943

Greece has been most severely affected by Axis occupation. Mass executions have taken place, especially where resistance to the invaders has continued; poverty and starvation are acute throughout the country; the death-rate has risen alarmingly; anti-semitic measures have been enforced, but with no Greek support; many priests have been killed, others have become leaders of resistance; labourers have been deported, and pro-Allied sympathizers imprisoned or shot; Greek law and government have disappeared entirely in certain areas; education has virtually ceased; and the press and radio are German controlled.

Zones of Occupation

From May 1941 until the fall of Mussolini at the end of July 1943 Greece was occupied by German, Bulgarian and Italian forces (Fig. 92). The Germans kept control of all key positions, especially airfields and ports; they maintained a general supervision of the Greek coasts, and, with the increasing sabotage on bridges and railways, they took over most of the railway lines in the north. Apart

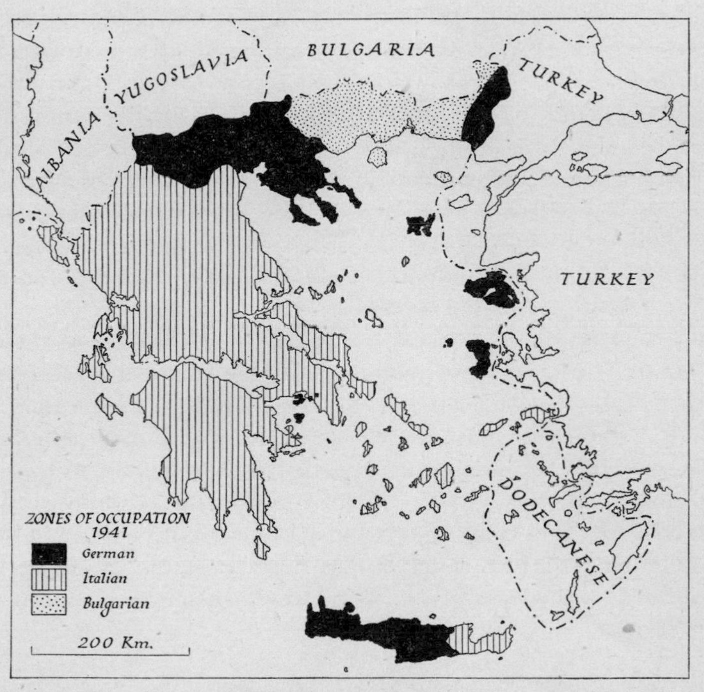

Fig. 92. The Occupation of Greece, 1941

Based on official sources.

from this general control, they also occupied five key regions: the frontier region with Turkey, along the right bank of the river Évros; the islands of Límnos, Lésvos and Khíos in the eastern Aegean; the greater part of Makedhonía, between the Strimón in the east and the Aliákmon in the west; the Athínai-Piraiévs district and the islands of the Saronic Gulf; and finally, central and western Kríti, which provided a base for the North African campaign.

The Bulgarians, anxious to fulfil their dreams of a 'Greater Bulgaria', occupied the territory between the Strimón on the west and the German-occupied Évros zone on the east. No formal statement of annexation has been made, but every form of Greek government has been swept away; the Greek gendarmerie and priests of the Orthodox Church have been expelled, and all teaching is given in Bulgarian. It is estimated that over 100,000 inhabitants of this region, who did not wish to claim citizenship of the 'Greater Bulgaria', have been removed.

The Italians occupied the greater part of Greece until July 1943, but in many districts their control was only nominal, partly because key positions were held by the Germans, and partly because of the rising power of the Greek patriots. Like the Bulgarians in western Makedhonía and Dh. Thráki, the Italians virtually annexed the Ionian islands. With the fall of Mussolini, unrest increased amongst the Italian troops; some were withdrawn, others were disarmed, and others clashed with German forces. By 24 September they had lost their grip on the last of the Ionian islands, and the Germans had recovered control throughout Greece, except, of course, for those regions held by Greek guerrillas.

During July, the Germans had announced that in view of the general war situation, and, in particular, the increasing activities of the guerrillas, a stronger occupation of Greece was necessary. As a result, German security forces were reinforced, and the supreme power, even in Bulgarian-occupied districts, was held by German authorities. Bulgarian troops took over a broad zone between the Strimón and the Axiós, except for a 20 km. zone around Thessaloníki. Their occupation was supposed to be purely a military one, but, nevertheless, Greek gendarmerie were ordered to withdraw west of the Axiós.

Greek Guerrillas

Certain areas of Greece, in particular, the mountainous districts of Ípiros, Makedhonía and Thessalía, have been completely liberated from enemy control and are living under guerrilla administration. In July 1943 there were said to be 40,000 armed and organized guerrillas in Greece, a number which has probably risen considerably since the fall of Italy. One of the largest groups is known as the National Liberation Front, or *Ethnikón Apeleftherotikón Métopon* (E.A.M.). It was the first movement in Greece organized in resistance to the occupying powers, and is composed chiefly of the Communist Party, the Agrarian Party, the Socialist Party, and the Republican Liberal Union. Another group, led by Colonel Zervas, is known as the E.D.E.S., and is made up largely of Royalists and Right wing elements in Greek politics. Unfortunately, these two rival organizations which had agreed to co-operate in the summer of 1943 were again fighting each other in the autumn. Both groups organize not only military resistance, but agricultural sabotage and strikes.

The Puppet Government in Greece

In setting up a puppet government, the Germans were faced with difficulties which they did not meet in other occupied countries. There was no important minority in Greece forming a dissatisfied national group; bankers and industrialists had traditionally pro-British sympathies; and, moreover, the Greeks had just emerged from five years of dictatorship and wished for the restoration of the Parliamentary regime. The Germans therefore exploited the bitter feud between Venizelists and anti-Venizelists, finding collaborationists amongst Generals and University Professors with anti-Venizelist sympathies. Obviously the puppet government could have no policy of its own, and its principal functions were to police the country, under alien supervision, and to break any anti-Axis organization. It attempted, with little success, to tackle the problems of famine and unemployment, and to stamp out the guerrilla movement. Numerous reconstructions have taken place since the first government was set up in May 1941, and the personnel was divided into two factions until the collapse of Italy, one mainly pro-Italian, the other mainly pro-German. Both were united, however, in their bitter antagonism to Bulgarian imperialistic aspirations.

Administrative and Social Changes

Police. The police were not at first disarmed by the Germans, but a certain amount of disarmament was later carried out by the Italians. Their duties were stated mainly to be control of curfew regulations, and of black-market and illicit trading, leaving the more administrative side of police work in the hands of the Italians. Even before the collapse of Italy, both the Greek and Italian police came under the control of the *Gestapo*.

The Judicial System. Like the rest of the Civil Service, the judicial system was completely disrupted by the invasion and by subsequent interference from the occupying powers and the puppet administration. Most judges and magistrates resigned or were dismissed, and over parts of Greece no civil law courts remain. German and Italian courts-martial dealt with all cases affecting the occupying forces, directly or indirectly. These courts dealt also with Civil Servants, public utility workers and those engaged in factories, airfields, hospitals, etc.

The Church. The Orthodox Church was the only organized force left in Greece in 1941, and it has done much to unite all elements in resistance. Primarily, however, it concerns itself with philanthropic and relief work. This has been especially noticeable in the attempt to alleviate the sufferings of the Jews. Many Jews have been arrested and deported to Poland, others are employed on forced labour in Bulgaria, and at the end of May 1943 it was estimated that only 5,000 Jews out of a pre-war population of over 40,000 remained in Thessaloníki. Many Orthodox priests have been put to death, others have joined guerrilla forces in the mountains. At the end of 1941, it was announced that the autonomous status of Áyion Óros was to be abolished, and that the province was to come directly under the Ministry of Religion.

Education. The requisitioning of school buildings, the acute shortage of teachers, the lack of books and necessary apparatus, the disruption of family life, famine, and the danger of epidemics have brought teaching virtually to a standstill. Here and there, educated persons have taught small groups of children, but for the most part the educational system has been completely broken. In those secondary schools which remained open, the teaching of German and Italian was made compulsory: French and English, which were the principal foreign languages taught, have been abolished. In the Bulgarian zone of occupation, not a single Greek school or Greek teacher remains, and all teaching is in Bulgarian.

The Universities have also suffered severely; the standard of entry was lowered, 'unnecessary' chairs were abolished, and there were frequent and long stoppages in the course of studies. Special German courses have been introduced and a chair of Italian History and Literature was founded. The University at Thessaloníki has been completely reorganized.

The Famine

Under normal circumstances, the Greeks grow only about 60 % of their total requirements in wheat, and are dependent upon imports for much of their necessary foodstuffs. Since the outbreak of war, the agricultural resources of the country have been greatly diminished, and the standard of living, always precariously low, has fallen to starvation level.

The famine began in August 1941, and reached its peak during the following winter. The pre-war figure for deaths in Athínai-

Piraiévs did not exceed 60 per day, but during the worst period of famine the number varied from 600 to 1,000 per day. Less conservative estimates have placed it as high as 2,000 per day. A small section of the population was able to supplement its rations by buying food at exorbitant prices, but the poor suffered terribly. Starvation has caused mass evacuation from the islands, and even in rural districts there is acute undernourishment. In the first two years of the occupation it was stated that some 300,000 deaths from starvation had occurred (1 in 25 of the population), and that the mortality rate throughout Greece had risen to six and a half times the normal figure. Children had been most severely affected by the famine, and in some of the worst districts the infantile mortality rate had risen to a peak of 90 %.

From January to June 1943, the food situation improved considerably, largely because of the import of Canadian and other foodstuffs carried by Swedish ships. Monthly shipments of 15,000 tons of Canadian wheat; 3,000 tons of pulses and 100 tons of milk have been allowed into the country since 1942, added to which there has been some help from neutral and Axis sources. But the imports fall considerably short of the estimated minimum monthly requirements of 25–30,000 tons of grain alone. The first organized countermeasures to the famine were undertaken by the Greek Red Cross, with supplies of foodstuffs received from Turkey. These were started in October 1941, but they remained grossly inadequate until Allied food shipments began to arrive at the end of the winter. Apart from the soup kitchens organized by the Greek Red Cross there were a number of independent philanthropic organizations providing milk and clothing for children. Subsequently, highly organized soup kitchens for children were started. A joint Swedish-Swiss Commission, organized by the International Red Cross, is now responsible for the distribution of daily rations to 2,000,000 people in Athínai and Piraiévs, Thessaloníki, Vólos, Pátrai and a few other large towns. The remainder of the population must maintain themselves on the small local production.

Within the last few months, it is stated that conditions have again deteriorated and the bread ration has fallen markedly. In the capital alone, it is estimated that 50 % of the child population, numbering some 125,000, cannot rely on being fed by their families.

There have been no serious epidemics, but the general weakening of health through malnutrition has been followed by a physical and mental enfeeblement, known as hypovitaminosis. Ulcers of the stomach, pellagra, scurvy, enteritis and dysentery have become extremely common, and organic resistance has fallen so low that the slightest illness becomes chronic (see p. 291).

The Greek Government in Cairo

After the fall of Kríti, the Greek government was set up in London, but in March 1943 it was removed to Cairo. A decree of 22 October 1941 stated that the King was to appoint the Prime Minister and, at his instance, the other Ministers. The competent Ministers must concur in the proposal of a law or a Royal Decree. The Legislative Powers would be exercised by means of emergency laws, issued at the instance of the Council of Ministers; and the Executive Power by means of Royal decrees, issued at the instance of the competent Ministers.

On 4 July 1943 the King broadcast that '...as soon as the security of our country warrants it and military conditions allow, free general elections for a Constituent Assembly will be carried out. These elections will be held within six months, as already decided by my Government. I am confident that no Greek will be found who will not respect the decisions of the Constituent Assembly: I shall be the first to respect them. All the relevant articles of the Constitution of 1911 are in force to-day, and will remain so until the Greek people expresses its sovereign will. As soon as it is possible to transfer the seat of the Government to Greek soil, the members of the present Government, as already announced by the Prime Minister, will submit their resignations, so that a Government may be formed which is fully representative of all parties and all the currents of the public opinion of the country.'

BIBLIOGRAPHICAL NOTE

1. The War of Independence has had many historians. Two very useful books are: C. W. Crawley, *The Question of Greek Independence* 1821–1833 (Cambridge, 1930); this contains a full bibliography of both unpublished and published sources; W. Miller, *A History of the Greek People* 1821–1831 (London, 1922).

2. The best short accounts of the history of Modern Greece are: W. Miller, *Greece* (London, 1928); J. Mavrokordato, *Modern Greece* 1800–1931 (London, 1931); E. S. Forster, *A Short History of Modern Greece* 1821–1940 (London, 1941).

3. The part played by Greece in the history of the Eastern Mediterranean is discussed in: J. A. R. Marriott, *The Eastern Question* (Oxford, 1917); A. J. Toynbee, *The Western Question in Greece and Turkey* (Oxford, 1922); G. F. Hudson, *Turkey, Greece and the Eastern Mediterranean* (Oxford, 1939).

4. Four war-time books may be mentioned: S. Casson, *Greece Against the Axis* (London, 1941). C. Mackenzie, *Wind of Freedom* (London, 1943). D. Powell, *Remember Greece* (London, 1941). *The Greek White Book*, published for the Royal Greek Ministry for Foreign Affairs (London, 1942).

Chapter VIII

GOVERNMENT, ADMINISTRATION AND LAW

THE CONSTITUTION

The constitutional history of Greece is complex, and ever since the bloodless revolution of 1843, the Greeks have been much exercised to make provision for democratic government. The first written Constitution of 1844 was framed to free Greece from the evils of absolute monarchy (see p. 203). It was superseded by that of 1864 which, with modifications introduced in 1911, remained in force until the establishment of the Republic in 1924. A Republican Constitution was passed in 1927 and was in process of revision when its fundamental basis was destroyed by the restoration of the Monarchy in 1935. The Constitution of 1864 (as revised in 1911) was then restored, pending revision, but internal dissension and external threat led to the establishment of the dictatorship of Metaxas in 1936. It is thus necessary to consider the development of the machinery of central government in historical perspective, with special attention to the Constitution of 1864 and that of 1927.

The Constitution of 1864

The foundations of Greek democracy were firmly established by this constitution. It stated that all powers emanated from the people, and it limited still further the power of the monarchy. Greece was established as a constitutional monarchy hereditary in the male line, or (in the case of extinction) in the female line, and both the King and the Heir Apparent had to be members of the Orthodox Church. Legislative power belonged to the King and the Chamber of Deputies. The Senate, which had been established in 1844, was abolished. Deputies were elected for four years by universal manhood suffrage,

Constitutions of Greece

Constitution	Main Provisions
Constitution of 1844	1. Constitutional Monarchy. 2. Independence from Constantinople of the Orthodox Church of Greec reasserted (as in 1833). [The Oecumenical Patriarch did no recognize the position until 1850.] 3. National Assembly bi-cameral < SENATE (*Yerousía*). / CHAMBER OF DEPUTIES (*Voulí*).
Constitution of 1864	1. Constitutional Monarchy. Executive power vested in the King, ex ercised by responsible Ministers appointed by him. 2. Independence of Orthodox Church of Greece reasserted (cf. 1844, 2) The practice of any religion permitted. 3. National Assembly uni-cameral. CHAMBER OF DEPUTIES elected for four years by direct manhoo suffrage. 4. All Greeks declared free and equal in the eyes of the law. 5. Freedom of the Press established. 6. Local authorities to be elected.
Revision in 1911 of Constitution of 1864	7. Quorum of Chamber of Deputies reduced from half plus one to one third of all its members. 8. Serving soldiers and sailors to be ineligible as deputies. 9. Security of tenure established for judiciary and civil servants. 10. Primary education declared free and compulsory. [First enacted 1833.] 11. 'Purist' Greek, *Katharévousa*, the language of the text of the Constitution, declared the official language and the medium of elementary education.
Constitution of 1927 (first drafted in 1925)	1. Republic (*Dhimokratía*). Executive power exercised by the Presiden through his responsible Ministers. President elected for 5 years by Senate and Chamber jointly. 2. Independence of Orthodox Church of Greece, and permission to practise any religion, reasserted (cf. 1864, 2): 3. National Assembly bi-cameral. SENATE. 120 members of over 40 years of age: serving soldiers, sailors and public servants ineligible. CHAMBER OF DEPUTIES. Elected for 4 years by universal manhood suffrage (cf. 1864, 3): serving soldiers, sailors and public servants ineligible (cf. 1911, 8). Quorum one-quarter of all members. April 1935 Constituent Act abolished Senate. 4. All Greeks declared free and equal (cf. 1864, 4) and liberty of person inviolable. 5. Freedom of speech and of the Press (cf. 1864, 5) and the right of public meeting affirmed. 6. Local authorities to be elected (cf. 1864, 6) and their powers increased. 7. Security of tenure established for judiciary and civil servants (cf. 1911, 9). 8. Primary education declared free and compulsory for all children for 6 years. Education to be conducted in the 'purist' language (cf. 1911, 10–11). 9. Council of State of 21 life-members, appointed by Council of Ministers, for matters of administrative law.
10 October 1935. Restoration of Constitution of 1911 (as a consequence of Restoration of Monarchy)	Provisions as Constitution 1864, Revised 1911 (see above), pending revision.
August 1936 (Metaxas's *coup d'état*, 4 August)	Articles of 1911 Constitution securing the liberties of the subject suspended, etc. Government by decree-law, pending replacement of parliamentary by corporative institutions.

and the voting was by secret ballot. Candidates for election must have attained their twenty-fifth year and voters their twenty-first. The executive power was vested in the King but was exercised by responsible ministers appointed by him. The independence of the Greek Orthodox Church was reasserted (see p. 332); it was declared the established church of Greece, but toleration was granted to all sects. All Greeks were declared free and equal in the eyes of the law; capital punishment for political offences and the penalty of the permanent deprivation of civil rights were abolished; the freedom of the Press was established. Local authorities were no longer to be nominated by the Minister of the Interior, but were to be elected.

Two defects were soon manifest in the Constitution. In the first place, the quorum for the Chamber of Deputies, fixed at a half plus one of the members, was so high that it allowed easy obstruction to bills, for the opposition merely stayed out of the Chamber. In the second place, the admission of serving soldiers and sailors as deputies allowed political measures, favoured by the military, to be backed by the threat of force. The frequent changes of government which thus occurred prevented any consistent foreign policy, and general dissatisfaction with the methods of government reached a head over the handling of the Cretan question (see p. 211). This, together with the constantly frustrated desire for army reform, led eventually to the formation in 1909 of the Military League, which became a focus of opposition to the Ministers. The discontented element in the Army and Navy was sufficiently powerful to coerce the Chamber, and free constitutional government existed only in name. Venizelos, summoned to Athínai as the political adviser of the League, saw the anomalous position and proposed the summoning of an Assembly for Constitutional reform.

The Revision of 1911

Revision of the non-fundamental articles of the Constitution of 1864 brought about important changes. The quorum of the Chamber of Deputies was reduced from a half plus one to one-third of all the members, and serving soldiers and sailors were declared ineligible as deputies. Both these were measures calculated to make for more stable government. A further reform of great significance was the establishment of a permanent judiciary and civil service. This was long overdue; ministries changed frequently, and, with each change, a complete dislocation of public services occurred all over the country, affecting the smallest functionary in the smallest village. The expropriation of the owners of large estates was carried through with special reference to the creation of peasant proprietors in the newly acquired province of Thessalía—a measure which did much to improve peasant conditions in the area and made for its strong allegiance to the Greek state. Elementary education was declared free and compulsory; 'purist' Greek or *katharévousa*, the language in which the Constitution was drawn up, was to be the medium of education; and the translation of the Scriptures into the 'popular' language or *Dhimotikí* or into any foreign tongue was forbidden. The adoption of *katharévousa*, from which Turkish and foreign words had been purged, was closely linked with the development of national consciousness (see p. 320).

Under this Constitution the administration was reformed, the army and navy were reorganized, and the lot of the peasants was improved. A period of progress and stability seemed to have begun, but almost immediately Greece was involved in war. The Balkan wars of 1912–14 strengthened the unity of Greece; there was little or no opposition to the Liberal Party of Venizelos; the Chamber of Deputies behaved as a responsible body; and the dynasty, its prestige increased by the successful military adventures of Constantine, seemed secure. Then came the war of 1914–18, and with it the internal conflict caused by the antagonism between Constantine and Venizelos. This culminated in the removal of the former in June 1917 and in the complete ascendancy of the latter under Allied influence (see p. 216).

From Monarchy to Republic

Since the war of 1914–18 the political life of the country has been dominated by the struggle between Venizelists and anti-Venizelists, complicated by the struggle between Republicans and Royalists, which though related was not quite the same thing. After the fall of Venizelos and the return of Constantine in December 1920 (see p. 219), the new Chamber, meeting in February 1921, voted large increases in the King's civil list and substituted the 'popular' language for the 'purist' form as the medium of instruction in elementary schools. The language question was becoming more and more bound up with party politics (see p. 297). The Chamber declared itself a National Constituent Assembly, and began to examine proposals for Constitutional reform which would strengthen the power of the Crown. While these were still being discussed came the defeat in Asia Minor, and also the revolutionary movement which preceded and followed the final abdication of Constantine in favour of George II n September 1922 (see p. 220). An attempt to return to constitu-ional government was interrupted by the rapid rise of the republican novement, which led in turn to the departure of King George and f Venizelos himself after a brief reappearance. The Republic pro-laimed on 25 March 1924 was ratified by plebiscite on 13 April (see . 222).

The National Assembly entrusted the drafting of the new Con-titution to a Commission of forty members. In June 1925, the work vas interrupted by the coup of General Pangalos, who was exasper-ted by the inefficiency and corruption of the administration. The National Assembly then delegated its constituent powers to a new Commission of thirty members, reserving only the right to ratify the ompleted work. The draft of 125 Articles was submitted to the Pangalos Government, which arbitrarily modified the text and pro-laimed a Constitution of 117 Articles on 30 September 1925. Having dissolved the Assembly and postponed the promised elections, Pangalos then suspended this unratified Constitution, proposed to emodel it on American lines with increased powers for the President, nd crowned his virtual dictatorship by getting himself elected as President in April 1926. On his overthrow in September, the original raft of 125 Articles was published; and the Chamber elected in November, acting as a constituent body, adopted a final text of 127 Articles on 2 June 1927 (see pp. 222–3).

The Constitution of 1927

The Constitution promulgated in 1925, and passed, after some nodification, in 1927, declared the Hellenic state to be a Parliamentary Republic. Greeks were declared equal before the law, and individual berty was inviolable. The right of public meeting was affirmed, as vas also that of freedom of speech and of the Press: only Greek itizens might publish newspapers. As in 1864, the Orthodox Church was declared independent and recognized as the established hurch, without prejudice to the practice of any other religion. As n 1911, translation of the Scriptures was forbidden, elementary ducation was to be free and compulsory and to be conducted in the purist' language. The Constitution endeavoured, as proposed in 911, to establish a permanent Civil Service, and judges of the three ighest courts, the *Areopagítai*, the *Efétai* (Lords Justices of Appeal) nd the *Protodhíkai* (puisne judges) were to be appointed for life. Decentralization of internal administration was provided (see p. 253), nd the building of refugee settlements was permitted on expro-

priated and unoccupied lands before compensation had been granted
The legislative power was to be exercised by the Chamber and th
Senate, and the executive power by the President through th
responsible ministers.

The President of the Republic was elected for five years by th
Chamber of Deputies and the Senate sitting in joint session: it wa
believed that the Senators and Deputies could better assess th
qualifications of a man for this position than the whole body o
citizens. No president might hold office for more than two con
secutive terms. He appointed and dismissed the Prime Minister
promulgated laws voted by the legislature and decreed laws durin
recess, if empowered to do so by the Chamber and subject to late
ratification. After a majority decision of the Senate, he might dissolv
the Chamber once, before its term had expired, but not twice for th
same cause. He represented the State in international affairs, and i
theory (but never in practice) he was the head of the Army and Navy
Hedged around by limitations, the presidential powers were not suc
as to make the office a prize for ambitious men. Respect for th
Constitution, dignity and freedom from self-seeking were necessar
qualities, and the office was held by elder statesmen of assure
position.

The Council of Ministers, with the Prime Minister presiding, wa
collectively responsible for the general policy of the government an
had to possess the confidence of the Chamber. Each Minister wa
individually responsible for what was done in his departmen
Ministers had access to both Senate and Chamber, but had the righ
to vote only in the body to which they belonged.

The Senate, abolished by the Constitution of 1864, was re
established on a broader basis in 1927 and was to consist of 12
members; ninety-two elected by the constituencies for nine yea
(one-third of the number being replaced every three years), eightee
nominated by professional bodies, and ten elected by the Chamb
and the Senate at the beginning of the first session of each legislatur
Senators had to be Greek citizens, eligible to vote and of forty yea
of age or over. Serving soldiers and sailors and paid public official
with the exception of University professors, were ineligible. Aft
being passed by the Chamber a bill was to become law unless rejecte
by the Senate within forty days. If rejected by the Senate, it becan
law if passed again, after an interval of not less than two months, b
an absolute majority of the whole Chamber; but within these tw
months, the Senate might call a joint meeting of both Chambers f

a final decision on the bill by majority vote of the whole number of Senators and Deputies. The Senate might also initiate and submit to the Chamber any measures except the budget, proposals for loans, and votes of credit. Any such financial measure had to be initiated in the Chamber of Deputies, and became law unless rejected by the Senate within a month; if so rejected, its fate was finally decided by a new vote of the Chamber of Deputies, which thus held the purse-strings. The Senate also sat as a tribunal to try cases of high treason or any other action against the safety and independence of the state.

The purpose in re-establishing the Senate was not primarily to add a conservative element or to represent privileged classes, but to ensure closer study of proposed legislation independently of snap votes in the Chamber. The difficulty was to find men suited for the position of Senators: able and active politicians preferred seats as Deputies. Moreover, Greek governments as a rule found it difficult enough to secure the passage of bills in a uni-cameral constitution, and the establishment of a second house gave still more opportunities for delay and deadlock. The first Senate under this constitution was elected in 1929, but the institution was abolished in 1935.

The Chamber of Deputies was elected by universal manhood suffrage by means of a secret ballot. The *nomoí* (departments) formed the constituencies, the number of Deputies returned from each being proportional to the population, one for every 16,000 inhabitants, with the proviso that the total number of Deputies should not be less than 200 nor more than 250. Deputies must be Greek citizens, aged twenty-five years or more; serving soldiers and sailors, paid public officials, mayors, and officials of privileged companies were ineligible. Officers of the Army or Navy who resigned in order to become Deputies might never return to their profession; every effort was made, strongly supported by public opinion, to guard against the political soldier. Deputies were elected for four years, though in practice the legislature rarely attained its full term. The session began in October for a period of not less than three nor more than six months. The quorum of the Chamber, already reduced in 1911, was again reduced and was fixed as one-quarter of the total number of Deputies. Each bill had to be given two readings, and the budget had to be introduced during the first two months of a session. A vote of want of confidence in the government could not be carried by the votes of less than two-fifths of the Deputies; Ministers might vote if they were members of the Chamber. To facilitate agreement between Chamber and Senate, a mixed Commission of Senators and Deputies might be formed.

A permanent mixed Commission on foreign affairs was set up at the beginning of the first session of each legislature. It also functioned during recesses and even after the dissolution of the Chamber. All ex-Premiers were ex-officio members of this Commission. The handling of foreign affairs is so difficult and crucial in Balkan states that the need for continuity and expert advice was understood.

The Council of State, suppressed in 1865, had been recreated on paper in 1911, but the Balkan wars and the war of 1914–18 prevented it from functioning. The Constitution of 1927 provided for the establishment, within a year, of a Council of State to consist of not more than twenty-one members, appointed for life by the Council of Ministers. Public officials, except professors of law, were ineligible. The duties of the Council, as further defined by law in 1935, were to settle administrative disputes, to draft administrative laws, to put into final form laws and decrees sent to it by the Chamber and the executive power, and to codify administrative law. The text thus codified had then to be ratified by a decree proposed by the Minister of Justice.

The Supreme Economic Council was established in 1930 to act in an advisory capacity on economic matters, and to recommend legislation to the government. It consisted of fifty-two members representing agriculture, industry, commerce and banking, communications and transport, consumers, the arts and sciences, and, finally, Greek economic organizations in the United States and Egypt. Members were appointed for six years, one-half resigning every three years. Deputies, Senators and public officials were ineligible.

The Revision of the Constitution of 1927

The Constitution of 1927 provided for the revision of non-fundamental articles after a period of five years, if it were judged necessary. The machinery for revision was purposely made complicated in an attempt to ensure that changes should be made only after careful examination. In 1932, a mixed Commission of Senators and Deputies was set up to consider the question of revision. Among many suggestions, the most important, which perhaps indicated the trend of current opinion, was the proposal for an article allowing the President to suspend certain fundamental rights and to resort to the use of armed force if security and public order were seriously threatened. None of the suggestions proposed by the Commission was carried out.

The work of drafting revisions was carried on in spite of rising monarchist sentiment, a sentiment which was perhaps more anti-Venizelist than pro-Glucksburg. There was a deadlock between the Populist (moderate royalist) majority in the Chamber and the Venizelist (liberal) majority in the Senate in opposition. Moreover, extreme royalists, like Metaxas, wished to suspend the republican Constitution, while Plastiras and the extreme republicans attempted a military coup in order to forestall a restoration of the monarchy. The collapse of this attempt (March 1935), and the momentary support given to it by Venizelos in Kríti, followed by republican abstention from the elections in June, helped to discredit the Republic.

The Restoration of the Monarchy

The moderate royalists in the new Chamber, yielding to the more extreme minority, declared in favour of a return to the Monarchy and the Constitution of 1911 (see p. 225); this was done in advance of the plebiscite that was to decide between the maintenance of the parliamentary Republic and the restoration of a parliamentary and constitutional Monarchy. Although the republicans disputed the validity of the proceedings, the plebiscite held on 3 November 1935 showed an overwhelming majority in favour of the Monarchy.

On his return to Greece, on 25 November 1935, King George II hoped, by means of an amnesty and a non-party government, to get an agreed revision of the revived Constitution of 1911. But the elections of January 1936 produced a Chamber so evenly divided in numbers that in April it acquiesced to the proposal of Metaxas to adjourn for five months. Meanwhile the Ministry was to govern by decree, but a permanent parliamentary Commission of forty Deputies, representing all parties in proportion, was to take over the legislative function of the Chamber.

The Dictatorship of Metaxas

Metaxas soon persuaded the King to give up the difficult attempt at constitutional rule (see p. 225). The decrees of 4 August 1936 dissolved the Chamber without fixing any date for new elections, proclaimed martial law, and suspended those articles of the Constitution of 1911 which guaranteed the liberty of the subject. On 6 August, Metaxas stated that the Constitution provisionally in force was still that of 1911, although it was generally admitted to be ill-adapted to existing conditions, and, indeed, a Revision Committee had already been sitting. On 15 August a new law brought the Press completely under government control, and in September severe penalties for propagating Communism were decreed. Metaxas then announced the reform of the Constitution. Parliamentary government was to be abolished and a corporative State was to be established. The *Nomárkhai* (Prefects) would govern the *Nomoí* (Departments) and the head of the government would be the head of the state. Strikes would be forbidden. A Chamber might emerge, as might a large state party. No such Chamber or party had emerged by the time of the death of Metaxas. After the *coup d'état* government was by decree-law, proposed by the head of the government and sanctioned by the King. The Cabinet retained the executive power, but was responsible only to the King and no longer to a popularly elected Assembly.

Note on the Electoral Method

The main changes in the electoral law of Greece since the war 1914–18, apart from various changes in the number of Deputies elected, were those relating to methods of election. In November 1926, despite strenuous opposition by all the old parties, by the Press and by the bulk of public opinion, the old system, by which one Deputy per 16,000 inhabitants was elected, was abandoned, and for the first time elections were held under a modified form of the Belgian system of proportional representation. The supporters of this system urged that its adoption would be a way of breaking up the large Venizelist and anti-Venizelist blocs, and of bringing into political life new parties and personalities. Those opposed to the idea preferred the old majority system, as tending to produce a strong government. The result of the 1926 election was a coalition government, with no effective opposition, and parliamentary life eventually became disorganized. In 1928, Venizelos persuaded the President to issue a decree-law abolishing proportional representation, and the 1928 election, held on the majority system, resulted in a victory for the Venizelists who commanded two-thirds of the votes in the Chamber. The question of the electoral method was the cause of much political dissension in 1932. Proportional representation was used in the elections in September of that year, which again resulted in a political impasse. It was not used in the elections of March 1933, or in those of June 1935, but it was reintroduced for the elections of January 1936. In April 1936, the Chamber passed a decree confirming the use of proportional representation as a provisional electoral system. Since the dissolution of the Chamber on 4 August of that year the question has remained in abeyance.

Political Structure

The political life of Greece is both intensely active and highly unstable: the changes from Monarchy to Republic and back again to Monarchy, the number and variety of political parties, and the short average life of the governments (there were forty-eight governments between 1920 and 1928), all bear witness to this fact. Political questions, of major or even minor importance, have often split the nation, hindering economic development, hampering social progress and even embittering family life. Through all the kaleidoscopic changes, and in spite of the five years' duration of the dictatorship of Metaxas, the Greeks have remained steadfast in their allegiance to true democracy.

Greek Ministers, as befits a democratic nation, have always been accessible. A Minister, in addition to his ordinary duties, received an endless stream of visitors in his office, often several at once, and quite informally. Tours through the provinces were frequent and, with their crowds, speech making, banquets and interviews, imposed a severe mental and physical strain. More recently, Ministers had, by force of circumstance, become less accessible, and could be interviewed only at certain hours.

As with Ministers so with Deputies, if to a less degree: a Deputy had always to be approachable to his constituents and much was expected of him in the way of procuring jobs. He had also to stand godfather to the children of constituents, and each godchild might cost him £1 or £2. Elections were often costly affairs, and a rich man might spend as much as £1 a vote in an expensive constituency like Piraiévs. Greek Prime Ministers, however, have not been accused of enriching themselves at the expense of the state, and most of them have lived and died poor.

Political Parties

Political parties in Greece tend to be formed by and to reflect the opinions of their leaders rather than, as in England, to be highly organized, semi-permanent groups with an elected head. At the general election of January 1936, the election which preceded the

Metaxas *coup d'état*, eleven parties won seats—four belonging to the Right, five of Liberal persuasion, an Independent Agrarian party and the Communist party. Of these, only four held more than ten seats:

Parties of the General Election, January 1936

	Seats
Right Wing Groups:	
Popular Party (Tsaldaris)	72
National Radical Union (Kondilis and Theotokis)	60
Party of Free Opinion (Metaxas)	7
Reform Group (Kotzananis)	4
	143
Liberal Groups:	
Liberals (Sofoulis)	126
Republican Coalition (Kafandaris and Papanastasiou)	7
Agrarian Party (Milonas)	4
Old Republicans (Koundoros)	3
New Liberals (Botzaris)	1
	141
Others:	
Independent Agrarians (Pangontsos)	1
Communists (Sckavainas)	15
	16
Total	300

The Right had two powerful parties, the *Popular Party* led by Tsaldaris with democratic conservatism as its platform, and the *National Radical Union* led by Kondilis, with more extreme royalist views than the populists, advocating the strengthening of the executive powers of the government. The other parties of the Right were relatively unimportant; the *Party of Free Opinion* under Metaxas stood during the later years of the Republic for immediate restoration of the Monarchy, and the *Reform Group* was chiefly interested in administrative reforms in Makedhonía.

The Liberal Group was dominated by the one powerful party, the *Liberals*, led by Sofoulis; this was the old Venizelist party, and had played the most prominent part in the establishment of representative government. Most of its leaders had been implicated in the rebellion against the royalist tendencies in 1935, but the party was not necessarily anti-royalist. The other Liberal parties were all small, holding only fifteen seats between them. The *Republican Coalition Party*, another name for the Progressive Party, advocated a policy of administrative decentralization; the *Agrarian Party* was interested in the confiscation of church property and social reforms in general; the *Old Republicans* were the republican diehards; and the *New Liberals* were a split from the main Liberal party.

The Right Wing, firmly entrenched in Attikí and the Pelopónnisos, and the Liberal groups, popular in the new provinces of northern Greece and in Kríti, were almost equally powerful; thus the Communists, with fifteen seats, held the balance between them, for the Independent Agrarian party had only one Deputy. This situation led to political deadlock, and bills and reforms supported by the Right were thrown out by the Liberals; much time was wasted in the Chambers in talk and by obstruction; disorderly scenes sometimes necessitated the suspension of sittings.

The Metaxas Regime

Under the Metaxas regime, political parties were not formally abolished, but they were in practice prevented from functioning, and, though Metaxas announced his intention of forming a National Government Party 'representing the people's healthy liberties', the will had to be taken for the deed. The regime was not strictly comparable to any other in Europe: it was in many respects authoritarian rather than totalitarian, and it was a non-party rather than a one-party system. But it did possess some of the worst features of totalitarianism, and men and women openly against the dictatorship were banished to the islands. Political representation in the traditional sense did not exist, but a new system of professional representation was emerging. The Greek peasants, forming approximately 70 % of the population, were to be represented through the agricultural co-operatives to which they must all belong: industrial workers were to be represented through their trade unions: and a similar type of representation was developing for the smaller professional and employer groups. The constitutional form, however, was still fluid in 1940.

Free political discussion was somewhat curbed by censorship of the newspapers and the surveillance of public meetings, but argument in private was, if less well informed, probably as freely indulged as ever. This predilection for political argument is certainly a most characteristic feature of Greek society; it may be in part due to ancient tradition, but it may also be due to the fact that Modern Greece, still politically youthful, has been faced with most difficult problems.

The Administration

Central Government

The government of the country was carried out by the departments of state; and although there has been more recently a tendency to allow greater local freedom, administration was still more centralized than in England. In theory Metaxas favoured a policy of decentralization, but he kept all matters relating to security in his own hands.

There were eleven Ministries when Metaxas came to power in August 1936, and no changes in their essential functions were made before the occupation of Greece in 1941. There were Ministries of Foreign Affairs, Interior, National Economy, Public Health and Immigration, Agriculture, Justice, Finance, Communications, Education and Religion, and Army, Marine and Air.

The Ministries of Foreign Affairs, the Interior, Justice, Finance, Education, Communications, the Army and Marine had long been established. The Ministry of the Interior was responsible for local administration in the provinces and in the capital; it also controlled the affairs of the *Khorofilakí* (Gendarmerie) and of the *Astinomía* (Town Police). The Ministry of Education included Ecclesiastical Affairs. The Army and the Navy were once separately administered; they were later combined and, together with the Air Ministry, formed one department. The Ministry of National Economy was established by the first Venizelist Government (1911) to encourage the development of national resources. Commerce, mines, industries, agriculture and forests were within its province. Technical education in these subjects also came under this Ministry and not under the Ministry of Education. Agriculture, including Forestry, became a separate department after the war of 1914–18. The Department of Health was also formed then, and was rapidly developed. Recently the Ministry of Railways was separated from the Ministry of Communications, but the latter kept control of Posts, Telegraphs and Telephones, and the responsibility for the building and upkeep of roads. Ministries of Press and Tourism and of Railways were established by Metaxas.

Sub-sections of the Ministries dealt with specialized branches of their work: thus archaeology formed a sub-section of Education, electric power a section of National Economy, and plant pathology a section of Agriculture.

Local Government

The Greek takes a strong interest in local government, and willingly assumes the responsibility for its administration. Even under Turkish domination much of the local administration remained in Greek hands. Thus the articles of the 1927 Constitution which provided for a future system of local administrative authority gave solid grounds for satisfaction, especially in the 'new' provinces of northern Greece where centralized control exercised from Athínai was particularly resented. The purpose of this decentralization was to make it easier for citizens to appeal to the authority of the state, so that local administrative problems might be solved locally and without delay. In Greece the word 'decentralization' does not imply, as it usually does, the giving of greater powers to the local elected bodies, but the concentration of greater powers in the hands of the local Agents of the Central Executive, i.e. the Governors-General and the Nomarchs (Prefects). Until 1930 there had been in the various Ministries in Athínai numerous committees composed of civil servants who had to give a preliminary ruling on any matter which was not of strictly local interest. In the Department of Trade and Industry, for example, there were seven different Committees and Commissions, each composed of fifteen to twenty senior officials. Venizelos pointed out that this committee system caused intolerable delay and weakened the sense of responsibility in members of the Committees. He carried through measures transferring certain powers from these Committees to the Ministers, who could in turn delegate them to the Governors-General. The Committees were to act as purely advisory bodies and the competent Minister would be fully responsible for all decisions taken. The Governors-General, with a staff of civil servants to advise them, were given fairly wide powers, and would also have to take decisions on their own responsibility. After the *coup d'état* of 1936, Metaxas continued this policy of 'decentralization'. A law of April 1938 transferred various powers from the Ministers to the Nomarchs, while in November of that year a further law dealt with the reorganization of the administrative units and their subdivisions. There was, however, at the same time a tendency for bodies nominated by the government to be substituted gradually for the locally elected communal and municipal councils.

The *Dhiamérisma* (pl. *dhiamerísmata*) (Fig. 93) is the largest administrative unit of Greece, but, except in the more recently acquired areas, it is of theoretical rather than practical importance. These divisions are ten in number and correspond roughly to the broad geographical regions. Four of them, however, Thráki (with eastern Makedhonía), western Makedhonía, Ípiros and Kríti, have an administrative reality; each is ruled by a Governor-General (Yenikós

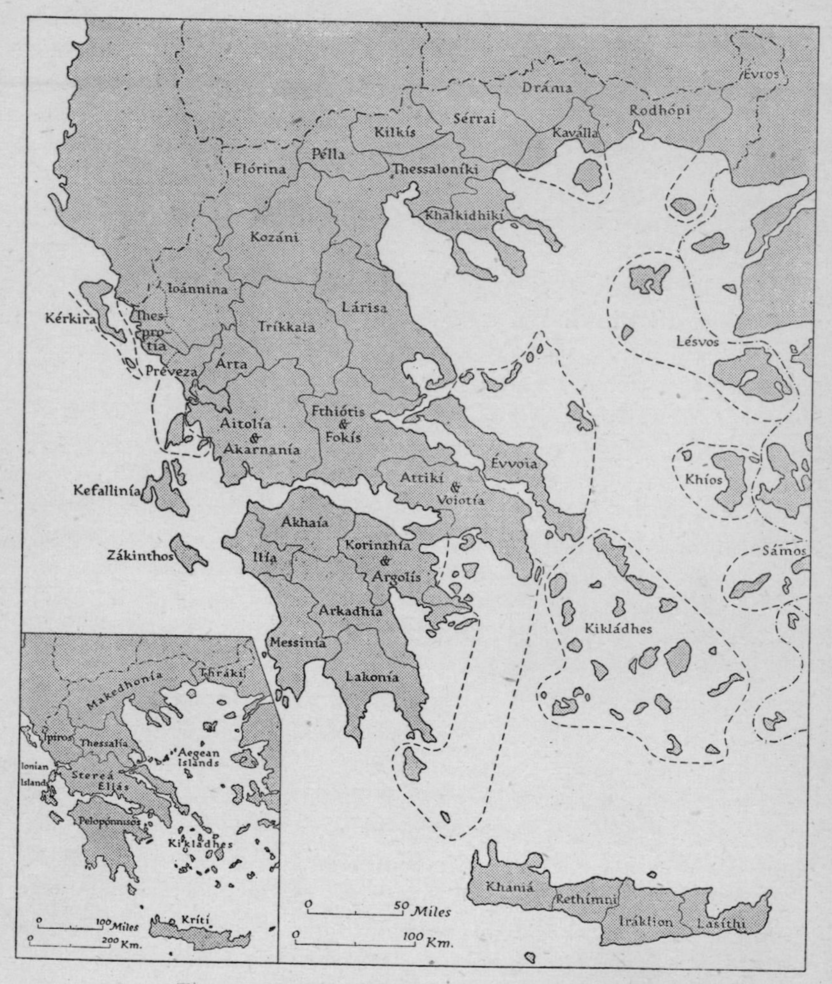

Fig. 93. The administrative divisions of Greece

Based on 1 : 1,000,000 G.S.G.S., Series 2758: Europe (1941), and the population census of 1928.

Greece is divided into ten *dhiamerísmata* or geographical regions as shown on the inset map, and into thirty-nine *nomoí* or departments. The *nomós* of Thesprotía was formed out of parts of Ioánnina and Préveza after 1936. A full list of these administrative regions and their populations is given in Appendix VIII, pp. 477–8.

Dhioikitís), nominated in Athínai, who holds ministerial rank. After the Metaxas *coup*, Athínai was also placed under a Governor-General with similar powers.

The *Nomós* (pl. *nomoí*) (Fig. 93), however, is the most important administrative unit. Since the reorganization of some of the boundaries in 1936, the nomes (*nomoí*) number 39, including that of Áyion Óros (Mount Áthos) which is an autonomous unit under the Greek government. The nomarch (*nomárkhis*) is the government official in charge of the administration of each nome. He is appointed by the Minister of the Interior and cannot be appointed to his native nome, to that of his wife, or to one in which he has exercised political rights during the three years preceding his nomination. This proviso is to try to ensure that the nomarch shall have no private interests to consider in dealing with local affairs.

It is the business of the nomarch to maintain public order and security, to administer the Health services,* to supervise prisons and hospitals and to maintain railways, roads, bridges and public buildings. He must enforce the education acts, collect rates and taxes and administer government funds. In 1938 the power of the nomarch was further increased; he was made the direct representative of the government and of the Governor-General of the *dhiamérisma*, superior to all civil, military and maritime authorities in his nome. He is the head of the police and port authorities, and can exercise disciplinary powers over civil servants within his area. Complaints against the acts of the local authorities are now to be dealt with by the nomarch rather than the Minister in Athínai; the relevant Minister is to confine himself to giving directions and supervision, but the decisions of the nomarch, if they transgress the law or a royal decree, can be the subject of appeal to the Governor-General or the Minister.

The preservation of archaeological remains is, in general, the duty of the nomarch, but the archaeological divisions of the country do not correspond exactly with the administrative divisions. In each archaeological district resides an *Éforos* (pl. *éforoi*), an inspector of antiquities, who is responsible to the Minister of Education for the conduct of excavations, and for the supervision of those carried out by foreigners. It is his duty to prevent illicit excavations and the illegal sale of antiquities and to visit and report on the ancient sites and museums of his district. In many cases the *éforos* is also the curator of the local museum.

* In recent years, Public Health Centres were being set up in each nome directly under the Department of Public Health (see p. 263).

The *Eparkhía* (pl. *eparkhíai*) is a subdivision of the nome, in which the functions of the nomarch are carried out by his local representative the *éparkhos*. These are old divisions which retain in most of Greece a historical significance only, but like the *dhiamerísmata*, they have been revived as real administrative units in northern Greece.

The *Dhímos* (pl. *dhímoi*) and the *Koinótis* (pl. *koinótites*) form the working subdivisions of the nomes. Originally the deme (*dhímos*) was the only subdivision, but since the reorganization of administrative units in 1912 the term deme was restricted to towns, usually the capitals of districts, which with their surrounding villages have a population of more than 5,000 inhabitants. There are seventy-three demes in all, few nomes having more than one or two. Attikí-Voiotía is an exception with fourteen demes and Argolís-Korinthía and Thessaloníki have five each. (See Appendix VIII.) The head of the deme is the *dhímarkhos*, who is assisted in his duties by a deme council and a committee elected by the council. The commune (*Koinótis*) is comparable to an English rural parish; it must possess a school and a population of more than 300 and is usually made up of a single small settlement with perhaps a few outlying cottages. Smaller settlements combine to form a commune, but in remote districts or small islands, small settlements if they own a certain amount of communal property rank as communes, even if they do not possess a school. There were over 5,600 communes in 1938. Each has a *proëdhros* and a council to conduct local business. Throughout the period of Turkish rule Greek local government had maintained its rights and responsibilities and the local officials and councils were elected. For a time after the establishment of the new kingdom in 1833 *dhímarkhoi* and the *proëdhroi* were nominated by the King or the nomarch, but in 1864 the right to elect them was restored to the inhabitants of the areas concerned. Until 1930, local officials were elected by universal manhood suffrage, but since then women of thirty years and over who can read and write also vote. The Constitution of 1927 laid down that 'only Greek citizens' were eligible for 'the public services' and expressly defined Greek citizens so as to include both sexes, maintaining that political rights can be conferred upon women by law. The size of the local councils varies in proportion to the total population. The officials are elected for four years; serving soldiers and sailors are ineligible, in order to prevent the military from becoming powerful in local government. The *dhímarkhos* or *proëdhros* is an important official; he is responsible for the registration of births and deaths, for drawing up and keeping up to date the lists of electors, and for making lists of those liable for military service. Matters of public health and public works within the deme or commune come within his control, and he is responsible to the nomarch for the local budget. The local finances are usually administered by the state except in the case of a very wealthy deme; but this is almost the only encroachment of the state on the independence of the local authorities over local affairs. In 1936 General Metaxas suspended the powers of some of these authorities, since they were strong enough to object forcibly to his autocratic regime.

The *Sinoikismós* (pl. *sinoikismoí*) is the smallest administrative unit in Greece; small hamlets, a collection of homes or even a single monastery may be so classed. There were 11,130 *sinoikismoí* in 1938.

The Administration of Áyion Óros

The twenty monasteries of Áyion Óros (Mount Athos) form a self-governing community under the Greek state, each monastery ranking as a *sinoikismós* (see above). The state has complete sovereignty over the territory, and all who take up residence there acquire Greek nationality without further formality. The state is represented by a civil Governor resident at Kariaí, and the few resident civil servants and police are under his orders. Ecclesiastically, Áyion Óros is under the direct jurisdiction of the Oecumenical Patriarchs. The lands of the monasteries within the peninsula are inalienable and exempt from taxation. Local administration is entirely in the hands of the twenty monasteries whose representatives form the Holy Community; a committee of four members, chosen in turn, forms the executive. The president of the committee is also the president of the Community; the sittings are held at the village of Kariaí, the seat of the government since the tenth century.

The Constitution of 1927 merely recognized as legal for Áyion Óros a way of government that was centuries old. In 1060, the Community was withdrawn from the authority of the Patriarch of Constantinople, and what amounted almost to a monastic republic was constituted. The Turks respected the privileged position of the monks, and the present Constitution differs only in detail from that drawn up in 1783, when the area was still under the suzerainty of the Sultan. The Constitution of 1927 forbade any alteration either of the system of government or of the number of monasteries on Áyion Óros.

The Legal System

Under the Turks the Greeks, in addition to their ecclesiastical institutions and a certain amount of local self-government, retained their judicial independence.

The Civil Law of Greece is based on Roman Law; in 1835 the Greeks adopted the Byzantine code with some modifications. Further modifications and new enactments, derived largely from the *Code Napoléon* and from German Law, were subsequently introduced. The Penal Code is based on the revised Bavarian system and is complete, methodical and humane. The Commercial Code is modelled on that of France.

Liberty of person and domicile are inviolate; no person can be arrested, no house entered, and no letter opened without a judicial warrant. The individual in Greece is protected from summary arrest and imprisonment, except *in flagrante delicto*, both by the Constitution of 1927 and by that of 1911 which was restored in 1935. When Metaxas came into power in 1936 those Articles of the Constitution which affected the liberty of the subject were illegally suspended and summary arrests were undoubtedly made.

The Courts

Justice is administered through two graded series of courts, criminal and civil. The personnel of the courts in the two series is often identical but juries are empanelled only in criminal cases.

The lowest criminal court is the *Ptaismatodhikíon* (pl. *ptaismatodhikía*), a police court which has as a rule only one magistrate. It can inflict short terms of imprisonment and small fines up to 600 drachmae. The *Plimmeliodhikíon*, the correctional tribunal, comes next in the scale, and there are two grades. By far the greater number sit with only one magistrate and have the power to sentence offenders to a maximum penalty of six months imprisonment or a fine of 6,000 drachmae. The higher court with three magistrates can impose heavier penalties and can quash the decisions of the courts with one magistrate. At this stage appeal can be made to appeal courts in each circuit. The *Kakouryiodhikíon*, the court of Assize, tries the more serious criminal cases except those of piracy or of political crime. These courts can inflict the maximum penalties within the law but there is a right of appeal.

The lowest civil court is the *Irinodhikíon* administered by a Justice of the Peace. It decides civil and commercial cases where no large sums are involved. The *Protodhikíon*, the Court of First Instance which corresponds with the Court of Assize, deals with the more serious offences against the civil and commercial code.

Above all these courts, both criminal and civil, are nine Courts of Appeal (sing. *Efetíon*, pl. *efetía*), one for each of the circuits of Athínai, Návplion, Pátrai, Kérkira, Lárisa, Thessaloníki, Thráki, the Kikládhes and the Aegean islands, and Kríti. Each has three members, but nine similar courts, each with five members, deal with crimes committed by state functionaries from Ministers downwards.

The Supreme Court of Appeal, still known by its ancient name of *Areopágos*, sits at Athínai. Its duty is to preserve the unity of the legal system and to quash all judgments contrary to the law of the land. It has two chambers; the first deals with cases judged by magistrates in Courts of Appeal and Courts of the First Instance, the second with appeals in criminal cases and appeals against judgment by military courts and tribunals.

The relationship of these courts to one another, and their numbers in 1937 are given below:

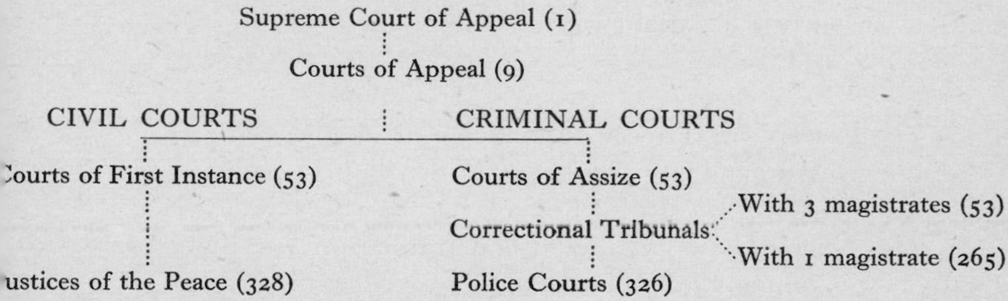

Supreme Court of Appeal (1)

Courts of Appeal (9)

CIVIL COURTS	CRIMINAL COURTS	
ourts of First Instance (53)	Courts of Assize (53)	
	Correctional Tribunals	With 3 magistrates (53)
		With 1 magistrate (265)
ustices of the Peace (328)	Police Courts (326)	

There is also a Maritime Court, and Courts of Arbitration have been set up to settle commercial and industrial disputes. The Council of State can be consulted in difficult cases and has the power to annul official decisions and acts contrary to the Law (see p. 246).

Sentences of all kinds are often completely or partially remitted, or the penalty is suspended for terms of one or more years. The death sentence is seldom carried out. The guillotine is the official method of execution, but its use was discontinued many years ago and shooting is the method now usually employed.

The Prisons

Prisons are either Correctional or Criminal. There are forty-five of the former, and eleven of the latter. The conditions prevailing in prisons were, until recently, bad. In the criminal prison at Návplion prisoners were herded together in a deep pit in the rock; visitors could walk round the edge and talk with them, or buy small objects which the prisoners spent their time in making. Food was mostly supplied by friends and relatives. This state of things is becoming obsolete and farm prisons are being established. The first rural prison was opened at Tírins many years ago, and there are now five others. If the penalty is less than a life sentence, the prisoner may choose to go to one of these farm prisons either as a farmer or as a craftsman. Prisoners are paid one-tenth of the district wage. Each day's work in the fields, 'under the sun', counts as two days towards his term, each day's work indoors, 'in the shade', as one and one-half days, and for good conduct one-third of the sentence is remitted. There are wardens and guards as at other prisons, but in addition there is a technical staff to direct the work of the farm and teach the prisoners modern agricultural methods. Kassándra in Khalkidhikí, for example, is a farm of over 8,000 ha. with accommodation for about 470 prisoners. Here, much work has been done in drainage and reclamation, and tractors and horses are now used to plough land that was once a malarial swamp.

The Police

There were in Greece two separate bodies—the *Khorofilakí* (Gendarmerie) and the *Astinomía* (Town Police); since 1938 a third body, the *Agrofilakí* (Rural Police), has also been established.

The *Khorofilakí* is organized and trained on a military basis and its duty is to maintain order in all Greece except in Athínai, Piraiévs, Pátrai and Kérkira which are policed by the *Astinomía*. The *Khorofilakí* is recruited by the voluntary enlistment for three years of men under 30, and many of these re-enlist when their term of service is over. Men between 19 and 25 years of age who enlist voluntarily and who hold a leaving certificate from a secondary school or a diploma of law become the non-commissioned and commissioned officers. The *Khorofilakí* was reorganized by a law of April 1938 and its administration was transferred from the Ministry of War to the Ministry of the Interior; thus, in accordance with the policy of decentralization the *Khorofilakí* is now under the control of the nomarch. According to the census of 1928 they numbered about 11,000, since when, particularly under the Metaxas regime, the force has much increased. In 1940 its strength was stated to be about 25,000 but this may be an over-estimate.

The *Astinomía*, a body created in 1923, is responsible for the maintenance of law and order in Athínai, Piraiévs, Pátrai and Kérkira, which were then the largest towns and ports of Greece. Its members, who number just over 4,000, direct traffic on the streets and assist customs' officers on the quays. The first training college for the *Astinomía* was at Kérkira, where it was organized on English lines, by General Sir F. Halliday. In 1938 the Director of the *Astinomía* stated that the government had raised the corps to the enviable position of defenders of the established order, and undoubtedly under Metaxas it became much more powerful.

The *Agrofilakí*, as distinct from the *Khorofilakí*, was established by a law of January 1938. It is administered by the Ministry of Agriculture and its members are appointed directly by the nomarch. They are often part time small farmers themselves and their work is largely concerned with the problems of a farming community, the settlement of field boundaries, the claims for straying animals, disputes about damage to vines and olives and the like. They could make suggestions to agricultural councils, by whom their work was to be supervised, and they were to be given time and a free hand to carry out their duties.

BIBLIOGRAPHICAL NOTE

No comprehensive account of the government and administration of Greece has been published in English, and most of this chapter has been compiled from official sources. On the other hand, the many Constitutions have been fully described in the numerous books on the history of Greece since the War of Independence. The most important of these are given in the bibliographical note to Chapter VII. Reference should also be made to J. A. Hawgood, *Modern constitutions since 1787* (London, 1939), and to K. Braunias, *Das parlamentarische Wahlrecht*, 2 vols. (Berlin, 1932).

Chapter IX

PUBLIC HEALTH, DISEASE AND HYGIENE

Health Administration and Services: Vital Statistics: Diseases: Hints on the Preservation of Health: Bibliographical Note

Health Administration and Services

The ten years preceding the Italian invasion of Greece in 1940 witnessed very great activity in the development of public health services. Ambitious and far-reaching schemes for improvement were begun and real progress was achieved. Progress would, however, have been more solid and much less intermittent had it not been for the clash of vested interests, frequent changes of government, and still more frequent changes of ministers who assumed charge of the Ministry of Health and Public Assistance.

This period of activity began in 1928. The very severe epidemic of dengue which afflicted Greece in that year had disclosed certain fundamental weaknesses in the structure of the health services. The Greek government invited the League of Nations to collaborate in their reorganization, and a commission of experts was sent to Greece. This commission elaborated a programme of reform which was adopted by the Greek government. The services of an English medical officer on the staff of the Health Organization of the League of Nations were obtained. One of the main recommendations concerned the creation of a School of Hygiene in Athínai, which began its work in 1931 under the direction of Dr Norman White.

When war broke out the administration was as follows: centralized control was exercised by the Ministry of Health and Public Assistance, and the minister was advised by a Supreme Health Council. The ministry had three departments:

(1) Department of Public Health, responsible for the prevention of infectious disease, including malaria, tuberculosis and venereal diseases; port health work; maternal and child welfare; medical treatment of the poor, and the supervision of hospitals and the medical profession.

(2) Department of Public Assistance, responsible for the protection of abandoned children, orphans and the poor; for philanthropic

organizations and public institutions, and for pensions and assistance to war victims.

(3) Department of Public Relief, concerned with unemployment, housing for the poorer classes, and the care of refugees.

The budget of the ministry for 1935–6 amounted to 733 million drachmae. The principal items of expenditure in million drachmae were:

School of Hygiene	4	Control of infectious disease	10
Prefectual health services	11	Control of malaria	11
Maternal and child welfare	1·6	Control of trachoma	1
Medical assistance	27·5	Control of venereal disease	9
Pensions and assistance to war victims	243	Anti-tuberculosis measures	38

In 1937 a special tax, levied in the form of a social welfare stamp, was imposed on tobacco and correspondence. The proceeds, which were estimated to be 500 million drachmae, were to be used exclusively for public health work and social welfare, and were to be additional to budget credits. Enlargement of certain hospitals and sanatoria and the creation of a school for the training of visiting and hospital nurses were among the first projects to be so financed.

Medical Services

Local Health Centres have been set up in each *nomós* and the time-honoured *nomiátros* (the doctor of the *nomós*) and his bureau thus replaced, though in some areas the change is as yet but nominal. These health centres, of which there are two grades, are responsible for all the health activities in the *nomoí*. There are seven grade A health centres staffed by a medical hygienist in charge, a deputy, three part-time medical practitioners, four visiting nurses and three sanitary inspectors; the majority of *nomoí* have grade B health centres with a technical staff of one medical hygienist and two sanitary inspectors.

Municipalities (*dhímoi*) must each appoint a health officer: if the officer appointed be insufficiently trained, he must take a special course at the School of Hygiene. Communes (*koinótites*) with an annual budget in excess of 400,000 dr. must appoint health officers under similar conditions. Only a very small number of communes do so as yet, and in most rural communes local practitioners are charged with such public health duties as circumstances permit.

When war broke out in 1940 the organization of these local health centres was still in the stage of development.

The School Medical Service is independent of the Ministry of Health: it is directly under the control of the Ministry of Education. The staff in 1938 consisted of fifty-two medical officers and three nurses. They are responsible for the regular medical inspection of schools and scholars, for the vaccination and revaccination of school-children and the protection of their health.

The Army and Navy Medical Services are under the control of their respective ministries. Selected officers of both services attend courses for the Diploma of Public Health at the School of Hygiene.

The Port Health Service at Piraiévs possesses equipment for the fumigation of ships.

Medical Schools and Hospitals

In 1938 practising physicians in Greece numbered about 6,500, of whom no less than 1,800 resided in Athínai-Piraiévs, which had a population of about a million. Most of the leaders of the medical profession have obtained their medical education, in whole or in part, in foreign universities, mostly in France or Germany. A few have been trained in Italy. Many of them are staunch protagonists of their respective schools; their scientific and professional outlook is that of the particular University in which they were trained, a fact which sometimes militated against the smooth working of schemes demanding combined effort. Many of the medical officers now occupying key positions in the public health service have been able to study conditions in other European countries or in the United States. They have been helped by travelling fellowships awarded by the Rockefeller Foundation or the Health Organization of the League of Nations.

The Medical Faculty of the University of Athens. This faculty provides a fairly high standard of medical education It confers the usual degrees and diplomas, and its teaching facilities in anatomy, physiology, pharmacology and pathology have been much improved during recent years. Modern buildings erected during the past ten years now house many of the departments.

The School of Hygiene, Athens. In 1938 the School of Hygiene had nine divisions: microbiology and serology; epidemiology and statistics; malariology and tropical diseases; public health; social hygiene; biochemistry and nutritional hygiene; school hygiene; sanitary engineering; metereology and climatology in relation to public health. In its early years the malariology and sanitary engineering divisions were directed by experts belonging to the staff of the

Rockefeller Foundation; the Foundation financed in very large part the activities of these divisions and later made contributions to the development of the school as a whole. In 1940 the school was staffed entirely by Greek experts.

The School of Hygiene is directly under the authority of the Ministry of Health. Its relations with the Medical Faculty of the University of Athens have been defined; professors at the head of the divisions of the school are nominated by the School Council, such nominations being approved by the Medical Faculty of the University before being ratified. The school holds post-graduate courses of training for medical officers of health. Courses of instruction are also held for sanitary inspectors.

The Ambelokípi Health Centre is attached to the School of Hygiene. This is a model local health service for the part of Athínai in which the School of Hygiene is situated, and it provides admirable facilities for the practical training of health officers and of public health nurses. Its activities include pre-natal work, maternity and child welfare work, school hygiene, dental care, control of communicable diseases including tuberculosis and venereal disease, sanitation, vital statistics, health education and propaganda.

The Hellenic Pasteur Institute is affiliated with the Pasteur Institute of Paris and had a French Director. For many years it has been an active centre of medical research; it manufactures serums and vaccines and provides anti-rabies treatment.

The Syngros Hospital for Venereal Diseases provides admirable teaching in this branch of medicine.

Other Medical Institutions under the direct supervision of the Ministry of Health include hygiene and bacteriological laboratories in Athínai and Thessaloníki, disinfecting stations at Athínai, Thessaloníki, Kérkira and Sámos, and an anti-rabic vaccination laboratory with a hospital in Athínai.

Training Schools for Nurses are attached to many hospitals: the Greek Red Cross Society possesses a large modern hospital in Athínai with an excellent school of nursing, and the Evangelismós Hospital, Athínai, also has a large training school.

Hospital Accommodation is provided by government institutions, the municipal health authorities and philanthropic societies. The philanthropic hospitals are among the best; the Greek Red Cross Hospital and the Evangelismós Hospital are both good, and the Madame Venizelos Maternity Hospital was a model of its kind.

Official Greek returns give the total number of hospitals of various types in 1939 as:

Type	Government		Municipal		Philanthropic		Total	
	Hospitals	Beds	Hospitals	Beds	Hospitals	Beds	Hospitals	Beds
General	21	1,557	22	2,265	28	2,011	71	5,833
Sanatoria (general and T.B.)	7	2,635	0	0	5	745	12	3,380
Venereal and skin diseases	6	598	0	0	0	0	6	598
Infectious diseases including leprosy	5	741	1	32	0	0	6	773
Total	39	5,531	23	2,297	33	2,756	95	10,584

From the above figures, hospitals for children, for women, lunatic asylums, ophthalmic and certain small special hospitals, have been excluded.

Sanitation

Standards of sanitation in Greece are low, though noteworthy improvements have been effected during recent years. The prevalence of intestinal infections is high and it is surprising that it has not been higher: Greece owes much to the sun. For the most part excreta disposal is primitive; unprotected water supplies are common; flies are very abundant.

Athínai and Piraiévs with a population in 1928 of nearly 700,000 were almost unique among European cities of comparable size, inasmuch as they possessed (until very recently if they do not still) no system for the disposal of sewage worthy the name. The soil was grossly contaminated from leaching cesspools. A rainstorm would convert certain roads into torrents, and in dry weather dust was dangerously offensive. Elaborate drainage and sewerage schemes were planned and discussed for many years; the problems involved were fundamentally not difficult, as the city is in close proximity to an almost tideless sea. The cost involved in carrying out the scheme was, however, high: for example, in certain refugee settlements near Piraiévs, which have been built on hard rock, the laying of drains might prove prohibitively costly. Ten years ago when the water supply of Athínai was altogether insufficient for the greatly increased population, conditions could hardly have been worse. Then Athínai

Plate 89. The Marathón Dam

The reservoir, started in October 1926 and completed in October 1929, provides Athínai with its water supply. It has a capacity of 1,448,000,000 cu. ft., or nearly 3 years' supply. The dam, 177 ft. high and 935 ft. long, is constructed of concrete masonry and is entirely faced with white marble.

Plate 90. Varlaam Monastery, Metéora

There were once twenty-four monasteries on these remarkable pinnacles of rock near Kal báka: to-day, only four remain. Varlaam monastery, founded in 1517, is now reached stone-cut steps.

Plate 91. Dhiónisos Monastery, Mount Athos

The convent is on the west coast of the Athos peninsula and was founded in 1375 by th Emperor, Alexis III. The monastic buildings are grouped around the church.

had its new water supply and a transformation was effected (Plate 89).

Greece is a country of extremes; from the public health point of view one can find examples of the worst and the best. The water supply of Athínai is one of the best. A narrow valley in the hills above Marathón has been converted into a lake by an imposing dam constructed of marble quarried on the spot. The water as it leaves the lake is of a high degree of purity, and near Athínai it is chlorinated and filtered before distribution. Athínai and Piraiévs are thus assured a plentiful and pure supply of water for many years, whatever the rate of growth of the city may be.

Other Greek cities have had urgent drainage and water-supply problems to solve. Some years ago the water supply of Pátrai was insufficient in quantity and was intermittent. Suction exercised by empty water pipes laid in proximity to sewers was responsible for grossly contaminated water, and consequent outbreaks of dysentery and other intestinal diseases were frequent.

The Sanitary Engineering Division of the School of Hygiene at Athens, by means of model installations in various parts of Greece, and by the instruction given to health officers and sanitary inspectors, has made a very valuable contribution to the public health services of Greece.

Health Conditions among Greek Refugees

A full account has been given elsewhere (see p. 368) of the overwhelming influx of Greek refugees into Greece during the later stages of, and after, the disastrous war with Turkey. They had arrived destitute for the most part, and no provision for their proper reception had been, or could have been, made. The prevalence of communicable diseases was high and the hygienic standards low, both in reception areas and in parts of the countries of origin of the refugees. Typhus fever, typhoid and the dysenteries threatened to become serious among them, under-nourished as they were and without adequate shelter. Tuberculosis also was rife. Mortality rates were high. On the whole, however, the crisis was surmounted with much less loss than could have been reasonably hoped for at the time.

One could find a good deal to criticize adversely from the health point of view in many of the settlements for which the Refugee Commission was responsible. It is unfortunate, for instance, that health considerations were not the determining factor in siting agricultural colonies, especially in Makedhonía, where malaria is so widely prevalent. Many settlements are located in areas in which adequate malaria control is difficult and costly, and numerous dispensaries must be maintained.

Vital Statistics

In the following table are given the birth-rates, general death-rates, and infant mortality rates for Greece for 16 years:

Year	General death-rate per 1,000 inhabitants	Birth-rate per 1,000 inhabitants	Deaths of infants under 1 year per 1,000 live births
1922	16·9	22·6	82
1923	17·8	19·9	92
1924	16·9	21·2	98
1925	15·2	26·9	90
1926	14·2	30·7	75
1927	16·6	29·3	100
1928	17·0	30·5	94
1929	18·4	29·0	111
1930	16·3	31·4	99
1931	17·8	30·9	134
1932	18·0	28·5	129
1933	16·9	28·8	123
1934	15·0	31·2	112
1935	14·9	28·3	113
1936	15·2	28·1	114
1937	15·2	26·4	121

It is not possible to extract from these figures any evidence of sustained improvement in health conditions during recent years. Further, the figures do not bear out the impressions of observers of the fluctuating health conditions in Greece during this period; thus the question as to the degree of reliance to be placed on these statistical returns calls for consideration. The year 1922 witnessed the beginning of the large-scale influx of refugees. One would have expected this to have been accompanied by considerably increased general death-rates. It is probable, however, that vital occurrences during these early years of refugee settlement were not registered with such completeness as they were during the last ten years. There was, moreover, a considerable amount of guess-work involved in estimating the populations on which the annual rates of the earlier years were calculated. Prior to the Greek census of 1928 the estimated number of refugees in Greece was given as 1,526,500. The census returns disclosed only 1,222,000. The relatively low infant mortality rates recorded between 1922 and 1928 are probably an indication that births were registered more meticulously than were deaths of infants: this is frequently the case, more especially with regard to male births. One is on safer ground in basing conclusions on the figures for the years 1928–37. These give an average annual death-rate of 16·5 ‰, and an average birth-rate of 29·4 ‰, with a tendency for both rates to fall. The excess of births over deaths therefore approximates to 13 ‰ per annum. The infant mortality rate varied around 115 ‰ live births per annum.

The mean Greek death-rate of 16·5 is lower than similar rates for the same period of time for Bulgaria 16·8, Yugoslavia 18·2 and Romania 20·3, but is about 50 % in excess of the death-rate for England and Wales. The birth-rate of 29·4 is almost the same as that of Bulgaria 29·1, but lower than that of Yugoslavia 31·7 and of Romania 33·3. The Greek birth-rate is double that of England and Wales. The Greek infant mortality rate of 115 per 1,000 live births compares favourably with those of Bulgaria 147, Yugoslavia 149 and of Romania 182, but is still double that of England and Wales.

Causes of Death

Below are tabulated the causes to which deaths in 1936 were attributed, according to the abridged international nomenclature of 1929.

In view of climatic conditions it is rather surprising to find the pneumonias heading the list of causes of death. The tuberculosis death-rate is also high. If influenza, fatal cases of which generally terminate with lung involvement, be included, no less than 25 % of the total deaths were ascribed to respiratory diseases. The death-rate ascribed to senility, 149 per 100,000, is, as in many other countries, unsatisfactorily high. In England and Wales deaths attributed to senility average about 41 per 100,000. Still more unsatisfactory is it to find nearly 9 % of the total deaths ascribed to unknown or ill-defined causes. This is indicative of the lack of skilled medical attendance in a considerable proportion of fatal cases of sickness. As in other Balkan and Mediterranean countries, the death-rate from diarrhoea and enteritis among children under two years of age is high. The high prevalence of these diseases is testimony of unhygienic conditions, contaminated water, tainted food, and flies. In 1936, the typhoid and paratyphoid death-rate was higher than that reported from any other European country.

Mortality by Cause in Greece during 1936

Causes of death (abridged international nomenclature)	Deaths	Rate per 100,000 inhabitants
Typhoid and paratyphoid fevers	1,511	21·9
Typhus fever	8	0·1
Smallpox	10	0·2
Measles	492	7·1
Scarlet fever	128	1·9
Whooping cough	1,381	20·1
Diphtheria	312	4·5
Influenza	2,963	43·0
Plague	0	0·0
Tuberculosis of the respiratory system	7,157	103·9
Other forms of tuberculosis	1,689	24·5
Syphilis	112	1·6
Malaria	5,181	75·2
Other infectious or parasitic diseases	3,843	55·8
Of which acute poliomyelitis	*60*	*0·9*
Of which cerebrospinal meningitis	*64*	*0·9*
Cancer and other malignant tumours	3,419	49·6
Tumours non-malignant or of unspecified nature	297	4·3
Chronic rheumatism and gout	91	1·3
Diabetes mellitus	310	4·5
Alcoholism (acute or chronic)	52	0·8
Other general diseases and chronic poisonings	932	13·5
Progressive locomotor ataxia and general paralysis of the insane	85	1·2
Cerebral haemorrhage, cerebral embolism and thrombosis	4,422	64·2
Other diseases of nervous system and of organs of special sense	2,065	30·0
Diseases of the heart	4,307	62·5
Other diseases of circulatory system	862	12·5
Bronchitis	897	13·0
Pneumonias	14,280	207·4
Other diseases of respiratory system (tuberculosis excepted)	1,547	22·5
Diarrhoea and enteritis	9,825	142·7
Of which under 2 years	*7,626*	*39·4**
Appendicitis	224	3·3
Diseases of liver and biliary passages	1,006	14·6
Other diseases of digestive system	2,060	29·9
Nephritis	4,105	59·6
Other diseases of genito-urinary system	822	11·9
Puerperal septicaemia	429	2·2*
Other diseases of pregnancy, child-birth and puerperal state	383	2·0*
Diseases of skin and cellular tissue and of bones and organs of locomotion	317	4·6
Congenital debility and malformations, premature birth and other diseases of early infancy	5,044	26·1*
Senility	10,273	149·2
Suicide	399	5·8
Homicide	399	5·8
Violent and accidental deaths (suicide and homicide excepted)	2,241	32·5
Causes of death not specified or ill-defined	9,125	132·5
Total	105,005	1,524·8

* Rates per 1,000 living births.

The table is taken from the *League of Nations: Annual Epidemiological Report* for the year 1938 (Geneva, 1941), p. 72.

The outstanding feature of the table is to find a death-rate of 75·2 per 100,000 attributed to malaria, a rate more than twenty times greater than the malaria death-rate of any other European country in 1936. It must be noted, however, that statistics of mortality of different countries are comparable only to a limited extent. Even when a uniform list of causes of death has been adopted, practice differs with regard to the classification of death certificates on which appear more than one cause of death, pre-eminence sometimes being given to contributory causes. Malaria infections contribute to the fatal issue of many diseases, and as a cause of invalidity malaria is without rival, but in a country with adequate medical assistance it is not pre-eminent as a direct cause of death.

Diseases

For geographical reasons we may think of Greece as a frontier country. It is not far from Egypt and the Levant, so that from time to time the country has suffered from serious epidemics of smallpox, plague, typhus and relapsing fever, diseases which are now rare or unknown in central or northern Europe. When political and economic conditions have been favourable the Greeks have been successful in excluding or controlling these epidemics: at other times, owing to wars and other calamities, the diseases have re-established themselves and spread. The epidemics have risen and fallen (but with a tendency to become less and less) several times in the present century. Every war tends to displace populations, destroy agriculture, limit commerce, and expose people to unfamiliar risks of disease: thus the Balkan wars and the war of 1914–18 were periods in and after which epidemic diseases probably tended to increase.

Malaria

Malaria in the Past. There is little doubt that for many centuries Greece and other Mediterranean countries have been seriously malarious: indeed, some scholars attribute the destruction of Greek and Roman civilization, at least in part, to malaria, or more particularly to virulent strains of the parasite which may have been imported from Africa. One may also feel some certainty that outbreaks of the disease have been an almost inevitable sequel of the innumerable wars which have been fought in this area. This effect of war is probably due in part to neglect of agriculture, destruction of food supplies and a consequent reduction of health and resistance, and in part to movement of soldiers or refugees, and the exposure of people to local strains of the malaria parasites, against which they have little immunity. Moreover, the soldier must often live and fight in unhealthy regions avoided by the civilian.

Coming to a more recent epoch, one may suppose that the Balkan wars led to an increase in malaria in Greece and the surrounding lands. The effects of the war of 1914–18 have been carefully recorded, at least in the British, French and German armies. The French and British landed at Thessaloníki in the late autumn of 1915, when the malaria season was almost past. Inadequate steps were taken to prepare for anti-malarial work on a large scale, and in particular the ordinary medical officers received little or no training. At the end of June 1916, the armies of Britain and France on the one side, and Bulgaria and Germany on the other, settled down in very malarious territory, including the valleys of the Axiós and Strimón. It proved impossible to control the *Anopheles*, owing to the vast areas of swamp and other breeding places: protection by nets and quinine even where practised was unsuccessful, and epidemics of malaria almost immobilized the armies during the summers of 1916–18. In the words of the official *History of the Great War*, malaria 'dominated the military and medical situations in Macedonia'.

The position was made still more serious in 1916 by the presence of large numbers of Greek refugees who had come down from the north in front of the Bulgars and who camped along the road from Thessaloníki to Lembét. They suffered from virulent malaria from which many of them died, and they were doubtless a source of infection to British and Allied forces.

In the British forces on the Macedonian front there were approximately thirty thousand admissions to hospital for malaria in 1916, seventy thousand in 1917 and sixty thousand in 1918. The peak month was October 1917, with 14,900 admissions. But it must be remembered that very many men, though sick, were not admitted to hospital, so that perhaps the above figures represent less than half the sickness. For comparative purposes the malaria rates (i.e. the number of admissions for malaria per thousand men per annum) are even more instructive.

Year	Macedonia	Egypt and Palestine	Mesopotamia	East Africa
1916	332	8	69	?
1917	353	45	94	2,880
1918	369	134	96	1,280

The figures show that about a third of the men in the Macedonian force were admitted to hospital for malaria each year: moreover, one should remember that the admissions are concentrated, and that most occur during about six months in summer and autumn, so that for that period the rate is very high indeed. The figures for Egypt and Palestine were much lower; on the other hand, those for East Africa were much higher, partly because the malaria season in that country extends throughout the year.

The malaria mortality (per thousand men per annum) in the British Force was 1·01 in 1916, 0·37 in 1917 and 0·31 in 1918; the figures seem to indicate an improvement in diagnosis and treatment. There was a considerable amount of blackwater fever, a complication of malaria. In the twelve months ending October 1918 there were 136 cases; of these, 85 % occurred from December to April, none in the summer months; the case mortality was 27 %.

The next historical event affecting malaria in Greece was the evacuation of the Greek population from the area round Smyrna. The immigrants were put to live in parts of Makedhonía and Thráki which had previously been populated by Turks and which happened to be very malarious. This, combined with breakdown of cultivation, lack of simple necessities, and general disorganization, resulted in great outbreaks of malaria, which was of a very grave and often fatal type. Among other things very many cases of blackwater fever occurred in the suburbs of Thessaloníki. Indeed, Thessaloníki was for several years the only place in the world in which one could be certain of seeing blackwater fever, and therefore became a place of pilgrimage for pathologists and students of this condition.

The control of *Anopheles* and malaria is nowadays much easier, because of our greater knowledge of the insect's biology, because of the discovery of the larvicidal effects of Paris Green and because anti-malarial oils are much more effective than they were 25 years ago. Moreover large areas of land have been drained, though it should not be forgotten that drainage canals are important breeding places of *Anopheles*. The anti-malarial work of Greece has been in part done by Greeks, in part inspired and financed by the Rockefeller Foundation.

Present Distribution of Malaria. With the possible exceptions of tuberculosis and infant diarrhoea, malaria is the most serious disease of Greece. There is no considerable area of the mainland which is free of it, and in many places the incidence is high and the amount of disability which it causes is great. On the islands, it is known that the incidence tends to be less than on the mainland: but malaria occurs in all the Ionian islands and in most of the Aegean islands except perhaps the very small ones. In Kríti the disease is found in all parts and is severe in the large cultivated plains. Much the same is true of Khíos and Lésvos; Thásos, Imbros and Síros are in general salubrious, though there are marshes or irrigated areas with malaria on each of them.

Wherever it occurs malaria produces far more cases of sickness than deaths, for which reason one would prefer statistics of morbidity rather than mortality; but in Greece malaria is not a notifiable disease, and in any case the man with fever rarely visits a doctor, so that information about morbidity is not very full. There was, however, a very valuable survey made throughout Greece, including the islands, in 1933 by Balfour of the Rockefeller Foundation and his colleagues, a year in which malaria was not above the average. They examined some 8,000 children in sixty-nine places, information from children being for technical reasons more valuable than that from adults: the spleen rate, that is to say the percentage of spleens found enlarged, is used as a measure of chronic malaria, and the parasite rate, that is to say the percentage of children in whose blood the malaria parasite was found, is also recorded. The results obtained may be summarized as follows:

Region	No. of places	Spleens		Bloods	
		No. examined	Rate %	No. examined	Parasite rate %
Makedhonía and Thráki	19	2,439	38	2,402	16
Ípiros	8	788	50	783	25
Stereá Ellás and Évvoia	14	2,095	36	2,112	17
Pelopónnisos	12	1,202	39	1,192	21
Kríti	6	330	40	262	16
Ionian Islands	4	265	18	265	6
Kikládhes	6	1,065	17	645	11
Total	69	8,184	35·6	7,661	17·4

Reclassifying the data in a different manner, these workers found that in thirty-one places with a population exceeding 1,000 the spleen rate was 27·8 % and the parasite rate 13·3 %: in thirty-eight villages, with less than 1,000 inhabitants, the rates were about twice as high, 56·7 and 27·7. The figures clearly demonstrate the gravity of the disease throughout Greece and its lower incidence in the Ionian islands and the Kikládhes.

The official figures for sickness due to malaria on the State Railways are also of considerable interest. In 1937–8, 19·7 % of the men on the Piraiévs-Platí line and 34·2 % of those on the lines radiating from Thessaloníki reported sick with malaria: in the two groups together, 27·6 % of 7,200 men were sick with malaria. These figures are rather lower than the average, which varies between 24 and 45 % for all the railways for the previous 5 years: it is noteworthy that in every year the rate is higher on the Thessaloníki lines than on that from the Piraiévs to Platí.

Another recent observer has studied a group of villages in eastern Makedhonía, some of them very malarious, others not. Making a single visit to each village in the malaria season and questioning the people, he reached the conclusion that on any one day just under 2 % of the population were incapacitated by the disease, and that in the most malarious villages about 5·6 % were incapacitated. If one takes the somewhat conservative guess that about two million of the population of seven million are malarious, and assumes a 2 % incapacity daily during a malaria season of 4–6 months, and a less incapacity in the other months, one obtains a striking idea of the total amount of sickness which is caused by this disease.

The official figures for malaria mortality give the following numbers of deaths from malaria and the death-rates per 10,000 inhabitants for all Greece, for country districts and for towns:

	Deaths			Rates per 10,000		
	Country	Town	All Greece	Country	Town	All Greece
1934	2,570	412	2,980	5·64	1·94	4·46
1935	3,080	522	3,600	6·64	2·42	5·30
1936	4,480	710	5,181	9·52	3·21	7·52
1937	2,880	490	3,365	6·07	2·18	4·83
1938	2,490	336	2,822	5·17	1·49	4·00

Putting these figures for deaths in other terms, one may say that in different years deaths directly due to malaria form from 3·0 to 7·7 of all deaths. Statistics are also available about the malaria deaths and death-rates (per 10,000 living) for separate districts. They need not be quoted at length: the interesting point is that the rates in 1938 were highest in Thráki (6·71), Makedhonía (6·30) and Ípiros (7·60). They were much lower in the rest of the mainland and in Kríti (1·46), and lowest of all in the Ionian islands (0·74) and the Kikládhes (0·41). For the same years, i.e. from 1934 to 1938, the malaria death-rates range from 0·2 to 0·5 for Athínai and Piraiévs: for Thessaloníki the figure is very much higher, between 2·9 and 7·7. There is no other large European city except Chisinau in Romania, which has reported a rate exceeding 1·0 in the same years. For other Greek towns the following malaria death-rates are available for 1937 only:

Population 50,000–100,000		Population 20,000–30,000			
Town	Malaria death-rate per 10,000	Town	Malaria death-rate per 10,000	Town	Malaria death-rate per 10,000
Kaválla	2·37	Sérrai	7·20	Mitilíni	0·88
Vólos	2·37	Komotiní	4·34	Kérkira	0·86
Pátrai	0·41	Dráma	4·29	Khaniá	0·83
		Kalámai	3·98	Iráklion	0·47
		Xánthi	3·77		

Once again the gravity of malaria in the north (Thessaloníki, Kaválla, Dráma, Sérrai) is apparent.

One may summarize the statistical evidence about sickness and deaths due to malaria by saying that it is a serious problem in all parts of Greece including the islands. There is evidence of several sorts indicating that malaria is most grave in the north (Makedhonía, Thráki, Ípiros), less so in Stereá-Ellás, the Pelopónnisos and Kríti, and still less so in the Ionian Islands and the Kikládhes. The city of Thessaloníki, as well as the surrounding provinces, is highly malarious.

It is also important to note that though malaria is much more prevalent close to large marshes, it is almost universal in its distribution. Even a hill village, which seems to be surrounded by an expanse of arid rocky slope, will have a spring or a trickle of water not far from it. This insignificant amount of water will be found to produce *Anopheles superpictus*, which comes into the village and is responsible for the local malaria. This type of 'hill malaria' prevails up to at least 1,200 m., above which there are very few villages.

Anopheles Mosquitoes. The distinction between malaria in the valleys and hills turns upon the biology of two species of mosquito—*A. maculipennis* and *A. superpictus*, which between them are responsible for all malaria in Greece and the Balkans. In general *A. maculipennis* breeds in water which is stagnant or moving slowly: it may breed in large marshes or ponds, or in small borrow pits and minute patches of water which have leaked from irrigation channels, and in the slower reaches of streams. It is difficult to define its breeding places because the insect is very general in its choice of water. This mosquito goes through the winter as an adult, great numbers of which may be found in houses and stables, where the females bite occasionally during the winter. The insects are in winter quarters from early November to early March. In summer one may find enormous numbers of adults in the same places, hundreds or even thousands in a small stable (a point in which it differs from most of the common *Anopheles* of Africa or Asia). The adults of these species fly at least 5 km. in numbers sufficient to cause outbreaks of malaria: this is well established and has been recorded in several places. They are generally most abundant in July or August.

It is important to realize that *A. maculipennis* is not a uniform species but is divided into 'biological races'. It may be unfortunate, but it is true, that these races cannot generally be distinguished either as adult or larva. They are best identified by the eggs, which are different even to the naked eye, and one must identify the races in a locality either by catching females and causing them to lay eggs or by collecting the eggs from the breeding places. This might appear to be an example of entomological finesse carried to absurd lengths; but the races are so different both in their choice of breeding place and in relation to malaria that it is a necessity to identify them.

The main practical point is that the race called *elutus* (or *sacharovi*) bites man for choice, and is a dangerous carrier of malaria. The other races which occur in the area (*typicus* and *subalpinus*) bite cattle for choice, though they are minor, but proved, carriers of human malaria. The difference is striking, for the proportion of *elutus* with infected salivary glands is generally 20 or 30 times greater than the proportion among other races in the same village. This has been shown in several places, notably in Greek Makedhonía, just south of the Bulgarian boundary, on a total of 30,000 dissections (Barber and Rice). It was also found that half the blood-filled *elutus* had fed on man: of the other races 5 % had fed on man, 95 % on cattle, horses, etc. But though the other local races of *maculipennis* (*typicus* and *subalpinus*) are relatively unimportant, they are known to produce malaria in several parts of the Balkans, so that one cannot regard them as harmless.

The larva of the dangerous race, *elutus*, will tolerate more salt than that of other races; indeed, it needs traces of salt and cannot tolerate very pure waters. For this reason its distribution tends to be coastal, though it has been found breeding up to 50 km. from the sea.

The second important species is *A. superpictus*. It may be found breeding in stagnant or slowly moving water, along with various races of *maculipennis*; but it most commonly occurs, in the absence of *maculipennis*, in mountain streams with rough rocky beds. The larva does not actually live in water which is moving rapidly but rather in sheltered spots, even very small ones, along the stream's edge. One also finds them in great numbers, in a stream which is nearly dry, among boulders or in films of water so shallow that the larvae cannot dive, but also in deeper water, especially if sand or dust is floating on the surface. They also occur commonly in small irrigation channels, and the little runnels leading to water mills. A common characteristic of nearly all breeding places is freedom from water plants. This species winters only in the adult state, and in the same places as *A. maculipennis*, but its winter sleep continues rather longer, and the females do not come out and lay eggs, even in the plains, till April, so that there are very few adults of the next generation till June.

The status of *superpictus* as carrier of malaria is now clear. There are areas where no other species occurs, and where malaria is abundant as in Mavríkion (Vóvoda) in Greece, parts of the Struma Valley in Bulgaria, and considerable parts of Cyprus. It is known to feed much on cattle and horses, the presence of which may be supposed to protect human beings.

Though the breeding places of *maculipennis* and *superpictus* overlap, one may to some extent distinguish:

Malaria of plains, mainly transmitted by *elutus* and to some extent by other races of *maculipennis* breeding in still water.

Malaria of hills, solely transmitted by *superpictus*, breeding in or along running water.

It is also true that, though both are widely distributed, *elutus* tends to predominate in the north, *superpictus* in the Pelopónnisos and islands.

The following other species of *Anopheles* occur in Greece: none of them is significant as a carrier of malaria: *A. algeriensis*, *bifurcatus*, *hyrcanus*, *marteri* (hill streams in north), *plumbeus* (water in holes in trees) and *italicus*.

The Control of Anopheles. The general principles of control are well known, but the following particular local points require emphasis:

(1) As the biological races of *A. maculipennis* are fundamentally different one must carry out egg surveys, and concentrate on the race *elutus*. There is no other basis for a satisfactory control.

(2) Females of both species (*maculipennis* and *superpictus*) fly very far, frequently going 5 km. in numbers sufficient to cause malaria.

This sometimes means that one cannot control breeding and must concentrate on other measures. The killing of adult mosquitoes by sprays is a rather new technique which would be particularly important if troops were moving into a new area during the breeding season of the mosquitoes.

(3) Both species pass the winter as an adult, females taking up their quarters in houses and occasionally transmitting malaria all through the winter. At this season no breeding is going on, so that measures for destroying larvae are without effect, but the hibernating adults should be killed with sprays.

(4) The second important species, *A. superpictus*, breeds mostly in running streams which become torrents in winter and spring. There are special engineering difficulties in dealing with water of this type, but the species may be brought under control by alinement of streams, by removing boulders and grass, by supplying alternative irrigation channels and keeping one dry, and by subsoil drains under beds of streams.

(5) In Greece and other Balkan lands rice fields are an important source of malaria-carrying *Anopheles*, and it is certainly necessary to control breeding among the growing rice. This is best done by shutting off the water at intervals, and for long enough to exterminate the larvae (i.e. two consecutive dry days in about every ten, depending on temperature, etc.). This always causes opposition from the cultivator but must be carried through. There is evidence from Portugal and from Bulgaria that this period of drying is not enough to harm the growing rice, indeed it is often beneficial, by killing weeds. The area under rice was slightly over 1,800 ha. in 1937: the most important districts are in Akarnanía, Aitolía, Messinía and Ípiros, and to a less extent in Makedhonía.

(6) In controlling malaria in Greece it is unnecessary to give attention to winter floods: the important thing is that possible breeding places should be under control by the end of May.

The Malaria Season. The season during which fresh cases of malaria occur depends in part on the biology of the mosquitoes. They are active and seeking blood from March or April till November, and malaria parasites (sporozoites) have been found in the salivary glands as early as 11 May. It seems clear that actual transmission is not common in May or even June, and that July, August and September are the months in which it most commonly occurs. After November, when the mosquitoes have gone into winter quarters, it is probable that transmission may occur, for the insects still occasionally bite man, and malaria sporozoites can be found in the salivary glands. The occasional transmission of malaria in winter is also borne out by the periodical examination of the blood of young infants: it is assumed that parasites found in their blood have generally been acquired after birth.

But apart from *Anopheles* there are many other factors which affect the season at which malaria is commonest in a human community. For one thing, the incubation period from the time when the man received the infection from the mosquito is very irregular and may extend to many months: for another there seems to be a tendency for the people infected in previous years to relapse in the hot months. It is certain that complaints at dispensaries, or admissions to hospital are much commoner in summer and autumn than at other seasons. The matter is further complicated by the fact that the different parasites have decidedly different seasons of abundance: thus benign tertian malaria (due to *Plasmodium vivax*) is abundant from May to October inclusive, with a peak in August, but subtertian malaria (*P. falciparum*) from August to December, with a peak in October.

It follows that the relative abundance of the different species of parasite depends on the season at which the human beings were examined. Balfour, quoting the results of some thousands of films from all parts of Greece, examined in summer and autumn, gives the following percentages:

P. vivax (benign tertian malaria)	34
P. falciparum (subtertian malaria)	33
P. malariae (quartan malaria)	31

But in spring and early summer the proportion of *P. vivax* (which is much more chronic) would be higher, and in times of epidemic malaria the proportion of *P. falciparum* would be greatly increased.

The general abundance of malaria varies greatly from year to year. If there has been heavy rain in spring, the breeding places are increased and remain full of water for many months: this will produce an increase of *Anopheles* and of malaria. There are doubtless many other effective factors, and it is only too probable that, owing to economic conditions, the war years will see a great increase in the disease and in the deaths which it causes.

Intestinal Diseases

There is no doubt that intestinal infections are much more prevalent in Greece, particularly in the latter half of the year, than they are in northern Europe. Lower hygiene standards, a lower standard of life generally and, to a less degree, climatic conditions, are sufficient to account for this. Statistical information regarding the prevalence of these diseases, and of notifiable infectious diseases in general, is not complete. The registration of cases of infectious diseases, and of the deaths they cause, was one of the responsibilities of the *nomiátros*, but this is now given to the local health centre. The completeness of registration of cases varies in different *nomoí*, but everywhere the returns of the *nomiátros* giving the number of deaths caused by infectious disease are uselessly incomplete. The figures published by the central statistical office concerning deaths from infectious diseases are obtained from registrars of births and deaths. These are commonly ten times higher than the figures recorded by the health authorities. The publication of both sets of figures causes needless confusion.

Typhoid and Paratyphoid Fevers. Cases of typhoid and paratyphoid fevers notified by Health Authorities in Greece, and the deaths attributed to these diseases by the Central Statistical Office numbered:

Year	Cases (Greek Health Authorities)	Deaths (Central Statistical Office)
1935	4,090	1,263
1936	5,462	1,511
1937	6,266	—

Accepting the figures published by the Central Statistical Office as the more accurate, and on the justifiable assumption that the case mortality rate of typhoid and paratyphoid fevers combined certainly did not exceed 20 %, there were upwards of 6,315 cases of these diseases in 1935 and of 7,555 cases in 1936. These are very conservative estimates, but even so they indicate a higher incidence than in any other European country.

Typhoid and paratyphoid death-rates per 100,000 inhabitants for the three largest cities are tabulated below. It is probable that corrections were not made for persons dying in hospitals who were not normally resident in municipal limits and who may have contracted the disease elsewhere:

	1934	1935	1936	1937
Athínai	13·6	16·8	13·9	18·5
Thessaloníki	15·5	16·2	19·1	13·6
Piraiévs	18·3	12·3	11·4	17·3

Such rates are lower than those for the country as a whole and are not unduly high for Mediterranean ports. As high, or higher rates are commonly reported from Barcelona, Marseilles, Toulon, Genoa and Palermo, for example. The rates for certain Near-East cities, Alexandria, Cairo, Baghdad and Beirut, in the same years were materially higher, generally above 20 and sometimes above 40. Rates in British and North American cities are rarely above 1·0, often 0·5–0·3.

Dysentery is widespread in Greece; both bacillary and amoebic forms of the disease occur, the former predominating. Deaths attributed to dysentery in 1935 numbered 1,535, in 1936 there were 1,822: the figures indicate a very high prevalence for a European country. Cases tend to be sporadic rather then epidemic, and are most numerous during summer and autumn. A very high prevalence of dysentery, and other intestinal infections, in Pátrai in 1932, was attributed to a grossly contaminated water supply: somewhat surprisingly a large proportion of the cases were found to be amoebic.

Enteritis and Diarrhoea, as elsewhere in southern Europe, are still a very serious cause of infant mortality and are indicative of low hygiene standards and maternal ignorance. From the table setting forth the causes of death in Greece in 1936 (see p. 270) it can be seen that of the total of 9,825 deaths attributed to enteritis and diarrhoea, no less than 7,626, or 77 %, occurred among children under two years of age.

Cholera has been absent for many years, but there were outbreaks in the Balkan wars (1912), and in Egypt more recently, though this disease was not observed among the refugees from Asia Minor in 1922–3. One must remember the possibility of cholera again appearing in Greece.

Mild Epidemic Jaundice (not due to paratyphoid) is not uncommon in countries in the eastern Mediterranean.

Tuberculosis

Tuberculosis in Greece usually causes more deaths than any other single condition except pneumonia and senility, and is therefore a serious problem. The death-rates have, however, fallen from 1·684 per thousand of the population in 1928, to 1·166 in 1938, rates almost twice as high as those in England. As in other countries, the rates are higher in urban than in rural districts, and in 1937 they were highest in Attikí and Voiotía (2·717) and Thessaloníki (1·948); medium in Kérkira (1·767) and the Kikládhes (1·028); lowest in Arkadhía

(0·570) and in Rethímni, Kríti (0·360). It is, however, recognized by the authorities that these figures understate the position, since deaths from tuberculosis must frequently be notified, in error, under other headings such as 'unknown causes', pleurisy, etc.

The pulmonary form, in which the disease attacks the lungs, is the most frequent, and is responsible for about 80 % of the deaths. Intestinal tuberculosis causes only about 4 % of deaths, and this fact confirms the statement made by one authority that tuberculous cows' milk is not common in the country. It is a Greek custom to boil milk before use.

Death from tuberculosis is relatively more frequent in males than in females, except at ages 10–19: this high rate in young adult girls is a common finding elsewhere. The peak of male deaths occurs in the age group 20–30, considerably earlier than in western Europe.

The death-rates do not give an accurate picture of the extent of the disease, and the figures of cases diagnosed during life are inaccurate. From experience in other countries it may be taken that the actual incidence of the disease is many times as great as the death-rates, perhaps even 10 times as great. This being so, and in view of the fact that the common pulmonary form is spread from person to person, especially within families, by tubercle bacilli contained in minute droplets of sputum or saliva expelled in the acts of coughing, sneezing or even talking, the high death-rates may be expected to fall but slowly, even under normal conditions. During and after the present war it may be taken as certain that the incidence will increase and the death-rates rise, as a result of under-nourishment and overcrowding.

The Typhus Group

In the Mediterranean area three distinct diseases, epidemic (exanthematous) typhus, murine typhus, and eruptive fever occur. In murine typhus the infection is normally among the rats, and is transmitted by fleas (generally *Xenopsylla cheopis*), either to rat, or occasionally to man. Human cases are therefore sporadic, and more frequent among those whose occupation brings them into contact with rats and their fleas. The disease is mild in man and the death-rate low.

On the other hand, in epidemic typhus, the micro-organism, *Rickettsia prowazeki*, is transmitted by lice directly from man to man, no rodent or other animal being involved. The disease tends therefore to occur, often as a great epidemic, among those who are infested with lice, particularly body lice, and to attack such people as prisoners, soldiers in the field, refugees, and the victims of famine or earthquake: among such the death-rate may be very high. Typhus is also frequent among medical staff, and those who deal with the clothes or bedding of the sick. The louse does not transmit the infection by its bite. The infectious material is the dried excrement of an infected louse, which enters the human body through scratches and cuts (and perhaps through the surface of the eye). The excrement, which remains infectious for many weeks, blows about, so that those who have not actually been bitten by a louse may contract the disease.

Exanthematous Typhus in epidemic form has always been a serious menace in Greece and other Balkan lands. Small numbers of cases are frequent, and great epidemics with enormous loss of life following earthquakes, failure of crops, wars and other calamities have occurred. There were very great epidemics in Serbia and Bulgaria, and rather lesser ones in Greece, in the last two Balkan wars and during and after the war of 1914–18. Perhaps the last occasion on which epidemics occurred in Greece followed the evacuation of the area around Smyrna in 1923. At that time very large numbers of destitute, underfed, poorly clothed refugees poured into Greece, till the refugees considerably outnumbered the native population in several places. There was particularly grave overcrowding in Athínai, Thessaloníki, Pátrai and Kérkira; there were verminous crowds on railway platforms, and typhus patients were found sharing a bed with lousy though healthy persons. The control of the lice and the disease was particularly difficult because few of the refugees possessed a change of garments. Many thousands of cases of typhus occurred, and the mortality among cases in hospital was about 10 %.

More recently the number of cases of typhus notified from Greece has ranged from forty to eighty per year. No distinction is made between the epidemic and the murine diseases, but one may assume that some at least of these are of the epidemic type which is probably much more frequent than the figures indicate, particularly in remote hill villages.

Typhus is not always easy to diagnose, and laboratories in countries in which it may occur must be prepared to carry out the Weil-Felix reaction. In exanthematous typhus this reaction (with *Proteus* X 19) is strongly positive at the end of the first week of the disease, sometimes sooner. Vaccination against typhus has been widely practised, but opinion is not unanimous as to its value.

Eruptive fever (fièvre boutonneuse; Mediterranean exanthematous fever) has been carefully studied in Athínai, where human cases are not rare: the disease also occurs at Vólos, Thessaloníki and in Kríti. Some twenty to thirty cases are notified annually, always in the warmer months. The infective agent is transmitted by the dog tick, *Rhipicephalus sanguineus.*

Relapsing Fever

As in other parts of the Mediterranean area, two distinct types of relapsing fever probably occur in Greece. The tick-carried type is properly an infection of rats and wild rodents. Occasionally, an infected tick bites a man, particularly one whose work brings him into close contact with rats: examples have been seen in workers in the grain trade, in piggeries, and also (in Palestine) in men who worked or lived in caves. The disease is therefore sporadic and uncommon in man. The second type due to *Spirochaeta recurrentis* which is transmitted by lice occurs only in human beings, and may produce large epidemics.

There is very little information about relapsing fever in Greece. The disease was epidemic in the Balkans and Turkey during and after the war of 1914–18, and was prevalent among the refugees entering Greece from Asia Minor in 1923, though it never formed so great a problem as typhus. Very small numbers of cases continued to be notified, the last being apparently in 1937. There is unfortunately reason to fear that under present conditions this disease, like typhus, may again become epidemic. The control of the disease is by the destruction of lice.

It should be remembered that it is difficult to distinguish relapsing fever from malaria except by the microscopic examination of a blood film: this examination is important, for the appropriate drugs are quite different.

Dengue

Dengue is an acute fever: like malaria it is transmitted by mosquitoes. The disease is not in itself serious, death being rare, though the patient is unfit for work for several weeks. But as dengue tends to occur in great epidemics, affecting a high proportion of the people at the same time, it may completely disorganize a community. Most of the individuals who have suffered are immune to fresh infection, so that a period of some years generally passes between epidemics.

The mosquito which transmits the infection is the yellow-fever mosquito, *Aedes argenteus*, a domestic insect, which breeds in small artificial collections of water, such as tubs, cisterns, jars, old bottles and tins, fonts and vases in cemeteries. Control of the insect is very difficult, for it entails house to house inspection and scrupulous attention to detail: a fairly effective measure is to make a piped supply of water available, so that people need no longer store water in the home. In Greece and similar countries this mosquito is common in towns and villages in summer: in winter it becomes rare, and seldom bites. There is evidence that the infection can persist through the winter in the mosquitoes, so that a winter campaign against the few remaining *Aedes* might ensure against the renewal of an epidemic.

Several great epidemics have occurred on the mainland of Greece and in some of the islands, Kríti, Síros for example. An outbreak started in the autumn of 1927 was very serious through the hot months of 1928, and was dying out in the following year. In 1928, it is estimated that there were 1,000,000 cases and 1,500 deaths in a total population of less than 7,000,000: 650,000 cases were in Athínai and Piraiévs, about 90 % of the population suffering. This pandemic was so serious as to cause disorganization of public services, shipping and railways. In that year the disease occurred very widely in Greece, including remote country areas, up to an altitude of about 600 m. It is significant that it did not occur in certain parts of western Makedhonía in which streams flow through the village, so that people do not store water and make breeding places for this mosquito inside their houses: also those parts of Athínai which have a piped supply suffered much less in this epidemic than the rest of the city in which the people have to depend on water carried in and kept in water pots.

It seems that there has been little or no dengue in Greece since 1929 (with the exception of an outbreak in 1935, the diagnosis being a matter of dispute), so that the population has probably lost much of its immunity. If therefore an outbreak occurred it might produce a very great epidemic. It is, moreover, probable that an outbreak anywhere in the eastern Mediterranean or Black Sea would involve the whole region. The military importance of the disease is obvious: large bodies of men not previously exposed to infection might be incapacitated for several months. No artificial means of immunizing man exists.

Yellow Fever

There is the possibility that yellow fever might be introduced by air either from Dakar to the western Mediterranean, or from West Africa through the Anglo-Egyptian Sudan, to Egypt and the Levant. There are two possible means of introduction: a man in the early stages of the disease might come in by air, and infect local mosquitoes, or infected mosquitoes might enter a plane in Africa and leave it in a place where yellow fever did not exist, the accidental carriage of mosquitoes and other insects by plane being well known to occur. In either event a very grave epidemic might be started in the Mediterranean, and maintained during summer months by the mosquito *Aedes argenteus*, which is locally abundant. There are a number of records of such outbreaks of yellow fever in Mediterranean countries. To reduce this risk it is essential to carry out careful control of *Aedes* in airports in the infected area, and in the Mediterranean; to carry out destruction of mosquitoes on planes in transit, methods being available; to be aware of the risk, so that if the disease were imported it would be detected and cases isolated.

Sandflies and Sandfly Fever

A number of species of sandfly (*Phlebotomus*) occur in Greece, not only on the mainland, but also in Kríti, and probably in all the other islands. Those most important to man are *P. papatasii*, *major*, *sergenti* and *perfiliewi* (*macedonicus*). All these insects breed, so far as we know, in similar places, the eggs being laid in cracks in walls or rocks, and perhaps in holes of rats, lizards, etc.: they sometimes breed in great numbers in newly erected walls, perhaps because they are still damp. The destruction of walls and houses by an earthquake has been followed by great increase in the sandflies, owing presumably to multiplication of breeding places, and it is reasonable to think that the same might follow bombardment. The sandflies themselves are active in the hot months, May to October, biting at dusk or in darkness, not flying more than a few score of yards, and not flying unless the air is still.

The control of sandflies is hardly practicable at present. One may often avoid them by sleeping in an exposed position, e.g. on a roof, and by clearing away bushes from around houses.

Sandfly fever is transmitted by the bite of these insects. It commonly gives three days' fever and three weeks' convalescence, so that it is not perhaps a serious matter. The disease doubtless occurs in all parts of Greece, during the summer months, and it attacks nearly all those who have not had it previously.

Leishmaniasis

Visceral leishmaniasis (infantile kala azar) is a relatively common disease in Greece, 210 cases being notified in 1937, and 320 in 1938. This is a matter of some consequence, for nearly all the infected children die unless they are correctly diagnosed and treated. The disease is very localized; groups of cases have been detected in Athínai and suburbs and in hill villages near Árgos. In Messinía, in 1935, 135 cases were seen in hill villages lying between 100 and 500 m. Fifty cases in a population of 30,000 are reported annually from Khaniá in Kríti, and the disease is known to occur in Spétsai and Ídhra. The disease is rare though not unknown in adults, and commonest in children of 2–5 years old. The parasite is transmitted by the bite of sandflies (probably *Phlebotomus major*). The parasite also occurs in dogs, in which indeed it is probably more frequent than it is in man.

Dermal leishmaniasis (oriental sore) is much less common, though there are foci in Kríti, at Athínai and at Neápolis, in south-eastern Pelopónnisos.

Plague

Plague is essentially a disease of rats, and is conveyed from rat to rat (and more rarely to man) by fleas, particularly *Xenopsylla cheopis*. Infected rats are carried by ships, and although modern methods limit the risk of infection from large ships, the small coastal boats are still dangerous. In most Mediterranean countries the disease tends to occur in ports and large towns, rather than in country districts.

In Greece there were many epidemics of plague during the nineteenth and early twentieth centuries; the epidemics visited Piraiévs, Kalámai, Pátrai, Thessaloníki, Síros, and many other places. In the ten years ending 1924 there were generally twenty to thirty human cases per annum, the majority occurring in summer. In 1924 there was a considerable outbreak, some 250 cases being notified from many parts of Greece, including the Ionian and Aegean islands. No cases have been notified from any part of Greece since 1930.

A survey of Athínai showed that the brown rat (*Rattus norvegicus*) is commoner than the black (*Rattus rattus*). Of 11,000 rat fleas, 84 % were *Xenopsylla cheopis*; the average number of fleas of this species per rat was 5·3. If the figure is normally so high, one may state that if plague was introduced there is every probability of its spreading through the rats and to man. The same species of flea is recorded from Kérkira, and is probably widely spread in other ports and cities.

Plague may persist among the rats of a town for long periods without giving rise to any human cases. This may happen quite commonly if *R. norvegicus* is the species concerned. *R. norvegicus* comes into much less intimate contact with man than does *R. rattus*. The systematic examination of a large number of rats caught in Athínai and Piraiévs, over a long period of time, failed to disclose any evidence of plague infection. The principal markets of Athínai, and some storehouses, are very heavily rat-infested, and the growth of the markets has failed to keep pace with the growth of the city. Should plague gain a foothold in Athínai, its eradication would be difficult and costly.

Venereal Diseases

Syphilis and gonorrhoea are doubtless prevalent, and lymphogranuloma inguinale (climatic bubo) is recorded from Athínai, Piraiévs and Síros. The Greek government maintains six venereal and skin hospitals (Athínai, 370 beds; Thessaloníki, 150 beds; smaller hospitals at Iráklion, Ioánnina, Khánia and Khíos).

Parasitic Worms

There are several parasitic worms such as *Ascaris*, and *Trichuris*, very common in countries in which the disposal of excrement is imperfectly carried out: they are doubtless common in Greece. It is also quite probable that the tapeworm of beef (*Taenia saginata*) and of pork (*T. solium*) occur. The hookworm (*Ankylostoma duodenale*) is almost certain to be present in moist coastal areas, especially if the land is irrigated: the infection is not likely to be heavy, or clinically significant.

The Bilharzia disease (due to *Schistosoma haematobium*) is almost certainly absent.

Diseases of the Eye

Diseases of the lids and conjunctiva are doubtless prevalent, particularly in summer. They are aggravated by the glare and dust, and to some extent spread by flies. It seems that several thousand cases of trachoma are treated annually in ophthalmic dispensaries, and that acute conjunctivitis is still more frequent. The amount of trachoma was greatly increased by the entry of destitute refugees from Asia Minor in 1922.

The Greek government maintains a small ophthalmic hospital on the island of Khíos: the university keeps fifty-five beds for ophthalmic cases in Athínai.

Other Infectious Diseases

Several other diseases are notifiable in Greece, apart from those common to childhood, which hardly call for comment. The number of cases or deaths notified in some recent years are as follows:

Disease		1935	1936	1937	1938
Anthrax	Deaths	167	154	—	—
Tetanus	Deaths	192	194	—	—
Undulant fever	Cases	31	23	54	69
	Deaths	7	16	—	—
Cerebrospinal meningitis	Cases	189	261	457	479
	Deaths	55	64	129	—
Smallpox	Deaths	9	10	—	—
Rabies	Deaths	18	15	—	—
Leprosy	Cases	21	41	31	—
	Deaths	14	11	—	—

Anthrax and Tetanus, two diseases associated with agriculture, often occur in human subjects: a similar frequence is noted in other countries in the eastern Mediterranean. Relative to the population both diseases are very many times more common in Greece than in England.

Undulant Fever, commonly acquired from uncooked milk, is not rare: there is evidence that much of it is of the *melittensis* type.

Smallpox, thanks to vaccination, is now rare and the situation might be regarded as safe. It should, however, be remembered that if the Greek health service is not successful in continuing to protect the population by vaccination, the risk of importation from surrounding countries, and of subsequent spread, is considerable.

Leprosy is evidently much more common than the above figures seem to suggest. The mortality figures mean little, as lepers frequently die from intercurrent disease. Even allowing for the fact that the patients live many years, it is difficult to reconcile twenty to forty notifications per year with the provision of 560 beds in special hospitals (Athínai, 178 beds; Spinalónga, 300; Karlóvasi and Khíos, smaller numbers).

Weil's disease (*Leptospirosis icterohaemorrhagica*) has been recorded, and the Leptospira has been recovered from rats in Athínai and Síros. One outbreak (thirty cases, three deaths) was traced to a water cistern, which had been infected by rats and which was used in a café. An infectious spirochaetosis resembling Weil's disease, but differing from it on bacteriological grounds, has also been described.

Tularaemia, it seems, has not been detected in Greece. In view of the fact that it has so often eluded notice, and as it has been detected in Turkey, the possibility of its occurrence should not be forgotten.

Miscellaneous Diseases

Deficiency Diseases, such as rickets, beri-beri, scurvy, pellagra, nutritional oedema, are not referred to in Greek health statistics. Malnutrition, however, is very much in evidence, especially in children, in many parts of rural Greece. The standard of living is miserable among the poorest classes; bread and olive oil, which is lacking in vitamins, form the staple food in many parts where very little milk and very little meat or fish are consumed. Deficiency diseases have undoubtedly become very serious since the occupation of Greece by the Germans.

Drug Addiction, it is understood, is serious; the working classes are said to favour hashish, the more well to do morphine, and cocaine addicts are numerous. It is stated that the public asylums house more than a thousand drug takers.

Biting Insects, other than those already referred to, include domestic mosquitoes, of which the most troublesome is *Culex pipiens*; it very commonly breeds in cess-pits, a point which should be remembered if much annoyance is being caused and the breeding place cannot be found. Bed bugs are extremely common in towns and villages, and fleas are troublesome in April and May.

The black spider (*Latrodectus* 13-*guttata*) almost certainly occurs in Greece. The bite may produce intense pain, and lead to loss of consciousness. The rigid, board-like abdomen has been mistaken for that due to peritonitis.

Mites. There is a small mite (*Pediculoides*), related to the itch mite, which occurs in barley and straw. It attacks the human skin, and causes serious eruptions in people who handle these materials. It is common in many sub-tropical lands, and Greece is a country in which it is particularly troublesome.

Myiasis. There is a large grey fly (*Wohlfahrtia magnifica*) which puts its maggots in wound and cuts, on man or animals. The maggots destroy tissues with great rapidity, and spread sepsis. This insect may occasion a considerable amount of serious injury. The larvae may readily be destroyed, in the tissues, by free irrigation with chloroform water, or by instilling chloroform dissolved in liquid paraffin. This is far more efficacious than swabbing with alcohol or iodine.

Snakes. The only poisonous snakes are vipers, which are quite common in uncultivated areas. The part bitten is likely to be intensely painful, swollen and discoloured, and a medical man will watch for evidence of gangrene or septic involvement.

Hints on the Preservation of Health

In Britain the private citizen hardly needs to take steps to preserve his health. The community sees to it that the water supply is fit to drink and the food up to standard. But in a Mediterranean country, the individual must know how to avoid needless disease, and may have to take active steps to keep himself and others in good health.

The following points are important:

(1) It is necessary to be vaccinated against smallpox and inoculated against typhoid, paratyphoid, and tetanus.

(2) In Greece malaria is widespread. To avoid malaria:

- (*a*) From the beginning of May to the end of November sleep under a mosquito net, carefully used, tucked in and kept in good repair. If sleeping on the ground, tuck the edge of the net under a ground sheet.
- (*b*) Avoid being needlessly bitten: do not leave legs or arms bare after sunset.
- (*c*) If possible kill mosquitoes in houses, or other dwellings, with fly spray.

Mosquito larvae in water are destroyed by various methods, oiling, using poisonous dusts, draining, etc.

If there is no doctor, treat a case of fever by making the man lie down, giving 10 grains of quinine and a dose of salts.

(3) In warm climates a frequent diarrhoea, or dysentery (which means the passage of blood and mucous, often with severe griping pains), or more serious infections such as typhoid fever, are very common in Europeans.

All these troubles are due to germs, which come from some other person's excrement and have been swallowed by the sufferer, perhaps in water, or milk, or uncooked food (raw fruit, salads, etc.).

To avoid these diseases:

(*a*) Inoculation against typhoid and paratyphoid is essential.

(*b*) Chlorinate or boil all water, *however clean it looks*, before you drink it or clean teeth in it.

(*c*) Never drink unboiled milk, or locally prepared mineral waters.

(*d*) Do not eat lettuces or other salad foods, which cannot be cleaned by reason of the folds.

(*e*) Soak fresh fruit, not overripe or damaged, in permanganate of potash before eating it.

(*f*) Try to make cooks and those who serve food wash their hands, and insist on cleanliness in the preparation of food.

(*g*) Burn all odd scraps of food.

(*h*) Keep latrines clean, and as far as possible fly-proof.

(*i*) Insist that latrines, and no other spots, are used.

(*j*) Keep warm at night.

In the absence of a doctor treat these troubles by rest (i.e. lying down, taking nothing but water for a day or so), warmth and a dose of salts.

(4) Typhus and relapsing fever, diseases transmitted by lice, are rare in Greece but epidemics do occur.

Frequent inspection should be made of the inner surface of undergarments. Lice and their eggs can be killed by running a hot iron along seams, or steeping shirts, vests, etc. in cresol before washing them.

BIBLIOGRAPHICAL NOTE

(1) Vital Statistics

The *Annuaire statistique de la Grèce*, 1939 (Athènes, 1940) gives marriage, birth and death-rates for the year 1938, together with retrospective tables. It also includes a special section on Public Hygiene which gives the causes of death by age and sex of the population in the different administrative areas of Greece. Details are given of the number and type of hospitals throughout Greece.

Publications of the Epidemiological Intelligence Service of the Health Organization of the League of Nations give, in convenient form, demographic data and statistics of notifiable diseases. The Annual Epidemiological Report (Geneva, 1941) contains corrected statistics in most cases up to the year 1938. A table gives for thirty-five countries the number of deaths and the death-rate for each rubric of the abridged International List of Causes of Death.

(2) Malaria

The effects of malaria on the armed forces in Macedonia during the war of 1914–18 are described in *History of the Great War, Medical Services, Diseases of the War*, vol. I (London, n.d.) and also in the *History of the Great War, Medical Services, General History*, vol. IV (London, 1924).

A very large number of specialist papers have been written on malaria in Greece. Amongst these are: M. C. Balfour, 'Malaria studies in Greece. Measurements of malaria, 1930–1933', *American Journal of Tropical Medicine*, vol. XV, pp. 301–30 (Baltimore, 1935); M. C. Balfour, 'Some features of malaria in Greece and experience with its control', *Rivista di malariologia*, vol. XV, pp. 114–31 (Roma, 1936); M. A. Barber, A. G. Mandekos and J. B. Rice, 'The seasonal incidence of malaria transmission in Macedonia', *American Journal of Hygiene*, vol. XXIV, pp. 249–67 (Baltimore, 1936); M. Bates and L. W. Hackett, 'The distinguishing characteristics of the populations of *Anopheles maculipennis* found in southern Europe', *VIIth International Congress of Entomology* (Berlin, 1938); H. P. Carr, A. G. Mandekos and M. A. Barber, 'Malaria studies in Greece. A survey of malaria morbidity in a region of East Macedonia', *Annals of Tropical Medicine and Parasitology*, vol. XXIX, pp. 399–405 (Liverpool, 1935); E. Martini, 'Die biologische Malariabekämpfung in Mazedonien', *Zeitschrift für angewandte Entomologie*, Bd. VII, pp. 225–86 (Berlin, 1921); G. Pandazis, 'La faune des Culicides de Grèce', *Acta Instituti et Musei zoologici Universitatis Atheniensis*, Tomus I, pp. 1–27 (Athínai, 1935); J. B. Rice and M. A. Barber, 'The varieties of *Anopheles maculipennis* in a region of Greek Macedonia', *Bulletin of Entomological Research*, vol. XXVIII, pp. 489–97 (London, 1937).

(3) Other Diseases

The following papers give specialist information on certain diseases: G. Blanc and J. Caminopetros, 'Recherches Expérimentales sur la dengue', *Annales de l'Institut Pasteur*, Tome XLIV, no. 4, pp. 367–436 (Paris, 1930); 'The dengue epidemic in Greece', *League of Nations Monthly Epidemiological Report of the Health Section of the Secretariat*, no. 9 (Geneva, 1928); G. Blanc and J. Caminopetros, 'Etudes épidémiologiques et expérimentales sur la fièvre boutonneuse, faites a l'Institut Pasteur d'Athènes', *Archives de l'Institut Pasteur de Tunis*, Tome XX, pp. 343–94 (Tunis, 1932); M. A. Gautier, 'Rapport de la Commission des epidemies en Grèce', *Grèce medicale*, Tome XXVI, pp. 1–26 (Syra, 1924); Sir Patrick Hehir, 'Typhus fever in Greek refugees', *Annals of Tropical Medicine and Parasitology*, vol. XVII, pp. 347–58 (Liverpool, 1923); C. Seyfarth, 'Ueber die Pest in Griechenland auf Grund einer Studienreise im Herbst 1924', *Münchener medizinische Wochenschrift*, no. 34, pp. 1428–31 (München, 1925); C. Seyfarth, 'Infektionskrankheiten und ihre Bekämpfung unter den Kleinasiatischen Flüchtlingen in Griechenland, Kreta und Korfu', *Zeitschrift für Hygiene und Infektionskrankheiten*, Bd. CIV, pp. 682–702 (Berlin, 1925).

Chapter X

EDUCATION

Historical Background: The Administration of Education: Primary Education: Secondary Education: Higher Education: The General Standard of Education: Learned Societies and Libraries: Bibliographical Note

Historical Background

Before the War of Independence, 1821–32, education and religion were firmly interwoven, for Mohammed II, the conqueror of Constantinople, had granted the Patriarch and bishops of the Greek Orthodox Church not only liberty of worship, but also the right to found and direct Greek schools. During the long period of subjection to the Turks, the village priests, though they could hardly read and write themselves, collected the children of their parishes, taught them the Greek alphabet and kept alive and vigorous the Greek language and culture.

The nationalists of the nineteenth century realized that education was a first need of the people, and in 1822 a Committee was set up at Návplion to organize state education. It proposed that free and compulsory primary education should be maintained by the *dhímos* (the local authority), and that secondary education, which was to be neither free nor compulsory, should be given in Hellenic schools and gymnasia. In 1828, Capodistrias put the scheme into practice: 71 demotic (primary) schools were opened, 18 Hellenic schools and 3 gymnasia.

In 1833 education was brought within a state system which remained much the same until 1928. Four years' attendance at a demotic school was made compulsory for all children from 6 to 10 years of age, and the subjects to be taught were religion, reading, writing and arithmetic, and, 'if possible', history and geography. Secondary education was organized in two stages: Hellenic schools offered a three-year course with teaching in ancient Greek, Latin, geography, history, mathematics and French, in addition to primary school subjects; gymnasia, a further three-year course (after 1840, a four-year course) in the same subjects, to prepare pupils for the University.

Teachers' training colleges were also established: intending teachers entered after their second year at a Hellenic school (i.e. after six years' education) and sat for their certificate after two years' training. In 1836, Otho founded the Polytechnic which was to give instruction in technical subjects and to have University status, and in 1837 the University of Athens, which soon became an intellectual centre for Greeks throughout the Near East.

Administrative and Social Problems

Development from these beginnings was slow and interrupted, and much of the framework remained an ideal rather than a reality. There was no lack of will to make use of the opportunities, but practical difficulties were great.

Poverty greatly hindered educational progress; there was a shortage of teachers, of school buildings and even of scholars. Teachers' salaries were a mere pittance, and, though public holidays were more numerous than in England and summer vacations were long, holidays did not allow sufficient consecutive time to earn much from other sources. The profession was therefore unattractive and of necessity it became in practice a part-time occupation, to the detriment of school work. Moreover, teachers were badly trained; the essential minimum requirements of education were often disregarded, especially during and immediately after the war of 1912–22. Poor educational qualifications lowered still further the standing of the profession, and thus increased the shortage. Secondly, school buildings were inadequate; most schools were housed in any available shed, however unsuitable it might be for the teaching of children. The Liberal government of 1911 began to build modern schools, but the work was interrupted by the first Balkan war. Finally, in spite of the law, many children failed to attend school. In times of economic depression it was essential that children should earn; in periods of war, shortage of adult male labour created a demand for child labour in the fields and in the factories. Moreover, secondary education did call for some fees, small it is true, but often more than parents could afford.

Political unrest and the absence of a permanent civil service also created serious difficulties. Teachers were civil servants, and their appointment and dismissal were in the hands of the Minister for Education. However mild their political views, they might find themselves at any time out of work or transferred to a remote village: in 1894, for example, a Minister told the Deputies that of 3,256 teachers, 1,092 had been transferred and 1,420 dismissed. In 1899, a Supreme Council of Education (*Anótaton Ekpedheftikón Simvóulion*) was set up to decentralize somewhat the control of education; various powers, hitherto in the hands of the Minister, were given to it, and schools were to be administered through 71 local boards. The right of dismissal, however, still remained with the government. In 1922, teachers were allowed to form a Trade Union, which sends two delegates to the Council and which has done much to improve the conditions of the profession.

The language question, which has become closely linked with party politics, has perhaps complicated educational development more than any other single factor. *Dhimotikí*, the language of the people, was considered a vulgar patois by a group of exiled Greeks who became prominent figures in the War of Independence. They favoured a so-called pure Greek, *katharévousa*, for use as a national language (see p. 320). It was originally laid down that all instruction in schools, even in the earliest stages, should be in *katharévousa*, so that pupils speaking *dhimotikí* at home had to learn the vocabulary and grammar of a language virtually new to them. In 1911 it was proposed to introduce *dhimotikí* as the medium of education in all primary schools; the proposal raised an outcry from the Royalists largely in a spirit of political opposition, from some professional men on grounds of prestige, and from some teachers who only knew the grammar of the *katharévousa*. In 1917, Venizelos adopted the proposal, but in 1920 when the Royalists came into power they forbade the use of *dhimotikí* in schools and made a public bonfire of the new text-books written in it. Chaos followed. Every change of government meant a change in the medium of primary education: in 1922, *dhimotikí* was reintroduced by Plastiras; in 1925, Pangalos forbade its use; in 1928, it was restored by the Coalition government with the proviso that *katharévousa* should be taught four hours weekly in the two top forms; in 1932, *katharévousa* was to be taught in all forms; in 1933, the two top forms were to be taught exclusively in *katharévousa*; and in 1936, Metaxas, always using *dhimotikí* himself, re-established teaching in the popular tongue throughout the primary schools and ordered the publication of an official grammar of the language.

The acquisition of new territories and new population, and the absence of any long period of peace in which to organize a comprehensive educational scheme, further hindered the progress of educational development. The new provinces acquired in 1913 had a school system rather different from the remainder of Greece, and numerous schools were subsidized by various Balkan nationalities, each interested in furthering its own political ends. A number of kindergarten schools had been opened by a Greek patriot society at the end of the nineteenth century, and these kindergarten schools were now increased in number, principally to give instruction to children brought up under foreign rule, whose parents did not even speak Greek. The reorganization of education in these new provinces was hardly complete at the outbreak of war in 1914, and on the conclusion of peace, the exchange of nationals between Bulgaria and Greece, and Turkey and Greece, had completely changed the make-up of the population (Fig. 108). The children of these immigrants, even the older ones, had received little education owing to the disturbed conditions in which they had grown up, and some of them belonged to families from the interior of Asia Minor who did not speak Greek. The need for kindergarten schools therefore remained, and in 1936 there were 651 kindergarten schools in Greece, mostly run on Montessori lines. Of these, 484 were in Makedhonía, 74 in Ípiros (60 in Ioánnina), 48 in Dhitikí Thráki, 20 in the *nomós* of Attikí-Voiotía, and of the 19 remaining, 9 were in Lárisa. This distribution exactly reflects the new settlements of Greek immigrants, established 1922–6 (Figs. 106 and 107).

Recent changes. Venizelos and Metaxas both introduced important changes: Venizelos worked to improve and extend educational facilities, Metaxas to curtail them.

Venizelos, in 1928, tried to make real the reforms of 1911 that re-affirmed the compulsory nature of primary education, raised the school-leaving age from 10 to 12 years, and consequently increased the number of forms in demotic schools from four to six. He unified the system of education in old and new Greece by changing the system in the old provinces: the Hellenic schools were abolished and gymnasia with four-year courses changed into gymnasia with six years. Education during the first two years in the gymnasia replaced that given in the Hellenic schools and directly continued the instruction of the demotic schools. The liberal government, even during the period of severe economic crisis, did not reduce expenditure on education; in fact, with increasing population expenditure rose.

Metaxas, however, when he came into power in 1936, curtailed the amount spent on education and made secondary and University education more costly and more difficult of entry. He increased secondary school fees and added two more classes to the gymnasium, so that pupils who intended to proceed to secondary education must make the decision at 10 years old. The Leaving Certificate examination was to be taken at 16 years of age and a University entrance examination two years later.

The Administration of Education

Education is largely subsidized, organized and controlled by the state. Private schools are permitted if they conform to the law, and Greek education owes much to the generous endowment of schools and colleges both by wealthy Greeks and by foreigners. Since 1929, foreigners have not been allowed to open primary schools: the ban was imposed to stop the appearance of more Catholic and Uniat schools.

The Minister of Education and Religion is responsible for the evolution and direction of educational policy, for the administration of education within the law, and for the control of expenditure. He has also the power of veto, though no power of initiative, in respect to the appointment and dismissal of teachers in schools and Universities.

The Council of Education (*Anótaton Ekpedheftikón Simvóulion*) has eighteen members: twelve of them must hold a degree in arts, two in mathematics, and two in physics. One member must be a teacher of physical training and one must represent the private schools. The Council appoints teachers after the nominations have been scrutinized by the Minister, controls promotions and transfers, and approves the text-books for use in schools.

Local education is under the direction of a local committee composed of the *nomárkhis*, the inspector of schools appointed to the *nomós*, a judge, a local secondary school teacher and a delegate from the primary school teachers of the *nomós*. This committee had disciplinary power and the right to propose the appointment and dismissal of teachers. Such proposals are sent to the Council of Education in Athens which transmits them to the Minister of Education for approval.

Primary Education

In 1937–8, there were 8,339 primary schools in Greece with 15,573 teachers (8,854 men and 6,719 women) and 985,018 pupils (531,735 boys and 453,283 girls).

The Primary or Demotic Schools

As a rule, demotic schools have six forms requiring a normal attendance of six years; the smallest rural schools have at least four classes, even if all four are taught by one teacher. Instruction is given throughout the school in religion, reading, writing and arithmetic, but the curriculum may also include the study of Greek history and geography, elementary natural history, drawing, singing and gymnastics.

Some 700 demotic schools have infant departments attached to them, but some kindergartens are independent. In 1938, there were 743 infant schools with 38,338 pupils and 781 teachers: most of these schools are in the new provinces.

Night Schools

There are only sixty-one night schools in Greece concerned with primary education, of which eighteen belong to the state and forty-three to private authorities: all the state schools, with the exception of two in Athens, are in northern Greece and twenty-four of the private ones are in the capital.

Secondary Education

The Gymnasia (*yimnásion*, pl. *yimnásia*)

The gymnasia are entered by public examination, taken by pupils at the age of 10 years, and they give a further six years' training before the Leaving Certificate is taken, and two more years before the entrance examination to the University is taken. In 1937 there were 304 gymnasia with 67,933 pupils.

The curriculum of the gymnasia during the first two years continues the general education on the same lines as in the primary schools, and begins instruction in ancient Greek, in mathematics, physics and hygiene. In the next four years there are, in theory, three parallel alternative courses: classical, practical (scientific) and commercial. The classical course is designed for pupils intending to go to the University and includes ancient Greek, Latin, mathematics with trigonometry and cosmography. The scientific course, intended primarily for those proceeding to the Polytechnic, has less advanced ancient Greek and Latin, but more advanced mathematics, and adds lessons in geography, mechanical drawing, physics and sometimes chemistry. The pupils following the commercial course study a little ancient Greek but no Latin, and are mainly instructed in mathematics, geography, elementary economics, political science and accountancy. Greek history is studied by all pupils throughout the school, and modern European history is taught in the last year.

The semi-gymnasia are schools which offer only the first two years' general course of the gymnasium; they are not considered wholly successful and many have been closed down, but in 1937 there were 161 schools with 5,618 pupils, mostly in small provincial towns.

Special Schools

Secondary schools for vocational training were attended in 1938 by over 30,000 pupils. A Junior Technical School is attached to the Polytechnic of Athens and has four-year courses in surveying, engineering and mechanical drawing. A school for cheese makers with twenty pupils is at Ioánnina, and a junior forestry school to train forestry inspectors at Vitína. Thirty agricultural schools have been established in centres widely distributed throughout Greece, and much of the recent progress in agricultural methods is due to the training they give. They have about 100 pupils and fulfil a great need in a country where agricultural practices are still relatively primitive. There were 113 commercial and industrial schools with nearly 14,000 pupils in 1938, a number which reflects the interest of the Greeks in commerce and trade. Military schools prepare boys for careers in the army, navy and air force and others train candidates for administrative posts in the civil service. Religious seminaries educate boys for the priesthood and a few schools give training for entry into the social services.

Private Schools

Many children, especially girls, of the wealthier classes attend private schools, some founded by Greeks, others by foreign enterprise. These schools are not bound by the state syllabus, but are visited by the state inspectors. In 1938, there were ninety private secondary schools in Greece with about 7,500 pupils; seventy-seven of the schools were in the *nomós* of Attikí-Voiotía. In Athens itself there are three famous schools for girls: the Volmerenge boarding school, a French school which was transferred to Athens from Návplion over a century ago; the High School founded in 1831 by an American clergyman, Dr Hill; and the Arsakeion School, opened in 1836 and endowed by and named after the benefactor, Arsakes. This last school has branches at Pátrai, Lárisa and Kérkira.

These schools have done much for the secondary education of girls and the training of intending teachers. In 1927, a residential school for boys, modelled on the English public school tradition, was opened at Spétsai. It was endowed by a Greek merchant, and the experiment was encouraged by Venizelos who hoped that it would educate boys to take, in due course, high posts in the government service.

Higher Education

Teachers' Training Schools

There are separate training colleges for kindergarten, primary and secondary school teachers, and there are also schools for teachers of physical training, music and other specialist subjects. Some intending primary school teachers receive both their general education and their training at the same school, others take part of a gymnasium course first, but all must have the equivalent of three years' instruction in a gymnasium and two years in a training school (*Dhidhaskáleion*). A kindergarten teacher must take a four-year course after the primary school stage. Not all secondary school teachers hold a University degree; some go directly after completing a full six-year course at a gymnasium and obtaining a Leaving Certificate to a teachers' training course of two years' duration; others qualify for the higher posts and take a three-years' University course, followed by a one-year training course.

Technical Colleges

Higher education in technical and special subjects is well provided. There is an Agricultural College in Athens which gives a three-year course with nine months' practical work; it has, in addition, an active research department. The School of Economics and Commerce, the Pandios School of Politics and the School of Fine Arts all have University status and give advanced courses of instruction.

The National Polytechnic of Athens is an old foundation, originally established in 1836, but there have been breaks in its history. It was re-established in 1887 and again in 1914. It offers technical instruction in a wide variety of subjects; the faculties of Civil, Mechanical and Electrical Engineering, Industrial Chemistry, and Architecture attract the most students. The Polytechnic has well-equipped laboratories and workshops, and in the session 1937–8 there were forty-seven professors and lecturers and 521 students working there.

The Universities

The Universities of Greece are modelled on the University systems of northern Germany and though in the early days many of the professors were foreigners, in recent years the great majority of University teachers have been Greek.

The University of Athens was founded as a state University in 1837. When the Ionian islands were ceded to Greece in 1864, the 'Ionian Academy', founded by Lord Guildford in 1824 as a centre of University education in the islands, was incorporated in the National University at Athens. A Greek merchant, Domboli, left funds in 1854 to accumulate for fifty-seven years which were then to be used to endow a University in the memory of Capodistrias. In 1911, these funds matured and the University of Athens received them, qualifying for the bequest by changing its name to the National and Capodistrian University. Technically, the University is divided into two, the National University receives a subsidy from the state, the Capodistrian University lives on the income from the Domboli bequest, but the two form a single academic whole, governed by a single Convocation. The Professors of each Faculty propose appointments for vacant posts to the Minister of Education, who has the right of veto but no right of initiative.

The University has fine buildings, a high standard of scholarship and five Faculties—Theology, Law, Medicine (including Pharmacy and Dentistry), Philosophy, Physical Science and Mathematics. In 1938 there were 218 professors and lecturers and 5,748 students. The normal University course is four years, except in Medicine (six years), and Law and Medicine attract the greatest number of students; in 1937 out of 1,679 students leaving, 913 sat for the law degree and 309 for medical degrees. Students are drawn from all over Greece and also from Cyprus, the Dodecanese and Egypt. Formerly, Athens attracted students from other Balkan countries, but the establishment of national universities has changed this; the opening of a University at Rhodes will also, no doubt, decrease the numbers of students from the Dodecanese.

The University of Thessaloníki was founded by the state in 1925 to meet the increasing needs of the country and especially those of the northern provinces. The University is administered by the Senate and the Economic (Rectorial) Council presided over by the Rector. The recommendations of these bodies are subject to the approval of the Minister of Education, who has the right of veto but not the right of initiative.

Work began the year after the formal foundation with the opening of the Faculty of Philosophy. The following year the Faculty of Science (made up of the Departments of Physics, Chemistry, Natural Sciences and Mathematics) and the Faculty of Law were opened. The School of Forestry has been transferred from Athens to Thessaloníki and a Faculty of Agriculture and Forestry constituted; recently, a Faculty of Veterinary Surgery has been added. A Chair of Balkan History was established in the Faculty of Philosophy, an excellent departure, as the study of Balkan problems in their historical setting is much needed. In 1937–8 there were seventy-six professors and lecturers and 1,582 students in the University. The students, largely drawn from the new provinces, would profit, it was felt, by the study of the applied sciences and local and modern aspects of history, law and literature. It was thought that the new University would gain by development along a line rather different from that of the capital. Thus, in Thessaloníki, the emphasis is on the more practical and technical aspects of the subjects. Attached to the University, yet administratively separate from it, there is a Meteorological and Climatological Institute founded in 1929, which is well placed to supplement the work carried out at the Royal Observatory in Athens.

Foreign Colleges

There are three foreign colleges offering facilities for higher education:

L'Institut Supérieur d'Etudes Françaises was established in 1905, under the patronage of the French Archaeological School. It offers courses similar to those available in a French university, and it enjoys great prestige in Greece. France has a strong cultural influence throughout the country and nearly all educated Greeks speak French.

The Athens College for Boys is one of an important group of American colleges in the Near East. It was opened in 1925 with the ultimate object of giving courses supplementary to those of the University of Athens, particularly in mechanical sciences and engineering.

The Institute of English Studies was established by the British Council in Athens in November 1938. It offered facilities to students of all ages and classes, and the syllabus ranged from beginners' classes to a teachers' training course. Of 4,000 students enrolled in 1940, 800 were of school age and 762 were members of an Advanced Division. It was hoped in a short time to separate off the Advanced

Division as a School of Higher English Studies with some 1,000 pupils doing work of University standard.

Other institutes were opened in 1939 and 1940 at Thessaloníki, Kaválla, Kérkira, Sérres, Kalámai, Xánthi and Komotíni, Pátrai, and Sámos. These institutes were very popular and, if continued, would certainly have exercised an important cultural influence in Greece. All the institutes were closed, with the schools, when the Italians invaded the country in 1941.

The General Standard of Education

Illiteracy in Greece is as yet common, which is not surprising in view of the difficulties which have faced Greek educationists. The exact degree of illiteracy is difficult to determine; figures exist, official and unofficial, but it must be recognized that they are little more than controlled guesses. Remembering their inadequacy the study of them does, however, bring out clearly two facts, the steady improvement in Greek education in the twentieth century and the regional variation in standard.

At the end of the nineteenth century it was said that less than half the population of Attikí could read and write, and that in most

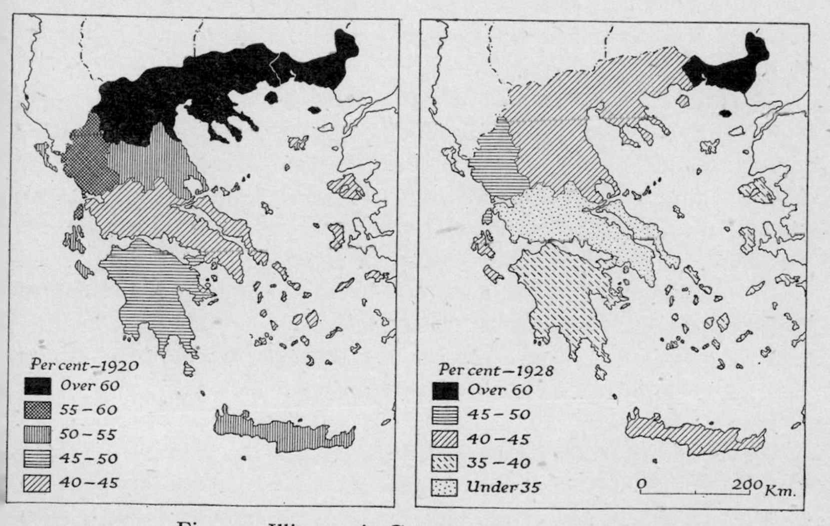

Fig. 94. Illiteracy in Greece, 1920 and 1928

Based on data from the *Annuaire Statistique de la Grèce*, p. 57 (Athènes, 1933). The figures show the percentage of the population over 8 years of age which was illiterate in 1920 and 1928.

regions 99 % of the women could neither read nor write. More recent figures show the fruits of the efforts made to encourage education. The 1928 census recorded 23·47 % men and 57·97 % women, or 40·91 % of the total population, over 8 years of age as illiterate. There is a striking difference in the proportion of women compared with men who cannot read and write. The education of girls lagged far behind that of boys; in the country women and girls do much of the manual labour in the fields, and in the towns girls of school age crowd the factories. Since 1890, women have been admitted to the University on the same terms as men. The education of girls of all classes shows steady improvement, and in 1938, 45 % of the pupils in primary schools were girls and in secondary schools 33 %. A decade earlier there were four times as many boys as girls in the primary schools, and in the secondary schools the proportion was even greater.

The standard of education varies throughout Greece (Fig. 94). In 1920 and in 1928, the percentage of illiterates was highest in the provinces of Dhitikí Thráki, Makedhonía, Ípiros, Thessalía, and in Kríti, that is, in regions most recently added to the Greek state. It was lowest in Stereá Ellás and Évvoia, largely owing to the high standard of education in the capital and in Attikí generally. Comparing the two maps for 1920 and 1928, the most striking fact is the great progress shown in Makedhonía and Thessalía, where illiteracy has decreased in less than a decade by more than 20 %. These are the regions where, between the two dates, Turkish peasants were replaced by Greeks from Asia Minor and Turkish Thrace, and the change indicates the better standard of education of the immigrant Greeks compared with the emigrant Turks. It may be that the same contrast in standards between Turks and Greeks accounts for the fact that in Dhitikí Thráki, where the Turks were exempted from compulsory emigration and therefore where few immigrant Greeks settled (few Turkish farms being left vacant), the percentage of illiteracy (over 60 %) in 1920 was the same as in 1928. This is the only region in Greece which showed no progress.

It is for the most part old people who cannot read and write and as these die and the younger generation, for whom education has been compulsory in fact and not merely in name, grows up, illiteracy is decreasing. It is judged that the average figure to-day may be nearer 30 than 40 %, with a still lower average among men.

Learned Societies and Libraries

There is a wide interest, not confined to academic circles, in archaeology, literature, history and science, and Athens has famous museums, good libraries, important scientific institutes and flourishing learned societies.

There are two Greek Archaeological Societies, and the Greeks have accomplished a great deal of work on both Classical and Byzantine sites. They have also allowed foreigners to establish archaeological schools and granted them permits to excavate. There are German, French, British, American and Italian Schools of Archaeology in Athens, all of them with important excavations to their credit. Many of their finds are to be found in the museums of Athens (see p. 425).

The Parnassos, founded in 1865, is the oldest literary society; it not only organizes lectures and discussions, but runs night schools for poor children, especially for the little boot-blacks. There is also a Byzantine Society, a Geographical Society, a Historical and Ethnological Society, and a Society for the Study of Political and Social Problems. An Academy, modelled on the French Academy, was founded in 1926. The Academy holds meetings and publishes the work of its members: in 1937 there were fifty-two Greek members, eighteen foreign associates and twenty-seven corresponding members.

The Royal Observatory of Athens was founded in 1843, and has Astronomical, Meteorological and Seismological Departments. The Geological Service of Greece was founded in 1919; geological surveys have been begun and some maps are published. The Geological Museum and the Zoological Museum are closely associated with the teaching departments of the University, but are also open to the public. *L'Institute Pasteur Hellénique*, also founded in 1919 and modelled on the French original, is doing good work.

Athens is also rich in libraries. The National Library, which includes the Public and the University Library, has been built up from several famous collections, some of them begun before the War of Independence; it contains over 400,000 volumes. The Library of the Chamber of Deputies was founded in 1844, but was burnt out in 1859 and rebuilt in 1875; it has 540,000 volumes and possesses perhaps the best collection of foreign works and a unique collection of newspaper files. The Schools of Archaeology possess good specialist libraries; the Finlay Library of the British School and the Gennedeion Library of the American School are especially rich in treasures.

BIBLIOGRAPHICAL NOTE

1. There is no up-to-date and comprehensive account in English of Greek education, and much of the information in this chapter is based on official sources. Three books may serve, however, to give a picture of the development of the educational system: (*a*) Ch. André, *Étude sur l'enseignement primaire en Grèce* (Athínai, 1905); (*b*) T. Haralambides, *Die Sculpolitik Griechenlands*, 1821–1935 (Berlin, 1935); (*c*) G. M. Wilcox, *Education in Greece* (New York, 1933).

2. Many general books on Greece include a short discussion of Greek schools and Universities. Of these, the most valuable are:

(*a*) P. F. Martin, *Greece in the Twentieth Century* (London, 1913).
(*b*) E. G. Mears, *Greece Today* (Stanford University Press, California, 1929).
(*c*) W. Miller, *Greek Life in Town and Country* (London, 1905).
(*d*) W. Miller, *Greece* (London, 1928).

The Near East Year Book, 1931–2, edited by H. T. Montagu Bell (London, 1931) and *Peace Handbooks*: vol. III, *The Balkan States*, part I, no. 18, 'Greece with the Cyclades and Northern Sporades', Foreign Office (London, 1920) also make short references to education in Greece.

3. Two useful papers are to be found in the *Educational Yearbook of the International Institute of Teachers' College, Columbia University* for 1926 and 1937 (New York, annual). Another valuable paper is J. Gennadius, 'A sketch of the history of education in Greece', in *World Federation of Education Associations Conference* (Edinburgh, 1925).

4. Detailed statistical information is given in the *Annuaire Statistique de la Grèce* (Athènes, annual).

Chapter XI

THE PEOPLE

THE ORIGIN OF THE GREEKS

The Classical Greeks

The coastlands and the islands of the Aegean were inhabited in pre-classical times by a relatively short dark people, with long narrow heads, usually regarded as 'Mediterranean' in type. It was these people who developed the Minoan civilization, based on Crete, between about 3000 and 1100 B.C. The mountain interior of the Balkans at this time seems to have been inhabited by tall broad-headed Illyrian peoples, who from early times may have mingled and inter-married with the 'Mediterranean' peoples of the coastlands of Greece.

Around about 2000 B.C., the Aegean world was invaded by the Achaeans whose origin is disputed. Some say they came from the steppes north of the Black Sea; others that they were the descendants of Illyrian peoples who had already been filtering southwards from the mountainous interior of the Balkans. In any case, they appear to have been tall and blond and more broad-headed than the 'Mediterraneans'.

From about 1600 B.C. onwards, they developed the Mycenaean civilization under the cultural stimulus of the Minoans. The Achaeans were followed, about the year 1100 B.C., by the Dorians from the north. These tall, blond, broad-headed people pushed south into the Peloponnese, where a Doric tongue, Tzakonian, can still be heard (see p. 322).

The Greeks of classical times were therefore descended from a fusion of two groups of peoples—long-headed 'Mediterraneans' and broad-headed newcomers from the north, but it is impossible to assess the relative proportions of these two groups. In any case, it is clear that considerable displacements of population must have taken place when the Achaeans and the Dorians came southward, and there has been much controversy about these matters.

Throughout classical times, the Greek lands received no new elements into their population. Indeed, the reverse occurred, for Greeks spread outward from the Aegean, and colonized far and wide in the Mediterranean and Black Seas (Fig. 72). Nor did the Roman period, in all probability, see much change in the composition of the Greek people, although a large number of slaves were imported from non-Greek lands. The Roman soldiers, merchants and civil servants settled mainly in the towns, and were not very numerous relative to the rest of the population. The Roman occupation, however, bequeathed one non-Greek element (the Vlachs) to the population of Greece and other Balkan lands (see p. 360 and Fig. 103).

The Barbarian invasions, that played so great a part in the break-up of the western provinces of the Roman empire, likewise did not much affect the population of the Greek lands. It is true that the Goths crossed the Danube, and raided into Greece after A.D. 250, and then again came on a larger scale after 378. But on the first occasion they withdrew; and, the second time, after spending some years in the peninsula, the Gothic horde marched north-westwards to Illyria and so to the west. The Greek people in the fifth century A.D. were, racially speaking, substantially what they had been in the fifth century B.C.

The Slav Immigration

From the sixth to the eighth centuries, the racial composition of the mainland Greeks underwent some change. To the north, the Slav peoples were expanding in all directions from their homeland around the Pripet marshes, and this widespread movement had great effect upon the population of the Balkan lands (see p. 157). Crossing the Danube, the Slavs, in conjunction with the Avars, began to raid Greek territory, and towards the end of the sixth century their raiding began to pass into settlement. Raiding and settlement continued throughout the seventh century; and, in the following century, after the plague which desolated Greece in 746, Slav settlement became particularly widespread, so much so that the interior of the Greek peninsula was known as Sclavinia (Fig. 77).

There has been much dispute about the Slav element in Greece, and the controversy entered an acute stage when, in 1830, the German scholar J. P. Fallermayer, in his *History of the Morea during the Middle Ages*, declared that the Slav and Albanian (see below) im-

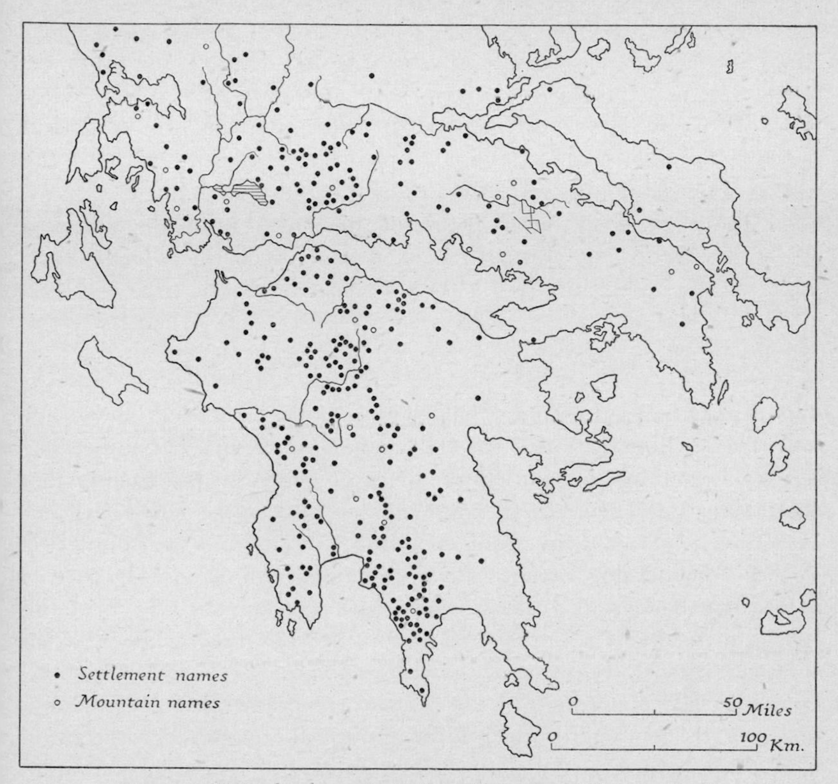

Fig. 95. Slavonic elements in the place-names of central and southern Greece

Based on J. Haliczer, 'The Distribution of Place-Names', *Geography*, vol. XXII, p. 202 (London, 1937).

The names are those of the 'Carte de la Grèce, 1:200,000' (Paris, 1852). Haliczer says: 'From the 1:200,000 map one gathers 228 Slavonic names in Peloponnesus and 128 in Middle Greece, apart from 22 mountain names and 14 river names' (p. 201). Many of these have since been replaced by others in accordance with Greek policy (see p. 446).

migrations into Greece had been so considerable that the modern inhabitants had 'not a single drop of Greek blood in their veins'. The controversy roused the diplomatic as well as the learned world, for many philhellenes, who were interested in the struggle for Greek independence, had laid great stress upon the illustrious ancestry of the Greeks. Since that time, the ideas of Fallermayer have been discussed at length, and, although they have been largely discredited, the fact remains that the Slavs must have made a considerable contribution to the peopling of Greece, as indeed can be seen from the numerous Slav place-names of the Greek mainland (Fig. 95). Apart from place-names, the only traces of the Slav immigration are a few customs and Slavonic types, seen mostly in the Pelopónnisos. But, of course, it is quite impossible to assess, in any statistical manner, the relative importance of classical and Slav elements in the modern Greek population. Whatever the racial position may have been, the Slavs, with the exception of those of Máni in the southern extremity of the Pelopónnisos, seem to have been easily assimilated linguistically and culturally by the Greeks.

The Frankish and Turkish Periods

The 'Franks' was a general term given to the crusaders and other westerners who partitioned the Byzantine empire in 1204, and whose states survived in Greece until the fifteenth century. But this medley of Italians and Frenchmen, Catalans and Navarrese, Germans and Flemings, never came in sufficient numbers to modify the population to any considerable extent. They remained, for the most part, a series of garrisons in a foreign land, and this was true even of the long-drawn-out Venetian occupation of parts of Greece. The Turkish occupation from the fifteenth century onwards likewise contributed no appreciable ingredient to the mass of the population. Negatively, however, the levy of tribute children and the contemporary emigration from Greece must have meant a considerable drain upon the Christian population. The bulk of the modern population of Greece is therefore descended from that of classical times, but has been appreciably modified, though to what extent it is impossible to say, by the Slav immigrations of the early Middle Ages. Many of the Albanians who settled in Greece during the Frankish and Turkish periods have also been assimilated into the Greek population (see p. 362).

But while the main body of the Greek people seems to have remained substantially unaltered since the end of the eighth century, local non-Greek elements have appeared, and these still form minorities within the present-day frontiers of Greece. Judged on a linguistic basis the main groups are Turks, Macedo-Slavs, Spanish Jews, Armenians, Vlachs, Albanians and Bulgars (see Chap. xii).

The Physical Characteristics of the Greeks

The modern Greeks, as one would expect from the history of the settlement of the region, conform to no one uniform physical type. Some have broad heads and some have narrow; some are tall and some are short; and though most Greeks are brunet in colouring, blue-eyed and even fair-headed individuals are to be seen.

The population seems to be on the average slightly built and of medium stature, perhaps a little above the European mean. The mountaineers of north-west Greece are taller than the southern Greeks, and in districts where the Albanian stock is dominant the people, especially the men, are markedly tall.

An examination of the head form indicates the heterogeneous racial character of the Greek. According to one authority 49% of a sample of the population examined were broad-headed and 34% long and narrow-headed. The variation of head form shows some regional differentiation; long narrow heads are most numerous in the Pelopónnisos, Attikí and Thessalía, while in Ípiros, in Arkananía, especially in the Akhelóös valley, and in the Ionian islands, broad and high heads are usual. In southern Évvoia and in Korinthía, where considerable Albanian immigration is recent, many people are broad-headed.

The Greek face is oval, rather narrow with a high forehead in most individuals, though round-faced types, reminiscent of the Slav population of the northern Balkans, occur. The nose is usually straight in profile with a narrow, high bridge, but some Greeks have aquiline noses, and a few decidedly turned up noses like the Slavs. In fact, again in face and nose form, an intermixture of types is clearly seen.

The majority of modern Greeks are decidedly brunet; their skin is sallow, their hair dark brown or black, and their eyes brown. But fairer types do occur, and blue or grey eyes are frequent especially in regions in which there is a strong Albanian element. Blue eyes with dark hair is a not uncommon combination even in eastern Greece and the islands. Fair-haired individuals are rare, one authority puts them as low as 1·5%, though another estimates them as 10% of the population. The Vlachs often have whiter skins than their neighbours, high complexions, and their hair is sometimes quite fair. This characteristic fairness differentiates dominant Vlach communities from the majority of Greeks in Thessalía, while their medium stature and slight build contrasts with the bigger physique of the peasants of Ípiros.

In general perhaps it may be said that the smaller, darker, and long-headed Greeks are more often seen in eastern Greece, in Thessalía, Voiotía, Attikí and the Pelopónnisos, while taller, fairer, broader-headed types are found in western Greece, but there are many exceptions to this statement. The physical types approximating most nearly to the ideal of Greek sculpture may perhaps be seen most often in Arkadhía and the islands.

THE GREEK LANGUAGE

The Greek language is spoken by about 93% of the inhabitants of the country (see p. 349). It has been developing slowly for nearly three thousand years, and it provides an unbroken link between Ancient Greece and the Greece of to-day. The main stages in the growth of the modern language from classical Greek are shown in a tabular form below. Despite the complicated history of the Greek language, Homer is far more intelligible to the modern Greek than Chaucer is to an Englishman.

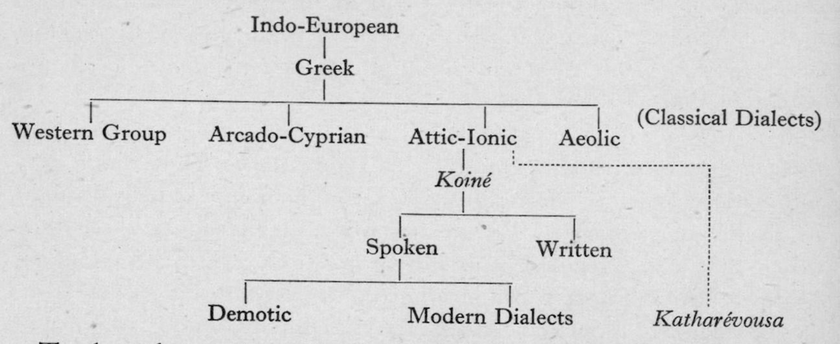

To-day, the modern Greek has a choice of three versions of his own language. These are (*a*) the spoken tongue ready at hand in the dialects which are the natural descendants of the spoken language of Hellenistic times; (*b*) the refined and unified language of literature and cultivated speech—this is the demotic, and it is founded on the first; and (*c*) the purist, *katharévousa*, the language of officialdom and the Church. There is no conflict between the first two; the one supplements the other and both are inevitably dependent on each other. The conflict exists between these two and *katharévousa*, and it is this conflict which accounts for the so-called 'bilingual' problem of Greece. This problem has been the source of considerable bitterness and strife.

Classical Greek

Origins

Greek belongs to the Indo-European family of languages, a family which includes Sanskrit, Italic, Germanic, Celtic, Balto-Slavonic and Indo-Iranian among its members. In many ways, Greek is the most outstanding representative of the parent language. For example, it has preserved in a remarkable manner the vowel qualities, the verbal system and the accentuation of the original stock. This is why Greek is of such great importance to the comparative philologist. Again, in its unbroken literary development from the eighth century B.C. to the present day the Greek language shows a unity which is unparalleled by any other Indo-European language.

It is generally assumed that Greek became detached from Indo-European during the third millennium B.C., and that about 2000 B.C. its speakers, who were then settled around the region of the upper Struma (Strímon), began their successive invasions of the country that is now Greece (see p. 130). The first invaders to move southwards found a diversity of peoples already in possession of the country. The impact of their several languages left its mark in the number of non-Indo-European words which are found in the early Greek vocabulary; these words are doubtless stray fragments of the group of languages spoken in the Aegean before the first Greek migrations. Thus, there are place-names like *Kórinthos*, *Imittós*, *Likavitós*, *Knossós* and *Parnassós*; names of many deities, such as *Athána* (*Athēna*), *Árēs*, *Artēmis* and *Apóllōn*; common words like *labírinthos* (labyrinth), *kipárissos* (cypress) and *pírgos* (citadel or rampart). These forms have an origin which is not Indo-European, but the number of such words is considerably less than was at one time estimated.

The Classical Dialects

Up to the fourth century B.C. there was no standard or common language in Greece. On the contrary, the successive waves of migration, geographical factors, varieties of religious customs and beliefs, and later, political divisions had all helped to produce a wide range of local differentiations in speech. These were to be found in every island and plain and city-state. It is difficult to trace the exact relationship between each of these dialects, for dialect frontiers seldom remain fixed. On the strength of documentary evidence, however, which goes back to inscriptions of the eighth century B.C., four main groups of dialects may be classified (Fig. 96). These were:

(i) *Aeolic* or *Central*, spoken in Aeolis, Lesbos, Boeotia and Thessaly.

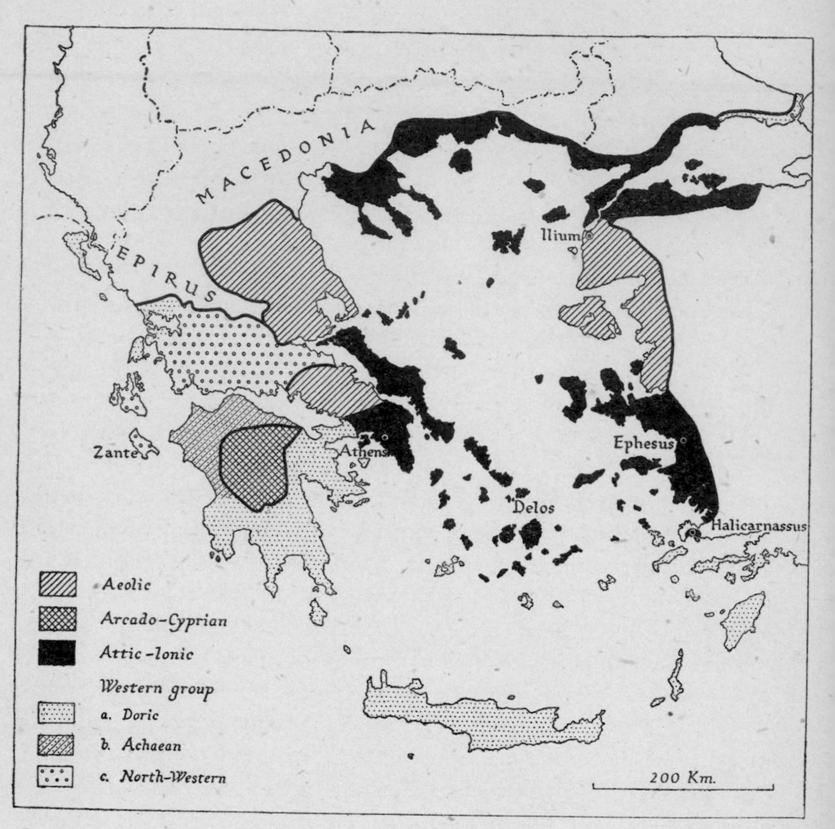

Fig. 96. Classical dialects

Based on C. D. Buck, *The Greek Dialects*, Plate V (New York, 1928).

The classical dialects contained many local variations, but they never showed any tendency to develop into separate languages. Of the four, the Western group was the most distinct, and the map suggests that, in relation to it, the other three loosely formed an eastern group. The dialects lost their individual identities in the Hellenistic period and were replaced by the *Koiné* or common Attic dialect which had become dominant with the growth of the political and social influence of Athens (see p. 133).

(ii) *The Western Group*: (*a*) Doric, including the speech of Messenia, Argolis, Laconia, Crete and the various Doric colonies. (*b*) The dialects of Achaia and Elis. (*c*) North-western Greek spoken in Epirus, Acarnania, Aetolia, Locris, Phocis and Phthiotis and in the islands of Cephalonia and Zante.

(iii) *Arcado-Cyprian*, spoken in Arcadia, Cyprus and probably Pamphylia.

(iv) *Attic-Ionic*, spoken in Attica, Euboea, Chalcidice, Ionia, the Cyclades and the colonies of Chalcis in Italy and Sicily.

Each of these dialects, except Arcado-Cyprian, in time attained a degree of literary eminence. There were many similarities among them but they remained essentially separate, and it was Attic that subsequently became the standard for all prose literature.

The Development of the Koiné

In the fourth century B.C. the classical dialects gradually lost their individual significance. After the conquests of Alexander the Great, the commercial and intellectual centres of Greek life were moving eastwards, where old-established Greek cities were still flourishing and where new cities were being founded. An ever-increasing number of Greek speakers began to appear in the non-Greek cities, and Greek culture quickly attained a dominating influence in the Levant: its position was not unlike that of French in the same area in modern times. As this influence became more widespread, it led to a superficial standardization which demanded, among other things, a standardized form of the Greek language to serve as a general instrument of communication. A synthesis of the major dialects might have produced this standard language, but the political, commercial and cultural supremacy of Athens emphasized the claims of the Attic dialect. In its literary forms, this dialect had been used by Aeschylus and Sophocles, Euripides and Aristophanes, Plato and Aristotle. It was now to become, in its spoken form and with several modifications, the language of the whole Greek world, and it was to flourish from the days of Alexander the Great to those of Justinian, that is, from the fourth century B.C. to the sixth century when the first signs of modern Greek began to appear.

Spoken Attic underwent many changes as it became a cosmopolitan language. Its structure, its vocabulary and indeed its pronunciation were affected by Ionic and Doric elements as well as by Macedonian and non-Greek forms from the East. A great number of people learnt it as a foreign language, and each foreign speaker doubtless contributed his share towards change and simplification.

The name *koiné diálektos* or 'common' Greek was given to the language as it emerged from these various changes. It continued to depart further and further from classical Attic, and it was for a long time far from uniform in all its usages among the various levels of society and from region to region. The *koiné* was rather slow in becoming the language of literature. Some writers consciously adhered as closely as possible to the traditional models of the classical period, and avoided the vulgarisms of ordinary speech. These writers were the 'Atticists', and among them were Fathers of the early Christian Church like Clement of Alexandria. The early Christian apologists had received a rhetorical training, and they thought that the new religion could best be defended against contemporary philosophy by employing the traditional literary idiom (a combination of written *koiné* and Attic), which has remained the official language of the Greek Church to the present day (see p. 324).

The most important written sources of early *koiné*, apart from private letters, reports and financial documents preserved in papyri, are the histories of Polybius and Diodorus, written in the second and first centuries B.C. respectively, the philosophical treatises of Epictetus, written in the first century A.D. and the New Testament and the Septuagint.

The development of *koiné* followed lines of simplification and regularization. Refinement and elegance were doubtless lost, but there were compensatory gains in directness and simplicity. The disappearance of the fixed quantities of vowels and syllables which had begun as early as the fifth century B.C. became complete; pitch accent was replaced by stress accent, and the rhythm of the language was transformed. Yet, although vowel quantities were levelled and although the main accent became one of intensity rather than of tone, the position of the accent and the syllabic length of words did not radically change.

The written form of this common language also had its variations, many of which were stylistic. But its later position as the language of government and education helped to maintain a useful balance between fixation and evolution throughout the area where the Greek language prevailed. It came to be widely adopted for works of science and philosophy. The Romans recognized its value for administrative purposes and no attempt was made to displace it by Latin. Some Latin idioms and several Latin words were borrowed into the language, but the reciprocal borrowing from Greek into Latin was more considerable. It is significant, however, that the *koiné* itself was not adopted as the official language of Christianity in the East as was Latin in the West. Thus the books of the New Testament, originally written in *koiné*, were at an early date translated into various languages. By the close of the Roman period the written language was in fact confined to Greek-speaking regions; these were mostly maritime and there was almost no penetration inland.

Though restricted, this written *koiné* survived the inroads of Islam and continued to be used by Byzantine prose writers to the fifteenth century. It was losing, however, its organic contact with the spoken *koiné*. It was no longer a *koiné* in the real sense, for it was probably unintelligible to the average person.

The Development of Modern Greek

The Growth of the Demotic Language

The spoken *koiné*, being a living speech, naturally varied from place to place and from one social stratum to another. Although a form of speech not greatly differing from the written standard may have been affected among the educated, a gap was growing between the written and spoken forms of the common dialect. This gap can be seen, for example, in the series of glossaries written during the third and fourth centuries A.D. giving the spoken equivalents of Atticized words and phrases. The spoken language, however, gradually crept into some literary forms and there arose a new body of literature belonging exclusively to the demotic language.

The earliest example of this gradual but ever-increasing process of demoticizing the written *koiné* is the 'Chronicle of Malalas', compiled as early as the sixth century of our era. Somewhat later there came the legends of the saints, then the chronicle of Theophanes and the romance of 'Barlaam and Josaphat', both earlier than the tenth century. These works contain much that was 'ancient and modern'—linguistic barbarisms arising out of the mixture of *koiné* and popular forms.

Between the tenth and sixteenth centuries, the popular language developed a resilient vigour which is displayed in its literature. The works of the emperor Constantine Porphyrogenitus and the collection of short poems called 'Digenis Akritas' belong to the tenth century. Everything which was intended to be circulated among the larger part of the public was written in the popular language—official

Byzantine deeds, popular chronicles and regulations to govern domestic economy. On a higher literary plane, although not entirely free of *koiné* traces, there was the 'Chronicle of the Morea', written in the late thirteenth century and giving a metrical account of the Frankish conquest of the Peloponnese (see p. 175). Above all, there were the ballads and folk-songs, which, though ageless in their themes, and though drawn from the common treasury of the Greek people, took their first literary shape in the popular language as late as the thirteenth century. It should be remembered that in Greece, as in many other countries, ballad literature was preserved by oral tradition. In Crete, during the sixteenth and seventeenth centuries, under Venetian rule, there was a further advance in the development of the popular language when native poetry and drama were given expression in an idiom of supple richness and crystal purity. An example of this is the epic 'Erotokritos and Arethousa' by Vitzenzos Kornaros of Sitia. A version of the Pentateuch in 'vulgar Greek', printed in Hebrew characters, had already been published at Constantinople in 1547 when the New Testament was translated into the popular tongue by Maximos, a monk of Gallipoli, and printed at Geneva in 1638. The attempt to circulate copies from Constantinople unfortunately ended in disaster.

The Creation of 'Katharévousa'

The gap between the written *koiné* and the popular or demotic language had reached its widest span by the eighteenth century. It was then that an attempt was made to bridge the gap by Adamantios Korais (1749–1833), a native of Chios. Korais, one of the greatest of Greek scholars, had been influenced by the doctrines of the French Revolution (see p. 194). He devoted himself to the cause of Greek independence and searched for a medium that would at once reveal the continuity of the Greek of his day with that of Ancient Greece and also express the idea of political unity for which he was striving. An admirer of ancient Greek and wholeheartedly in sympathy with what was its modern development, Korais endeavoured to make the best of both the learned and colloquial worlds. He tried to effect a compromise and produced an amalgam of strange ingredients: Attic, Byzantine and modern elements were mixed and given a markedly French colour. An artificial Greek was thus manufactured; the political and literary influence of Korais was later to give it dignity and authority.

When Greece recovered its independence in 1832, the need was at once felt for a language which could be employed both for the transaction of government business and as an aid to the assimilation of modern cultural influences by the regenerated nation. The compromise language of Korais was ready at hand and it possessed several expedient advantages. Thus there came into being *katharévousa*, the official language of modern Greece. It is essentially an artificial language, just as many other written languages are artificial compromises. *Katharévousa* has suffered, however, from the effects of pseudo-learning and from grave misconceptions of the ideal of linguistic purity. By the middle of the nineteenth century, the mild and well meant compromise of Korais had developed into an efficient but uncompromizing machinery of government. Since then, the *katharévousa* has held sway over public offices and printing presses, over the army and the law courts, over the secondary schools and the universities.

The *katharévousa* is not a completely uniform language; it has several varieties, differing not in principle but in the degree of elimination of foreign words and the substitution of ancient words. Yet seldom are any of these varieties actually spoken in their entirety, although the written *katharévousa* shows its influence on public and formal speeches.

The Demotic Renascence

Towards the beginning of the nineteenth century the Greek folk-songs had been collected and a study of their language showed that below the dead literary language and across the dialectal divisions' a common poetical language, pulsating with life, had unobtrusively been evolving for many centuries. The task of collecting folk-songs was in Greece, as elsewhere, the first sign of a quickened consciousness of the vital power of the vernacular. A new 'school' arose, consisting mainly of poets at the outset, to uphold the claims of the popular language. It should not be forgotten, of course, that although they went along diverging linguistic paths, both Korais and these demotic writers had been stimulated by the same patriotism (see p. 194). It was in the Ionian islands, which were not annexed to Greece until 1864, that the demotic renascence began. There, Solomos (1789–1856), a Zakinthian nobleman, wrote eloquently in defence of the popular language and handled it with exquisite skill in his poems. He was followed by Valaoritis (1824–57) who borrowed prodigally from the vocabulary of the ballads and folk-songs, and sang of Greek independence in the same way as the ballads had extolled klephtic heroism (see p. 189). The number of books written in demotic has steadily increased. It was soon discovered that the demotic could be used to express all the complexities of modern life and it became a medium of prose. Ioannis Psicharis (1854–1929) was the vigorous leader of the demotic supporters, and his greatness lies not so much in his own written works as in those of the men he inspired.

The Modern Dialects

The spoken *koiné* of Hellenistic times had its local variations. Out of these variations there developed dialects. The process continued throughout the Byzantine period, but the unity of the Byzantine empire prevented the dialects from breaking up into separate languages as in the case of Latin, whose dialect variations have become the Romance languages of to-day. With the fall of the empire however, the differences in the spoken *koiné* were accentuated, and it is around later modifications of those dialects that modern Greek revolves.

The dialects of to-day are not, of course, directly derived from the classical dialects which began to disintegrate in the fourth century B.C (see p. 317); they are local derivations from the colloquial hellenistic *koiné*. But there is one striking exception; this is the Tzakonian dialect which is found to the north-west of Leonídhion in south-eastern Arkadhía. This dialect, preserved within a small maritime area, retains marked proofs of its origin from the ancient Doric.

Although the position of the dialects has been constantly undermined since the introduction of *katharévousa*, they still show sligh variations in pronunciation, construction and vocabulary. Nearly every district has words which are peculiar to itself. Thus islands like Skíros have a considerable number of words which are not easily intelligible elsewhere. In the Pelopónnisos, too, the Maniates, who live along the south-eastern shore of the Gulf of Messínia between the Taïyetos mountains and the sea, speak a dialect of marked peculiarities.

It will be difficult to show the exact distribution of dialect area until the results of various linguistic surveys have been finally correlated. A tentative attempt has been made to divide them into eastern and western groups, with the line of 24 degrees longitud marking the approximate division. Thus the dialects of Asia Minor Cyprus, the Dodecanese, Khíos, Náxos, Kríti and some of th Kikládhes form the eastern group. It would be dangerous, however to exaggerate the strength of the regional variations in speech and t attempt too rigid a demarcation of dialect boundaries. Differences in pronunciation and idiom, though more noticeable in some areas than others, are often slight. As a result, modern Greek has not those marked variations which are found, for example, in France between standard French and the patois.

Loan-words

There is a varying proportion of loan-words in the Greek dialects of to-day. Turkish words were once common enough in most of them, but they have nearly all disappeared, although hybrid forms hold on tenaciously in those areas which were the last to be united to Greece—in Makedhonía, Thessalía and Ípiros. In the Ionian islands the long Italian connexion has left a legacy of Italian words. The dialect of Kríti also has Italian borrowings in addition to traces of Arabic influence. The patois of the cosmopolitan Greeks of Athínai is now almost a distinct dialect, deeply affected by words and idioms from French and English.

It is rather surprising, however, that the demotic language, after the unbroken series of cultural fusions, infiltrations and dominations which has accompanied its development, does not show a more formidable word-list of borrowings. Latin words, though relatively few, are the most numerous; they are terms from military life, legal and administrative terms and the names of weights and measures. Italian words come next in point of time and frequency; they deal mainly with maritime features and most of them are derived from the medieval *portolani*, or books of navigation, which were the standard guide-books for mariners. Traces of Slav and Albanian are now scanty apart from place-name forms (Fig. 95). Most remarkable of all, only a few ordinary words remain to testify to the long years of Turkish domination. All the Turkish administrative terms which found their way into Greek have disappeared, while the influence of Greek still persists in Turkey, if only in the name of Istanbul itself. Turkish names of physical features still linger, especially the names of small rivers and hills; but although they are being slowly and systematically removed from Greek official maps it is not easy to state to what extent they are disappearing from native speech. More recently, terms of elegance and refinement have come from French, and terms of sport and recreation have been borrowed from English. The tendency of the modern language, however, is to make expedient and temporary borrowings from other languages, and to eliminate them when native synonyms have been found; they are usually taken from the storehouse of the ancient language. In this way some portion of the Greek vocabulary is constantly emerging from the melting pot, and it is thus that the demotic language continually enriches itself.

The Present Linguistic Position

The constitutions of 1911 and 1927 expressly forbade the translation of the New Testament into demotic Greek without the consent of the Orthodox Church and the Patriarch of Constantinople. Again, it was not until 1927 that the demotic was officially allowed to be taught in elementary schools, and then, at the fifth year, from three to four hours per week had to be devoted to the study of *katharévousa*. The demotic is not officially allowed in the *gymnasia*. Opposition to the recognition of the popular language has varied in strength in different governments; in general, it has been opposed by the conservatives and upheld by the more progressive parties.

The greatest living Greek writer, Costis Palamas, writes both poetry and prose in the popular language. The demotic is indeed becoming the medium for all kinds of imaginative and creative literature, and it is gradually finding its way into learned journals. Again, there are compromisers among the supporters of *katharévousa*; these are the moderates, whose style is a compromise between the popular and purist forms. Among them the varieties of the *katharévousa* differ from writer to writer.

The slow ascendancy of the popular language has not been without hard struggle, and it is not by any means a complete ascendancy. On both sides there is naturally a genuine enthusiasm for the Greek language. By the extreme purists, classical Greek (i.e. Attic) is held with something of the veneration with which the Quorān is held by Moslems, and they regard demotic Greek as a rather degraded form little better than a patois and inadmissible in standard literature. The purists have had distinguished scholars on their side, and the literature written in *katharévousa* is not without its worthy representatives. To the supporters of the popular language, however, the demotic is the only living form of Greek; it is not chaotic but in the true line of organic development from the *koiné*. Its natural simplicity and the ease with which it can be learnt and used, it is argued, are in themselves powerful reasons for its general adoption.

The language problem in Greece remains unsolved, but an increasing number of the supporters of *katharévousa* are slowly being converted to the cause of the demotic tongue. The question is nothing new in Greek history; it is an exaggerated dualism which in a smaller degree is common to the majority of languages. Thus, the classical literature of Greece was written in a form which could not have been understood by the uneducated classes, and for centuries the language of the greatest writers was far removed from the speech of the lower classes. The conflict in Greece between the purist and the popular language has therefore been a perpetual one.

The Greek Language outside Greece

It was estimated in 1939 that there were about 1,675,000 Greek speakers outside Greece. Excluding the speakers of Greek in Turkey, and those in western Europe and the U.S.A., the outliers of Greek speech may be divided into two broad groups. To the first belong Cyprus, the Dodecanese and southern Albania, regions which have preserved strong cultural links with Greece, and where, in recent years, there has developed a 'national consciousness' with marked political aspirations. The second group consists of outliers whose significance is mainly historical and linguistic and which have now no political and little cultural contact with Greece; these outliers are to be found in Soviet Russia, in Italy and in Corsica.

Cyprus

Greek has been the predominant language in Cyprus since the fourteenth century B.C. when the island was colonized by Greeks from the mainland. Throughout its history Cyprus has maintained its close ties of language, religion and sentiment with Greece (see p. 221). In 1931, out of a population of about 350,000, there were 280,000 Greek speakers. Although English is the official language, Greek is recognized for administrative and legal purposes, and the *katharévousa* is taught in the schools. The dialect of Cyprus contains a strong admixture of French, Italian and Turkish words, all testifying to the successive occupations of the island. Since the thirteenth century there has been a strong literary tradition in the island. To-day there is a flourishing school of local poets, notably Lipertis and Palaisis, using the dialect for literary purposes.

The Dodecanese

With the exception of some Italians, a small colony of Jews in Rhódhos (Rhodes) and a few Turks in Rhódhos and Kos, the 136,000 inhabitants of the Dodecanese in 1937 were Greek speakers. The Greek dialects show little variation from island to island, but the dialect of Astipália, which was repopulated from Tínos in 1413 shows marked peculiarities. Educated persons in the islands can read and write the *katharévousa*, but since the Italian occupation both this and the demotic have been discouraged. Since 1937, Greek has been taught only as an optional language for two or three hours a week.

Albania

Article III of the Treaty of London, 1913, delimited the international frontier between Albania and Greece. The district of Ioánnina was assigned to Greece, while those of Gjinokaster (Argyrokastro), Korçë (Koritza) and Himarë (Chimarra) were included in Albania (Fig. 104).

Before Greece became an independent kingdom in 1832 there seems to have been the freest intercourse between the Tosks (those speaking the southern Albanian dialect) and the Greeks. Though the majority of the Tosks turned Mussulman, the large Christian minority were Orthodox, and their bishops were appointed by, and were under the control of, the Patriarch at Constantinople. Their Turkish governors, even Ali Pasha himself, used the Greek language for purpose of government; and, as the Albanian language was seldom written, Greek was the language used also for purposes of commerce and for such education as there was. Furthermore, after the overthrow of Ali Pasha in 1822, when south Albania fell more completely under Turkish domination than ever it had been before, the Turks not only permitted but even encouraged Greek propaganda in order to check the development of any national feeling, and at the same time prohibited the use of the Albanian language in schools and the appearance of Albanian newspapers. The result was the almost complete disuse of the native language south of the River Kalamas [Thíamis], even by Albanians of pure extraction; while north of that river as far as Argyrokastro most of the Tosks were (and are) bilingual, speaking Greek for public purposes and Albanian only in their home life when it was needed, since in many cases their women had no acquaintance with Greek.*

At the Peace Conference in February 1919 a 'Committee on Greek Territorial Claims' was appointed to make recommendations. No action was taken on this report, and after numerous proposals and

* *Peace Handbooks:* vol. III, *The Balkan States*, part I, no. 17, 'Albania', pp. 62–3, Foreign Office (London, 1920).

most complicated negotiations, the Conference of Ambassadors, on 9 November 1921, confirmed the 1913 frontier, and sent out a Delimitation Commission. The Greeks did not finally evacuate 'fourteen villages' near Korçë until October 1924. In the meantime, Albania had been admitted to the League of Nations, and had asked for a Commission of Enquiry. This made its final report on 18 April 1923.

Professor Sederholm of Finland, who was on the League of Nations Commission of Enquiry in 1921–3, estimated the total number of Greek speakers as between 35,000 and 40,000.* Of these, some 33,000 were in the prefecture of Gjinokaster, and there were practically no Greek speakers in Korçë. By 'Greek speakers', he understood those who spoke Greek at home.

At the time of the occupation of Albania by Italy in April 1939, the Albanians recognized within their country a Greek minority of some 20,000 persons. This minority enjoyed not only all the rights of Albanian citizenship, but also other privileges. They had their own schools, were represented on the local councils, and had their own members in the Albanian parliament.

Tenedos and Imbros

Both Tenedos (Bozcaada) and Imbros (İmroz Adasi), with populations of 6,000 and 6,762 respectively, belong to Turkey but they are predominantly Greek-speaking.

Soviet Russia

There are two varieties of Greek speech in Soviet Russia, namely the dialect of Rostov on Don and that of Mariupol.

Greek has been spoken around Rostov since the time of the empire of Trebizond (see p. 168) when there was a prosperous corn trade between the southern Ukraine and Trebizond. In the eighteenth century many Greek emigrants left Pontus, the stretch of the southern Black Sea coast extending from Sinop to Trebizond, and settled on the shores of the Sea of Azov. There were further movements in the nineteenth century. To-day there are about 100,000 Greek speakers around Rostov and they speak a Pontic dialect closely similar to the dialect which used to be spoken around Gümüshkhane (Argyropolis) in Turkey. It is estimated that about 6,000 of the more educated speak the demotic of Greece which, since 1926, has replaced the *katharévousa* in the Greek schools at Rostov. Books in both Pontic

* *League of Nations Official Journal*, 4th year, p. 493 (Geneva, 1923).

and demotic are published, though at present the former is more frequently used. A reformed phonetic spelling is employed for both Pontic and demotic. There are considerable traces of Turkish and Russian in the vocabulary of the Pontic dialect of Rostov.

It is estimated that there are about 80,000 Greek speakers between Mariupol and Stalino in the Donetz basin. Their dialect, however, is not Pontic and it differs greatly from any other of the modern Greek dialects. Colonies had been founded by the Greeks on the northern shores of the Black Sea, in pre-classical times, and although contact was maintained throughout the Byzantine period, they gradually fell before Tartar and Turkish invaders, the last colony at Cherson being dispersed in the fifteenth century. In the eighteenth century, when Greek emigration from Turkey into Russia was encouraged (see p. 193), the scattered remnants of Greek speakers already in Russia were brought together and settled in Mariupol. The Greek speakers are now distributed among fifteen villages, and while there are local variations in the dialect there is a common basis, with a demotic admixture, for the language of the local press. There is a considerable number of Tartar and Russian words in the Mariupol dialect.

Italy

Greek dialects are spoken in the Terra d'Otranto and Calabria regions of southern Italy. According to the returns of the 1921 Italian Census, there were 16,033 Greek-speakers in the Terra d'Otranto, mainly around Lecce, and 3,639 speakers in Calabria, to the east of Reggio and mainly in the commune of Bova. The number of speakers in Calabria has shown a steady decline, but the language is holding on tenaciously in the Terra d'Otranto. Despite the considerable influence of Italian words and constructions, these dialects are unmistakable remnants of the Greek spoken in the flourishing colonies of Magna Graecia in southern Italy and Sicily, and traces of Doric characteristics are still discernible. Later movements from Byzantium between the seventh and eleventh centuries further strengthened the hold of the language in these regions. To-day, however, although intermarriage with Italians has been rare, the two linguistic groups are not only Italian in everything except speech, but they are also mutually unacquainted.

Corsica

In 1675 about one thousand refugees from Maina came to Paomia near Cargèse in Corsica (see p. 190). After a compulsory move to

Ajaccio, the colony returned to Cargèse where it has remained since 1775. The smallness of the community, which now numbers about four hundred, constant intermarriage with Corsicans, and the loss of the Greek liturgies as a result of secession from the Orthodox Church, have been the main causes of the disappearance of the Greek language in Corsica. Thus, in 1926, only two families regularly spoke Greek. All the members of the colony speak the Corsican dialect of Italian, while only a few of the older members can speak their mother tongue. Their speech, although it has been greatly affected by Corsican, retains marked affinities with the dialect of Maina.

RELIGION: THE ORTHODOX CHURCH

According to the census of 1928, over 96% of the Greek people were members of the Orthodox Church (see p. 349). About 2% were Moslems, comprising mainly those Turks of Dhitikí Thráki who were exempt from the exchange of populations, but also including the Albanian Moslems and the Pomaks (see p. 363 and p. 355). Over 1% were Jews, mainly resident in Thessaloníki (see p. 356), although the Chief Rabbi lived in Athínai. Next came Roman Catholics who numbered about 0·5% of the total population, and who, with their own bishops, were found mostly in the Ionian islands and the Kikládhes (Síros, Tínos, Náxos and Thíra). For the most part they are descendants of Italian families who settled here in Venetian and Genoese times (see p. 184). The Protestant body (mainly Evangelical) is very small, although there has been an English Church in Athínai since 1838. To sum up: membership of the Orthodox Church is virtually a badge of Greek nationality. So closely identified are Church and nationality that during the Balkan Wars of 1912–14, when both Greece and Bulgaria claimed Macedonia, each estimated the ethnic character of the area in terms of membership of the Greek and Bulgarian Orthodox Church respectively. Then again, after the war of 1914–18, the exchange of Greek and Turkish populations was carried out on a religious basis (see p. 380).

General Characteristics

Even when they have ceased to believe in the Christian creed, Greeks seldom take the trouble openly to break away from the Church, which, on her side, makes no attempt to interfere with their private lives. However indifferent in practice, they retain their affection for an institution which has always identified itself with the national cause. Under Ottoman domination every little Greek community in Asia Minor, Thrace, Macedonia, the Aegean islands or the Greek peninsula had its Orthodox Church presided over by a priest, whose patriotic fervour for a reborn Greece controlling all the areas of Greek settlement in the eastern Mediterranean contributed largely to the foundations of modern Greece.

The Greek is not deeply religious. His conception of religion consists of keeping the prescribed fasts, which are rigorous and exacting; assisting at the Liturgy, especially in Holy Week and during the great festivals; supporting the clergy and charitable activities in his parish; and occasionally going on a pilgrimage. These pilgrimages to local shrines on the Saints' days often bring large groups of people from surrounding villages to some remote chapel or well: some shrines have a national rather than local importance, and on the appropriate Saint's day people flock there from all over Greece. Fasting during Lent is most carefully practised by the more devout Greeks; in addition to meat, they will not eat eggs or drink wine, and since fish is scarce in all parts of inland Greece, and scarcer than would be expected on the coast, the diet is very nearly restricted to bread and olives. Towards the end of Lent the effects of fasting are apparent; people look thin and pale, and lack energy. It is little wonder then, that after the midnight service ending with a procession through the village, Easter Day is a day of feasting.

Historical Outline

The first three centuries of the Christian era saw the development that culminated in the official recognition of Christianity by the Roman empire in A.D. 313. Before the fourth century was over, Byzantium had become the capital of the eastern half of the empire, and the minor bishop of Byzantium had become the Patriarch of Constantinople (see p. 155). A Church Council of 381 gave Constantinople precedence over the older patriarchates of Antioch, Alexandria and Jerusalem, and placed it second only to the bishopric of Rome.* The early history of the Eastern Church was a chequered one, varied internally by schisms and heresies, and externally by changes in its frontiers. In the south it lost large provinces to Islam

* For the early history of the Eastern Churches, see the N.I.D. Handbook on *Turkey*, vol. I, pp. 397–9 (1942).

in the seventh century, while to the north it gained by the conversion of the Bulgars, the Serbs and the Russians in the ninth and tenth centuries.

Throughout these years, and during succeeding centuries also, relations with the Church in the west were difficult. The division of the Roman Empire had prepared the way for a separation of the churches, and the differing histories of the east and west Mediterranean basins hastened the process of differentiation. Misunderstandings passed into disputes that ended in complete disruption. Frequent breaks between the two churches culminated in a final separation in 1054, and all subsequent attempts at reunion were unsuccessful.

Under the regime of the Turks, the Church was used as an instrument of government, and the Patriarch at Constantinople occupied an important place in the Ottoman system of administration. No attempt was made at wholesale conversion to Islam. It is true that many Christian churches, even St Sophia itself, were converted into mosques wherever Moslems were numerous, but the fact remains that the Turkish regime was, generally speaking, a tolerant one, at least as far as exercise of religion was concerned (see p. 186). Compared with the other peoples of the Balkan lands, the position of the Greeks was extremely favourable. The terms 'Greek' and 'Christian' became synonymous in the Turkish empire, a situation that was later fraught with difficulties when the rising feeling of Slav nationality in the Balkans began to assert itself against Greek predominance.

During the War of Independence (1821–32) the relations of the Greeks to Constantinople changed, for many were suspicious of a Patriarchate in Turkish territory, and the arrival of a Catholic king and his regency in 1833 helped to sever the bonds that connected the Church in Greece with Constantinople. An attempt was made to weaken the power of the Church generally; thus some 300 monasteries were dissolved and their property secularized; and, in particular, the severance with Constantinople was formally declared in 1833. By this act, the Church in Greece became autocephalous with the king as its supreme head. Church government was invested in a Holy Synod consisting of a royal commissioner and five senior ecclesiastics, the senior in time of ordination being president. This arrangement was confirmed by the constitution of 1844, but although this confirmed administrative separation, it recognized an 'inseparable dogmatic union with the Great Church of Constantinople'. The independence of 1833, however, had never been acknowledged by the Patriarch, and agreement was not reached until 1850–2 when the Patriarch recognized the Holy Synod with the archbishop of Athens as its president, on condition that the 'Great Church' at Constantinople should provide the sacred oil for anointing, and should be consulted on important questions of dogma. The constitution of 1864 again confirmed this arrangement and, while declaring the Orthodox Church to be the religion of the state, allowed complete toleration to all other sects. Despite this toleration in principle, the Orthodox Church has been bitterly opposed to the Macedonian Orthodox who use the Slavonic liturgy, and especially to the two or three thousand Catholics of the Byzantine rite (Uniates) who came with the refugees from Turkey into Greece in 1922–3.

The territory of the independent church expanded with that of the kingdom. After the union of the Ionian islands (which had hitherto been dependent upon the Patriarchate), the Ionian sees were united with the Church of Greece in 1866; the Thessalian were likewise added after 1881. When the third great extension of Greece took place after the Balkan Wars of 1912–13, the status of dioceses of the new territories remained under discussion until 1928 when, by arrangement with the Patriarchate, they were included within the Church of Greece. Kríti remained independent alike of Athínai and Constantinople except that its metropolitan was appointed by the Patriarchate; the religious affairs of the island are governed by a synod of the seven bishops of Kríti under the presidency of the archbishop of (Candia) Iráklion. The authority of Constantinople has thus continued to decline, until the archbishop of Athínai is now a more important personage than the Patriarch. The authority of the Patriarch was also limited in the rest of the Balkan lands. Since 1870, there has been a Bulgarian Exarch, and also Serbian and Romanian Patriarchs since 1922 and 1925 respectively. There has even been discussion at times about the advisability of retaining the Patriarchate in İstanbul (Constantinople), but sentimental and historical reasons weigh heavily in its favour.

From the time of its independence, the Church in Greece has been involved in the politics of the country; and the constitutional relations of Church and state, and the composition of the Holy Synod, have been changed a number of times as various shades of political opinion have been in power. The numbers of the Holy Synod have varied too, according to the political tendencies of the moment, but, apart from the royal commissioner, one-half its members have been elected from the 'old' (i.e. pre-1913) and one-half from the 'new' provinces. All members, chosen in rotation from the bishops, hold office for one year, and sit permanently at Athínai under the life presidency of the archbishop of Athínai. The number of bishoprics in 1941 was sixty-four, but the number of bishops is constantly varying. The bishops meet once in every three years in a 'Holy Community'. When the occasion arises, this elects the archbishop and also the bishops, subject to the approval of the king; it also decides on any legislation to be submitted to the government. The Church deals with the state through the Ministry of Education and Ecclesiastical Affairs. This Ministry has a separate section to deal with problems affecting other denominations. Since the latter half of the nineteenth century there has been some anti-clerical feeling in Greece, for the Church, as a great landowner, has been a conservative force against the policy of agrarian reform and the more liberal trends of the times.

The Secular Clergy

The secular clergy in the country are often drawn from the poorest classes, and in the past have had as a rule but little education. Before 1909, the lower clergy were paid out of the offerings of their congregations, and the bishops by the state. But in that year a General Ecclesiastical Fund was established from the surplus revenues of the monasteries and churches, and from this fund the bishops and clergy were paid; but, even so, the lower clergy have continued to be very poorly paid. As opposed to the monastic clergy, they are usually married, and supplement their tiny incomes by cultivating small properties, by keeping a shop, or by taking on any village post, varying from that of blacksmith to that of schoolmaster. In 1931, when a law was passed fixing the salaries of the lower clergy, some priests were even found working in mines. A determined attempt has recently been made to improve the education of the clergy, and the Metropolitan of Athínai now tries to appoint only those who hold a diploma of one of the theological seminaries. Until a few years ago, the Rhizareion School in Athínai, founded in 1843 by two brothers from Ípiros, was the only institution for the higher education of the clergy, but now theological seminaries run on similar lines have been established in several provincial centres.

The Monastic Clergy

There were in 1937 some 202 monasteries in Greece (including twenty in Áyion Óros) and just over 5,000 monks. Convents of women numbered fifty-three with nearly 1,000 nuns. Since 1909 the surplus revenues of the monasteries have been taken to pay for the maintenance of the bishops and lower secular clergy, and there is a general view that the monastic funds are better used to improve the material position and education of the clergy than in the upkeep of the monasteries. In 1926 it was proposed by the government that all monks under 50 years of age should be dismissed. The Holy Synod of 1926, though not consenting to go so far, ruled that novices should be discharged, and no further additions permitted. The number of monasteries and of monks has therefore declined markedly in recent years, and many of the smaller monasteries have been completely closed. The famous monasteries of Metéora in Thessalía, perched on isolated pinnacles and formerly reached only by vertical ladders or rope-cages worked by a pulley, have been reduced to four, with only a few monks in each (Plate 90).

All the high positions of the Church are in the hands of the regular (monastic) clergy; the bishops are usually chosen from the monastic orders, and thus the monastic life has become a necessary stepping stone to a career in the Church. Those who reach such positions are often learned theologians or men of ability in other respects; but in general the standard of learning in the monasteries is not high. According to western ideas of monasticism, the monks are very easy-going, especially in the idiorrhythmic monasteries (see below). They do not study, preach, or have schools or hospitals, and, as most of their property is farmed out, they have little to do except assist at the long Church offices. Manual work is done by lay brothers, or ordinary lay servants. Observance of the monastic rule, which is universally that of St Basil, varies a good deal, and, if in some monasteries it is relaxed, in others, especially in Áyion Óros, the true monastic fervour and discipline are maintained.

The monasteries offer hospitality to travellers, and this hospitality can best be appreciated in the lesser and more remote houses, where the traveller, after long hours of walking or riding in the summer heat through a treeless countryside, arrives in the evening at a picturesque rambling building with gardens, trees and running water, built round a cool courtyard with the church in the centre. He will be courteously received, conducted to the guest room, and, later, a meal, with a carafe of the monastery wine, will be provided. On leaving next morning no payment will be asked for, but it is correct to leave an offering in the Church. At some of the large monasteries, hostels have been built, and regular visitors are taken, as at the historic monastery of Megaspílaion.

Áyion Óros (Mount Athos)

A unique community, consisting entirely of monks, inhabits the most easterly of the three peninsulas of Khalkidhikí. The peninsula, named Aktí or Athos, is joined to the mainland by an isthmus, and consists of a narrow ridge rising at its seaward end to the conical peak of Mount Athos. It forms the administrative district of Áyion Óros, commonly called Mount Athos, an autonomous republic under Greek sovereignty. In 1937 there were 3,466 monks, including those not ordained, living in twenty monasteries along the shores of the peninsula, or perched on its flanks, or set astride the ridge, deep in chestnut woods. Some are like country houses, some like vast hotels, others like fortresses, and one, at least, with its seven tiers of soaring balconies is like a monastery in Tibet: everything here is medieval and Byzantine, and time seems to have stood still (Plate 91).

The legends of the monks attribute the first religious settlements on the peninsula to the time of Constantine (A.D. 307–37), but the hermitages are first mentioned in historical documents of the ninth century. Under a constitution, approved by the Emperor Constantine IX in 1045, women and female animals were, and still are, excluded from the Holy Mountain. The capture of Constantinople by the Franks in 1204 brought pillage and ruin to the communities of Áyion Óros, but with the restoration of the Byzantine empire in the middle of the thirteenth century (see p. 171), the monasteries again became prosperous. The monks submitted to the Turks after the capture of Salonica in 1430 (see p. 185), and the Turks respected the special privileges of the monks in return for the payment of tribute. Khalkidhikí remained under Turkish rule until 1913. When Makedhonía was acquired by Greece in that year, the ancient constitutional rights of Áyion Óros were recognized, and the constitutional position of the republic was fully defined in the Constitution of 1928 (see p. 257).

The government of the republic sits at Kariaí, the capital, a small town above the port where steamers call. Affairs are managed by the Holy Community consisting of twenty monks, one from each monastery, but there is also a resident lay representative of the Greek government, and four police. A visitor must present himself before the Community with a letter of introduction and obtain a permit before he can be received at any of the monasteries. Provided with this permit he is hospitably and courteously received.

Of the twenty monasteries on the peninsula, eighteen are Greek inhabited by Greeks from all parts of the Greek world, one is Serbian, one Bulgarian, and until lately there was a large Russian community. Each of the twenty monasteries is a little republic in itself: the coenobitic monasteries (*koinóvia*), each under the rule of an abbot (*igoúmenos*) elected by the brethren, are subjected to severe discipline; the brethren are clothed alike, take their meals (usually limited to bread and vegetables) in the refectory, and possess no private property. The idiorrhythmic monasteries (*idiórrithma*) are governed by a board of two or three wardens (*epítropoi*) elected for a certain number of years; they are less strict in rule, and the monks are allowed to keep their private property. Dependent on the monasteries are twelve monastic settlements (*skétai*), some of considerable size, in which a still more ascetic mode of life prevails; and there are also several hundred sanctuaries (*kellía*) and hermitages (*askitíria*). Formerly, the monasteries, in addition to their farms in Greece, had properties in Romania and other countries, but these have now been lost to them, and even many of their farms in Khalkidhikí have been expropriated for the benefit of the refugees.

The monasteries once possessed a priceless collection of classical manuscripts, but many were destroyed by the Turks during the War of Greek Independence, and others were lost through the neglect and vandalism of the monks. It is even stated that the parchment of some was used as bait for fishing. More were destroyed by fire when the library of Simónos Pétra was burnt down in 1891 and that of St Paul in 1905. Yet others have been sold to visitors and are now dispersed; some are in libraries in Paris and Moscow. The monasteries do, however, still contain treasures of many kinds. Some of the muniment rooms have a marvellous series of documents, the study of which might throw much light on the social life and ecclesiastical history of the Near East from the middle of the tenth century. Many of the manuscripts are finely illuminated. In addition to these, the monasteries possess historic objects and precious reliquaries of interest, together with ikons, vestments, mosaics, mural paintings, frescoes and jewellery of great beauty.

SOCIAL CONDITIONS

The Greeks have a very marked sense of their individuality and an intense patriotic zeal. Their sense of equality, too, is very strong; titles of nobility survive only in the Ionian islands, and here they mean very little. There are, indeed, a few old families, proud of their descent, but nothing that can be described as a nobility. The only princes are of the blood royal and that blood is not Greek. It is expressly laid down in the Constitutions of 1864, 1911 and 1927 that no titles of nobility or distinction may be awarded to Greek citizens. The dominant class is the bourgeoisie, which has greatly increased in numbers and political power since the early days when the Greek Kingdom was almost entirely a land of peasants. It is from the ranks of the bourgeoisie that the politicians and the civil servants are largely drawn.

Despite the importance of the bourgeois element, Greece is mainly an agricultural country as the following table of occupations shows:

Category	Total	Total %
Agriculture	1,293,398	53·56
Stock rearing and hunting	167,302	6·93
Fishing	14,941	0·62
Mining and quarrying	6,340	0·26
Manufacturing	429,831	17·80
*Transport and communications	106,758	4·42
Banking, broking, etc.	22,937	0·95
Commerce	185,560	7·68
Personal service	57,570	2·38
Liberal professions	85,969	3·56
Public service	44,472	1·84
Total gainfully employed	2,415,078	100·00
Total population	6,204,684	

* Including 34,000 sailors.

Based on 1928 census returns, from *Annuaire Statistique de la Grèce*, 1937 (Athènes, 1938).

Thus, just over 60% of the working population are engaged in agriculture. Moreover, throughout country districts, women and children who are not counted as gainfully employed also assist in this work. The agricultural nature of the Greek economy is shown also in the relative proportion of town and country dwellers. According to the 1928 census, 67% of the population lived in settlements of under 5,000 inhabitants. On the other hand, a feature of the last two decades has been a strong drift from the countryside to the towns, a movement reflected not only in the rapid growth of the few urban centres but in the steadily increasing numbers engaged in industry and commerce.

Country Life

The vast majority of the people are small peasant proprietors. By the Agrarian Reform Law of October 1924, large estates were expropriated; their owners were compensated, but in general were allowed to retain no more than 30 ha. (74 acres), the remainder being distributed to landless farm-hands and to refugees. 'Old Greece' was already a land of small-holdings, and this new measure chiefly affected the Turkish *Tchifliks* (the big estates) of the newly acquired northern provinces (see p. 385). The work of expropriation was almost completed by 1939, with the result that the average holding for the whole of Greece was as low as 3 ha. A feature of the new agrarian regime was the growth of the co-operative movement, particularly amongst the areas of refugee settlement in northern Greece (see p. 251). By 1939 there were more than 5,000 Co-operatives in the whole country.

Both Venizelos and Metaxas showed themselves alive to the necessity of increasing the productivity of the country and improving the economic standing of the peasant. Thus the Metaxas Government had drawn up a ten-year plan which would have involved the expenditure of some 7,324 million drachmae, or approximately 14 million pounds sterling. It envisaged the draining of large areas of swamp and lake, the building of new roads and railways, and the construction of harbours, quays and docks. Some progress had been made along these lines before the outbreak of war in 1940, and work of this nature would do much to improve economic and social conditions in Greece. This is especially the case in country districts, many of which lack anything approaching adequate communication with each other and with the towns.

Nevertheless, in spite of the agrarian reforms, the financial help given by Co-operatives and the bold schemes envisaged by the Greek governments, the general standard of living in the countryside is low. Many a peasant in addition to cultivating his small plot fulfils some village function and acts as shopkeeper, postman, policeman, blacksmith, cobbler or other essential craftsman.

Settlement in Greece is predominantly in the form of villages, which are usually distinguished from towns by possessing under

3,000 inhabitants. Isolated farms are rare. For the most part, the villages are widely separated, especially in mountainous districts, where they are approached only by the roughest of mountain paths. Thus a peasant's fields are often far from his home, and a traveller approaching a village at sunset will fall in with a procession of peasants on horses, mules, ox-carts or donkeys returning from their work.

The village may be compact in form, like many that originated from the Turkish *Tchiflik*: on the other hand, it may be a simple aggregation of houses laid out more or less to suit the site and the converging roads; the village of the plain showing a tendency to a grid pattern, that of the hillside an unplanned growth. But whatever their differences in history or site, almost all villages have a central market square and a church, round which the houses cluster. In Makedhonía and Thráki, where the majority of refugees were settled, many of the villages are new and bear all the marks of planned building—a central square with the church, the school and the administrative buildings, and for the most part rectangular streets. The houses are small but modern, and the whole gives an effect of cleanliness, efficiency and prosperity. The influx of refugees and the clearing and draining of land for their settlement has improved the social conditions in these areas. The immigrant Greeks were on the whole accustomed to higher standards of living in Asia Minor than the peasants of northern Greece, and their energy and enterprise and more modern methods of farming set a standard for rural Greece. In the Ionian islands the standard of living is also relatively high, and a village like Stavrós in Itháki, most of whose inhabitants have prospered in South Africa or Australia, resembles a garden city with its white villas set among vineyards and olives, overlooking the sea. In the Máni of southern Pelopónnisos, as a legacy of its turbulent history, the inhabitants live in towers, in which the living room is on the first floor and is reached by a ladder drawn up at night.

The ordinary house in a village is a very simple affair of one story and two or three scantily furnished rooms; the family may sleep on rugs spread on the floor of the living room. More prosperous families live in houses of two stories. The type of house also varies according to the district, and the materials available. In the plains of Thessalía poor mud-brick houses are the rule, in the mountains solid constructions of stone with wide verandahs and stone-tiled roofs, in the islands of the Archipelago rough-cast walls and flat roofs, both dazzling with whitewash. The interiors of the island houses are spotlessly clean, and often gay with coloured dishes and embroideries.

The return of emigrants to their native homes is a noticeable feature of the life in many villages, particularly in the Pelopónnisos. They have made some money, perhaps in the United States, and are either back for a holiday, or they have returned for good. In the latter case they may buy some property, build a house, or start a store. Since the restrictions on immigration, many have not been able to return to America, and remain in Greece dissatisfied and unable to settle down. Too often they have lost their native peasant breeding, and have acquired a poor imitation of American manners. The peasant who has remained in his native surroundings is industrious, sober and thrifty, on the whole contented with his lot, which, however, he is anxious to improve, especially for his children. His ambition is achieved when he has sent one or more of his sons to the nearest secondary school, from which they will later emerge as black-coated members of society. Discontent with the monotony of life in these remote villages is easily to be understood in the case of people with quick intelligence and plenty of enterprise, and emigration and the attractions of town life have had the usual effect of causing a shortage of labour for agricultural work. The monotony is relieved by festivals of the Church, by fairs, weddings and funerals. At most gatherings dancing forms part of the entertainment; the dance is either a rather sedate round dance, the *Sirtó* or *Tráta*, in which a number of dancers, usually of the same sex, take part holding hands (Plate 92); or the more lively Albanian fling, danced by three or four people, one of whom executes a series of leaps and pirouettes. The national music is primitive and rather monotonous.

The peasants spend little on food or dress. Bread, made of barley and unleavened, olives and cheese are the principal diet, supplemented by dried fruit such as figs, or in season, fresh fruit and herbs seasoned with oil. Meat is rarely eaten and is usually goat, mutton or chicken. The principal meal may be at midday or in the evening, according to circumstances. They drink local wine, probably from their own grapes. Good water is highly prized and the peasants are real connoisseurs of its taste and quality. In pastoral districts, milk, especially curdled sheep's milk (*giaourti*), is drunk.

The national costume, of which the *foustanella* (a white pleated skirt or kilt reaching to the knee) is characteristic, is worn by peasants throughout Greece, but more especially in the mountains. In its elaborate form, as worn by the royal bodyguard in Athínai on gala

Plate 92. A country dance

One of the most common dances in country districts is the *Sirtó* or *Tráta*, a rather sedate round dance.

Plate 93. A street in Pírgos

The narrow paved streets of coastal towns are often in shadow and contrast strongly with the tall white buildings in the sun.

Plate 94. Greek peasant women near Dhelfoí (Delphi)

Plate 95. *Eftsones*

The national costume of Greece is the heavily pleated *foustanella*, tasselled fez, embroidered vest, white woollen tights and pompon slippers. The costume is worn by the royal bodyguard (*eftsones*).

days, it is very splendid with its heavily braided silk jacket, red-tasselled cap and red upturned shoes with black pompoms. White homespun leggings, reaching above the thighs, protect the legs, and at the waist is a broad leather belt with a pouch for carrying arms, tobacco and small possessions (Plate 95). In the country a black overcoat with a velvet collar and a small black skullcap form part of the costume. Where the *foustanella* is not worn, peasants and shepherds wear homespun trousers and in winter a goat-hair cape or coat with a hood. In the plains, the usual costume is a kind of blouse with a short skirt attached, and dark homespun gaiters; a handkerchief covers the head or, in summer, a wide straw hat. A great many peasants, however, wear European jacket and trousers of rather poor quality. In the islands of the Archipelago, a more or less universal costume is a pair of wide baggy breeches of blue cotton or cloth coming well below the knee, black stockings, a short jacket and red fez. The Cretan costume is quite distinctive. Women's dress varies according to districts. Though their everyday dresses sometimes carry embroidery, as among the Albanian women of Attíki, most peasant women possess special costumes, reserved for festivals and the like. These may be most elaborate, and districts, islands and villages have their own styles, many of the utmost distinction and beauty. The costume worn by the women of Skíros is justly famous.

Town Life

There are in Greece, according to the 1928 census, seventy-five towns of between 5,000 and 20,000 people, containing 10% of the population, and only twenty-two towns of over this size, accounting for a further 24% of the total population. Of these, Athínai (459,211), Piraiévs (251,659) and Thessaloníki (244,680) can alone claim the distinction of being large cities, Pátrai falling far behind with 64,636 inhabitants.

Most of the coastal towns and those of the islands differ considerably in plan and aspect from those of the interior. As with most of the maritime towns of the Mediterranean coasts they are very closely built and their narrow paved lanes are dark in contrast with the whiteness of the tall, flat-roofed buildings. The ground floors are occupied by the shops which are often connected in arcades: the market place, if there is one, is small. Yet unlike the small towns of Italy or Spain, those of Greece lack monuments of architectural interest, cathedrals and the like; their charm lies in their incomparable setting of sea or mountains, and their picturesque beauty is frequently enhanced by the remains of a medieval fortress or walls, at the foot of which the town is spread (Plate 87).

The inland towns are quite different. Normally they are built on a grid plan, with broad tree-lined streets and a considerable market place. The houses, apart from those containing the shops, are largely concealed from the streets by walls enclosing small gardens. They are for the most part two-storied buildings of stone or sun-dried brick, with low-pitched roofs of slate or curved red tiles. Other towns, of Turkish origin, are of a pattern common to the whole Balkan Peninsula. The older central part is always closely built with narrow winding streets. The lower walls of the houses on the street side are windowless, for the houses open only on to enclosed courts. The covered bazaars form the exception, the booths being widely open to the street but closed completely by shutters at night. The occupants of these tend to be segregated by trades. The rows of uniform cottages, built under government supervision to house the refugee population, are a modern feature of many towns, whether of Greek or Turkish origin.

Both in pattern of settlement and way of life, little distinction can be made between the smaller provincial towns, such as Thívai, and the larger villages. Town life is more accelerated perhaps but it is seldom gay. Formerly the shadow theatre was all that was available by way of amusement; now there may be a cinema. Greeks, however, do not require more elaborate amusements than perhaps playing cards in a café, gambling or merely talking, usually about politics. A feature of life in summer in the small towns is the evening promenade, when the whole population paces slowly to and fro across the principal square or the quayside till a late hour, while family groups sit at the café tables placed in the open. That about one person to every forty gainfully employed in Greece should be engaged in personal service, i.e. in hotels, restaurants, cafés, bars, etc., is a clear indication of Greek social life.

In the larger towns of course, such as the industrial centres of Piraiévs and Lávrion, or in large commercial towns like Pátrai with its arcades and busy shops, or in Thessaloníki with its hotels built on western European models, its University and cosmopolitan crowds, or even in Athínai itself, much more is offered in the way of entertainment. Cinemas, theatres and concerts are of a high standard. Very late hours are kept in the summer, and few Greeks dine before 9.30; the short hours of sleep at night are offset by the afternoon siesta, and office hours are curtailed. Yet even in Athínai, which in many respects does not differ greatly from other European capitals, the ordinary Athenians—as distinct from the cosmopolitan element—the professional classes, government officials and business men, have simple tastes and spend little on amusements or recreations. Sports, however, have captured the young, and tennis, football, and athletics of all kinds are taken up with enthusiasm; the hiking movement, too, has spread rapidly amongst the youth in Greece.

Social Legislation

The standard of living among the labouring classes in Greece has always been very low, more particularly in the large towns, where the increase in wage level has by no means kept pace with the very rapid rise in the cost of living. In Athínai, for instance, costs had risen about ten times above the 1914 level by 1923, and again doubled in the last two decades. Yet by the terms of the social insurance scheme of 1934, which with subsequent modifications was in force at the largest urban centres in 1939 (see p. 344), the minimum wage for industrial workers was as low as 55 dr. (about 2*s*.) per day in Athínai, 52 dr. in Thessaloníki and 50 dr. in the other towns. Female workers were to receive not less than 35 dr. in the capital. This scale, though an improvement on minimum wages often paid before the law was passed, still represents but a pittance even in Greece.

In a country where the economy is predominantly agricultural, and where the people have such a strong sense of their individuality, it is not surprising to find that the Trade Union movement has not been a powerful weapon in improving the wage level of the labourers. Nor have strikes and lock-outs played any large part in settling labour disputes. Yet even before the Balkan Wars, strikes were not unknown in Greece; they were, however, short-lived, non-violent and easily settled. With the development of industry, the Trade Union movement grew steadily, strikes became more frequent, and a law of 1920 affirmed the right to strike. The next few years saw frequent if sometimes minor strikes in the larger towns. A law of 1926 established the principle of voluntary conciliation and arbitration, and by 1929 arbitration commissions had been set up in some of the larger towns, their decisions being binding for three months. Within a few years the character of strikes had changed, and they were being used as a political, rather than as a purely industrial weapon. After the Metaxas *coup d'état*, however, strikes were virtually forbidden and voluntary

Trade Unionism in Greece came to an end. The reorganized *General Confederation of Labour* was to be the only representative organization of labour, and any Union refusing to affiliate was no longer recognized.

Social legislation in Greece is comparatively recent; yet even so it has often been in advance of public opinion. The introduction of holidays with pay, an eight-hour day for miners, various factory acts, and special legislation to safeguard women and children, were passed in 1911-12. A law of 1914 established the six-day week, and in this year too a Workmen's Compensation Act was passed. By 1924 the eight-hour day had been enforced in most industries, except those of seasonal activity, and by 1936 it covered all but the textile industry.

The first comprehensive social insurance scheme was introduced as late as 1922; it provided a fairly complete insurance system to be applied to all wage-earners. Even then it was not generally enforced, and in 1934 a new Act was passed, which laid down the general principles of universal compulsory insurance to cover sickness, maternity, accident, invalidity, old age and survivors' risks (see p. 343). All these insurances were covered by a single joint contribution by employer and employee. Afraid of arousing opposition in a country where wages were notoriously low, the government fixed the joint contribution at 3·6% of the basic wage, intending later to raise it to about 8%. Benefits were correspondingly low, and many of the voluntary schemes already in existence offered better terms. The Act applied to all wage-earners, not already insured under existing schemes, who resided in towns or villages where there were branches of the Central Insurance Institute. The application of the Act was several times postponed, and it was not until December 1937 that it came into force in Athínai and Piraiévs; the next year it was in operation in Thessaloníki and some 310,000 workers were so covered; in 1939 it was further extended to cover wage-earners in Pátrai, Vólos and Kalámai.

As yet there is no general scheme for compulsory unemployment insurance, but in 1936 some 48,000 persons were insured by subsidized voluntary schemes.

BIBLIOGRAPHICAL NOTE

A. *The Origin of the Greeks.*

A summary of the racial history of Greece is given in C. S. Coon's *The Races of Europe*, pp. 142–6 (New York, 1939). Two useful accounts of the Balkan peoples in general are: J. Ancel, *Peuples et Nations des Balkans* (Paris, 1930); E. Pittard, *Les Peuples des Balkans* (Paris, n.d.). Two books are particularly useful for a scholarly assessment of the evidence relating to the Slav immigration into Greece: J. B. Bury, *A History of the Late Roman Empire*, 395–800 A.D., 2 vols. (London,

1889); J. B. Bury, *A History of the Eastern Roman Empire*, A.D. 802–867 (London, 1912).

See also the other historical works indicated on p. 153.

B. *The Greek Language.*

(i) For the general history of the classical language the best work is A. Meillet's *Aperçu d'une histoire de la langue grecque* (Paris, 1935). In English, there is an excellent account by B. C. Atkinson, *The Greek Language* (London, 1933).

(ii) Within a short compass, N. Bachtin's *Introduction to the Study of Modern Greek* (Cambridge, 1935) is valuable and stimulating. There is a comprehensive survey of the organic continuity of the language in P. S. Costas's *An Outline of the Development of the Greek Language* (Chicago, 1936).

(iii) The distribution of the modern dialects is discussed at length by R. M. Dawkins, 'The dialects of modern Greece', *Transactions of the Philological Society*, 1940, pp. 1–38 (London). For Tzakonian, there is an admirable account in H. Pernot's *Introduction à l'étude du dialecte Tsakonien* (Paris, 1934).

(iv) A historical description of the conflict between the popular language and the 'katharévousa' is given by P. Vlasto, *Greek Bilingualism and some Parallel Cases* (Athens, 1933).

(v) The dialects of Rostov and Mariupol are described by R. M. Dawkins in 'The Pontic dialect of modern Greek in Asia Minor and Russia', *Transactions of the Philological Society*, 1937, pp. 15–52 (London). There is a detailed study of the Greek dialects spoken in southern Italy in G. Rohlfs's *Scavi linguistici nella Magna Grecia* (Roma, 1933). A short account of the Greek colony at Cargèse in Corsica is given by R. M. Dawkins, *Byzantinisch-Neugriechische Jahrbücher*, vol. V, pp. 371–9 (Athen, 1927). The statement on Greek-speaking peoples in southern Albania has been taken almost entirely from two official publications: *Peace Handbooks: The Balkan States*, part I, no. 17, 'Albania', vol. III, Foreign Office (London, 1920), and a report by J. J. Sederholm in the *League of Nations Official Journal*, 4th year, pp. 491–510 (Geneva, 1923). For a further account see E. P. Stickney, *Southern Albania or Northern Epirus in European International Affairs*, 1912–23 (Stanford, Cal. 1926).

C. *Religion.*

A general outline of the history of the Greek Orthodox Church may be obtained from one of the following: H. F. Tozer, *The Church and the Eastern Empire* (London, 1897); W. F. Adeney, *The Greek and Eastern Churches* (Edinburgh, 1908); A Fortescue, *The Orthodox Eastern Church* (3rd ed., London, 1911).

There is a chapter on the situation up to 1928 in W. Miller's, *Greece*, pp. 200–14 (London, 1928). For some aspects of Greek monasticism, see (i) F. W. Hasluck, *Athos and its Monasteries* (London, 1924); and (ii) R. M. Dawkins, *The Monks of Athos* (London, 1936). Relevant articles in James Hastings's *Encyclopædia of Religion and Ethics*, 13 vols. (Edinburgh and New York, 1908–26), should also be consulted.

D. *Social Conditions.*

A brief survey of the rural economy, the effects of agrarian reform and the development of the Co-operative movement in Greece is given by M. B. Simonide, 'L'économie rurale grecque et la crise de la guerre mondiale', pp. 161–87 of *Les Effets Économiques et Sociaux de la Guerre en Grèce*, edited by André Andréadès. This forms the Greek section of *Histoire Économique et Sociale de la Guerre Mondiale*, Publ. de la Dotation Carnegie pour la Paix Internat., Section d'écon. et d'hist. (Paris and New Haven, 1928). Another article in the same volume, pp. 189–222, by D. Kalitsounakis is 'Législation ouvrière et sociale grecque pendant et après la guerre'. This gives a short account of social legislation in Greece from 1909 to 1923.

There are, of course, very many travel books which describe the manners and customs of the Greeks.

Chapter XII

MINORITIES

General Summary: Turkish-speaking Peoples: The Macedo-Slavs: The Pomaks: The Jews: The Armenians: The Vlachs: The Greek Orthodox Albanians: The Albanian Moslems: The Gipsies: Bibliographical Note

General Summary

According to the census of 1928, minorities of religion or language in Greece represented about 7% of the total population (6,204,684). Of the foreign speakers, the great majority of the men are bilingual with Greek as a second language, and an increasing number of women can also speak or understand Greek. The main elements of language and religion are shown in the table on p. 349, but this does not indicate the large Albanian element in the heart of Greece (Fig. 97). Many of these Albanians, however, had long been assimilated, and those still speaking Albanian were Greek Orthodox in religion, and formed an integral and prosperous part of the Greek nation. In no sense did they constitute a minority.

It is in the north of Greece, outside the limits of the old kingdom of 1881, that minority problems have confronted the Greek government (Fig. 97). In this northern area, acquired as late as 1913–20, there was much ill feeling between the various ethnic elements, and the military operations of the years 1912–22 were accompanied by substantial displacements of population, which are summarized on p. 351. Various agreements in 1913–14 between Turkey and the Balkan powers had provided for voluntary exchanges of population, and the Treaty of Neuilly in 1919 between Greece and Bulgaria also provided for a voluntary exchange which brought 46,000 Greeks in exchange for about 92,000 Bulgarians. A more drastic remedy was found in the compulsory exchange of population between Greece and Turkey provided for in the Convention of Lausanne (January 1923). The exchange of some 390,000 Moslems for over one million Greeks not only reduced the Turkish population of Greece to a small body in Dhitikí Thráki (Western Thrace), but also provided a great mass of settlers to people these northern provinces with Greek patriots (see p. 394). No exchange took place with Albania, and some 18,598 Albanian Moslems remained in Greek territory according to the Greek census of 1928.

The minority question had been most acute in Macedonia. The nature of its inextricable tangle of Greeks, Bulgars, Turks and others may be seen from the fact that the area has given rise to the culinary term 'macédoine'. But now, after the exchanges, the 'Macedonian

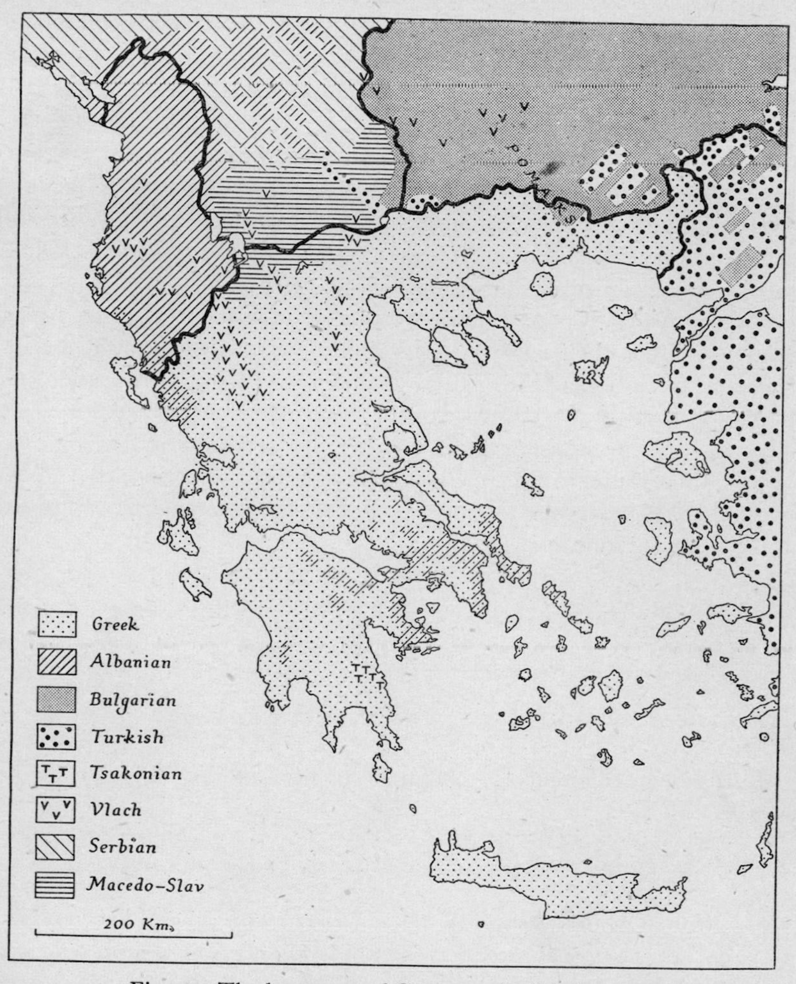

Fig. 97. The languages of Greece and adjoining areas

Based mainly on (1) *South-East Europe: Ethnographical Map*, G.S.G.S., No. 3703*a* (1918); (2) map in *Greek Refugee Settlement* (League of Nations, Geneva, 1926); (3) *Grande Atlante del Touring Club Italiano*, plate 16 (3rd ed. Roma, 1933); (4) *A Gazetteer of Greece*, Fig. 2 (P.C.G.N. London, 1942).

The distribution of Vlachs is based on the G.S.G.S. map and differs from that of Fig. 103.

Question', which had become so chronic a disturber of the peace, was greatly simplified if not completely solved. The great experiment of exchanging populations caused much personal hardship and regret, but at least it brought a partial solution to one of the most critical danger spots on the continent of Europe. The Vlachs were left, but they formed a minor element, too small and scattered to become an acute minority problem. The Macedo-Slavs of Greece, too, despite the Bulgar affinities of their language, had chosen to remain.

In accordance with the main peace treaties after the war of 1914–18, certain countries agreed to special minority treaties which were to operate under the guarantee of the League of Nations. Thus by article 46 of the Treaty of Neuilly (27 November 1919), 'Greece accepts and agrees to embody in a Treaty with the Principal Allied and Associated Powers such provisions as may be deemed necessary by these Powers to protect the interests of inhabitants of that State who differ from the majority of the population in race, language or religion'. The Greek Minorities Treaty was accordingly signed on 10 August 1920.*

In addition to these minority elements among the citizens of Greece, there were, at the census of 1928, 73,338 people of non-Greek nationality in Greece. These were divided among the various nationalities as follows:

Turks	22,373	Russians	3,329
Italians	14,598	Frenchmen	2,367
Albanians	7,193	Germans	1,429
British	6,908	Bulgars	1,238
Yugoslavs	4,797	Romanians	1,106
Americans (U.S.A.)	3,692	Others	4,308

Source: *Annuaire Statistique de la Grèce*, 1931, p. 78 (Athènes, 1932).

This foreign element is discussed from a demographic point of view in vol. II.

Turkish-speaking Peoples

The Ottoman Turks first acquired a footing on European territory in 1356; by 1461 they were masters of the Greek mainland; and by 1566 they were also in control of the Aegean islands. Except for the brief Venetian occupation of the Peloponnese (1685–1718), they remained in control of almost the whole area, until the Greek War of Independence (1821–32). After this, successive acquisitions of territory by the Greeks, added Thessalía (1881), Ípiros and Make-

* *League of Nations Treaty Series*, vol. XXVIII, pp. 243–65 (Geneva, 1924).

The Population of Greece by Language and Religion (according to the 1928 Census)

Languages	Total	Christians			Moslems	Jews	Other religions	Without religion
		Greek Orthodox	Roman Catholic	Protestant				
Greek	5,759,523	5,716,100	27,747	3,867	2,623	9,090	15	81
Foreign	445,161	245,429	7,435	5,136	123,394	63,701	30	36
Turkish	191,254	103,642	327	760	86,506	17	1	1
Macedo-Slav	81,984	81,844	68	11	2	58	—	1
Spanish	63,200	28	58	41	72	62,999	—	2
Armenian	33,634	31,038	1,136	1,432	16	10	2	—
Koutzovlach	19,703	19,679	9	2	3	10	—	—
Albanian	18,773	95	59	17	18,598	3	1	—
Bulgar	16,775	20	—	—	16,755	—	—	—
Romani	4,998	3,853	—	1	1,130	—	14	—
Russian	3,295	3,177	49	14	3	40	—	12
Italian	3,199	98	2,878	18	1	203	—	1
English	2,098	201	274	1,605	1	15	—	2
Others	6,248	1,754	2,577	1,235	307	346	12	17
Total	6,204,684	5,961,529	35,182	9,003	126,017	72,791	45	117

Source: *Annuaire Statistique de la Grèce*, 1931, p. 52 (Athènes, 1932).

dhonía (1913) and Dhitikí Thráki (1920) to the Greek state. Despite the long period of their political domination, the Turks contributed but little, ethnographically speaking, to the mass of the Greek population. Where they settled, mainly in the north, they remained a distinct minority, separated by the barriers of language and religion.*

When Thessalía was added to Greece in 1881, the Turkish officials disappeared, and most of the Turkish landowners sold their estates and left the country. To the north, the acquisition of Makedhonía in 1913 and of Dhitikí Thráki in 1920 meant the addition of large numbers of Turks. This Turkish element, however, was greatly reduced by the exchange of population between Greece and Turkey under the Convention of Lausanne (1923) which ended the Greco-Turkish war. Altogether, some 390,000 Turks were exchanged for well over one million Greeks (see p. 378). It is difficult to obtain exact figures because of the disturbed political condition of the area during 1912–24, but the estimates on p. 351 probably give a fair picture of the changing situation.

At the census of 1928 there were 191,254 Turkish-speaking people in Greece. Of these, some 103,642 were Orthodox, who, for the most part, were refugees from Asia Minor; their language was Turkish, but they had remained Greek in sentiment as well as in religion. The remainder of the Turkish-speaking peoples in 1928 consisted almost entirely of the Moslems of Dhitikí Thráki, who had been exempted from the exchange. These remained conscious of their Turkish nationality, but there is no evidence that they formed a discontented minority under Greek rule, or that the Turkish government was dissatisfied at the way the Greek government treated them. Their rights were protected by treaty, which allowed questions of family law and personal status to be regulated in accordance with Moslem usage. In 1924, there were some 300 mosques in Dhitikí Thráki and 128 Moslem schools, to which certain subsidies were given by the state; by 1933, the schools numbered 305. Five weekly Turkish newspapers were published in Xánthi and Komotiní. Until January 1936, the Thracian Moslems voted as a separate electoral college, electing four Deputies.

* Before 1923 there were a few Greek-speaking Moslems in Greece. They were known as the 'Valakhadhes' and they lived mainly in the valley of the upper Aliákmon (Vistritsa). Some authorities have derived the name from Vlachs, but a more likely derivation seems to be from the Turkish 'V'alláhi' (By God), because that was the only Turkish they knew. Their origin is obscure; one can merely instance the analogous case of the Bulgarian-speaking Moslems (Pomaks).

Migrations to and from Macedonia, Western Thrace (Dhitikí Thráki) and Eastern Thrace, 1912–24

Based on A. A. Pallis, 'Racial Migrations in the Balkans during the years 1912–1924', *Geographical Journal*, vol. LXVI, pp. 315–31 (London, 1925).

Macedonia

1912 10,000 Moslems from Macedonia before the armies of the Balkan allies.
1913 15,000 Bulgars mainly from the neighbourhood of Kilkís, with the retreating Bulgarian army.
5,000 Greeks from Bulgaria into Greek Macedonia after the Treaty of Bucharest.
5,000 Greeks from the Caucasus into Macedonia.
5,000 Greeks from Serbian Macedonia (area taken from Bulgaria).
1913–14 40,000 Greeks into Macedonia from Western Thrace (Bulgarian).
1914 100,000–115,000 Moslems into Turkey from Macedonia in consequence of Young Turk propaganda.
80,000 Greeks from Eastern Thrace and 20,000 from Asia Minor into Macedonia at the time when Turkey was demanding the Aegean islands.
1916 The Bulgars occupied Macedonia, and transported 36,000 Greeks from Macedonia to Bulgaria.
1918 Of the above, only 17,000 returned after the armistice of 1918.
1918–19 When the Greek army took Western and Eastern Thrace, some 140,000 Greeks returned to these areas from Macedonia.
1919–20 55,000 Greeks took refuge in Macedonia from south Russia and the Caucasus.
1919 1,000 Russians, mainly from Wrangel's army, arrived in Macedonia.
1919–24 27,000 Bulgars from Macedonia to Bulgaria consequent on the Convention of Neuilly.
1922–4 After the Smyrna disaster, and under the Convention of Lausanne, upwards of 700,000 Greeks into Macedonia from Asia Minor and Eastern Thrace.
1923–4 Following the Convention of Lausanne, 348,000 Moslems left Macedonia.

Western Thrace

1913 70,000 Greeks fled from Thrace before the Bulgars.
49,000 Moslems left Thrace in accordance with a Turco-Bulgarian Convention of 1913.
1919 51,000 Greeks returned to Western Thrace.
1920–4 125,000 refugees entered Western Thrace (5,000 Greeks from Caucasus, 116,000 Greeks from Turkey, and 4,000 Armenians and Caucasians).

Eastern Thrace

1912 104,000 Moslems fled before the advance of the Bulgarian army.
1913 2,000 Bulgars fled on return of Turkish army.
1913 49,000 Moslems came in, exchanged from Bulgarian Thrace.
47,000 Bulgars left in exchange for Moslems.
1914 115,000 Greeks expelled from Eastern Thrace.
1914 132,000 Moslems came in from the areas ceded to Greece, Serbia and Bulgaria.
1915–16 85,000 Greeks and 17,000 Armenians deported from Eastern Thrace.
1918–20 133,000 Greeks came in after Armistice of Mudros.
1922–4 186,000 Greeks and 7,000 Armenians escaped from Eastern Thrace and were replaced by 70,000 Moslems from Greece.

Ethnic composition of Makedhonía and Thrace, 1912–24

	Total number			Percentages		
	1912*	1920	1924†	1912	1920	1924
Greek Makedhonía:						
Greeks	513,000	577,000	1,277,000	43	52	89
Bulgars	119,000	104,000	77,000	10	9	5
Moslems‡	475,000	350,000	2,000§	39	31	0
Others‖	98,000	91,000	91,000	8	8	6
Total	1,205,000	1,122,000	1,447,000	100	100	100
Western Thrace:						
Greeks	87,000	68,000	189,000	36	36	62
Bulgars	35,000	35,000	23,000	15	18	7
Moslems‡	111,000	84,000	84,000¶	47	44	28
Others‖	4,000	4,000	8,000	2	2	3
Total	237,000	191,000	304,000	100	100	100
Eastern Thrace:**						
Greeks	253,000	186,000	0	44	36	0
Bulgars	50,000	1,000	1,000††	9	0	0
Moslems‡	223,000	300,000	370,000	40	59	95
Americans	24,000	7,000	0	4	1	0
Others‖	19,000	19,000	19,000	3	4	5
Total	569,000	513,000	390,000	100	100	100

Source: A. A. Pallis, 'Racial Migrations in the Balkans during the years 1912–1924', *Geographical Journal*, vol. LXVI, p. 330 (London, 1925).

* On the eve of the Balkan wars.
† At the end of the year.
‡ Includes Turks, Pomaks, Albanians, Valakhades and Moslem Gipsies.
§ Albanian Moslems exempted from the exchange (see p. 381).
‖ Jews, Vlachs, Uniates, Albanians, Foreigners.
¶ This figure is too low; see A. A. Pallis, 'The Greek Census of 1928', *Geographical Journal*, vol. LXXIII, p. 546 (London, 1929).
** Allotted to Greece in 1920, but reacquired by Turkey in 1922.
†† This figure for Bulgars seems unduly low.

The Macedo-Slavs

The Bulgars entered the Balkan lands somewhat later than the Slavs, and, towards the end of the seventh century, they established themselves south of the Danube; here they mixed with the Slav population already in the area, and so formed the empire of Bulgaria (see p. 160). Like the Slavs, the Bulgars raided southwards into the Byzantine empire, and this raiding passed into settlement; so that they, too, came to form an important element in the population of Macedonia and Thrace. Unlike the Slavs of peninsular Greece, however, the Slavs and Bulgars of these northern areas were not ıssimilated by the Greeks, and they remained culturally and linguistically distinct throughout later times, to form a complicating 'actor in the 'Macedonian Question' of the nineteenth and twentieth :enturies.

During the nineteenth century, this Christian population in Macedonia and Thrace consisted largely of mixed elements of undefinable origin for whom the different Balkan governments and their

Fig. 98. The Bulgarian Exarchate, 1870–1912

ased on D. Rizoff, *Die Bulgaren in ihren historischen, ethnographischen und olitischen Grenzen*, map 31 (Berlin, 1917).

: is interesting to compare this with Fig. 88 showing the limits of Bulgaria as roposed by the Treaty of San Stefano in 1878, and with Fig. 99 showing the :hnographic limits of Bulgarians according to a Bulgarian source.

ational churches contended fiercely, especially after the creation of ıe Bulgarian Exarchate in 1870 (Fig. 98). Some remained, as they ad always done, under the Greek Patriarch, others accepted the new ulgarian Exarch, while yet others acknowledged the Serbian Iational Church. The speech of the Macedo-Slavs can be understood y both Serbs and Bulgarians, though on the whole it is nearer ulgarian in character. Thus, the Macedonians, like Bulgarians, use the suffix article; and words which in 'Macedonian' have an *l*, hav it also in Bulgarian while it is omitted in Serb: e.g. Macedonian *bel* (white), Bulgarian *belo* and Serb *beo*.

With the break-up of the Turkish empire in Europe after the secon Balkan War of 1913, Serbia (afterwards Yugoslavia) acquired norther and central Macedonia, and southern Macedonia went to Greec (Fig. 90). The Serbs insisted on the Serbian character of the Slavoni population of this area; Bulgaria, however, insisted that it wa Bulgarian. The conflict between Serbian and Bulgarian claims is we illustrated by the different maps showing the ethnography of the are Figs. 99 and 100 represent the views of a Bulgarian and Serbia geographer respectively; Fig. 101 shows a British interpretation of th ethnography of the same area. As far as Macedonia is concerned th three views are brought together on Fig. 102. It is really impossible however, to draw any lines because Macedo-Slav is not one dialec but a group of similar dialects. Perhaps it would be true to sa that the Macedo-Slavs pass by scarcely perceptible grades from th Bulgarians of eastern Macedonia to the Serbians north of Skoplj (Usküb).

After the war of 1914–18, Greece and Yugoslavia were confirme in their division of Macedonia; and, in order to clarify the ethno graphic position, Greece succeeded in getting inserted in the Treat of Neuilly (1919) a provision for an optional exchange of population with Bulgaria. About 92,000 Bulgarians in Greece and some 46,00 Greeks in Bulgaria opted to emigrate, and the exchange was effecte under the control of a commission (see p. 369). There remained i Greece, according to the Greek census of 1928, some 81,844 Orthodo Slavs who spoke 'Macedonian' (*Makedonski*), but Bulgarian esti mates put their number as high as 300,000. They lived in the are adjoining the Yugoslav frontier (Fig. 97), and they had been un willing to leave their homes. Bulgaria claimed them as Bulgars, an pointed to the fact that they were once included in the Bulgaria Exarchate (Fig. 98). But the Greek government maintained tha all elements with Bulgarian affinities, sentimental, national o religious, had emigrated; those who stayed behind, having done s voluntarily, were regarded as Greek in sentiment. It even maintaine that the Macedo-Slavs did not want their own schools, which the could have if they wished. The schools in the area appear, therefore to have been Greek. Despite protests made from Bulgarian quarter the Macedo-Slavs of Greece were ecclesiastically under the juris diction of the Patriarch at Constantinople until 1928, when they wer

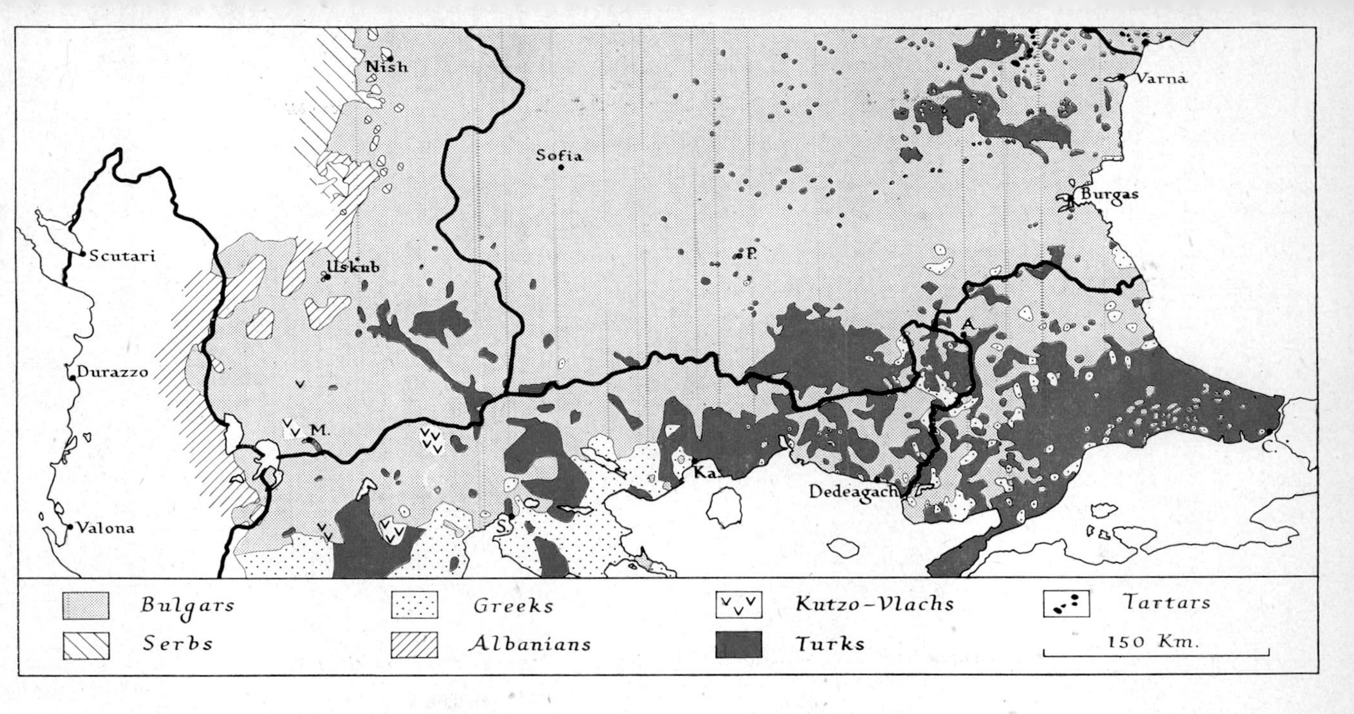

Fig. 99. A Bulgarian view of the ethnography of northern Greece, 1912

Based on A. Ischirkoff, 'Ethnographische Karte des Bulgarentums auf der Balkanhalbinsel im Jahre 1912', *Petermanns Mitteilungen*, vol. LXI, pp. 339–43 (Gotha, 1915).

The present-day international frontiers are shown. It is interesting to compare this with Fig. 98 showing the Bulgarian Exarchate of 1870, and with Fig. 88 showing the proposed frontiers of Bulgaria at the Treaty of San Stefano in 1878. *A*, Adrianople; *C*, Constantinople; *Ka*, Kavalla; *M*, Monastir; *P*, Plovdiv; *S*, Salonica.

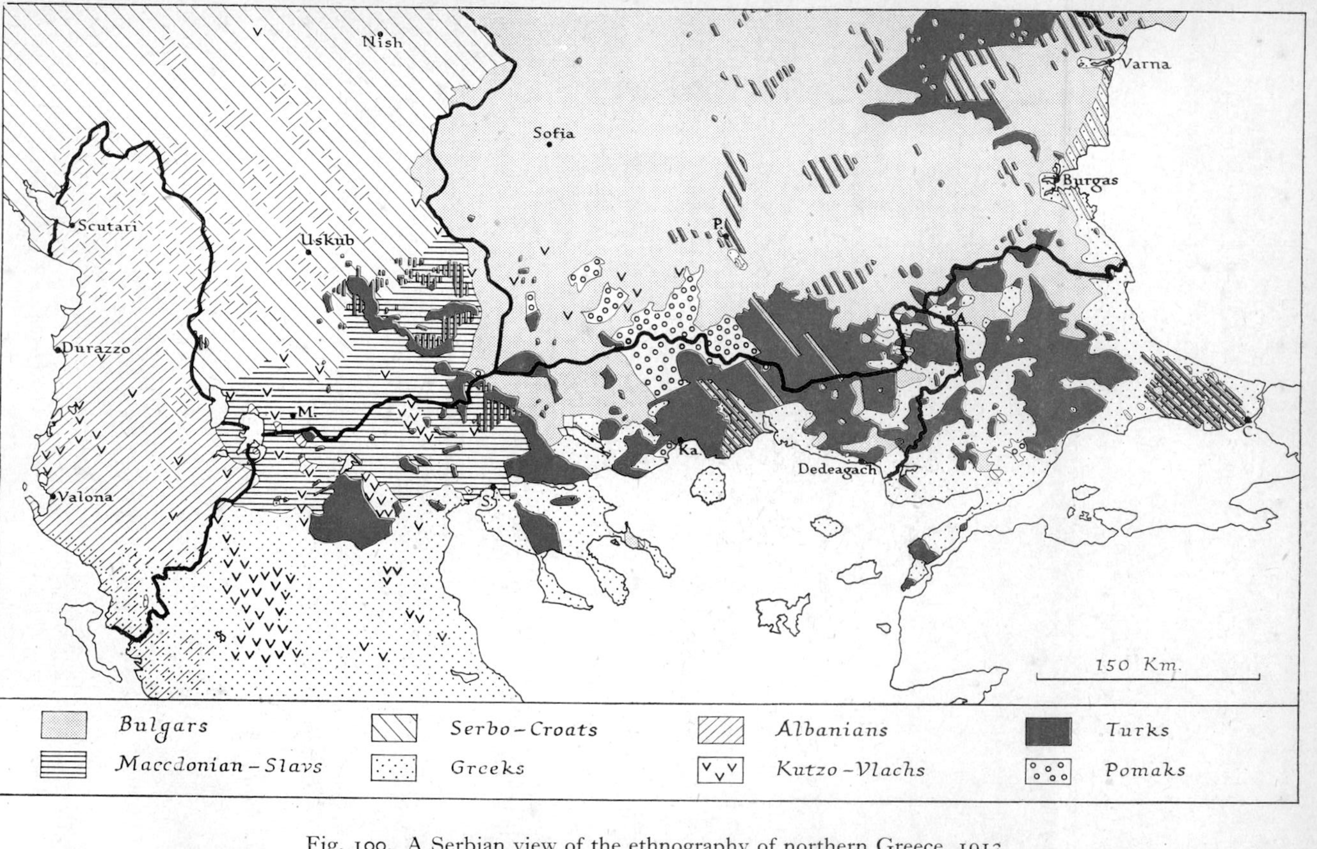

Fig. 100. A Serbian view of the ethnography of northern Greece, 1913

Based on J. Cvijić, 'Die ethnographische Abgrenzung der Völker auf der Balkanhalbinsel', *Petermanns Mitteilungen*, vol. LIX, pp. 113–18 (Gotha, 1913).

ncluded within the Church of Greece itself (see p. 332). There was officially no restriction on the language in which religious services might be held. Greek was usual, but it is probable that sermons were often preached in 'Macedonian', as about 70% of the priests belonged to the villages in which they officiated.

It is difficult to assess the national feelings of the Macedo-Slavs. Many of them may really have accepted, or even welcomed, the Greek schools. On the other hand, there may have been some who, while not leaving for Bulgaria, remained Bulgar at heart.

The Pomaks

The Pomaks are Bulgarian-speaking Moslems, most of whom live within the Bulgarian frontier, but there are some on Greek territory. About 102,000 were included in the Bulgarian census of 1926, and 16,755 in the Greek census of 1928. Their villages, which lay in the Rhodope Mountains, north of Dráma, were such obstinate centres of Bulgarian and Christian feeling under Turkish rule that, in the seventeenth century, the Grand Vizier Mohamed Kiuprili invaded the area, razed their churches to the ground, massacred great numbers of them, and converted the remainder to Islam.* The policy was very successful; the Pomaks became the bulwarks of Islam, and it is they who were the authors of the notorious 'Bulgarian atrocities' of 1876. The name 'Pomak' signifies 'helper', i.e. auxiliaries to the Turkish armies.

After the Balkan Wars of 1912–13, most of them were included in Bulgarian territory, but some were included in Greek territory and so they remained after the treaty settlements of Neuilly (1919) and Sèvres (1920). As Bulgarians and as Moslems they were involved in the voluntary exchange of populations with Bulgaria after 1919, and with the compulsory exchange with Turkey after 1923. Dhitikí Thráki, however, was exempted from the principle of compulsion (see p. 380), and the Pomaks of that area were allowed to remain in Greek territory (Fig. 97). In 1933, the Turkish press, seconded by that of Greece, complained that the Pomaks of Bulgaria were being oppressed by the Bulgarian authorities; some were even said to be taking refuge in Greece from Bulgaria. It is to be presumed,

* One authority has declared them to be former Christians who followed the Bogomil heresy, but who preferred Islam to the practices and persecution of both the Greek Orthodox and the Roman Catholic Churches—Sir Edwin Pears, *Turkey and its Peoples*, pp. 148–56 (London, 1911).

however, that, as between Bulgaria and Greece, Pomak sympathizers would favour Bulgaria. In 1941, Bulgaria's annexations included the Pomak areas of Greece (see p. 234).

THE JEWS

Jews in small numbers were established in Greece at the time of St Paul, but no clear indication of their distribution is available for over a thousand years after this. About 1160, the Jewish traveller Benjamin of Tudela found flourishing colonies at Thebes (2,000), Salonica (500), Almyros (400), Corinth (300) and Chalcis (200), and there were many smaller communities elsewhere.

The real influx of Jews into Greek lands did not come until towards the end of the fifteenth century. Large numbers of Sephardic Jews, expelled from Spain in 1492 and, attracted by the toleration offered them by the Turks, settled in and around Salonica. They were joined in the following century by the Maraños from Spain and Portugal—Jews who had been forced to adopt Christianity, outwardly at any rate. All the newcomers spoke a modified form of Castilian Spanish; this tongue, used by the Jews of Greece and other eastern Mediterranean lands, is known as 'ladino', and it has a considerable literature. In addition to a mingling of Portuguese dialects, it contains a strong mixture of Slav, Latin, Greek, Turkish and Arabic ingredients. Most of the Jews of modern Greece are bilingual, with Greek as a second language; many also speak French for business purposes.

Under Ottoman rule, the Jews were very prosperous, and when the Greeks occupied Thessaloníki in 1913, several thousands fled and many more left after the great fire of 1917. But in 1920 they still formed more than half of the population of the city, and consisted of a prosperous banking, business and professional element, together with a number of artisans and shopkeepers and a large number of dockers, labourers, masons and tobacco and silk growers. With the Graeco-Turkish exchange of population, their condition changed for the worse. The influx of over 100,000 Greek refugees reduced the Jewish element in the city to some 16%, and both Jewish business interests and Jewish workers had to stand up to intense competition.

An unusual Jewish sect, formerly centered at Salonica, were the Dönmeh. It was started in the seventeenth century by Shabbethai Levi, and its followers, while conforming to many Jewish practices adopted Islam. Their number has been variously estimated, but may

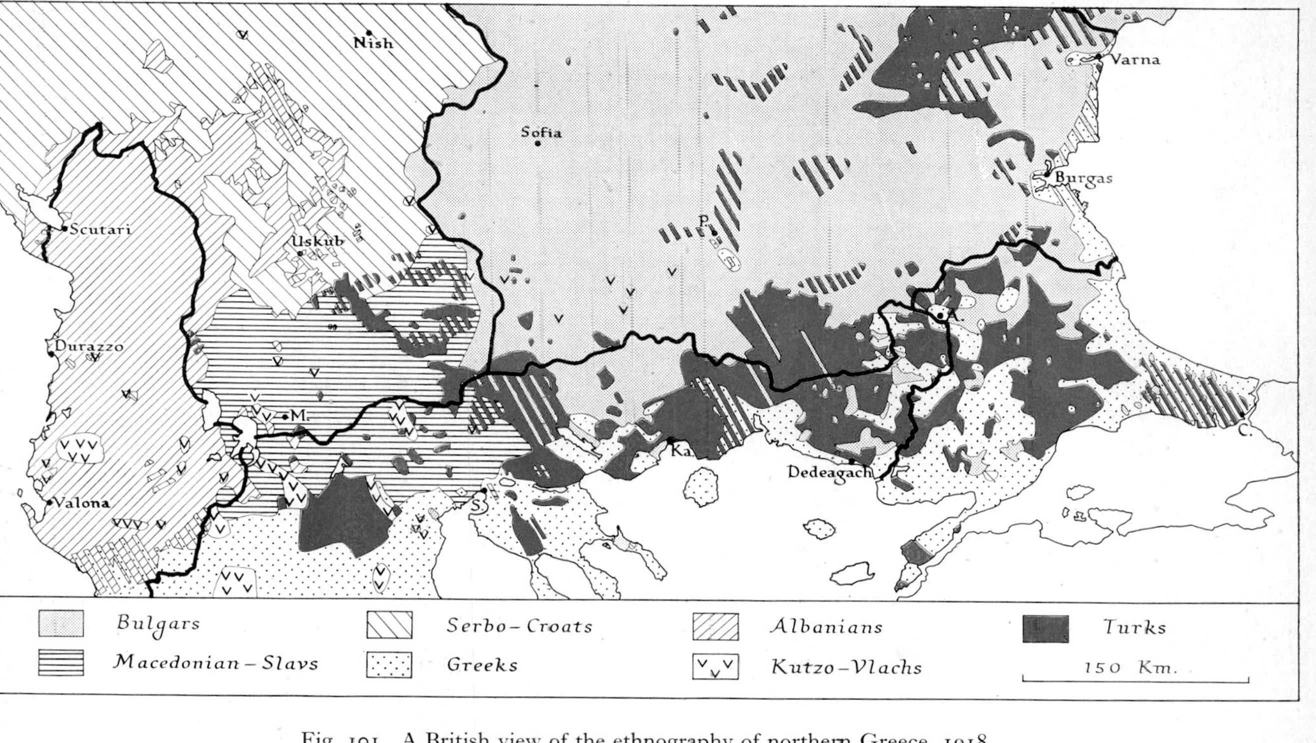

Fig. 101. A British view of the ethnography of northern Greece, 1918

Based on *South East Europe: Ethnographical Map*, G.S.G.S., no. 3703*a* (1918).

The present-day international frontiers are shown. *A*, Adrianople; *C*, Constantinople; *Ka*, Kavalla; *M*, Monastir; *P*, Plovdiv; *S*, Salonica.

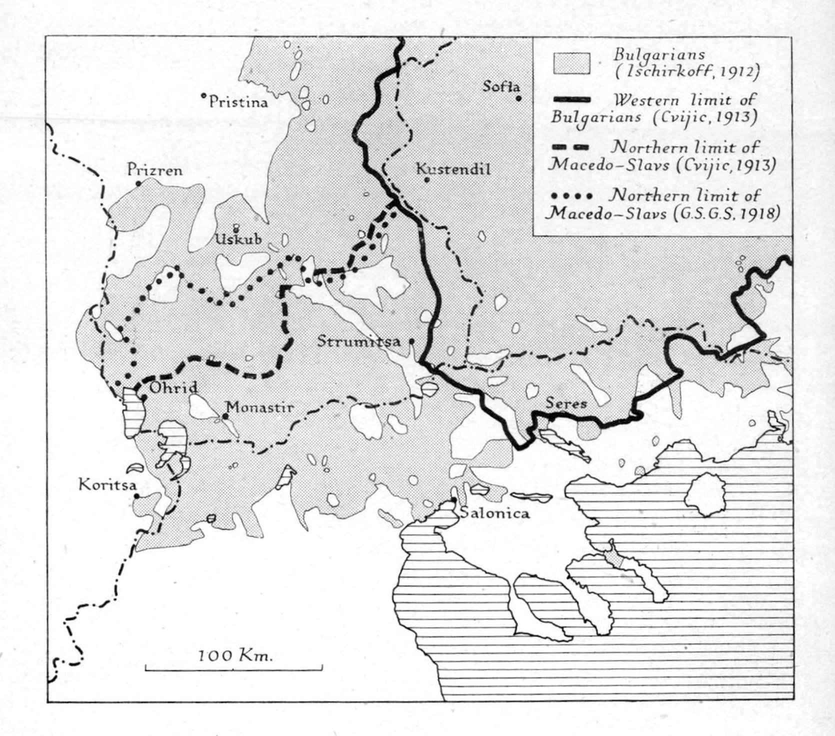

Fig. 102. Conflicting interpretations of ethnic distributions in Macedonia, 1912–20

Based on (1) A. Ischirkoff, 'Ethnographische Karte des Bulgarentums auf der Balkanhalbinsel im Jahre 1912', *Petermanns Mitteilungen*, vol. LXI, pp. 339–43 (Gotha, 1915); (2) J. Cvijić, 'Die ethnographische Abgrenzung der Völker auf der Balkanhalbinsel', *Petermanns Mitteilungen*, vol. LIX, pp. 113–18 (Gotha, 1913); (3) *South East Europe: Ethnographical Map*, G.S.G.S., no. 3703*a* (1918).

have been about 5,000–10,000. They have now been dispersed, and are found mainly in İstanbul and İzmir (Smyrna).

The Greek census of 1928 put the number of Jews in Greece at 72,791. The greater number of these were Spanish Jews (62,999) living mainly in Thessaloníki; but there were also a few thousand at Kaválla, and some hundreds at Flórina, Dráma and Sérrai. Outside Makedhonía, the Jews were almost entirely Greek speaking and were scattered throughout the country. Most of them were artisans, small shopkeepers and industrial workers; a few were professional men. The Jewish colony at Athínai itself may have numbered as many as 3,000.

There have been occasional anti-Semitic riots in Greece, notably after the cession of the Ionian islands in 1864, when the Jews of Kérkira (Corfu) and Zákinthos (Zante) were forced to emigrate, and in 1931 when riots broke out in Thessaloníki. But, in general, the Jews have been treated tolerantly, and the Greek government has never encouraged anti-Semitism. Under a law of 1890, any town with at least fifty Jewish families received an annual subsidy for the needs of their religion. Jewish schools were also allowed, subject to the right of state supervision. Thus at Thessaloníki in 1924, there were fourteen Jewish high schools and twenty-six Jewish elementary schools. There was also a flourishing Jewish press in the city. From 1923 to 1933 the Jews of Thessaloníki voted as a separate electoral college, returning two Deputies, but this system was abolished at their own request. The Greek Minorities Treaty included a special clause by which Jews should not be placed under any disability by reason of their refusal to attend courts of law or transact legal business on their Sabbath. There was, however, considerable Jewish complaint about the Sunday Rest Law in Greece. The Greek government did not readily admit Jewish refugees from Nazi Germany.

Since the Axis occupation in the spring of 1941, the German authorities are reported to have taken various measures against the Jewish community in Thessaloníki. Some Jews have been imprisoned in camps, some have been deported to Poland, and others have been enrolled for road-making (see p. 236).

The Armenians

Before the war of 1914–18, the Armenians lived partly in Turkey (in Cilicia and in the north-east), partly in the Caucasian provinces of Russia, and partly in north-west Persia. The Turkish Armenians were subjected in 1894–6, 1904 and 1909 to massacres which aroused protests from Christian Europe. From 1915 onwards, vast numbers were expelled from their dwellings in Turkey. Many perished or were massacred; others sought refuge abroad, mainly in Russia, Syria, Mesopotamia and Greece. It was estimated in 1925 that about 45,000 Armenians had come to Greece with the refugees from Asia Minor; one-half were peasants from central and western Anatolia, the other half were townsmen, mainly artisans and small shopkeepers. Many of them emigrated to the Soviet Republic of Erivan, but at the census of 1928 there were still 33,634 Armenian speakers left in Greece; 31,038 of these were stated to be Orthodox, which apparently meant that they belonged to the Monophysite Armenian Church. They had their own churches and schools (Plate 102).

Since 1928, further emigration has reduced their numbers; and some of those that remained have been absorbed in industry and have taken Greek nationality. In 1927 all Armenians under the age of 22 had been granted Greek citizenship, but this policy was suspended in 1928 when the Soviet government decided to accept Armenian immigrants. In 1936, all who had been registered under the Law of 1927 had their naturalization cancelled, and Greek citizenship was extended only to limited categories of Armenians. The Greek unwillingness to naturalize Armenians has been explained by the difficulties faced in absorbing the Greek refugees themselves. By 1938, upwards of 25,000 Armenians, not yet naturalized, were said to remain in Greece. About 10,000 of these were still completely unabsorbed and were living in huts on the outskirts of Athínai.

The Vlachs (Plates 96, 99)

At the census of 1928 there were 19,703 Vlach speakers in Greece, although some estimates have placed their number at many times this figure. They are for the most part nomadic shepherds and herdsmen, and are to be found principally in the Píndhos mountains, though Vlach villages are scattered throughout the Balkans (Fig. 103). In winter the Vlachs of the Píndhos take their flocks down into the plains of Ípiros, Thessalía and Makedhonía; and in modern Greek the word 'vlachos' signifies a shepherd. Their language is a dialect of Romanian with an admixture of Greek, Slav, Turkish and Albanian words. All the men and many of the women are bilingual, with Greek, Bulgarian, Albanian or Serbian as their second language. Most of them belong to the Orthodox Church. The hellenized or semi-hellenized Vlachs between Grevená and the pure Vlach villages of the Píndhos are known as 'Kupatshari'. Some Vlachs have taken to trade, and families of Vlach descent are numerous in Thessalian villages as weavers of frieze cloth and makers of rough jewellery, and as small general shopkeepers and itinerant traders; many have become carriers (*kiradjis*). These have been almost completely hellenized, but the nomadic groups still retain their distinct customs and their tongue. Some Vlachs are also to be found in the great cities of Greece (e.g. in

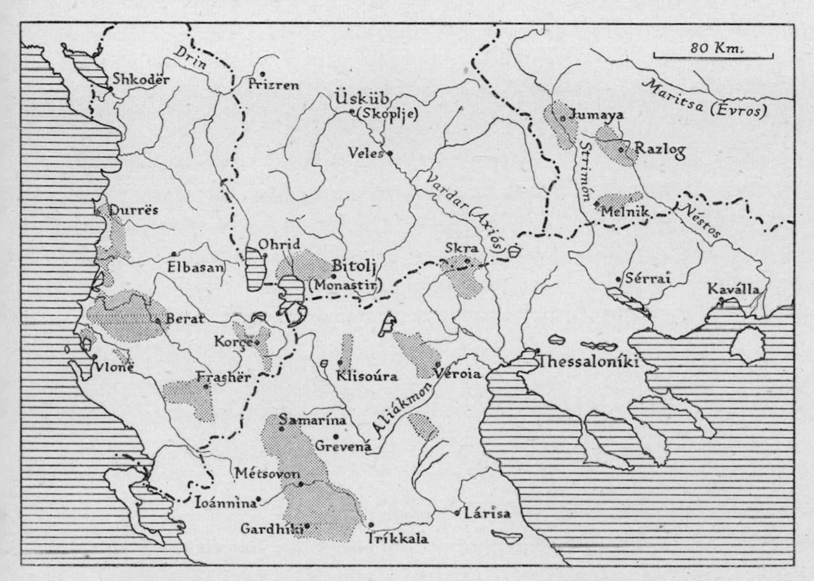

Fig. 103. The distribution of the Vlachs in Balkan lands

Based on A. J. B. Wace and M. S. Thompson, *The Nomads of the Balkans*, p. 206 (London, 1914).

Different authorities give varying ideas about the exact distribution of the Vlachs; this map, for example, differs in detail from the distribution of Vlachs as given on Fig. 97.

Thessaloníki and Sérrai), and have shown great business ability. One of the richest modern millionaires, M. Averof, who presented Greece with her only heavy cruiser, was a Vlach.

The name 'Vlachs' or 'Wallachs' was applied to them by their neighbours; its origin is identical with the English 'Wealh' or 'Welsh' (i.e. stranger), and is a Slavonic version of a general term used by Teutonic peoples to describe Roman provincials in the fourth and fifth centuries. The Vlachs, however, call themselves 'Aromani', i.e. Romans, and are also known as 'Tzintzars' and 'Koutsovlachs'. These last two are nicknames. 'Tzintzar' is derived from the numerous sibilant sounds in the Vlach tongue, thus the Romanian 'cinci' (five) is 'tsintsi' in Vlach. The origin of 'Koutsovlach' has been disputed, but the general opinion is that it means 'lame Vlach', with reference either to their speech or to their subsidiary relation to the main body of Romanians. They are also called 'Macedo-Romans' in contrast to the Daco-Romans north of the Danube.

The origin of the Vlachs is obscure and has given rise to much dispute, but it is now generally admitted that they are descended from Roman colonists and latinized provincials in the areas north and south of the Danube, and that, as their language suggests, they are akin to the Romanians. Their existence may be inferred from records as early as the sixth century in date, but the first definite mention of them is not until the year 976. During the next two centuries reference to them becomes frequent, but they were intermingled with other peoples in such a way that it is difficult to form any clear idea of their distribution. Several districts were called after them in the Middle Ages; thus 'Great Vlachia' was the name given to Thessaly and southern Macedonia, and 'Little Vlachia' to Acarnania and Aetolia, while there were Vlachs also in Bulgaria and to the north. These last were involved in the revolt against the Byzantine empire which led to the establishment of the second Bulgarian empire of 1186–1258 (see p. 161).

In the eleventh-century *Strategicon* of Cecaumenos, there is a description of the Vlachs around Trikkala and Larissa in Thessaly. Their mode of living then seems to have been very similar to what it is to-day; from April to September they lived with their flocks in the mountains and descended to the plains only in winter. There is also reference in the same account to the appointment of a Byzantine official to administer the Vlachs. Towards the end of the eleventh century, the southern Vlachs were again mentioned by the Byzantine historian Anna Comnena who referred to nomadic folk 'commonly called Vlachs' in the mountainous region of Thessaly. Benjamin of Tudela, about 1170, described them thus: 'Here are the confines of Wallachia, a country of which the inhabitants are called Vlachi. They are as nimble as deer and descend from their mountains into the plains of Greece committing robberies and taking booty. Nobody ventures to make war on them, nor can any king bring them to submission.' Under the Frankish regime, in the thirteenth century, these Vlachs of Thessaly emerged for a time as an independent

Plate 96. Vlach peasant woman

In all country districts throughout Greece women still spin their own wool (Plate 94). The photograph shows a Vlach woman of Vísani, a small village in Ípiros. She is wearing Vlach costume.

Plate 97. Albanian weavers in Greece

Most of the Albanians in Greece are Greek-speaking, but some of the women still speak Albanian in the home.

Plate 98. A gipsy settlement

There are several established camping spots for gipsies travelling through Greece. The most important are found at Marathón, Thívai Graviá and Samarína, near Kalabáka. The photograph shows a settlement on the slopes of Mt Párnis, not far from Athínai.

Plate 99. Vlach winter dwellings

The Vlachs usually pasture their flocks on lowlands during the winter, moving to the uplands in summer. The photograph was taken in August on the plain of Marathón.

principality; but when the line of Vlach princes became extinct in 1318, their territories were divided between the Byzantine empire and the Catalan duchy of Athens (see p. 173). Although they never again achieved political independence, the Vlachs have maintained their separate identity throughout subsequent political changes. Under the Turkish regime they paid tribute, and in the seventeenth and eighteenth centuries, many Vlachs were to be found engaged in commerce in the towns of the Turkish empire.

During the nineteenth century a nationalist movement, with cultural aspiration, gained some strength among the Vlachs, as among the other small peoples of Europe. This movement was encouraged from Romania, especially after the union of Moldavia and Wallachia in 1861; schools were started, amongst other places at Janina and Salonica; increasingly large sums appeared in the Romanian budget as subsidies for Vlach education, and Vlach periodicals were printed at Bucharest; but the Vlachs were too scattered to form a coherent self-conscious minority. In 1881, with the acquisition of Thessalía from the Turks, the most compact group of Vlachs passed into Greece. In 1905 the Sultan recognized the remaining Vlachs of the Turkish empire as a separate ecclesiastical unit with a national liturgy, no longer subject to the Greek Patriarchate. This separate recognition was resented at Athínai, and relations were broken off for a time between Greece and Romania.

In 1913, after the Balkan wars, Greece, like Serbia and Bulgaria, made an agreement with Romania, granting autonomy to Vlach schools and churches in Greek territory. Romania, moreover, was allowed to subsidize these institutions, under Greek supervision, and this arrangement has never been abrogated. Religious services continued to be conducted in Vlach; and, by the Greek Minorities Treaty of 1920, the Vlachs of the Píndhos were confirmed in their religious and scholastic autonomy under the control of the Greek state.

After the war of 1914–18, when Greek refugees from Turkey settled in Ípiros and Makedhonía, the amount of land available to the Vlachs for grazing was greatly reduced, and much of their stock had to be killed or sold. Many of them therefore emigrated to Romania, encouraged by the Romanian government, whose policy it was to settle them in the southern Dobrudja; these emigrants have been estimated at something under 30,000. This movement has continued on a small scale, so that by 1939 there probably were in Greece somewhat fewer than the 19,703 Vlach speakers enumerated in the census of 1928.

During the autumn of 1940 there were rumours that Italian propaganda had stirred up anti-Greek feeling among the Vlachs of the Píndhos, and reports from Romania in 1941 stated that some Vlachs had been arrested by the Greek government. In the spring of 1942, Romania also showed its interest in the Greek Vlachs by promising to send food into Greece for their relief.

The Greek Orthodox Albanians

The Albanians, next to the Slavs, form the most important group of settlers that have affected the ethnic composition of the Greeks. They are representatives of an obscure Illyrian stock, who were surrounded by the southward movement of the Slavs during the sixth, seventh and eighth centuries. In the middle of the fourteenth century, they began to expand southwards towards Acarnania and Aetolia and even into Thessaly, where the Vlachs had hitherto formed the bulk of the population. About this time also (*c.* 1350) the Byzantine rulers of the Peloponnese strengthened their army by recruiting large numbers of Albanians (Tosks). These mercenaries were followed by Albanian colonists who settled upon the waste lands of the province, where their descendants still remain to this day. Albanian settlers were also invited to settle in Attica and Boeotia by the Catalan rulers of the duchy of Athens (*c.* 1380) and by their Florentine successors. Early in the fifteenth century, the Venetians, too, were attracting Albanian settlers to Euboea by offering them grants of uncultivated land.

During the latter half of the sixteenth century, some Albanians were settled in the Aegean islands as part of a scheme of colonization formed by the Turks. The Turks also settled Albanians on the ravaged lands of the Peloponnese after the expulsion of the Venetians in 1718. Albanians were employed in the Turkish armies and were used to quell the insurrection in the Peloponnese in 1770. For some years after this, Albanian bands wandered over Greece causing great disorder, but they were put down in 1779; some were exterminated but others were induced to settle as colonists.

This considerable body of Albanians settled in various parts of the Greek lands. Though retaining their own customs and language they lived on good terms with the Greeks, and were ardent patriots in the War of Independence. Early in the nineteenth century their number was estimated by Leake at about 200,000 (see p. 196). At the Greek census of 1907, there were said to be 53,000 Albanians out of a total population of some two and half million people. Neither the census of 1913 nor that of 1921 classified the population by language. The census of 1928 reckoned almost all the Orthodox Albanians as Greeks, and they were, indeed, a prosperous and integral part of the Greek nation whose independence they had helped to establish. Some estimates have placed this Albanian element as high as 200,000, and even 350,000. The Albanians call themselves 'Skipetar' but are called 'Arvanitae' by the Greeks. They are to be found mainly in the country district of Attikí, Voiotía, Mégara, in the north-east of the Pelopónnisos, and in the islands of Salamís, Póros, Ídhra, Spétsai, Ándros, and southern Évvoia (Fig. 97). Though Albanian by descent they are Greek by national consciousness, and cannot be regarded as a national minority. They have not been difficult to assimilate, especially in the towns; and they have almost entirely lost their language in the Pelopónnisos. Elsewhere, Albanian is usually spoken in the home, the men, and also some of the women, being bilingual.

The Albanian Moslems

Quite a different category of Albanians are those in the more recently acquired provinces bordering upon Albania. Most of them live in Ípiros; the remainder live in western Makedhonía. The majority of them are Moslems. In western Makedhonía, some 2,000 Moslems were exempted from the Greek-Turkish exchange of populations on the ground that they were of Albanian origin. Some were villagers from the neighbourhood of Kastoría just south of Flórina; others were landed proprietors from Thessaloníki and Véroia. The census of 1928 gave 18,598 Albanian-speaking Moslems in the whole of Greece, according to which, therefore, there can have been only about 16,000 or so in Ípiros. Other estimates, however, suggest that the figure for Ípiros was as high as 33,000, while some estimates put the figure even higher than this. The big discrepancy may in part be explained by the fact that language was taken as the criterion in the census, and that many Albanian Moslems may have returned themselves as Greek speakers. The political frontier between Albania and Greece was decided in 1921 only after much discussion and the balancing of conflicting claims (Fig. 104).

The Albanians of Ípiros are commonly known as the Chamurian Moslems, and belong to the Cham branch of the south Albanian Tosks. They inhabit the coastal district of Chamuria, opposite Kérkira, near the Albanian frontier. There are also said to be some

Christian Chams, but their number is uncertain. The Albanian Moslems were exempted from the Graeco-Turkish exchange, and the Greek government has interfered neither with their language nor

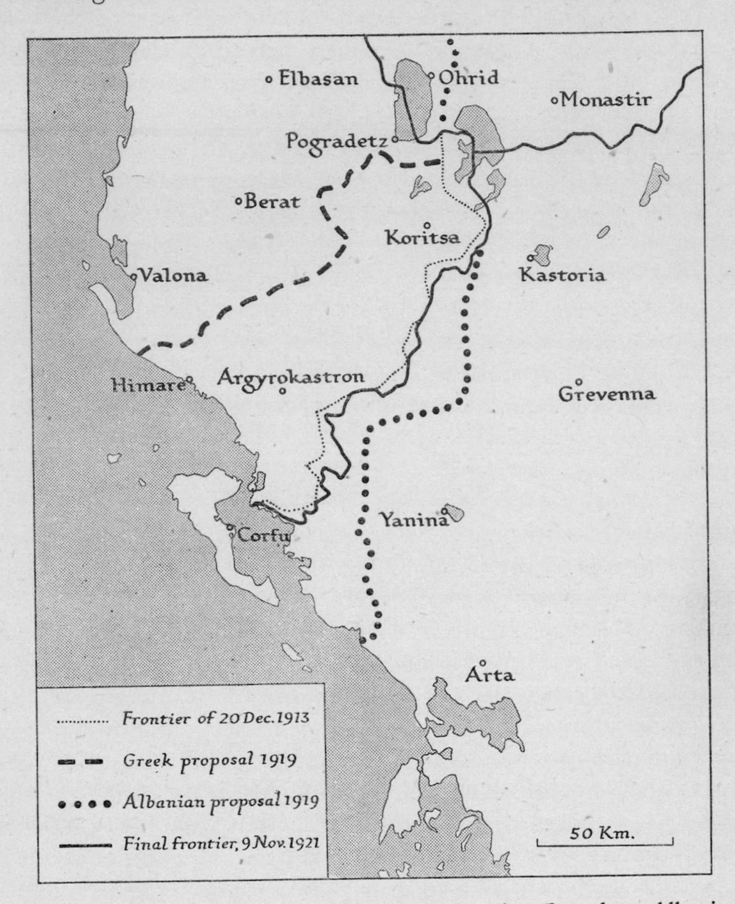

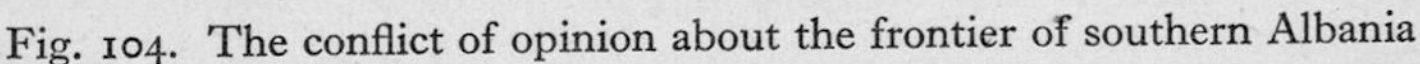

Fig. 104. The conflict of opinion about the frontier of southern Albania

Based on (1) Edith Pierpont Stickney, *Southern Albania or Northern Epirus in European International Affairs*, 1912–1923, pp. 96, 108 and 109 (Stanford, Cal., 1926), and (2) H. W. V. Temperley, *A History of the Peace Conference of Paris*, vol. IV, p. 338 (London, 1921).

There were other claims differing in detail, but the above is sufficient to show the divergence of opinion. The Italian proposal in 1919 followed the 1913 line, but earlier Italian proposals (1912–13) had included more Greek territory in Albania. The Albanian proposal was that of the Provisional Albanian government. In the north, the Greek-Albanian frontier of 1913 ran to the west of Lake Megáli Préspa, but, at the demarcation of the boundary in the field by an international commission, the frontier was drawn through the lake; other small modifications were also made elsewhere.

their religion. It is true that no special schools were provided for them, but religious instruction has been given in Albanian in all state schools attended by the minority. Their national consciousness is difficult to gauge. The Albanian government has regarded them as a minority and has taken the same interest in their welfare as the Greek government has taken in the Greek minority on the other side of the frontier. In the summer of 1940 there were Italian stories that the Chamurian Albanians were being oppressed by the Greeks, and there were Greek replies that Albanians and Greeks were living in complete harmony.

The Gipsies

There have been gipsies in Greece since the end of the eleventh century when they crossed the Bosphorus into Europe, the descendants of migratory bands who had set out from north-west India at least before the seventh century A.D. The earliest written record of them in Greece, however, is a reference to their presence outside Candia in Crete in 1322. By the fifteenth century they had spread throughout the Balkan peninsula and had become settled north of the Danube, in Transylvania and Wallachia. There were further movements westward from Greece in the sixteenth century, mainly because Turkish incursions were becoming more frequent and pressing. The extent of this westward movement is seen, for example, in Catalonia, where, at the end of the sixteenth century, the names 'gipsy' and 'Greek' were synonymous.

In the seventeenth century, attempts were made to settle the gipsies of the Ottoman empire on the land or in the towns. Many of those who were not serving in the Turkish armies were forced to adopt a sedentary life, and gipsy quarters gradually grew in the larger towns. Since then the sedentary gipsies of Greece have adopted the language and religion of the country, and they have, on the whole, been assimilated into the national way of living. A much larger number, however, has remained nomadic and unassimilated.

Modern Greek distinguishes between the two groups. The nomad gipsies are called *athinganoi*, a name derived from that of an heretical tribe living around Phrygia in the ninth century. The collective appellation 'athinganoi', through its variant 'atzigan' is the origin of German 'Zigeuner' and English 'tinker'. The sedentary group is called *gyphtoi*: both 'gyphtoi' and 'gipsies' are traces of the erroneous belief in the Egyptian ancestry of these people. The gipsies call themselves 'Rom' and their dialect 'Romani', both probably derived from the name 'Romaoi' which the Byzantine Greeks applied to themselves. The Romani dialect spoken by the Greek gipsies is the oldest and purest European Romani hitherto recorded; it contains the greatest percentage of the vocabulary of the parent Indian language, and the proportion of loan-words is strikingly small. On the other hand, there is a considerable proportion of Greek words in the speech of western European gipsies.

The presence of both sedentary and nomad gipsies in Greece makes it extremely difficult to give an accurate estimate of their number in the country, and the information derived from official statistics is often contradictory to that supplied by unofficial observers. According to the Greek census of 1928, there were 4,998 Romani (Tzigane) speakers, of whom 3,853 were members of the Orthodox Church, and 1,130 Moslems. It should be borne in mind that many sedentary gipsies have, as in countries outside Greece, lost their Romani speech and would therefore not be included in this return. On the other hand, nomad gipsies are known to be elusive when official censuses are taken. It was estimated that there were from 60,000 to 80,000 gipsies in Makedhonía alone in 1924, and an authoritative estimate places the number of gipsies in Greece in 1936 as high as 100,000. In considering these estimates, however, it is important to remember that Greece still serves as a temporary centre for gipsies migrating to other Balkan countries and to Turkey.

The most important gipsy quarters for sedentaries are those at Athínai and Thessaloníki. The sedentary gipsies are in great demand as harvesters, and most of them follow a variety of regular occupations such as basket making, iron working, and brick and tile making. The largest number of nomads is found in Makedhonía, but there are also large camping areas in Thessalía, in Fthiótis, in Voiotía, in the Alfiós valley, in Ilía near Pírgos and in Kríti. The nomad gipsies usually make a living out of basket making, broom making, sieve making, horse dealing, bear taming and fortune telling. They are continually on the march, despising their sedentary comrades, and always regarded with suspicion by the Greek peasants (Plate 98).

BIBLIOGRAPHICAL NOTE

1. There is no full treatment of the minorities of Greece within one volume in English, but C. A. Macartney's *National States and Minorities*, pp. 529–30 (London, 1934), provides a statistical summary with comment, and there are a number of books dealing with individual minorities.

2. For a list of books dealing with the Graeco-Turkish and Graeco-Bulgarian exchanges of population, and their consequences for Greece, see p. 396.

3. The complicated ethnic situation in Macedonia has given rise to a large number of books. A convenient introduction to the complexity is given in (1) *Peace Handbooks*: vol. IV, *The Balkan States*, part II, no. 21, 'Macedonia', Foreign Office (London, 1920); and (2) G. Weigand, *Ethnographie von Makedonien* (Leipzig, 1924). The following should also be consulted, though they were written before the exchanges of populations had simplified the problem: H. N. Brailsford, *Macedonia: Its Races and their Future* (London, 1906) (this is pro-Bulgarian). J. Cvijíc, *Questions balkaniques* (n.d. Paris and Neuchatel) (this is pro-Serbian); M. Paillarès, *L'Imbroglio Macédonien* (Paris, 1907) (this is pro-Greek).
See also the historical works indicated on p. 238.

4. A short account of the Armenian refugees in Greece may be found in Sir John Hope Simpson's *The Refugee Problem*, pp. 407–10 (London, 1939).

5. The following deal with the Vlachs, and each is accompanied by a distribution map: A. J. B. Wace and M. S. Thompson, *The Nomads of the Balkans* (London, 1914); G. Weigand, *Die Aromunen*, 2 vols. (Leipzig, 1894–5); A. Rubin, *Les Roumains de Macédoine* (Bucarest, 1913).

6. Short accounts of the Spanish Jews of Greece will be found in articles on Dönmeh, Greece, Salonica in (1) *The Jewish Encyclopedia*, 12 vols. (New York and London, 1901–6); and (2) Vallentine's *Jewish Encyclopedia*, edited by A. M. Hyamson and A. M. Silbermann (London, 1938).

7. Some information about the gipsies of Greece will be found in M. Block, *Zigeuner* (Berlin, 1936).

8. The history of the Albanian element in Greece will be found in W. Miller, *The Latins in the Levant*, passim (London, 1908). There is also a useful paper by F. H. Hasluck, 'Albanian Settlements in the Aegean Islands', in the *Annual of the British School at Athens*, vol. XV, pp. 223–8 (London, 1909). An account of the Graeco-Albanian claims in the north is given by E. P. Stickney in *Southern Albania or Northern Epirus in European International Affairs*, 1912–23 (Stanford, Cal., 1926).

Chapter XIII

THE EXCHANGES OF POPULATIONS

Introduction

The Graeco-Bulgarian Exchange: The Convention of Neuilly (November 1919); The Mixed Commission; The Settlement in Greece; The Settlement in Bulgaria

The Graeco-Turkish Exchange: The Disaster of Smyrna; The Convention of Lausanne (January 1923); The Mixed Commission; The Settlement in Greece; The Settlement in Turkey

Bibliographical Note

Introduction

Of all the changes brought about by the treaty settlements following the war of 1914–18, few are so interesting as the exchanges of populations between Greece and Turkey and between Greece and Bulgaria. There are many examples in past history of wholesale transplantations of population from one area to another, but these exchanges in the 1920's were unique in that they represented attempts to solve difficult minority problems, and also because they both tried to ensure that the transferred populations were adequately compensated. The Graeco-Turkish exchange was the more striking, partly because it involved over one million Greeks from Turkey and nearly 400,000 Moslems from Greece, and partly because the exchange was compulsory in character. The voluntary Graeco-Bulgarian exchange, on the other hand, involved only 92,000 people from Greece and 46,000 from Bulgaria, but it provides an equally outstanding example of the mechanism by which exchange was effected. If similar exchanges are ever contemplated for other regions, these two examples must inevitably provide useful information about the problems inherent in such radical measures.

Both exchanges were the culmination of a series of movements that had begun with the last phase of the break-up of Ottoman power in Europe. The military operations in Balkan lands during the years 1912–22 were, moreover, accompanied by substantial displacements of population that are summarized on p. 351. Further, it must be remembered that the idea of exchange was not in itself a new product of the post-war world of 1919, for there was already a precedent in two pre-war agreements.

The treaty between Bulgaria and Turkey in September 1913 formulated for the first time the idea of an 'authorized reciprocal exchange' between the Bulgarian and Moslem minorities within 15 km. of the common frontier. In fact, most of these people had already moved during the Turco-Bulgarian war, and the object of this treaty was to prevent them from returning, and to compel the remaining minorities to move also. A Mixed Commission, which met at Adrianople in November 1913, provided for the valuation and liquidation of the properties of the emigrants. Altogether 48,570 Moslems from Bulgaria were involved, and 46,764 Bulgarians from Turkish Thrace. The liquidation was, however, never carried out, for in October 1914 Turkey entered the war, and the work of the Commission was discontinued.

In the meantime, the 'Young Turk' government, imbued with ideals of nationality and of 'Turkey for the Turks', sought to force a similar agreement upon Greece. Early in 1914, it expelled 115,000 Greeks from Eastern Thrace and 150,000 from the western coastlands of Asia Minor; some 50,000 Greeks from the latter area were also deported into the interior of Anatolia. The Greek government protested and, after some negotiation, an agreement was reached in May upon the following points: (1) that a voluntary exchange should be initiated between the Greeks of Thrace and western Asia Minor and the Moslems of Makedhonía and Ípiros; (2) that a Mixed Commission should be appointed to supervise the exchange, and to value and liquidate the property of the emigrants; (3) that the Commission was to consist of four members appointed by the two governments, together with a neutral arbitrator. The Commission first met at Smyrna in June 1914, but its work was suspended when Turkey entered the war in October.

Both agreements were indications of what was to follow when the confusion of 1914–18 was over, and they may be regarded as the forerunners of the Graeco-Bulgarian Convention of Neuilly in 1919 and the Graeco-Turkish Convention of Lausanne in 1923.

The Graeco-Bulgarian Exchange

The Convention of Neuilly (*November* 1919)

The Treaty of Neuilly between the Allied Powers and Bulgaria, on 27 November 1919, provided for 'the reciprocal and voluntary emigration of persons belonging to racial minorities', and on the same day the Greek and Bulgarian plenipotentiaries signed a Convention to put this measure into effect. It was hoped that Serbia would join in the Convention, but this hope was not realized.

The Convention of Neuilly was not as important as that of Lausanne because far fewer people were involved, but the main scheme was the same—the emigration of minorities with their moveable property, and the liquidation of their immoveable property all to be carried out under the supervision of a Mixed Commission whose neutral members were to be nominated by the League of Nations. As under the Lausanne Convention, the benefits of liquidation were also to include former emigrants, but no limiting date was fixed, and the Mixed Commission was left to decide this point. But there were differences between the two Conventions. The Lausanne Convention provided for compulsory exchange on a religious basis (see p. 380). The Graeco-Bulgarian exchange, on the other hand, was to be purely voluntary, and this voluntary character was repeatedly stressed. Moreover, no definite test, religious or otherwise, was laid down; the right of emigration and liquidation was extended to all 'racial, religious or linguistic minorities', provided they claimed Greek or Bulgarian affinities respectively. Then again the Convention of Neuilly did not go into such technical details as that of Lausanne; the broad lines only were laid down, and the details were left to be discussed and decided by the Mixed Commission itself. The Convention was ratified by both parties on 9 August 1920 and the Mixed Commission was constituted on 18 December 1920. It consisted of four members—a Bulgarian, a Greek and two neutral (from Belgium and New Zealand).

The Mixed Commission

The work of the Mixed Commission fell into three stages:

(1) The preparatory period, December 1920–December 1922. (The sittings were discontinued from December 1922–February 1923.)

(2) The supervision of the migrations, February 1923–December 1924.

(3) The liquidation of properties, from January 1925 onwards.

This chronological division is not strictly valid, for some of the problems of one stage often lingered on to be settled subsequently, but still the division does serve to indicate the main phases of the work of the Commission.

(1) *Preparatory Work.* During the preparatory stages, much time was wasted on discussion about the interpretation of the Convention and in working out 'Rules of Emigration and Liquidation'. Whether an applicant belonged to a 'racial, religious or linguistic minority' was left to be settled by the mayor of the commune in which the applicant lived; the mayor was to provide a certificate to this effect, subject, of course, to the right of appeal by the applicant to the Commission itself. Difficulties arose over the property of communities (hospitals, convents, schools, churches, etc.) whose members emigrated, and this question was ultimately decided by reference to the Permanent Court of International Justice (1930). The Commission had also to decide how far back to extend the right of liquidation to former emigrants; and, after some discussion, it fixed the date at 18 December 1900. Thus it attempted to do justice to the various migrations (and their associated abandonment and confiscation of properties) that had taken place during the past generation of unrest in the Balkan lands.

An important point to be decided was the period during which the benefits of the Convention should remain available. The time limit was first put at two years from 18 December 1920, but this was successively extended until it was placed at 31 December 1924, and even after this, certain extensions were allowed. A declaration of emigration was 'a solemn and irrevocable' act which could only be cancelled in exceptional cases. An application for liquidation was to be filed, according to prescribed form, at the same time or later.

(2) *The Supervision of Emigration.* After this period of preparation, the work of the Commission was interrupted for three months following the Smyrna disaster, from December 1922 to February 1923, and its sittings were discontinued, an interruption, says S. P. Ladas, that was 'in no way justified'. But at any rate in March the Commission started upon the labour not only of supervising and facilitating migration, but also of ensuring the voluntary character of all movements; this latter was a most important function in view of the general atmosphere of suspicion prevailing among the minorities of both countries. For some years after the institution of the Commission both minorities, especially the Bulgarian minority in Greece,* showed little desire to move, and it seemed doubtful whether any

* The Macedonian Revolutionary Organization brought pressure on the Bulgarian minority to remain. The organization had worked for forty years to secure Bulgarian preponderance in Macedonia and Thrace, and was therefore anxious to maintain the Bulgarian element in the area.

emigration of significance would take place. The collection of declarations to migrate had begun in November 1922 just at the moment when refugees from Asia Minor and Eastern Thrace came pouring into Greece. Up to June 1923, only 197 Greek families in Bulgaria had opted to move, and the corresponding figure for Bulgarian families in Greece up to July 1923 was only 166.

The situation on the northern frontier of Greece at this time was very confusing. Many Bulgarians along the railway line from Komotiní to Dedéagach (Alexandroúpolis) in Western Thrace had been deported to Thessalía and the Greek islands for military reasons, and were not brought back until the end of 1923, after the Treaty of Lausanne with Turkey had dissipated the threat of war in the north. Some Bulgarians had escaped to Bulgaria at this time. Those that remained in Makedhonía and elsewhere were soon overwhelmed by the flood of refugees from Turkey that were now being settled in Greece, and conflicts inevitably arose between the Bulgarian minority and the newcomers. Indeed, it was asserted that the settlement of the Greek refugees 'in districts with Bulgarian populations inevitably resulted in the flight of the latter',* and that the Greek authorities had 'hastened the departure of Bulgarians from Macedonia and Thrace'. In the meantime, bands of Bulgarian brigands (*komitadjis*) were crossing the frontier, and the Bulgarian minority in Greece, rightly or wrongly, was suspected of helping in the confusion and disorder. The general result of the atmosphere of hostility was to force many Bulgarians in eastern Makedhonía and Thrace to leave, and applications to emigrate rose quickly. In the month of July 1923, some 288 families asked to leave; the figure for August was 349. As the Bulgarian government had not created a department to deal with the settlement of these newcomers, they were more or less left to look after themselves, and soon they appeared in the Greek villages of south-eastern Bulgaria. The Greek minority, faced with this hostility in Bulgaria, began to think more favourably of moving to Greece. In July there were 365 family applications, and in August there were a further 313.

Throughout these months, the Mixed Commission was making every effort to secure fair treatment for the minorities of the two countries. Thus it intervened to assist the Bulgarians of Thrace who had returned from deportation to find their homes and lands occupied by Greek refugees. Hitherto, Western Thrace (Dhitikí Thráki) had

* C. A. Macartney, etc., *Survey of International Affairs*, 1925, vol. II, p. 29[illegible] (Oxford, 1928).

been excluded from the Convention because technically it was not yet part of Greece, but on 26 October 1923 it was included within the benefits of liquidation and the full formalities were waived. Efforts were made to distribute the refugees of both countries in the best possible way and to ensure that prospective emigrants were not dispossessed before they had harvested their crops.

During these years, the work of the Commission was continually hindered by the difficult relations between Greece and Bulgaria. Each government protested against the other's treatment of minorities. In July 1924, the massacre of some Bulgarians at the Greek village of Tális on the Graeco-Bulgarian frontier led to bitter feeling, and, frightened by these events, an increasing number of Bulgarians left Greece. On the other hand, in November, some Greeks in the Bulgarian village of Stanimaka were killed in a fray; and there were other 'incidents' in Bulgaria also. Amidst this excitement and ill-will on both sides, the Commission was continually occupied, though not with much success, in emphasizing the voluntary character of the exchange. In July, for example, it had been forced to suspend declarations of emigration for three months lest they might be due to fright or undue pressure. In October of the following year (1925) a frontier incident at Demir-Kapu in the Belashitsa Mountains, 12 km. south-west of Petrich, resulted in local fighting which nearly provoked a war between the two countries. The swift intervention of the League of Nations helped to smooth out matters, and Greece agreed to pay damages of £45,000.

Throughout these alarms, and indeed because of them, migration continued, and claims for liquidation were filed. According to figures issued in May 1929, some 92,000 Bulgarians had taken advantage of the benefits of the Commission. Of these, some 39,000 had left Greece before the establishment of the Commission in 1920. On the other hand, 46,000 Greeks from Bulgaria participated, and 16,000 of these were 'former emigrants'. The net movement that took place during 1923–8 involved, therefore, 53,000 Bulgarians and 30,000 Greeks.

(3) *The Liquidation of Properties*. The period for filing declarations of emigration expired in December 1924, and from January 1925 onward the most important work of the Commission started. The liquidation of the property of the emigrants involved the most complicated economic and legal considerations. Sub-Commissions were set up in various parts of Greece and Bulgaria, each consisting of a Greek and a Bulgarian and a neutral president. The activities

of these Sub-Commissions were co-ordinated at three centres—Sofiya, Thessaloníki and Komotiní. For the work of appraisal a staff of surveyors, foresters, architects and agriculturalists was employed. The total personnel of the Commission grew from 77 in 1924 to 380 in 1927, but was reduced to 222 in 1929.

The stages in the liquidation of a property were as follows. After an application had been made, one of the Sub-Commissions verified the existence of the property; then it was surveyed; next, its resources in fields, forests and buildings were valued. These details were assembled and verified for each village at one of the three centres of Sofiya, Thessaloníki and Komotiní. They were then submitted to the Mixed Commission for final approval. 'The neutral members were never able to obtain a unanimous vote on the liquidation of any village.'* Of the amount due to an emigrant 10% was then paid in cash and the rest in 6% bonds. The Bulgarian government was responsible for the payment of bonds issued to refugees from Greece, and vice versa. The difference in the total amounts then became the debt of one government to the other. Difficulties arose over the payment of the bonds, but these were settled in December 1927 by an arrangement known as the Kaphandaris-Molov Agreement, called after the Finance Ministers of the two countries. The following statistics, furnished by the Greek government, show the position up to 13 October 1930:

Greeks from Bulgaria

			$	
Claims liquidated	16,800	Value	8,920,000	
Claims awaiting liquidation (approx.)	1,000	Value	500,000	(approx.)
	17,800		$9,420,000	

Bulgarians from Greece

			$	
Claims liquidated	28,100	Value	20,311,821	
Claims awaiting liquidation (approx.)	1,300	Value	1,300,000	(approx.)
	29,400		$21,611,821	

Source: Charles B. Eddy, *Greece and the Greek Refugees*, p. 223 (London, 1931).

In the settlement of the financial problems, which caused much friction between the two countries, the Mixed Commission received great assistance from the Financial Committee of the League of Nations. By 1932 the work of the Commission was over. It had been

* Stephen P. Ladas, *The Exchange of Minorities, Bulgaria, Greece and Turkey*, p. 271 (New York, 1932).

able to perform a task which the Graeco-Turkish Mixed Commission was to find impossible (see p. 382). M. André Wurfbain has summed up its work by saying that, 'although often threatened with failure, it never broke down, and it did effectively succeed in assuring to the emigrants the indemnities due to them'.*

The Settlement in Greece

The settlement of the immigrants from Bulgaria in Greece came under the supervision of the Greek Refugee Settlement Commission, and the main features of its work are described below (see p. 384). The arrival of some 46,000 Greeks from Bulgaria was, of course, only a small item when compared with that of over one million refugees from Turkey. On the other hand, the departure of 92,000 people to Bulgaria not only released property for the use of the Commission but also considerably simplified the ethnic situation in northern Greece. Eastern Makedhonía was more or less cleared of Bulgarian elements. Moreover, under the Graeco-Turkish exchange, the Bulgarian Moslems (Pomaks) of the area left for Turkey. Only a small body of Pomaks (some 16,755 in 1928) remained in the north-west of Dhitikí Thráki, where the Moslem population was not exchanged (see p. 380). The other people with Bulgarian affinities that remained in northern Greece were the Macedo-Slavs of central and western Makedhonía. They numbered some 82,000 and spoke 'Macedonian' (see p. 354).

The Settlement in Bulgaria

The problem confronting Bulgaria was much smaller than that in Greece, but the plight of the refugees was no less terrible, despite the relief work carried on by Red Cross and other societies. Moreover, the post-war settlement had reduced the territory of Bulgaria, and the 92,000 arrivals from Greece were not the only refugees who had to be settled in this reduced area. According to Bulgarian figures of 1926, some 220,000 refugees of Bulgarian affinity had entered the country since 1913, and there were also 20,000 Armenian and 30,000 Russian refugees. It appears that by 1926 about one-half of these had been absorbed, and in September of this year the Bulgarian government appealed to the League of Nations for help in raising a loan for the settlement of the remainder. The result was a 7% loan

* A. Wurfbain, *L'Échange Gréco-Bulgare des minorites ethniques*, p. 179 (Lausanne, 1930).

of £2,400,000 (£1,750,000 from Great Britain, and the rest from Holland, Italy and Switzerland), and of $4,500,000 from the U.S.A.

In the meantime, the Council of the League appointed a 'Commissioner for the settlement of Refugees in Bulgaria' (M. René Charron), and it was agreed that a plan for settlement should at once be drawn up, and the Commissioner should make quarterly reports on the progress of the work. No adequate arrangements for settlement yet existed, and, consequently, a General Directorate was set up by the Bulgarian government in December 1926. It was found that the number of families to be assisted was 31,271 comprising some 125,000 people. The total area covered by the plan was 175,000 ha. (about half the size of Cornwall); and, on this, small agricultural holdings were to be established. Many difficulties at once arose over the distribution of land. The communes resisted the attempts of the government to take away vacant land for the purposes of settlement; and frequently the local inhabitants had already taken possession of the properties left by the Greek emigrants. In many places, boundaries were in dispute, and there was no proper land register in existence. Before the land could be divided up, therefore, it had to be measured, and the work of surveying was entrusted at first to the Bulgarian Geographical Institute, and later to a private group of engineers. This work of surveying was carried out only with great difficulty and amidst much local hostility. The final appraisal of the land distributed was begun in May 1929 by a Land Valuation Committee.

Division of land was only part of the problem. Houses had to be erected; livestock and seed had to be distributed; ploughs and other agricultural implements had to be provided; adequate water supplies had to be secured. Many areas were marshy, and drainage works and anti-malarial campaigns had to be initiated. In some areas, roads had to be made, and a railway was built from Rakovski to Mastanli, now Momchilgrad (to the north of Komotiní in Greece), in order to open up areas for settlement. Along the coast of the Black Sea, the fisheries had hitherto been mainly in the hands of Greeks; refugees were now established here, and boats and gear provided for them. The cost of all these facilities was charged individually against the refugees, and arrangements were made for them to refund their debts over a period of years. Bulgarian emigrants from Greece who had received Bulgarian state bonds in return for property left in Greece were allowed to use these in repayment.

It had originally been laid down in the Protocol of the League of Nations that, as a rule, refugees should not be settled within a zone of 50 km. from the Greek, Yugoslav and Romanian frontiers. Over one-half of the country was thus to be closed to settlement; but many refugees had already settled in this area and their establishment could be completed at only a small cost. After many conferences, the principle of the 50 km. zone was maintained, but exceptions were allowed in certain areas where the re-establishment of refugees would

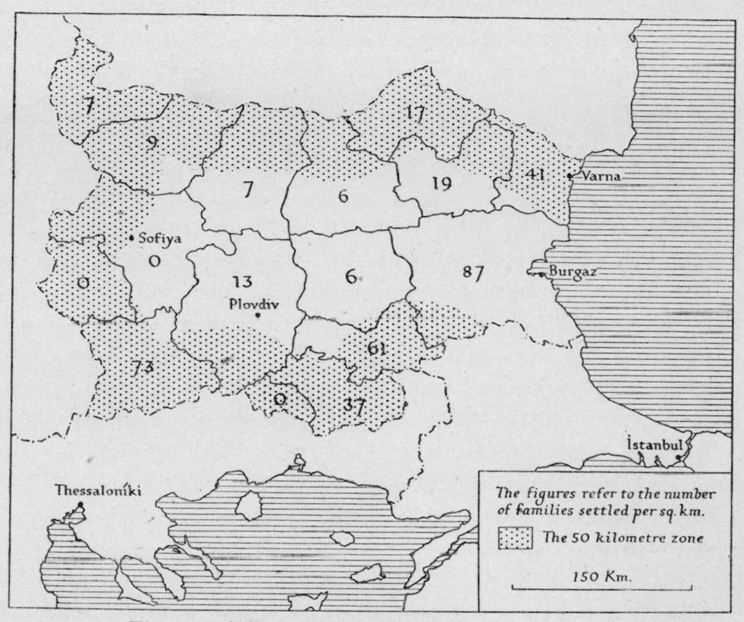

Fig. 105. The settlement of refugees in Bulgaria

Based on (1) *League of Nations Official Journal*, November 1930, p. 1566 (Geneva); and (2) *Annuaire Statistique du Royaume de Bulgarie*, 1931, pp. 22–3 (Sofia, 1931). The information, contained in the sixteenth report of the Commissioner of the League of Nations, covers four years of the work of settlement to 15 August 1930. Altogether, 28,342 families were settled during this period.

involve waste of money. Fig. 105 shows the progress of the settlement up to August 1930, by which time the main work was done. Over one-half of the refugees had been settled in the district of Burgaz near the Black Sea coast. The remainder had been accommodated in the north along the Danube, in the Deli Orman region of the north-east, where water-supply schemes and the evacuation of former Turkish inhabitants made settlement possible, in the Plovdiv and Arda basins of south central Bulgaria, and in the Struma valley.

Despite all the difficulties involved, the net result of the settlement brought great benefit to the Bulgarian state. The distress of the refugees was relieved. Political conditions along the frontiers were greatly improved, and the dangers of 'Komitadji' raids into neighbouring countries were wiped out. Finally, the economic condition of Bulgaria was greatly improved by the extension of its arable lands, and by the new works of health and communication. The many advance repayments made by the refugees indicated the success of their settlement. The Black Sea area, in particular, desolate in 1926, had become productive and densely populated by 1929. The economic statistics for the country as a whole tell their own story of improvement.

The Graeco-Turkish Exchange

The Disaster of Smyrna

Before 1922 the Greek subjects of Turkey numbered something over one and a half millions. Geographically, they fell into the three main groups: (1) those living in Thrace, in Constantinople, and on the shores of the Sea of Marmora; (2) those along the western coastlands of Asia Minor, especially around Smyrna; and (3) those living at various centres along the southern shores of the Black Sea, and more particularly around Trebizond. There were also two smaller groups; one in Cappadocia, around Caesarea, and the other in Cilicia around Tarsus and Mersina. Altogether they formed an extremely prosperous group in the Turkish empire, pre-eminent in commerce and industry, and successful also in agriculture. They naturally found bitter opposition from the rising Turkish Nationalist Party which aimed not only at constitutional reform but at creating a 'Turkey for the Turks'.

With the outbreak of the Graeco-Turkish war in March 1921, the hinterland of Smyrna passed quickly into the hands of the Greek forces, who advanced inland to within sixty miles of Angora. But the tide of battle turned, and the Greek army was defeated and forced to retreat. As it drew back towards the coast, the local Greeks fled with it in a disorganized mass. When the Turks reached Smyrna itself in September 1922, there were appalling scenes of horror, and the confusion was heightened by a disastrous fire that destroyed the greater part of the town. All the Greeks who could escape, fled, and it has been estimated that upwards of 800,000 people left the shores of Asia Minor within the space of a few days. They arrived at the islands or mainland of Greece in whatever ships and boats could be found, seaworthy or not. They were without food or clothes, were frequently covered with vermin, and brought with them various diseases, including typhus fever. This vast number of refugees was further increased when, by the armistice signed at Mudania in October, the Greeks were obliged to evacuate Eastern Thrace within fifteen days. Thus more were added to the already overwhelming throngs on Greek territory (Plate 100).

The plight of Greece after the disaster of Smyrna won widespread sympathy. The League of Nations, through Dr Nansen's relief organization, did much to help. The American National Red Cross and the American Near East Relief organization, too, played a great part in dealing with the situation in Greece and Asia Minor respectively.

The Convention of Lausanne (January 1923)

With the complete triumph of the Turks, the Allies called a conference in November 1922 at Lausanne to negotiate a peace. The urgent question of minorities was at once raised. On the one hand, there were the Greeks of Asia Minor and Eastern Thrace, both those who had fled and those who had remained behind; there were also those Turks living on Greek soil, especially in Makedhonía and Dhitikí Thráki. Three solutions of the problem were possible. The Greek refugees might have been sent back; but to this solution the nationalist Turkish government was completely opposed. It wished even to expel those Greeks (numbering some half a million) who were still left in Asia Minor, and so to create a homogeneous Turkish state with no important minority within its frontiers. An alternative solution, the maintenance of the *status quo*, found no favour with the Greeks who wished to expel the Turks of Makedhonía and Dhitikí Thráki so as to provide lands for the settlement of the refugees. A third possibility was that of compulsory exchange, and this was adopted by the Convention of Lausanne in January 1923. There has been much dispute about how the idea of compulsory exchange arose, but, at any rate, the idea of exchange itself was not new. In June 1914 a Graeco-Turkish Convention had arranged for the exchange of some 200,000 Greeks in return for an equal number of Moslems from Ípiros and Makedhonía; but nothing had come of this agreement owing to the outbreak of war.

The word 'compulsory' had not been mentioned in the Convention of 1914, but now the Turks at once insisted upon compulsion. The

Greeks, doubting the capacity of their country, weakened by the years of warfare, to absorb so vast a mass of new inhabitants, pointed to the inequality of a measure which would force Greece to accept some 1,300,000 people in return for about 390,000 Turks. Lord Curzon, representing Great Britain, opposed compulsion on the ground that the results of such a transference had not been fully considered by the Turks who, he held, 'would lose more than they would gain'; and he feared the disturbance of economic life, likely to follow from 'this gigantic transference of population, for which there is no precedent in modern times'. The French, too, were not in favour of compulsion. But no argument would move the nationalist Turks. Moreover, compulsion had one great advantage; it obviated delays and enabled measures to be taken promptly without the endless difficulties that were likely to arise if evacuation were voluntary. If the agricultural population was to move at all, it had to move quickly in order that cultivation should not be delayed.

In the end, faced by the determination of the Turks, the conference gave way, and compulsory exchange was agreed upon. By the Convention of Lausanne, signed on 30 January 1923:

(*a*) Greece renounced the right to send back the Greek Orthodox population which had left Asia Minor and Eastern Thrace.

(*b*) Greece agreed to compulsory emigration of members of the Greek Orthodox Church still resident in Turkey with the exception of those established (*établis*) in Constantinople before 30 October 1918.

(*c*) Turkey agreed to compulsory emigration of Moslems from Greece, with the exception of those established in Dhitikí Thráki, to the east of the frontier laid down by the Treaty of Bucharest in 1913.

The exchange was to take place after 1 May 1923, but any persons who had migrated since 18 October 1912 were also included within its scope. The basis of exchange was to be religious, not linguistic; every member of the Greek Orthodox Church was to leave Turkey, and all Moslems were to leave Greece. Consequently, Greek Moslems, Greek Roman Catholics and Greek Protestants were allowed to remain in Turkey, while Turkish-speaking members of the Greek Church were expelled. Conversely, any Turks who had adopted Christianity were allowed to stay in Greece, while Greek-speaking Moslems were expelled; those Moslem Bulgars (Pomaks) of north-eastern Makedhonía who had not gone to Bulgaria were also included in this definition of exchangeables. The Turks, therefore,

Plate 100. The exodus of Greeks from Smyrna

With the defeat of the Greek armies in Turkey in Autumn 1922, the Greek refugees, in complete disorder, were directed to almost any harbour along the west coast of Asia Minor.

Plate 101. Refugees in Athínai (Athens)

The photograph shows the interior of the municipal theatre, Athínai, where for a long time each box housed a family of refugees.

Plate 102. Armenian potters

Those refugees who settled in urban centres frequently took up their old work. The photograph shows Armenians making pottery and enamel ware, known as *Kioutahia*. The carpet-making industry also grew rapidly with the settlement of urban refugees.

Plate 103. A refugee village in Dhitikí Thráki (Western Thrace)

The village, in course of construction, is typical of many of the new settlements that grew up in northern Greece to meet the needs of the agricultural communities.

did not succeed in completely eliminating Greeks from Turkey, but their purpose was fulfilled; Greek nationalism as a political force was now obliterated from Turkish soil, and the few Greeks who remained no longer presented any serious minority problem.

Two exceptions to the Convention of Lausanne were subsequently made. Under the Treaty of Lausanne, a different document from the Convention and not signed until July, the islands of Imbros and Tenedos were handed over to Turkey, but their Greek inhabitants were exempted from exchange. Another subsequent arrangement was the exemption of the Albanian Moslems in north-west Greece who were allowed to remain in their homes. There was also considerable discussion about the definition of the word *établis* as applied to the Greeks of İstanbul (Constantinople), and over the question of the Patriarchate; the Turkish government several times expressed a desire for a complete exchange, but this was always met by a Greek refusal. Agreement, however, was reached about the status of the Greeks in İstanbul in 1925, and again in 1930; and the Patriarchate was allowed to remain on the understanding that it concerned itself solely with religious matters. It was estimated in 1931 that İstanbul contained about 100,000 Greeks out of a total population of some 700,000.

The Mixed Commission

The Convention of Lausanne had provided for the setting up of a Mixed Commission to supervise the transfer of populations. This comprised four representatives of Greece and of Turkey respectively, and three neutrals (a Dane, a Spaniard and a Swede) from whom a chairman was chosen. They first met at Athínai on 8 October 1923, and, with the exception of a short visit to Thessaloníki, remained there until June 1924 when they moved to Constantinople. A secretariat was set up, and Sub-Commissions, each consisting of a Turk, a Greek, and a neutral president, were organized to deal with the details of different areas. The personnel of the Commission varied from time to time as the various Sub-Commissions were created or discontinued, but in June 1924 the total personnel was about 150.

The people to be exchanged by the two countries fell into three categories: (1) the large number of refugees, chiefly the 800,000 Greeks from Asia Minor and those from Eastern Thrace, (2) the Greeks, numbering about half a million, still left in Asia Minor, and (3) the 390,000 or so Turks in Greece, not including, of course, the Moslems of Dhitikí Thráki and the Albanian Moslems. The Greek refugees were, for the most part, women, children and older people. It was therefore decided that those of their men folk who had remained behind must form the first category of people to be moved, otherwise it would be difficult to settle families on the land. Accordingly, the able-bodied men of the Orthodox Church were first removed from Turkey; and afterwards the Moslems were removed from Greece. By May 1925, about 580,000 people had been transferred, comprising some 190,000 Greeks and 390,000 Moslems. The disproportion between the number of Greeks who were expected to be moved and the number of passports issued through the Commission is accounted for by the high death-rate after the Greek disaster in Asia Minor, and by the additional numbers who had taken flight before the Commission began its work.

The Convention of Lausanne had provided that emigrants should be free to take away their moveable possessions of every kind, but this provision was of little value to the majority of the Greek refugees who had of necessity brought very little with them in their flight across the Aegean. They could, however, hope to receive some compensation, for Article 14 of the Convention had stated that 'the emigrant shall in principle be entitled to receive in the country to which he emigrates, as representing the sums due to him, property of a value equal to and of the same nature as that which he has left behind'. The Mixed Commission was given power to value and liquidate any property (moveable or immoveable) so left behind. Each proprietor was then to receive a statement of the sum due to him; this was to be credited to him in his new country, while his property itself was to be placed at the disposal of the state in which it lay. The total values of all the Greek and Turkish properties, respectively, were to be established by the Commission, and any difference was to be reckoned as a debt owed by one state to the other.

This scheme, however, was never carried out, and there were long and complicated negotiations about the value of the properties left behind by the exchangeables in each country. The physical difficulties of valuation were very great, especially since many of the Greek villages in Asia Minor had been destroyed during the campaign of 1921–2; their existing worth was small, and there was, therefore, much discussion about the date to be adopted in the determination of values, for the Convention itself had not specified a date. Then again, the complicated character of Turkish land law made the ownership of abandoned properties doubtful in many cases. The Moslems who left Greece, on the other hand, had departed in an orderly fashion, and their properties were at once taken over without being allowed to deteriorate; but, even so, it was frequently impossible to reconcile the widely differing estimates of their value. Thus the following values were given for the Moslem farm of Koula in Makedhonía:*

Turkish estimate	5,150,000	drachmae
Greek estimate	61,250	„
Neutral estimate	183,750	„

To these difficulties over 'exchangeables' were added complications about the property of non-exchangeables in İstanbul and Dhitikí Thráki, and about Turkish nationals who held property in Greece and Greek nationals who held property in Turkey.

The net result of the long-drawn-out and frequently suspended negotiation was the Convention of Ankara on 10 June 1930. This finally recognized that it was impossible to decide whether the aggregate value of the property left in Turkey was greater or less than that left in Greece, and that it was impossible to decide whether Greece owed money to Turkey or vice versa. The new Convention therefore declared that the property left by the Greek 'exchangeables' from Turkey should pass in complete ownership to the Turkish government, and that the property of Moslem 'exchangeables' should likewise pass to the Greek government. The various points in dispute about the property of 'non-exchangeables' were also settled, and Greece agreed to pay the sum of £425,000 to the Mixed Commission for the purpose of indemnifying the people concerned. Many Greeks felt that this payment was unjust, but the Greek government was anxious to get rid of the difficult atmosphere of these years of negotiation; it hoped that friendly relations with Turkey would result in a general political and economic benefit, and indeed this hope was amply fulfilled in the years that followed.

As far as the individual 'exchangeables' were concerned, both Greek and Turkish governments, in view of Article 14 of the Convention of Lausanne, were now left under a moral obligation to use the property left behind to compensate their respective settlers (see pp. 391, 394). The other claims for compensation, to be paid out of the £425,000 provided by the Greek government, were dealt with by the Mixed Commission until it was dissolved in 1934.

* S. P. Ladas, *The Exchange of Minorities: Bulgaria, Greece and Turkey*, p. 556 (New York, 1932).

The Settlement in Greece

The large number of Greek refugees, the urban character of so many of them, and the fact that so much of the land available for settlement was barren or marshy, meant that the Greeks were not able to deal with the problem of settlement unaided. They therefore applied to the League of Nations for help, and a Refugee Settlement Commission was set up with four members, two Greeks, one Englishman and one American as chairman. This was an autonomous body invested by the Greek government with full executive powers, and responsible to the Council of the League of Nations to which it submitted quarterly reports. The personnel of the Commission, which reached a maximum of about 2,000 in 1928, was almost entirely Greek, and was supplied largely by the Ministries of Agriculture, Public Welfare, Public Health and by the National Bank of Greece. An initial advance of £1,000,000 was made by the Bank of England in August 1923 to meet the immediate needs of the Commission and to enable the work of settlement to be started at once. Later, with the approval of the League an international 7% loan of £12,300,000 was issued (December 1924)—£7,500,000 in London, £2,500,000 in Athínai and £2,300,000 in New York. Early in 1928, further loans of £9,000,000 (some at 6%, some at 4%) were made to the Greek government, and one-third of this was also assigned to the Commission, making a total of £15,300,000. The actual amount received by the Commission, however, was considerably less because most of the bonds had been issued below par.

One of the difficulties that faced those who grappled with the problem of settlement was the lack of statistics. A census of refugees in Greece, made in April 1923 before the Settlement Commission had started work, placed their number at 847,931. But others arrived after this not only from Turkey but from Bulgaria, Russia and elsewhere. By the general census of May 1928, the total, excluding Armenians, numbered 1,221,849, of whom 151,892 had sought refuge in Greece before the disaster of Smyrna. The total figure was made up as follows:

From Turkey	1,104,216
From Russia	58,526
From Bulgaria	49,027
From Albania, Serbia, Dodecanese, etc.	10,080

The Armenians numbered 33,634 in 1928 (see p. 358). None of these figures can be regarded as accurate because no data were available for births, deaths and emigration among the refugees since their arrival. There is no way therefore of deducing the original number of refugees; the figure 1,300,000 is sometimes given, of whom 200,000 were probably in a position to support themselves. The remainder probably comprised about 650,000 agricultural and 450,000 urban refugees, although estimates of these proportions have varied considerably.

Agricultural Settlement. A start had already been made by the Greek government itself, and the Commission, when it met for the first time at Thessaloníki in November 1923, took over these beginnings. The government promised to assign not less than 500,000 ha. of land to the Commission, and the refugees were to be settled on this upon a self-supporting basis. By 1929, the total land so assigned amounted to 861,010 ha. This land belonged to three categories: (1) land belonging to the state; (2) land vacated by the exchangeable Turks; (3) land expropriated according to the agrarian reform laws.

It must be remembered that while the Commission was performing its task, Greece was engaged in carrying out a programme of agrarian reform in favour of small tenant farmers. By the Agrarian Reform Law of October 1924, large estates were broken up; and their owners were permitted to retain 30 ha. (74 acres), the remainder being distributed to native tenants or to refugees. The Commission was, therefore, engaged upon a double task—it participated in agrarian reform as well as settled refugees.

The great bulk of the agricultural refugees were placed in Makedhonía and Dhitikí Thráki (Figs. 106, 107), which was the part of Greece with the greatest potentialities for settlement, especially with the aid of drainage and irrigation works. Moreover, most of the Moslems and Bulgarians who left Greece were from Makedhonía, and thus the large estates (*tchifliks*), formerly in the ownership of the Turkish ruling class, were now available for occupation by peasant proprietors. Other refugees were settled in Kríti, Thessalía, Ípiros, Évvoia and to a very small extent in Pelopónnisos (see table on p. 387). A general idea of the refugee element in the population of Greece can be obtained from Fig. 106.

The Commission as a rule allotted land to groups of families rather than to individuals. The ideal was to regroup together the refugees coming from each village in Turkey, but this could not always be realized. Each group of families elected councils which allotted shares to its constituent families. The family share (for a family of four members) varied according to the quality of the soil and the nature of the cultivation. In the cereal lands of Makedhonía and Dhitikí Thráki it averaged about 3·5 ha. (8⅔ acres). In Thessalía the holdings were smaller; in Ípiros larger; in the fertile lands of the

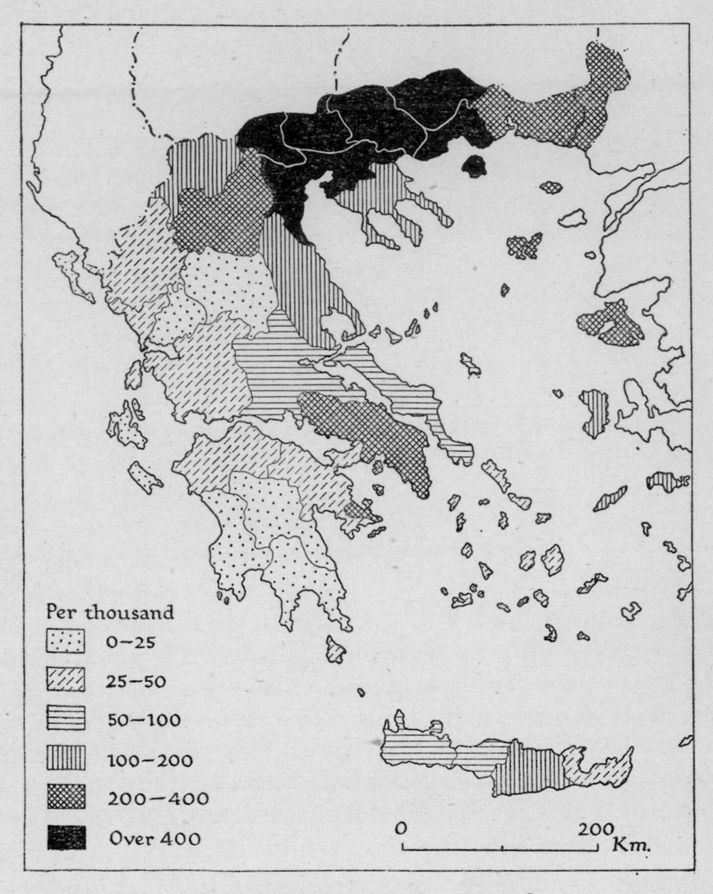

Fig. 106. Refugees in Greece, 1928

Based on data from *Annuaire Statistique de la Grèce*, 1931, p. 30 (Athènes, 1932). The figures show the number of refugees per thousand inhabitants in each *nomós*. The heavy shading over the whole of Attikí is misleading, since almost all the refugees are concentrated in and around Athínai.

Évros (Maritsa) valley they were only about 1·5 ha.; and in the tobacco districts of Makedhonía and Dhitikí Thráki they varied between about 0·9 and 2·0 ha. To the cattle-breeding groups in the mountain districts of the northern provinces, holdings of about

The Settlement of the Greek Refugees

From Charles B. Eddy, *Greece and the Greek Refugees*, p. 169 (London, 1931).
There are slight discrepancies between the figures in this table and the more accurate statistics of the 1928 census.

Provinces	Area in sq. km.	Population 1920	Population 1928	Refugees 1928	Refugees %	Established by R.S.C.			Per cent. of refugees established by the R.S.C.
						Rural	Urban*	Total	
Stereá Ellás and Evvoia	24,996	1,136,183	1,592,842	306,193	19·0	15,543	52,208†	67,751	22
Thessalía	13,354	438,408	493,213	34,659	7·0	7,628	6,728‡	14,356	40
Ionian Islands	1,926	198,070	213,157	3,291	1·4	—	780	780	—
Kikládhes	2,580	122,347	129,702	4,782	4·0	—	816	816	—
Pelopónnisos	22,283	934,094	1,053,327	28,362	2·7	3,236	4,980	8,216	—
Makedhonía	34,893	1,078,748	1,412,477	638,253	45·0	427,297	21,204§	448,501	70
Ípiros	9,351	292,954	312,634	8,179	2·5	4,190	608	4,798	—
Aegean Islands	3,848	260,058	307,734	56,613	19·0	2,965‖	1,712	4,677	8
Kríti	8,289	346,584	386,427	33,900	9·0	19,316	1,720	21,036	62
Dhitikí Thráki	8,706	209,443	303,171	107,607	35·0	71,293	18,856¶	90,149	84
Totals	130,199	5,016,889	6,204,684	1,221,849**	19·7	551,468	109,612	661,080	54

* Numbers obtained by multiplying the number of houses (27,403) by 4.
† 47,664 in Athínai and Piraiévs. Excess families are not counted, for there were more than one family in some houses.
‡ 5,848 in Vólos.
§ 4,372 in Thessaloníki.
‖ In Límnos only.
¶ 4,748 in Komotiní and 4,820 in Xánthi.
** Of which 151,892 arrived before September 1922.

8–10 ha. per family were granted. One of the difficulties encountered in this allotment was the absence of adequate maps. A provisional distribution of land had first to be made, and surveys had then to be undertaken before the final allotment could be made and the debt of each refugee fixed.

But allotment of land was only one part of the problem. Homes had to be provided. Over 50,000 houses had been left behind by Moslems and Bulgarians, but at least 10,000 of these were in dire need of repair, and over another 50,000 had to be built in order to house the 130,000 families who settled in Makedhonía and Dhitikí Thráki. Nor was this all. Animals, sheds, ploughs, carts, furniture, had to be provided, and also maintenance while the first season's crop was growing. Then again, public utilities had to be created; hospitals, schools and churches had to be built; wells had to be sunk; health services and agricultural and veterinary stations had to be established; water supply and sanitary services had to be provided; roads and bridges had to be constructed; drainage and irrigation works had to be carried out. The large-scale drainage works, started in the valleys of the Axiós and the Strimón, not only provided more land for cultivation but helped in the fight against malaria so prevalent in the region; the death-rate from malaria in the early years of the settlement was very high. Then again, experiment had to be made with various types of wheat to find out which suited the country. The Australian wheat 'Canberra', among others, proved very successful because it ripens in Greece before the period in which the burning *livas* wind destroys the harvests. Nor was this village settlement entirely concerned with agriculture, for on the coasts of Khalkidhikí and the shores of the Gulf of Évvoia, fishing communities were established and equipped with boats and appliances.

The successive quarterly reports of the Commission show increasing progress, and, in 1929, Sir John Campbell, the vice-chairman of the Commission, summed up the results of the work in Makedhonía and Dhitikí Thráki in these words:

'The aspect of the country has entirely changed. Everywhere one sees the cheerful red roofs of the colonization settlements. Where formerly vast uncultivated plains stretched, there are now flourishing villages, full of bustling activity, and showing obvious signs of comfort, and in many cases of prosperity. The whole countryside is awake and alive with new life. The refugees are working with admirable energy and courage'* (Plate 103).

* *League of Nations Official Journal*, June 1930, p. 712 (Geneva).

The agricultural statistics tell their own story. The production of wheat in Greece rose from about 250,000 tons in 1922 to 450,000 tons in 1928. The production of silk from silkworms rose from 50,000 to 160,000 boxes; the yield of tobacco likewise increased from 25,000 to 61,000 tons. It was the same with other commodities.

Urban Settlement. The Greek community of Asia Minor had included a large and prosperous urban element of bankers, merchants, shopkeepers and artisans for whom there were no ready business openings in Greece. The settlement of urban refugees was therefore a more complicated problem than that of agricultural refugees, and the Commission did not originally include the urban element within its scope, but concentrated upon 'the establishment of refugees in productive work', i.e. upon land settlement. The Greek government grappled with the urban problem itself, and the Commission did not undertake to help in this sphere until the beginning of 1925. It was then found impracticable to settle the urban refugees on the land nor was it possible to provide them with urban occupations by any large-scale planning. All that could be done was to facilitate their absorption into the existing urban life of Greece. The Commission therefore restricted its efforts to two main lines of activity.

(1) It lent financial support to the construction of permanent quarters for the housing of the urban element. When the swarm of refugees had come into Greece in the autumn of 1922, Athínai Piraiévs and Thessaloníki had provided the greatest number of convenient shelters (schools, theatres, warehouses, etc.). Building work was accordingly undertaken mainly in these three cities. Athínai and Piraiévs seemed the places where new industries would most likely be established; and Thessaloníki, as the centre for an expanding agricultural hinterland, promised many urban possibilities. The situation by 1928 is summed up in the following table:

	Total population in 1920	Total population in 1928	Refugees 1928
Athínai	292,991	459,211	129,380
Piraiévs	133,482	259,659	101,185
Thessaloníki	170,321	244,680	117,041

Source: Charles B. Eddy, *Greece and the Greek Refugees*, p. 116 (London, 1931).

Note. The figures for Athínai and Piraiévs do not include the population of the closely connected suburbs of Fáliron and of Kallithéa (the latter having a population of over 25,000 in 1928, of whom 15,516 were refugees). At Thessaloníki, the Moslems had departed between 1920 and 1928.

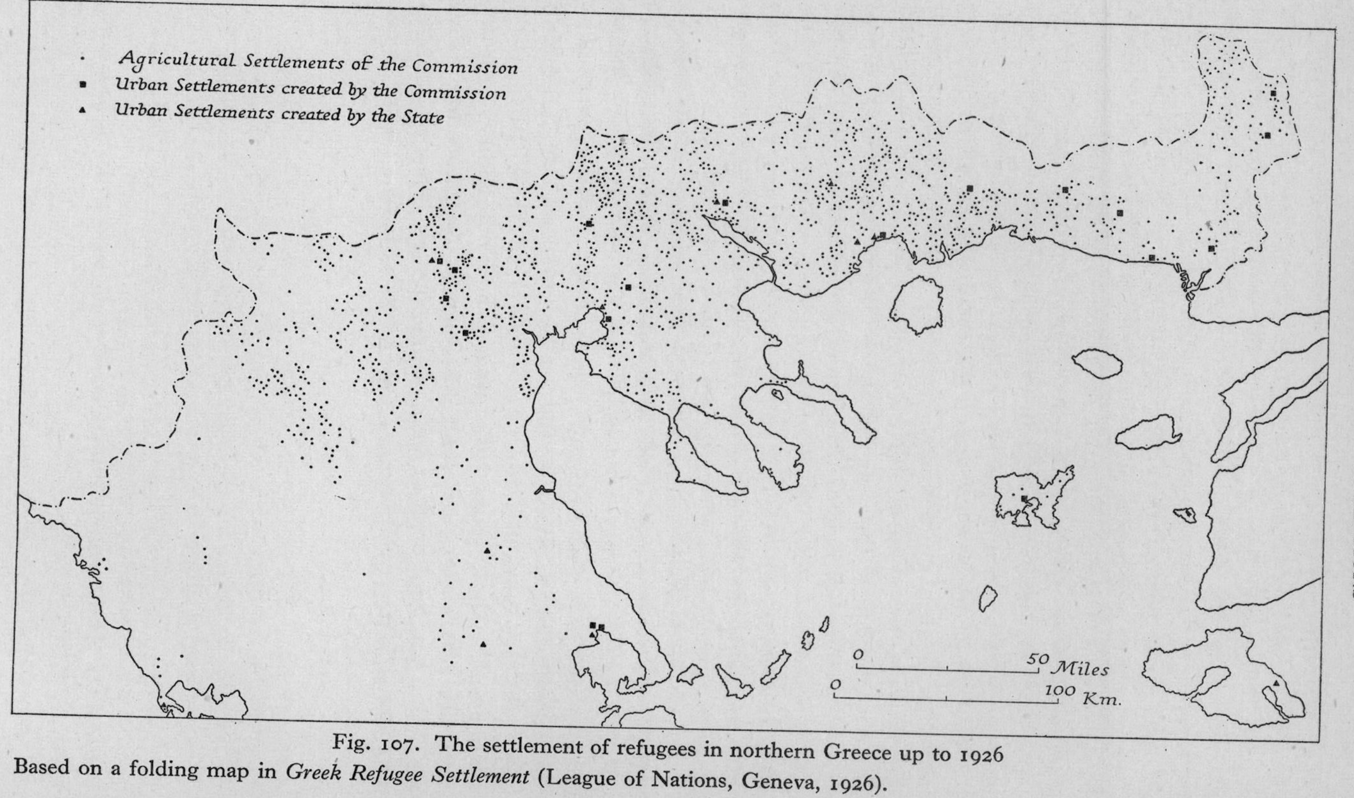

Fig. 107. The settlement of refugees in northern Greece up to 1926

Based on a folding map in *Greek Refugee Settlement* (League of Nations, Geneva, 1926).

But, of course, urban quarters were also erected in many of the smaller towns of Greece where openings appeared or where beginnings were found in the buildings left by Turkish and Bulgarian emigrants. Altogether urban quarters were erected in eighty-six other towns ranging from Pátrai (the fourth city in Greece) to small communities with less than 5,000 inhabitants.

(2) In the second place, the Commission also lent financial support to certain outstanding arts and crafts which utilized the traditional skill of the refugees and which promised an assured return for money lent; these crafts were mainly the making of carpets, embroideries, silks, pottery, silver-ware and enamelled articles. Moreover, the urban element included many people who had been prominent in banking, shipping, commerce and in the liberal professions in Turkey, and now they brought to Greece their great ability and in some cases their capital. The result was a new spirit that permeated the commercial life of Greece. Thus the production of woollen stuffs and fabrics rose from 1,700,000 yd. in 1922 to 2,600,000 yd. in 1925; and the production of cement from 37,000 to 60,000 tons. In the carpet and weaving industries the number employed rose from 4,000 in 1923 to 11,000 in 1928 (Plate 102).

The end of the Settlement Commission. Early in 1929 the Commission reported to the League of Nations that its final liquidation could take place in the following year, as its funds would soon be exhausted, and the main work of settlement was over. Arrangements were made for the transference of its responsibilities to the Greek government, and the Commission ceased to exist on 31 December 1930. During the period of winding up, the Greek Chamber passed a series of measures designed to maintain and increase the agricultural progress that was being made; and, amongst other measures, a General Directorate of Agriculture and the Agrarian Bank of Greece were established.

One of the questions important in the final straightening of the affairs of the Commission was that of the indemnities payable to the immigrants by the Greek Government. In view of the breakdown of the provisions of the Convention of Lausanne, the Government had assumed a moral responsibility for compensation. The value of the property abandoned in Turkey was assessed by special commissions composed of refugee natives from the same district as the claimants; exaggerated assessments were revised by a superior council. On the other hand, the Moslem urban property left in Greece was turned over in 1925 to the National Bank of Greece which issued bonds to the urban refugees on account of their claims. The bonds were redeemable at par as the property was sold by the bank. But these bonds were insufficient to cover the claims, and the government had to contract a number of internal loans in order to meet the indemnities.

The rural refugees received their compensation in a similar way, except that practically all the claims were settled through the Commission itself; these agricultural refugees were debited with the value of their new lands at an average rate of 4,000 drachmae per hectare (£4. 6*s.* 0*d* per acre) of cultivable land; this was the price at which the State had indemnified those whose land had been expropriated under the Agrarian Law of 1924.

When they received compensation, the refugees were able to start repaying their debts, and from 1927 onwards these repayments showed a considerable increase. In the agricultural areas, the system of repayment was organized by forming the rural communities into co-operative societies whose members were jointly responsible for their debts. In 1930, the Commission, in anticipation of its end, made agreements with the state by which the debts of agricultural refugees were to be collected by the Agricultural Bank of Greece, and those of urban refugees by the National Bank of Greece. In taking over the work of the Commission, the Greek state was assuming no unfamiliar duties. It had laid the foundation for the work of settlement, and it had been mainly responsible throughout for the settlement of urban refugees. Now, the completion of the agricultural settlement was added to its urban responsibilities. In praising the leadership and co-ordination provided by the Commission, it must not be forgotten that the state itself had dealt with nearly one-half the total number of refugees (see table on p. 387).

The settlement had very great consequences for the life of Greece. Against the suffering caused by the uprooting of population, and the evils attendant upon the overcrowding of cities by poor people, must be set two great benefits, economic and political. On the one hand, there was a great increase in both agricultural and industrial production. This stimulus, coming as it did after the disaster of 1922, was a most important factor in restoring the vitality of the country. The League of Nations report summed up the situation by saying: 'The work of settlement has been of great moral effect. It has restored confidence in the country, it has re-established faith in the heart of a people where dismay and demoralization once reigned. The economic restoration has quite naturally brought about the

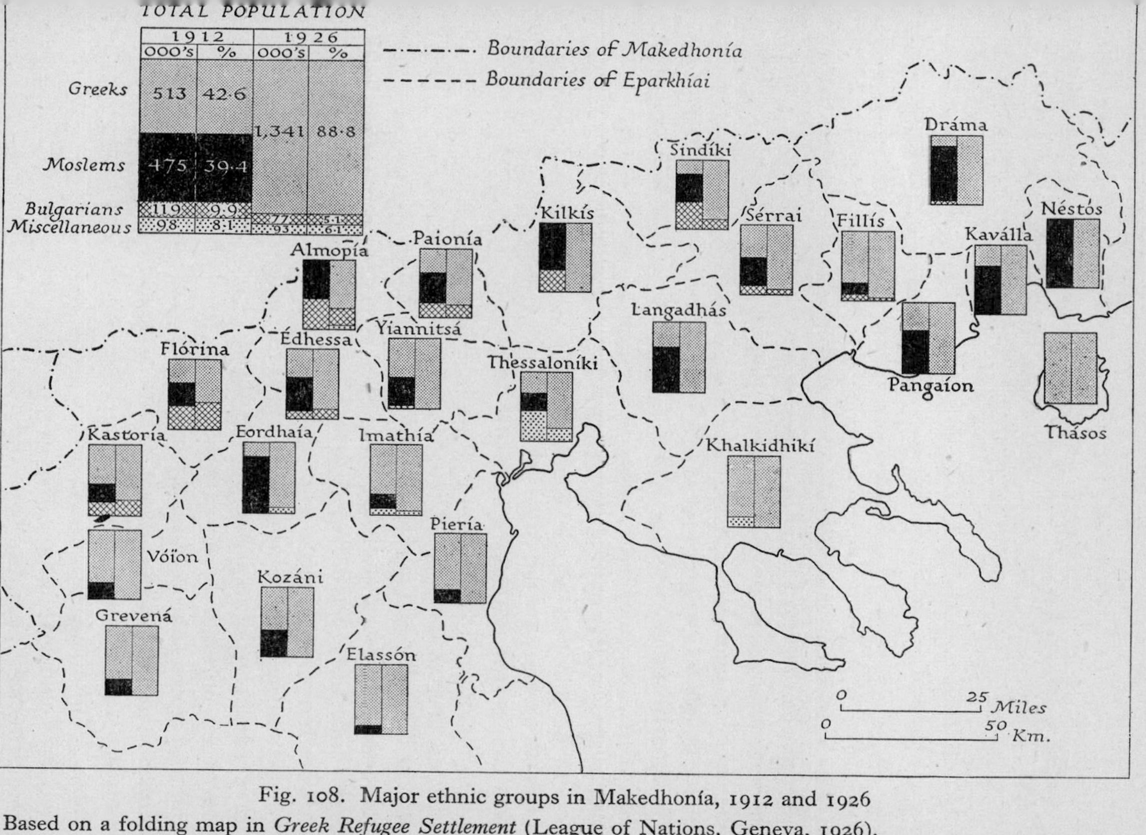

Fig. 108. Major ethnic groups in Makedhonía, 1912 and 1926

Based on a folding map in *Greek Refugee Settlement* (League of Nations, Geneva, 1926).

The main feature of the map is the disappearance of the Moslem element. There is also a reduction in the number of Bulgarians in many eparchies; 'Macedo-Slavs' are included under the heading 'Bulgarians'. The large rectangle shows the changes in the ethnic composition of Makedhonía as a whole.

moral regeneration of the whole country.'* On the other hand, there were political consequences, for the exchanges altered the ethnographic map of Makedhonía in a radical fashion (Fig. 108). The emigration of the large Moslem population (and also of the smaller Bulgar element) left Greek Makedhonía almost wholly Greek. The complicated 'Macedonian Question', which had so perplexed European diplomacy ever since 1870, was now, at any rate, considerably simplified.

The Settlement in Turkey

The settlement in Turkey followed different lines from that in Greece. In the first place, Turkey was not a member of the League of Nations, and, in any case, the Turks were resolved on avoiding dependence upon foreign loans. Accordingly, the Turkish government raised the whole cost of settlement from its own resources. A Department of Settlement and Tribes had been established in 1913, but, now, faced with the exchange of 1923, the Turks established a Ministry of Reconstruction, Exchange and Settlement with a staff to supervise settlement. This was replaced in 1924 by a Department of Settlement under the Ministry of the Interior, and this department was later transferred to the Ministry of Health.

In the second place, the numbers were much smaller than in Greece, and, despite the destruction of the war of 1922–3, the Turks had at their disposal ample land and farm buildings to accommodate the newcomers in Eastern Thrace and Asia Minor. According to the figures of the Mixed Commission, some 388,146 Moslems were transferred from Greece, but, apart from these of Greece, other Moslems were also moving into Turkey. This movement had been proceeding since the loss of subject territories in Europe in 1878; it had been particularly active since the First Balkan War (see table on p. 351); and it continued after 1923. One estimate places the number of immigrants (other than Greeks) from Eastern Europe between 1921 and 1929 at 190,000. The Turkish census of 1927 put the total number settled up to date at 434,079, but this only included people 'exchanged under convention'. Figures issued by the Turkish Department of Statistics gave the number settled during 1921–8 as 463,534. About 38% of these were settled in Eastern Thrace; and about 42% on the western coastlands of Asia Minor—that is, in the area vacated by the Greek population (Fig. 109).

* *Greek Refugee Settlement*, p. 206 (Geneva, 1926).

The Turkish settlement was different from that of Greece in yet a third way. Nearly 90% of the immigrants were cultivators, and they were at once able to occupy the land and farmsteads left by the Greeks. They were given land, seed, cattle and implements, subject to an agreement for repayment, but since the Turkish Settlement Law of 1925 most of these advances are not recoverable; between 1921 and 1930, some £1,539,511 was spent on settlement. The exchange had thus deprived Turkey of those Greek merchants who had been mainly responsible for the foreign trade of the country and

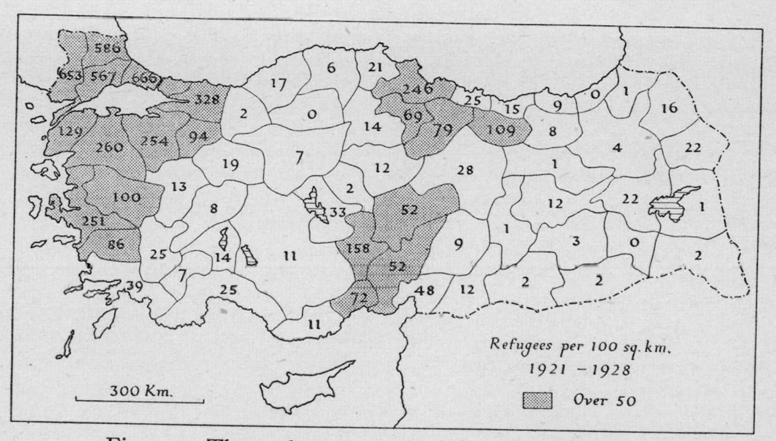

Fig. 109. The settlement of refugees in Turkey, 1921–8

Based on (1) S. P. Ladas, *The Exchange of Minorities: Bulgaria, Greece and Turkey*, p. 711 (New York, 1932); and (2) *Recensement général de la population*, 1927, pp. ii–xvii (Ankara, 1927).

The information, issued by the Turkish Department of Statistics, gave the number of people settled from 1921 to 1928 as 463,534. Of these, 388,146 from Greece were exchanged by the Mixed Commission, whilst a few thousand had left Greece on their own initiative. The remainder were Moslem emigrants or refugees from other countries.

for so many of its industries. The carpet, the fig and the olive-oil industries, for example, seemed irreparably damaged, but the last two, at any rate, have more than recovered. Against the economic loss must be set the political gain resulting from the disappearance of the Greek minority, and the vigour which the new nationalistic order was bringing with it. Nor did settlement stop with the establishment of the exchangeables from Greece, for immigration from eastern Europe continued; in 1936 there were some 30,000 arrivals; in 1937, some 31,000. Turkey, with plenty of land available, could take them, and the Turkish government in June 1938 announced a five-year plan which envisaged the establishment of about one million Turks from Bulgaria, Romania and Yugoslavia on productive farmlands in Asia Minor.

BIBLIOGRAPHICAL NOTE

1. A detailed account of both the Graeco-Bulgarian and the Graeco-Turkish exchanges is given in *The Exchange of Minorities: Bulgaria, Greece and Turkey*, by Stephen P. Ladas (New York, 1932). The appendices of this give the texts of the various conventions that governed the migrations. The *Official Journal* of the League of Nations is an important primary source of information.

A short summary of the two exchanges is included in *The Refugee Problem* by Sir John Hope Simpson (Oxford, 1939). He has also written a summary of the settlement in Greece—'The work of the Greek Refugee Settlement Commission', *Journal of the Royal Institute of International Affairs*, vol. VIII, pp. 583–604 (London, 1929). Sir John was vice-chairman of the G.R.C. from January 1927 to December 1930. An account of the Graeco-Turkish exchange can be found in C. A. Macartney, *Survey of International Affairs*, 1925, vol. II, pp. 257–79 (Oxford, 1928). There is also an account of the Convention of Ankara in Arnold J. Toynbee's *Survey of International Affairs*, 1930, pp. 157–68 (Oxford, 1931).

2. A summary of the work of the Greek Refugee Settlement Commission up to 1926 is given in an official publication by the League of Nations—*Greek Refugee Settlement* (Geneva, 1926); a French text was also published.

This may be supplemented by the later account in Charles B. Eddy's *Greece and the Greek Refugees* (London, 1931). Mr Eddy was Chairman of the G.R.C. from October 1926 to December 1930.

An excellent geographical survey of the consequences of the Settlement can be found in J. Ancel, *La Macedoine, son évolution contemporaine* (Paris, 1930).

3. The Graeco-Bulgarian exchange has been described by André Wurfbain in *L'Échange Gréco-Bulgare des minorités ethniques* (Lausanne, 1930). For Graeco-Bulgarian relations see (i) C. A. Macartney, *Survey of International Affairs*, 1925, vol. II, pp. 288–309 (Oxford, 1928); and (ii) Arnold J. Toynbee, *Survey of International Affairs*, 1931, pp. 345–53 (Oxford, 1932). The preliminaries to the Bulgarian Refugees' Loan are discussed in Arnold J. Toynbee, *Survey of International Affairs*, 1926, pp. 209–22 (Oxford, 1928).

4. A statistical summary of the changes of population in Greece is given in two papers by A. A. Pallis: (1) 'Racial Migrations in the Balkans during the Years 1912–24', *Geographical Journal*, vol. LXVI, pp. 315–31 (London, 1925); (2) 'The Greek Census of 1928', *Geographical Journal*, vol. LXXIII, pp. 543–8 (1929). Mr Pallis was one of the Greek members of the G.R.C. from September 1925 to December 1930.

Appendix I

MAPS AND CHARTS OF GREECE

Historical Introduction

The Greeks have made many attempts to survey their country in detail, but even to-day there is no map on a scale larger than 1:400,000 which covers the whole of Greece. This is not surprising when one considers the difficult mountainous regions which make up so much of their territory, the large tracts of marshland, the numerous islands, the frequent wars which have interrupted Greek survey work and shifted the national frontiers, the objections raised by Popular Representatives against cadastral surveys requiring the demarcation of commune boundaries, and the lack of adequate and long-continued financial support necessary for a comprehensive survey. On the other hand, the numerous wars fought on what is now Greek soil made detailed surveys of certain regions a necessity. Thus from 1916 to 1918 British, French, Italian, Serbian and German field companies produced excellent large-scale maps of northern Greece. Secondly, very accurate maps were needed for the demarcation of frontiers, and good strip maps exist for the country on either side of the old Turkish frontiers and the present boundaries with Albania, Yugoslavia, Bulgaria and Turkey. Thirdly, a strong stimulus to Greek cartography was provided by the settlement of large numbers of refugees on the plains of Makedhonía and Thráki (see p. 388). Ignorance of the extent and precise boundaries of the agricultural holdings, which covered an area of 7,000 sq. km., was an obstacle to be overcome by cadastral surveys on a scale not smaller than 1:5,000.

For early maps of the mainland a considerable debt is owed to French, Austrian and German cartographers, and for charts of the coasts and islands to the British Admiralty. The first scientific attempt to survey Greece was made by the French *Dépôt de la Guerre*, which in 1852 published the *Carte de la Grèce* on a scale of 1:200,000. The twenty sheets of the map are not contoured, the hachuring of the physical features is sometimes inaccurate, and the roads, railways and settlements are obviously out of date, but the survey has provided the basis for many of the subsequent maps of this region. In 1880 the Austrian Staff Map 1:300,000 was published by the *K.u.K. Militärgeographisches Institut*, but apart from extending the area of the survey and making corrections to roads and railways it added nothing to the earlier French map, and, in fact, copied many of its numerous mistakes. Nevertheless, for parts of the difficult terrain north of the Gulf of Kórinthos it remained the best map until the area was resurveyed and mapped by the Greeks within the last decade. In 1916 the *Austrian Staff Map* 1:200,000, also published by the *K.u.K. Militärgeographisches Institut*, was needed until the 1930's to complete the cover for Thessalía and Árta, acquired in 1881, for Makedhonía and Ípiros in 1913–14 and for Dhitikí Thráki in 1919–20. Though a big improvement on any previous map of these regions it is very much out of date and often faulty in the representation of relief features.

Apart from the work carried out by foreign governments, detailed surveys of small areas have from time to time been undertaken by various scientific authorities. Thus, as early as 1881, Curtius and Kaupert, working for the *Kaiserl. deutsche archäeologische Institut*, published the first of twenty-one sheets of Attikí and Salamís on a scale of 1:25,000: the map was a very great advance on anything which had preceded it. The German geographer, Philippson, who travelled extensively in central and southern Greece, made considerable additions and corrections to earlier maps, without making a complete survey. His map of the Pelopónnisos,

1:300,000, was published in 1892, and the four sheets stood as the best map of this area until after the war of 1914–18.

Large-scale maps of individual islands owe their origin to a variety of sources: many are based upon surveys made by the British for the Admiralty Charts, but their detail and accuracy are limited to coastal regions; some of the better maps, the result of careful surveys, appear in scientific journals not easily accessible, as for example the map of Samothráki, 1:50,000, by D. Jaranoff in the *Bull. de la Société Bulgare de Géographie* (Sofia, 1938), while others have been produced by the islanders themselves and can lay no great claim to accuracy. Detailed description of island maps will appear in a later volume.

Description of Maps

The maps of Greece are described in the following order:

A. Greek government topographical maps.
B. Maps issued by the Geographical Section of the British General Staff.
C. Greek Admiralty charts.
D. British Admiralty charts.
E. Miscellaneous maps.
F. Atlases.

In each group the maps are listed in order of scale, those on a large scale coming first. The following particulars are given where possible for each series:

(1) Authority responsible for its production.
(2) Date of production, with subsequent revisions.
(3) Number of published sheets in the series—to the latest available date for Greek government maps and to June 1943 for G.S.G.S.
(4) Size of sheets, measured to the margin of the area mapped.
(5) Projection. This is stated only for small scale maps. (In general Greek official maps are on a simple conical projection.)
(6) Meridian of origin (Athínai, Greenwich, Paris, Ferro): Grid and/or graticule.
(7) Scale. (This is only stated when the unit of measurement is exceptional.)
(8) Marginal information.
(9) Use of colour.
(10) Method of representation of relief.
(11) Details of roads, railways and other information.

A short note is sometimes added on the value of the map, its legibility and accuracy.

A. Greek Government Topographical Maps

Geodetic Surveys

The government department primarily responsible for the geodetic survey of Greece and the production of official maps is the *Greek Army Geographical Service*, referred to throughout the text as G.A.G.S. Before the war of 1914–18 it was known as the *Greek Army Cartographical Service* (G.A.C.S.). Some maps have been published for specific purposes under the direction of the Ministry for Air and the Ministry of Communications: Greek Admiralty surveys and charts are under the *Hydrographic Service of the Royal Marine.*

The triangulation of Greece has been computed on the spheroid of Bessel. Work was started in 1889, and by 1919 trigonometrical points of the first order had been established in peninsular Greece, and the Northern Sporádhes, the Kikládhes and Kérkira had been linked to the mainland. Perhaps the greatest work was undertaken between 1920 and 1932 with the measurement of the arc of the meridian from the frontier of Yugoslavia to Kríti. Subsequent surveys have linked Makedhonía, Thráki, and Bulgaria, the southern Ionian islands and the Dodecanese to the main Greek network. By 1936 there were 152 trigonometrical points of the first order.

A marble pillar near the Royal Observatory at Athínai serves as the origin of the geodetic triangulation. The accepted co-ordinates of this pillar are lat. 37° 58′ 20″.10, long. 0° 00′ 00″.00, and all published latitudes and longitudes are based upon these values. In 1927 a new and accurate value of 37° 58′ 18″.68, was published for the latitude, but as yet it has not been used in any computations affecting the triangulation and mapping of the country. The final longitude of the Pillar has been published as 23° 42′ 58″.815 (1 hr. 34 m. 52.065 s.) east of Greenwich. The fundamental azimuth of the triangulation system is the Geodetic Pillar-Párnis, 359° 46′ 13″.3 (north round to east).

The projections in general use in Greece are: (1) An azimuthal projection for the topographical work on the ground, developed by M. Hatt, Chief Hydrographer to the French Navy. (2) A conical projection, used for the compilation of field sheets and the publication of maps. The parallel of origin is 38° N lat. and no use is made of a scale factor.

(1) 1:20,000

These maps have been published by G.A.G.S. and G.A.C.S. for the following regions:

(*a*) Attikí, 29 sheets (G.A.G.S.), 1925–33.
(*b*) Lárisa, 6 sheets (G.A.G.S.), 1926–39 [2 sheets not dated].
(*c*) Elassón, 1 sheet (G.A.C.S.), not dated.
(*d*) Kórinthos: Khártis Frourás, 1 sheet (G.A.G.S.), 1932.
(*e*) Pátrai: Khártis Frourás, 3 sheets (G.A.G.S.), 1933.
(*f*) Thessaloníki, 4 sheets (G.A.G.S.), 1938.

The sheets usually measure 43 × 55 cm. Meridian of origin Athínai; margin is divided into minute intervals and a kilometre grid is normal. Printed in black, though some of the 29 sheets of the Attikí-Voiotía region are coloured, using red for settlements and roads (three categories), blue for sea, rivers and marshes, brown for contours, and green for woodland of different types. Contours are at 20 m. intervals, every 100 m. accentuated; spot heights in black; cliffs shown by close hachures. Railways (two categories) are in black.

The series is very clear, even when not coloured, and useful in providing detail of some of the most important areas in Greece.

(2) 1:50,000

Published by G.A.G.S. 1934–41 in 64 sheets, measuring 42 × 54 cm. The series covers small sections of the Greek frontiers with Albania, Yugoslavia and Bulgaria. Meridian of origin Athínai; graticule at 30 min. intervals; kilometre grid in red. A few sheets are printed wholly in grey, but the majority have brown contours at 20 m. intervals, every 100 m. accentuated. Water in blue; other features, including land utilization, railways (broad and narrow gauge) and settlements are in black. Administrative centres of nomes and eparchies, demes and communes are distinguished by different size and type of lettering: roads, sometimes shown in red, are classified as motor roads, roads under construction (and abandoned), cart-tracks with or without stone foundations, and mule tracks, easy or difficult.

The chief merit of the map lies in its detail, but although most of the surveys were revised 1932–3, up-to-date accuracy of many sheets is questionable, especially of those based on the Austrian 1:200,000.

Further sheets have been published on this scale by the Greek General Staff or the Geographical or Cartographical Services. They are very limited in extent and for the most part are enlargements of the Greek 1:75,000 sheets. The information is very much out of date. The regions mapped are:

(*a*) Dhomokós-Velestínon. 5 sheets (Greek General Staff), not dated but before 1906. Meridian of origin Paris: margins divided into 5 min. intervals. Contours every 20 m., spot heights; railways, roads and settlements.

(*b*) Sérvia, Sarandáporos-Dheskáti. 1 sheet (G.A.C.S.), not dated. Meridian of origin Athínai: margins divided into minute intervals. Contours every 20 m.; spot heights; railways, roads (three categories) woods, settlements.

(*c*) Kirlí Dervén Sórovits-Kaïlária. 1 sheet (G.A.C.S.), not dated. Detail as in (*b*).

(*d*) Lárisa area. 8 sheets (G.A.G.S.), 1917–18. Reproduction of Greek 1:75,000 (see A 3).

(*e*) Mesolóngion. 1 sheet (G.A.G.S.), not dated but before 1933. Detail as in (*b*).

(3) 1:75,000. *Khártis Ellinikoú Vasilíou*

Published by G.A.C.S. and G.A.G.S. Based on a trigonometrical and topographical survey on a scale of 1:20,000 which was started in 1889, interrupted by war with Turkey and re-begun in 1901. The first dated sheet did not appear until 1908. The photographic reduction of the earlier survey sheets to 1:75,000 and their engraving and reduction was undertaken by the *Militärgeographisches Institut* of Wien (Vienna), where the work was carried out in conjunction with the Greek military officers responsible for the survey. Each sheet of the original survey, from which the published sheets are reduced, forms a spherical trapezium of 6 min. of longitude and 6 min. of latitude. The map when completed would have comprised 120 sheets, but in 1927 when only 24 sheets had been published, it was decided to abandon the project. Subsequently, however, a large undated sheet of Athínai kai Perikhóra was issued on this scale.

Each sheet covers an area between 15 min. of latitude and 30 min. of longitude, 47×57 cm., reckoned from the meridian of origin Athínai. Margins divided into minute intervals and a graticule is formed by lines at 5 min. intervals. Most sheets are coloured; contours are in grey or brown, roads (four categories) are red and water blue. Railways (three categories) and names are in black.

Relief is shown by contours at 10 m. intervals, by spot heights and by grey hill shading. Blue shading of decreasing tone value is used to indicate depths from 0–2, 2–5, 5–10 and over 10 m. Over this depth submarine contours with a 10 m. interval are given to 60 m. Cartographic methods, however, vary considerably from sheet to sheet.

(4) 1:100,000. *Epitelikós Khártis tis Elládhos*

The first sheet was published by G.A.G.S. in 1925 and almost the whole of the mainland has now been mapped (Fig. 110). By 1941 there were 79 published sheets. A disadvantage of the series is that the edges of the sheets do not join accurately, owing to the azimuthal projection employed. The scale error, however, amounts to not more than 1:300,000, because of the limited extent of the field of each projection. The diagonals are free from scale errors and bearings from the centre are correct.

Each sheet covers an area between 30 min. of longitude and 30 min. of latitude (42×56 cm.); east and west edges lie at multiples of 30 min. east or west of the meridian of origin Athínai; north and south edges lie at multiples of 30 min. north or south of the 38th parallel. Margins are divided into minute intervals and the central lines of latitude and longitude are carried across the sheet.

Relief is shown by brown contours at 20 m. intervals, every 100 m. accentuated; spot heights in black; cliffs and sands in brown. Red is used for roads and tracks (five categories), bridges (three types) and for antiquities; blue for water, green for woods, vineyards and meadows. All other features are in black. Railways of standard and narrow gauge are distinguished, and there is a vast amount of miscellaneous information which does much to make the map difficult to read. It is the only official publication on a large scale which covers most of the country. All names are in Greek orthography (see p. 447).

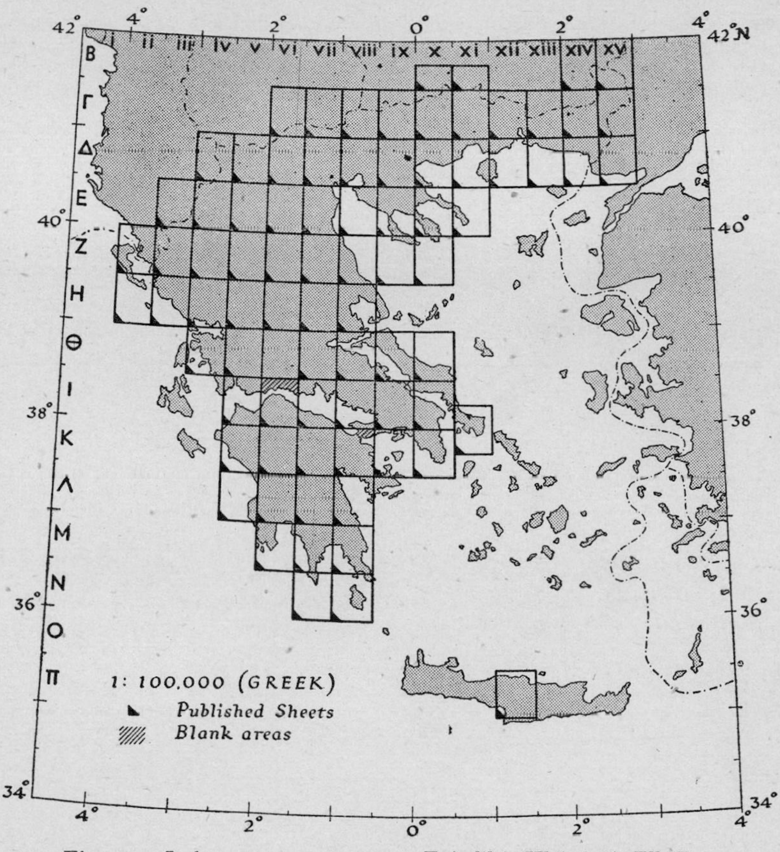

Fig. 110. Index map to 1 : 100,000, *Epitelikós Khártis tis Elládhos*

Sheet Θ V1 and two further sheets of Kríti have been completed since 1941.

(5) 1:200,000. *Carte Normale Aéronautique Internationale*

Single sheet 42 × 55 cm., published by G.A.G.S. in 1932. It covers Thessaloníki and gives inset plans of airfields at Thessaloníki, Sérrai and Kateríni.

Relief is shown by brown contours, brown hill shading and black spot heights. Roads (two categories) in red; railways (two categories) in black; woods and marshes in green; coast line and water in blue. A key to the use of symbols is given in Greek and English.

(6) 1:400,000. *Yenikós Khártis tis Elládhos*

Eleven sheets 45 × 56 cm., published by G.A.G.S. 1923–38, covering almost the whole of mainland Greece (Fig. 111). Drawn on a simple conical projection (standard parallel 38° N): meridian of origin Athínai. Margins of each sheet are divided into 10 min. intervals and lines of latitude and longitude are carried across the map every degree.

Relief is shown by grey contours at 200 m. intervals, every fifth contour emphasized; spot heights in black; grey hill shading is used effectively. Lakes, rivers and marshes are in blue; woods in green; roads (three categories) in red and railways (two categories) in black. All settlements except small villages are named. The quality of the different sheets varies, but the map is usually clear, especially in the north. A further advantage is that almost all the Pelopónnisos is on a single sheet.

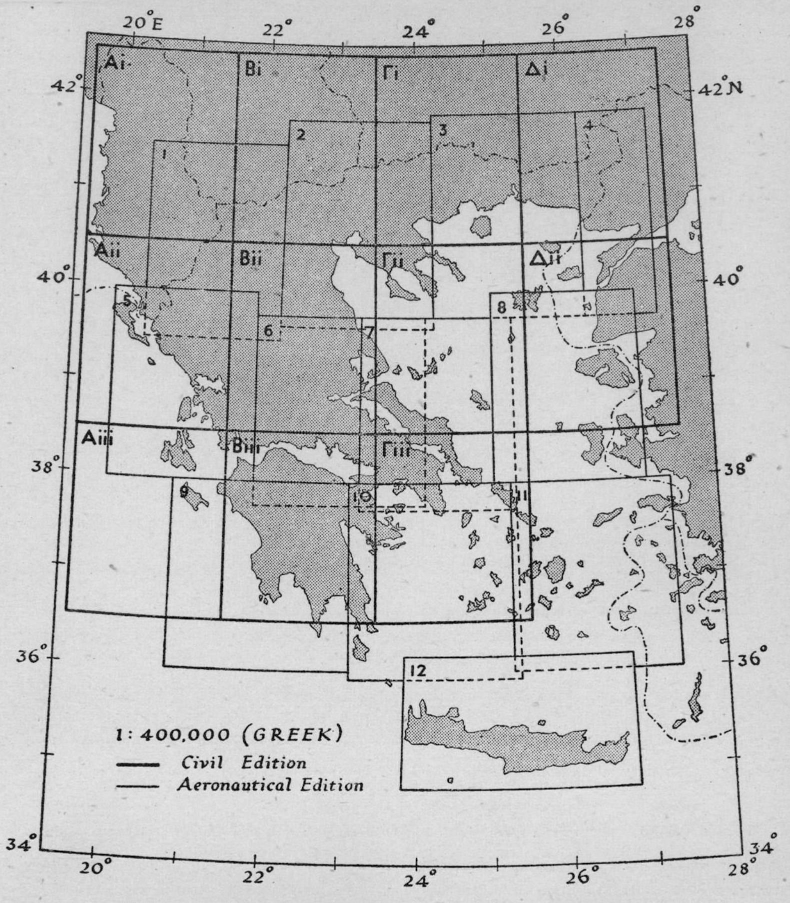

Fig. 111. Index map to Greek official 1 : 400,000 maps

The civil edition is the *Yenikós Khártis tis Elládhos*. Names and titles on the 12 sheets of the *Carte Aéronautique* are given in Greek and French.

(7) 1:400,000. *Carte Aéronautique*

Twelve sheets, varying considerably in size, produced by G.A.G.S. 1932–5, for the Ministry of Air (Fig. 111). Mercator's projection; meridian of origin Greenwich.

Margins of each sheet are divided into 2 min. intervals and meridians and parallels are carried across the sheet at 20 min. intervals.

Relief is shown by brown contours at 20 m. intervals, by pecked lines at 500 and 1500 m. and by layer tinting of three shades of brown; submarine contours of 10 and 20 m. are usually marked; mountain peaks are indicated by open triangles with their approximate heights, and hachuring is used for cliffs.

Hydrographical features are shown in blue, wooded country in green, roads (two categories) and railways (two categories) in black. Aeronautical details are in red, plans and photographs of airports and seaplane bases are inset on appropriate sheets. Names are given both in French and Greek (see p. 447).

Many places have been shown in wrong positions, others are wrongly named; but the map is valuable since it is the only official publication which covers the whole of Greece. The P.C.G.N. has issued a circular correcting the numerous errors of spelling and position of towns.

(8) 1:500,000. *Khártis Odikoú Dhiktíou Elládhos*

Six sheets, published by the Ministry of Communications, 1936. All principal settlements are marked and roads and railways are both divided into two categories. Some sheets are layer coloured, all are contoured. The aim of the map is to show the road network of Greece.

(9) 1:750,000. *Sidhirodhromikón Dhiktíou tis Elládhos*

Two sheets, published by the Greek Ministry of Communications in 1930, show the railway system of Greece. Roads are in black, water in blue and railways in red, divided into four categories according to gauge. In a panel on the southern sheet, railway stations on each route are listed with their distances in km. from the terminus. There are also inset maps of the Athínai-Piraiévs district.

(10) 1:1,000,000. *Carte Normale Aéronautique Internationale*

Single sheet, 54 × 44 cm. published in 1935 for the Ministry of Air. It is said to be based on the Greek 1:100,000. Meridian of origin Greenwich, and lines of latitude and longitude are carried across the map at degree intervals. Colour is used effectively—red for roads (two categories) and railways (two categories), green for woods, blue for water and the names of hydrographical features. Relief is shown by spot heights and by layer colouring, the divisions being 200, 500 and subsequent intervals of 500 m. Lines of magnetic variation and aeronautical details are in black. Names are transliterated into French and a key to the symbols employed is also given in French.

(11) 1:1,000,000. Europe—Aviation

Two sheets 81 × 55 cm. published by G.A.G.S. in 1936. Meridian of origin, Paris.

Relief is shown by layer colouring, divided by the 200, 500, 1,000 and subsequent 1,000 m. contours. Detail of colour, relief, communications and miscellaneous information is similar to that of A 8.

B. Maps Issued by the Geographical Section of the British General Staff

The production of accurate large-scale maps of Greece for English use is extremely difficult. The inadequate cover provided by the Greeks themselves, the inaccuracy of some of their work and the difficulties presented by Greek orthography make the problem complex. Moreover the two principal series issued by G.S.G.S., Series 4087 and Series 4088 (1940), were prepared in a very short space of time, so that there are mistakes in the transference and transliteration of names (see p. 448). Spot heights too, vary considerably from the Greek originals. G.S.G.S. make it clear that these maps are provisional editions.

(1) 1:100,000. Series 4087: The Balkans

Topographical series based on official maps of the Balkan countries, compiled, drawn and printed by the Ordnance Survey, 1940. Thirty-eight provisional sheets of Greece, 60 × 60 cm. (Fig. 112). The series does not cover western Stereá Ellás,

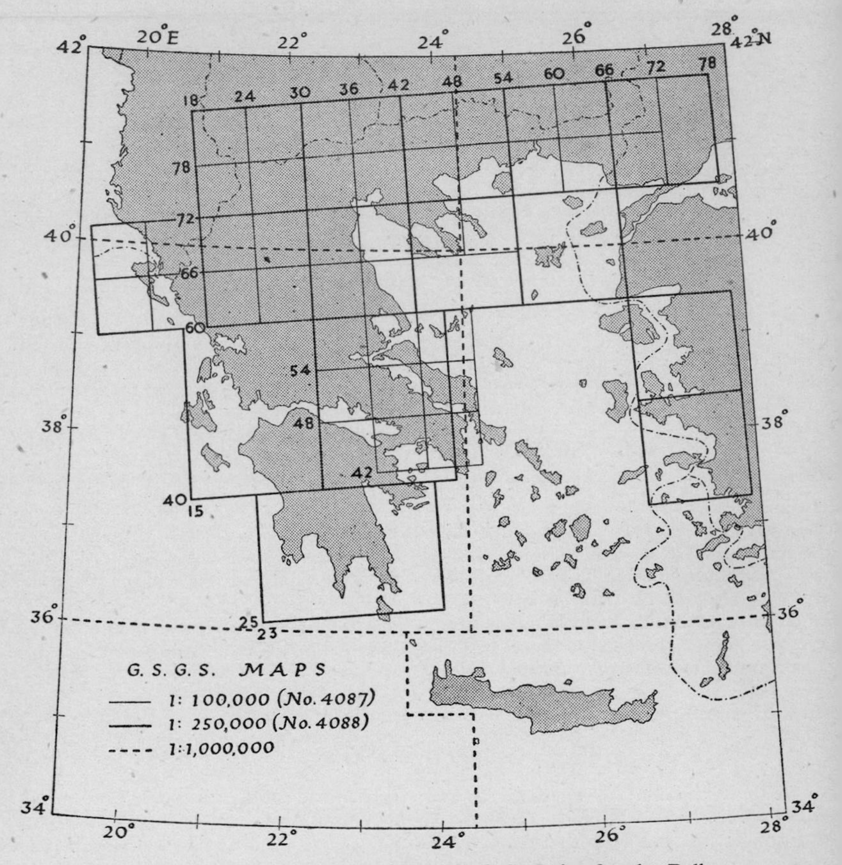

Fig. 112. Index map to the chief G.S.G.S. series for the Balkans

Pelopónnisos and the Greek islands. Kilometre grid, numbered in margins in blue. Outer margin divided into minute intervals of latitude and longitude. Meridian of origin Greenwich.

Relief is shown by contours in red at 50 m. intervals where the information is available, every fifth emphasised. Spot heights in black and cliffs in hachures. Water in blue, trees in green; roads (three categories) and telegraphic communications in red; tracks and paths, railways (four categories) and other miscellaneous information in black. A note on pronunciation is given in the margin.

A second edition of a few sheets was published in 1941, incorporating information from later Greek sheets and military authorities. Brown is used instead of red for contours and roads, but all other detail is the same as above. The spelling of place-names is more accurate than on the provisional edition (see p. 448).

Topographical inaccuracies are all too frequent, and the map should not be relied upon for detailed work. It is being replaced by copies of the 1:100,000 *Epitelikós Khártis tis Elládhos* (A 4), made by 512 (A. Fld. Svy.) Coy. R.E., 1941–. The relief on these sheets is much more accurate: place-names are transliterated (see p. 449).

(2) 1:100,000. Series 2832: Greece

Five sheets, Attikí (2), Lárisa, Fársala, Ayiá, published by the War Office, 1917–18. Those of Attikí are based on the 1:100,000 *Karte von Attica*, by E. Curtius and J. A. Kaupert, 1900; the others upon the Greek 1:75,000 G.A.C.S. 1909–11. The sheets vary in size. Graticule drawn at 5 min. intervals, numbered and lettered to form a grid. Meridian of origin Greenwich.

Relief is shown by contours in brown at 40 m. intervals, every 200 m. accentuated. Cliffs indicated by brown hachures; spot heights in black. Water in blue; woods in green; roads (four categories) and railways (two categories) in black. All other miscellaneous detail in black. Marginal information includes a glossary of words likely to appear on Greek maps and a note on pronunciation of Greek.

(3) 1:100,000. Lower Mesta Karasu (Néstos)

Single sheet, 16 × 30 cm. based on air photographs and published by the Ordnance Survey 1918. Contours in black, water in blue, woods in green. Settlements, roads (two categories), cart-tracks, footpaths and the one railway in black.

(4) 1:250,000. Series 4088: The Balkans

Topographical series based on various official and unofficial maps, of the Balkan countries. Twenty-nine provisional sheets, 48 × 48 cm., of which only twelve concern Greece (Fig. 112). Compiled, drawn and heliographed by the Ordnance Survey 1940. In 1941, three further sheets, 60 × 80 cm., were produced by the 512 (A. Fld. Svy.) Coy. R.E. and heliographed by the Ordnance Survey. They complete the series for the mainland of Greece. Ten-kilometre grid, numbered in blue. Latitude and longitude (sexagesimal from Greenwich) given for each corner of three layer sheets; margins of earlier sheets divided into minute intervals.

Relief is shown by contours in brown at 100 m. intervals, every fifth emphasized; on later sheets interval is 200 m. Spot heights are frequently inaccurate. Water in blue; trees in green; roads (three categories) and telegraphic communications in red; railways (two categories) in black. Settlements are in solid black and are often wrongly named. Names are very infrequent.

(5) 1:250,000. Series 2097: The Balkans and Asia Minor

Six sheets of northern Greece, published by the War Office, 1908–16. Detail similar to B 4. In 1922 certain sheets of this series were issued, with the new Greco-Bulgarian Frontier superimposed.

(6) 1:500,000. Series 4072–4072*a*: Europe and N. Africa (Air)

Compiled and drawn at the War Office, 1940, printed by the Ordnance Survey. Eight sheets, 55 × 67 cm. complete the cover for Greece. Conical orthomorphic projection; graticule divisions 10 min. of latitude and longitude. Outer margins divided into sections of 10 statute miles, lines of equal magnetic declination are drawn across the map at 30-min. intervals. Local mean times as compared with G.M.T. are given in blue.

Relief is shown by brown contours, layer-tinting in purple and black spot heights. Water in blue, woods in green, roads (two categories) in brown, railways (three categories) in black. Miscellaneous information in black.

(7) 1:1,000,000. Series 2758: Europe

Five sheets, K 34, K 35, J 34, J 35, I 35, each covering an area between 4 degrees of latitude and 6 degrees of longitude. J 35 has a serial No. 2555. Compiled, drawn and printed at the Ordnance Surveys from a variety of official and unofficial sources. There have been numerous editions to date of each sheet, from the first editions of 1915–16. Modified Polyconic projection: graticule at degree intervals; meridian of origin Greenwich. Margins divided into 5 min. intervals.

Relief is shown by green contours at 100 and 200 m., then at 200 m. intervals, with layer colouring in green and brown. Spot heights in black. Roads (three categories) in red, railways (three categories) in black; towns of five orders of importance by different symbols; water in blue.

An unlayered edition of this series, with contours in brown, has also been published.

(8) 1:1,000,000. Series 2758: Europe (Air)

Five sheets of this series were published by the War Office in 1939. On them detailed aeronautical information supplied by the Air Ministry has been superimposed in blue.

(9) 1:1,000,000. Series 3884 and 3884*a*: Railways in Greece and Albania

A single sheet, 91 × 64 cm. (north margin) and × 70 cm. (south margin) first published at the War Office in 1939; second edition with railways corrected in 1941. Based upon G.S.G.S. Series 2758. Modified Polyconic projection; graticule at degree intervals. Meridian of origin Greenwich. Railways are shown on the revised sheet in seven categories in red—normal gauge with double or single line, single line being doubled, under construction or projected; narrow gauge, narrow gauge being converted to normal gauge, under construction or projected. Rivers and marshes are in blue; towns are graded in five orders of importance. No other information is given.

(10) 1:1,000,000. Series 2664: Maps of the Balkan States

Single sheet, published by the War Office, 1915, showing the 1912 Frontiers, corrected to October 1915. Miscellaneous details, settlements, roads, railways, etc.

C. Greek Admiralty Charts

The government department responsible for Admiralty surveys and charts is the *Hydrographic Service of the Royal Marine* which has built up a considerable reputation for accuracy, despite the limited means at its disposal. Charts numbering 1–12 and 14–48 were published in Athínai between 1917 and 1939, almost all of which have been corrected to 1939. They vary considerably in size and scale, and in the policy adopted for place-names (see p. 447). The meridian of origin is Greenwich and on charts covering large areas the margins are divided into minute intervals. As with the British Admiralty charts, Mercator's projection is used, lines being carried across the sheet at each degree. Insets of port plans, anchorages and panorama sketches of coasts are numerous.

Land is coloured yellow; directional lights are usually marked by yellow circles with a red centre; all other detail is in black. Relief is indicated on large scale charts by closely spaced contours, or more probably by form-lines, the vertical interval varying from chart to chart and often from place to place on the same chart: the heights of coastal peaks are given in metres. No reliance should be placed on the accuracy of land information. On small scale charts the coastal lands are closely hachured. Soundings are in metres and there is a close network of readings offshore. There is no uniformity in the choice of submarine contours, except in showing the 5 m. line on all charts of anchorages. A conversion table from metres to feet and fathoms is printed on most sheets. Rivers, marshes, roads, railways and settlements are shown by appropriate symbols, but detail is limited to a narrow coastal belt.

The following list gives the number of each chart, followed by the title, transliterated by the P.C.G.N. system. Insets are shown by the use of brackets and the scale is given only once, unless there is lack of uniformity (Fig. 113):

(1) Stilís Harbour, 1:10,000.
(2) Vólos Harbour; Pteleón Bay; Vathoúdhi Bay, 1:20,000.
(3) Salamís Arsenal and Keratsiní Bay, 1:10,000.
(4) Préveza Straits and Bay, 1:10,000.
(5) Návplion Harbour, 1:5,000.
(6) Evrípos Channel, 1:25,000. (Vatónda Bay; Evrípos Strait; Stenó and Mikró-Vathí Bays; Levkandí Bay; Búrji Channel, 1:10,000.)
(7) Mesolóngion Lagoon and Bay, 1:50,000.
(8) Tínos Harbour; Síros Harbour, 1:10,000; Foínix Bay, 1:20,000.
(9) Levkás Canal, 1:10,000. (Visilikí Bay, 1:10,000, Vlikhón Bay, 1:25,000.)
(10) Amvrakía Gulf, 1:50,000. (Vónitsa Bay, 1:20,000.)
(11) Coasts of Greece, 1:1,000,000.
(12) Goumenítsa Bay, 1:20,000.
(13) Not published.
(14) Alexandroúpolis Bay, 1:10,000.
(15) Aïvali Bay and Mosko island, 1:40,000.
(16) Gulf of Thessaloníki, 1:40,000. (Thessaloníki Harbour, 1:7,500; Thessaloníki Bay, 1:20,000.)
(17) Mégara Strait, 1:20,000.
(18) Zakínthos Harbour; Katákolon Harbour; Killíni Harbour, 1:10,000; Kalámai Harbour, 1:6,666.
(19) Domvraína and Posidhonía Gulfs, 1:50,000. (Kórinthos-Posidhonía, 1:10,000.)
(20) Krionéri Bay; Pátrai Harbour, 1:10,000.
(21) Atalándi-Oreoí Channel, 1:50,000. (Likhádes Islands, 1:20,000; Maliaic Gulf, 1:50,000.)
(22) Piraiévs and Fáliron Bay, 1:10,000.
(23) Kímolos Straits; Mílos Bay, 1:20,000.
(24) Áyios Nikólaos, Kéa; Koutalá Bay; Livádhi Bay; Loutrá Bay; Mérikha Bay, 1:10,000; Áyios Stéfanos, 1:20,000.
(25) Náxos Bay, 1:15,000; Míkonos Bay, 1:20,000.
(26) Gávrion Bay; Ándros Harbour; Kórthion Harbour, 1:20,000.
(27) Póros Strait and Harbour, 1:10,000.
(28) Kástron-Límnos; Áyios Pávlos; Kondiá, 1:10,000.
(29) Aíyina Straits, 1:10,000. (Angístri Channel, 1:10,000.)
(30) Kástro Bay-Sífnos, 1:5,000; Kamáres Bay; Vathí Bay; Kondós Bay; Fáros Bay; Platíyialos Bay, 1:10,000.
(31) Vathí Bay; Karavostási Bay; Tres Klisiés; Íos Harbour; Manganári Bay, 1:10,000.
(32) Elevsís Gulf, 1:20,000.
(33) Strimón Gulf, 1:20,000; Stavrós Bay; Elevthéron Bay; Stratónion Bay, 1:10,000.
(34) Páros Harbour and Andíparos Straits; Mármara, Tsipído, Trío Bays; Náousa Bay; Despotikó Bay, 1:20,000.
(35) Athínai Gulf, 1:50,000.
(36) Khaniá Harbour, 1:5,000; Iráklion Harbour, 1:10,000; Réthimnon Bays, 1:15,000; Soúdha Bay, 1:20,000.

(37) Athínai Gulf and Attikí Coasts, 1:75,000.
(38) Psará Bay; Khíos Harbour, 1:10,000.
(39) Mitilíni; Eressós Anchorage; Plomárion Harbour; Sígri Harbour; Garbía; Yéras Harbour, 1:20,000.
(40) Gulf of Pátrai, 1:100,000. (Krionéri Bay; Návpaktos Bay; Monastiráki Bay; Pápas Cape; Killíni Harbour; Aíyon Bay; Pátrai Harbour, 1:20,000; Mesolóngion Canal and Harbour, 1:25,000; Petalás Harbour; Oxiá Bay, 1:50,000.)
(41) Pílos Bay, 1:20,000.
(42) Spétsai Anchorage and Khéli Harbour, 1:25,000. (Ídhra Harbour, Áyios Nikólaos, 1:5,000.)

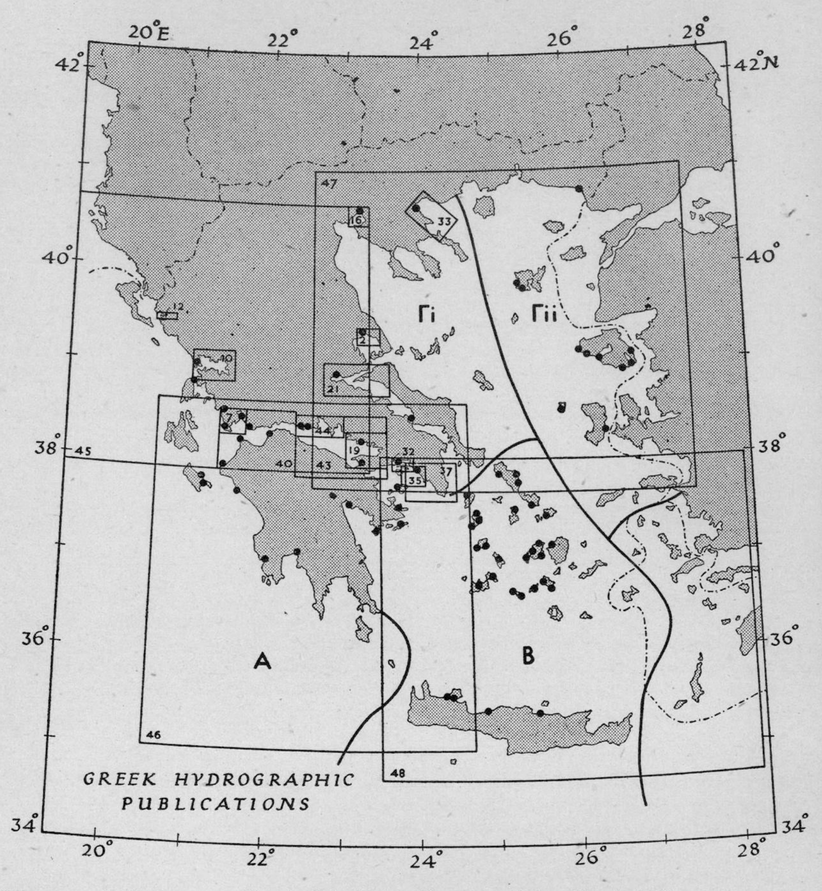

Fig. 113. Index map to Greek Admiralty Charts and the Greek Sailing Directions

The boundaries of the areas described in each of the four volumes of the Greek Sailing Directions, *Navtiliakí Odhiyíi ton Ellinikón Aktón* (Ploïyós), A, B, Γi and Γii are indicated by the heavy curved lines. The rectangles show the areas covered by the larger sheets of Greek government charts. The black dots locate the more important port plans shown on these charts (see pp. 407–9).

(43) Kórinthos, Gulf and Isthmus, 1:100,000. (Xilókastron Anchorage; Sikionía Anchorage; Vrakháti Anchorage, 1:20,000; Kórinthos Isthmus; Loutráki Bay, 1:25,000.)
(44) Itéa Gulf, 1:25,000. (Áyios Ioánnis, 1:10,000; Eratiní Bay and Pánormos Bays; Vídhavis Bay, 1:20,000; Andíkira Bay, 1:50,000.)
(45) North West coasts of Greece, 1:500,000.
(46) South West coasts of Greece, 1:500,000.
(47) North East coasts of Greece, 1:500,000.
(48) South East coasts of Greece, 1:500,000.

D. British Admiralty Charts

A complete list of British charts of the Greek coasts, together with an index map, is given in the *Catalogue of Admiralty charts and other Hydrographic Publications* (London, annual). The earliest charts were first published in 1843, and by 1900 all the coasts had been surveyed, though not in detail. Numerous new editions or large corrections have been made from time to time. In recent years British charts have been corrected mainly from the hydrographic surveys carried out by the Greeks: most have been corrected to 1939.

Apart from their value for navigation the charts show topographical details of the mainland and islands which are not always to be found on Greek official maps. Thus, chart 1556 (Gulf of Vólos) on a scale of 1:109,000 is very well hachured and is useful in showing the relief of the Pílion region. The peninsula south from Pílion is not shown on the Greek, 1:100,000. It must be remembered however, that the accuracy of any of these charts is determined largely by that of the original survey and the frequency with which they are revised. The transliteration policies which have been adopted from time to time for use on these charts is discussed on p. 448.

E. Miscellaneous Maps

General and Topographical Maps

(1) 1:10,000. Greek-Yugoslav Border: Devdelija Area

Eight sheets, 30 × 50 cm. published by the *Armée d'Orient Aéronautique Militaire* in 1916. Kilometre grid. Very little detail shown: no contours; rivers marked and valleys hachured; sands and marshes indicated. Roads (two categories), railways and settlements are most important features of the map.

(2) 1:20,000. Salonica Army Map: British, French and Italian Surveys for Macedonian Campaign

Published by British, French and Italian Topographical Services, 1916–19. There are 169 sheets of varying sizes. Kilometre grid. Contours in brown at 20 m. intervals, every fifth emphasized; spot heights in black. Water in blue; roads of all types, railways and settlements in black. Names are transliterated, and geographical terms may be in any one of the three languages.

(3) 1:25,000. Northern Greece, including Serbian-Grecian boundary

Published by the German-Bulgarian Topographical Survey, 1916–18. Seventy-four sheets, 55 × 55 cm. Kilometre grid. Contours in brown at 10 m. intervals; frequent spot heights. Roads, railways, rivers and settlements in black. Place-names are in Cyrillic, with transliterations.

(4) 1:25,000. Part of the Serbian-Grecian boundary

Published by the Serbian Topographical Section, 1918. Twelve sheets of varying sizes. Kilometre grid. Contours in brownish red, every 20 m. Rivers in blue, roads, railways and settlements in black. Place-names are in Cyrillic.

(5) 1:25,000. Greece

Surveyed and reproduced by 512 (A. Fld. Svy.) Coy. R.E. 1941. Fourteen sheets, based on Greek 1:50,000 (G.A.G.S.) and partly revised from air photographs. They cover an area west from the Gulf of Thérmai to Véroia. Kilometre grid. Contours in brown at 100 m. intervals, though occasionally 20 m. contours are inserted; spot heights in black. Rivers, marsh and sea in blue; canals, roads, railways and settlements in black. The utilization of the land is also shown.

Fourteen strip maps, of the Édhessa-Véroia area were issued by the Field Survey in 1941. They are based on air photographs.

(6) 1:25,000. *Karten von Attika*

Published by E. Curtius and J. A. Kaupert for the *Kaiserl. deutsche archäeologische Institut*, 1881–93. Twenty-one sheets, 47 × 44 cm. Meridian of origin Ferro. Contours at 20 m. intervals and hachures are in brown; spot heights in black; depths offshore given in metres. Water in blue, roads and railways in black. The map was the result of the first detailed scientific survey to be made of a large area in Greece. It is beautifully produced. In addition to these 21 sheets, four special sheets of Athínai-Piraiévs were published on a scale of 1:12,500.

(7) 1:50,000. Salonica Army Map: British, French, Serbian, Italian and Greek surveys for Macedonian Campaign

Published by the Topographical Services of the countries mentioned above. Sixty-six sheets. Kilometre grid. Details of the series as in E (2).

(8) 1:50,000. *Khártis Ellinikoú Vasilíou*

A French enlargement of the Greek 1:75,000 (G.A.G.S.) by the *Service Topographique des A.A.O.*, 1917–18. Eighteen sheets of the Lárisa area and Kérkira. Names transliterated and generic part of compound place-names translated into French.

(9) 1:50,000. *Khártis Ellinikoú Vasilíou*

Enlargements and reproductions of the Greek 1:75,000 (G.A.C.S.) by the R.E. Printing Section, G.H.Q., B.S.F. No. 256, 1917. Four sheets—Ayiá, Lárisa, Témbi, Tírnavos. Names are transliterated and an English key to the use of symbols has been added.

(10) 1:50,000

Reproductions of the Greek 1:50,000 (G.A.G.S.) by 512 (A. Fld. Svy.) Coy. R.E., 1938–41. Eight sheets, kilometre grid. Contours in blue-grey or brown; water in blue; roads in red and other features in black. All names are transliterated. Cartographical details as given in A (2).

(11) 1:50,000

Provisional reproductions in grey of forty-four Greek 1:50,000 (G.A.G.S.) sheets by the Survey Directorate. G.H.Q., M.E.F. Kilometre grid. Red overprinting of a few key names, transliterated phonetically. Details as in A (2).

(12) 1:50,000. *Die Ebene von Argos*

Published by Dr H. Lehmann, in *Zeit. Ges. Erdkunde* (Berlin, 1931). Single sheet, 53 × 55 cm. Kilometre grid; meridian of origin Greenwich. Contours at 25 m. intervals, every fourth emphasised; spot heights; depths offshore in metres and submarine contours at 10, 25 and subsequent intervals of 25 m.; cliffs hachured. Land utilization shown. Names transliterated into German.

(13) 1:50,000. Survey of the Struma Valley and Plain of Philippi

Six sheets of various sizes, surveyed and published by Messrs Sir J. Jackson, Ltd., 1922 for the Greek government. The object of the survey, which was made by tacheometer, carefully controlled by triangulation, was the preliminary to engineering works to prevent flooding. The map, plotted from detailed sheets on a scale of 1:10,000, is gridded and coloured. Contours are in dotted lines; railways, roads and woods in appropriate symbols. The drainage pattern is clearly shown.

(14) 1:100,000. *Karten von Attika*

Published by E. Curtius and J. A. Kaupert, Berlin, 1900. Eleven sheets, 23 × 22 cm. Meridian of origin Ferro. Contours at 25 m. intervals, every fourth emphasized. Roads (three categories), railways (two categories) in black. Woods shown.

(15) 1:100,000. *Übersichtskarte von Attika, mit den antiken Namen*

Published by E. Curtius and J. A. Kaupert, Berlin, no date, but about 1903. Single sheet, 71 × 89 cm. Not contoured and other details as above. Ancient names are overlaid in red italics.

(16) 1:100,000. *Attikí*

Published by K. Grigouras, Athínai, 1933. Single sheet, based on original work and air photographs by K. Grigouras and P. Kalapothakis. Meridian of origin Athínai. Contours in brown; settlements and roads (two categories) in red; railways and miscellaneous information in black.

(17) 1:200,000. *Carte de la Grèce* (Romanized)

Published by the *Dépôt de la Guerre*, Paris, 1852. Twenty sheets based on the first scientific survey of Greece. Meridian of origin Paris: graticule at 25 min. intervals. Relief is shown by very close hachuring in black, which masks all details of roads and settlements and makes the map very difficult to read.

(18) 1:200,000. *Generalkarte von Mitteleuropa*

Published by the *K.u.K. Militärgeographisches Institut, Wien.* First edition produced 1906, with revisions up to 1937. Each sheet, 43 × 54 cm., covers one degree of latitude and longitude. Meridian of origin Ferro. Margins divided into min. intervals, and lines of latitude carried across the map at 15 min. intervals. The sheets are numbered and indexed by giving the central latitude and longitude for each sheet. Relief is occasionally shown by brown contours at 50, 100 and then every 100 m., with light brown hill-shading. Usually, however, brown hachures and black spot heights are employed. Water in blue, woods in green, roads (six categories) and railways (four categories) in black. Different symbols are used to distinguish relative sizes of towns.

There is a Greek edition of those sheets relevant to Greece, issued in 1910–12, but it shows very few improvements.

(19) 1:200,000. Demilitarized Zone in Thrace: recorded on Greek maps dated 1920–1923

Published by the Thracian Demilitarized Zone Commission, 1924. Two sheets, Xánthi, Demotika; 41 × 55 cm. Meridian of origin Ferro. Contours, roads (three categories), railways and settlements in black.

(20) 1:400,000. Greece

Reproduction of Greek 1:400,000 *Yenikós Khártis tis Elládhos* by 512 (A. Fld. Svy.) Coy. R.E. 1941. The map is gridded, and names are transliterated. Topographical terms are translated. For details see A (6).

(21) 1:500,000. *Khártis tis Elládhos*

Published by K. Grigouras and C. Papamandellos, Athínai, 1929. Six sheets, 54 × 59 cm. Meridian of origin Athínai; graticule at degree intervals. Contours at 200 m. intervals in brown; spot heights. Water in blue, roads (two categories) in red, railways and settlements in black. Names in Greek.

Copies of this map have been published for English use, with names transliterated and the generic part of names translated.

(22) 1:600,000. *Ellás*

Published by K. Grigouras and P. Kalapothakis, Athínai, 1934. Two sheets. Meridian of origin Athínai; contours, chief towns, railways (two categories) and air-routes. The chief purpose of the map is to show administrative boundaries. It is now out of date.

(23) 1:1,000,000. *Néos Politikós Khártis tis Elládhos*

Single sheet published by M. Saliveros, Athínai, 1936. In Greek; Meridian of origin Athínai.

(24) 1:1,250,000. *Khártis tis Megális mas Elládhos*

First edition was published in 1920 by M. Saliveros, Athínai; a revised edition was issued in 1931. The map shows chief towns, railways and spot heights, and is coloured to show administrative divisions.

(25) 1:1,750,000. Greece

A single sheet, 60 × 50 cm., published by John Bartholomew and Son, Ltd. (Edinburgh, 1943). Margins divided into degree intervals (latitude sexagesimal from Greenwich); meridians and parallels drawn across the map to form a graticule.

Relief is shown by black dotted contours at 100, 300, 500, 1,000, 2,000 and 3,000 m.: layer tinting in seven shades of green and brown: spot heights in black in feet. Sea and lakes in blue; roads (two categories) in brown; railways (standard, metre and narrow gauge) in brown; canals in black pectinate line; boundaries (three types) in purple.

All names are given in their official forms, adopting the P.C.G.N. policies for the transliteration of Greek and Cyrillic orthography. Geographical terms are translated into English. This is the folding map at the end of Vol. II.

(26) 1:2,000,000. Greece and the Aegean

Plate 48 of *The Times Survey Atlas of the World*, published by 'The Times' (London, 1920) and prepared by J. G. Bartholomew. The plate, 33 × 20 cm., has a graticule formed by meridians and parallels (sexagesimal from Greenwich) at degree intervals.

Relief is shown by black dotted contours at 100, 300, 500 with subsequent intervals of 500–3,000 m.: layer tinting in eight shades of green and brown, submarine contour at 100 fm., spot heights in feet in black. Lakes in blue; sea in two shades of blue. No roads are marked; railways in black (double and single lines). International frontiers (1920) in broad red band; administrative boundaries in thinner red lines.

(27) 1:2,000,000. Italy and the Balkans

A single sheet, 96×71 cm., published by John Bartholomew and Son, Ltd. (Edinburgh, 1940). Detail is very much the same as in E, 26, though revised in places. Roads in red (two categories); international frontiers in solid purple; boundaries, pre-1940, in purple pecked line.

The map is clear, attractive and of considerable value for general use.

Communication Maps

(1) 1:50,000. *Route de Bralo à Itea*

Published by the *Service Topographique des A.A.O.*, 1918. Two sheets, kilometre grid, graticule at 5 min. intervals. Meridian of origin Athínai. Contours at 20 m. intervals in brown, every fifth accentuated; spot heights. Rivers in blue, railways, roads and settlements in black. Woods and cultivated land are marked. Names transliterated into a French form.

(2) 1:200,000. *Évvoia-Voiotía*

Published by the Hellenic Tourist Bureau in 1932. A gridded sheet, layer coloured, showing railways (two categories) in black and roads (three categories) in red.

(3) 1:500,000. *Carte Routière: Athènes-Salonique-Coula*

An undated sheet published by C. A. Contogonis for the *Automobile et Touring Club de Grèce*, before 1930. Contours are in brown at 500 m. intervals; spot heights in black. Water in blue, railways in black and roads (two categories) in red. Bridges are marked and distances are given in kilometres along the principal roads from Athínai.

(4) 1:600,000. *Autostrassenkarten*

Sheet 90 and parts of sheets 82 and 83 published by Freytag and Berndt Wien, 1931–40. Relief is only indicated by spot heights and road gradients. Rivers, coastline and sea in blue; woods in green; sailing routes in brown pecked lines. Principal roads in yellow (four categories) with distances from chief centres and gradients printed alongside. Lesser roads shown in brown. Names are in Greek script with a transliteration into a German form in brackets.

(5) 1:1,000,000. *Carte du Réseau des Routes Principales de la Grèce*

An undated sheet 70×62 cm., published by C. A. Contogonis, Athínai, *c.* 1934 for the *Automobile et Touring Club de Grèce*. No grid or graticule. Sea in blue; rivers, outline, chief towns and railways in black. Motor roads in red with distances in kilometres from chief centres. Sea routes are marked with distances in kilometres between ports.

(6) 1:1,000,000. Greece and Albania

Single sheet, reproduced by G.S.G.S. 3884 (see B. 9) by 512 (A. Fld. Svy.) Coy. R.E., 1941. Railways are shown in three categories only.

Frontier Maps

(1) 1:25,000. *Frontière Gréco-Bulgare* (*Traité de Neuilly*, 27 November, 1919)

Published by the *Commission de délimitation*, 1921. Thirty-seven sheets; meridian of origin Paris. The map is contoured and shows all settlements and roads. The same authority published a detailed description of the frontier to accompany the map.

(2) 1:25,000. *Carte de la Frontière Gréco-Turque*, 1925–6

Ten sheets, dated 1928, were published by the *Commission de délimitation*, 1925–26. Each sheet measures 56 × 74 cm. Margins divided into minute intervals; contours every 10 m. in black, water in blue, roads (two categories), and settlements in red, railways, vegetation and miscellaneous details in black. Names are in a transliterated form.

(3) 1:50,000. *Carte de la Nouvelle Frontière Turco-Grecque* 1881—*executée pour la commission de délimitation*

Fourteen sheets, linographed by the Int. Dept., War Office, 1881. Meridian of origin Paris. Each sheet, 58 × 44 cm., maps a narrow zone on either side of the frontier. Contours in brown at 20 m. intervals; rivers in black, woods differentiated by appropriate symbols. Names are transliterated into a French form.

(4) 1:50,000. *Carte de la Frontière Turco-Héllenique indiquant le tracé arrêté sur le terrain par la Commission Internationale de* 1897–8

Fourteen sheets, heliozincographed at the Ordnance Survey, 1898. The sheets are based on those of 1881 (3), revised by Greek and Turkish officers.

(5) 1:50,000. *Carte de la Frontière Gréco-Albanaise*

Published by the *Comm. Int. de délimitation des frontières de l'Albanie*, 1925. Seven sheets; meridian of origin Paris. Contours at 20 m. intervals, spot heights. Roads and tracks differentiated. Names transliterated.

(6) 1:400,000. Map to illustrate the rectification of the Turco-Greek frontier in 1897

Single sheet, published by the Int. Dept., War Office, 1898. The boundary is shown as delimited in 1881 (3) and the rectification made in 1897 (4).

Maps and Plans in Guide Books

(1) *Les Guides Bleus—Grèce*

Published by the *Librairie Hachette* (Paris, 1935). There are forty-one maps on varying scales, mostly in colour. In addition, there are seventy-seven plans of archaeological sites and modern towns.

(2) *Baedeker's Greece*

Published by K. Baedeker (Leipzig and London, fourth revised edition, 1909). It includes twenty-four plans of archaeological sites and modern towns, on scales varying from 1:1,500 to 1:25,000. There are also fifteen maps of regions most frequented by tourists, and a 'Travelling Map of Greece, 1:1,000,000' which extends north to the Greco-Turkish frontier of 1881.

F. Atlases

(1) *Atlas Climatique de la Grèce*

The Atlas was produced by E. G. Mariolopoulos and A. N. Livathinos (Athènes, 1935) and includes coloured maps (often very generalized) of each climatic element for Greece and the surrounding seas. Names and keys to the use of symbols are given in French and Greek.

(2) *Khártis Attikís*

Published by 'Elevtheroudakis' (Athínai, 1923). A map of Attikí on a scale of 1:100,000, backed with linen 70 × 90 cm., and cut up into 30 sections. Bound in a cover, 14 × 20 cm., with 48 pages of gazetteer. The margins of the map are divided into minute intervals; graticule at 10 min. intervals and the resulting rectangles numbered and lettered to form a key to gazetteer.

Relief is shown by brown contours at 25 m. intervals, every second emphasized; by brown hill shading and by spot heights. Water in blue, woods in green, roads and tracks (four categories) and railways (two categories) in black.

(3) *Hellas-Pelopónnisos. Atlas de poche à l'usage des tourists*

Published by K. Grigouras (Athínai, 1936). A map of Attikí and Pelopónnisos, on a scale of 1:400,000 cut up into six sections and bound in a cover (25 × 17 cm.) with a general map, a plan of Athínai and 23 pages of illustrated description of places of interest. The map is poorly printed and shows roads and railways, with relief represented by crude shading. Names are in both Greek and Roman orthography.

Appendix II

GAZETTEER OF ANTIQUITIES

The Gazetteer, which includes the principal archaeological sites in Greece (Figs. 114 and 115), is arranged in alphabetical order. The name of the site is given in the conventional English spelling and is usually followed in brackets by the name of the modern settlement, transliterated according to the P.C.G.N. system. In some instances, however, there is no conventional English name, and in these cases the name of the modern settlement makes the only heading. Throughout the text, personal names and well-known archaeological terms are given in the conventional spelling.

Aegina (Aíyina)

Island in the Saronic Gulf. Reached by steamer from Piraiévs in 2 hr. The steamer touches at Aíyina the capital, where remains of the ancient ports are visible. To the north, a single column marks the site of the *Temple of Aphrodite* (fifth century B.C.), built above an earlier sanctuary. Immediately to the east, a strongly fortified prehistoric town, continuously occupied throughout the Bronze Age, has recently been excavated. In the north-east corner of the island (2½ hr. by mule track) the *Temple of Aphaea*, famous for its situation and its sculptures, stands on a terrace, surrounded by pines. It was built of local stone to commemorate the Battle of Salamis (480 B.C.); twenty of its columns are standing. The sculptures from the pediments were bought in 1812 by Prince Louis of Bavaria and transported to Munich. On the left of the track to the temple, about 1 hr. from the town, are the ruins of many chapels, monasteries and houses, all that is left of Palaiokhóra, the medieval town where the inhabitants used to take refuge when attacked by pirates. On the mountain peak (Óros) which dominates the island stood an open-air altar of Zeus. The path to the summit goes by an ancient *Sanctuary of Aphaea*, of which the terrace wall is a fine example of Hellenic masonry.

Amphissa (Ámfissa)

In Fthiótis-Fokís; on the road from Itéa to Brálos. Reached by steamer from Piraiévs to Itéa; or by road from Athínai via Livádhia. There are extensive and well-preserved remains of the great medieval fortress (mostly Catalan), and of several churches.

Andravídha

In Ilía; station on the railway between Pátrai and Pírgos. The old capital of the Frankish princes of Achaea was here. There are remains of the choir of their Gothic *Cathedral of Santa Sophia*, in which the Frankish parliament often met.

Árgos

In Argolís; 4 km. from the sea at the head of the Gulf of Argolís. Reached by train or road from Athínai. To the south of the town are the remains of a well-preserved Greek *Theatre*, and of some remarkable Roman mosaics; to the north, on a low hill (Aspís), are the remains of an Hellenic fortress and sanctuary. The *Citadel* (Lárisa), partly Byzantine, partly Venetian and partly Turkish, rests on the original Hellenic foundations; traces of the Mycenaean circuit wall and gateway have also been found. Árgos was completely destroyed by Ibrahim Pasha in the Greek War of Independence, and since then has been overshadowed by Návplion.

Heraeum of Árgos, the renowned sanctuary of Hera, lies on the road to Návplion, 2 hr. from Árgos. The ruins, of which little more than foundations remain, are partly those of the oldest Greek temple known and partly of a later temple (420 B.C.), which contained the colossal gold and ivory statue of a goddess, by the sculptor Poliklitos. The temples stand on terraces, approached by flights of steps, and the whole complex of temples, propylaea, porticoes and other buildings, backed by the rugged mountains of Argolís, must have been highly impressive.

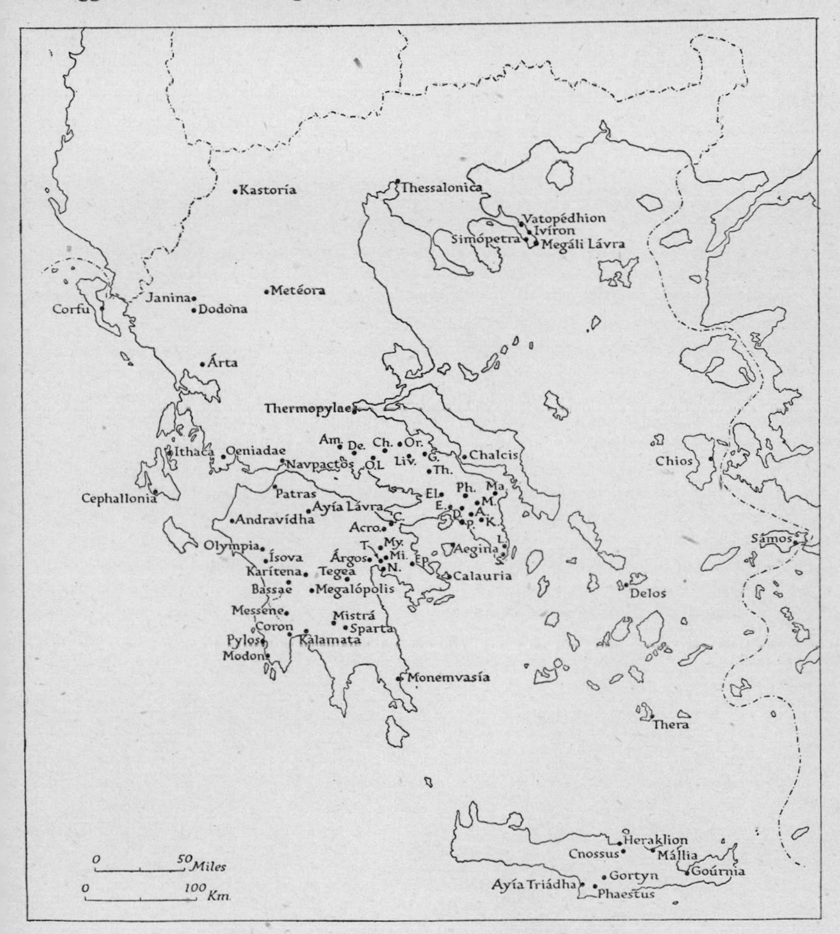

Fig. 114. Archaeological sites in Greece

The map shows the position of only those places mentioned in the Gazetteer, and is not intended to show all archaeological sites. For a key to the abbreviations see Fig. 115.

ÁRTA

In Árta; on the road from Agrínion to Ioánnina. There are few ancient Greek remains, but the thirteenth- and fourteenth-century Byzantine churches are of great interest. Among these, the church of *Panayía Parigorítissa* is remarkable for certain structural peculiarities, for its numerous cupolas, its elaborate ornamental brickwork, and its sculptures in Italian style; the church of *Áyios Vassílios* for its brickwork, and *Ayía Theodhóra* for the cenotaph of St Theodora, wife of Michael II, despot of Epirus.

ATHENS (ATHÍNAI)

In Attikí. Though a great number of the many buildings that once adorned the most renowned of Greek cities have ceased to exist, more ancient buildings have survived in Athínai than in any other place in Greece, and among them the Parthenon is held by many to be the most perfect piece of architecture in the world. The principal group of remains is on the Acropolis (Fig. 116), where four outstanding examples of Greek architecture in its best period can be studied; the other remains are scattered over a fairly wide area lying mostly to the north of the Acropolis, or along its southern flank (Fig. 117).

The Acropolis (Plate 77)

The present entrance to the Acropolis, at the foot of the steps leading to the Propylaea, is through the *Beulé gate*, named after a French archaeologist who extricated it from the middle of a Turkish bastion. The gateway is Byzantine, but the flanking pylons date from the fourth century A.D.

Originally a Mycenaean stronghold, like Mycenae or Tiryns, the Acropolis was surrounded by a wall of 'cyclopaean' masonry, of which remains are visible here and there, especially in the south-west corner behind the south wing of the Propylaea. The entrance to the stronghold was by a gateway on the north approached by a ramp. Just within the entrance stood the Mycenaean palace.

The four principal buildings still on the Acropolis date from the second half of the fifth century B.C., and formed part of the programme of Pericles for beautifying Athens. They are the Erechtheum on the north side, the Parthenon or Temple of Athena, the Propylaea or monumental western entrance, and the Temple of Athena of Victory (Athíne Níki). But the present rather bare appearance of the Acropolis gives an imperfect idea of what it really looked like, for there were other less conspicuous buildings, shrines of various gods and goddesses and above all a forest of votive statues. Among these towered the great bronze *statue of Athena Promachus*, 9 m. in height, which was transported to Constantinople in the sixth century A.D.

The Erechtheum replaced an earlier shrine and was the holiest spot on the Acropolis; for here, the contest for Attica between Athena and Poseidon had, it was believed, taken place, and here the sacred olive tree had sprouted from the ground. The present building is distinguished by its elegant Ionic columns and delicate detail, and by the famous porch supported by figures of standing maidens. The second figure from the west is a reproduction in plaster of the original, bought by Lord Elgin and now in the British Museum (Plate 78).

The Parthenon replaced two earlier temples and was built 447–432 B.C. Owing to the steep fall of the rock to the south, most of it rests on a substructure, and the ground to the south has been raised to its present level by means of a filling. The depth of this filling is as much as 15 m. at the southern edge, where it is contained by an ancient wall built by Cimon about 470 B.C. (Plate 79).

The temple is in the Doric style, of Pentelic marble. The celebrated sculptor Phidias directed the work of the building, and also made the colossal statue of Athena, to house which the temple was destined; the whole undertaking was under the general control of Pericles himself. Apart from the excellence of its proportions, the aesthetic impression produced by the Parthenon is due in part to a skilfully calculated curvature in the construction of steps and architrave, and in part to the exterior columns. These have the normal *éntasis* (swelling) and are not strictly vertical since their axes are inclined inwards. The purpose of these refinements was mainly to correct the optical illusion which long straight lines would have produced. The gables (pediments) at either end were filled with figures sculptured n the round; below the cornice were panels (metopes) sculptured in relief, and round the outside of the temple proper (*sīkos*) just below the roof ran a continuous frieze of processional figures, also sculptured in relief. To form a conception of the exterior of the temple, when complete, it must be remembered that the metopes and many architectural details were enhanced by polychromy, the favourite colours

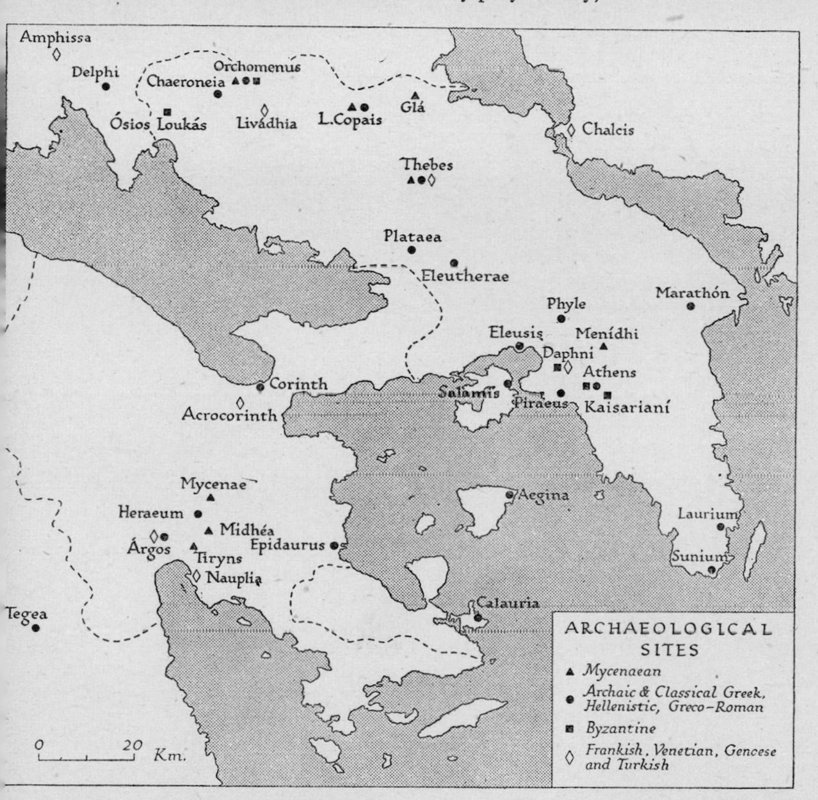

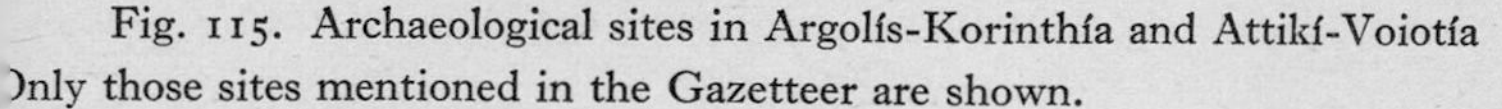
Fig. 115. Archaeological sites in Argolís-Korinthía and Attikí-Voiotía
Only those sites mentioned in the Gazetteer are shown.

being rather bright red and blue. The temple itself, that is, the core of the building, as distinct from the colonnades (peristyle) that surrounded it, was divided by a wall into two parts, an eastern and a western, each with a pillared portico. The eastern part was subdivided by rows of columns into three naves; at the end of the central nave, almost reaching to the roof, stood the huge gold and ivory statue of Athena, the work of Phidias. It was taken to Constantinople in A.D. 426. The western part probably contained the temple treasure. On its western wall can be seen traces of paintings dating from the time when the Parthenon was used as a Christian Church. It was converted to this use in the sixth century, and it remained in Orthodox hands until 1209, when the Franks adopted it as their cathedral. After the

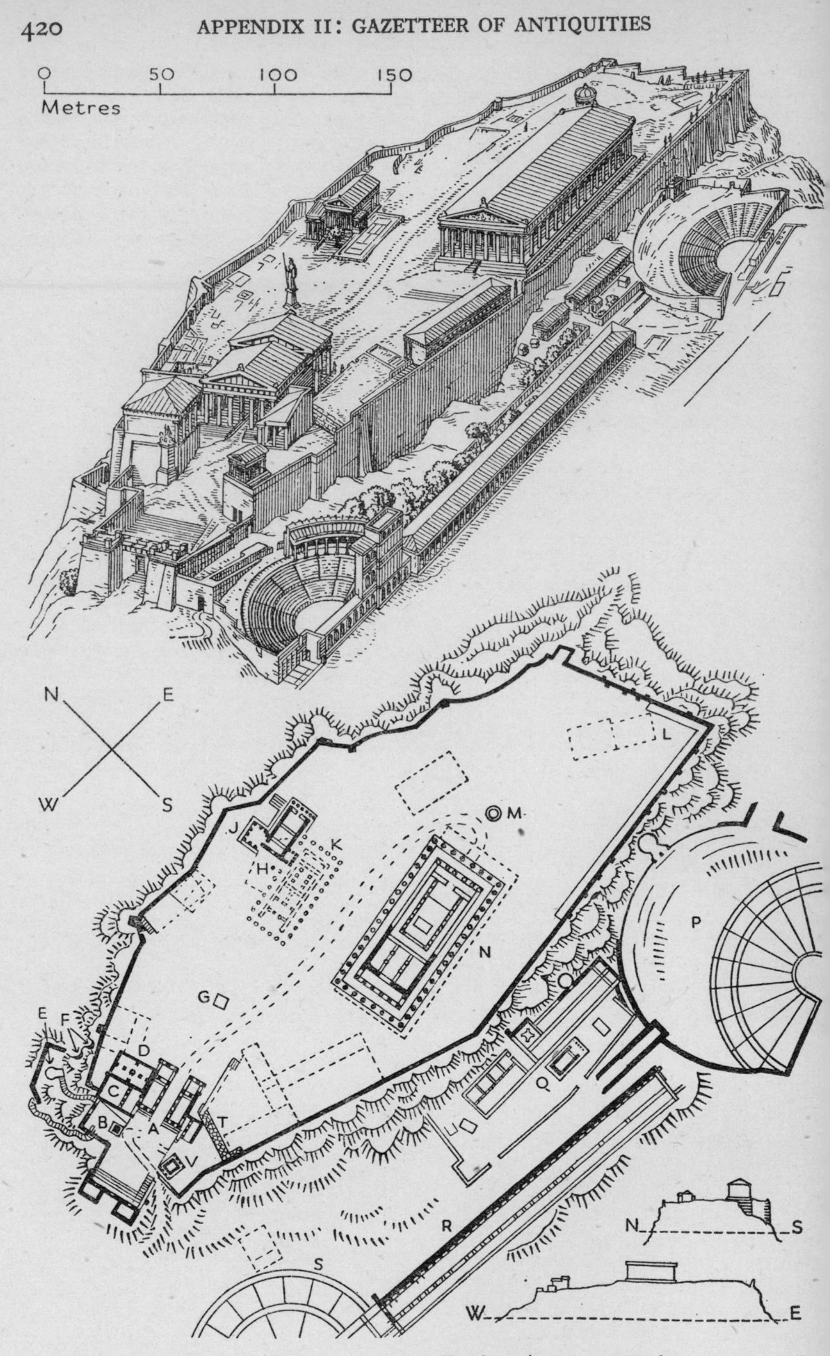

Fig. 116. For Legend and Explanation see opposite

Turkish conquest, it became a mosque, and a minaret was added in the south-west angle, but part was being used as a powder magazine in 1687, at the time of the siege of the Acropolis by the Venetians under Morosini; and it was then that a mortar fired by the Venetian artillery exploded the magazine and reduced the building to its present ruinous condition. Further damage was done by Morosini when he tried to remove part of the sculptures in the western gable, and most of what was left of the sculptures and frieze, and fifteen of the metopes were removed by Lord Elgin, who had bought them from the Turkish government in 1816, and sold to the British Museum for £35,000. Careful repairs and reconstruction have been going on since 1834, and the last of the columns of the north side was re-erected in 1930.

The Propylaea. A monumental entrance to the Acropolis from the west consists of two porticoes, an eastern and a western, with a central columned space between them. The western portico is flanked with wings and had a façade of six Doric columns; the central space had two rows of Ionic columns flanking an inclined ramp which allowed the passage of processions through the entrance; a transverse wall separated the central space from the eastern portico, which otherwise resembled the western. The Propylaea were begun in 437 B.C. and almost finished when the Peloponnesian War broke out. Made of Pentelic marble, they rank with the Parthenon as a major creation of Greek architecture.

The Temple of Athena of Victory. Standing on a tall platform to the south of the steps leading to the Propylaea, this elegant little shrine was built to house a statue of Athena. It was destroyed in 1682 by the Turks and reconstructed from the ancient fragments in 1835. It has two Ionic porticoes, and a sculptured frieze runs round the upper part of the building. The north and west sides of this frieze are reproductions from casts, the originals having been removed by Lord Elgin. On the parapet stood a balustrade composed of marble plaques with exceptionally beautiful reliefs, some of which are in the Acropolis Museum.

South of the Acropolis

Spread along the foot of the Acropolis on the south slope, there are several ancient buildings, of which the *Theatre of Dionysus* at the east end and the *Odeum of Herodes Atticus* at the west end are the most impressive. The theatre occupies roughly the site of at least two earlier wooden theatres, in the second of which the plays of the great Athenian dramatists, Aeschylus, Sophocles and Euripides, and of the comic poet Aristophanes had been produced. A stone theatre was begun in 400 B.C., but stage, orchestra and seats were later frequently remodelled, the position

---

Legend to Fig. 116

Fig. 116. Reconstruction and plan of the Acropolis

Based on drawings from (1) H. Luckenbach, *Kunst und Geschichte*, pp. 41–2 (München and Berlin, 1920); (2) Sir Banister Fletcher, *History of Architecture*, p. 77 (London, 1896, 10th ed. 1938).

A, Propylaea
B, Pedestal of Agrippa
C, Pinacotheca
D, Roman cistern
E, Clepsydra
F, Caves of Apollo and Pan
G, Statue of Athena Promachus
H, Sacred Olive tree
J, Erechtheum
K, Old Temple of Athena
L, Platform for votive statues
M, Roman temple
N, Parthenon
P, Theatre of Dionysus
Q, Aesculapium
R, Stoa of Eumenes
S, Odeum of Herodes Atticus
T, Mycenaean wall
V, Temple of Athena of Victory

of the orchestra was altered and the stage brought forward on three occasions. The remarkable sculptures on the face of the stage date from Nero's alteration but were again used in the final alteration of A.D. 224–5. The lower rows of seats also date from the Roman period; among them special seats for distinguished persons are noteworthy, that for the priest of Dionysus in the centre with its beautiful sculptured ornament, and others with inscriptions. The imperial box was added by the Emperor Hadrian. The theatre held about 20,000 spectators.

At the west end of the slope, *the Odeum*, named after Herodes Atticus, a rich benefactor of Athens, who built it in A.D.161, was used for concerts and theatrical displays. The stage building with its three storied wings and elaborate façade is essentially Roman in character. It was transformed into a redoubt by the Turks, cleared by Greek archaeologists in the middle of the last century, and is now occasionally used for plays and concerts. The conspicuous monument on the ridge to the south of the Acropolis is the *Tomb of Philopappos*, a Syrian benefactor of Athens in the first century A.D.

West of the Acropolis

About 300 m. to the west is the *Pnyx*, a rocky hill, where citizens met in assembly and were addressed by the great Athenian orators of the fifth and fourth centuries B.C. The tribune from which the orators spoke is cut out of the rock, and the ground in front of it, which sloped away, was artificially banked up to form the auditorium and contained by a semicircular wall. A quorum was constituted by 5,000 citizens, but a far larger number could be accommodated.

The hill immediately to the north-west of the Acropolis is the *Areopagus*, where the ancient court of that name held its sittings. Its functions were partly political, partly judicial. As a political court it guarded the constitution, as a judicial court it tried cases of treason and corruption. A crevasse surrounded by a railing marks the *Sanctuary of the Eumenides*, goddesses of the lower world and avengers of murder. Originally, murderers could claim asylum here pending their trial by the court. The traditional site where the court held its sittings is marked by some cuttings in the rock. St Paul's famous speech to the Athenians was delivered 'in the middle of the Areopagus', and an annual pilgrimage is made here on 29 June.

North of the Acropolis

The earliest *Agora* (market-place) lay south of the Acropolis, but later the flat ground to the north-west was used. This large area was in process of excavation by American archaeologists when war broke out in 1939, and numerous buildings and monuments had already been disengaged from the accumulated debris and the complex of modern streets and houses which had risen above it. It has already been possible to identify many of them. Some of the buildings had never been buried, such as the *Portico of Attalus*, a long colonnade with shops built in the second century B.C. by Attalus II, king of Pergamon in Asia Minor, and the *Portico of the Giants*, an inexplicable monument in which square Roman pillars, sculptured in front in the form of giants or tritons have been added to an earlier building.

The *Roman market*, to the east of the Agora, is a large enclosed quadrangle entered from the west by a monumental gateway. Between the columns of the façade of the gateway three passages led into a hall, thence into a second hall and so into the marble-flagged quadrangle. An inscription at the entrance shows that the oil market was held in the halls. An arcade, of two storeys, ran round the quadrangle; behind the arcade were shops. On the east side was a second gateway similar to that on the west. Conceived and executed as a whole, the planned and orderly lay-out of the Roman market is in strong contrast to the haphazard medley of buildings of all kinds and periods which the old Agora had become.

The *Tower of the Winds*, so called from the symbolic figures sculptured on each face, is a curious octagonal building just east of the Roman market. In reality it was an hydraulic clock built by a certain Andronicus in the first century B.C.

The *Library of Hadrian* is a large quadrangle, a little to the north and in line with the Roman market. A colonnade ran round the four sides. The library building was in the east side, the principal entrance in the west. In the centre of the quadrangle a kind of pavilion was later erected, which was later transformed into a Byzantine church.

The *Theseum* (Plate 80), or the *Temple of Hephaestos*, named after the patron of artisans, stands on a low hill overlooking the Agora to the east. It was built about 450 B.C., and is the most complete Greek temple in existence, but having none of the subtle structural refinements of the Parthenon, it produces a cold and formal impression. The metopes on the east front and four on each side have remained in place, but are badly disfigured: so too is part of the frieze. Traces of the polychrome decoration can be seen, notably on the roof of the colonnade at the east end. The building has suffered from being turned into a church.

About 300 m. north-west of the old Agora are the remains of two gateways, the *Sacred Gate*, and the *Dipylon Gate*, which stood at the points where two converging roads, one the sacred way to Eleusis, the other the road to the Academy, entered the city through the outer circuit wall. The ground at the sides of these roads for some distance outside the wall was used as the cemetery, in accordance with ancient custom. The later graves of ordinary folk were put above earlier ones, but richer or more distinguished persons had sculptured tombstones, many of which can still be seen in position. The best are those that line a road branching left from the Sacred Way, a short distance outside the Sacred Gate. Here there is no grave earlier than the fourth century B.C., but that part of the cemetery beside the road to the Academy has not yet been cleared and it is known that great Athenians, Pericles, and others of the fifth century, were buried in this ground. The whole cemetery was in use for many hundreds of years, and was of considerable extent. At present, the entrance is from Piraiévs Street.

East of the Acropolis

About 300 m. south-east of the Acropolis rise the huge columns of the *Temple of Olympian Zeus* (Plate 106). Begun in 175 B.C. under the direction of Antiochus IV, king of Syria, the Temple was finished by the Roman Emperor Hadrian in A.D. 131. Only sixteen columns remain of the 104 which formed the colonnade; the thirteen columns standing in a group formed the south-east corner. The temple was one of the largest in the world.

The Arch of Hadrian, an ornamental structure erected to mark the supposed limits of the city of Theseus, stands a few yards distant from the north-west corner of the enclosure of the temple of Zeus, with which, however, it has no architectural connection.

In a side street between this arch and the Acropolis is the elegant *Monument of Lysicrates*, a small circular temple of the fourth century B.C. erected to commemorate a victory in a singing contest by a choir of boys. A delicately sculptured frieze runs round the monument. At the beginning of the nineteenth century it still formed part of the library of a Franciscan convent, where Lord Byron was fond of lodging.

The Walls

For a great part of its history Athens has been a walled city (Fig. 117). As early as the sixth century B.C. the quarters round the Acropolis were enclosed within a circuit wall. This was destroyed by the Persians in 480 B.C., and two years later Themistocles built a new wall, enclosing a much larger area. This later wall, of brick on a stone foundation, was built in such haste that material from other buildings, bases of statues and any odd scraps of stone lying at hand were incorporated in it. Traces of it can be seen on the ridges south of the Acropolis, and on either side of the Dipylon Gate. It was subsequently restored on many occasions, but retained substantially the same line, at least as late as the sixth century A.D. The *Frankish* circuit wall was very short and extended only north of the Acropolis. The *Turkish* wall was much longer, but its line did not correspond with that of any of the previous walls.

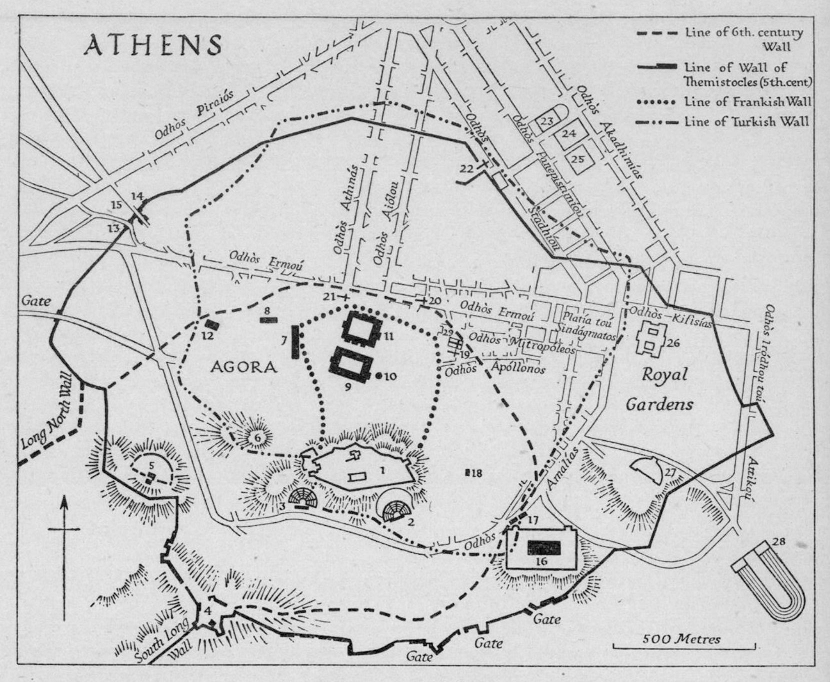

Fig. 117. Athens

Based on plans in *Les Guides Bleus-Grèce*, pp. 11 and 20 (Paris, 1935).

Classical Monuments: 1, Acropolis; 2, Theatre of Dionysus; 3, Odeum of Herodes Atticus; 4, Tomb of Philopappos; 5, Pnyx; 6, Areopagus; 7, Portico of Attalus; 8, Portico of the Giants; 9, Roman Market; 10, Tower of the Winds; 11, Library of Hadrian; 12, Theseum Temple of Hephaestus; 13, The Sacred Gate; 14, The Dipylon Gate; 15, Cemetery; 16, Temple of Olympian Zeus; 17, Arch of Hadrian; 18, Monument of Lysicrates. *Byzantine Churches:* 19, The Old Cathedral (Áyios Elevthérios); 20, Church of Kapnikaréa; 21, Church of Our Lady of the Great Monastery; 22, Church of Saints Theodore. *Modern Buildings:* 23, University Library; 24, University; 25, Academy; 26, Royal Palace; 27, Záppion; 28, Stadium; 29, New Cathedral.

The Long Walls

Built in 461 B.C., the Long Walls ran in parallel straight lines, *c.* 225 m. apart, to join the circuit wall of Athens to those of Piraeus and Phaleron. Pericles built a third wall between them in 450 B.C., which eventually took the place of the

Phaleron wall. The northern joined the circuit wall just west of the Observatory, and its line can here be traced for a short distance; the southern joined the circuit wall at the Monument of Philopappos.

Byzantine Athens

Hidden away in its streets and squares the city possesses a few Byzantine churches, small because Byzantine churches tend to be small, and also because, in the Byzantine period, Athens was a small and unimportant provincial town. The churches are, nevertheless, of some interest and considerable charm. In the square off Metropole Street (Odhòs Mitropóleos), dwarfed by the modern cathedral, is the tiny ninth-century chapel of *Áyios Elevthérios*, interesting for the numerous reliefs taken from more ancient Hellenic or Byzantine buildings, and built into its walls (Plate 83). Facing the Monastiráki station of the Athínai-Piraiévs railway is the eleventh-century church of *Our Lady of the Great Monastery*, with fine capitals. *Saints Theodore* (Áyioi Theódhoroi) in a square off Stadium Street (Odhòs Stádhiou) is the best preserved, and, in its present form, also dates from the eleventh century. In the middle of Hermes Street (Odhòs Ermoú) is the church known as *Kapnikaréa*, dating from the twelfth century (Plate 84).

Frankish and Venetian Athens

Remains of this period scarcely exist. The small ruined church at the north-west foot of the Acropolis, however, is Frankish. The Parthenon was used as a Catholic church, and the Florentine dukes of Athens had their palace in the Propylaea; a square tower near the south wing was built by them and not pulled down until 1875.

Turkish Athens

The mosque in the corner of the square by the Monastiráki station is one of the few remains left of the Turkish period. Turkish handiwork was largely destructive and the Acropolis, which they used as a fortress, suffered much. The streets and houses on the north slopes of the Acropolis retain their picturesque Turkish character.

Modern Athens

Of the modern public buildings, some of those built in the nineteenth century are interesting, if not always successful experiments in the adaptation of classical forms. The principal examples are the University, the Academy and the National Library, forming a group in University Street, the old Royal Palace in Constitution Square (Platía toú Sindágmatos), and the Záppion standing in the large public park south of the palace. South-east of the Záppion the Stadium occupies the site of the ancient building, in which the Panathenaic games were held, but in its present condition, it is almost entirely modern, having been restored in 1895.

Museums

The *National Museum* in Patissia Road (Odhòs Patissíon) is first in size and importance. It is especially rich in Mycenaean objects, including the famous treasure from the shaft graves at Mycenae, in gigantic Attic vases intended to stand above graves, and in early Greek sculpture. Of the classical period two bronze statues recently recovered from the sea are noteworthy; so, too, are fragments from the temple of Athena at Teyéa, original works of the fourth century B.C. by the renowned sculptor, Scopas. There is also a rich collection of Greek vases of all periods, as well as jewellery, terra-cottas and small objects.

The *Acropolis Museum* lies east of the Parthenon. It is reserved for antiquities found on the Acropolis, and contains interesting sculptures from the ancient temple of Athena Polias, and other early temples; also a series of figures of maidens recovered from the debris of temples destroyed by the Persians in 480 B.C. These statues were offerings, and in no sense portraits, but are none the less full of character and charm, and illustrate remarkably the development of Greek sculpture in the sixth century B.C.

The *Byzantine Museum* in Cefissia Road (Odhòs Kifisías) is chronologically arranged to illustrate the development of Byzantine art, and is principally of an ecclesiastical character. The ikons are especially good.

The *Numismatic Museum* occupies a wing of the Academy building in University Street (Odhòs Panepistimíou).

The *Benaki Museum*, in Coumbaris Street (Odhòs Koumbári), has a good collection of Byzantine, Moslem and Greek pottery, textiles and miscellaneous works of art.

The *Historical Museum* (Patissia Road) contains objects connected with the War of Independence.

The mosque in Monastiráki Square possesses a good collection of modern Greek textiles and peasant art.

ATHOS (ÁYION ÓROS) (Plate 91)

In Khalkidhikí; the most easterly of the three peninsulas. Reached by steamer from Thessaloníki to the port of Dhafní; or by road to Políyiros, thence by track to Ierissós, which lies just outside the limits of the Holy Mountain. Permits to visit the monasteries, which must be presented on arrival at Karíai, the capital, can be obtained through the Archbishop at Athínai, or Thessaloníki, or the Minister of Education. Many of the monasteries date from the tenth century and are rich in objects of beauty and historic interest. From the north-west the principal monasteries are: *Vatopédhion*, with valuable MSS; *Ivíron* with a rich library; *Megáli Lávra*, situated at the eastern extremity of the peninsula, with its fortress-like buildings and fine frescoes; *Simópetra*, on the south coast, chiefly remarkable for its situation on an isolated rock, above which the monastery rises like a block of flats with galleries at each floor overhanging the precipice.

AYÍA LÁVRA

In Akhaía; reached from Kalávrita, terminus of the mountain railway from Dhiakoptón. The present buildings are modern, but the monastery was founded in the tenth century and contains some sixteenth-century wall paintings by Catanello. Its special claim to renown is that it was here that Yermanos, archbishop of Patras, raised the standard of revolt against the Turks in 1821. The standard is preserved in the monastery.

AYÍA TRIÁDHA

In Kríti; on the same ridge as Phaestus but about 4 km. farther west. Remains of a Minoan palace, considerably smaller than those of Phaestus or Cnossus. Most of the structure, consisting of a complex of rooms, porticoes, magazines and flights of steps, built on an L-shaped plan is dated 1900–1700 B.C.; it was destroyed, though not completely, about 1450 B.C., probably by the Achaeans, who seem, however, to have reconstructed it, building a large megaron (hall) and various rooms in the eastern wing. The rich finds from the site, notably three ceremonial vases in carved steatite, are in the museum at Iráklion.

BASSAE (Plate 81)

In Messinía; reached by track from Andrítsaina in 2½ hr. The temple stands in isolated mountain surroundings of great beauty. It was built by Iktinos, architect of the Parthenon, about 420 B.C., to the honour of Apollo in gratitude for deliverance from a plague. Except for the roof the temple is almost complete, but the frieze which ran round the inner part, and the metopes which decorated the exterior, were bought by the British government in 1812, and are now in the British Museum. The temple is of the Doric order, but there is an isolated column inside, the earliest example of the Corinthian order (Fig. 73).

Calauria (Póros)

Island, off the north-east coast of Argolís. Reached by daily steamers from Piraiévs. On the east coast of the island are the remains of a sixth-century temple, famous as the headquarters of a maritime league. The great orator Demosthenes sought asylum here in 322 B.C., and to avoid capture poisoned himself. The temple is very ruinous but, for beauty of situation, is only surpassed by that at Aíyina.

Cephallonia (Kefallinía)

One of the Ionian islands; reached by steamer from Pátra to Argostólion the capital. Ancient remains are few but the museum exhibits the contents of some late Mycenean tombs; while Latin rule has left its monuments principally at *Kástro*, the ruined Venetian capital. Evidence of British occupation at Argostólion is provided by statues of Napier and Lord Guilford and various buildings dating from that period.

Chaeroneia (Khairónia)

In Voiotía; reached by rail from Athínai, or by road via Livádhia. In the neighbourhood took place the famous battle between the Greeks and Macedonians in 338 B.C., in which Demosthenes took part on the Greek side, and Alexander the Great on the Macedonian; here also in 86 B.C. the Roman Sulla defeated the generals of Mithridates of Pontus in Asia Minor; and on the same spot the Franks under the duke of Athens were decisively defeated by the Catalans in A.D. 1311. On the left of the railway, just before Khairónia station is reached, a mound marks the spot where the Macedonians who fell in the battle of 338 B.C. were buried; the Thebans who fell in the same battle were commemorated by a colossal stone lion, the fragments of which were recently collected and put together. The restored monument now stands at the village of Khairónia next to the museum. In the museum are finds from numerous prehistoric sites in the neighbourhood.

Chalcis (Khalkís)

In Évvoia; on the narrowest part of the channel between the island and the mainland. Reached by rail, road or sea from Athínai. In the waters of the strait Agamemnon assembled the Achaian fleet before sailing to Troy. The Venetians occupied the island in 1210, and held it till 1470 when Chalcis was besieged and captured by the Turks after a heroic resistance. A terrible massacre followed. Almost all the Venetian remains have been done away with, but there is Frankish work in the church of Ayía Paraskeví, a Byzantine church transformed into a Gothic cathedral. The Venetian Governor's palace is now the prison. In the small museum are interesting Frankish and Venetian sculptured slabs with armorial bearings, and on the opposite side of the channel is the Turkish fortress of Karababa.

Chios (Khíos)

Island off the Turkish coast; reached by regular steamer from Piraiévs. Khíos has from the earliest times produced distinguished writers. Homer himself, it was claimed, was a Chiote, as was in more modern times the reformer of the Greek language, Korais (see p. 320), whose library is in the town. The island has had a troubled history and has suffered many changes of masters. Traces of its most affluent period, under the Genoese, are numerous, especially in the *Kástro*, which guards the entrance to the port. In the small Museum is a collection of a distinctive class of early Greek pottery (sixth century B.C.) found on the island and probably made there. To the east of the town the monastery of *Néa Moní* contains original frescoes of the eleventh century.

CNOSSUS (KNOSSÓS) (Fig. 118)

In Kríti; reached by road from Iráklion (5 km.). The Minoan place of Cnossus was discovered by Sir Arthur Evans towards the end of the nineteenth century. It is the largest and most impressive of the Minoan palaces and was the centre of the Minoan civilization, and whatever historical facts may lie behind the legend

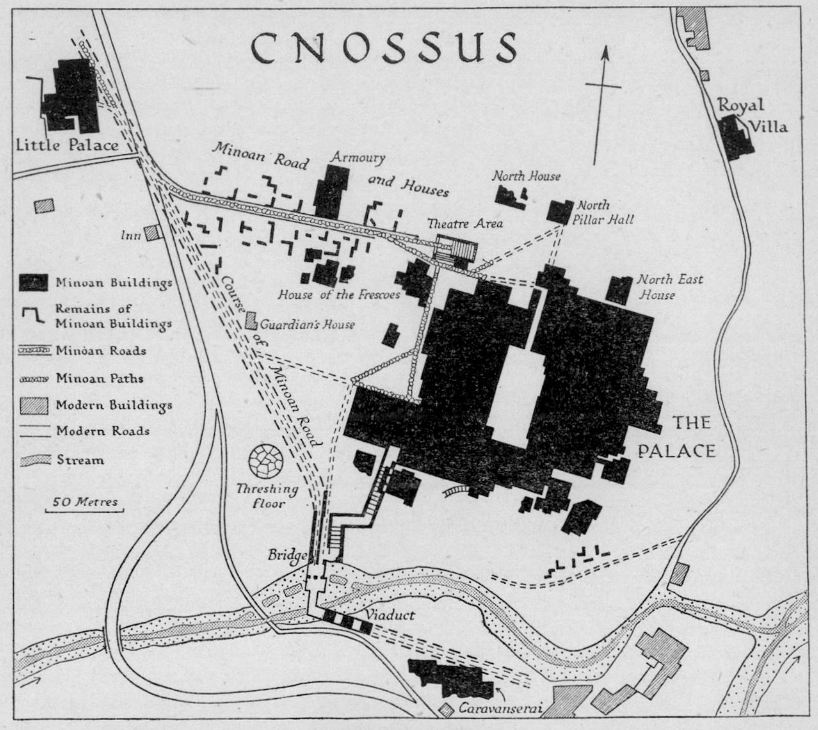

Fig. 118. Cnossus

For detailed plans of the Minoan palace, reference should be made to Sir Arthur Evans, *The Palace of Minos at Knossos*, vol. II, part 2, plan B (London, 1928).

of Minos, Theseus, Ariadne and the Minotaur must be associated with it. The existing palace, a complex of rooms, corridors and magazines grouped round a large quadrangle, dates mostly from the sixteenth century B.C., but an earlier palace, of which the beginnings go back some four hundred years, had preceded it. Its destruction by earthquake determined the construction of a larger more splendid palace. This new palace was itself partially destroyed by earthquake, after it had stood for perhaps one hundred years, and was then rebuilt on the old lines. About 1450 B.C. another earthquake occurred, followed, fifty years later, by a final destruction, this time by enemies, probably Achaeans from mainland Greece. The palace was never rebuilt, but the ruins were partially inhabited for perhaps the next two hundred years.

A certain amount of reconstruction was done by Sir Arthur Evans, and at various points restored copies of the original frescoes have been placed on the walls. Thus a better idea of a Minoan palace can be formed here than at any of the other palaces, but the plan is so complex and there are so many small rooms that in order to understand the remains, a more complete description is required than can be given here (see p. 428). North-west of the palace is the *Theatre Area* and the *Little Palace*, to the north-east the *Royal Villa*, and to the south-west the *viaduct* which carried the road across the ravine to the *Caravanserai* where, it is supposed, travellers were accommodated. A little to the south of the 'caravanserai', below the modern road, is the *House of the High Priest* with a stone altar and church-like plan, and beyond, the *Royal Temple Tomb*, an unusually interesting monument consisting of a sepulchral chamber, belonging to the last days of the palace. About 3 km. north of the palace in a field to the west of the ravine is the *Tomb of Isopata*, a square tomb which had a corbelled vault and a fore-hall approached by a stone-lined dromos (passage). The tomb was built about 1500 B.C. and was in use for at least one hundred years. To judge by the splendour of its contents, which included fine rapiers and a set of Egyptian alabaster vases, it may well have been a royal tomb.

A visit to the palace should be supplemented by a visit to the museum at Iráklion, where most of the finds from Cnossus are exhibited.

CORFU OR CORCYRA (KÉRKIRA)

The most northerly of the Ionian islands, reached by steamer from Piraiévs and the port of call for steamers bound for or returning from Italy. In the town of Kérkira the most interesting monument is the *Old Fort*, to the north of the harbour, built by the Venetians in 1550. There are also many buildings dating from the British occupation (1814–64).

South of the modern town in ancient Corcyra there are the remains of an archaic *Temple of Artemis* on the peninsula of Palaiópolis. The remarkable pediment from this temple, representing a colossal gorgon, and other mythical figures is in the museum. Many spots on the island are imaginatively associated with the Homeric story of Odysseus and Alcinous, King of Phaeacia. St Spirídon is the patron saint of Kérkira, and his relics, first brought to the island in 1489, are carried in procession through the streets four times a year.

CORINTH (PALAIÁ KÓRINTHOS)

In Argolís-Korinthía; reached by road from Néa Kórinthos (7 km.), or from the station of Examíllia (2½ hr. walk). The importance of Corinth in all periods of Greek history is explained by its position, which commands both the land route from central Greece to the Pelopónnisos and the sea route from east to west. Even before Mycenaean times the district was comparatively densely populated, and the Mycenaeans themselves had a port on the gulf a little west of Néa Kórinthos. In Hellenic times the prosperity of Corinth began as early as the eighth century, and in the seventh and following centuries the Corinthians were producing and exporting vases, bronzes and other objects of art on a large scale, but the principal wealth was derived from levying toll on merchandise between the East and West. This prosperity declined as a result of Athenian competition. In 140 B.C., having become involved in conflict with Rome, Corinth was completely destroyed by Mummius. Julius Caesar recolonized the place with Italians and a second period of prosperity followed. The present remains are almost all of Roman date and belong to the time when Corinth had the reputation of being the most splendid as well as the most frivolous city in Greece. It was sacked by successive waves of barbarians and the population took refuge on Acrocorinth, which, in the Middle Ages, passed successively into the hands of Normans, Franks, Florentines, Byzantines, Turks, Venetians and again Turks in 1715. It was recovered by the Greeks in 1821. The modern village of Palaiá Kórinthos occupies only part of the ancient city which was of vast extent. It is here that the American School of Classical Studies at Athínai has been conducting successful excavations for many years. The area of the excavations is dominated by the *Temple of Apollo*, built in the sixth century B.C. The seven standing columns belong to the west front and south-west corner. The Roman market-place which was roughly square in shape and surrounded by porticoes lay to the south of the temple, and was reached by a paved road leading from the port of Lechaeum on the Gulf. The entrance was a monumental *Propylaea*, at the approach to which, on the right-hand side, was a long portico with shops. Just east of the entrance is the famous *Peirene fountain* which was fed by spring water from Akrokórinthos. The water flowed through a rock-cut underground tunnel into a large reservoir, whence it passed into basins.

Just within the Propylaea on the west was an imposing structure which served as a façade to a large basilica standing above the portico with shops. It is known as the *Captives' Façade*, on account of the sculptured figures of barbarian captives that adorned its upper storey. The basilica itself is perhaps that in which St Paul stood before Gallio. The curious oblique terrace wall to the west of the Captives' Façade has two openings for staircases, one of which communicated with a very ancient sacred spring, the other with an oracular shrine.

North-west of the market-place are three buildings of interest: the *fountain of Glauce*, in construction rather like that of Peirene, and connected by a conduit with a source at the base of Akrokórinthos; the *Odeum* built by Herodes Atticus, and the *Theatre*, with traces of Roman paintings, showing engagements between gladiators and wild beasts. West of the market is a *Villa* with an especially fine and well-preserved mosaic of Roman date.

In the museum are pre-Mycenaean and Mycenaean vases from prehistoric sites in the neighbourhood, portrait statues and sculptured fragments from the many buildings.

Acrocorinth (*Akrokórinthos*)

Reached by mule track from Palaiá Kórinthos (1 hr.) to the gateway, thence to the summit (¾ hr.). Acrocorinth was originally fortified in Hellenic times and subsequently by Byzantines, Franks, Venetians and Turks. Traces of the handiwork of all these are visible in the imposing fortifications, which are, however, substantially Venetian. Within the circuit wall are the ruins of a small town, which took the place of Corinth, abandoned by its inhabitants in the Middle Ages. The site of the temple of Aphrodite is on the higher of the two summits.

CORON (KORÓNI)

In Messinía; reached by road or steamer from Kalámai. There are magnificent remains of this once important Venetian station.

DAPHNI (DHAFNÍ)

In Attikí; on the road to Elevsís, 8 km. from Athínai. A monastery was erected here in the fifth century A.D., on the site of an ancient temple of Apollo, but the present church dates from the eleventh century. The Franks introduced Cistercian monks in 1211, who remained until the Turkish conquest, and Frankish elements can be discerned in the building. The church is a fine example of Byzantine architecture, but the splendid mosaics are its chief glory (Plate 82).

Delos (Dhílos)

One of the Kiklȧdhes; reached by steamer from Piraiévs to Míkonos, thence by boat. Delos was originally a religious centre and in legend was the birthplace of Apollo. Throughout much of its varied history it was dependent on Athens, and the Delian festival, held every four years, was an Athenian festival. From 315 to 166 B.C., however, the island was independent, and the sanctuary acquired a pan-Hellenic character. In 166 B.C. the island again passed under Athenian domination and Delos was declared an open port. Its commerical importance, as a clearing house for the trade passing between the Levant and Italy and Greece, then overshadowed its religious significance. This period of prosperity passed away and Delos never fully recovered from its destruction by Mithridates in 28 B.C. It is now uninhabited. The remains are of special interest, since it is here possible, as nowhere else in Greece (except possibly at Ólinthos), to form an idea of a large Hellenic town.

The religious city, situated immediately east of the landing place, consists of a market-place and two porticoes, between which an avenue lined with votive sculpture led north to the sacred enclosure. Just within the Propylaea or gateway of the enclosure stood the colossal statue of Apollo. The *Temple of Apollo* itself was begun in the middle of the fifth century but was not finished till the fourth. It is flanked on the north by the smaller *Temple of the Athenians*, and an archaic temple of the sixth century. Beyond is a group of treasuries. East of the temple is a long narrow building of unusual plan, and along the north side of the enclosure the *Portico of Antigonus*, a king of Macedonia.

The *Sacred Lake* is the district north of the sanctuary, flanked on the south by the *Market of the Italians*, a large colonnaded quadrangle. East of the lake on a terrace is a row of stone lions, interesting examples of archaic animal sculpture; north of the lake are houses, shops and the *Palaestra* (wrestling place). The stadium and gymnasium lie about 350 m. to the north-east.

Mt Cynthus. On the way to the summit is a group of buildings erected by foreigners, Syrians and Egyptians; nearby is the *Temple of Hera*; next, the sacred cave, and on the summit a sanctuary of *Zeus and Athena*.

The residential quarter lies on the west flank of Mt Cynthus and extends to the harbour. At its south-west extremity is the *Theatre*; below, a complex of streets, lanes, houses and shops. Two of the houses—the *House of the Trident* and the *House of Dionysus*, contain admirable mosaic floors. The *House of the Dolphins* and the *House of Masks*, both in the Theatre quarter, also have good mosaics. Somewhat to the south of the residential quarter are the quays, warehouses and shops, where merchandise, much of it in transit, was handled.

The museum contains many archaic statues, and an interesting collection of vases from the Heraeum.

Delphi (Dhelfoí) (Fig. 119)

In Fthiótis-Fokís; reached by road from Athínai via Thívai and Livádhia, or by steamer to Itéa, thence by road. It was the seat of the famous oracle of Apollo which was habitually consulted by Greeks from all parts of the Greek world, both on affairs of the highest importance and on quite trivial matters. A host of buildings, temples, treasuries, statues, a theatre, a gymnasium and a stadium sprang up in connexion with the sanctuary, and games were celebrated every four years. The ravine of the Papadía, a tributary of the Xiropótamos (Pleistos), separates the main sanctuary on the west from the gymnasium and the sanctuary of Athena on the east.

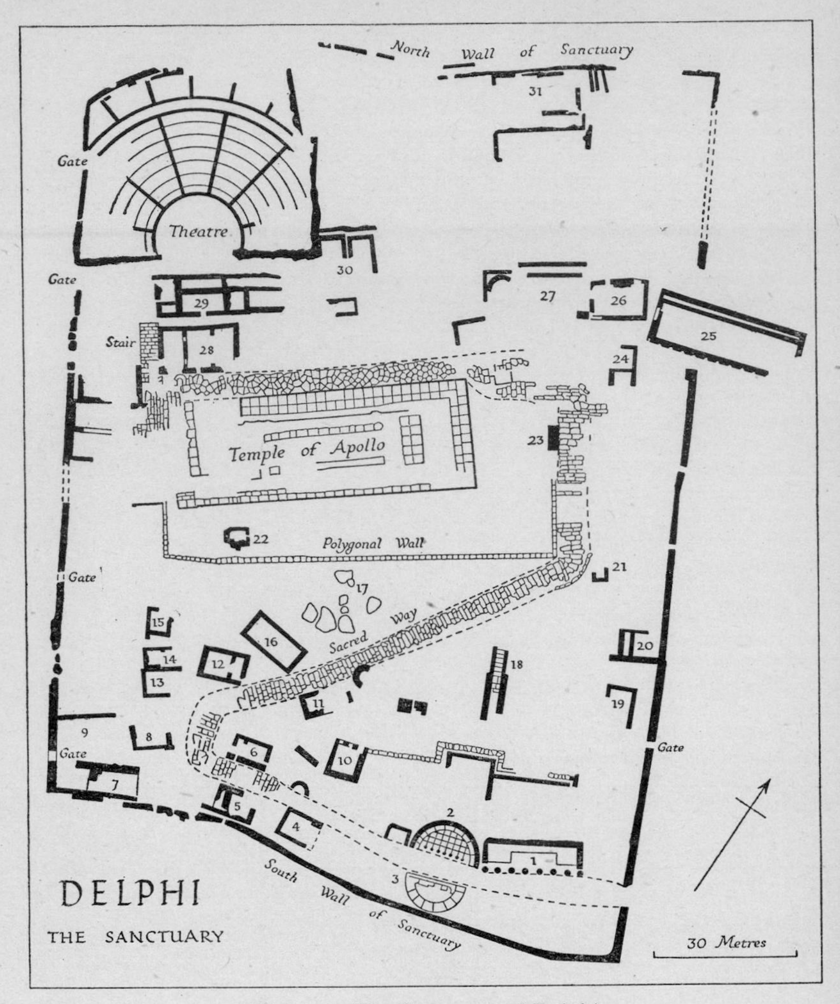

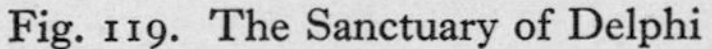

Fig. 119. The Sanctuary of Delphi

Based on a plan in *Les Guides Bleus-Grèce*, p. 238 (Paris, 1935).

1, Ex-voto of the Spartans; 2, Ex-voto of the kings of Argos; 3, Ex-voto of Epigonoi of Argos; 4, Treasury of the Sicyonians; 5, Treasury of the Siphnians; 6, Treasury of the Cnidians; 7, Treasury of the Thebans; 8, Treasury of the Boeotians; 9, Ex-voto of the Liparians; 10, Treasury; 11, a Treasury; 12, Treasury of the Athenians; 13, Treasury of the Potidaeans; 14, Treasury of the Syracusians; 15, Treasury of Agylla; 16, Hall of the Councillors; 17, The Sanctuary of the Oracle; 18, a Staircase; 19, Treasury of the Cyrenians; 20, a Treasury; 21, Treasury of the Corinthians; 22, Temple of the Muses; 23, Altar of Apollo; 24, Treasury of Acanthus; 25, Portico of Attalus (late a Roman cistern); 26, Heroon of Neoptolemus; 27, Precinct of Neoptolemus; 28, Shrine of Alexander; 29, Stage of Theatre; 30, Treasuries; 31, Lesche of Cnidians.

The Sanctuary proper lies on the slopes above the Livádhia road, in an enclosure entered from the south-east corner. From here, the *Sacred Way* wound up the hillside to the great *Temple of Apollo*. On either side of the Way were buildings, trophies and *ex-votos*. The votive statuary erected by various cities to commemorate victories over other cities is just within the entrance. Beyond began the *Treasuries*, among which those of the *Sicyonians* and *Siphnians* (on the left) and of the *Cnidians* (on the right) are conspicuous for their beautiful sculptures. Beyond the bend of the Way on the left, the *Treasury of the Athenians* has been restored and re-erected (1904–6). Passing the hall where the guardians of the sanctuary held their meetings and the site of the original oracle, the road turns northwards just below the angle of the magnificent supporting wall to the entrance of the *Temple of Apollo*. The Temple, standing on a colossal platform, dominated the sanctuary. It was built in the fourth century B.C. immediately over the subterranean chamber, in which stood the Pythian tripod at the spot where the priestess gave her oracular responses. The temple replaced two earlier structures, of which the first was destroyed by fire in 548 B.C. and the second was shattered by an earthquake in 373 B.C. In the north-west corner of the enclosure is the *Theatre*. Belonging to the fourth century with later restorations, it is well preserved, and has been used in recent years in an attempt to revive the Delphic festival. Outside the enclosure, to the north-west, is the *Stadium*.

The *Gymnasium* and attendant buildings form the second main group and lie on the south side of the road to the east of the ravine. Just to the north is the famous *Spring of Kastalia*, where visitors to the sanctuary purified themselves before entering.

The Sanctuary of Athena is the third principal group of remains and lies in an enclosure (Marmaria) on the right of the road to Livádhia. Here between an earlier and later temple of Athena stood a beautiful little round building, or *Thólos*, an Attic work of the fifth century B.C. (Plate 104).

The museum. In addition to the sculptures recovered from the Treasuries and figures from the pediments of the old Temple of Apollo, from the Thólos and other buildings, the museum possesses the famous bronze *Charioteer*, one of the most perfect of Greek works of art (Plate 107).

Dodona (Dhodhóna)

In Ípiros; reached by road from Ioánnina as far as Kosmíra, thence by track (2 hr.). Famous sanctuary of Zeus and seat of the most ancient oracle in Greece whose utterances were delivered in the rustling of the leaves of the sacred oak. The site is much overgrown, but the theatre can be identified as well as the walls of the acropolis and some traces of the sanctuary itself.

Eleusis (Elevsís)

In Attikí; reached by road or by rail from Athínai (20 km.). Celebrated sanctuary of Demeter (Ceres) and her daughter Core (Proserpine). According to the legend, the king of Eleusis helped Demeter in her search for Core who had been carried off by Hades (Pluto). Demeter showed her gratitude by presenting the king with a grain of wheat, thus teaching him the art of agriculture. The Mysteries recalled this event. Their exact nature is unknown, but the festivals connected with them, which were, in fact, initiation ceremonies, took place in autumn every year and included processions along the Sacred Way between Athens and Eleusis. Greeks from all parts attended these festivals. The remains are of many periods and represent successive enlargements of the Telesterion (main hall) in which the mysteries were celebrated, and extensions or enhancements of the sacred enclosure into which none but the initiated was admitted. The earliest Telesterion was pre-

Hellenic. The actual building is mostly of the fourth century B.C.; the rearrangement of the interior colonnades and the addition of rock-cut seats were made in Roman times. The grand *Propylaea*, the two triumphal arches and the *Temple of Demeter* are also of Roman date. On the slopes of the Acropolis, remains of a prehistoric town have been found. There is a small but interesting museum.

Eleutherae (Elevtheraí)

In Attikí; on the right of the Athínai-Thívai road, 50 km. from Athínai. Remains of an Hellenic fortress which guarded the southern entrance of the pass over Mt Kithairón. This is one of the best preserved Greek fortresses.

Epidaurus (Epídhavros)

In Argolís; reached by road from Návplion (30 km.). It is the site of a famous sanctuary of Asclepius, the god of healing, to which sick persons resorted from afar. The sanctuary was at the height of its popularity in the fourth century B.C. and continued to flourish during the Roman period, when it acquired the character of a health resort. A Sacred Way led south from the port of Epidaurus to the monumental entrance of a sacred enclosure. Within stood the *Temple of Asclepius*, built in the fourth century and containing a gold and ivory statue of the god. A few steps to the west was a round building with an interior and an exterior colonnade, which, to judge from surviving architectural fragments, must have been of exceptional elegance. North of the Temple are long colonnades, under which the sick slept, waiting for healing to take place during sleep. At the east end of the colonnades was the bath, and immediately north of this a bath of Roman date and a library. The ruins include a palaestra, a gymnasium, a vast hotel, a stadium and the best preserved of all Greek theatres (Plate 105). In the museum are collected architectural and other fragments from the site, but those from the pediments of the temple of Asclepius have been transferred to the National Museum in Athínai.

Glá

In Voiotía; on the north-east of Lake Kopaïs. Reached from Thívai by road or rail to Alíartos, thence by the canal bank to the village of Topólia, from which Glá is 25 min. distance on foot. The remains of a pre-Hellenic (Mycenaean?) fortress and palace stand on what was formerly an island. A wall, constructed of enormous blocks of stone, encircles the ruins and closely follows the indentations of the former shoreline. It is from 5 to 7 m. thick and is preserved to a height varying from 2 to 6 m.: four gates are clearly recognized. The palace, which is L-shaped, consists of a complex of rooms and corridors, and was protected by a symmetrically planned fortress, which must have been of great strength, but of which only the foundations remain. Regarded as a whole the fortress of Glá is a magnificent example of pre-Hellenic architecture, comparable to Mycenae and Tiryns, but owing to the lack of literary evidence, its history and identity remain completely obscure.

Gortyn (Górtin)

In Kríti; reached by road from Iráklion (50 km.). Remains of an ancient city with a temple of Apollo; the *Odeum* (Roman) was converted into the Christian basilica of St Titus (sixth century), but an inscription of great interest to students of Greek law, which had been carved on the interior wall of the apse of the basilica, was allowed to remain in position in the Christian church. It dates from the fifth century A.D. and is known as the 'Law of Gortyn'.

Plate 104. Sanctuary of Athena, Delphi

The ruins of the Tholos, a circular building of the fifth century B.C., are in the foreground.

Plate 105. The theatre of Epidaurus, end of fourth century B.C.

This is the best preserved of all ancient Greek theatres, holding 14,000 spectators. The acoustic properties are remarkable.

Plate 106. The Temple of Olympian Zeus

This group of columns formed the south-east corner of the colonnade. The temple was completed by the Emperor Hadrian in A.D. 131.

Plate 107. The bronze charioteer, Delphi

The figure formed part of a group which included a chariot drawn by four horses, and a boy holding the bridles. It was dedicated about 480 B.C.

Goúrnia

In Kríti; on the north coast. Reached by road from Iráklion (80 km.), or by coasting steamer to Pakhiámmos. The site shows a more or less complete Minoan town, which has been carefully excavated so that streets, houses and the general lay-out can be studied. The period is roughly 1400–1300 B.C.

Heraklion (Iráklion)

In Kríti; on the north coast. Reached by frequent steamers from Piraiévs. The harbour works bearing the lion of St Mark on sculptured plaques, a stone fountain in the principal square, and the walls of the town are all Venetian. Elsewhere, though the minarets have been destroyed, there are many Turkish features. The museum is admirably arranged and contains most of the archaeological finds made in Kríti.

Ísova

In Messinía; on the south bank of the Alfiós. Reached by the new road from Andrítsaina to Olímbia. There are fairly well-preserved remains of a Frankish monastery, much used by the Frankish knights and their retinues as a halting place on the way between the court of Sparta and the port of Glarentza. The remains include parts of two churches, which are interesting as being among the very few surviving Gothic buildings in Greece.

Ithaca (Itháki)

One of the Ionian islands; reached by steamer from Pátrai. Recent excavations by the British School at Athínai have virtually established the claim of Ithaca as the legendary home of Odysseus, though there is still lack of agreement about the sites mentioned in Homer's *Odyssey*. The palace of Odysseus was almost certainly at Pilikáta near the village of Stavrós, in the north of the island. There is a small museum at Stavrós, in which many of the finds from this part of the island are exhibited. A second museum, not yet completed, is at Vathí, where finds made in the southern half by the British School can be seen. A statue of Sir Thomas Maitland on the quay at Vathí and the good roads recall the British occupation (1814–64).

Janina (Ioánnina)

In Ípiros; on the west shore of Lake Ioánnina. This picturesque town has few monuments of interest, though its history has been full of incident. There are five monasteries on an island in the lake, all dating from the thirteenth century and containing some good frescoes. In that of *Pandelëímon*, which can be visited, Ali Pasha was assassinated in 1822. It was he who set Janina ablaze when it was besieged by Ismail in 1820, and it was during this fire that the schools for which the town was renowned were completely destroyed. The memory of Ali Pasha is recalled by a mosque on the Kástro, and his tomb enclosed by a beautiful ironwork grille can be seen.

Kaisarianí

In Attikí; at the foot of Imittós. Reached by road from Athínai (7 km.). Small monastery built on the site of a temple of Aphrodite, where a spring of excellent water was held to have miraculous properties. Both in antiquity and in the Middle Ages the water was conducted to Athens in pipes; to-day it is transported in barrels and sold in the streets. The church dates from the tenth century, and has some good frescoes of the seventeenth century.

Kalamata (Kalámai)

In Messinía; terminus of the Athínai-Pelopónnisos railway. *Frankish castle* with Venetian additions in which William II, Villehardouin, the fourth Prince of

Achaea, died in 1278. In the town is an interesting church (The Holy Apostles), Byzantine in origin, to which a church in Italian style has been added.

Karítena

In Arkadhía; reached by road from Trípolis via Vitína or Megalópolis. An important Frankish castle, guarding the Alfiós valley, is well preserved. So, too, is the Frankish bridge over the Alfiós below the town.

Kastoría

In Flórina; reached by road from the station of Amíndaion on the Thessaloníki-Flórina railway. The town has a great number of churches, interesting both as examples of a provincial style of architecture, and for the decorative brickwork or frescoes. Most are of the basilica type and are not later than the eleventh century. The following are specially noteworthy; Áyioi Anárgiroi, Áyios Stéfanos, Panayía Korbelítissa, a miniature church of great charm and interest, and Tón Taxiárkhon, which dates from the fourteenth century.

Laurium (Lávrion)

In Attikí; reached by road from Athínai (53 km.) or by railway (66 km.). Silver and lead were extracted here in antiquity, so that the mines were famous and on them the wealth of Athens was based. The old workings can be visited at various points. Those in the Berzéko valley are perhaps the most interesting. They can be reached from a point, Kamáriza, on the main road about 5 km. from Lávrion. Shafts leading to the workings, underground galleries and the cisterns used for washing the minerals can be seen.

Livádhia

In Voiotía; on the road from Thívai to Ámfissa. Famous in antiquity for the oracle of Trophonius, to consult which it was necessary to descend into the bowels of the earth and drink the waters of Lethe. The site of the oracle lay in the gorge of the river Érkina (to the south of the modern town), where there are many springs, variously identified, and traces of a sanctuary with votive niches cut in the rock. In the Middle Ages and in Turkish times Livádhia was a place of considerable importance. The ruins of the castle built by the Catalans, rise above the town.

Maina (Máni)

District in Lakonía; reached by road from Spárti via Yíthion to Areópolis or by coasting steamers, which touch at various ports in the peninsula. The villages can be reached only by the roughest of tracks. The Máni is a unique part of Greece, and has always been a region of unrest (Chapter VI). In this grim country the houses are built like towers, the paths are more stony than anywhere else in Greece, and for drinking water the Maniotes depend on rain water collected in cisterns. The architecture of the churches shows interesting local peculiarities.

Mállia

In Kríti; reached by the coast road from Iráklion, eastwards as far as the village of Mállia, then by track a farther 3 km.; or by steamer to Khersónnisos. Remains of a Minoan palace built round a central court. On the west side are sanctuaries and official apartments, a loggia, and the Grand Staircase; on the east a long portico and the storerooms, with store-jars *in situ*; on the north a hypostyle chamber, a smaller court, and two entrances; from here a paved road led towards the sea The palace was first built *c.* 2000 B.C., altered *c.* 1600 B.C., and finally abandoned *c.* 1400 B.C.. Its history thus resembles that of Cnossos and Phaestus.

Marathón (Plate 85)

In Attikí; reached by road from Athínai (37 km.). Scene of the decisive battle in which the Athenians under Miltiades defeated a much larger Persian force, which had disembarked in the bay (490 B.C.). The spot where the fighting was most intense is marked by a tumulus under which the ashes of the fallen Athenians were buried. Funerary vases were found with the ashes, and obsidian arrowheads were collected on the surface of the tumulus. The tumulus is some 5 km. from the modern village of Marathón.

Megalópolis

In Arkadhía; reached by rail or road from Trípolis. Founded by Epaminondas the Theban in 372 B.C. as a capital city in which were to be collected the inhabitants of the cities of Arcadia. The experiment was a failure, but the extensive remains are impressive and include walls, a fine theatre of Roman date, assembly hall and other buildings in idyllic surroundings, on either side of the river Dhávia. Megalópolis was excavated by the British School at Athínai, 1890–3.

Menídhi

In Attikí; on the right of the road to Menídhi village, 9 km. from Athínai is a large stone-built Mycenaean 'beehive tomb'.

Messene (Messíni)

In Messinía; reached by rail from Kalámai. The city was constructed to be the capital for the Messinians, who were freed from the long Spartan domination by the decisive battle of Leuktra in 371 B.C. It was surrounded by a wall, an outstanding example of Greek military architecture, and the Arcadian Gate in the northern sector is an especially fine piece of work. The wall also enclosed the acropolis on Mt Ithómi, now occupied by a small hermitage but formerly by a sanctuary of Zeus. Within the city walls are remains of the theatre, a large temple and other buildings.

Metéora (Plate 90)

In Thessalía; reached from Kalabáka, terminus of the Vólos-Kalabáka railway, or by road from Tríkkala. The monasteries are remarkable for their amazing situation. In the troubled times of the fourteenth century certain hermits sought safety on the almost inaccessible summits of a group of detached perpendicular rocks, each some 450 m. high, which rise from the plain north of Kalabáka. These hermitages grew in course of time to monasteries. Once numbering twenty-four, they are now reduced to four, with about thirty monks in all. Until recently some could only be visited by means of vertical ladders attached to the face of the rock, or by rope cages, worked by windlasses, and used by the monks to transport supplies from below. These perilous means of access have now been replaced by stairs cut in the rock. The monasteries used to possess valuable treasure and libraries, which have now been dispersed either by sale or theft. Yet much of interest still remains in the way of architecture, frescoes, etc.

Midhéa

In Argolís; reached by road from Návplion to the village of Plataníti (2½ hr.). The remains of Mycenaean fortifications are perhaps the best in Greece. At the neighbouring village of Dhéndra is a Mycenaean 'beehive' tomb, recently excavated. The particularly rich finds are in the museum at Návplion.

Mistrá

In Lakonía; reached by road from Spárti (8 km.). On this rocky spur of Mt Taïyetos the first Frankish prince of Achaia built a strong castle, which fell to the Greeks not long afterwards. It became the centre of Greek resistance to the Franks, and an important town sprang up on the slopes. The remains include the Frankish castle, the Byzantine city grouped round the palace of the Greek Despot of the Morea, and a suburb strung out along the lower slopes. A series of Byzantine churches, a convent, and a monastery, all dating from the fourteenth and fifteenth centuries and many possessing admirable contemporary frescoes, unfortunately long neglected, make Mistrá unique for the study of Byzantine art.

Modon (Methóni)

In Messinía; on the west coast. Reached by road from Kalámai or Kiparissía. Like neighbouring Coron it was an important Venetian station, finally relinquished in 1715. The Venetian fortifications, which are well preserved, rest at many points on ancient Greek foundations.

Monemvasía (Plate 86)

In Lakonía; on the east coast. Reached by road from Spárti, or by coasting steamer from Piraiévs. The rocky promontory, some 275 m., bears a certain resemblance to Gibraltar and is connected with the mainland by a causeway. A place of great importance in the Middle Ages both as a trading station and a fortress, it changed hands many times. The Venetian fortifications still surround the town, and the Acropolis, churches and houses have Venetian elements. On the Acropolis is a ruined Byzantine church of the fourteenth century, resembling that of Dhafní.

Mycenae (Mikínai)

In Argolís; reached by rail or road from Athínai. It was the centre of Mycenaean power in Greece and the residence of Agamemnon, the supreme king. Though influenced by Cretan models, the palace, like that of Tiryns, was on the mainland plan, built around a megaron, not round a large open court. The site has suffered from the later building of a temple, but the massive circuit walls are well preserved. The principal entrance is through the famous *Lion Gate*. Just within the Gate, and surrounded by a circle of upright slabs, are the *Shaft Graves*, where Schliemann made his sensational discoveries, 1874–6. The objects found, which included gold masks, gold-mounted weapons, gold ornaments, objects of ivory, alabaster and other vases, are in the National Museum at Athínai. Outside the citadel are the great 'beehive' tombs, of which the *Treasury of Atreus* (Plate 73) is the supreme monument of Mycenaean architecture. It is a high-vaulted circular tomb sunk in the hill-side and approached by a long stone-lined passage (*dhrómos*). A small chamber opens out of the vault. The carved pilasters which once adorned the façade (from which other decorative features are also missing) are in the British Museum. The masonry of the tomb consists of thirty-three rings of stone, each smaller in diameter than the one below it. The faces of the stones are cut and fitted in such a way that a continuous parabolic curve is produced from floor to apex, where a single cap stone closes the final ring. There are eight other 'beehive' tombs at Mycenae, in which the same method of construction has been used, but the masonry is less perfect. Next in point of excellence is the so-called *Tomb of Clytemnestra*, near the Lion Gate, but in every case, except that of the Treasury of Atreus and one other, the domes have collapsed. In addition to the stone-built tombs there are many rock-cut tombs, approached by rock-cut passages.

Naupactus (Návpaktos)

In Aitolía; on the Gulf of Kórinthos. Reached by road from Athínai via Ámfissa or by steamer from Pátrai. This ancient Greek city was strategically important as guarding the entrance to the Gulf of Kórinthos. The Venetian fortifications of the town and its tiny harbour are well preserved and strikingly picturesque.

Nauplia (Návplion) (Plate 88)

In Argolís at the head of the Gulf of Návplion; reached by daily steamer from Piraiévs, or by train via Árgos. Nauplia, the ancient port of Árgos, was strongly fortified by the Venetians, and the remains are among the finest in Greece. They include sections of the town walls, a fort on the island of Boúzi at the entrance to the harbour, and in the town the large building now used as a museum. The fortifications of the citadel of Itch-Kalé and of Palamede which dominate the town are partly Venetian, partly Turkish. Outside the church of St Spirídon, Kapodistrias, the first President of Greece, was assassinated in 1831. From 1829 to 1834 Návplion served as the capital of Greece and the seat of government.

On the road to Epídhavros, 2 km. to the east, is the convent of Ayía Moní, built on the site of an ancient sanctuary of Ira. The convent church is a beautiful example of a small Byzantine church of the twelfth century.

Oeniadae (Oiniádhai)

In Akarnanía; reached by road from Aitolikón (ferry over the Aspropótamos). Unusually well-preserved remains of a Greek walled city. The circuit wall with towers and gates is *c.* 8 km. long: inside are the remains of a theatre and houses and harbour works (the place was formerly on the sea) built by Philip V of Macedon in the third century B.C. On the acropolis is a large gateway of the sixth century B.C. with a true arch and key-stone, a form of construction almost unknown in Greek architecture and perhaps due indirectly to Italian influence.

Olympia (Olímbia)

In Ilía; reached by train from Pátrai via Pírgos. The fame of this great sanctuary was hardly less than that of Delphi, and like Delphi, it was a centre where statesmen, athletes and pilgrims from all parts of the Greek world assembled, especially at the time of the quinquennial celebrations of the Games. The place was almost exclusively a sanctuary, having no permanent population, except that of priests and others who managed its affairs, and these were housed outside the limits of the sanctuary. The cult of Zeus, with which Olympia was primarily associated in historical times, actually replaced earlier pre-Achaean cults: it lasted from at least 776 B.C., the year of the first Olympiad, from which dates were reckoned by the Greeks, to the final destruction of the temple by order of Theodosius II in A.D. 426.

The excavations which have extricated a large part of the ruins from the silt of the river Alfiós have been in the hands of German archaeologists since 1875. They have uncovered the whole of the area of the *Sacred enclosure* and many adjacent buildings (Fig. 120). At the north-west corner of the enclosure (Altis) are two of the most ancient monuments on the site; the *Temple of Hera* (Plate 74), a temple of the seventh century B.C. which replaced two previous temples, and the *Pelopeion*, a pentagonal enclosure within which stood an altar of Pelops, a legendary Achaean hero. The temple of Hera had an unusual plan, being so arranged that there were five chapels on each side of the interior. It was in one of these that the famous *statue of Hermes*, believed to be the original work of the sculptor Praxiteles, was found. East of the Heraeum is a pretentious monument erected by Herodes Atticus, on which is exhibited twenty-four statues, of which fifteen were of himself or members of his family. East of this monument is a terrace with a row of treasuries, erected by various states as at Delphi. Architectural fragments from these, some of great beauty, are in the museum. Farther east, but outside the Enclosure is the stadium, and to the south of it the hippodrome. Within the Enclosure, near its south-west corner, and dominating all, is the *Temple of Zeus.* It was finished in 456 B.C. and was in the Doric style. It rests on a huge stone substructure and the fragments of columns give some idea of the scale of the building, destined to hold the colossal statue of Zeus, the work of Phidias. A marble and bronze balustrade surrounded the statue, which was lighted only by the light from the doorway. An embroidered purple curtain, the gift of Antiochus IV,

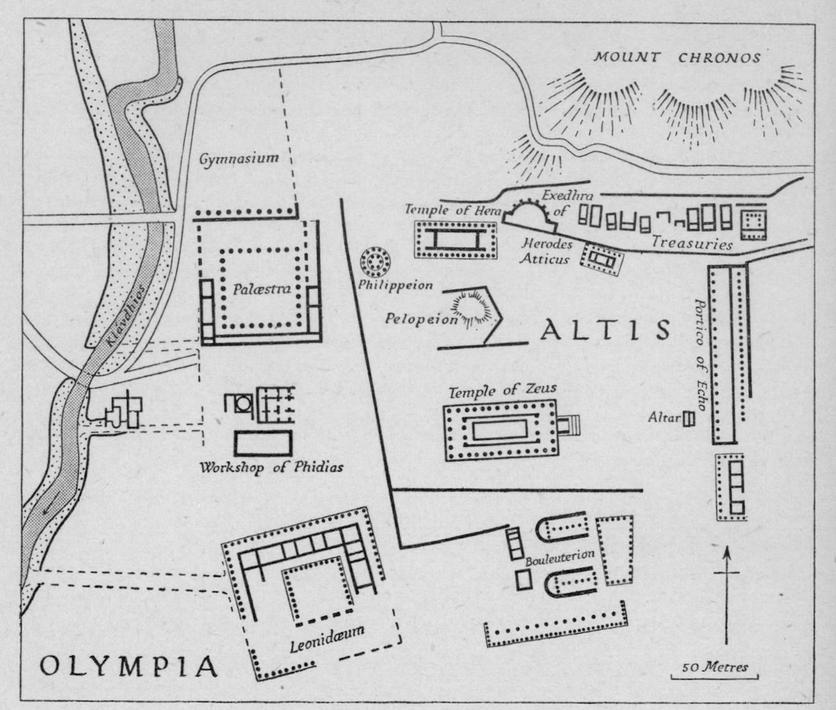

Fig. 120. Olympia

Based on a plan in *Les Guides Bleus-Grèce*, p. 340 (Paris, 1935).

king of Syria, normally hung in front of it. The statue was of gold and ivory, the throne of ebony was enriched with gold, ivory and precious stones. It remained at Olympia till Theodosius II had it removed to Constantinople, where it was destroyed by fire in A.D. 475. Plate 75 shows a panel from the *Temple of Zeus.*

A row of statues stood in front of the eastern approach to the temple, others to the north and south. The long row of columns running along the east wall of the Enclosure form part of the *Portico of Echo.*

Outside the Enclosure, on the south and west, stood various large buildings. To the south was the *Bouleuterion*, where the Olympic Senate sat, in the south-west corner the vast *Leonidaeum* in which distinguished visitors were probably housed; on the west side the *Studio of Phidias*, in which the model of the Statue of Zeus was made and which had the same dimensions as the chamber (*sikos*) of the temple itself. North of this is the *Palaestra*, where the wrestling events took place, and farther north the gymnasium.

In the *museum* outstanding sculptures are those from the pediments of the temple of Zeus, held by many to be the most splendid of all examples of Greek sculpture; the metopes of the same temple; sculptures from the Treasuries; a colossal painted head of Hera, probably from the temple statue; the victory of Paeonius, which stood in front of the Temple of Zeus; and finally the Hermes, long accepted as an original by Praxiteles, but now regarded by many as a Roman copy.

ORCHOMENUS (ORKHOMENÓS)

In Voiotía; reached by train to Livádhia station thence by road (8 km.). One of the centres of Mycenaean civilization, Orchomenus possesses the remains of a magnificent 'beehive' tomb similar to those of Mycenae and elsewhere, but with one exceptional feature: the walls and ceiling of the small inner chambers are not plain, but carved with elaborate patterns of spirals, rosettes, and palmettes. To the west of the tomb, lower down the slopes, are the remains of the Greek Orchomenus, a city which flourished from the seventh to the fourth century B.C. High up the slope are the remains of the later Greek city built by Philip II of Macedon, the father of Alexander the Great, enclosed within a circuit wall and culminating in a small acropolis. Extremely interesting remains of a series of prehistoric settlements have been found underlying the earlier Greek city. Another building of interest is the little Byzantine church of Skripoú, a little north-east of the 'beehive' tomb. It is comprised partly of ancient fragments collected from a temple of the Graces which stood here, and is one of the earliest examples in Greece of a church built on the plan of a Greek cross. It is, moreover, precisely dated by an inscription (874) which is the case with very few Byzantine churches in Greece. A well-known archaic statue, now in the National Museum, was found here.

ÓSIOS LOUKÁS

In Voiotía; reached from Livádhia by track in 5 hr. Byzantine monastery dedicated to a local hermit. The present church dates from the eleventh century and is famous both for its architecture and its superb mosaics, comparable to those of Dhafní.

PATRAS (PÁTRAI)

In Akhaía; reached by train from Athínai or steamer from Piraiévs. Pátrai enjoyed periods of prosperity in Roman, Byzantine and Frankish times but not many remains of the past have survived. The principal are a Roman Odeum built of brick, and a citadel partly Venetian, partly Turkish, in which are incorporated fragments of early temples. St Andrew preached here and the Church of St Andrew is built over a spring, with which, in pagan times, oracular powers were associated.

PHAESTUS (FAISTÓS)

In Kríti; reached by road from Iráklion. The Minoan palace is second only in importance to that of Cnossus, which it resembles in its general lay-out. Most of the existing palace belongs to the sixteenth century B.C., but it stands on the site of an earlier palace built about 2000 B.C. On the west of the Great Court are the official quarters, storerooms opening off a corridor, and guest rooms. Farther west, at a lower level, forming part of the earlier palace, was a wide paved court or arena, with seats for spectators, and, in its north-east corner, a sanctuary or chapel. All this was covered in and levelled when the second palace was built. Access to the new palace was up a wide flight of steps (east of the chapel) which led through a vestibule to a kind of *megaron*. The north wing was composed of a complex of rooms and courtyards, connected by a narrow passage with the central court, and forming, it is supposed, the private apartments. Though resembling Cnossus, Phaestus is more regular in plan and is built of finer materials, more carefully worked. It has been excavated by an Italian archaeological mission.

PHYLE (FILÉ)

In Attikí; reached by road from Athínai to the village of Khasía, thence by track (2 hr.). Fortress on the shortest route to Thívai; one of several that guarded the frontier between Attikí and Voiotía. It was built in the fourth century B.C. About half the walls and one tower are well preserved: the masonry is excellent.

PIRAEUS (PIRAIÉVS)

In Attikí; the port of Athínai. In spite of its overwhelming modernity, Piraiévs has many ancient remains, which, however, are not all easy to find. The most noteworthy are: traces of an inner and outer wall enclosing on the land side the western arm of the Outer and Central Harbours; a gate with round flanking towers, adjoining the State Railway station; a wall which can be followed round the peninsula of Áktion, from the entrance of the Outer Harbour almost to the Zéas Harbour; the Harbour of Zéas itself, in which remains of dry docks, and slipways for hauling up triremes can be seen; the Hellenistic theatre (second century) close by; the Harbour of Mounikhías with more dry docks; the principal gate of the city where the road to Athens passed through; and adjoining it a small portion of the northern of the *two Long Walls* that united Piraeus with Athens. The name of the Outer Harbour in the Middle Ages was Portoleone, derived from a colossal stone lion which stood at the entrance (hence, the modern Greek name Limín Leóntos). The lion was removed to Venice by Morosini in 1687.

PYLOS OR NAVARINO (PÍLOS)

In Messinía; reached by road from Kiparissía, on the Pírgos-Kalámai line, or direct from Kalámai. The modern town is at the south of the bay, and its official name, Pílos, is inappropriate. Ancient Pylos was at the north-west corner of the bay where the acropolis is now crowned by the ruins of a Franco-Venetian castle (Palaiókastro). The site of Homeric Pylos, the long-disputed Pylos of Nestor, is likely to be determined by recent excavations which have revealed the existence of a large Mycenaean palace on a hill 7 km. north of ancient Pylos. Beehive tombs, already discovered in the neighbourhood and the traditional name of 'Cave of Nestor' at Pílos itself point in the same direction. The long island of Sfaktiría, which partially closes the bay on the west, became famous in Greek history when, during the Peloponnesian War the Athenians blockaded a Spartan detachment and compelled them to surrender. The spot where the Spartans made their last stand is on the peak at the north end of the island, where there are traces of an ancient fort. Navarino again became famous in 1827, when a Turkish admiral with a fleet of ninety-nine ships, lying in the bay, provoked an engagement with an allied fleet (British, French and Russian) of seventy-seven ships under Admiral Codrington. The battle ended in the complete destruction of the Turkish fleet, and, indirectly to the granting of independence to Greece. Turkish vessels, sunk in the engagement, can still be seen below the water. At various points south of the island, and on adjacent islets, are memorials to foreigners of various nationalities who fell in the service of Greece. Above the modern town is a large fortress, partly Venetian, partly Turkish.

SÁMOS

Island off the west coast of Turkey; reached by regular steamer from Piraiévs. The ancient remains are concentrated in the south-west of the island in the neighbourhood of Tigáni and at the Heraeum, 7 km. to the west. At Tigáni the circuit wall of the ancient city is well preserved; there is also a theatre and an interesting tunnel about 900 m. long, constructed by order of the tyrant Polycrates in the sixth century B.C., by which water was conducted to the city. At the Heraeum, or sanctuary of Hera, are the foundations of a great temple, built above an earlier temple, but never finished; of the great altar; of buildings of Hellenistic and Roman dates, and of an early Christian basilica. The people of Samos were famous in the seventh and sixth centuries B.C. for their skill as metallurgists, architects and sculptors. The museum at Tigáni contains some especially fine examples of sculpture of that period, as well as several Roman portraits.

Sparta (Spárti)

In Lakonía; reached by road from Trípolis, or from the port of Yíthion. The remains of ancient Sparta lie to the north of the modern town, among olive groves. The remains of the circuit wall are of Roman date; the theatre is of the second and first centuries B.C. On a terrace north of the theatre are the remains of the temple of *Athena of the Bronze House*, in which Pausanias, king of Sparta, took refuge in 477 B.C. Leonidas, who led the Greeks at Thermopylae, was a Spartan, and a fine head and torso of a warrior in marble found near this spot may possibly represent him. It was found during the British excavations and is now in the National Museum at Athínai. Near the bridge over the Evrótas on the Trípolis road is a very ancient sanctuary of Artemis, to which in Roman times a small theatre was added so that the ceremonies associated with the cult could be more easily witnessed. The excavation of this site and of ancient Sparta in general has been the special activity of the British School at Athínai. The finds are mostly in the local museum, but a collection of carved ivories, found at the temple of Artemis, is in the National Museum at Athínai.

Sunium (Soúnion)

In Attikí, reached by road from Athínai, via Lávrion. The ancient acropolis guarding the entrance to the Gulf of Évvoia, was fortified with a circuit wall and towers. At the edge of the cliff stood the sanctuary of Poseidon, god of the sea, surrounded by a wall which was entered by a pillared gateway. The temple itself, of which twelve columns are still standing, was built by Pericles in the fifth century B.C. to replace an earlier temple, destroyed by the Persians. Though in ruins, the position of the temple makes it impressive.

Tegea (Teyéa)

In Arkadhía; reached by road from Trípolis (5 km.). The village of Palaio-episkopí occupies the site of the ancient city, of which parts of the circuit wall and theatre are preserved. The most impressive relic, however, is the temple of Athena, situated at the neighbouring village of Piáli. It was built about 350 B.C., and the sculptures were by the renowned Scopas: fragments of these sculptures are in the National Museum at Athínai.

Thebes (Thívai)

In Voiotía; reached by rail or road from Athínai. A place of great importance in Greek history and for long the rival of Athens. Scanty remains of a Mycenaean palace underlie the present town, and there are Mycenaean rock-cut tombs on the slopes. At the south-east edge of the hill are the foundations of a *temple of Apollo* and a gateway at the point where the outer circuit wall joined the circuit wall of the Mycenaean acropolis. During the Middle Ages Thebes was a flourishing town and the capital of the Frankish duchy of Athens, but all that remains of this period is a fine tower, part of the Frankish castle of St Omer. A museum adjoins the tower.

Thera (Thíra)

Island in the southern Kikládhes; reached by steamer from Piraiévs. Thera was a colony of the Dorians (ninth century B.C.), whose settlement and religious centre was in the south-east of the island, on a ridge overlooking the sea. The remains are strung out along this ridge. At the southern end of the ancient city of Thera are grouped earlier buildings, approached by a long terrace; most of these are connected with the *Sanctuary of Apollo*, whose festival was celebrated by dances of young men. The northern part is occupied by the later, or Ptolemaic city (300–145 B.C.), with streets, houses, a theatre and baths.

Thermopylae (Thermopílai)

In Fthiótis-Fokís; on the road from Thívai to Lamía, via Atalándi. The pass, once a narrow passage between rocks and sea, has been held on many occasions against invading armies. Perhaps the most famous occasion was in 480 B.C., when Leonidas with a handful of Spartans and Thespians held it against the Persian host under Xerxes. The position was turned and Leonidas was killed, but the survivors retired to a small hill in the middle of the pass and died fighting to the last man. A stone lion now marks the spot. The sites of the various incidents of the fighting have been identified by recent excavations.

Thessalonica (Thessaloníki)

In Thessaloníki; the city, founded in 316 B.C., owes its name to Thessalonike, the sister of Alexander the Great, and wife of Cassander, one of Alexander's generals. It became the capital of Roman Macedonia, and its position on the *Via Egnatia* assured its prosperity and importance as long as direct communication between Rome and Constantinople was possible and desired. The modern road, which bears the same name and follows the old Roman road, runs parallel to the sea front through the centre of the city. It is spanned near the eastern city wall by the *Arch of Galerius* (fourth century A.D.), on which the much-worn sculptured reliefs represent Roman victories over the Persians.

The *ancient walls* built in the sixth century A.D., and since then frequently altered and repaired, rest in part on Hellenistic foundations and still surround the acropolis and a great part of the city. The section along the sea front has been destroyed, but its southern limit is marked by a round tower (*The White Tower*).

Thessaloníki possesses some famous churches. *Áyios Yióryios*, close to the Arch of Galerius is, by origin, a Roman rotunda of the fourth century A.D., and the two probably formed part of the same building scheme. The rotunda was converted into a church in the fifth century and adorned with remarkable mosaics, still surviving, though sadly disfigured. It was turned into a mosque in 1591 and a minaret was added: after the Greeks occupied Thessaloníki in 1912 it again became a Christian church. *Áyios Dhimítrios* is a basilica of the fifth century with five naves separated by columns; until 1917 it possessed some of the earliest and finest Christian mosaics. The church was then almost entirely destroyed by fire, but a few of the mosaics survived. *Áyia Paraskeví*, built in the fifth century, is an interesting church on the plan of a Syrian basilica, and has some beautifully carved capitals. The church of *Áyia Sofía*, distinguished by its dome, also has some remarkably fine mosaics, in the dome and in the apse. Those in the dome are held to be of the eleventh century, but the date of the mosaic in the apse, as well as of the construction of the church, are more doubtful. The little *church of the Apostles* in the north-west corner of the town is a beautiful example of ornamental brickwork. It was built in the fourteenth century.

TIRYNS (TÍRINS)

In Argolis; reached by road or rail from Návplion (3 km.) or from Árgos (7 km.). The remains of a Mycenaean palace, comparable to that of Mycenae, but better preserved and more compact, are situated on a low hill by the side of the road. Even before Mycenaean times the site was occupied and, as early as the third millennium, a large circular building stood on the summit. Between 2000 B.C. and 1600 B.C. fortification began, and was gradually extended throughout the following Mycenaean period. The ramparts, which include the lower ground to the north, the staircase and postern gate on the west, the *Grand Entrance* on the east and the existing palace, all belong to the end of the Mycenaean period. Traces of the earlier palace have almost completely disappeared. The *casemates* built in the thickness of the wall on the south and south-east are remarkable. The average thickness of the walls is from 8 to 10 m., and the original height is estimated to have been about 10 m. The palace was approached from the east side by a ramp, which led to a kind of terrace, thence westwards through a pillared porch into a large court; on the north of this a second porch led into a smaller court surrounded by porticoes, where stood the altar of sacrifice. The palace proper lay to the north of this court. The principal apartment, as is usual on the mainland as opposed to Cretan palaces, is the *megaron*, entered from the smaller court through a vestibule and antechamber. The roof of the megaron was supported on four central columns standing round a circular hearth. The walls were adorned with frescoes. Behind and round the megaron lay the complex of rooms forming the rest of the palace, baths, womens' apartments, etc. In the side of the hill to the east is a 'beehive' tomb, and several rock-cut tombs.

Appendix III

THE PLACE NAMES OF GREECE

Introduction

The problem of transcribing Greek place names is difficult for the following reasons:

(i) The geography and history of Greece became best known through the writings of people using the Latin and not the Greek language as their medium, with the result that many important places are now hardly recognized by their Greek names outside Greece. Thus Attikí, Évvoia, Évripos, Ípiros, Ólimbos, Imittós, Ídhi are unfamiliar, whereas the Latin forms Attica, Euboea, Euripus, Epirus, Olympus, Hymettus, Ida are in common use.

(ii) The conventional English forms of Greek place names have evolved not only from the latinized forms of the original Greek names, but also from forms introduced from other sources: for example, the Crusaders learnt Frankish names for Greek places and spread their use in England.

(iii) Greek orthography (spelling and characters) has changed very little from classical times, but changes in pronunciation have been considerable. The strict transliteration of the written name therefore gives a very different result from the phonetic rendering of the same name as pronounced in Greece to-day.

(iv) In compound place names (e.g. Korinthiakós Kólpos) the specific part (Korinthiakós derived from Kórinthos) must be combined in number, gender and case with the generic part (Kólpos). This calls for exact knowledge of the language, and the variation in the case ending of the specific part may make the name unrecognizable to the non-linguistic reader. But even with this knowledge, if the generic part of the name is translated, grammatical combination with the specific part is sometimes impossible. For instance, Orfanóu in Kólpos Orfanóu is the genitive of a nominative form which has been lost. A slightly different example of this difficulty is Saronikós Kólpos, where Saronikós is the adjectival form of an unknown noun.

(v) Two widely diverse forms of the Greek language are in use in Greece to-day, the *katharévousa* (purist speech) and *dhimotikí* (demotic or popular speech) (see p. 314).

Place names which appear with official status in a government publication are usually given in a form which is in accordance with the spirit of *katharévousa*; for example, ancient names are restored, foreign names are translated where possible into a *katharévousa* form of Greek, and demotic spellings are made to conform with those dictionaries favouring *katharévousa*. It must be remembered that places are very frequently known locally by their demotic names or by colloquial alternatives, and that these forms will most probably not appear in official publications.

(vi) Maps issued by the Greek government are the chief and sometimes the only sources for the official forms of place names. But the whole of Greece has not been surveyed in detail and there are broad stretches of country for which no large-scale maps exist. Moreover, even where there is map-cover on a scale of 1:100,000, the less important features of the physical landscape are not always named. For this reason it is not possible to transliterate the official Greek form in every case.

A further difficulty arises from the fact that official maps are not always in agreement concerning the spelling of names. For example, a village near Kórinthos is given the variant forms of Examíllia (1:100,000, Sheet VIII K) and Examília (1:400,000, Civil Edition, Sheet B iii). The authority for both maps is the Army Geographical Service.

Official Systems of Spelling and Transliteration

The principles followed by certain official bodies in the spelling of Greek place names are given below:

(1) *Greek Government Charts*

The Greek Hydrographic Service tends to give an official status to a demotic or colloquial form as an alternative to the *katharévousa* form. Place names are written in Greek characters. Charts which were published after 1928 give a sub-title in which English geographical terms are used. These sub-titles may be in one of two forms; the terms may be combined with a transliterated form of the place-name (e.g. Port of Herakleon—1936) or the whole of the sub-title may be given in an anglicized form (e.g. Bays of Crete Island—1936).

(2) *Greek Army Geographical Service*

(*a*) 1:100,000, *Epitelikós Khártis tis Elládhos*. This series provides the most complete set of detailed surveys, but it does not cover the whole country. Demotic and colloquial forms rarely appear. The new or revised edition of each sheet substitutes Greek names for many of those place names which were formerly Turkish, Bulgarian or Albanian.

(*b*) 1:400,000. *Carte Aéronautique*. This is the only official Greek survey which covers the whole of Greece (12 sheets published in Athínai, 1932–5). The titles and sub-titles of each sheet are given both in Greek and in French. The key to the map is also given in both languages. On the map itself the names of large settlements are always given in a French form of transliteration and in some cases in Greek within brackets beneath the French name. It has not been possible to determine fully the system used in selecting towns which are named in both languages. The names of small settlements and of geographical features are given only in Greek.

(3) *Permanent Committee on Geographical Names (P.C.G.N.)*

The principles adopted in 1941 by the P.C.G.N. for Greek nomenclature are briefly:

(*a*) All geographical names in modern use are rendered in a new transliteration (see 3 (*e*)).

(*b*) The position of the Greek accent, which is a stress accent, is preserved in the transliterated name. It is placed on the last vowel of the stressed syllable, e.g. Návplon, Itháki, Platí.

(*c*) The names of ancient sites and ancient names in historical context are rendered in the classical transliteration (see 3 (*e*)).

(*d*) In compound place names the generic part is given in the new transliterated form of the Greek term, e.g. Ólimbos Óros (Mount Olympus); Korinthiakós Kólpos (Gulf of Corinth). *Glossaries: I, Modern Greek* (London, 1942) gives English renderings of these Greek geographical terms.

(*e*) Both the new transliteration system and the system of classical transliteration have been issued in the P.C.G.N. circular *Transliteration of Greek* (London, 1941), and later on pp. xxx–xxxiv of the P.C.G.N. *Glossaries: I, Modern Greek* (London, 1942). The new transliteration (see p. 452) replaces the system appearing on pp. 51–4 of the R.G.S. *Technical Series*, No. 2 (London, 2nd edition, 1933).

The P.C.G.N. has also produced *A Gazetteer of Greece* (London, 1942) which is a list of the names of all inhabited places and of all important geographical features which appear on Greek maps of Greece. It should be noted that except for the *Carte Aéronautique*, 1:400,000, Greece is not completely covered by Greek official sheets or detailed charts, and the list of names in the Gazetteer is not therefore complete. Official names are printed in thick type and are transliterated according to the principles of the new transliteration. The official name is not necessarily in common or even in local use in Greece. The official source of the names of inhabited places is the census publications of the Greek Ministry of Economics, of which the most complete and accessible publication is *Population de la Grèce d'après le recensement du* 15–16 *Mai* 1928 (Athènes, Deúxième Edition, 1935). In this work place names are given both in Greek orthography and in a French transliterated form. The official sources for names of land features are the maps of the Greek Army Geographical Service; and of hydrographic features, the charts and publications of the Hydrographic Service of the Royal Hellenic Navy.

(4) *British Admiralty Sailing Directions*

The new transliteration (P.C.G.N. 1941) is used for all place names throughout the *Mediterranean Pilot*, vol. IV, 7th edition, 1941. In the index to the *Pilot* two forms appear: the name as it appears on the Admiralty Charts and the name as it is rendered by the new transliteration (P.C.G.N. 1941). A most useful list of official names and terms with some of their alternative Greek names is also given in App. V, p. 429. The alternative names are often in a demotic form. The same policy has been followed in the new edition of the *Mediterranean Pilot*, vol. III, 7th edition, 1943.

In compound place names the generic part has in all cases been translated into English—thus it is Gulf of Kórinthos, not Korinthiakós Kólpos. This practice avoids the confusion which might arise from the variation of case ending of the specific part and makes the place name more intelligible to the English reader. This follows a suggestion made by the secretary of the P.C.G.N. for use in 'popular prose-context', provided that it is carried out with care by experts. Although all names have been rendered in the new transliteration (P.C.G.N. 1941) the note 'System of Orthography' in *Mediterranean Pilot*, vol. IV (7th edition, 1941), pp. xiii–xvi states that the R.G.S. II (1921) system has been adopted. This is evidently an oversight, the note having survived from the previous edition of 1929. Barely a single name has a form common to both editions.

(5) *British Admiralty Charts*

A system of transliteration was first adopted for use on Admiralty Charts in 1886, and there have been numerous emendments from time to time. It is therefore possible to find the same name spelt in two different ways on charts which were published in different years; e.g. Kaufkalida Island on Ch. 207, west coast of Morea (first published in 1867) and Kauphkalida Island on Ch. 1800, Malta to Cape Malea (first published in 1894). It must be remembered that it is only feasible to alter the spelling of names which appear on a chart when a new edition of that chart is decided upon. For charts of the Greek coasts and seas this happens infrequently, and there cannot therefore be immediate uniformity of method in the transliteration of place names throughout the series.

In 1921, the R.G.S. II system of transliteration was adopted, the rules for which may be seen on pp. xvii–xx of the *Mediterranean Pilot*, vol. III (6th edition, London, 1929). In 1941 the Hydrographic Department approved the new transliteration system of the P.C.G.N. and on charts showing major corrections since that date, place names have been made to conform with the P.C.G.N. system, e.g. Chart 1676, Gulf of Pátrai (1892, revised 1904, with major corrections 1941).

On all charts the generic element of compound place names is given in English, e.g. Gulf of Pátrai, Mesolóngion Lake, Cape Pápas, River Fídharis.

(6) *Geographical Section, British General Staff* (*G.S.G.S.*)

Since 1940 G.S.G.S. has issued two series of maps which largely cover Greek territory, No. 4087 on the scale of 1:100,000 and No. 4088 on the scale of 1:250,000. Both series show the same policy in the transliteration of names. The generic element of compound place names for hydrographical features has been translated into English, a policy which was followed in order to conform with the Admiralty practice. For land features, however, the generic part is given in a transliterated form of the Greek word. Owing to the short time available for the production of the maps in 1940 little care could be taken in the transliteration of names and numerous mistakes occur. For instance, in the name Thermaïkós Kólpos (No. 4087 Sheet C. 3066) Kólpos has been translated and the adjectival form Thermaïkós has been retained in place of the noun Thérmai. Thus a new place name Gulf of Thermaïkós has arisen. The actual spelling shows an attempt to render place names as pronounced in Greece, but it differs both from previous systems of transliteration and from the P.C.G.N. system. In 1941 G.S.G.S. approved the P.C.G.N. new transliteration and maps published in this year, and subsequently, were more accurate (e.g. No. 4087, Sheet C. 4866, 2nd edition, 1942). The spelling of place names on future and revised editions will agree with the forms given in the P.C.G.N. Gazetteer.

The inherent difficulties of Greek orthography have prevented G.S.G.S. from publishing exact photographic reproductions of any Greek official maps.

(7) 512 (*A. Fld. Svy.*) *Coy. R.E.*, 1941

Numerous maps of Greece on scales varying from 1:25,000 to 1:400,000 have been produced by this authority (see p. 405). For the most part the generic part of compound place names has been translated, even when combined with a Greek adjectival form. This policy has again led to error, as in Thermaïkos Gulf or in Megali Spring (*mégas*, *megáli*, *méga* = big). On occasions it is the adjectival part of a compound place-name that has been translated, with curious results, e.g. 'Big Keserli' (Méga Keserlí), 'Small Sanda' (Mikrí Sánda): or even the whole name has been translated when comprised of recognisable words—e.g. 'old castle' for Paliókastro, 'small fields' for Khorafákia. The lack of consistency is evident even from study of a single sheet, e.g. 1:100,000 Δ VI. The transliteration system is sometimes literal and sometimes phonetic: Sfendamni or Sphentamni; Georgios or Yeoryios (*sic*).

Abbreviations are never expanded, which leads to further difficulties, particularly with an inflected language. Thus Ay. may stand for Áyios, Ayía, Áyion, Ayíou, or Áyioi, while Prph. is not immediately recognisable as Profítis.

In the most recent (1943) sheets there appears to be more consistency: the tendency is to keep the Greek form of compound place names, e.g. Kolpos Gardhikíou, Oros Maínalon. The transliteration is more phonetic and approaches closely to that adopted by the P.C.G.N.

The Spelling of Place names in this Handbook

(*a*) The new transliteration (P.C.G.N. 1941) is used for all place names where the official Greek form is known. Nearly all of these names are included in the *Gazetteer of Greece* mentioned above. Where the official Greek form is not known, it has been necessary to use the conventional English spelling. The only exception to this rule is in the name, Athínai, where the conventional English form, Athens, has frequently been used.

(*b*) Geographical terms are given in English, e.g. Gulf of Kórinthos, not Korinthiakós Kólpos. This practice has been followed in order to conform with that pursued by the Hydrographic Department of the Admiralty in the *Mediterranean Pilot* and on charts revised since 1941. It is a hybrid form with serious disadvantages, and it is not always possible to find the nominative of the specific part.

(*c*) Adjectival forms of place names have been avoided wherever possible, except when used in a historical context. For example, Gulf of Kórinthos is used rather than Corinthian Gulf, and Plain of Voiotía rather than Boeotian Plain. An exception must be made, however, in the case of those compound place names where there is no known nominative of the specific part. For example, in Saronikós

Kólpos, Saronikós is the adjectival form of an unknown noun. Gulf of Saronikós is therefore grammatically incorrect, and although the difficulty might be avoided by the use of Gulf of Áiyina, this is a colloquial use and is not accepted as official. It has, therefore, been thought best to use Saronic Gulf, which follows the practice adopted in the *Admiralty Sailing Directions*. A similar example is Maliakós Kólpos which must be rendered as Maliaic Gulf.

In a historical context, the conventional English spelling of the adjectival form is used. For example, the 'Cretan' question, not the 'Kritikon' question, which would involve coining a new form. This conventional spelling has been used occasionally elsewhere in the Handbook, in order to avoid clumsy and un-English forms.

(*d*) In a historical context the names of towns, villages and sites are given in the classical system of transliteration, and where first mentioned the new transliteration form (P.C.G.N.) is also given in brackets. Both forms are given in the index.

(*e*) Names which have acquired archaeological significance, e.g. Acropolis, Hippodrome, are given in their English classical form, and not in the transliterated form Akrópolis, Íppodhrómion.

(*f*) Personal names are given in the conventional English spelling and follow the accepted standard of the leading libraries.

Conclusion

It is evident that many of the place names as spelt in the present Handbook cannot be regarded as stabilized. The system of transliteration is largely based upon a phonetic rendering of a speech which is undergoing continuous change; place-names are being revised with each new edition of the Greek source maps and it is almost certain that many demotic forms will be accepted eventually as official, or at least as alternatives to the *katharévousa* forms. Moreover, if agreement is to be reached on a standard international form, the generic element of compound place-names will not necessarily be in English.

Appendix IV

NOTE ON THE GREEK ALPHABET

The Semitic, the Greek and the Roman alphabets all have simple straight-line capital letters suitable for carving in stone. They are clearly related to one another; the Greek is derived from the Semitic, the Roman from the Greek. The origin of the Semitic alphabet is unknown. It has been alternatively suggested that both the Semitic and Greek alphabets were developed independently from a primitive set of signs in common use all over the eastern Mediterranean, for commercial purposes in Minoan times. There is, however, much doubt as to the significance of these signs.

The names of the Greek letters afford strong evidence that the Greek alphabet is derived from the Semitic and is not a parallel development from a common source. The Hebrew names of the letters, aleph, beth, gimel, daleth, etc., are obviously the same as the Greek names, álfa, víta, gámma, dhélta, etc. Seventeen of the twenty-two Hebrew letter names are words describing common objects, while their Greek equivalents are meaningless as Greek words: thus the Semitic alphabet is considered the parent of the Greek.

The names of the Greek letters are not, however, identical with the Hebrew; the vowel terminations suggest that the Greek names are derived from an Aramaic form. It is probable, therefore, that the Greek was borrowed not directly from the Phoenicians but, perhaps much earlier, along with Babylonian weights and measures, from the Aramaic-speaking peoples of southern and western Asia Minor. The Achaeans, seafarers in the Aegean as early as the fifteenth century B.C., were in touch with peoples of the eastern and western shores and may have brought the alphabet to Greece. Since Greek communities were relatively isolated from each other, it is easy to believe that more than one borrowing and more than one adaptation of the alphabet took place. Two slightly different forms became common in Greece: the western or Chalcidian alphabet and the eastern or Ionic alphabet. The Greeks made certain changes and additions to the Semitic alphabet. They set aside some symbols to represent vowel sounds: the Semitic breathing marks aleph for álfa, he for épsilon, and the letters cheth for éta and yod for ióta were so used. In the eastern alphabet íta became a vowel, but in the western it remained a breathing. They added χ, φ and ω to their alphabet; the origin of these signs is obscure. Many of the other letters underwent considerable adaptation of form and sound. By the fourth century B.C. the western and the eastern alphabets had been more or less amalgamated, and the letters in their present form were in use throughout Greek lands.

The Roman alphabet was derived from the Greek alphabet. The Greek colonists took the western form of the Greek alphabet to Sicily and southern Italy, and the Etruscans, migrating to Italy about the ninth century B.C., carried, it is thought, a closely related form from Asia Minor. This form had been obtained from Greece before the Greek alphabet was clearly differentiated into its eastern and western types. The Roman alphabet in use to-day in northern and western Europe arose from the fusion of these two forms.

The Greek Alphabet

Script	Print	Name		International phonetic symbol	Classical transliteration	P.C.G.N. transliteration
A a	Α α	ἄλφα	álfa	a, ʌ	a	a
B ϐ	Β β	βῆτα	víta	v	b	v
G γ	Γ γ	γάμμα	gámma	g, ɣ; j; ŋ	g; n	g; y; n
D δ	Δ δ	δέλτα	dhélta	ð	d	dh, d
E ε	Ε ε	ἔψιλον	épsilon	ε, e	e	e
Z ʒ	Ζ ʒ	ʒῆτα	zíta	z	z	z
H n	Η η	ἦτα	íta	iː, i	i	i
Θ,ϑ ∂	Θ θ	θῆτα	thíta	θ	th	th
J,ʃ ι	Ι ι	ἰώτα	ióta	iː, i	i	i
K u	Κ κ	κάππα	káppa	k	k	k
Λ,Ꞥ. λ	Λ λ	λάμβδα	lámvdha	l, ʎ	l	l
M,Ⅿ. μ	Μ μ	μῦ	mi	m	m	m
N,Π. ν	Ν ν	νῦ	ni	n, ɲ	n	n
Ξ,Ξ. ʒ	Ξ ξ	ξῖ	xi	ks	x	x
O o	Ο ο	ὄμικρον	ómikron	ɔ	o	o
Π. π,ω	Π π	πῖ	pi	p	p	p
P ϱ	Ρ ρ	ῥῶ	ro	r	r	r
Σ σ,ς,ѕ	Σ σ, ς	σῖγμα	sígma	s	s	s, ss
T τ	Τ τ	ταῦ	taf	t	t	t
V υ	Υ υ	ὔψιλον	ípsilon	iː, i; v, f	y; u	i; v
Φ φ	Φ φ	φῖ	fi	f	ph	f
X x	Χ χ	χῖ	khi	x, ç	ch	kh
Ψ y	Ψ ψ	ψῖ	psi	ps	ps	ps
Ω ω	Ω ω	ὠμέγα	oméga	ɔ	o	o

Appendix V

THE PRONUNCIATION OF MODERN GREEK

Modern Greek uses relatively few sounds and the majority of them are not difficult for an Englishman.

Vowels

Seven vowels and five apparent diphthongs are used to denote vowel sounds in writing, but several of them are pronounced alike:

Greek	α	αι, ε	η, ι, υ, ει, οι, υι	ο, ω	ου
English	*a*	*e*	*i*	*o*	*oo*
Phonetic	ɑ, ʌ	e, ɛ	iː, i	ɔ	u

The vowel sounds are pure as in Italian, but their nearest English equivalents are:

a	as in *attention*, or *u* as in *sup*
e	if stressed as *ei* in *vein*, if unstressed as *e* in *bed*
i	,, ,, *i* ,, *machine*, ,, ,, *i* ,, *sit*
o	between *au* in *autumn* and *o* in *cross*. Never as the diphthong *ow* in *now*
oo	as in *food*.

αυ and ευ are pronounced *av* and *ev* except before unvoiced consonants (θ, κ, ξ, π, σ, τ, φ, χ, ψ) when they become *af* and *ef*,

e.g. Ναύπλιον pronounced *Náf-plion*;* Πειραιεύς pronounced *Pir-e-éfs*, but Εὔβοια pronounced *Évv-i-a*.

When two vowels coming together in a word are pronounced separately, the second vowel is marked by a diæresis (¨):

e.g. καϋμένος (burnt) pronounced *ka-i-ménos* not *kav-mén-os*
'Αχαΐα ,, *Akh-a-í-a* ,, *Akh-é-a*.

When two vowels come together in different words in a sentence, it is customary in speech, and sometimes in writing, to drop one of them. In some cases the two words are then joined together:

e.g. κατ' ἔτος for κατὰ ἔτος (annually, every year)
τὤνα ,, τὸ ἕνα (the one).

The omitted letter is indicated by the apostrophe (').

Consonants

The consonants, except γ and χ, have English sound equivalents:

Greek	β,	δ,	ζ,	θ,	κ,	λ,	μ,	ν,	ξ,	π,	ρ,	τ,	σ,	φ,	ψ.
English	*v*,	*th*,	*z*,	*th*,	*k*,	*l*,	*m*,	*n*,	*ks*,	*p*,	*r*,	*t*,	*s*,	*f*,	*ps*.
Phonetic	v,	ð,	z,	θ,	k,	l, ʎ,	m,	n, ɲ,	ks,	p,	r,	t,	s,	f,	ps.

* Imitated pronunciation must not be confused with transliteration (see p. 447).

δ and θ are clearly distinguished.

θ (θ) is pronounced as *th* in *thick, thought.*

δ (ð) " " *th* " *this, the,* except between ν and ρ, when it is pronounced *d.*

e.g. Ἄνδρος pronounced *Án-dros*, δένδρον (*tree*) pronounced *thén-dron.*

κ (k) before ε, αι, η, ο, ει, οι, is a sound between an English *k* and *h*, something like *k* in *key* but much softer:

e.g. Κιθαιρών pronounced *Khith-e-rón.*

κ is a more guttural sound resembling γ when it is the initial letter of a word following one ending with ν.

e.g. ἑκατὸν καΐκια (a hundred caïques) pronounced *eka-tón gha-í-kia.*

γ and χ are sounds absent from English and they are very difficult for an Englishman to make correctly.

γ (ɣ) is in general a guttural sound very like the French guttural *r*, and softer than *g* in *gun.*

e.g. Γαλλία (France) pronounced *Ghall-ía.**

Exceptions:

(ŋ) (i) before γ, κ, ξ, χ as *n* in *finger.*

e.g. λαγκάδα (pass, gorge) pronounced *lan-gátha.*

γκ at the beginning of a word, however, is hard as *g* in *go.*

e.g. γκρεμνός (cliff, precipice) pronounced *grem-nós.*

(g) (ii) after γ as *g* in *go.*

e.g. 'Αγγλικός (English) pronounced *Ang-li-kós.*

(j) (iii) before αι, ε, ι, η, υ, ει, οι as *y* in *yes.*

e.g. Γύθειον pronounced *Yí-thi-on.*

χ (x) is very similar in sound to *ch* in Scottish *loch* or German *doch*, but

(ç) before αι, ε, ι, η, υ, ει, οι it is softer as *ch* in German *dich.*

Some sounds are absent from Greek and if needed in Greek transliteration of foreign words are represented by letter combinations:

μπ gives *b* (b).

[Medially μπ is pronounced *mb* and occurs in Greek words.]

ντ initially gives *d* (d).

[Medially ντ is pronounced *nd* and occurs in Greek words.]

τσ gives *ch* (ʧ) as in *church.*

τ3, ντ3 gives *j* (ʤ) as in *jump.*

* The use of *gh* to represent γ is conventional; no combination of English letters gives the right sound.

Breathings

The rough (ʽ) and smooth (ʼ) breathing marks, which in Ancient Greek distinguished words beginning with an aspirate (ʽ) from those without (ʼ), are still placed in writing on all initial vowels. In Modern Greek they do not affect the pronunciation—the initial letter h has been dropped: e.g. ἅγιος (holy) pronounced *á-yos*. In foreign words, usually Turkish, an initial aspirate is represented by χ:

e.g. χάνι (inn) pronounced *háni*.

Accents

Modern Greek has a stress accent only and this cannot be placed further from the end of the word than the antepenultimate syllable, or the penultimate when the last vowel was originally long. The distinction between long and short vowels is no longer made in pronunciation (see p. 453), but in determining the accentuation η, ω, and the apparent diphthongs normally count as long; ε and ο short; and α, ι, υ may be either long or short.

Three accents are used:*

(i) the *acute* (ʹ), which may stand on any of the last three syllables.

(ii) the *grave* (`), which may only be placed on the last syllable. It is used instead of the acute when a word with an acute accent on the last syllable is in the middle of a sentence or phrase and is not followed by a punctuation mark: e.g. τὸ μικρὸ ρέμμα (the little stream) not τό μικρό ρέμμα.

(iii) the *circumflex*, which may only be placed on the last or the penultimate syllable: on the last only when it is long, and on the penultimate only when it is long and the last is short. The circumflex and the acute accent are not distinguished in pronunciation.

Since long and short vowels are no longer distinct in sound, the rules of accentuation are often broken in popular speech, especially when a word changes its accent from rule in declension:

e.g. Ἅγιος (masc.), Ἁγία (fem.) is correct, and Ἁγία is always written by educated Greeks but Ἅγια often said.

It will be found therefore, that the accent as placed on names on the official maps is not always that given by the local inhabitants. Nevertheless correct stress accent is very important if the speaker wishes to be readily understood. There are many words in common use which are distinguished in speaking only by their stress:

e.g. καλός (good), *kalós* and κάλος (corn, i.e. on the toe), *kálos*.
πολύς (much), *polís* ,, πόλις (city), *pólis*.

A few monosyllables have no accent—those in common use are: ὁ, ἡ, οἱ, αἱ (the; masc. and fem., sing. and plural), pronounced *ō, ī, ī, ē*. εἰς (in or into) pronounced *īss*.

Ióta Subscript

ῃ (and ῳ in literary forms) is sometimes written with an iota subscript, indicating that the vowel was once followed by ι. It is not pronounced:

e.g. νὰ γράφῃς (that you may write) pronounced *ná ghráfis*.

Punctuation

The signs are the same as in English except the question mark, which is (;), and the semi-colon, which is (·).

* In P.C.G.N. transliteration all accents are marked (ʹ).

Appendix VI

MODERN GREEK—ENGLISH GLOSSARY

The words given in the Glossary are those most commonly found on Greek maps and charts and those used as place-names or forming elements in the place-names. It will be noted that a very large number of the place-names of Greece are descriptive in form, and thus the same name occurs again and again in different parts of the country. Pírgos (a tower), Panayía (a holy place), Stavrós (a cross) are village names found all over Greece, while Neokhórion (new village), Palaiokhórion (old village) and Palaiókastron (old fortress) occur in almost every region. Xerovoúni (dry mountain), Mavrovoúni (black mountain), Aspropótamos (white river) are very common, and similar examples could be cited indefinitely. Another favourite practice is to use the names of the saints and prophets. Mountain peaks and villages especially are frequently named in this way: Profítis Ilías (Prophet Elias), Áyios Ioánnis (St John), Áyios Nikólaos (St Nicholas), Ayía Paraskeví (Good Friday), to give only a few, are so common that they have almost ceased to serve their purpose as names, since they are no longer distinctive beyond a very local range.

The selection of words in this Glossary has been taken largely from the Permanent Committee on Geographical Names (P.C.G.N.) publication *Glossaries: 1. Modern Greek* (London, 1942), and the spellings and accents are as given in this source. The *Short Glossary of Greek* (London, 1943), published by G.S.G.S., has also been used, in addition to various dictionaries and grammars. The meanings given are the nearest translation of the word, used in a geographical sense.

Dictionaries

(1) The standard dictionary in Greek is the Ἱστορικὸν Λεξικὸν τῆς Νέας Ἑλληνικῆς (Athens, 1933–). Only a few volumes are as yet published.

(2) A. Kyriakides, *Modern Greek-English Dictionary* (2nd ed., Athens, 1909). It is a useful work, and includes a Cypriot vocabulary.

(3) M. Constantinides, *Modern Greek-English Dictionary* (Athens, 1910). This is the most comprehensive of the smaller dictionaries: all the words given are in current use, and *katharévousa* forms, rarely used in conversation, and demotic forms, used only in popular speech, are marked.

(4) A. N. Jannaris, *A Concise Dictionary of the English and Modern Greek Languages* (London, 1st ed. 1895: 8th reprint, 1943). A very useful and scholarly English-Greek dictionary; *katharévousa* and demotic forms are distinguished: most words given are common to literary use and conventional speech.

(5) I. Kykkotis, *English-Greek and Greek-English Dictionary* (London, 1942). Published in a library form (including a short grammar) and in a pocket edition. The vocabulary is less extensive than that of (2), (3) or (4), but is up-to-date, and more demotic in character.

Grammars

(6) M. Gardner, *A Short and Easy Modern Greek Grammar* (London, 1892). This is out of print, but is very practical and scholarly. It includes a good list of idiomatic phrases.

(7) A. Thumb, *Handbook of the Modern Greek Vernacular*, translated by S. Angus (Edinburgh, 1912). This very scholarly work, which includes grammar, texts (some of which are in local dialects) and glossary, is suitable for advanced students.

(8) K. Petraris, *A Handbook of the Modern Greek Spoken Language*, translated by W. H. D. Rouse (London, 1921). A translation of the manual composed in German on the Gaspey-Otto-Sauer method. It contains exercises, and is very useful, but not readily obtainable.

(9) I. Kykkotis, *Modern Greek* (*Self-Taught*) (London, 1941). This is a short up-to-date grammar, in which special attention is paid to modern popular usage. It has a short but valuable vocabulary.

(10) *A Modern Greek Manual for Self-Tuition* (Trubner's Language Manuals, edited by J. H. Freese) (London, 1920). This includes grammar, exercises, vocabulary and texts.

(11) N. Anastassiou, revised by L. Joannidis, *Modern Greek Self-Taught* (Marlborough's Self-Taught Series) (London, 1932). It is essentially a phrase-book, but a short grammar is included.

In the glossary which follows, ancient words which have fallen out of common use and artificial compounds are marked *k* (*katharévousa*). Such words are rarely used in ordinary speech, and after them alternative or demotic forms, preferable for colloquial use, have been given.

The following abbreviations have been used:

Alb.	Albanian	*lit.*	literally
attrib.	attributive	*mil.*	military
Bulg.	Bulgarian	*naut.*	nautical
cf.	compare (*confer*)	*nav.*	naval
d.	demotic (δημοτική)	*pl.*	plural
It.	Italian	*topog.*	topographical
k.	*katharévousa* (καθαρεύουσα)	*Turk.*	Turkish
Lat.	Latin		

Greek	P.C.G.N. Transliteration	English
A		
ἀβαθ-ής, ής, ές	avath-ís, ís, és	shallow
'Αγγλικ-ός, ή, όν	Anglik-ós, í, ón	English
Ἅγ-ιος, ία, ιον, *masc. pl.* Ἅγιοι	Áy-ios, ía, ion, *m. pl.* Áyioi	Saint, Holy, *d.* Ἅη
ἀγκάλη	angáli	bight, open bay
ἀγορά	agorá	market, market place
ἄγρ-ιος, ία, ιον	ágrios, ía, ion	wild
ἀγροικία	agroikía	farmhouse
ἀγρός	agrós	field, *d.* χωράφι
ἀγωγή	agoyí	conduit
ἄδεια	ádhia	permit, authorization
ἀδιάβατ-ος, ος, ον	adhiávatos, os, on	impassable, unfordable
ἀέρας, *d.*	aéras	air, cf. ἀήρ; wind, cf. ἄνεμος
ἀεροδρόμιον	aërodhrómion	aerodrome
ἀζιμούθ, *Arabic*	azimúth	azimuth
Ἅη, *d.*	Áï	Saint
ἀήρ, *k.*	aír	air, *d.* ἀέρας
αἱμασιά	aimasiá	dike, stone wall
ἀκατοίκητ-ος, ος, ον	akatoíkitos, os, on	uninhabited
ἄκρον	ákron	extremity
ἀκτή	aktí	coast, *commonly* παραλία
ἀλάτι, *d.*	aláti	salt
ἀλμύρα	almíra	salt-marsh
ἁλυκή	alikí	salt-pan
ἀλῶνι	alóni	threshing-floor
ἀμμόλοφος	ammólofos	sand-hill

GREEK	P.C.G.N. TRANSLITERATION	ENGLISH
ἄμμος	ámmos	sand
ἀμμουδιά	ammoudhiá	sandy shore
ἀμπέλι, *pl.* ἀμπέλια, *d.*	ambéli, *pl.* ambélia	vine, vineyard
ἄμπωτις	ámbotis	ebb tide
ἀνά	aná	by, on, at intervals of
ἀνάκτορα	anáktora	palace
'Ανατολή	Anatolí	East
ἀνεμόμυλος	anemómilos	windmill
ἄνεμος	ánemos	wind, *d.* ἀέρας
ἀνθρακωρυχεῖον	anthrakorikhíon	coal-mine
ἄνθραξ	ánthrax	coal, *d.* κάρβουνο
ἄνοιξι, *d.*	ánoixi	Spring
ἄντα, *Turk.*	áda	island
ἀντλία	andlía	pump
ἄνω	áno	up, upper, *commonly* ἐπάνω, *d.* ἀπάνω
ἀξιωματικός	axiomatikós	officer
ἀπαγορεύεται	apagorévetai	forbidden, *as* '*entrance* forbidden'
'Απηλιώτης, *k.*	Apiliótis	East Wind, *d.* Λεβάντε
ἄπνοια	ápnoia	calm (of wind)
ἀπό	apó	from
ἀποβάθρα	apováthra	landing stage, wharf
ἀποθήκη	apothíki	store
ἀποκρύπτεται	apokríptetai	hidden, *as* 'hidden *rock*'
ἀπολυμαντήριον	apolimandírion	cleansing-station
ἀποξηρανθ-είς, εῖσα, έν	apoxiranth-ís, ísa, én	drained, dried up
ἀπόστασις	apóstasis	distance
ἀποστολή	apostolí	mission
ἀπότομ-ος, ος, ον	apótom-os, os, on	steep
ἀραι-ός, ά, όν	arai-ós, á, ón	sparse
ἀριθμός	arithmós	number
ἀριστερ-ός, ά, όν	arister-ós, á, ón	left, *as* 'left *hand*'
ἀρχαιολογικ-ός, ή, όν	arkhaioloyik-ós, í, ón	archaeological
ἀσβεστόλιθος	asvestólithos	limestone, *commonly* ἀσβεστόπετρα
ἀσβεστόπετρα	asvestópetra	limestone
ἀσμάκι, *from Turk.* azmak	asmáki	seasonal torrent, overflow channel
ἄσπρ-ος, η, ο, *d.*	áspr-os, i, o	white
ἀστραπή	astrapí	lightning
ἀστυνομία	astinomía	police (urban)
ἀστυνόμος	astinómos	police officer (urban)
ἀσύρματος	asírmatos	wireless
ἀτμόπλοιον	atmóploion	steamer, *d.* βαπόρι
ἀτραπός, *k.*	atrapós	footpath, *d.* μονοπάτι
αὐλάκι, *d.*	avláki	channel, ditch
αὖλαξ	ávlax	channel, ditch
αὔρα	ávra	breeze
αὐτοκίνητον	avtokíniton	motor-car
ἀφετηρία	afetiría	*topog.* bench-mark

B

GREEK	P.C.G.N. TRANSLITERATION	ENGLISH
βαθμός	vathmós	degree
βάθος	váthos	depth
βάλτος, *d.*	váltos	marsh
βαμβάκι	vamváki	cotton
βαμβακόφυτον	vamvakófiton	cotton-plant

Greek	P.C.G.N. Transliteration	English
βαπόρι, *d.*	vapóri	steamer
βάρκα	várka	a rowing boat
βαρ-ύς, εῖα, ύ	var-ís, ía, í	heavy
βασιλικ-ός, ή, όν	vasilik-ós, í, ón	royal
βάσις	vásis	base, base line
βελονοειδ-ής, ής, ές	velonoïdh-ís, ís, és	needle-like (e.g. of pines)
βέλος	vélos	needle of compass
βενζίνη	venzíni	oil-fuel, motor boat
βῆμα	víma	platform, step
βιβάρι, *from Lat.* vivarium	vivári	fishery, *d.* διβάρι
βίγκλα *or* βίγλα	víngla *or* vígla	look-out place
βιομηχανία	viomikhanía	industry
Βλαχικ-ός, ή, όν	Vlakhik-ós, í, ón	Vlach
βόδα, *Serbo-Croat*	vóda	spring, water
βολή	volí	range, shooting practice
βόρβορος	vórvoros	ooze
βορειν-ός, ή, ό, *d.*	vorin-ós, í, ó	northern
βόρ-ειος, εία, ειον	vór-ios, ía, ion	northern
Βορράς, *k.*	Vorrás	North; North Wind, *d.* Μπόρα or Τραμοντάνα
βοσκή	voskí	pasture, *d.* λειβάδι
βουνό, *pl.* βουνά, *d.*	vounó, *pl.* vouná	hill, mountain
βράχος, *pl.* βράχοι	vrákhos, *pl.* vrákhoi	rock
βροντή	vrondí	thunder
βροχή, *d.*	vrokhí	rain
βρύσις	vrisis	spring, running water, *d.* βρύση
βρυσοῦλα	vrisoúla	small spring
βυθισμέν-ος, η, ον	vithismén-os, i, on	submerged
βυθομέτρησις	vithométrisis	*naut.* sounding
βύθος	víthos	bottom
βωμός	vomós	altar

Γ

Greek	P.C.G.N. Transliteration	English
γάλα	gála	milk
γαλακτοκομεῖον	galaktokomíon	dairy
γαλήνη	galíni	calm (of water)
Γαλλικ-ός, ή, όν	Gallik-ós, í, ón	French
Γαρμπής, *d.*	Garbís	South-west Wind, *k.* Λίβας
γενί, *Turk.*	yení	new
γενικ-ός, ή όν	yenik-ós, í, ón	general, universal
γέρανος	yéranos	crane
Γερμανικ-ός, ή, όν	Yermanik-ós, í, ón	German
γέφυρα	yéfira	bridge
γεωγραφικ-ός, ή, όν	yeografik-ós, í, ón	geographical
γεώδ-ης, ης, ες	yeódh-is, is, es	earthy
γεωργικ-ός, ή, όν	yeoryik-ós, í, ón	agricultural
γῆ	yi	earth
γιαλός, *d.*	yialós	shore
Γιουγοσλαυϊκ-ός, ή, όν	Yugoslavik-ós, í, ón	Yugoslav
γκιόλ, *Turk.* göl	gol	lake
γκρεμνός, *d.*	gremnós	cliff, precipice
γλυκ-ός, ή, ό, *d.*	glik-ós, í, ó	sweet
γλυκ-ύς, εῖα, ύ	glik-ís, ía, í	sweet

GREEK	P.C.G.N. TRANSLITERATION	ENGLISH
γλῶσσα	glóssa	tongue, language
γοῦρνα, *d.*	goúrna	*topog.* trough
Γραικός *or* Γρέγος, *d.*	Graikós *or* Grégos	North-east Wind, *k.* Μέσης
γράμμα	grámma	letter (of the alphabet), epistle
γραμμή	grammí	line
γραφεῖον	grafíon	office
γυμνάσιον	yimnásion	place of exercise, high school
γυμν-ός, ή, όν	yimn-ós, í, ón	bare
γωνία	gonía	angle, corner

Δ

GREEK	P.C.G.N. TRANSLITERATION	ENGLISH
δαλιάνι, *from Turk.* dalyan, *better* νταλιάνι	daliáni	lagoon
δάσος	dhásos	wood, grove
δένδρον	dhéndron	tree
δεξαμενή	dhexamení	dry dock, cistern, reservoir, *d.* στέρνα
δεξ-ιός, ιά, ιόν	dhex-iós, iá, ión	right, *as* right *hand*
δεύτερον λεπτόν	dhévteron leptón	second (of time *or* arc), *sometimes represented by symbol* δ
δημαρχεῖον	dhimarkhíon	town-hall
δῆμος	dhímos	deme (subdivision of an eparchy); the public
δημοτικ-ός, ή, όν	dhimotik-ós, í, ón	popular
διά	dhiá	for, through, by
διαβατ-ός, ή, όν	dhiavat-ós, í, ón	traversable, fordable
διάβρωσις	dhiávrosis	erosion
δίαιτα	dhíaita	*topog.* regular course (of a river)
διαμέρισμα	dhiamérisma	division (administrative region)
διάπλους	dhiáplous	passage (for ships)
δίαυλος	dhíavlos	strait
διβάρι, *d.*	dhivári	fishery
διεθν-ής, ής, ές	dhiethn-ís, ís, és	international
διέλευσις	dhiélevsis	passing through
δικαστήριον	dhikastírion	law-court
δίοδος	dhíodhos	passage
διόπτευσις	dhióptevsis	*naut.* bearing
διοχέτευσις	dhiokhétevsis	drainage
διπλ-ός, ή, ό, *d.*	dhipl-ós, í, ó	double
διώρυγμα, *form of* διώρυξ	dhiórigma *or* dhiórix	canal
δόκιμος	dhókimos	apprentice, *nav.* midshipman
δραχμή, *pl.* δραχμαί	dhrakhmí, *pl.* dhrakhmaí	drachma (coin)
δρομολόγιον	dhromolóyion	itinerary, time table
δρόμος	dhrómos	road
δρυμός	dhrimós	thicket
δρύς	dhrís	oak
δύσβατ-ος, ος, ον	dhísvat-os, os, on	rough (of roads)
Δυσμαί	Dhismaí	West
δυτικ-ός, ή, όν	dhitik-ós, í, ón	western

Ε

GREEK	P.C.G.N. TRANSLITERATION	ENGLISH
ἔαρ, *k.*	éär	Spring, *d.* ἄνοιξι
ἕδρα	édhra	seat (of government)
ἐθνικ-ός, ή, όν	ethnik-ós, í, ón	national

Greek	P.C.G.N. Transliteration	English
εἶδος	ídhos	type, sort
εἰς	is	into, to
εἰσαγωγή	isagoyí	import, introduction
εἰσιτήριον	isitírion	ticket
εἴσοδος	ísodhos	entrance
εἴσπλους	ísplous	entrance (for ships)
ἐκ	ek	from, out of
ἑκατέρωθεν	ekatérothen	from either way
ἐκβολή, *pl.* ἐκβολαί	ekvolí, *pl.* ekvolaí	mouth (of a river)
ἔκδοσις	ékdhosis	edition, publication
ἐκκλησία	ekklisía	church
ἐκσκαφή	ekskafí	excavation
ἔκτασις	éktasis	area, extent
ἐλαία	elaía	olive, olive tree
ἐλάχιστ-ος, η, ον	elákhist-os, i, on	least, minimum
ἐλεύθ-ερος, έρα, ερον	elévth-eros, éra, eron	free
Ἑλληνικ-ός, ή, όν	Ellenik-ós, í, ón	Greek
ἕλος	élos	marsh, *d.* βάλτος
ἐμπορικ-ός, ή, όν	emborik-ós, í, ón	commercial
ἐμπόριον	embórion	trade
ἐν	en	in
ἐνέργεια	enéryia	energy
Ἐνετικ-ός, ή, όν	Enetik-ós, í, ón	Venetian, *d.* Βενέτικος
ἐξαγωγή	exagoyí	export
ἔξαρσις	éxarsis	elevation
ἐξέδρα	exédhra	jetty
ἐξοχή	exokhí	country (as opposed to town)
ἐξοχικ-ός, ή, όν	exokhik-ós, í, ón	rural
ἔξω	éxo	outer, outside
ἐπί	epí	against, for, to
ἐπιγραφή	epigrafí	inscription
ἐπικίνδυν-ος, ος, ον	epikíndhin-os, os, on	dangerous
ἐπισκευή	episkeví	repair
ἐπιτρεπόμεν-ος, η, ον	epitrepómen-os, i, on	allowed, permitted
ἐπιφάνεια	epifánia	surface
ἐποχή	epokhí	season
ἐργασία	ergasía	work, employment
ἔργον, *pl.* ἔργα	érgon, *pl.* érga	work
ἐρείπιον, *pl.* ἐρείπια	erípion, *pl.* erípia	ruin
ἐρυθρ-ός, ά, όν, *k.*	erithr-ós, á, ón	red, *d.* κόκκινος
ἐσωτερικ-ός, ή, όν	esoterik-ós, í, ón	internal
Ἐτησίαι, *k.*	Etisíai	Etesian or Trade Winds, *d.* Μελτέμια
ἐτήσ-ιος, ία, ιον	etís-ios, ía, ion	annual
ἔτος	étos	year, *d.* χρόνος
εὔβατ-ος, ος, ον	évvat-os, os, on	easily traversable
εὔριπος	évripos	tidal channel
Εὖρος, *k.*	Évros	South-east Wind, *d.* Σιρόκος
εὖρος	évros	width
ἐφόδιον, *pl.* ἐφόδια	efódhion, *pl.* efódhia	supply, victuals

Z

Greek	P.C.G.N. Transliteration	English
ζεστ-ός, ή, ό, *d.*	zest-ós, í, ó	hot
ζευγάρι	zevgári	pair
ζεῦγμα	zévgma	*naut.* boom

Greek	P.C.G.N. Transliteration	English
Ζέφυρος, *k.*	Zéfiros	West Wind, *d.* Πονέντε
ζώνη	zóni	zone
ζῷον, *pl.* ζῷα	zóön, *pl.* zóa	animal
Η		
ἤ	i	either, or
ἡγεμονικ-ός, ή, όν	iyemonik-ós, í, ón	governmental
ἠλεκτρικ-ός, ή, όν	ilektrik-ós, í, ón	electric
ἥλιος	ílios	sun
ἡμέρα	iméra	day
ἡμιονικ-ός, ή, όν	imionik-ós, í, ón	suitable for mule traffic
ἥμισ-υς, εια, υ	ímis-is, ia, i	half
ἠπειρωτικ-ός, ή, όν	ipirotik-ós, í, ón	continental
Θ		
θάλασσα	thálassa	sea
θέατρον	théatron	theatre
θεῖον	thíon	sulphur
θέρετρον	théretron	summer-quarters
θερμοκρασία	thermokrasía	temperature
θέρος, *k.*	théros	Summer, *d.* καλοκαίρι
θέσις	thésis	position
θόλος	thólos	vault, dome, cf. τροῦλλος
θύελλα, *k.*	thíella	storm, *commonly* τρικυμία
θυννεῖον	thinníon	tunny-fishery
Ι		
ἰαματικ-ός, ή, όν	iamatik-ós, í, ón	medicinal
ἱερόν	ierón	temple
ἰλύς	ilís	mud, *d.* λάσπις
Ἰουδαϊκ-ός, ή, όν	Ioudhaïk-ós, í, ón	Jewish
ἱππικόν	ippikón	cavalry
ἱπποδρόμιον	ippodhrómion	race-course
ἰσθμός	isthmós	isthmus
ἴσιωμα, *d.*	ísioma	level ground
ἰσοβαθής, *pl.* ἰσοβαθεῖς	isovathís, *pl.* isovathís	submarine contour-line
ἰσοδιάστασις	isodhiástasis	contour-interval
ἴσ-ος, η, ον	ís-os, i, on	equal, even
ἰσοϋψής, ἰσοϋψεῖς	isoïpsís, *pl.* isoïpsís	contour-line
ἱστός	istós	flag-staff, mast
Κ		
κάβος *d., from It.* capo	kávos	cape
καὶ	kai	and
καΐκι, *d., from Turk.* kaik	kaḯki	boat, caique
καινούργ-ιος, ια, ιο, *d.*	kainoúry-ios, ia, io	new
καιρικ-ός, ή, όν	kairik-ós, í, ón	weather, *as* weather-*conditions*
καιρός	kairós	weather
κακ-ός, ή, όν	kak-ós, í, ón	bad
καλαμών, *d.* καλαμιά	kalamón, kalamiá	reed bed
καλλιέργεια	kalliéryia	cultivation
καλοκαίρι, *d.*	kalokaíri	Summer

GREEK	P.C.G.N. TRANSLITERATION	ENGLISH
καλ-ός, ή, όν	kal-ós, í, ón	good, well
καλύβι, *pl.* καλύβια	kalívi, *pl.* kalívia	hut
καλώδιον	kalódhion	cable
κάμπος, *d.*	kámbos	field, cf. ἀγρός, χωράφι; plain, cf. πεδιάς, πεδίον
καμπύλη	kambíli	contour, curve
καπνοδόκος	kapnodhókhos	chimney
καράβι, *d.*	karávi	ship
καραβοφάναρο, *d.*	karavofánaro	lightship
κάρβουνο, *d. from It.* carbone	kárvouno	coal
καρποφόρ-ος, ος, ον	karpofór-os, os, on	fruit-bearing
κατά	katá	according to, during
καταβόθρα	katavóthra	swallow-hole, chasm, *d.* χώνος
καταιγίς	kataiyís	hurricane
κατακόρυφ-ος, ος, ον	katakórif-os, os, on	vertical
κατάλληλ-ος, ος, ον	katállel-os, os, on	suitable
καταρράκτης	katarráktis	waterfall, cascade
κατάστρωμα	katástroma	levelled place, *naut.* deck
κατάφυτ-ος, ος, ον	katáfit-os, os, on	planted ground
κάτεργον	kátergon	pontoon
κάτω	káto	lower, down
κατῳκημέν-ος, η, ον	katokimén-os, i, on	inhabited
κέντρον	kéndron	centre
κεραμεῖον	keramíon	pottery, tile works
κεφάλι, *d.*	kefáli	headland
κίνδυνος	kíndhinos	danger
κίνησις	kínisis	movement
κινητ-ός, ή, όν	kinit-ós, í, ón	moved, driven
κλεισοῦρα	klisoúra	pass, defile
κλῖμα	klíma	climate
κοιλάς	koilás	natural hollow, valley
κοιν-ός, ή, όν	koin-ós, í, ón	common
κοινότης	koinótis	commune (subdivision of a deme)
κοίτασμα	koítasma	deposit, bed, layer
κοίτη	koíti	bed (of a river)
κόκκιν-ος, η, ο, *d.*	kókkin-os, i, o	red
κόλπος	kólpos	gulf
κόλπωσις	kólposis	wide bay
κοντά, *d.*	kondá	near
κορυφή	korifí	peak, summit
κρατήρ	kratír	crater
κράτος	krátos	state (political)
κρεμαστ-ός, ή, όν	kremast-ós, í, ón	hanging
κρημνός	krimnós	cliff, precipice, *d.* γκρεμνός
κρήνη, *k.*	kríni	fountain, *commonly* πηγή
κρητιδικ-ός, ή, όν	kritidhik-ós, í, ón	chalky
κρύ-ος, α, ο, *d.*	krí-os, a, o	cold
κρυπτή	kriptí	hidden place
κτῆνος, *pl.* κτῆνα	ktínos, *pl.* ktína	beast, *pl.* cattle
κύκλος	kíklos	circle
κυκλωνικ-ός, ή, όν	kiklonik-ós, í, ón	cyclonic
κυματοθραύστης, *k.*	kimatothrávstis	breakwater, *d.* μῶλος
κύρ-ιος, ία, ιον	kír-ios, ía, ion	chief, sir, Mr, madam, Mrs
κώμη	kómi	large village
κωμόπολις	komópolis	provincial town

Λ

Greek	P.C.G.N. Transliteration	English
λαγγάδα, *d.* λαγκάδα	langádha	pass, deep valley
λαζαρέτο, *d. from It.* lazzaretto	lazaréto	quarantine station, *k.* λοιμοκαθαρτήριον
Λεβάντε, *d.*	Levánde	East Wind, *k.* Ἀπηλιώτης
λειβάδι, *d.* λιβάδι	levádhi	meadow, cf. λειμών; pasture, cf. βοσκή
λεκάνη	lekáni	basin
λέμβος	lémvos	boat, *d.* καΐκι
λεμβουργεῖον	lemvouryíon	boat-building yard
λεύκη	lévki	poplar
λευκόλιθος	levkólithos	magnesite
λευκ-ός, ή, όν, *k.*	levk-ós, í, ón	white, *d.* ἄσπρος
λευκοσίδηρος	levkosídhiros	tin
Λίβας, *k.*	Lívas	South-west Wind, *d.* Γαρμπής
λιθάρι, *d.*	lithári	ashlar, stone, *k.* λίθος
λιθόκτιστ-ος, ος, ον	lithóktist-os, os, on	built of stone
λιμάνι, *d.*	limáni	harbour, haven, port
λίμνη	límni	lake
λιμνοθάλασσα	limnothálassa	lagoon
λίπασμα	lípasma	fertilizer
λόγῳ	lógo	on account of
λούτζα, *d.*	loútza	clearing (among trees)
λουτρόν, *pl.* λουτρά	loutrón, *pl.* loutrá	bath, *d.* μπάνιο
λοφίσκος	lofískos	hillock
λόφος	lófos	hill (*strictly* a long low ridge)

Μ

Greek	P.C.G.N. Transliteration	English
μαγγάνιον	mangánion	manganese
μαγούλα, *d.*	magoúla	mound
Μαΐστρος, *d.*	Maïstros	North-west Wind, *k.* Σκίρων
μακρ-ός, ά, όν	makr-ós, á, ón	long
μάλ, *def.* μάλι, *Alb.*	mál, máli	mountain
μάνδρα	mándra	sheepfold, *d.* στάνη
μάρμαρον	mármaron	marble
μαῦρ-ος, η, ο, *d.*	mávr-os, i, o	black
μεγάλ-ος, η, ο, *d.*	megál-os, i, o	big, great
μέγαρον	mégaron	hall
μέγ-ας, άλη, α	még-as, áli, a	big, great, *d.* μεγάλος
μέγιστ-ος, η, ον	méyist-os, i, on	greatest, maximum
μέλ-ας, αινα, αν, *k.*	mél-as, aina, an	black, *d.* μαῦρος
Μελτέμια, *d. from Turk.* meltem	Meltémia	Etesian *or* Trade Winds
μέρος	méros	part
μεσαῖ-ος, α, ον	mesaí-os, a, on	middle, *commonly* μέσος
μέση	mési	average, mean
μεσημβρία	mesimvría	South, cf. Νότος; mid-day, *d.* μεσημέρι
μεσημβρινόν	mesimvrinón	meridian
μεσημέρι, *d.*	mesiméri	mid-day
Μέσης, *k.*	Mésis	North-east Wind, *d.* Γραικός *or* Γρέγος
μέσ-ος, η, ον	més-os, i, on	middle
μετά	metá	with, after
μεταλλεῖον	metallíon	mine
μετάξι	metáxi	silk

GREEK	P.C.G.N. TRANSLITERATION	ENGLISH
μετεωρολογικ-ός, ή, όν	meteoroloyik-ós, í, ón	meteorological
μετόχιον	metókhion	farm-buildings
μέτρον, *pl.* μέτρα	métron, *pl.* métra	measure, metre
μέχρι	mékhri	until
μή	mi	not (in subordinate clauses), cf. οὔ
μηδενικόν, *k.*	midhenikón	zero, *commonly* μηδέν
μῆκος	míkos	length, longitude
μήν	min	month
μηνιαῖ-ος, α, ον	miniaí-os, a, on	monthly
μητρόπολις	mitrópolis	cathedral
μηχανή	mikhaní	machine
μικρ-ός, ά, όν	mikr-ós, á, ón	small
μικρ-ός, ή, ό, *d.*	mikr-ós, í, ó	small
μικτ-ός, ή, όν	mikt-ós, í, ón	mixed
μίλιον, *pl.* μίλια	mílion, *pl.* mília	mile
μνῆμα	mníma	tomb
μνημεῖον	mnimíon	monument
μονή	moní	monastery
μονοπάτι, *d.*	monopáti	foot-path, *k.* ἀτραπός
μουσεῖον	mousíon	museum
μουτσάρα, *Vlach*	moutsára	marsh
μπαΐρ, μπαΐρι, *from Turk.* bayir	baír, baíri	hill
μπάνιο, *d. from It.* bagno	bánio	bath
μπάρα, *Serbo-Croat*	bára	swamp
μπατάκ, *Turk.*	baták	swamp
μπογάζι, *from Turk.* boğaz	bogázi	strait
Μπόρα, *d.*	Bóra	North Wind (Βορρᾶς, Τραμοντάνα)
μπουνάρ, *Turk.*	bunár	source, spring
μπουρούν, *attrib.* μπουρνοῦ, *Turk.*	burún, burnú	cape
μυλαύλαξ	milávlax	mill-stream
μύλος	mílos	mill
μύτη	míti	nose, cape
μυχός	mikhós	*naut.* head of a gulf
Μωαμεθανικ-ός, ή, όν	Moamethanik-ós, í, ón	Mohammedan
μῶλος, *d.*	mólos	breakwater, mole

N

GREEK	P.C.G.N. TRANSLITERATION	ENGLISH
νάρκη	nárkhi	mine, *nav.*
ναυάγιον	naváyion	wreck
ναυπηγεῖον	navpiyíon	ship-yard
ναύσταθμος	návstathmos	naval-base
ναύτης	návtis	sailor
ναυτικ-ός, ή, όν	navtik-ós, í, ón	naval
ναυτιλία	navtilía	navigation
ναυτών, *pl.* ναυτῶνες	navtón, *pl.* navtónes	naval barracks
νεκροταφεῖον	nekrotafíon	cemetery
νερό, *d.*	neró	water
νέφος	néfos	cloud
νεώριον	neórion	dock, dockyard
νησάκι, *pl.* νησάκια, *d.*	nisáki, *pl.* nisákia	islet
νησί, *pl.* νησιά, *d.*	nisí, *pl.* nisiá	island
νησίς, *pl.* νησίδες	nisís, *pl.* nisídhes	islet, *d.* νησάκι

GREEK	P.C.G.N. TRANSLITERATION	ENGLISH
νῆσος, *pl.* νῆσοι	nísos, *pl.* nísoi	island, *d.* νησί
νομαρχία	nomarkhía	office of provincial governor
νομός	nomós	nome (Greek province)
νοσοκομεῖον	nosokomíon	hospital
νότ-ιος, ια, ιον	nót-ios, ia, ion	southern
Νότος	Nótos	South, cf. Μεσημβρία; South Wind *d.* Ὄστρια
ντάγ, *Turk.*	dag	mountain
νταλιάνι, *from Turk.* dalyan	daliáni	lagoon
ντερβένι, *from Turk.* derbent	dervéni	mountain pass
ντερέ, *attrib.* ντερεσί, *Turk.*	deré, deresí	stream, valley
ντόλ, *Bulg.*	dol	ravine, valley
νύχτα, *d.*	níkhta	night

Ξ

GREEK	P.C.G.N. TRANSLITERATION	ENGLISH
ξενοδοχεῖον	xenodhokhíon	hotel
ξέν-ος, η, ον	xén-os, i, on	foreign, strange, a guest
ξενών	xenón	guest-house
ξέρα, *d.*	xéra	reef, cf. σκόπελος; sunken reef, cf ὕφαλος
ξερ-ός, ή, ό, *d.*	xer-ós, í, ó	dry, parched
ξέχωμα	xékhoma	excavation, *commonly* ἐκσκαφή
ξηρά	xirá	land, dry land
ξηρόβαλτος	xiróvaltos	dried-up marsh
ξύλιν-ος, η, ον	xílin-os, i, on	wooden
ξύλον	xílon	wood, timber

O

GREEK	P.C.G.N. TRANSLITERATION	ENGLISH
ὁδός	odhós	street
οἰκία *k.*	oikía	house, *d.* σπίτι
ὅλ-ος, η, ον	ól-os, i, on	whole, all
ὁμαλ-ός, ή, όν	omal-ós, í, ón	level
ὄμβρ-ιος, ία, ιον, *k.*	ómvr-ios, ía, ion	rainy, *d.* βροχερός
ὁμίχλη	omíkhli	mist
ὅμοι-ος, α, ον	ómoi-os, a, on	same
ὀνομασία	onomasía	designation, name
ὀπή	opí	opening
ὀπίσω	opíso	behind
ὀπωροκῆπος, *k.*	oporokípos	orchard
ὁρατ-ός, ή, όν	orat-ós, í, ón	visible
ὀργυιά	oryiá	fathom (6 ft.)
ὀρειν-ός, ή, όν	orin-ós, í, ón	mountainous
ὀρθ-ός, ή, όν	orth-ós, í, ón	upright
ὁριζοντογραφία	orizondografía	ground-survey
ὅριον	órion	boundary-line
ὁρμητήριον	ormitírion	starting-point, base
ὁρμίσκος	ormískos	cove, small bay
ὅρμος	órmos	cove, bay
ὄρος, *pl.* ὄρη	óros, *pl.* óri	mountain, *d.* βουνό
ὅρος, *pl.* ὅροι	óros, *pl.* óroi	boundary, term
ὀροσειρά	orosirá	mountain-range

GREEK	P.C.G.N. TRANSLITERATION	ENGLISH
όσημον	orósimon	landmark
υγμα	órigma	ground dug up *or* dug out
υζών, *k.*	orizón	rice-plantation, *d.* ρίζι
υχεῖον	orikhíon	working (mine *or* quarry)
τρεον	óstreon	oyster
στρια, *d.*	Óstria	South Wind, cf. Νότος
	ou	not, *d.* δέν
ρανός	ouranós	sky
ετός	okhetós	drain
θος	ókhthos	bank (of a river)
ύρωσις	okhírosis	fortification
λαι-ός, ά, όν	palai-ós, á, ón	old
λη-ός, ά, ό, *d.*	pali-ós, á, ó	old
λίρροια	palírroia	tide
ρά	pará	more than; near, cf. ἐγγύς, κοντά
ραγωγή	paragoyí	production
ρακείμεν-ος, η, ον	parakímen-os, i, on	*topog.* neighbouring
ραλία	paralía	coast
ρατηρητήριον	paratiritírion	observation-post, *d.* σκοπιά
διάς, *k.* πεδίον	pedhiás, pedhíon	plain, *d.* κάμπος
ζικόν	pezikón	infantry
ζοπόρος	pezopóros	pedestrian
ζός	pezós	pedestrian
λαγος	pélagos	open sea, high sea
ρα	péra	beyond, yonder
ραμα	pérama	ferry
ρασμα, *d.*	pérasma	crossing
ρί	perí	about, around
ριβόλι, *d.*	perivóli	garden
ριοχή	periokhí	district
ριπλοῦς	periploús	circumnavigation
ριστατικ-ός, ή, όν	peristatik-ós, í, ón	emergency—*as* emergency-*light*
ριτοίχισμα	peritoíkhisma	enclosure
ρίφραγμα	perífragma	fence
ρίχωρα	períkhora	surroundings
τρα	pétra	rock, cf. βράχος; stone, cf. λίθος, λιθάρι
τρέλαιον	petrélaion	petroleum
τροκοπειό, *d.*	petrokopió	quarry
ύκη	pévki	pine
γάδι, *d.*	pigádhi	well
γή	piyí	spring, cf. βρύσις; fountain, cf. κρήνη
λός	pilós	clay
αγί, πλάϊ, *d.*	playí, pláï	side
αγιά, *d.*	playiá	slope
ατεῖα	platía	public place, square
άτος	plátos	breadth; latitude, *sometimes represented by symbol* φ
ατ-ύς, εῖα, ύ	plat-ís, ía, í	broad
ατύφυλλ-ος, ος, ον	platífill-os, os, on	deciduous (*lit.* broad-leaved)
εύσιμ-ος, ος, ον	plévsim-os, os, on	navigable
ῆθος	plíthos	multitude

GREEK	P.C.G.N. TRANSLITERATION	ENGLISH
πληθυσμός	plithismós	population
πλήμμη	plímmi	high water
πλημμύρα	plimmíra	flood
πλημμυρίς	plimmirís	high tide
πλοηγία	ploïyía	pilotage
πλοηγός	ploïgós	pilot
πλοιάριον	ploiárion	small craft
πλοῖον	ploíon	ship, *d.* καράβι
πλοῦς	plous	sailing
πόδι, *pl.* πόδες	pódhi, *pl.* pódhes	foot (measure)
ποιμήν, *k.*	poimín	shepherd
πόλις	pólis	city, town
πολ-ύς, λή, ύ	pol-ís, lí, í	many
Πονέντε, *d.*	Ponénde	West Wind, *k.* Ζέφυρος
πορεία, *d.*	poría	course
πορθμεῖον	porthmíon	ferry-boat, flying-bridge
πορθμός	porthmós	narrows of a strait, where it can be easily crossed or bridged
πόρος	póros	ford
πόρτο, *d.*, *from Lat.* portus	pórto	small harbour
πόσιμ-ος, ος, ον	pósim-os, os, on	drinkable
ποταμός	potamós	river
πουρνάρι	pournári	holm-oak
πράσ-ινος, ίνη, ινον	prás-inos, íni, inon	green
πρό	pro	before, in front of
προάστειον	proástion	suburb
προβλής	provlís	pier
προβολεύς	provolévs	searchlight
προβολή	provolí	projection *as map*-projection
προεξοχή, *k.*	proexokhí	promontory, cf. ἀκρωτήριον
πρόϊ, *Alb.*	próï	river
προκυμαία, *k.*	prokimaía	*naut.* mole, *d.* μῶλος
προλιμήν	prolimín	outer harbour
προξενεῖον	proxeníon	consulate
πρός	pros	to, towards
πρόσκαιρ-ος, ος, ον	próskair-os, os, on	temporary
προσοχή	prosokhí	attention, care
πρόχωμα	prókhoma	earthwork
πρωΐ	proí	morning (*lit.* early)
πρωτεύουσα	protévousa	capital, *as* capital *city*
πρῶτον λεπτόν	próton leptón	minute (of time *or* arc)
πυξίς	pixís	mariner's compass
πῦρ, *k.*	pir	fire, *d.* φωτιά
πυραμίς	piramís	pyramid
πύργος	pírgos	tower
πυριτιδαποθήκη	piritidhapothíki	powder-magazine
πυριτιδοποιεῖον	piritidhopoiíon	powder-factory
πυροβολεῖον	pirovolíon	battery (of guns)
πυρσός	pirsós	beacon
πυρσωρίς	pirsorís	floating-beacon

Ρ

GREEK	P.C.G.N. TRANSLITERATION	ENGLISH
ῥάχη	rákhi	ridge
ῥέκα, *Bulg.*	réka	stream
ῥέμα, ῥέμμα, *d.*	réma; rémma	current, stream

GREEK	P.C.G.N. TRANSLITERATION	ENGLISH
ῥεῦμα	révma	current, stream
ῥηχία	rikhía	low water
ῥύαξ	ríax	brook
ῥυμουλκόν	rimoulkón	tug-boat
Ρωμαϊκ-ός, ή, όν	Romaïk-ós, í, ón	Roman
Ρωσσικ-ός, ή, όν	Rossik-ós, í, ón	Russian

Σ

GREEK	P.C.G.N. TRANSLITERATION	ENGLISH
σανατόριον	sanatórion	sanatorium
σεισμός	sismós	earthquake
σελήνη, *k.*	selíni	moon, *d.* φεγγάρι
σέλλωμα	sélloma	*topog.* saddle
σημάδι, *d.*	simádhi	mark, sign
σημαία	simaía	flag
σήμανσις	símansis	signal
σημαντήρ	simandír	buoy
σημείωσις	simíosis	note, notice
σῆραγξ	síranx	tunnel
σίδερο, *d.*	sídhiro	iron
σίδηρος	sídhiros	iron
σιδηρ-οῦς, ᾶ, οῦν, *k.*	sidhir-oús, á, oún	iron
Σιρόκος, *d.*	Sirókos	South-east Wind, *k.* Εὖρος
σκάλα, *d.*	skála	small port, quay, stairway
σκάφη	skáfi	trough, *naut.* skiff
σκευή	skeví	equipment
σκήτη	skíti	hermitage
Σκίρων, *k.*	Skíron	North-west Wind, *d.* Μαΐστρος
σκληρ-ός, ά, όν	sklir-ós, á, ón	hard
σκόπελος	skópelos	reef, *d.* ξέρα
σκοπιά, *d.*	skopiá	observation-post
σκοτειν-ός, ή, όν	skotin-ós, í, ón	dark
σμύρις	smíris	emery
Σορόκος, *form of* Σιρόκος	Sorókos	South-east Wind
σοῦ, *Turk.*	su	water, river
σοῦδα	soúdha	ditch (*obs., surviving in names*)
σπήλαιον, σπηλιά, *d.*	spílaion, spiliá	cave
σπίτι, *d.*, *from Lat.* hospitium	spíti	house
στάδιον	stádhion	stade (*just over* 200 *yd.*)
σταθερ-ός, ά, όν	stather-ós, á, ón	fixed, steady
στάθμη	státhmi	level *as sea*-level
σταθμός	stathmós	station
στάνη, *d.*	stáni	sheepfold
στάσις	stásis	halt
σταῦλος	stávlos	stable
σταυροδρόμι, *d.*	stavrodhrómi	cross-roads
σταυρός	stavrós	cross
σταφιδάλωνα	stafidhálona	drying-ground for currants
στενόν	stenón	pass, cf. κλεισοῦρα, λαγγάδα; strait, cf. δίαυλος
στεν-ός, ή, όν	sten-ós, í, ón	narrow
στενωπός	stenopós	narrow pass
στέρνα, *d.*, *from It.* cisterna	stérna	cistern, reservoir

Greek	P.C.G.N. Transliteration	English
στήλη	stíli	column, pillar, post
στηλίς	stilís	small mast
στοά	stoá	colonnade
στόμα	stóma	mouth
στρατιώτης	stratiótis	soldier
στρατιωτικ-ός, ή, όν	stratiotik-ós, í, ón	military
στρατόπεδον	stratópedhon	camp
στρατός	stratós	army
στρατών, *pl.* στρατῶνες	stratón, *pl.* stratónes	barracks
στρόβιλος	stróvilos	eddy, whirlpool
στρογγυλ-ός, ή, ό, *d.*	strongil-ós, í, ó	circular, round
στῦλος	stílos	pillar, post (*strictly* column)
συγκοινωνία	singoinonía	communication
σύμβλεγμα	símblegma	group, cluster
συμφώνως	simfónos	in agreement with
συναγωγή	sinagoyí	synagogue
συνεργεῖον	sineryíon	workshop
συνοικία	sinoikía	settlement
συνοικισμός	sinoikismós	settlement
σύνολον	sínolon	total
σύνορον	sínoron	frontier
σύνταγμα	síndagma	regiment, constitution
σύρμα	sírma	wire
σύρτις	sírtis	quick-sand
σφαγεῖον	sfayíon	slaughterhouse
σχεδιάγραμμα	skhedhiágramma	sketch-plan
σχέδιον	skhédhion	plan
σχέσις	skhésis	relation
σχῆμα	skhíma	plan, figure, form
σχισμή	skhismí	cleft
σχιστόλιθος	skhistólithos	slate
σχιστ-ός, ή, όν	skhist-ós, í, ón	split
σχολεῖον, σχολή	skholíon, skholí	school

T

Greek	P.C.G.N. Transliteration	English
ταμεῖον	tamíon	treasury
ταμπάκικο, *d.*, *from Turk.* tabak	tabákiko	tannery
ταμποῦρι, *from Turk.* tabur	tabúri	entrenchment
τάξις	táxis	class, rank
τάς, *Turk.* taş	tash	rock
τάφος	táfos	grave, tomb
τάφρος, *d.*	táfros	trench
ταχυδρομεῖον	takhidhromíon	post-office
ταχύτης	takhítis	speed
τεῖχος	tíkhos	wall
τέλμα	télma	swamp
τελματώδ-ης, ης, ες	telmatódh-is, is, es	swampy
τέλος	télos	end
τελωνεῖον	teloníon	customs-house
τελωνοφυλακεῖον	telonofilakíon	customs-office
τέμενος	témenos	precinct
τέναγος	ténagos	pond, fen

GREEK	P.C.G.N. TRANSLITERATION	ENGLISH
τεπέ, *Turk.*	tepé	hill
τεχνητ-ός, ή, όν	tekhnit-ós, í, ón	artificial
τεχνικ-ός, ή, όν	tekhnik-ós, í, ón	technical
τηλεγραφεῖον	tilegrafíon	telegraph-office
τηλεφωνεῖον	tilefoníon	telephone-office
τιμή	timí	price
τμῆμα	tmíma	department, section
τοῖχος	toíkhos	wall
τοννοδέτη	tonnodhéti	mooring-stake
τόννος	tónnos	ton
τόξον	tóxon	arc, range, trajectory
τοπικ-ός, ή, όν	topik-ós, í, ón	local
τοπογραφικ-ός, ή, όν	topografik-ós, í, ón	topographical
τόπος	tópos	place
τορπίλλη	torpílli	torpedo
τοῦβλο, *d.*	toúvlo	brick
τουβλοποιεῖον	touvlopoiíon	brick-works
τοῦζλα, *Turk.*	túzla	salt-pan
τοῦμπα, *d.*	toúmba	tumulus, mound
Τραμοντάνα, *d.*	Tramontána	North Wind, cf. Βορρᾶς, Μπόρα
τραν-ός, ή, όν	tran-ós, í, ón	large, perspicuous
τράπεζα	trápeza	table, bank (for money)
τριγωνισμός	trigonismós	survey, triangulation
τρίγωνον	trígonon	triangle
τρικυμία	trikimía	storm
τροῦλλος	troúllos	dome
τρόχαλος	trókhalos	cairn
τροχιά	trokhiá	track
τρῦπα, *d.*	trípa	hole
τσιφλίκ, τσιφλίκι, *from Turk.* çiftlik	chiflík, chiflíki	farm-buildings
τσοῦκα, *Alb.*, *Bulg.*	chúka	peak
τυροκομεῖον, *k.*	tirokomíon	cheese-dairy
τώρα, *d.*	tóra	now

Y

GREEK	P.C.G.N. TRANSLITERATION	ENGLISH
ὑγειονομεῖον	iyinomíon	port health-office
ὑγρασία	igrasía	moisture
ὑγρ-ός, ά, όν	igr-ós, á, ón	wet
ὑδαταγωγός	idhatagogós	water-conduit
ὑδραγωγεῖον	idhragoyíon	water-conduit
ὑδρεῖον	idhríon	pipe-line
ὕδρευσις	ídhrevsis	water-supply
ὑδρογραφικ-ός, ή, όν	idhrografik-ós, í, ón	hydrographical
ὑδροκίνητ-ος, ος, ον	idhrokínit-os, os, on	water-driven
ὑδρόμυλος	idhrómilos	water-mill
ὑδροπλάνον	idhroplánon	sea-plane
ὑδρορρόη	idhrorróï	water-spout
ὑπάλληλος	ipállilos	employee, official
ὑπάρχ-ων, ουσα, ον	ipárkh-on, ousa, on	existing
ὑπέρ	ipér	above, for
ὑπό	ipó	by, under
ὑποβρύχιον	ipovríkhion	submarine boat
ὑπόγ-ειος, ειος, ειον	ipóy-ios, ios, ion	underground

Greek	P.C.G.N. Transliteration	English
ὑποθαλάσσ-ιος, ιος, ιον	ipothaláss-ios, ios, ion	submarine
ὑπόνομος	ipónomos	sewer
ὑπόστεγον	ipóstegon	hangar
ὑπουργεῖον	ipouryíon	ministry, government department
ὑφάλμυρ-ος, α, ον	ifálmir-os, a, on	brackish
ὕφαλος	ífalos	sunken reef, *d.* ξέρα
ὕφαυλαξ	ífavlax	side-channel
ὕφεσις	ífesis	depression, diminution
ὕφορμος	íformos	roadstead
ὑψηλ-ός, ή, όν	ipsil-ós, í, ón	high, *d.* ψηλός
ὑψομετρικ-ός, ή, όν	ipsometrik-ós, í, ón	hypsometric
ὕψος	ípsos	height (altitude)
ὕψωμα	ípsoma	height (elevated ground), *d.* ψήλωμα

Φ

Greek	P.C.G.N. Transliteration	English
φάβρικα *from It.* fabrica, *better* φάμπρηκα	fábrica	factory
φανός	fanós	light, apparatus giving light
φαράγγι, *d.*	farángi	gorge
φάρος	fáros	lighthouse
φεγγάρι, *d.*	fengári	moon
φθινόπωρον	fthinóporon	Autumn
φθισιατρεῖον	fthisiatríon	sanatorium for tuberculosis
φόρος	fóros	toll
φορτηγ-ός, ός, όν	fortig-ós, ós, ón	transport, *as* transport-*vehicle*
φοῦρνος, *d.*	foúrnos	oven
φράγμα	frágma	barrage, weir
φρέαρ	fréär	well, *d.* πηγάδι
φρενοκομεῖον	frenokomíon	lunatic-asylum
φρούριον	froúrion	fort
φῦκι, *d.*	fíki	sea-weed
φυλακή	filakí	prison
φυλάκιον	filákion	sentry-post
φυλακεῖον	filakíon	guard-house
φύλλον	fíllon	leaf, sheet (of a map)
φῶς	fos	light
φωτογραφικ-ός, ή, όν	fotografik-ós, í, ón	photographic
φωτοσημαντήρ	fotosimandír	light-buoy

Χ

Greek	P.C.G.N. Transliteration	English
χάλιξ	khálix	gravel
χαλκός	khalkós	copper
χαμηλ-ός, ή, όν	khamil-ós, í, ón	low
χανδάκι, *d.*	khandháki	ditch
χάνι, *d., from Turk.* han	kháni	inn
χαράδρα	kharádhra	ravine
χάρτης	khártis	chart, map
χειμάδιον	khimádhion	winter-hut
χείμαρρος	khímarros	torrent
χειμεριν-ός, ή, όν	khimerin-ós, í, ón	winter, *as* winter-*quarters*
χειμών	khimón	Winter
χερσόνησος	khersónisos	peninsula
χιλιόμετρον	khiliómetron	kilometre

Greek	P.C.G.N. Transliteration	English
χιών	khión	snow
χοιραδώδ-ης, ης, ες	khoiradhódh-is, is, es	shallow with rocks awash
χοιράς	khoirás	rock awash
χονδρ-ός, ά, όν	khondr-ós, á, ón	coarse, thick
χούνη	khoúni	gully
χουνί	khouní	funnel
χρῆσις	khrísis	use
χρόνος, *d.*	khrónos	year
χρώμιον	khrómion	chromium
χῶμα	khóma	soil
χώνος, *d.*	khónos	swallow-hole, chasm
χώρα	khóra	country; main town of an island
χωράφι, *d.*	khoráfi	field
χωρητικότης	khoritikótis	tonnage
χωρίον	khoríon	village, *d.* χωριό
χωροσταθμικ-ός, ή, όν	khorostathmik-ós, í, ón	levelling, *as* levelling-*station*
χωροφυλακή	khorofilakí	police (rural)
χωροφύλαξ	khorofílax	policeman (rural)

Ψ

Greek	P.C.G.N. Transliteration	English
ψευδάργυρος	psevdháryiros	zinc
ψηλ-ός, ή, ό, *d.*	psil-ós, í, ó	high, tall
ψήλωμα, *d.*	psíloma	height (elevated ground)
ψῆφος	psífos	pebble
ψιλ-ός, ή, όν	psil-ós, í, ón	thin

Ω

Greek	P.C.G.N. Transliteration	English
ὤμορφ-ος, η, ο, *d.*	ómorf-os, i, o	beautiful
ὥρα	óra	hour
ὡραῖ-ος, α, ον	oraí-os, a, on	beautiful
ὡριαῖ-ος, α, ον	oriaí-os, a, on	hourly
ὡρολόγιον	orolóyion	clock
ὡρονομικ-ός, ή, όν	oronomik-ós, í, ón	emitting a time signal

Appendix VII

NOTE ON PLANT NAMES

The botanical names of the plants mentioned in chapter IV are given below with a common English name where one exists and, when known, the modern Greek name. Many plants seem to have no name in common use in modern Greek; the usual answer given to a request for the name of a flower is λουλοῦδι (*louloúdhi*), which merely means a wild flower. Many flowers of very different kinds go by the name of ἄγριος κρίνος (*ágrios krínos*); the wild lily and many creeping and trailing plants, as well as the *Clematis cirrhosa* L. to which it properly applies, are called περικοκλάδα (*perikokládha*). The country people call many red flowers—poppies—παπαρούνα (*paparoúna*), and especially give this name to the red anemone, *Anemone coronaria* L.

The names of some plants, however, especially those useful to man or commonly dominant in the vegetation types, differ very little from the classical Greek forms. This is particularly true of the Cretan variants.

Botanical name	English name (if any)	Modern Greek name (where known)
I. TREES:		
Pinus halepensis Mill.	Aleppo pine	ἡ παραλία πεύκη (*paralía pévki*)
P. Pinea L.	Stone pine	ἡ κουκκουναριά (*koukkounariá*) or ἡ στροφίλια (*strofília*)
P. nigra Arn.	—	ἡ μαύρη πεύκη (*mávri pévki*)
Abies cephalonica Loud.	—	τὸ ἔλατο (*élato*)
A. Apollinis Link.	—	—
Fagus sylvatica L.	Beech	ἡ ὀξυά (*oxiá*)
Aesculus Hippocastanum L.	Horse chestnut	—
Castanea sativa Mill.	Chestnut	ἡ καστανιά (*kastaniá*)
Carpinus orientalis Mill.	—	—
C. Betulus L.	Hornbeam	—
Fraxinus excelsior L.	Ash	ἡ μελιά (*meliá*)
F. Ornus L.	Manna-ash	—
Platanus orientalis L.	Oriental plane	ὁ πλάτανος (*plátanos*)
Populus nigra L.	Black poplar	—
P. alba L.	White poplar	ἡ λεύκη (*lévki*)
Salix sp.	Willow	ἡ ἰτεά (*iteá*)
Quercus Ilex L.	Holm oak	ἡ ἀριά (*ariá*)
Q. Aegilops L.	Valona oak	ἡ βαλανιδιά (*valanidhiá*)
Q. coccifera L.	Kermes oak or Prickly oak	τὸ πρινάρι (*prinári*) or τὸ πουρνάρι (*pournári*)
Q. lanuginosa Thuill.	—	ἡ δρῦς (*drís*)
Q. conferta Kit.	—	ἡ δρῦς (*drís*)
Q. sessiliflora Salisb.	Sessile oak	ἡ δρῦς (*drís*)
Q. Cerris L.	Turkey oak	ἡ δρῦς (*drís*)
Q. macedonica DC.	Macedonian oak	ἡ δρῦς (*drís*)
Rhus Coriaria L.	Sumac	τὸ σομακί (*somakí*)
Cercis Siliquastrum L.	Judas tree	ἡ κότσικας (*kótsikas*)
Ostrya carpinifolia Scop.	Hop hornbeam	—
Pyrus communis L.	Wild pear	ἡ ἀχλαδιά (*akhladhiá*)
Tilia microphylla Vent.	Lime	ἡ φλαμουριά (*flamouriá*)

Botanical name	English name (if any)	Modern Greek name (where known)
Agave americana L.	Agave	ἡ ἀθάνατος (*athánatos*)
Opuntia Ficus indica Mill.	Prickly pear	ἡ φραγκοσυκιά (*frangosikiá*)
Olea europaea L.	Olive	ἡ ἐληά (*eliá*)
Ficus Carica L.	Fig	ἡ συκιά (*sikiá*)
Prunus Amygdalus Stokes	Almond	ἡ ἀμυγδαλιά (*amygdhaliá*)
Juglans regia L.	Walnut	ἡ καρυδιά (*karidhiá*)
Punica Granatum L.	Pomegranate	ἡ ροϊδιά (*roïdhiá*)
Ceratonia Siliqua L.	Carob	ἡ ξυλοκερατιά (*xilokeratiá*) or ἡ χαρουπιά (*kharoupiá*)

II. Brushwood Plants:

Botanical name	English name (if any)	Modern Greek name (where known)
Nerium Oleander L.	Oleander	ἡ πικροδάφνη (*pikrodháfne*)
Laurus nobilis L.	Bay tree	ἡ δάφνη (*dháfne*)
Arbutus Unedo L.	Strawberry tree	τὸ κούμαρο (*koúmaro*)
Vitex Agnus-castus L.	Chaste tree	ἡ λυγαριά (*ligariá*)
Myrtus communis L.	Myrtle	ἡ μυρτιά (*mirtiá*)
Pistacia Lentiscus L.	Lentisk	ἡ μαστιχιά (*mastikhiá*)
Spartium junceum L.	Spanish broom	τὸ σπάρτο (*spárto*)
Erica arborea L.	Tree heath	—
E. verticillata Forsk.	(A heather)	ἡ ἐρείκη (*eríki* or *ríki*)
Calycotome villosa Link.	(A gorse-like plant)	ἡ ἀσπάλαθος (*aspálathos*), ἡ ἀσφάλακλος (*asfálaklos*), τὸ ἀσπάλακτρο (*aspálaktro*) — Cretan name
Buxus sempervirens L.	Box	ἡ πύξος (*píxos*)
Pistacia Terebinthus L.	Terebinth	ἡ τερέβινθος (*terévinthos*)
Juniperus excelsa Bieb.	—	ἡ ἄρκευθος (*árkevthos*)
J. drupacea Lab.	—	ἡ ἄρκευθος (*árkevthos*)
J. Oxycedrus L.	—	ἡ ἄρκευθος (*árkevthos*)
Jasminum fruticans L.	—	ἡ ἰάσμη (*iásmi*)
Prunus laurocerasus L.	Cherry laurel	—
Clematis cirrhosa L.	—	ἡ περικοκλάδα (*perikokládha*) [a name given to many other climbing plants]
Smilax aspera L.	—	ἡ ἀκρέvατος (*akrévatos*) or ἡ ἀρκουδόβατος (*arkoudóvatos*)
Hedera Helix L.	Ivy	ὁ κισσός (*kissós*)
Poterium spinosum	—	ἡ στιβίδα (*stivídha*)
Coridothymus capitatus Reichb.	Cretan thyme	τὸ θυμάρι (*thimári*)
Origanum onites L.	Marjoram	τὸ ριγάνι (*rigáni*)
Cistus salvifolius L.	Cistus	ἡ κουνούκλα (*kounoúkla*)
C. creticus L.	Cistus	ἡ κουνούκλα (*kounoúkla*)
C. monspeliensis L.	Cistus	ἡ κουνούκλα (*kounoúkla*)
C. parviflorus Lam.	Cistus	ἡ κουνούκλα (*kounoúkla*)
Lavendula Stoechas L.	French lavender	ἡ λεβάντα (*levánta*)
Genista acanthoclada DC.	(A gorse-like plant)	—
Stachys cretica L.	—	—
Satureia Thymbra L.	Savory	ἡ θρούμπη (*throúmbi*)
Thymelaea hirsuta Endl.	—	τὸ θερόκαλο (*therókalo*), ἡ φινοκαλιά (*finokaliá*), Crete
T. Tartonraira All.	—	ἡ κολοφοῦσα (*kolofoúsa*)
Phlomis fruticosa L.	Jerusalem sage	ἡ σφάκα (*sfáka*)
Paliurus Spina-Christi Mill.	Christ's thorn	τὸ παλιοῦρι (*palioúri*)
Cotinus coggygria Scop.	Wigtree or Venetian sumac	—
Syringa vulgaris L.	Lilac	ἡ πασχαλιά (*paskhaliá*)
Berberis vulgaris L.	Common barberry	—

Botanical name	English name (if any)	Modern Greek name (where known)
Prunus nana Stokes	—	—
Viburnum Lantana L.	Wayfaring tree	—
Juniperus communis L.	Juniper	τὸ ἀρδίτσι (*ardhítsi*)
Daphne oleoides Schreb.	—	—
Prunus prostrata Lab.	—	—

III. Marsh and Sand-Dune Plants:

Botanical name	English name (if any)	Modern Greek name (where known)
Dunes and Pebble-beach Plants:		
Cakile maritima L.	Sea Rocket	—
Eryngium maritimum L.	Sea Holly	—
E. creticum Lam.	—	—
Medicago marina L.	—	—
Euphorbia Peplis L.	—	—
Polygonum maritimum L.	—	—
Salsola Kali L.	Saltwort	—
Cyperus Kali Murbeck	—	—
Matthiola tricuspidata R.Br.	—	—
Salicornia fruticosa L.	Glasswort or Marsh samphire	—
Salt-marsh Plants:		
Carex divisa Huds.	—	—
Pancratium maritimum L.	Sea-lily	ὁ κρίνος τῆς θαλάσσης (*krínos tis thalássis*)
Marsdenia erecta R.Br.	—	—
Lavatera cretica L.	—	—
Linum maritimum L.	—	—
Euphorbia pubescens Vahl.	—	—
Spergularia salina J. & C. Presl	Sandwort spurrey	—
Frankenia hirsuta L.	—	—
Limonium virgatum Fourr.	—	—
L. vulgare Mill.	Sea lavender	—
Goniolimon collinum Boiss.	—	—
Juncus acutus L.	—	—
Echinophora tenuifolia L.	—	—
Freshwater Marsh Plants:		
Typha angustifolia L.	Bulrush	τὸ βροῦλο (*vroúlo*)
Alisma Plantago-aquatica L.	Water plantain	—
Scirpus Tabernaemontani C. C. Gmel.	—	—
S. maritimus L.	—	—
S. Holoschoenus L.	—	—
Cyperus longus L.	Galingale	ἡ κύπερις (*kíperis*)
Juncus bufonius L.	Toad rush	—
Phalaris arundinacea L.	Reed grass	—
Iris pseudacorus L.	Yellow flag	—
Orchis palustris Jacq.	—	τὸ σαλέπι (*salépi*)
Lythrum Salicaria L.	Purple loosestrife	—

Appendix VIII

TABLE OF GREEK ADMINISTRATIVE REGIONS

Dhiamerísmata and Nomoí	Area in sq. km. 1938	Number of: (31 Dec. 1938)				Population: 1928 Census		Population estimates 31 Dec. 1938		Absolute increase population 1928–38	% increase population 1928–38
		Eparkhíai	Dhímoi	Koinótites	Sinoikismoí	Total	Pop. per sq. km.	Total	Pop. per sq. km.		
Stereá Ellás	*25,132·4*	*22*	*19*	*924*	*1,753*	*1,601,396*	*63·72*	*1,799,169*	*70·59*	*197,773*	*12·35*
Aitolía-Akarnanía	7,746·8	6	2	308	573	220,055	28·41	255,862	33·03	35,807	16·27
Attikí-Voiotía	6,697·4	7	14	185	459	1,033,221	154·27	1,144,330	170·86	111,109	10·75
Évvoia	4,296·5	4	2	159	340	154,449	35·95	179,523	41·78	25,074	16·23
Fthiótis-Fokís	6,391·7	5	1	272	381	193,671	30·30	219,454	34·33	25,783	13·31
Pelopónnisos	*21,643·2*	*22*	*13*	*1,294*	*2,307*	*1,044,773*	*48·27*	*1,185,046*	*54·75*	*140,273*	*13·43*
Argolís-Korinthía	4,628·7	5	5	180	361	165,766	35·81	190,184	41·09	24,418	14·73
Arkadhía	4,327·0	4	1	244	369	166,141	38·40	187,327	43·29	21,186	12·75
Akhaïa	2,956·1	3	2	226	414	190,422	64·42	213,291	72·15	22,869	12·01
Ilía	2,146·9	1	2	154	227	130,201	60·65	148,554	69·19	18,353	14·10
Lakonía	3,763·8	4	1	157	404	129,927	34·52	148,499	39·45	18,572	14·29
Messinía	3,820·7	5	2	333	532	262,316	68·66	297,191	77·78	34,875	13·30
Kikládhes	*2,649·5*	*7*	*1*	*114*	*437*	*129,702*	*48·95*	*146,987*	*55·48*	*17,285*	*13·33*
Kikládhes	2,649·5	7	1	114	437	129,702	48·95	146,987	55·48	17,285	13·33
Ionian Islands	*1,947·0*	*7*	*3*	*238*	*558*	*213,157*	*109·48*	*231,510*	*118·91*	*18,353*	*8·61*
Zákinthos	407·9	1	1	46	76	40,492	99·27	44,750	109·71	4,258	10·52
Kérkira	637·7	2	1	97	229	106,251	166·62	114,620	179·74	8,369	7·88
Kefallinía	901·4	4	1	95	253	66,414	73·68	72,140	80·03	5,726	8·62
Thessalía	*13,487·8*	*10*	*4*	*491*	*787*	*493,213*	*36·57*	*562,020*	*41·67*	*68,807*	*13·95*
Lárisa	7,622·8	7	2	223	407	278,465	36·55	312,272	40·97	33,807	12·14
Tríkkala	5,865·0	3	2	268	380	214,748	36·62	249,748	42·58	35,000	16·30

TABLE OF GREEK ADMINISTRATIVE REGIONS (*cont.*)

Dhiamerísmata and Nomoí	Area in sq. km. 1938	Number of: (31 Dec. 1938)				Population: 1928 Census		Population estimates 31 Dec. 1938		Absolute increase population 1928–38	% increase population 1928–38
		Eparkhíai	Dhímoi	Koinótites	Sinoikismoí	Total	Pop. per sq. km.	Total	Pop. per sq. km.		
Makedhonía	*34,602·5*	*26*	*15*	*1,074*	*2,095*	*1,411,769*	*40·80*	*1,686,479*	*48·74*	*274,710*	*19·46*
Dráma	3,497·3	1	1	64	197	111,572	31·90	139,583	39·91	28,011	25·11
Thessaloníki	6,309·0	4	5	168	378	472,823	74·95	539,697	85·54	66,874	14·14
Kaválla	2,169·2	4	1	77	144	118,432	54·60	139,309	64·22	20,877	17·63
Kilkís	2,507·5	2	1	71	229	73,139	29·17	95,593	38·12	22,454	30·70
Kozáni	6,214·9	4	1	245	351	165,059	26·56	202,849	32·64	37,790	22·89
Pélla	2,802·5	3	2	86	157	93,908	33·51	117,990	42·10	24,082	25·64
Sérrai	4,056·5	4	1	129	255	181,457	44·73	216,569	53·39	35,112	19·35
Flórina	3,502·7	2	2	160	215	125,722	35·89	152,809	43·63	27,087	21·55
Khalkidhikí	3,203·5	2	1	74	148	64,799	20·23	82,080	23·17	12,423	17·83
Áyion Óros	339·4	—	—	—	21	4,858	14·31				
Ípiros	*9,552·5*	*10*	*4*	*604*	*811*	*312,634*	*32·73*	*363,041*	*38·00*	*50,407*	*16·12*
Árta	1,741·1	1	1	69	107	52,664	30·25	62,462	35·88	9,798	18·60
Thresprotía	1,594·1	3	1	129	179	55,357	34·73	64,191	40·27	8,834	15·96
Ioánnina	5,066·1	4	1	304	379	137,529	27·15	159,020	31·39	21,491	15·63
Préveza	1,151·2	2	1	102	146	67,084	58·27	77,368	67·21	10,284	15·33
Kriti	*8,378·8*	*20*	*4*	*544*	*1,489*	*386,427*	*46·12*	*441,687*	*52·71*	*55,260*	*14·30*
Iráklion	2,561·0	7	1	180	416	144,921	56·56	162,978	63·64	18,057	12·46
Lasíthi	1,910·6	4	1	83	262	61,813	32·35	75,914	39·73	14,101	22·81
Rethímni	1,507·7	4	1	133	286	67,674	44·89	76,141	50·50	8,467	12·51
Khaniá	2,399·5	5	1	148	525	112,019	46·68	126,654	52·78	14,635	13·06
Aegean Islands	*3,900·6*	*7*	*5*	*208*	*367*	*307,734*	*78·89*	*337,986*	*86·65*	*30,252*	*9·83*
Lésvos	2,165·9	4	2	101	149	161,557	74·59	177,214	81·82	15,657	9·69
Sámos	833·1	2	1	49	141	70,497	84·62	77,858	93·46	7,361	10·44
Khíos	901·6	1	2	58	77	75,680	83·94	82,914	91·96	7,234	9·56
Dhitikí Thráki	*8,585·5*	*8*	*5*	*126*	*526*	*303,879*	*35·39*	*354,889*	*41·34*	*51,010*	*16·79*
Évros	4,233·9	5	3	64	202	124,417	29·39	151,260	35·73	26,843	21·58
Rodhópi	4,351·6	3	2	62	324	179,462	41·24	203,629	46·79	24,167	13·47
Total all Greece	129,879·8	139	73	5,617	11,130	6,204,684	47·77	7,108,814	54·73	904,130	14·57

From the *Annuaire Statistique de la Grèce*, 1939, p. 30 (Athènes, 1940).

For an account of the administrative units, see pp. 253–7.

Appendix IX

CLIMATIC TABLES

1. The meteorological stations.
2. Principal climatic elements.
3. Average monthly temperatures (° C.), 1900–29.
4. Absolute maximum and minimum temperatures.
5. Percentage frequency of days of frost, 1900–29.
6. Average monthly rainfall in mm., 1894–1929.
7. Average number of rain days, 1894–1929.
8. Percentage frequency of days on which snow falls.
9. Frequency of thunderstorms.
10. Relative humidity. Average monthly figures for 1900–29.
11. Mean hours of sunshine, 1900–29.

Table 1. *The meteorological stations*

Station	Class*	Latitude	Longitude	Height in m.	Station	Class*	Latitude	Longitude	Height in m.
Flórina	C	40° 48′	21° 26′	620	Kalávrita	C	38° 02′	22° 07′	724
Thessaloníki	B	40° 40′	22° 58′	39	Athínai	A	37° 58′	23° 43′	107
Kozáni	B	40° 18′	21° 47′	667	Ándros	B	37° 50′	24° 55′	44
Límnos	B	39° 53′	25° 04′	3	Zákinthos	B	37° 47′	20° 53′	6
Ioánnina	B	39° 40′	20° 52′	466	Sámos	B	37° 44′	27° 00′	91
Lárisa	B	39° 39′	22° 25′	76	Pírgos	C	37° 41′	21° 27′	29
Kérkira	B	39° 37′	19° 55′	27	Návplion	B	37° 34′	22° 49′	11
Tríkkala	B	39° 33′	21° 46′	114	Trípolis	B	37° 31′	22° 23′	661
Vólos	B	39° 22′	22° 56′	6	Síros	B	37° 26′	24° 56′	32
Árta	B	39° 10′	20° 58′	57	Kiparissía	B	37° 15′	21° 40′	114
Mitilíni	B	39° 06′	26° 35′	10	Náxos	B	37° 06′	25° 24′	7
Préveza	C	38° 58′	20° 45′	5	Spárti	B	37° 05′	22° 25′	193
Lamía	B	38° 54′	22° 26′	83	Kalámai	B	37° 02′	22° 05′	31
Skíros	B	38° 54′	24° 33′	57	Yíthion	B	36° 45′	22° 23′	28
Khalkís	B	38° 28′	23° 37′	12	Mílos	B	36° 43′	24° 25′	172
Levádhia	C	38° 27′	22° 52′	151	Thíra	B	36° 25′	25° 24′	229
Mesolóngion	B	38° 23′	21° 26′	4	Kíthira	B	36° 09′	23° 00′	166
Khíos	B	38° 22′	26° 10′	9	Khaniá	B	35° 30′	24° 02′	14
Pátrai	B	38° 15′	21° 44′	17	Melidhónion	C	35° 23′	24° 09′	104
Aíyion	C	38° 15′	22° 15′	68	Iráklion	B	35° 19′	25° 06′	36
Argostólion	B	38° 10′	20° 30′	13	Anóyia	B	35° 16′	24° 54′	776
Dhekélia	C	38° 08′	23° 45′	479	Ierápetra	C	35° 00′	25° 45′	3

* A. Station with a complete set of self-recording instruments. B. Station with a mercury barometer, hygrometers and a rainfall gauge. C. Station with a hygrometer and rainfall gauge.

Stations with rainfall gauges only are not given in this list but are marked on Fig. 53.

Table 2. *Principal climatic elements. Average Annual Figures*

Station	Height in metres	Temp. air °C.	Relative humidity %	Dominant wind	Cloudiness	Rainfall mm.	Days of rain	Days of snow per 1,000	Days frost per 1,000	Days thunder per 1,000
Thessaloníki	39	16·1	66·8	SW	4·5	486·1	93·4	13·4	6·2	57·3
Ioánnina*	466	14·6	70·4	NW	5·0	1,195·4	137·1	13·3	11·4	90·8
Lárisa	76	16·3	69·2	E	4·5	518·4	97·8	10·7	4·3	19·9
Kérkira	27	17·9	73·2	S	3·9	1,171·6	97·1	1·6	13·8	42·2
Tríkkala	114	16·3	67·0	W	5·2	738·3	116·5	17·9	2·0	36·2
Árta	57	17·3	71·7	E	4·2	1,080·1	101·2	2·3	13·0	61·4
Mitilíni*	10	17·2	73·7	N	3·4	658·8	75·5	3·3	6·1	37·0
Lamía	83	17·3	—	E	4·5	583·9	85·6	9·2	1·4	12·7
Khalkís	12	18·1	65·8	N	4·3	432·3	86·1	9·6	4·4	21·8
Pátrai	17	18·2	68·8	W	3·8	707·2	103·0	1·6	10·3	43·6
Athínai	107	17·5	59·8	NE	4·0	383·9	81·9	9·7	7·0	40·6
Zákinthos	6	18·7	57·6	NW	3·2	1,114·8	100·4	2·2	16·9	32·7
Návplion	11	18·3	64·6	N	3·6	495·1	67·2	4·7	1·8	23·0
Trípolis	661	14·4	66·3	SW	4·0	808·9	107·7	24·9	9·0	13·8
Náxos	7	18·7	—	N	4·7	380·2	72·2	5·7	5·9	29·6
Spárti	193	17·5	65·2	N	3·9	818·6	85·8	6·0	4·8	34·8
Kalámai	31	19·0	67·0	N	3·7	839·2	91·4	0·8	5·0	28·0
Thíra	229	17·3	67·9	N	3·8	357·3	55·6	4·9	10·3	27·0
Kíthira	166	18·7	64·6	W	3·6	616·4	43·1	1·0	3·9	7·5
Iráklion*	36	19·1	65·1	NW	4·0	510·2	96·8	11·0	5·3	21·9

Figures in general are based on observations for the period 1900–29; rainfall figures on observations for the period 1894–1929. They have been taken from E. G. Mariolopoulos, *The Climate of Greece* (Athínai, 1938): the text is in Modern Greek.

* Stations with observations for shorter periods.

Table 3. *Average monthly temperatures* (° C.), 1900–29

Station	Height in metres	Jan. ° C.	Feb. ° C.	Mar. ° C.	Apr. ° C.	May ° C.	June ° C.	July ° C.	Aug. ° C.	Sept. ° C.	Oct. ° C.	Nov. ° C.	Dec. ° C.	Year ° C.	Year ° F.
Flórina	620	0·8	1·7	5·6	9·2	15·5	18·9	23·0	22·3	17·9	12·6	7·2	1·8	11·4	52·5
Thessaloníki	39	5·6	6·7	10·4	14·6	19·3	23·6	26·3	25·9	22·3	17·2	11·4	7·6	15·9	60·6
Kozáni	667	2·2	3·1	6·8	9·9	16·7	20·3	23·7	23·2	18·8	13·2	7·5	3·9	12·5	54·5
Ioánnina	466	5·1	6·3	9·4	12·9	17·1	20·7	24·1	24·6	24·7	15·3	10·1	6·5	14·4	57·9
Lárisa	76	5·4	7·1	10·5	14·8	19·4	24·2	27·2	26·8	22·4	16·8	11·3	7·3	16·1	61·0
Kérkira	27	10·4	10·8	12·5	15·3	19·2	23·1	25·8	26·0	23·1	19·0	15·2	12·1	17·7	63·8
Tríkkala	114	5·5	7·0	10·7	15·1	19·5	24·1	27·3	27·0	22·5	16·5	10·9	7·2	16·2	61·1
Vólos	6	7·6	8·7	11·2	15·3	19·4	23·4	26·6	26·3	23·3	17·8	13·6	9·3	16·9	62·4
Árta	57	8·5	9·4	11·9	15·3	19·4	23·2	26·5	26·9	23·2	18·2	13·2	10·0	17·1	62·7
Mitilíni	10	8·5	8·4	11·3	15·1	19·4	23·7	26·6	26·2	22·6	18·1	13·7	10·4	17·0	62·5
Préveza	5	9·5	10·2	12·7	15·4	19·1	22·7	25·4	25·7	23·1	18·9	14·6	11·2	17·4	63·3
Lamía	83	7·6	8·9	11·5	15·3	19·8	24·6	27·4	27·0	23·0	18·2	12·7	9·7	17·1	62·7
Khalkís	12	9·0	9·5	11·8	15·8	20·2	24·8	27·4	27·3	23·8	19·2	15·2	10·9	17·9	64·2
Mesolóngion	4	9·9	10·6	12·8	16·2	20·2	24·1	26·9	27·1	24·1	19·5	14·9	11·5	18·2	64·7
Pátrai	17	10·1	10·7	12·7	16·0	20·0	23·9	26·9	27·0	23·9	19·1	14·8	11·8	18·1	64·5
Aíyion	68	9·8	10·2	12·2	15·4	19·2	23·3	26·4	26·7	23·7	18·8	14·5	11·6	17·7	63·8
Argostólion	13	11·0	11·3	13·0	15·8	19·4	23·3	25·9	26·1	23·7	19·5	15·7	12·6	18·1	64·5
Dhekélia	479	5·8	6·3	8·2	12·0	16·2	20·1	23·2	23·3	19·8	15·6	11·1	7·9	14·1	57·3
Athínai	107	9·1	9·5	11·5	14·9	19·3	23·7	26·9	26·7	23·3	19·0	14·3	11·0	17·4	63·3
Ándros	44	10·5	10·7	12·4	15·6	19·4	23·6	26·1	26·0	22·9	19·3	15·4	12·2	17·8	64·0
Zákinthos	6	11·4	11·5	13·1	15·4	20·0	23·9	26·8	27·0	24·0	19·9	16·0	13·1	18·5	65·2
Návplion	11	10·0	10·6	12·6	15·7	19·5	24·4	27·2	27·0	23·7	19·5	15·1	11·8	18·1	64·5
Trípolis	661	5·1	6·0	8·5	12·4	16·4	20·7	24·2	24·2	20·4	15·1	10·4	7·1	14·2	57·5
Síros	32	11·4	11·6	13·1	16·2	19·9	24·1	26·6	26·5	23·5	19·9	16·1	13·1	18·5	65·2
Kiparissía	114	11·0	11·4	13·1	16·0	19·5	23·1	25·7	26·3	23·6	19·6	15·8	12·8	18·2	64·7
Náxos	7	12·4	12·6	13·9	16·4	19·4	22·9	24·9	25·1	23·0	20·1	16·9	14·1	18·5	65·2
Spárti	193	8·8	9·5	11·6	15·1	19·2	23·5	27·0	27·2	23·7	18·6	13·8	10·5	17·4	63·3
Kalámai	31	11·2	11·6	13·5	16·4	19·1	24·1	27·0	27·4	24·6	20·3	16·1	13·0	18·7	65·6
Thíra	229	10·5	10·7	12·1	14·7	18·1	21·9	24·4	24·5	21·9	18·8	15·3	12·4	17·1	62·7
Kíthira	166	11·1	11·5	13·0	15·5	18·9	23·0	26·4	26·9	24·5	20·6	16·4	13·1	18·3	64·9
Khaniá	14	11·3	11·7	13·2	15·8	19·3	22·3	25·7	25·7	22·8	19·7	16·0	13·0	18·1	64·5
Iráklion	36	12·2	12·3	14·0	16·8	20·0	23·8	26·1	26·3	23·7	20·8	17·3	14·0	19·0	66·2
Anóyia	776	7·1	6·8	9·2	13·2	16·3	21·0	22·5	22·4	19·4	16·2	12·8	9·0	14·7	58·4

Table 4. *Absolute maximum and minimum temperatures*

Station	Height in metres	Absolute maxima		Date	Absolute minima		Date	Range		Period of observations
		° C.	° F.		° C.	° F.		° C.	° F.	
Flórina	620	—	—	—	−23·0	−9·5	4. 2. 1929	—	—	1926–1931
Thessaloníki	39	41·6	106·8	10. 7. 1927	− 9·5	14·9	8. 2. 1911	51·6	91·9	1894–1929
Kozáni	667	40·8	105·4	12. 7. 1916	−19·0	−2·2	9. 2. 1929	59·8	107·6	1915–1920
Ioánnina	466	40·8	105·4	12. 8. 1922	− 9·9	14·2	27. 1. 1924	60·7	91·2	1915–1929
Lárisa	76	45·0	112·9	12. 7. 1916	−13·0	8·6	6. 1. 1905	58·0	104·3	1894–1929
Kérkira	27	38·8	101·8	12. 8. 1922	− 5·0	22·9	11. 2. 1911	43·8	88·9	1894–1929
Tríkkala	114	44·5	112·0	12. 7. 1916	−19·0	−2·2	26. 1. 1907	63·5	114·2	1894–1929
Vólos	6	41·0	105·8	5. 7. 1912	− 7·0	19·3	2. 2. 1911	48·0	86·5	1894–1929
Árta	57	44·2	111·5	{24. 8. 1911 22. 6. 1916}	− 8·9	15·9	4. 3. 1913	53·1	95·6	1894–1929
Mitilíni	10	41·6	106·8	6. 7. 1916	− 5·8	21·5	9. 2. 1929	47·4	85·3	1915–1929
Lamía	83	44·3	111·7	20. 7. 1894	− 8·2	17·2	26. 12. 1907	52·5	94·5	1894–1929
Khalkís	12	44·2	111·5	12. 7. 1916	− 7·0	19·3	18. 2. 1911	51·2	92·2	1894–1929
Mesolóngion	4	40·5	104·9	3. 8. 1908	− 5·2	22·6	27. 1. 1898	45·7	82·3	1894–1929
Pátrai	17	41·7	107·0	24. 8. 1911	− 5·0	22·9	4. 2. 1909	46·7	85·1	1894–1929
Aíyion	68	40·2	104·3	24. 8. 1911	− 4·0	24·7	11. 2. 1911	42·2	79·6	1904–1921
Argostólion	13	43·0	109·3	24. 8. 1911	− 3·3	26·0	27. 1. 1898	46·3	83·3	1894–1929
Dhekélia	479	40·4	104·7	23. 7. 1902	− 8·8	16·1	9. 2. 1911	49·2	88·6	1900–1915
Athínai	107	43·0	109·3	21. 6. 1916	− 5·5	22·0	26. 1. 1924	48·5	87·3	1894–1929
Ándros	44	42·0	107·5	5. 7. 1912	− 3·0	26·5	27. 1. 1898	45·0	81·0	1894–1929

Zákinthos	6	39·2	102·5	31. 7. 1928	− 1·0	30·2	10. 2. 1911	40·2	72·3	1894–1929
Sámos	91	35·0	95·0	4. 9. 1906	− 3·8	25·1	23. 1. 1907 24. 1. 1907	38·8	70·9	1904–1907
Návplion	11	42·5	108·4	12. 7. 1916	− 4·0	24·7	27. 2. 1928 27. 12. 1928	46·5	83·7	1894–1929
Trípolis	661	48·0	118·3	6. 8. 1896 12. 8. 1896	−17·0	1·4	26. 1. 1907	65·0	116·9	1894–1929
Síros	32	40·0	104·0	31. 8. 1911 6. 7. 1916	− 2·0	28·4	26. 1. 1924 10. 11. 1920	42·0	75·6	1894–1929
Kiparissía	114	39·5	103·1	13. 5. 1903	− 3·0	26·5	16. 1. 1901	42·5	76·6	1900–1929
Náxos	7	36·8	98·3	5. 7. 1912	− 1·2	29·8	26. 1. 1898	38·0	68·5	1894–1929
Spárti	193	43·5	110·2	12. 8. 1896 12. 7. 1916	− 6·3	20·6	24. 2. 1894	49·8	89·6	1894–1929
Kalámai	31	45·0	112·9	—. 6. 1916	− 3·4	25·8	27. 2. 1928 27. 12. 1928	48·4	87·1	1894–1929
Thíra	229	39·9	105·6	18. 7. 1917	− 4·8	23·3	27. 2. 1928	44·7	82·3	1894–1929
Kíthira	166	39·0	102·2	17. 7. 1895	− 2·0	28·4	11. 2. 1911	41·0	73·8	1894–1929
Khaniá	14	41·5	106·6	8. 6. 1916 19. 6. 1916	− 1·0	30·2	11. 2. 1920	42·5	76·4	1915–1929
Iráklion	36	45·7	114·2	16. 6. 1914	0·1	31·8	28. 2. 1928	45·6	82·4	1909–1929
Anóyia	776	37·3	99·1	13. 7. 1916	− 5·0	22·9	10. 2. 1920	42·3	76·2	1915–1929

Table 5. *Percentage frequency of days of frost*, 1900–29

Station	Height in metres	Nov.	Dec.	Jan.	Feb.	Mar.	Apr.	Nov.-Apr.
		%	%	%	%	%	%	%
Thessaloníki	39	5·0	12·4	18·5	25·6	6·2	0	11·3
Kozáni	667	20·7	39·7	50·6	71·8	25·2	2·3	30·3
Ioánnina	466	9·4	26·2	33·1	28·1	7·6	0	17·4
Lárisa	76	7·5	25·9	45·6	31·8	10·2	0·3	20·2
Kérkira	27	0·1	0·5	2·3	3·8	0·5	0	1·2
Tríkkala	114	8·8	27·3	43·4	32·6	10·2	0·3	20·4
Vólos	6	0·8	1·9	13·7	8·0	1·2	0	4·3
Árta	57	1·9	10·8	17·4	15·4	2·7	0·3	8·1
Mitilíni	10	0·2	2·9	8·4	14·3	2·7	0	4·8
Préveza	5	0·3	0·7	2·7	1·5	0	0	0·8
Lamía	83	2·9	7·1	16·1	16·2	3·6	0·3	7·7
Khalkís	12	0·9	1·5	7·2	9·5	1·8	0·5	3·6
Mesolóngion	4	0·1	0·9	2·7	3·0	0·2	0	1·2
Pátrai	17	0·2	0·2	3·2	3·3	0·3	0	1·2
Aíyion	68	0	0·6	2·7	3·4	0	0	1·1
Argostólion	13	0	0·3	1·7	2·0	0·1	0	0·7
Dhekélia	479	9·4	26·2	33·1	28·1	7·6	0	17·4
Athínai	107	0·3	1·4	4·4	4·4	0·4	0·0	1·8
Ándros	44	0·1	0	1·7	2·9	0·1	0	0·8
Zákinthos	6	0	0	0·2	0·3	0	0	0·1
Návplion	11	0·4	1·8	4·5	6·4	0·6	0	2·3
Trípolis	661	10·2	26·4	42·5	36·2	20·8	3·6	23·3
Síros	32	0	0	0·8	1·4	0·1	0	0·4
Kiparissía	114	0	0·1	1·1	1·3	0·5	0	0·5
Náxos	7	0	0	0	0	0·1	0	0·0
Spárti	193	0·7	2·5	9·6	9·2	1·9	0·1	4·0
Kalámai	31	0	0	1·2	2·3	0·3	0	0·7
Thíra	229	0	0·1	0·5	2·1	0·4	0	0·5
Kíthira	166	0	0·1	0·7	1·6	0·1	0	0·4
Khaniá	14	0	0	0·2	0·8	0	0	0·2
Iráklion	36	0	0	0	0·5	0	0	0·1
Anóyia	776	0·8	1·8	6·5	12·1	3·8	0·6	4·3

Table 6. *Average monthly rainfall in mm.*, 1894–1929

Station	Jan.	Feb.	Mar.	Apr.	May	June	July	Aug.	Sept.	Oct.	Nov.	Dec.	Year mm.	Year in.
Thessaloníki	35·4	31·6	38·1	42·1	52·9	34·6	25·2	23·5	32·6	58·5	64·4	47·1	486·1	19·1
Ioánnina	121·6	126·3	104·5	96·9	106·1	79·8	26·7	14·1	58·8	132·5	155·8	172·3	1,195·4	47·1
Lárisa	48·8	42·8	37·2	37·1	53·1	34·0	23·0	19·1	26·4	64·7	71·7	60·5	518·4	20·4
Kérkira	159·2	139·1	93·4	79·9	48·1	26·1	6·8	18·5	62·7	176·3	161·0	200·5	1,171·6	46·1
Tríkkala	96·0	69·3	65·6	47·9	68·2	33·7	16·3	16·6	27·9	98·7	102·3	95·8	738·3	29·1
Vólos	49·8	56·1	40·7	32·6	41·4	29·4	14·6	23·0	32·6	64·6	74·8	55·2	514·8	20·3
Árta	144·3	124·4	103·0	76·4	66·0	28·2	10·4	11·4	42·3	146·6	153·4	173·7	1,080·1	42·5
Mitilíni	108·1	103·3	71·0	67·9	26·8	5·4	2·1	1·5	9·4	51·1	90·4	121·0	658·0	25·9
Lamía	67·4	64·9	53·2	35·3	42·5	36·7	15·8	16·0	23·9	76·0	76·0	76·2	583·9	23·0
Khalkís	66·0	51·0	38·0	26·4	23·9	15·0	3·4	6·3	27·1	41·2	62·0	72·0	432·3	17·0
Levádhia	103·9	80·9	68·4	35·3	51·7	31·6	8·8	19·3	31·5	63·6	111·0	126·5	732·3	28·8
Mesolóngion	100·9	81·6	72·3	46·4	37·9	16·4	4·7	5·7	19·5	96·5	122·3	133·2	737·4	29·0
Khíos	128·7	98·4	63·0	20·7	16·2	8·0	1·6	2·0	24·9	78·2	123·3	163·8	728·7	28·7
Pátrai	97·5	78·2	66·7	51·8	34·0	16·9	3·9	5·1	27·7	93·7	112·6	119·5	707·2	27·8
Aíyion	77·0	63·6	58·5	30·1	32·7	7·2	1·4	4·7	14·9	65·1	106·8	102·0	564·0	22·2
Argostólion	127·1	103·2	78·6	45·1	27·2	14·8	4·6	10·9	27·9	128·7	130·7	173·5	873·3	34·4
Athínai	53·4	40·3	30·4	19·9	20·6	16·4	4·4	7·8	16·0	40·0	66·2	68·5	383·9	15·1
Kórinthos	66·9	48·2	35·9	25·9	20·6	15·1	5·1	4·7	22·5	44·7	60·5	54·6	404·7	15·9
Ándros	126·4	103·9	68·6	28·2	18·7	10·5	1·3	1·6	12·2	41·7	89·0	134·2	636·2	25·0
Zákinthos	181·6	133·8	87·5	54·7	30·0	8·4	2·3	10·8	35·3	129·5	206·9	234·0	1,114·8	43·9
Pírgos	128·8	102·6	73·0	51·5	33·0	13·7	1·2	11·9	21·5	99·8	131·9	164·4	833·3	32·8
Návplion	70·8	55·5	46·4	22·2	25·1	16·3	4·3	10·8	23·4	60·7	67·2	92·4	495·1	19·5
Trípolis	125·8	88·9	68·5	54·4	50·1	36·8	15·6	15·1	25·8	78·3	120·2	129·3	808·9	31·8
Síros	102·4	66·2	48·4	26·5	17·3	4·9	0·8	2·6	8·9	14·5	75·2	92·6	487·4	19·2
Kiparissía	130·7	100·2	63·8	50·2	41·7	11·2	0·9	6·9	29·7	85·8	140·5	165·9	827·5	32·6
Náxos	80·0	58·2	35·0	22·3	16·4	2·8	0·4	0·6	5·8	27·7	53·8	77·2	380·2	15·0
Spárti	126·3	90·1	72·5	44·0	47·0	31·0	10·9	17·3	35·3	77·8	114·5	152·0	816·6	32·0
Kalámai	141·3	106·2	71·3	51·9	43·4	13·9	3·8	10·0	24·5	90·8	123·6	158·5	839·2	33·0
Thíra	76·7	48·8	32·4	21·0	12·9	1·8	0·2	0·2	6·8	23·5	54·7	78·2	357·3	14·1
Kíthira	124·9	83·1	54·3	20·0	11·6	4·9	1·3	2·2	16·1	53·8	103·8	140·4	616·4	24·3
Khaniá	128·7	100·5	67·0	28·9	15·3	2·4	0·6	3·2	32·2	37·7	121·7	168·7	706·9	27·8
Iráklion	85·7	71·6	45·6	27·2	22·5	1·7	1·0	7·0	17·8	38·5	99·6	92·0	510·2	20·1
Anóyia	215·2	172·8	119·0	54·3	62·6	6·2	2·0	14·1	17·0	70·8	157·3	232·4	1,123·6	44·2

Table 7. *Average number of raindays*, 1894–1929

Station	Jan.	Feb.	Mar.	Apr.	May	June	July	Aug.	Sept.	Oct.	Nov.	Dec.	Year
Thessaloníki	7·8	8·3	8·8	8·9	10·3	7·9	4·6	3·9	5·6	8·6	9·1	9·4	93·4
Ioánnina	12·9	13·4	13·5	13·1	14·4	9·8	5·9	3·9	7·8	12·3	14·5	15·6	137·1
Lárisa	9·8	9·2	8·7	9·0	10·2	7·6	4·7	3·7	5·0	9·2	10·1	10·6	97·8
Kérkira	12·5	11·6	10·1	9·4	6·1	4·2	1·4	1·6	4·6	10·4	10·8	14·5	97·1
Tríkkala	12·5	11·0	10·6	9·9	10·8	8·6	4·9	3·8	6·3	11·4	12·9	13·8	116·5
Vólos	9·8	9·4	9·0	7·8	7·3	6·3	2·7	2·7	4·6	8·0	10·5	10·0	87·9
Árta	11·7	11·0	11·0	10·2	8·7	5·3	2·2	1·9	5·1	9·9	11·0	13·3	101·2
Mitilíni	11·1	10·4	6·5	6·5	5·5	2·8	1·2	0·4	2·1	7·5	8·5	12·9	75·5
Lamía	10·4	9·2	8·4	6·8	6·9	5·3	2·7	2·4	4·8	7·9	9·7	11·1	85·6
Khalkís	11·9	10·1	9·0	6·4	6·1	4·9	1·9	2·0	3·6	7·6	10·6	11·9	86·1
Levádhia	9·1	8·3	7·6	4·4	6·5	3·9	2·0	2·1	2·6	6·3	8·8	10·2	71·5
Mesolóngion	12·6	12·1	10·9	9·2	8·0	4·6	1·2	1·9	4·6	9·9	12·2	14·2	101·4
Khíos	13·5	10·2	10·3	6·0	4·5	1·6	0·5	1·1	3·2	7·0	12·4	15·0	85·3
Pátrai	12·5	11·6	10·8	10·0	8·1	5·1	1·3	1·9	4·7	10·7	12·1	14·3	103·0
Aíyion	10·4	9·6	9·0	7·7	6·8	3·2	1·1	1·6	3·4	8·4	11·9	10·7	83·8
Argostólion	12·8	11·7	9·6	6·7	4·5	2·9	0·6	1·0	3·7	9·3	11·1	13·6	87·6
Athínai	10·8	9·3	8·9	7·2	7·0	4·9	1·6	1·8	3·3	6·6	10·0	10·9	81·9
Kórinthos	4·8	4·9	3·5	3·5	3·3	1·3	0·4	0·9	2·5	4·2	5·1	5·8	40·2
Ándros	12·6	11·6	8·3	5·0	4·3	1·8	0·7	0·8	1·8	5·4	9·0	12·1	73·3
Zákinthos	13·8	12·5	10·5	8·0	6·0	3·6	0·8	1·4	4·4	9·9	13·1	16·5	100·4
Pírgos	10·0	11·3	8·1	6·8	4·6	2·4	0·5	1·0	2·1	7·1	10·1	12·1	76·1
Návplion	9·1	8·3	6·9	4·7	5·0	3·4	1·3	1·3	2·7	6·4	8·1	10·0	67·2
Trípolis	12·8	12·4	11·4	9·3	9·5	6·9	3·6	3·0	4·6	8·4	11·6	14·0	107·7
Síros	11·6	9·8	7·6	4·6	4·2	1·3	0·3	0·4	1·4	4·8	8·2	10·7	64·8
Kiparissía	13·0	10·3	8·9	6·9	5·0	2·2	0·6	1·0	2·8	7·3	11·7	14·0	83·6
Náxos	12·1	10·9	7·9	5·2	4·7	1·8	0·4	0·4	1·8	5·1	8·4	12·6	72·2
Spárti	10·5	9·9	9·1	7·0	7·7	4·2	1·8	2·4	3·9	7·3	10·2	11·8	85·8
Kalámai	12·7	11·3	9·4	7·8	6·9	3·7	1·4	1·7	3·9	7·8	10·9	14·0	91·4
Thíra	10·7	8·6	6·5	3·9	2·8	0·9	0·1	0·1	1·2	3·8	7·1	9·9	55·6
Kíthira	7·7	6·1	4·8	2·0	1·6	0·6	0·3	0·4	1·1	3·8	6·0	9·1	43·1
Khaniá	17·2	15·8	11·7	8·4	5·0	1·4	0·1	0·6	4·6	6·7	12·9	18·5	103·0
Iráklion	18·0	15·0	12·1	7·5	6·3	1·8	0·1	0·7	1·9	7·1	9·7	16·2	96·8
Anóyia	22·2	17·9	15·1	10·1	8·6	2·6	0·5	1·6	4·4	10·3	15·1	21·2	129·7

A 'rain day' is one on which more than 0·1 mm. of rain falls.

Table 8. *Percentage frequency of days on which snow falls*

Station	Nov.	Dec.	Jan.	Feb.	Mar.	Apr.	Year
	%	%	%	%	%	%	%
Thessaloníki	1·3	2·0	5·5	5·0	2·3	0·3	1·4
Kastoría	4·0	7·4	11·6	10·7	3·9	0·7	3·2
Kozáni	3·7	7·7	12·9	13·2	5·5	0·7	3·8
Kónitsa	1·0	3·2	7·4	6·1	4·2	1·0	1·9
Métsovon	7·3	12·9	19·7	23·6	17·1	6·0	7·4
Kalabáka	1·0	5·0	6·8	8·2	3·5	0·3	2·1
Ioánnina	1·0	2·9	3·2	5·0	3·5	0	1·4
Lárisa	1·0	1·6	4·2	5·1	1·3	1·0	1·1
Kérkira	0	0·3	1·0	0·7	0	0	0·2
Tríkkala	1·3	1·9	7·4	8·7	2·3	0·1	1·8
Vólos	0	1·3	3·2	4·5	1·3	0·1	0·9
Almirós	0·3	1·6	2·9	3·6	1·6	0	0·8
Árta	0	0·3	1·0	0·9	0·3	0	0·2
Skópelos	0·7	0·6	2·3	4·3	1·3	0·3	0·8
Dhomokós	2·7	2·6	10·0	10·0	3·2	0·3	2·4
Mitilíni	0	1·0	1·6	1·4	0	0	0·3
Préveza	0·3	0·6	1·0	0·7	0	0	0·2
Istiaía	0	2·3	2·9	3·9	2·3	0	1·0
Lamía	0·3	1·3	4·2	4·0	1·3	0	0·9
Karpenísion	6·0	9·0	22·6	20·0	12·3	3·3	6·2
Skíros	0·3	1·9	3·9	5·7	1·9	0·3	1·2
Levkás	0·3	0·6	1·0	0·4	0·3	0	0·2
Kími	2·0	1·6	2·3	5·0	2·3	0·3	1·1
Agrínion	0·1	0·1	0·7	0·4	0·1	0	0·1
Eptálofon	2·0	8·4	14·2	13·9	12·9	2·3	4·5
Lidhoríkion	0·1	1·0	3·5	5·0	2·7	0·7	1·1
Khalkís	0·3	1·6	4·2	4·6	1·0	0·3	1·0
Levádhia	0·7	1·0	3·5	3·6	2·3	0	0·9
Návpaktos	0	0·3	1·6	0·4	0	0	0·2
Mesolóngion	0	0·1	0·6	0·4	0·1	0	0·1
Khíos	0·3	2·3	3·5	2·5	1·0	0	0·8
Thívai	1·0	1·3	1·9	5·0	1·6	0·1	0·9
Pátrai	0	0·1	1·6	0·6	1·2	0	0·2
Aíyion	0·3	0·3	1·6	1·3	0	0	0·3
Argostólion	0·3	0·3	0·6	1·0	0·1	0	0·2
Dhekélia	1·7	4·2	16·1	11·4	6·8	2·0	3·5
Káristos	0	1·3	1·6	6·1	1·0	0	0·8
Athínai	0·7	2·3	4·5	4·6	2·6	0·1	1·2
Kórinthos	0·3	0·3	0·6	1·4	0·3	0	0·2
Ándros	0·1	1·6	3·5	3·8	1·0	0	0·8
Zákinthos	0	0·3	0·3	1·0	0·3	0	0·2
Aíyina	0	0·3	1·0	1·8	0·3	0	0·3
Pírgos	0·1	0·0	0·6	0·7	0·0	0	0·1
Dhimitsána	1·0	3·9	10·6	17·5	8·4	2·0	3·6
Návplion	0·7	0·6	1·6	2·5	0·3	0	0·5
Trípolis	1·3	3·2	10·0	10·0	4·8	1·0	2·5
Síros	0·1	0·1	5·2	1·9	3·7	0·6	0·5
Megalópolis	0	0·1	0·6	0·7	0·1	0	0·1
Leonídhion	0	0·3	1·3	1·1	0	0	0·2
Náxos	0·1	0·6	2·3	2·6	1·0	0	0·6
Spárti	1·0	0·6	2·2	2·4	0·6	0·1	0·6
Kalámai	0	0	0·3	0·6	0·1	0	0·1
Yíthion	0·7	0·6	0·3	0·4	0·3	0	0·2
Mílos	0·3	0·0	1·3	3·2	0·6	0	0·5
Thíra	0·1	0·3	1·9	2·7	1·0	0	0·5
Kíthira	0	0·1	0·3	0·7	0	0	0·1
Khaniá	1·0	1·6	3·5	3·2	1·0	0·3	0·9
Melidhónion	0·3	2·6	3·2	5·0	1·6	0·3	1·1
Iráklion	1·0	1·6	6·8	13·6	5·5	1·0	2·5
Sitía	0	0·3	1·6	1·0	0·3	0	0·3
Ierápetra	0	0	0·3	0·6	0·6	0	0·2

Table 9. *Frequency of thunderstorms*

[Average number of thunderstorm days per 1,000]

Stations	Jan.	Feb.	Mar.	Apr.	May	June	July	Aug.	Sept.	Oct.	Nov.	Dec.	Year
Thessaloníki	10·8	11·8	10·8	25·4	139·8	193·7	102·9	82·9	57·1	27·6	20·6	3·1	57·3
Kozáni	0	0	7·2	12·5	60·5	100·0	46·6	46·6	18·5	20·2	20·0	3·2	28·1
Ioánnina	23·7	25·4	45·2	93·3	180·6	157·8	111·8	88·2	106·6	118·6	91·1	45·2	90·8
Lárisa	0·0	3·8	9·2	11·9	39·2	48·8	35·7	25·4	15·5	19·6	14·3	5·7	19·9
Kérkira	47·8	44·0	35·8	41·4	33·6	35·6	21·1	26·7	52·9	82·3	68·9	63·4	46·2
Tríkkala	15·1	14·2	12·9	14·4	74·2	98·9	57·0	46·2	30·0	35·5	24·4	11·8	36·2
Vólos	6·5	14·4	14·0	16·1	51·6	83·3	53·8	44·1	31·1	49·5	23·3	5·4	32·8
Árta	48·4	43·6	45·2	66·7	79·6	92·2	50·5	29·0	56·7	89·2	78·9	55·9	61·4
Mitilíni	32·3	50·9	34·5	64·4	55·9	31·1	17·2	4·3	17·8	45·2	37·8	51·6	37·0
Lamía	1·8	5·9	5·4	5·6	10·8	42·6	8·9	19·7	16·7	26·9	1·9	3·6	12·5
Skíros	17·1	39·1	26·6	15·6	24·7	31·2	17·1	26·6	29·4	39·9	33·3	24·7	27·1
Khalkís	10·0	12·9	13·3	5·8	33·6	49·4	22·2	14·5	27·6	33·4	27·6	11·1	21·8
Mesolóngion	37·6	37·7	25·8	50·0	58·1	43·3	17·2	16·1	41·4	74·2	63·3	54·8	43·3
Khíos	83·5	83·2	68·3	43·1	57·0	29·4	9·5	22·8	56·9	68·9	70·6	81·6	56·3
Pátrai	30·1	41·3	41·9	47·8	45·2	63·3	17·2	24·7	37·8	75·2	65·6	33·3	43·6
Aíyion	21·2	33·4	14·3	9·3	26·8	40·7	26·9	16·1	18·5	41·2	46·3	28·7	26·9
Argostólion	33·4	34·1	35·8	18·5	15·5	17·3	6·0	6·0	14·8	41·8	48·1	47·8	26·7
Dhekélia	25·8	39·4	34·5	13·3	86·0	97·8	53·8	40·9	62·2	47·3	53·3	32·3	48·8
Athínai	28·1	29·0	25·9	28·1	64·1	73·3	42·4	36·4	50·0	77·0	64·8	41·0	46·7
Ándros	17·8	18·4	11·1	8·0	8·9	8·0	2·2	0·0	12·6	22·2	12·6	25·6	12·3
Zákinthos	47·3	35·4	23·7	23·3	18·3	23·3	4·3	12·9	16·7	62·4	65·6	60·2	32·7
Sámos	16·0	11·5	7·1	13·0	32·0	60·0	0	19·0	7·0	65·0	10·0	10·3	50·7
Návplion	15·6	12·2	5·6	9·2	28·9	68·9	28·9	15·6	20·7	40·5	13·8	14·5	23·0
Trípolis	9·7	10·0	6·5	6·7	18·3	38·9	18·3	7·5	5·6	18·3	11·1	12·9	13·8
Síros	31·2	25·9	22·6	7·8	20·4	5·6	6·5	7·5	12·2	36·6	40·0	46·2	22·6
Kiparissía	35·3	28·6	18·4	20·6	23·0	15·4	4·6	4·6	19·0	52·2	34·9	50·7	25·8
Náxos	41·9	47·2	37·6	21·1	29·0	12·2	11·8	8·6	17·8	33·3	52·2	41·9	29·6
Spárti	22·2	32·9	23·4	23·2	59·0	59·8	23·4	22·2	33·3	42·3	35·6	35·8	34·8
Kalámai	16·1	22·1	16·1	22·9	34·3	41·7	14·1	14·1	35·4	38·3	48·1	34·3	28·0
Thíra	29·0	36·6	30·1	20·0	23·7	7·8	2·1	2·1	14·4	47·3	67·8	43·0	27·0
Kíthira	9·7	8·7	3·2	3·4	6·4	3·3	0·0	1·6	5·0	12·9	28·3	8·1	7·5
Khaniá	43·0	42·4	28·0	22·2	15·6	2·0	0·0	0·0	28·8	60·2	44·4	77·4	30·3
Melidhónion	88·8	57·5	40·3	20·8	44·4	12·5	0·0	4·0	16·7	104·8	83·3	88·8	47·9
Iráklion	33·3	37·0	34·5	15·3	19·4	4·4	0·0	0·0	4·4	47·3	33·3	38·7	21·9
Anóyia	58·1	50·9	32·3	37·8	38·7	15·6	2·2	2·2	31·1	88·2	66·7	73·1	41·4

Table 10. *Relative humidity. Average monthly figures for* 1900–29

Station	Jan.	Feb.	Mar.	Apr.	May	June	July	Aug.	Sept.	Oct.	Nov.	Dec.	Year
	%	%	%	%	%	%	%	%	%	%	%	%	%
Thessaloníki	74·0	73·1	69·3	66·5	65·1	59·5	54·2	55·6	61·2	71·6	74·2	76·9	66·8
Ioánnina	77·0	76·6	73·4	67·2	68·2	63·9	58·0	58·4	65·5	76·7	79·2	80·8	70·4
Lárisa	81·5	77·7	73·2	67·6	66·3	58·8	53·2	52·8	60·9	74·2	81·2	83·2	69·2
Kérkira	76·1	75·1	74·4	74·8	73·2	71·3	65·9	66·2	70·4	76·6	76·7	77·7	73·2
Tríkkala	79·2	76·3	70·9	65·4	64·8	56·4	49·5	49·7	58·1	73·4	80·0	80·8	67·0
Vólos	77·4	77·3	75·2	70·6	70·3	65·2	60·3	60·9	64·4	75·6	80·0	81·0	71·5
Árta	76·8	75·0	73·7	73·3	70·2	67·2	61·6	61·3	67·4	75·8	78·0	79·5	71·7
Mitilíni	85·2	82·6	77·6	74·0	69·6	63·7	59·3	61·5	68·6	73·5	81·8	86·6	73·7
Khalkís	76·3	75·3	72·1	63·9	59·8	56·1	51·0	52·6	59·2	69·6	75·0	78·2	65·8
Mesolóngion	72·9	72·3	69·9	69·4	66·8	64·9	60·2	60·4	63·0	70·3	74·3	76·4	68·4
Pátrai	75·0	73·5	71·4	69·1	67·0	65·6	59·0	59·6	62·4	72·0	74·6	76·8	68·8
Athínai	71·0	70·1	66·2	60·0	54·9	50·9	43·2	44·3	51·0	63·2	70·0	72·6	59·9
Ándros	75·3	75·1	71·7	67·8	63·3	60·3	58·3	59·3	64·1	69·7	76·5	78·7	68·3
Zákinthos	72·1	71·5	71·4	68·9	64·0	62·2	57·6	58·9	62·8	71·3	74·9	75·3	67·6
Návplion	74·8	72·6	69·4	64·5	61·8	58·2	47·6	54·4	57·7	68·3	74·7	76·1	64·6
Trípolis	79·6	77·5	71·4	64·4	61·5	57·7	48·9	48·4	57·7	70·2	77·8	80·4	66·3
Síros	70·3	69·4	67·3	64·4	60·8	57·3	52·4	54·7	60·0	67·5	71·8	72·9	64·1
Kiparissía	73·8	72·3	70·8	68·9	67·4	66·3	61·8	61·7	65·8	70·4	72·2	74·6	68·8
Spárti	75·7	73·2	70·3	64·7	61·9	57·2	49·2	49·9	57·5	68·7	76·3	78·1	65·2
Kalámai	73·3	71·7	69·3	67·2	64·9	61·5	55·3	57·6	62·5	71·2	73·6	75·3	67·0
Thíra	71·9	72·3	70·0	68·3	66·8	64·0	59·0	59·6	65·4	70·0	72·9	74·1	67·9
Kíthira	71·3	71·1	69·0	66·4	60·4	59·5	54·2	53·7	58·7	65·7	72·3	72·4	64·6
Khaniá	73·0	71·2	68·9	67·1	65·4	61·9	57·3	59·2	62·9	69·9	72·9	75·2	67·1
Iráklion	69·4	68·0	65·8	62·8	63·1	62·4	59·1	60·8	63·1	66·0	68·7	72·0	65·1
Anóyia	74·6	75·1	69·8	63·9	63·1	56·3	52·1	53·4	59·7	69·6	71·2	77·6	65·6

Table 11. *Mean hours of sunshine*, 1900–29

Station	Jan.	Feb.	Mar.	Apr.	May	June	July	Aug.	Sept.	Oct.	Nov.	Dec.	Year
Thessaloníki	128	129	169	199	227	295	365	349	266	175	140	112	2,555
Kozáni	125	126	159	210	196	291	359	326	250	145	111	92	2,390
Ioánnina	114	114	137	154	195	263	353	351	276	155	105	99	2,316
Lárisa	132	123	170	201	244	285	367	347	228	190	117	116	2,520
Kérkira	138	138	192	213	284	330	412	376	276	197	132	122	2,810
Tríkkala	108	105	140	162	204	254	335	330	239	159	96	96	2,228
Árta	132	126	173	185	248	307	388	359	276	194	135	123	2,646
Mitilíni	136	144	214	244	283	369	428	405	332	218	160	120	3,053
Lamía	124	117	155	197	252	306	374	354	261	180	115	117	2,552
Khalkís	106	109	170	217	265	319	400	370	283	194	118	103	2,654
Mesolóngion	133	127	170	197	247	314	395	370	286	201	136	126	2,702
Pátrai	134	133	181	204	268	336	418	382	301	208	136	126	2,827
Aíyion	128	130	177	208	268	336	413	382	294	208	130	123	2,797
Argostólion	146	139	199	240	308	353	421	391	301	222	152	136	3,008
Dhekélia	128	133	188	232	304	348	408	378	298	239	136	127	2,919
Athínai	134	141	192	237	261	316	362	341	273	211	145	125	2,737
Ándros	98	100	162	228	290	362	417	382	298	205	112	94	2,748
Zákinthos	156	157	221	248	320	362	420	386	305	226	161	145	3,107
Návplion	150	142	199	240	285	335	398	365	290	222	158	148	2,932
Trípolis	129	115	185	220	277	326	384	356	286	208	137	130	2,753
Síros	107	115	173	228	281	361	410	385	301	212	134	110	2,817
Kiparissía	129	122	173	200	267	334	409	380	290	202	134	119	2,759
Náxos	83	85	140	184	241	329	396	176	286	177	98	86	2,481
Spárti	145	137	185	220	272	329	387	364	283	205	137	134	2,798
Kalámai	139	137	192	220	276	369	409	380	298	212	143	134	2,909
Thíra	102	104	162	211	280	367	431	404	334	230	132	186	2,943
Khaniá	115	126	185	246	306	365	424	392	308	216	139	121	2,943
Iráklion	115	102	159	230	275	369	419	387	301	207	127	113	2,804
Anóyia	100	99	151	215	262	360	410	379	289	196	130	122	2,713

Appendix X

GREEK COINAGE, WEIGHTS AND MEASURES

Coinage

Greece entered the Latin Monetary Union in 1868, and until 1910 the drachma was equal in value to the franc of France, Belgium and Switzerland, and the lira of Italy. The present monetary unit is the drachma (*dhrakhmí*, pl. *dhrakmaí, d.-és*), which is divided into 100 lepta (*leptón*, pl. *leptá*). Owing to the unsatisfactory financial position of the country, the currency consists almost entirely of paper. What coins there are, are of small denominations and consist of nickel, or nickel and silver. The rate of exchange was fixed in 1936 at 540–550 drachmae to the £ sterling, and remained at this level until 1939.

Weights and Measures

The metric system of weights and measures was officially introduced into Greece in 1898 and became compulsory in 1922. The issue of a decree in 1926 to enforce this system indicates the tenacity with which the people clung to the weights and measures to which they were accustomed. The following Greek units are still used; the stremma has been altered in value to bring it into line with the metric system:

Length.	1 pique (*píkhi*, pl. *píkhai, d.-es*)		=0·64 m.	=25·2 ins.
Area.	1 stremma (*strémma*, pl. *strémmata*)		=1,000 sq. m.	=0·247 acre.
Capacity.	1 oke (*oká*, pl. *okádhes*)		=1·33 l.	=2·35 pints.
	300 drachms (*dhrámi*, pl. *dhrámia*)		=1 l.	=1·76 pints.
	1 bushel (*koilón*, pl. *koilá*)=22 okes of wheat, 17 okes of barley.			
	The barrel (*varrélla*, pl. *varréllai, d.-es*) for wine or oil has a capacity which varies from district to district.			
Weight.	1 drachm		= 3·2 grm.	= 0·11 oz.
	1 oke	=400 drachms	= 1·28 kg.	= 2·8 lb.
	1 kantari (*kantári*, pl. *kantária*) 1 statir (*statír*, pl. *statíres*)	= 44 okes	=56·32 kg.	=124·16 lb.
	18 kantari or 800 okes	=approx. 1 English ton.		
	The Venetian pound (150 drachms or 0·48 kg. or 1·06 lb.) is used in the currant trade.			

The following are the Greek names of the units of the metric system:

Length.	*Khiliostómetron* (pl. *khiliostómetra*), millimetre. *Ekatostómetron*, centimetre. *Métron*, metre. *Khiliómetron*, kilometre.
Area.	*Tetragonikón métron*, square metre. *Ektárion* (pl. *ektária*), hectare. *Tetragonikón khiliómetron*, square kilometre.
Volume.	*Kivikón métron*, cubic metre.
Capacity.	*Lítra* (pl. *lítrai, d.-es*), litre. *Ekatólitron* (pl. *ekatólitra*), hectolitre.
Weight.	*Khiliostógrammon* (pl. *khiliostógramma*), milligram. *Grammárion* (pl. *grammária*), gram. *Khiliógrammon*, kilogram. *Metrikós tónos* (pl. *metrikoí tónoi*), metric ton.

CONVERSION TABLES

Metric and British Units

It is customary to think of the 'metre' and the 'yard' as representing unalterable units of length. This is not so. The metre was originally intended to be the 10,000,000th part of the earth's meridional quadrant. But the accurate determination of this length proved to be extremely difficult—partly for technical reasons, and partly because of different conceptions of the 'figure of the earth'. In view of these difficulties it became necessary to define the length of the metre in terms of suitable metal bars measured under specified conditions of temperature, pressure, humidity, etc. Similar standard bars were also used to define the length of other units such as the yard. As all these metallic standards are subject to change, conversion tables differ according to the date of comparison between different bars. The tables that follow are based on the comparison between the yard and the metre made in 1895. This made 1 metre equivalent to 39·370113 in.

Metric System. List of Prefixes

Deca means ten times.
Hecto means a hundred times.
Kilo means a thousand times.

Deci means a tenth part of.
Centi means a hundredth part of.
Milli means a thousandth part of.

In abbreviations the Decametre, etc., is Dm., and the decimetre, etc., dm.

Note on 'Nautical', 'Geographical' and 'Statute' miles

A British 'nautical mile' is the length of the minute of the meridian at any given latitude, and is therefore a variable unit. It is given in feet for Clarke's 1880 spheroid by the formula

$$60771{\cdot}1 - 30{\cdot}7 \cos 2 \text{ Lat.}$$

This is the sea mile of the scale of latitude and distance of the Admiralty Charts. From the above formula it will be found to vary from 6,046·4 ft. at the equator to 6,107·8 ft. at the poles, being 6,077·1 ft. at latitude 45°.

The so-called 'international nautical mile' of 1,852 m. or 6,076 ft. is the length of the minute of the meridian at latitude 45° on the international spheroid. This corresponds to the 6,077 ft. for Clarke's spheroid.

A 'geographical mile' is a fixed unit, being defined by some as the length of a minute of the equator and by others as that of the minute of the meridian at latitude 45°. According to the former definition its value on Clarke's spheroid is 6,087 ft. and according to the latter 6,077 ft. The round figure 6,080 is usually adopted for the purposes of ordinary navigation.

The British 'statute mile' measures 5,280 ft.

List of Conversion Tables

Table 1. *Length*

Nautical mile	Statute mile	Kilometre	Metre	Yard	Foot	Inch	Centimetre
1	1·152	1·853	1853	2027	6080*	72,960	185,300
0·8684	*1*	1·60934	1609·34	1760	5280	63,360	160,934
0·5396	0·621372	*1*	1000	1093·61	3280·84	39,370·1	100,000
0·0005396	0·0006214	0·001	*1*	1·09361	3·28084	39·3701	100
0·0004934	0·0005682	0·0009144	0·914399	*1*	3	36	91·4399
0·0001645	0·0001894	0·0003048	0·3048	0·33333	*1*	12	30·48
0·0000137	0·0000158	0·0000254	0·0254	0·02778	0·083333	*1*	2·54
0·0000054	0·0000062	0·00001	0·01	0·0109361	0·032808	0·393701	*1*

* This is the customary British practice, and not the 'international nautical mile', which Great Britain has not adopted.

Table 2. *Area*

Square mile	Square kilometre	Hectare	Acre	Square metre	Square yard
1	2·58998	258·998	640	2,589,980	3,097,600
0·386103	*1*	100	247·106	1,000,000	1,195,990
0·003861	0·01	*1*	2·47106	10,000	11,959·9
0·0015625	0·0040469	0·404685	*1*	4046·85	4840
0·00000039	0·000001	0·0001	0·000247	*1*	1·19599
0·00000032	0·00000084	0·0000836	0·000207	0·836126	*1*

Table 3. *Yield per Unit Area*

Tons per acre	Metric tons per hectare	Quintals per hectare
1	2·51071	25·1071
0·398294	*1*	10
0·0398294	0·1	*1*

Table 4. *Volume and Capacity*

Kilolitre	Cubic metre	Cubic yard	Bushel	Cubic feet	Imp. gall.	Litre	Pint
1	1·000027	1·30799	27·4969	35·3157	219·976	1000	1759·80
0·999973	*1*	1·30795	27·4962	35·3148	219·970	999·973	1759·75
0·764532	0·764553	*1*	21·0223	27	168·178	764·532	1345·43
0·0363677	0·0363687	0·0475685	*1*	1·28435	8	36·3677	64
0·028316	0·028317	0·037037	0·778602	*1*	6·22882	28·3160	49·8306
0·0045460	0·0045608	0·0059461	0·125	0·160544	*1*	4·54596	8
0·001	0·001000	0·001308	0·027497	0·035316	0·219976	*1*	1·75980
0·0005682	0·0005683	0·0007433	0·015625	0·020068	0·125	0·56824	*1*

Table 5. *Weight*

Ton	Metric ton or millier	Quintal	Kilogram	Pound
1	1·01605	10·1605	1016·05	2240
0·984207	*1*	10	1000	2204·62
0·0984207	0·1	*1*	100	220·462
0·0009842	0·001	0·01	*1*	2·20462
0·0004464	0·0004536	0·004536	0·453592	*1*

Table 6. *Temperature: Equivalents of Fahrenheit and Centigrade Scales*

°F.	°C.	°F.	°C.	°F.	°C.	°F.	°C.	°F.	°C.	°F.	°C.
100	37·7	79·25	26·25	58	14·4	37·4	3	17	−8·3	−4	−20
99·5	37·5	79	26·1	57·2	14	37	2·7	16·25	−8·75	−5	−20·5
99	37·2	78·8	26	57	13·8	36·5	2·5	16	−8·8	−5·8	−21
98·6	37	78	25·5	56·75	13·75	36	2·2	15·8	−9	−6	−21·1
98	36·6	77	25	56	13·3	35·6	2	15	−9·4	−6·25	−21·25
97·25	36·25	76	24·4	55·4	13	35	1·6	14	−10	−7	−21·6
97	36·1	75·2	24	55	12·7	34·25	1·25	13	−10·5	−7·6	−22
96·8	36	75	23·8	54·5	12·5	34	1·1	12·2	−11	−8	−22·2
96	35·5	74·75	23·75	54	12·2	33·8	1	12	−11·1	−8·5	−22·5
95	35	74	23·3	53·6	12	33	0·5	11·75	−11·25	−9	−22·7
94	34·4	73·4	23	53	11·6	32	0	11	−11·6	−9·4	−23
93·2	34	73	22·7	52·25	11·25	31	−0·5	10·4	−12	−10	−23·3
93	33·8	72·5	22·5	52	11·1	30·2	−1	10	−12·2	−10·75	−23·75
92·75	33·75	72	22·2	51·8	11	30	−1·1	9·5	−12·5	−11	−23·8
92	33·3	71·6	22	51	10·5	29·75	−1·25	9	−12·7	−11·2	−24
91·4	33	71	21·6	50	10	29	−1·6	8·6	−13	−12	−24·4
91	32·7	70·25	21·25	49	9·4	28·4	−2	8	−13·3	−13	−25
90·5	32·5	70	21·1	48·2	9	28	−2·2	7·25	−13·75	−14	−25·5
90	32·2	69·8	21	48	8·8	27·5	−2·5	7	−13·8	−14·8	−26
89·6	32	69	20·5	47·75	8·75	27	−2·7	6·8	−14	−15	−26·1
89	31·6	68	20	47	8·3	26·6	−3	6	−14·4	−15·25	−26·25
88·25	31·25	67	19·4	46·4	8	26	−3·3	5	−15	−16	−26·6
88	31·1	66·2	19	46	7·7	25·25	−3·75	4	−15·5	−16·6	−27
87·8	31	66	18·8	45·5	7·5	25	−3·8	3·2	−16	−17	−27·2
87	30·5	65·75	18·75	45	7·2	24·8	−4	3	−16·1	−17·5	−27·5
86	30	65	18·3	44·6	7	24	−4·4	2·75	−16·25	−18	−27·7
85	29·4	64·4	18	44	6·6	23	−5	2	−16·6	−18·4	−28
84·2	29	64	17·7	43·25	6·25	22	−5·5	1·4	−17	−19	−28·3
84	28·8	63·5	17·5	43	6·1	21·2	−6	1	−17·2	−19·75	−28·75
83·75	28·75	63	17·2	42·8	6	21	−6·1	0·5	−17·5	−20	−28·8
83	28·3	62·6	17	42	5·5	20·75	−6·25	0	−17·7	−20·2	−29
82·4	28	62	16·6	41	5	20	−6·6	−0·4	−18	−21	−29·4
82	27·7	61·25	16·25	40	4·4	19·4	−7	−1	−18·3	−22	−30
81·5	27·5	61	16·1	39·2	4	19	−7·2	−1·75	−18·75	−23	−30·5
81	27·2	60·8	16	39	3·8	18·5	−7·5	−2	−18·8	−23·8	−31
80·6	27	60	15·5	38·75	3·75	18	−7·7	−2·2	−19	−24	−31·1
80	26·6	59	15	38	3·3	17·6	−8	−3	−19·4	−24·25	−31·25

Table 7. *Pressure: Equivalents of Millibars, Millimetres of Mercury, and Inches of Mercury at 32° F. in Latitude 45°*

Mercury in.	Millibars	Mercury mm.	Mercury in.	Millibars	Mercury mm.	Mercury in.	Millibars	Mercury mm.	Mercury in.	Millibars	Mercury mm.	Mercury in.	Millibars	Mercury mm.
27·02	915	686·3	27·82	942	706·6	28·62	969	726·8	29·41	996	747·1	30·21	1,023	767·3
27·05	916	687·1	27·85	943	707·3	28·65	970	727·6	29·44	997	747·8	30·24	1,024	768·1
27·08	917	687·8	27·88	944	708·1	28·67	971	728·3	29·47	998	748·6	30·27	1,025	768·8
27·11	918	688·6	27·91	945	708·8	28·70	972	729·1	29·50	999	749·3	30·30	1,026	769·6
27·14	919	689·3	27·94	946	709·6	28·73	973	729·8	29·53	1,000	750·1	30·33	1,027	770·3
27·17	920	690·1	27·97	947	710·3	28·76	974	730·6	29·56	1,001	750·8	30·36	1,028	771·1
27·20	921	690·8	28·00	948	711·1	28·79	975	731·3	29·59	1,002	751·6	30·39	1,029	771·8
27·23	922	691·6	28·03	949	711·8	28·82	976	732·1	29·62	1,003	752·3	30·42	1,030	772·6
27·26	923	692·3	28·05	950	712·6	28·85	977	732·8	29·65	1,004	753·1	30·45	1,031	773·3
27·29	924	693·1	28·08	951	713·3	28·88	978	733·6	29·68	1,005	753·8	30·48	1,032	774·1
27·32	925	693·8	28·11	952	714·1	28·91	979	734·3	29·71	1,006	754·6	30·51	1,033	774·8
27·35	926	694·6	28·14	953	714·8	28·94	980	735·1	29·74	1,007	755·3	30·53	1,034	775·6
27·38	927	695·3	28·17	954	715·6	28·97	981	735·8	29·77	1,008	756·1	30·56	1,035	776·3
27·41	928	696·1	28·20	955	716·3	29·00	982	736·6	29·80	1,009	756·8	30·59	1,036	777·1
27·44	929	696·8	28·23	956	717·1	29·03	983	737·3	29·83	1,010	757·6	30·62	1,037	777·8
27·46	930	697·6	28·26	957	717·8	29·06	984	738·1	29·86	1,011	758·3	30·65	1,038	778·6
27·49	931	698·3	28·29	958	718·6	29·09	985	738·8	29·89	1,012	759·1	30·68	1,039	779·3
27·52	932	699·1	28·32	959	719·3	29·12	986	739·6	29·92	1,013	759·8	30·71	1,040	780·1
27·55	933	699·8	28·35	960	720·1	29·15	987	740·3	29·94	1,014	760·6	30·74	1,041	780·8
27·58	934	700·6	28·38	961	720·8	29·18	988	741·1	29·97	1,015	761·3	30·77	1,042	781·6
27·61	935	701·3	28·41	962	721·6	29·21	989	741·8	30·00	1,016	762·1	30·80	1,043	782·3
27·64	936	702·1	28·44	963	722·3	29·24	990	742·6	30·03	1,017	762·8	30·83	1,044	783·1
27·67	937	702·8	28·47	964	723·1	29·26	991	743·3	30·06	1,018	763·6	30·86	1,045	783·8
27·70	938	703·6	28·50	965	723·8	29·29	992	744·1	30·09	1,019	764·3	30·89	1,046	784·6
27·73	939	704·3	28·53	966	724·6	29·32	993	744·8	30·12	1,020	765·1	30·92	1,047	785·3
27·76	940	705·1	28·56	967	725·3	29·35	994	745·6	30·15	1,021	765·8	30·95	1,048	786·1
27·79	941	705·8	28·59	968	726·1	29·38	995	746·3	30·18	1,022	766·6	30·98	1,049	786·8

INDEX

PRINTED UNDER THE AUTHORITY OF H.M. STATIONERY OFFICE
AT THE UNIVERSITY PRESS, CAMBRIDGE